CRITICAL THINKING

A STUDENT'S INTRODUCTION

THIRD EDITION

Gregory Bassham

William Irwin

Henry Nardone

James M. Wallace

King's College

**McGraw-Hill
Higher Education**

Boston   Burr Ridge, IL   Dubuque, IA   New York   San Francisco   St. Louis
Bangkok   Bogotá   Caracas   Kuala Lumpur   Lisbon   London   Madrid   Mexico City
Milan   Montreal   New Delhi   Santiago   Seoul   Singapore   Sydney   Taipei   Toronto

McGraw-Hill
Higher Education

Published by McGraw-Hill, an imprint of The McGraw-Hill Companies, Inc., 1221 Avenue of the Americas, New York, NY 10020. Copyright © 2008. All rights reserved. No part of this publication may be reproduced or distributed in any form or by any means, or stored in a database or retrieval system, without the prior written consent of The McGraw-Hill Companies, Inc., including, but not limited to, in any network or other electronic storage or transmission, or broadcast for distance learning.

This book is printed on acid-free paper.

2 3 4 5 6 7 8 9 0 DOC/DOC 0 9 8

ISBN: 978-0-07-340734-0
MHID: 0-07-340734-8

Editor in Chief: *Emily Barrosse*
Publisher: *Lisa Moore*
Sponsoring Editor: *Mark Georgiev*
Marketing Manager: *Pamela S. Cooper*
Editorial Assistant: *Marley Magaziner*
Production Editor: *Carey Eisner*
Manuscript Editor: *Margaret Moore*
Design Manager: *Andrei Pasternak*
Cover Designer: *Andrei Pasternak*
Art Editor: *Emma Ghiselli*
Photo Research: *Brian J. Pecko*
Production Supervisor: *Richard DeVitto*
Composition: *11/12.5 Bembo by ICC Macmillan*
Printing: *45# New Era Matte Plus, R. R. Donnelley & Sons*
Cover: *Front cover, Royalty-Free/Corbis; Back cover, © Goodshoot/Alamy.*

Credits: The credits section for this book begins on page C-1 and is considered an extension of the copyright page.

Library of Congress Cataloging-in-Publication Data

Critical thinking : a student's introduction / Gregory Bassham . . . [et al.].—3rd ed.
    p. cm.
  Includes bibliographical references and index.
  ISBN-13: 978-0-07-340734-0
  ISBN-10: 0-07-340734-8
  1. Critical thinking—Textbooks. I. Bassham, Gregory, 1959–
B809.2.C745 2008
160—dc22   2007015071

The Internet addresses listed in the text were accurate at the time of publication. The inclusion of a Web site does not indicate an endorsement by the authors or McGraw-Hill, and McGraw-Hill does not guarantee the accuracy of the information presented at these sites.

www.mhhe.com

To Enrico, Eric, Nicole, Dylan,
Catherine, Daniel, and Kate

CONTENTS

CHAPTER 2   Recognizing Arguments   30

CHAPTER 3   Basic Logical Concepts   55

CHAPTER 4   Language   90

CHAPTER 5   Logical Fallacies—I   124

CHAPTER 6   Logical Fallacies—II   145

CHAPTER 7   Analyzing Arguments   171

CHAPTER 12   Finding, Evaluating, and Using Sources   340

CHAPTER 13   Writing Argumentative Essays   389

PREFACE

The first edition of *Critical Thinking: A Student's Introduction* grew out of our conviction that a critical thinking text that works—that produces real, measurable improvement in students' critical reasoning skills—must have two essential features:

- It must be a text that our increasingly gadget-oriented students actually *read*.
- It must provide abundant, class-tested exercises that give students the practice they need to develop as maturing critical thinkers.

In revising *Critical Thinking: A Student's Introduction* for this edition, we've tried to remain faithful to this original vision. Many passages have been rewritten to make the book clearer and (we hope) more engaging and accessible. In addition, hundreds of new exercises have been added to give students even more opportunities to hone their critical reasoning skills.

OVERVIEW OF THE TEXT

Critical Thinking: A Student's Introduction is designed to provide a versatile and comprehensive introduction to critical thinking. The book is divided into seven major parts:

1. *The Fundamentals:* Chapters 1–3 introduce students to the basics of critical thinking in clear, reader-friendly language.
2. *Language:* Chapter 4 discusses the uses and pitfalls of language, emphasizing the ways in which language is used to hinder clear, effective thinking.
3. *Fallacies:* Chapters 5 and 6 teach students how to recognize and avoid twenty of the most common logical fallacies.

4. *Argument Analysis and Evaluation:* Chapters 7 and 8 offer a clear, step-by-step introduction to the complex but essential skills of argument analysis and evaluation.

5. *Traditional Topics in Informal Logic:* Chapters 9–11 offer a clear, simplified introduction to three traditional topics in informal logic: categorical logic, propositional logic, and inductive reasoning.

6. *Researching and Writing Argumentative Essays:* Chapters 12 and 13 provide students with specific, detailed guidance in producing well-researched, properly documented, and well-written argumentative essays.

7. *Practical Applications:* Chapters 14 and 15 invite students to apply what they have learned by reflecting critically on two areas in which *un*critical thinking is particularly common: the media (Chapter 14) and pseudoscience and the paranormal (Chapter 15).

The text can be taught in a variety of ways. For instructors who stress argument analysis and evaluation, we suggest Chapters 1–8. For instructors who emphasize informal logic, we recommend Chapters 1–6 and 9–11. For instructors who focus on writing, we suggest Chapters 1–6 and 12 and 13. And for instructors who stress practical applications of critical thinking, we recommend Chapters 1–6 and 14 and 15.

STRENGTHS AND DISTINCTIVE FEATURES OF THE TEXT

There are a number of features that set this text apart from other critical thinking texts:

- A versatile, student-centered approach that covers all the basics of critical thinking—and more—in reader-friendly language
- An abundance of interesting (and often humorous or thought-provoking) classroom-tested exercises
- An emphasis on active, collaborative learning
- A strong focus on writing, with complete chapters on using and evaluating sources (Chapter 12) and writing argumentative essays (Chapter 13)
- An emphasis on real-world applications of critical thinking, with many examples taken from popular culture, and complete chapters on the media and pseudoscientific thinking
- An extensive treatment of critical thinking standards, hindrances, and dispositions
- A clear and detailed discussion of the distinction between deductive and inductive reasoning

- An abundance of thought-provoking marginal quotes, as well as "Critical Thinking Lapses"—outrageous errors in reasoning and thinking
- For the student, an Online Study Guide that includes detailed chapter outlines, tutorials, quizzes, definitions of key terms, and Web links at *www.mhhe.com/bassham3*
- For the instructor, a password-protected Web site at *www.mhhe.com/bassham3* offers a user-friendly Instructor's Manual that includes complete answer keys, teaching tips, sample tests and quizzes, PowerPoint presentations, and a computerized test bank

WHAT'S NEW TO THE THIRD EDITION

In preparing this edition, we have been greatly aided by suggestions from users and reviewers of the previous editions. The major changes in this edition are these:

- An expanded and reorganized chapter on evaluating arguments (Chapter 8) integrates the material more fully with preceding chapters.
- Many new essays for class discussion and analysis appear in Chapters 7 and 8.
- A new chapter on moral and legal reasoning is available to course adopters on the Instructor's part of the book's Web site.
- Many new marginal quotes and boxed passages have been added, including "Pop Culture Connection" boxes that draw on themes in popular culture to illustrate points in the text.
- Several chapters have been streamlined, including those on writing argumentative essays and pseudoscientific thinking.
- Many new and updated exercises and examples have been added throughout the book.
- Both the Instructor's Manual and student online support resources have been considerably expanded.

ACKNOWLEDGMENTS

For helpful comments and suggestions leading to this third edition, we wish to thank Dan Barwick (Alfred State College), Corine Sutherland (Golden West College), Christopher H. Pearson (University of Washington), and Perry Hardison (Alamance Community College). We are also grateful to David Baggett, Chris Blakey, Meaghan Godwin, Sean Martin, Dwayne Mulder, and

Frank Williams for sharing their thoughts and queries about the book. Our continued thanks to reviewers of the previous editions: David Bowen, James Brooks, Barbara Carlson, B. Steve Csaki, Rory Conces, David Detmer, Andrew Dzida, Thomson Faller, Barbara Forrest, Mary Elizabeth Gleason, Claude Gratton, Jann James, Leemon McHenry, Tom MacMillan, Marty Most, Nikolas Pappas, and Ted Schick.

It is a pleasure to pay tribute to the skilled and courteous people at McGraw-Hill who guided us through the production process, especially former philosophy and religion editor Jon-David Hague, manuscript editor Margaret Moore, production editor Carey Eisner, editorial assistant Marley Magaziner, and development editor Beth Ebenstein.

Finally, thanks to our families for putting up with our endless piles of index cards and generously giving us the time to write. Your love and support made all the difference.

CHAPTER 1

INTRODUCTION TO CRITICAL THINKING

This book is about the power of disciplined thinking. It's about learning to think for yourself and being your own person. It's about the personal empowerment and enrichment that result from learning to use your mind to its fullest potential. In short, it's about critical thinking.

Critical thinking is what a college education is all about. In many high schools, the emphasis tends to be on "lower-order thinking." Students are simply expected to passively absorb information and then repeat it back on tests. In college, by contrast, the emphasis is on fostering "higher-order thinking": the active, intelligent evaluation of ideas and information. This doesn't mean that factual information and rote learning are ignored in college. But it is not the main goal of a college education to teach students *what to think*. The main goal is to teach students *how to think*—that is, how to become independent, self-directed thinkers and learners.

> Learning without thinking is useless.
> —Confucius

WHAT IS CRITICAL THINKING?

Often when we use the word *critical* we mean "negative and fault-finding." This is the sense we have in mind, for example, when we complain about a parent or a friend who we think is unfairly critical of what we do or say. But *critical* also means "involving or exercising skilled judgment or observation." In this sense critical thinking means thinking clearly and intelligently. More precisely, **critical thinking** is the general term given to a wide range of cognitive skills and intellectual dispositions needed to effectively identify, analyze, and evaluate arguments and truth claims; to discover and overcome personal prejudices and biases; to formulate and present convincing reasons in support of conclusions; and to make reasonable, intelligent decisions about what to believe and what to do.

Put somewhat differently, critical thinking is disciplined thinking governed by clear intellectual standards. Among the most important of these intellectual standards are **clarity, precision, accuracy, relevance, consistency,**

> The purpose which runs through all other educational purposes—the common thread of education—is the development of the ability to think.
> —Educational Policies Commission

1

logical correctness, completeness, and **fairness.**[1] Let's begin our introduction to critical thinking by looking briefly at each of these important critical thinking standards.

CRITICAL THINKING STANDARDS
Clarity

Before we can effectively evaluate a person's argument or claim, we need to understand clearly what he or she is saying. Unfortunately, that can be difficult because people often fail to express themselves clearly. Sometimes this lack of clarity is due to laziness, carelessness, or a lack of skill. At other times it results from a misguided effort to appear clever, learned, or profound. Consider the following passage from philosopher Martin Heidegger's influential but notoriously obscure book *Being and Time:*

> Temporality makes possible the unity of existence, facticity, and falling, and in this way constitutes primordially the totality of the structure of care. The items of care have not been pieced together cumulatively any more than temporality itself has been put together 'in the course of time' ["mit der Zeit"] out of the future, the having been, and the Present. Temporality 'is' not an *entity* at all. It is not, but it *temporalizes* itself. . . . Temporality temporalizes, and indeed it temporalizes possible ways of itself. These make possible the multiplicity of Dasein's modes of Being, and especially the basic possibility of authentic or inauthentic existence.[2]

That may be profound, or it may be nonsense, or it may be both. Whatever exactly it is, it is quite needlessly obscure.

As William Strunk Jr. and E. B. White remark in their classic *The Elements of Style,* "[M]uddiness is not merely a disturber of prose, it is also a destroyer of life, of hope: death on the highway caused by a badly worded road sign, heartbreak among lovers caused by a misplaced phrase in a well-intentioned letter. . . ."[3] Only by paying careful attention to language can we avoid such needless miscommunications and disappointments.

Critical thinkers not only strive for clarity of language but also seek maximum clarity of thought. As self-help books constantly remind us, to achieve our personal goals in life we need a clear conception of our goals and priorities, a realistic grasp of our abilities, and a clear understanding of the problems and opportunities we face. Such self-understanding can be achieved only if we value and pursue clarity of thought.

Precision

Detective stories contain some of the most interesting examples of critical thinking in fiction. The most famous fictional sleuth is, of course, Sherlock Holmes, the immortal creation of British writer Sir Arthur Conan Doyle.

Everything that can be said can be said clearly.

—Ludwig Wittgenstein

Confusion has its costs.

—Crosby, Stills, and Nash

Clarity is not a mere embellishment of the intellect; it is the very heart of intellectual virtue.

—Charles Larmore

In Doyle's stories Holmes is often able to solve complex mysteries when the bungling detectives from Scotland Yard haven't so much as a clue. What is the secret of his success? An extraordinary commitment to *precision*. First, by careful and highly trained observation, Holmes is able to discover clues that others have overlooked. Then, by a process of precise logical inference, he is able to reason from those clues to discover the solution to the mystery.

Everyone recognizes the importance of precision in specialized fields such as medicine, mathematics, architecture, and engineering. Critical thinkers also understand the importance of precise thinking in daily life. They understand that to cut through the confusions and uncertainties that surround many everyday problems and issues, it is often necessary to insist on precise answers to precise questions: What exactly is the problem we're facing? What exactly are the alternatives? What exactly are the advantages and disadvantages of each alternative? Only when we habitually seek such precision are we truly critical thinkers.

Really valuable ideas can only be had at the price of close attention.
—Charles S. Peirce

Accuracy

There is a well-known saying about computers: "Garbage in, garbage out." Simply put, this means that if you put bad information into a computer, bad information is exactly what you will get out of it. Much the same is true of human thinking. No matter how brilliant you may be, you're almost guaranteed to make bad decisions if your decisions are based on false information.

A good example of this is provided by America's long and costly involvement in Vietnam. The policymakers who embroiled us in that conflict were not stupid. On the contrary, they were, in journalist David Halberstam's oft-quoted phrase, "the best and the brightest" of their generation. Of course, the reasons for their repeated failures of judgment are complex and controversial; but much of the blame, historians agree, must be placed on false and inadequate information: ignorance of Vietnamese history and culture, an exaggerated estimate of the strategic importance of Vietnam and Southeast Asia, false assumptions about the degree of popular support in South Vietnam, unduly optimistic assessments of the "progress" of the war, and so on. Had American policymakers taken greater pains to learn the truth about such matters, it is likely they would not have made the poor decisions they did.

Critical thinkers don't merely value the truth; they have a *passion* for accurate, timely information. As consumers, citizens, workers, and parents, they strive to make decisions that are as informed as possible. In the spirit of Socrates' famous statement that the unexamined life is not worth living, they never stop learning, growing, and inquiring.

No one can navigate well through life without an accurate map by which to steer. Knowledge is the possession of such a map, and truth is what the map gives us, linking us to reality.
—Tom Morris

Relevance

Anyone who has ever sat through a boring school assembly or watched a mudslinging political debate can appreciate the importance of staying focused on relevant ideas and information. A favorite debaters' trick is to try to distract an

audience's attention by raising an irrelevant issue. Even Abraham Lincoln wasn't above such tricks, as the following story told by his law partner illustrates:

> In a case where Judge [Stephen T.] Logan—always earnest and grave—opposed him, Lincoln created no little merriment by his reference to Logan's style of dress. He carried the surprise in store for the latter, till he reached his turn before the

jury. Addressing them, he said: "Gentlemen, you must be careful and not permit yourselves to be overcome by the eloquence of counsel for the defense. Judge Logan, I know, is an effective lawyer. I have met him too often to doubt that; but shrewd and careful though he be, still he is sometimes wrong. Since this trial has begun I have discovered that, with all his caution and fastidiousness, he hasn't knowledge enough to put his shirt on right." Logan turned red as crimson, but sure enough, Lincoln was correct, for the former had donned a new shirt, and by mistake had drawn it over his head with the pleated bosom behind. The general laugh which followed destroyed the effect of Logan's eloquence over the jury— the very point at which Lincoln aimed.[4]

Lincoln's ploy was entertaining and succeeded in distracting the attention of the jury. Had the jurors been thinking critically, however, they would have realized that carelessness about one's attire has no logical relevance to the strength of one's arguments.

> *No tedious and irrelevant discussion can be allowed; what is said should be pertinent.*
>
> —Plato

Consistency

It is easy to see why consistency is essential to critical thinking. Logic tells us that if a person holds inconsistent beliefs, at least one of those beliefs must be false. Critical thinkers prize truth and so are constantly on the lookout for inconsistencies, both in their own thinking and in the arguments and assertions of others.

There are two kinds of inconsistency that we should avoid. One is *logical inconsistency,* which involves saying or believing inconsistent things (i.e., things that cannot both or all be true) about a particular matter. The other is *practical inconsistency,* which involves saying one thing and doing another.

Sometimes people are fully aware that their words conflict with their deeds. The politician who cynically breaks her campaign promises once she takes office, the TV evangelist caught in an extramarital affair, the drug counselor arrested for peddling drugs—such people are hypocrites pure and simple. From a critical thinking point of view, such examples are not especially interesting. As a rule, they involve failures of character to a greater degree than they do failures of critical reasoning.

More interesting from a critical thinking standpoint are cases in which people are not fully aware that their words conflict with their deeds. Such cases highlight an important lesson of critical thinking: that human beings often display a remarkable capacity for self-deception. Author Harold Kushner cites an all-too-typical example:

> Ask the average person which is more important to him, making money or being devoted to his family, and virtually everyone will answer *family* without hesitation. But watch how the average person actually lives out his life. See where he really invests his time and energy, and he will give away the fact that he really does not live by what he says he believes. He has let himself be persuaded that if he leaves for work earlier in the morning and comes home more tired at night, he is proving how devoted he is to his family by expending himself to provide them with all the things they have seen advertised.[5]

> *We must not be like those who can astonish their onlookers by their skill in syllogistic argumentation, but who when it comes to their own lives, contradict their own teachings.*
>
> —Plato

> *There is a difference between knowing the path and walking the path.*
>
> —Morpheus, in *The Matrix*

Speaking of Inconsistency . . .

Philosophy professor Kenneth R. Merrill offers the following tongue-in-cheek advice for writers. What kind of inconsistency does Merrill commit?

1. Watch your spelling. Writters who mis-pele a lott of words are propperly re-guarded as iliterate.
2. Don't forget the apostrophe where its needed, but don't stick it in where theres no need for it. A writers reputation hangs on such trifle's.
3. Don't exaggerate. Overstatement always causes infinite harm.
4. Beware of the dangling participle. Forget-ting this admonition, infelicitous phrases creep into our writing.
5. Clichés should be avoided like the plague. However, hackneyed language is not likely to be a problem for the writer who, since he was knee-high to a grasshopper, has built a better mouse-trap and has kept his shoulder to the wheel.
6. Keep your language simple. Eschew sesquipedalian locutions and fustian rhetoric. Stay clear of the crepuscular—nay, tenebrific and fuliginous—regions of orotund sonorities.
7. Avoid vogue words. Hopefully, the writer will remember that her words basically impact the reader at the dynamic inter-face of creative thought and action. To be viable, the writer's parameters must enable her to engage the knowledge-able reader in a meaningful dialogue—especially at this point in time, when people tend to prioritize their priorities optimally.
8. Avoid profane or abusive language. It is a damned outrage how many knuckle-dragging slobs vilify people they disagree with.[6]

Critical thinking helps us become aware of such unconscious practical incon-sistencies, allowing us to deal with them on a conscious and rational basis.

It is also common, of course, for people to unknowingly hold inconsis-tent beliefs about a particular subject. In fact, as Socrates pointed out long ago, such unconscious logical inconsistency is far more common than most people suspect. As we shall see, for example, many today claim that "morality is rela-tive," while holding a variety of views that imply that it is not relative. Critical thinking helps us recognize such logical inconsistencies or, still better, avoid them altogether.

Logical Correctness

Intelligence means a person who can see implications and arrive at conclusions.

—Talmud

To think logically is to reason correctly—that is, to draw well-founded conclu-sions from the beliefs we hold. To think critically we need accurate and well-supported beliefs. But, just as important, we need to be able to reason from those beliefs to conclusions that logically follow from them. Unfortunately, illogical thinking is all too common in human affairs. Bertrand Russell, in his classic essay "An Outline of Intellectual Rubbish," provides an amusing example:

I am sometimes shocked by the blasphemies of those who think themselves pious—for instance, the nuns who never take a bath without wearing a bathrobe

• Critical Thinking Lapse •

The human race are masters of the ridiculous. There was actually a story in our newspaper of a man who was bitten on the tongue while kissing a rattlesnake. He decided to try a nonscientific remedy he heard about to counteract a snakebite. So he wired his mouth to a pickup truck battery and tried to jump-start his tongue. It knocked him out and he ended up in the hospital, where he lost part of his tongue and one lip.[7]

Man is the Reasoning Animal. Such is the claim. I think it is open to dispute. Indeed, my experiments have proven to me that he is the Unreasoning Animal. Note his history. . . . His record is the fantastic record of a maniac.

—Mark Twain

all the time. When asked why, since no man can see them, they reply: "Oh, but you forget the good God." Apparently they conceive of the deity as a Peeping Tom, whose omnipotence enables Him to see through bathroom walls, but who is foiled by bathrobes. This view strikes me as curious.[8]

As Russell observes, from the proposition

1. God sees everything.

the pious nuns correctly drew the conclusion

2. God sees through bathroom walls.

However, they failed to draw the equally obvious conclusion that

3. God sees through bathrobes.

Such illogic is, indeed, curious—but not, alas, uncommon.

Completeness

In most contexts, we rightly prefer deep and complete thinking to shallow and superficial thinking. Thus, we justly condemn slipshod criminal investigations, hasty jury deliberations, superficial news stories, sketchy driving directions, and snap medical diagnoses. Of course, there are times when it is impossible or inappropriate to discuss an issue in depth; no one would expect, for example, a thorough and wide-ranging discussion of the ethics of human genetic research in a short newspaper editorial. Generally speaking, however, thinking is better when it is deep rather than shallow, thorough rather than superficial.

It is only when there is completeness and exhaustiveness that there is scholarship.

—Hsün Tzu

Fairness

Finally, critical thinking demands that our thinking be fair—that is, open-minded, impartial, and free of distorting biases and preconceptions. That can be very difficult to achieve. Even the most superficial acquaintance with history and the social sciences tells us that people are often strongly disposed to resist unfamiliar ideas, to prejudge issues, to stereotype outsiders, and to identify truth with their own self-interest or the interests of their nation or group. It is probably unrealistic to suppose that our thinking could ever be completely free

It is not much good thinking of a thing unless you think it out.

—H. G. Wells

of biases and preconceptions; to some extent we all perceive reality in ways that are powerfully shaped by our individual life experiences and cultural backgrounds. But as difficult as it may be to achieve, basic fair-mindedness is clearly an essential attribute of a critical thinker.

> *Close-mindedness means premature intellectual old age.*
> —John Dewey

Exercise 1.1

I. Break into groups of four or five. Choose one member of your group to take notes and be the group reporter. Discuss your education up to this point. To what extent has your education prepared you to think clearly, precisely, accurately, logically, and so forth? Have you ever known a person (e.g., a teacher or a parent) who strongly modeled the critical thinking standards discussed in this section? If so, how did he or she do that?

II. Have you ever been guilty of either practical inconsistency (saying one thing and doing another) or logical inconsistency (believing inconsistent things about a particular topic or issue)? In small groups think of examples either from your own experience or from that of someone you know. Be prepared to share your examples with the class as a whole.

The Benefits of Critical Thinking

Having looked at some of the key intellectual standards governing critical reasoning (clarity, precision, and so forth), let's now consider more specifically what you can expect to gain from a course in critical thinking.

Critical Thinking in the Classroom

When they first enter college, students are sometimes surprised to discover that their professors seem less interested in how they got their beliefs than they are in whether those beliefs can withstand critical scrutiny. In college the focus is on higher-order thinking: the active, intelligent evaluation of ideas and information. For this reason critical thinking plays a vital role throughout the college curriculum.

> *The main aim of education is practical and reflective judgment, a mind trained to be critical everywhere in the use of evidence.*
> —Brand Blanchard

In a critical thinking course, students learn a variety of skills that can greatly improve their classroom performance. These skills include

- understanding the arguments and beliefs of others
- critically evaluating those arguments and beliefs
- developing and defending one's own well-supported arguments and beliefs

Let's look briefly at each of these three skills.

To succeed in college, you must, of course, be able to *understand* the material you are studying. A course in critical thinking cannot make inherently difficult material easy to grasp, but critical thinking does teach a variety of skills that, with practice, can significantly improve your ability to understand the arguments and issues discussed in your college textbooks and classes.

> We don't want you to axiomatically accept the conventional wisdom on a particular subject. Indeed, your first instinct should be to question it.
>
> —John J. Mearsheimer

In addition, critical thinking can help you *critically evaluate* what you are learning in class. During your college career, your instructors will often ask you to discuss "critically" some argument or idea introduced in class. Critical thinking teaches a wide range of strategies and skills that can greatly improve your ability to engage in such critical evaluations.

You will also be asked to *develop your own arguments* on particular topics or issues. In an American Government class, for example, you might be asked to write a paper addressing the issue of whether Congress has gone too far in restricting presidential war powers. To write such a paper successfully, you must do more than simply find and assess relevant arguments and information. You must also be able to marshal arguments and evidence in a way that convincingly supports your view. The systematic training provided in a course in critical thinking can greatly improve that skill as well.

Critical Thinking in the Workplace

> There is nothing more practical than sound thinking.
>
> —Foundation for Critical Thinking

Surveys indicate that fewer than half of today's college graduates can expect to be working in their major field of study within five years of graduation. This statistic speaks volumes about changing workplace realities. Increasingly, employers are looking not for employees with highly specialized career skills, since such skills can usually best be learned on the job, but for employees with good thinking and communication skills—quick learners who can solve problems, think creatively, gather and analyze information, draw appropriate conclusions from data, and communicate their ideas clearly and effectively. These are exactly the kinds of generalized thinking and problem-solving skills that a course in critical thinking aims to improve.

Critical Thinking in Life

Critical thinking is valuable in many contexts outside the classroom and the workplace. Let's look briefly at three ways in which this is the case.

First, critical thinking can help us avoid making foolish personal decisions. All of us have at one time or another made decisions about consumer purchases, relationships, personal behavior, and the like that we later realized were seriously misguided or irrational. Critical thinking can help us avoid such mistakes by teaching us to think about important life decisions more carefully, clearly, and logically.

Second, critical thinking plays a vital role in promoting democratic processes. Despite what cynics might say, in a democracy it really is "we the people" who have the ultimate say over who governs and for what purposes. It is vital, therefore, that citizens' decisions be as informed and as deliberate as possible. Many of today's most serious societal problems—environmental destruction, nuclear proliferation, religious and ethnic intolerance, decaying inner cities, racial prejudice, failing schools, spiraling health-care costs, to mention just a few—have largely been caused by poor critical thinking. And as Albert Einstein once remarked, "The significant problems we face cannot be solved at the level of thinking we were at when we created them."

Third, critical thinking is worth studying for its own sake, simply for the personal enrichment it can bring to our lives. One of the most basic truths of the human condition is that most people, most of the time, believe what they are told. Throughout most of recorded history, people accepted without question that the earth was the center of the universe, that demons cause disease, that slavery was just, and that women are inferior to men. Critical thinking, honestly and courageously pursued, can help free us from the unexamined assumptions and biases of our upbringing and our society. It lets us step back from the prevailing customs and ideologies of our culture and ask, "This is what I've been taught, but is it *true*? In short, critical thinking allows us to lead self-directed, "examined" lives. Such personal liberation is, as the word itself implies, the ultimate goal of a *liberal* arts education. Whatever other benefits it brings, a liberal education can have no greater reward.

> *Citizens who think for themselves, rather than uncritically ingesting what their leaders tell them, are the absolutely necessary ingredient of a society that is to remain truly free.*
> —Howard Kahane

BARRIERS TO CRITICAL THINKING

The preceding section raises an obvious question: If critical thinking is so important, why is it that *un*critical thinking is so common? Why is it that so many people—including many highly educated and intelligent people—find critical thinking so difficult?

The reasons, as you might expect, are quite complex. Here is a list of some of the most common barriers to critical thinking:

- lack of relevant background information
- poor reading skills
- bias
- prejudice
- superstition
- egocentrism (self-centered thinking)
- sociocentrism (group-centered thinking)
- peer pressure
- conformism
- provincialism
- narrow-mindedness
- close-mindedness
- distrust in reason
- relativistic thinking
- stereotyping
- unwarranted assumptions
- scapegoating
- rationalization

- denial
- wishful thinking
- short-term thinking
- selective perception
- selective memory
- overpowering emotions
- self-deception
- face-saving
- fear of change

Let's examine in detail five of these impediments—egocentrism, sociocentrism, relativistic thinking, unwarranted assumptions, and wishful thinking—that play an especially powerful role in hindering critical thinking.

Egocentrism

Egocentrism is the tendency to see reality as centered on oneself. Egocentrics are selfish, self-absorbed people who view their interests, ideas, and values as superior to everyone else's. All of us are affected to some degree by egocentric biases.

Egocentrism can manifest itself in a variety of ways. Two common forms are self-interested thinking and self-serving bias.

One cannot think clearly about what one is wrapped up in.
—Holmes Rolston

Self-interested thinking is the tendency to accept and defend beliefs that harmonize with one's self-interest. Almost no one is immune from self-interested thinking. Most doctors support legislation making it more difficult for them to be sued for malpractice; most lawyers do not. Most state university professors strongly support tenure, paid sabbaticals, low teaching loads, and a strong faculty voice in university governance; many state taxpayers and university administrators do not. Most factory workers support laws requiring advance notice of plant closings; most factory owners do not. Most American voters favor campaign finance reform; most elected politicians do not. Of course, some of these beliefs may be supported by good reasons. From a psychological standpoint, however, it is likely that self-interest plays at least some role in shaping the respective attitudes and beliefs.

Admit your faults. I would if I had any.
—Milton Berle

Self-interested thinking, however understandable it may seem, is a major obstacle to critical thinking. Everyone finds it tempting at times to reason that "this benefits me, therefore it must be good"; but from a critical thinking standpoint, such "reasoning" is a sham. Implicit in such thinking is the assumption that "What is most important is what *I* want and need." But why should I, or anyone else, accept such an arbitrary and obviously self-serving assumption? What makes *your* wants and needs more important than everyone else's? Critical thinking condemns such special pleading. It demands that we weigh evidence and arguments objectively and impartially. Ultimately, it demands that we revere truth—even when it hurts.

Self-serving bias is the tendency to overrate oneself—to see oneself as better in some respect than one actually is. We have all known braggarts or know-it-alls who claim to be more talented or knowledgeable than they really are. If you are like most people, you probably think of yourself as being an unusually self-aware person who is largely immune from any such self-deception. If so, then you too are probably suffering from self-serving bias.

Studies show that self-serving bias is an extremely common trait. In one survey one million high school seniors were asked to rate themselves on their "ability to get along with others." *Not a single respondent rated himself below average in such ability.*[9] Other surveys have shown that 90 percent of business managers and more than 90 percent of college professors rate their performance as better than average. It is easy, of course, to understand why people tend to overrate themselves. We all like to feel good about ourselves. Nobody likes to think of himself or herself as being "below average" in some important respect. At the same time, however, it is important to be able to look honestly at our personal strengths and weaknesses. We want to set high personal goals, but not goals that are wildly unrealistic. Self-confidence grounded in genuine accomplishment is an important element of success. Overconfidence is an obstacle to genuine personal and intellectual growth.

> *The one thing that unites all human beings, regardless of age, gender, religion, economic status, or ethnic background, is that, deep down inside, we all believe that we are above-average drivers.*
>
> —Dave Barry

EXERCISE 1.2

Are you overconfident in your beliefs? Here's a simple test to determine if you are. For each of the following ten items, provide a low and a high guess such that you are 90 percent sure the correct answer falls between the two. Your challenge is to be neither too narrow (i.e., overconfident) nor too wide (i.e., underconfident). If you successfully meet the challenge, you should have 10 percent misses—that is, exactly one miss.[10]

	90% Confidence Range	
	LOW	HIGH
1. Martin Luther King's age at death	_____	_____
2. Length of Nile River (in miles)	_____	_____
3. Percentage of African Americans in the United States	_____	_____
4. Number of books in the Old Testament	_____	_____
5. Diameter of the moon (in miles)	_____	_____
6. Weight of an empty Boeing 747 (in pounds)	_____	_____
7. Current population of California	_____	_____
8. Year in which Wolfgang Amadeus Mozart was born	_____	_____
9. Air distance from London to Tokyo (in miles)	_____	_____
10. Deepest known point in the ocean (in feet)	_____	_____ [11]

> He who knows most, knows best how little he knows.
>
> —Thomas Jefferson

Sociocentrism

Sociocentrism is group-centered thinking. Just as egocentrism can hinder rational thinking by focusing excessively on the self, so sociocentrism can hinder rational thinking by focusing excessively on the group.

Sociocentrism can distort critical thinking in many ways. Two of the most important are group bias and conformism.

Group bias is the tendency to see one's own group (nation, tribe, sect, peer group, and the like) as being inherently better than others. Social scientists tell us that such thinking is extremely common throughout human history and across cultures. Just as we seem naturally inclined to hold inflated views of ourselves, so we find it easy to hold inflated views of our family, our community, or our nation. Conversely, we find it easy to look with suspicion or disfavor on those we regard as "outsiders."

Most people absorb group bias unconsciously, usually from early childhood. It is common, for example, for people to grow up thinking that their society's beliefs, institutions, and values are better than those of other societies.

> Custom and example have a much more persuasive power than any certitude obtained by way of inquiry.
>
> —René Descartes

➤ Pop Culture Connection ◄

Poker and Critical Thinking

Poker players fall victim to critical thinking barriers like wishful think-ing and self-serving bias just like anybody else.[12] One barrier that can be particularly costly to poker players is overconfidence. Overconfi-dent players think that they're better, or luckier, than they actually are. This often leads them to play with far superior opponents, to stay in too many hands, and to bet recklessly. The result: players who over-rate their abilities quickly become ATMs for their tablemates.

Poker legend Doyle Brunson tells a cautionary tale about the dan-gers of overconfidence. A cocky New Yorker calling himself "Rochester Ricky" and flashing a big bankroll walked into a Fort Worth poker par-lor. Around the table sat Amarillo Slim, Puggy Pearson, Johnny Moss, Sailor Roberts, Brunson himself, and a couple of Texas businessmen. Two things quickly became apparent. Though he knew his game, Rochester hadn't played much no-limit poker, and he hadn't a clue he was playing against some of the best no-limit Hold'em poker talent in the world.

Rochester didn't realize that strategies that work well in limit games (for example, calling frequently and bluffing cautiously) often backfire in no-limit games. His parting words as he gathered up the paltry remnants of his $10,0000 bankroll were "If you guys are ever in Rochester, don't bother to look me up. You won't see me playing Hold'em against Texans as long as I live."[13]

As the great American philosopher Clint Eastwood said, "A man's got to know his limitations."

Consider this exchange between eight-year-old Maurice D. and the well-known Swiss scientist and philosopher Jean Piaget:

Maurice D. (8 years, 3 months old): If you didn't have any nationality and you were given a free choice of nationality, which would you choose? *Swiss nationality.* Why? *Because I was born in Switzerland.* Now look, do you think the French and the Swiss are equally nice, or the one nicer or less nice than the other? *The Swiss are nicer.* Why? *The French are always nasty.* Who is more intelligent, the Swiss or the French, or do you think they're just the same? *The Swiss are more intelligent.* Why? *Because they learn French quickly.* If I asked a French boy to choose any na-tionality he liked, what country do you think he'd choose? *He'd choose France.* Why? *Because he was born in France.* And what would he say about who's nicer? Would he think the Swiss and the French equally nice or one better than the other? *He'd say the French are nicer.* Why? *Because he was born in France.* And who would he think more intelligent? *The French.* Why? *He'd say that the French want to learn quicker than the Swiss.* Now you and the French boy don't really give the same answer. Who do you think answered best? *I did.* Why? *Because Switzerland is always better.*[14]

To those who would investigate the cause of existing opinions, the study of predispositions is much more important than the study of argument.

—W. E. H. Lecky

Although most people outgrow such childish nationalistic biases to some extent, few of us manage to outgrow them completely. Clearly, this kind of "mine-is-better" thinking lies at the root of a great deal of human conflict, intolerance, and oppression.

Conformism refers to our tendency to follow the crowd—that is, to conform (often unthinkingly) to authority or to group standards of conduct and belief. The desire to belong, to be part of the in-group, can be among the most powerful of human motivations. As two classic experiments demonstrate, this desire to conform can seriously cripple our powers of critical reasoning and decision making.

In the first experiment, conducted in the 1950s by Solomon Asch, groups of eight college students were asked to match a standard line like the following

————————————

with three comparison lines such as these:

A ————————

B ————————————

C ——————————

When fifty million people say a foolish thing it is still a foolish thing.

—Anatole France

In each group, only one of the eight participants was unaware of the true nature of the experiment; the other seven were confederates working in league with the experimenter. In each case the single true subject was seated at the end of the table and asked to answer last. In some trials the seven confederates unanimously gave the correct answer (B); in others they unanimously gave an incorrect answer. The results: When no pressure to conform was present, subjects gave the correct answer more than 99 percent of the time. When faced with the united opposition of their peers, however, almost one-third (32 percent) of the subjects refused to believe their own eyes and gave answers that were obviously incorrect!

When all think alike, then no one is thinking.

—Walter Lippmann

Another famous experiment was conducted by Stanley Milgram in the 1960s.[15] In Milgram's experiment, subjects were asked to administer a series of increasingly severe electrical shocks to people whom the subjects could hear but couldn't see. (In fact, no actual shocks were given; the shock "victims" were actually confederates who merely pretended to be in pain.) Subjects were told that they were participating in a study of the effects of punishment on learning. Their task was to act as "teachers" who inflict progressively more painful shocks on "learners" whenever the latter failed to answer a question correctly. The severity of the shocks was controlled by a series of thirty switches, which ranged in 15-volt intervals from 15 volts ("Slight Shock") to 450 volts ("XX Danger: Severe Shock"). The purpose of the study was to determine how far ordinary people would go in inflicting pain on total strangers, simply because they were asked to do so by someone perceived to be "an authority."

The results were, well, shocking. More than 85 percent of the subjects continued to administer shocks beyond the 300-volt mark, long after the point at which they could hear the victims crying out or pounding on the walls in pain. After the 330-volt mark, the screaming stopped, and for all the subjects knew, the victims were either unconscious or dead. Despite that, nearly two-thirds (65 percent) of the subjects continued to administer shocks, as they were instructed, until they had administered the maximum 450 volts.

The lesson of these studies is clear: "Authority moves us. We are impressed, influenced, and intimidated by authority, so much so that, under the right conditions, we abandon our own values, beliefs, and judgments, even doubt our own immediate sensory experience."[16] As critical thinkers, we need to be aware of the seductive power of peer pressure and reliance on authority and develop habits of independent thinking to combat them.

> *Man is born to think for himself.*
> —Denis Diderot

Unwarranted Assumptions and Stereotypes

An **assumption** is something we take for granted, something we believe to be true without any proof or conclusive evidence. Almost everything we think and do is based on assumptions. If the weather report calls for rain, we take an umbrella because we assume that the meteorologist is not lying, that the report is based on a scientific analysis of weather patterns, that the instruments are accurate, and so forth. There may be no proof that any of this is true, but we realize that it is wiser to take the umbrella than to insist that the weather bureau provide exhaustive evidence to justify its prediction.

Although we often hear the injunction "Don't assume," it would be impossible to get through a day without making assumptions; in fact, many of our daily actions are based on assumptions we have drawn from the patterns in our experience. You go to class at the scheduled time because you assume that class is being held at its normal hour and in its same place. You don't call the professor each day to ask if class is being held; you just assume that it is. Such assumptions are *warranted,* which means that we have good reason to hold them. When you see a driver coming toward you with the turn signal on, you have good reason to believe that the driver intends to turn. You may be incorrect, and it might be safer to withhold action until you are certain, but your assumption is not unreasonable.

Unwarranted assumptions, however, are unreasonable. An *unwarranted* assumption is something taken for granted without good reason. Such assumptions often prevent our seeing things clearly. For example, our attraction for someone might cause us to assume that he or she feels the same way and thus to interpret that person's actions incorrectly.

One of the most common types of unwarranted assumptions is a **stereotype.** The word *stereotype* comes from the printing press era, when plates, or stereotypes, were used to produce identical copies of one page. Similarly, when we stereotype, as the word is now used, we assume that individual people have all been stamped from one plate, so all politicians are alike, or Muslims, or African Americans, professors, women, and so forth. When we form an opinion of someone that is based not on his or her individual qualities but, rather, on his or her membership in a particular group, we are assuming that all or virtually all members of that group are alike. Because people are not identical, no matter what race or other similarities they share, stereotypical conceptions will often be false or misleading.

Typically, stereotypes are arrived at through a process known as *hasty generalization,* in which one draws a conclusion about a large class of things (in this case, people) from a small sample. If we meet one South Bergian who is rude, we might jump to the conclusion that all South Bergians are rude. Or we might generalize from what we have heard from a few friends or read in a single news story. Often the media—advertisements, the news, movies, and so forth—encourage stereotyping by the way they portray groups of people.

Critical thinking demands that we become aware of our own thinking, including our assumptions. A *conscious* assumption is one of which we are aware: We know that we are taking something for granted. We might stop and say, "I'm going to assume that this weather report is accurate" or "I'm assuming that we have class today." Of course, it would not be possible to uncover every assumption that informs our thinking. You have made countless assumptions since you awoke this morning. And being conscious of an unwarranted assumption does not justify it; saying, "I'm aware of my tendency to stereotype" does not justify stereotyping.

The assumptions we need to become most conscious of are not the ones that lead to our routine behaviors, such as carrying an umbrella or going to class, but the ones on which we base our more important attitudes, actions, and decisions. If we are conscious of our tendency to stereotype, we can take measures to end it.

> General notions are generally wrong.
>
> —Mary Worthley Montague

EXERCISE 1.3

I. Read this story and answer the questions that follow.

When it happened, a disturbing mix of feelings bubbled inside you. It sickened you to watch the boat slip beneath the waves and disappear forever; so much work had gone into maintaining it and keeping it afloat, but at least everyone was safe in the tiny lifeboat you'd had just enough time to launch. You secretly congratulated yourself for having had the foresight to stock the lifeboat with a few emergency items, such as a small amount of food and water, but you knew that a boat built to hold three, maybe four people wasn't going to survive too long with such an overload of passengers.

You looked around at your companions: the brilliant Dr. Brown, whose cleverness and quick wit had impressed you on many occasions; Marie Brown, pregnant and clearly exhausted from the climb into the lifeboat; Lieutenant Ashley Morganstern, a twenty-year veteran who'd seen the most brutal sorts of combat; the lieutenant's secretary and traveling companion, whose shirt you noticed for the first time bore the monogram *LB,* but whom everyone called, simply, "Letty"; and Eagle-Eye Sam, the trusted friend who'd been at your side for many years as you sailed the oceans in your precious, now-vanished boat and whose nickname came from his ability to spot the smallest objects seemingly miles away at sea.

Seeing the fear on your passengers' faces, you tried to comfort them: "Don't worry; we'll be fine. They'll be looking for us right away. I'm sure of it." But you weren't so sure. In fact, you knew it wasn't true. It might be days before you were found, since you'd had no time to radio for help. Rescuers probably wouldn't be dispatched until Friday, five days from now, when your failure to show up in port would finally arouse concern.

On the third day, your passengers showed increasing signs of frustration, anger, and fear. "Where are they?" Marie cried. "We can't go on like this!"

You knew she was right. *We can't,* you thought, *not all of us anyway.*

On the fourth day, the food was completely gone, and just enough water remained to keep perhaps three people alive for another day, maybe two. Suddenly, things got worse. "Is that water?!" Marie screamed, pointing a shaking finger at the bottom of the lifeboat. Horrified, you looked down to see a slight trickle of water seeping in at the very center of the boat. Dr. Brown grabbed a T-shirt that was lying in the bottom of the boat and used it like a sponge to absorb the water, wringing it out over the side and plunging it into the invading water again and again. But it was no use; the water began to seep in faster than Brown could work.

"We're too heavy," the lieutenant insisted without emotion. "We've got to lighten the load. Someone has to get out and swim."

"Swim?!" Marie gasped in disbelief. "Are you insane?! There are sharks in these waters!"

"Who's it going to be, Captain?" the lieutenant asked almost coldly, staring you square in the eye. "Which one of us swims?"

"Me. I'll go," you say, swinging your leg out over the side of the boat.

"No," Letty insisted. "You're the only one who knows how to navigate. If you go, we'll all die. You must choose one of us to sacrifice."

And so you did.

A. Answer the following questions individually.
   1. Which one did you choose? Why? Why didn't you choose the others?
   2. As you read, you probably imagined what the characters looked like. From the image you had of them, describe the following characters in a few sentences:
      The Captain
      Dr. Brown
      Marie Brown
      Lieutenant Ashley Morganstern
      Letty
      Eagle-Eye Sam
   3. Do you think Dr. Brown is related to Marie Brown? If so, how?
B. Now form groups of three and complete the following tasks:
   1. Compare your responses to question 1 in part A. Discuss the reasons for your decisions. Is there any consensus in the group?
   2. Do you all agree on the relationship between Dr. Brown and Marie Brown?
   3. What evidence is there in the story to support your answer for question 3 in part A? Is it possible that they are related in another way or not at all?

4. Look at your portraits of Dr. Brown. How many assumptions did you and your group members make about the doctor's gender, age, appearance, and profession? What evidence in the story supports your image of the doctor? If your images are similar, what do you think accounts for that similarity? Are your mental images similar to ones we normally see in the media, for example?

5. Look at your portraits of the other characters. First, what similarities do you find among your group's members? Second, what evidence is there in the story to support your assumptions? Are other assumptions possible? Finally, where do you think your mental images came from?

II. In groups of three or four, name and explain a stereotypical conception people may have had about you over the years. Note how that stereotypical conception keeps others from coming to know you more accurately. Turn your page over and exchange papers with other members of your group. See if the other members can determine which stereotype description goes with what member of your group.

Relativistic Thinking

Virtually every college professor has had at least one conversation like the following:

Janie: Professor X, I don't understand why you gave me a D on this paper.

Prof. X: Well, as I noted in my written comments, you state your opinions, but you don't offer any reasons to back them up.

Janie: Do you mean you gave me a low grade because you disagree with my opinions?

Prof. X: No, not at all, Janie. You received a low grade because you didn't give any reasons to support your opinions.

Janie: But isn't everyone entitled to his or her own opinion? And can anyone ever really prove that his or her opinion is right and everyone else's is wrong? Why, then, do I have to give reasons for my opinions when I'm entitled to hold them and no one can prove that they're wrong?

Janie, here, has fallen into the trap of *relativistic thinking*. It is crucial to understand why this is a trap, because once one has fallen into it, it is very difficult to see any point in studying critical thinking at all.

Relativism is the view that truth is a matter of opinion. There are two popular forms of relativism: subjectivism and cultural relativism. **Subjectivism** is the view that truth is a matter of individual opinion. This is the view Janie apparently holds. According to subjectivism, whatever an individual believes is true, *is* true for that person, and there is no such thing as "objective" or "absolute" truth, i.e., truth that exists independent of what anyone believes. For example, suppose Bobby believes that abortion is wrong and Alice believes that abortion is not always wrong. According to subjectivism, abortion is always wrong for Bobby and not always wrong for Alice. Both beliefs are true—*for them*. And truth *for* one individual or another is the only kind of truth there is.

The other common form of relativism is **cultural relativism.** This is the view that truth is a matter of social or cultural opinion. In other words, cultural relativism is the view that what is true for person A is what person A's culture or society believes is true. Drinking wine, for example, is widely considered to be wrong in Iran but is not generally considered to be wrong in France. According to cultural relativism, therefore, drinking wine is immoral in Iran but is morally permissible in France. Thus, for the cultural relativist, just as for the subjectivist, there is no objective or absolute standard of truth. What is true is whatever most people in a society or culture believe to be true.

Relatively few people endorse subjectivism or cultural relativism in the pure, unqualified forms in which we have stated them. Almost everybody would admit, for example, that $1 + 1 = 2$ is true, no matter who might be ignorant or deluded enough to deny it. What relativists usually claim, therefore, is not that all truth is relative, but that truth is relative in some important domain(s). By far the most common form of relativism is *moral relativism.* Like relativism generally, moral relativism comes in two major forms: moral subjectivism and cultural moral relativism. **Moral subjectivism** is the view that what is morally right and good for an individual, A, is whatever A believes is morally right and good. Thus, if Andy believes that premarital sex is always wrong, and Jennifer believes that it is not always wrong, according to moral subjectivism premarital sex is always wrong for Andy and is not always wrong for Jennifer.

The other major form of moral relativism is **cultural moral relativism,** the view that what is morally right and good for an individual, A, is whatever A's society or culture believes is morally right and good. Thus, according to cultural moral relativism, if culture A believes that polygamy is wrong, and culture B believes that polygamy is right, then polygamy is wrong for culture A and right for culture B.

Cultural moral relativism is a very popular view today, especially among the young. There are two major reasons people seem to find it so attractive. One has to do with the nature of moral disagreement, and the other concerns the value of tolerance.

Ethics, obviously, is very different from math or science. In math and science, there are arguments and disagreements, but not nearly to the extent there are in ethics. In ethics there is widespread disagreement, the disagreements often go very deep, and there seems to be no rational way to resolve many of them. What this shows, some people conclude, is that there is no objective truth in ethics; morality is just a matter of individual or societal opinion.

Another reason people find cultural moral relativism attractive is that it seems to support the value of tolerance. Throughout history, terrible wars, persecutions, and acts of religious and cultural imperialism have been perpetrated by people who firmly believed in the absolute righteousness of their moral beliefs and practices. Cultural moral relativism seems to imply that we must be tolerant of other cultures' moral beliefs and values. If culture A believes that polygamy is wrong, and culture B believes that it is right, then culture A must agree that polygamy is right for culture B, no matter how offensive the practice may be to culture A.

Despite these apparent attractions, however, there are deep problems with cultural moral relativism, as the following exercise (adapted from a set of role-playing scenarios developed by Professor Grant H. Cornwell[17]) will illustrate.

EXERCISE 1.4

In groups of four or five, choose a group reporter to take notes and be the group spokesperson. Read and discuss one of the following case studies as assigned by your instructor.

Case 1

Definition: A cultural moral relativist is one who maintains the following thesis:

Whatever members of a culture believe is morally right and good is morally right and good for them.

You are a member of culture C studying cultures A and B. You are a committed cultural moral relativist, i.e., you maintain wholeheartedly the relativist thesis.

Culture A is a pacifist culture and believes that it is always morally wrong to commit a violent act against another human being for any reason.

Culture B is a militaristic and slaveholding culture. Its members believe that it is morally good and right to invade, subjugate, and enslave other cultures. While you are observing them, culture B invades culture A.

DISCUSSION QUESTIONS

1. What can you consistently believe with regard to the morality of culture A? The morality of culture B? Specifically, as a consistent moral relativist, can you criticize or condemn the morality of culture A? Of culture B?

2. What can you consistently do with regard to culture B's invasion and attempted subjugation of culture A?

Case 2

Definition: A cultural moral relativist is one who maintains the following thesis:
Whatever members of a culture believe is morally right and good is morally right and good for them.

You are a member of culture B and a committed cultural moral relativist, i.e., you maintain wholeheartedly the relativist thesis.

Culture B is a militaristic and slaveholding culture. A majority of its members believe that it is morally right and good to invade, subjugate, and enslave other cultures.

Culture A is a pacifist culture. A majority of its members believe that it is always wrong to commit any act of violence against another human being for any reason.

Culture B believes that it is morally wrong for culture A to practice pacifism.

Culture B invades culture A. Its aim is to subjugate and enslave members of culture A and force some of them to participate in gladiatorial bouts for the amusement of members of culture B.

DISCUSSION QUESTIONS

1. Is there any logical inconsistency in being a cultural moral relativist and also belonging to culture B? (*Hint:* Consider not only what culture B believes is right and good for its own members to do but also what it believes is right and good for other cultures to do.) If so, which beliefs, precisely, are inconsistent?

2. What can you consistently believe with regard to the morality of culture A? The morality of culture B? Specifically, as a consistent moral relativist, can you criticize or condemn the morality of culture A? Of culture B?

3. What can you consistently do with regard to culture B's invasion and attempted conquest of culture A?

Case 3

Definition: A cultural moral relativist is one who maintains the following thesis:

Whatever members of a culture believe is morally right and good is morally right and good for them.

Culture B consists of two subcultures: the Alphas and the Betas. The Alphas are a ruling majority group. They believe that it is morally right to randomly select a young child for sacrifice at the beginning of each year. The Betas are an oppressed minority group with its own distinctive cultural, moral, and religious practices. Betas believe strongly that child sacrifice is morally wrong.

You are a member of culture B and a Beta. You are also a committed cultural moral relativist, i.e., you maintain wholeheartedly the relativist thesis.

Culture A is a pacifist culture. Members of this culture believe that it is always wrong to commit any act of violence against another human being for any reason.

The Alphas believe that it is morally right to impose their beliefs and values on culture A. They believe that it is a moral atrocity that culture A does not sacrifice children, and they believe that they have a moral duty to use whatever means are necessary to change the beliefs of culture A and have its members comply with this practice.

Culture B invades culture A and begins its program of subjugation and indoctrination.

DISCUSSION QUESTIONS

1. Is it possible for an individual to belong to more than one culture at the same time? If so, does this pose any logical difficulty for the cultural moral relativist?

2. Is there any logical difficulty in being a moral relativist and belonging to culture B? (*Hint:* Consider not only what culture B believes is right and good for its own members to do but also what it believes is right and good for other cultures to do.)

3. What can you consistently believe with regard to the morality of culture A? The morality of culture B? Specifically, as a consistent moral relativist, can you criticize or condemn the morality of culture A? Of culture B?

4. What can you consistently do with regard to culture B's invasion and attempted subjugation of culture A?

5. Suppose that sometime in the future the Betas become the majority subculture in culture B, and a majority of culture B comes to believe that child sacrifice is wrong. Can this be described as "moral progress" from the standpoint of cultural moral relativism? Why or why not?

These cases highlight several serious problems with cultural moral relativism.

1. *Relativism makes it impossible for us to criticize other cultures' customs and values, even those that intuitively seem to us to be terribly wrong.* We can no longer say, for example, that a particular culture is wrong to practice slavery or child sacrifice, as long as that culture believes that those practices are morally right.

2. *Relativism makes it impossible for us to criticize our own societies' customs and values.* Suppose you personally oppose racial segregation, but a majority of your society supports it. According to relativism, you must change your mind and agree that racial segregation is right in your society. In fact, if relativism is true, anyone who criticizes majority values is *always wrong.* Total conformity to majority opinion is required.

3. *Relativism rules out the idea of moral progress.* Moral values can change, but if relativism is true, they can never become better or worse, for relativism implies that what is right for a society is what that culture believes is right *at that time.* Thus, a relativist cannot say, for example, that the abolition of slavery or laws outlawing gender discrimination represented moral progress in the United States.

4. *Relativism can lead to conflicting moral duties.* There are several ways in which a relativist might find himself stuck with conflicting moral beliefs and duties. Cases 2 and 3 highlight two ways in which this can occur:[18]
    a. *When a relativist is a member of a society that holds beliefs that conflict with moral relativism* (cases 2 and 3). If your society believes, for

example, that child sacrifice is absolutely and objectively right, then you too, as a moral relativist, must believe that child sacrifice is absolutely and objectively right, for whatever moral beliefs your society holds, you must hold as well.

b. *When a relativist belongs to two or more cultures and those cultures hold mutually inconsistent moral beliefs* (case 3). Can a person belong to two different cultures at the same time? It is hard to see why not. An Amish farmer living in Ohio, for instance, would seem to be a member of both an Amish culture and a larger American one. If such dual membership is possible, however, conflicts can clearly occur between the two cultures' moral codes. And given relativism's claim that what is right for a person is whatever his or her culture believes is right, this could lead to conflicting moral duties.

Thus, cultural moral relativism has consequences that make it very difficult to accept. In addition, however, it can be shown that the two main reasons people are attracted to cultural moral relativism—ethical disagreement and the value of tolerance—are not good reasons at all.

First, does the fact that there is deep disagreement in ethics show that there is no objective moral truth—that ethics is just a matter of opinion? Hardly. Think about another area in which there is deep, pervasive, and seemingly irresolvable disagreement: religion. People disagree vehemently over whether God exists, whether there is an afterlife, and so forth; yet we don't conclude from this that there is no objective truth about these matters. It may be difficult to *know* whether God exists. But *whether* he exists is not simply a matter of opinion. Thus, deep disagreement about an issue does not show that there is no objective truth about that issue.

Second, as the cases in Exercise 1.4 make clear, cultural moral relativism does not necessarily support the value of tolerance. Relativism tells us that we should accept the customs and values of our society. Thus, if you live in an *intolerant* society, relativism implies that you too should be intolerant.

Does this mean that cultural moral relativism has nothing at all to teach us? No. The fact that people disagree so much about ethics does not show that moral truth is simply a matter of opinion, but it should make us cautious and open-minded regarding our own ethical beliefs. If millions of obviously decent, intelligent people disagree with you, how can you be sure that your values are the correct ones? In this way relativism can teach us an important lesson about the value of intellectual humility. But we don't need relativism—which is a false and confused theory—to teach us this lesson. We can learn it just by opening our hearts and minds and thinking critically about the challenges of living an ethical life.

> *Good and ill have not changed since yesteryear; nor are they one thing among Elves and Dwarves and another among Men. It is a man's part to discern them, as much in the Golden Wood as in his own house.*
>
> —Aragorn, in J. R. R. Tolkien's *The Lord of the Rings*

Wishful Thinking

Once, as a Little Leaguer, one of the authors was thrown out at the plate in a foolish attempt to stretch a triple into a home run, possibly costing the team the game. Angry and disappointed, he refused to believe that he had really been thrown out. "I was safe by a mile," he said plaintively to his disbelieving coaches and teammates. It was only years later, when he was an adult, that he could admit to himself that he really had been out—out, in fact, by a mile.

Have you ever been guilty of wishful thinking—believing something not because you had good evidence for it but simply because you wished it were true? If so, you're not alone. Throughout human history, reason has done battle with wishful thinking and has usually come out the loser.

People fear the unknown and invent comforting myths to render the universe less hostile and more predictable. They fear death and listen credulously to stories of healing crystals, quack cures, and communication with the dead. They fantasize about possessing extraordinary personal powers and accept uncritically accounts of psychic prediction, levitation, and ESP. They delight in tales of the marvelous and the uncanny, and they buy mass-market tabloids that feature headlines such as "Spiritual Sex Channeler: Medium Helps Grieving Widows Make Love to their Dead Husbands."[19] They kid themselves into thinking, "It can't happen to me," and then find themselves dealing with the consequences of unwanted pregnancies, drunk-driving convictions, drug addiction, or AIDS.

> *The easiest thing of all is to deceive one's self; for what a man wishes, he generally believes to be true.*
>
> —Demosthenes

> *A man hears what he wants to hear and disregards the rest.*
>
> —Paul Simon

> *The universe is what it is, not what I choose that it should be.*
>
> —Bertrand Russell

EXERCISE 1.5

I. Have you ever been guilty of self-interested thinking, self-serving bias, group bias, conformism, or wishful thinking? Without embarrassing yourself too much, discuss these critical thinking lapses in groups of three or four, then share with the class whatever examples you'd like to discuss.

II. This textbook gives a number of examples of self-interested thinking, self-serving bias, group bias, conformism, and wishful thinking. Jot down at least two additional examples of each of these five critical thinking hindrances. Divide into groups of three or four, discuss your examples with the group, and share what you think are the best examples with the class as a whole.

CHARACTERISTICS OF A CRITICAL THINKER

So far in this chapter, we have discussed (1) the nature of critical thinking; (2) key critical thinking standards such as clarity, precision, accuracy, and fairness; (3) the benefits of critical thinking; and (4) some major impediments to critical thinking, including egocentrism, sociocentrism, relativistic thinking, unwarranted assumptions, and wishful thinking. With this as background, we are now in a position to offer a general profile of a critical thinker. The following list contrasts some of the key intellectual traits of critical thinkers with the relevant traits of uncritical thinkers.[20]

Critical Thinkers . . .	*Uncritical Thinkers . . .*
Have a passionate drive for clarity precision, accuracy, and other critical thinking standards.	Often think in ways that are unclear, imprecise, and inaccurate.
Are sensitive to ways in which critical thinking can be skewed by egocentrism, sociocentrism, wishful thinking, and other impediments.	Often fall prey to egocentrism, sociocentrism, relativistic thinking, unwarranted assumptions, and wishful thinking.
Understand the value of critical thinking, both to individuals and to society as a whole.	See little value in critical thinking.
Are intellectually honest with themselves, acknowledging what they don't know and recognizing their limitations.	Pretend they know more than they do and ignore their limitations.
Listen open-mindedly to opposing points of view and welcome criticisms of beliefs and assumptions.	Are close-minded and resist criticisms of beliefs and assumptions.
Base their beliefs on facts and evidence rather than on personal preference or self-interest.	Often base beliefs on mere personal preference or self-interest.
Are aware of the biases and preconceptions that shape the way they perceive the world.	Lack awareness of their own biases and preconceptions.
Think independently and are not afraid to disagree with group opinion.	Tend to engage in "groupthink," uncritically following the beliefs and values of the crowd.
Are able to get to the heart of an issue or a problem, without being distracted by details.	Are easily distracted and lack the ability to zero in on the essence of an issue or a problem.
Have the intellectual courage to face and assess fairly ideas that challenge even their most basic beliefs.	Fear and resist ideas that challenge their basic beliefs.
Pursue truth and are curious about a wide range of issues.	Are often relatively indifferent to truth and lack curiosity.
Have the intellectual perseverance to pursue insights or truths despite obstacles or difficulties.	Tend not to persevere when they encounter intellectual obstacles or difficulties.

Character is destiny.
—Heraclitus

To become a criti-
cal thinker is not,
in the end, to be
the same person
you are now, only
with better abili-
ties; it is, in an
important sense,
to become a dif-
ferent person.
—Gerald Nosich

A course in critical thinking is like most other things in life: You get out of it what you put into it. If you approach critical thinking as a chore—a pointless general education requirement you need to get out of the way before you can turn to more "relevant" courses in your major—a chore it will be. On the other hand, if you approach critical thinking as an opportunity to learn habits of disciplined thinking that are vital to success in school, in your career, and in your life as a liberally educated person, critical thinking can be a rewarding and even transformative experience. The choice is yours. Good luck and enjoy!

EXERCISE 1.6

I. Review the list of critical thinking traits on page 27, then write a 250-word essay in which you address the following questions: Which of the traits listed do you think is your strongest critical thinking trait? Why? Which is your weakest? Why? What could you do to improve in this latter regard? Be specific and realistic.

II. In groups of three or four, define the following critical thinking traits: intellectual honesty, open-mindedness, fair-mindedness, intellectual courage, and intellectual perseverance. (See the list of critical thinking traits on page 27 for some broad hints.) Give an example of each.

III. In groups of three or four, think of examples, either from your experience or from your knowledge of current events or history, of individuals who possess, or did possess, the quality of intellectual courage to an unusual degree. What about them leads you to think of them as being especially intellectually courageous? Do the same for the qualities of open-mindedness, intellectual honesty, and intellectual perseverance. Be prepared to share your group's best examples with the class.

IV. Read W. K. Clifford's essay "The Ethics of Belief" and William James's essay "The Will to Believe" (both widely available on the Internet). Write a 750-word essay in which you address the following questions: Is it always wrong to believe something for which one lacks sufficient evidence? Is "faith" inconsistent with critical thinking?

SUMMARY

1. *Critical thinking* is the general term given to a wide range of cognitive skills and intellectual dispositions needed to effectively identify, analyze, and evaluate arguments and truth claims; to discover and overcome personal prejudices and biases; to formulate and present convincing reasons in support of conclusions; and to make reasonable, intelligent decisions about what to believe and what to do. It is disciplined thinking governed by clear intellectual standards that have proven their value over the course of human history. Among the most important of these intellectual standards

are clarity, precision, accuracy, relevance, consistency, logical correctness, completeness, and fairness.

2. Critical thinking is beneficial for many reasons. It can help students do better in school by improving their ability to understand, construct, and criticize arguments. It can help people succeed in their careers by improving their ability to solve problems, think creatively, and communicate their ideas clearly and effectively. It can also reduce the likelihood of making serious mistakes in important personal decisions, promote democratic processes by improving the quality of public decision making, and liberate and empower individuals by freeing them from the unexamined assumptions, dogmas, and prejudices of their upbringing, their society, and their age.

> *To learn is to face transformation.*
> —Parker J. Palmer

3. Major barriers to critical thinking include egocentrism, sociocentrism, unwarranted assumptions, relativistic thinking, and wishful thinking.

   Egocentrism is the tendency to see reality as centered on oneself. Two common forms of egocentrism are self-interested thinking (the tendency to accept and defend beliefs that accord with one's own self-interest) and self-serving bias (the tendency to overrate oneself).

   Sociocentrism is group-centered thinking. Two common varieties of sociocentrism are group bias (the tendency to see one's culture or group as being better than others) and conformism (the tendency to conform, often unthinkingly, to authority or to group standards of conduct and belief).

   Unwarranted assumptions are things we take for granted without good reason. Often, unwarranted assumptions take the form of stereotypes. *Stereotypes* are generalizations about a group of people in which identical characteristics are assigned to all or virtually all members of the group, often without regard to whether such attributions are accurate.

   Relativistic thinking is thinking that is based on the idea that there is no "objective" or "absolute" truth because truth is simply a matter of opinion. The most popular form of relativism is *moral relativism,* which holds that what is morally right and good varies from individual to individual (*moral subjectivism*) or from culture to culture (*cultural moral relativism*).

   Wishful thinking is believing something because it makes one feel good, not because there is good reason for thinking that it is true.

4. Critical thinkers exhibit a number of traits that distinguish them from uncritical thinkers. Among the most important of these traits are a passionate drive for clarity, precision, accuracy, and other intellectual standards that characterize careful, disciplined thinking; a sensitivity to the ways in which critical thinking can be skewed by egocentrism, wishful thinking, and other psychological obstacles to rational belief; honesty and intellectual humility; open-mindedness; intellectual courage; love of truth; and intellectual perseverance.

CHAPTER 2

RECOGNIZING ARGUMENTS

As we saw in the previous chapter, critical thinking is centrally concerned with *reasons:* identifying reasons, evaluating reasons, and giving reasons. In critical thinking, passages that present reasons for a claim are called *arguments.* In this chapter we explore the concept of an argument and explain how to distinguish arguments from nonarguments.

WHAT IS AN ARGUMENT?

When people hear the word *argument,* they usually think of some kind of quarrel or shouting match. In critical thinking, however, an argument is simply a claim defended with reasons.

Arguments are composed of one or more premises and a conclusion. **Premises** are statements in an argument offered as evidence or reasons why we should accept another statement, the conclusion. The **conclusion** is the statement in an argument that the premises are intended to prove or support. An **argument,** accordingly, is a group of statements, one or more of which (called the premises) are intended to prove or support another statement (called the conclusion).

A **statement** is a sentence that can be viewed as either true or false.[1] Here are some examples of statements:

Red is a color.

Canada is in South America.

God does not exist.

Abortion is morally wrong.

Shrek II is a better movie than *Pirates of the Caribbean.*

Some of these statements are clearly true, some are clearly false, and some are controversial. Each of them is a statement, however, because each can be prefaced with the phrase "It is true that" or "It is false that."

Four things should be noted about statements. First, a sentence may be used to express more than one statement. For example, the grammatical sentence

> Roses are red and violets are blue

expresses two distinct statements ("Roses are red" and "Violets are blue"). Each of these is a statement because each is capable of standing alone as a declarative sentence.

Second, a statement can sometimes be expressed as a phrase or an incomplete clause, rather than as a complete declarative sentence. Consider the sentence

> With mortgage interest rates at thirty-year lows, you owe it to yourself to consider refinancing your home. (radio ad)

Grammatically, this is a single declarative sentence. The speaker's intent, however, is clearly to defend one assertion ("You owe it to yourself to consider refinancing your home") on the basis of another ("Mortgage interest rates are at thirty-year lows"). The fact that we have to rephrase the sentence slightly to make this explicit should not obscure the fact that two statements are being offered rather than one.

Third, not all sentences are statements, that is, sentences that either assert or deny that something is the case. Here are some examples of sentences that are not statements:

> What time is it? (question)
> Hi, Dad! (greeting)
> Close the window! (command)
> Please send me your current catalog. (request)
> Let's go to Paris for our anniversary. (proposal)
> Insert tab A into slot B. (instruction)
> Oh, my goodness! (exclamation)

None of these is a statement because none of them asserts or denies that anything is the case. None says, in effect, "This is a fact. Accept this; it is true." Consequently, sentences like these are not parts of arguments.

Finally, statements can be about subjective matters of personal experience as well as objectively verifiable matters of fact. If I say, for example,

> I feel a slight twinge in my left knee

this is a statement because it is either true or false (I might be lying, after all), even though other people may have no way of verifying whether I am telling the truth.

Not all sentences, however, are as they appear. Some sentences that look like nonstatements are actually statements and can be used in arguments. Here are two examples:

> Alyssa, you should quit smoking. Don't you realize how bad that is for your health?
>
> *Commencement address:* Do not read beauty magazines. They will only make you feel ugly. (Mary Schmich)

The first example contains a rhetorical question. A **rhetorical question** is a sentence that has the grammatical form of a question but is meant to be understood as a statement. In our example, the person asking the question isn't really looking for information. She's making an assertion: that smoking is very bad for one's health. This assertion is offered as a reason (premise) to support the conclusion that Alyssa should quit smoking.

The second example includes an **ought imperative,** that is, a sentence that has the form of an imperative or command but is intended to assert a value or ought judgment about what is good or bad or right or wrong. Grammatically, "Do not read beauty magazines" looks like a command or suggestion. In this context, however, the speaker is clearly making an assertion: that you *shouldn't* read beauty magazines. Her statement that reading such magazines will only make you feel ugly is offered as a reason to support this value judgment.

How can we tell when a sentence that looks like a command or suggestion is really an ought imperative? The key question to ask is this: Can we accurately rephrase the sentence so that it refers to what someone should or ought to do? If we can, the sentence should be regarded as a statement.

Consider two further examples. Suppose a drill sergeant says to a new recruit,

> Close that window, soldier! It's freezing in here!

In this context it is clear that the sergeant is issuing an order rather than expressing an ought judgment ("You *ought* to close that window, soldier!"). On the other hand, if one roommate were to say to another,

> Don't blow-dry your hair in the tub, Bert! You could electrocute yourself!

it is likely that the roommate is expressing an ought judgment ("You *shouldn't* blow-dry your hair in the tub!"), rather than issuing an order or making a mere suggestion.

As these examples make clear, it is always important to consider the context in which an expression is used. A sentence such as "Eat your vegetables" might be a command (nonstatement) in one context and an ought imperative (statement) in another.

To recap: Imperative sentences are not statements if they are intended as orders, suggestions, proposals, or exhortations. They are statements if they are intended as pieces of advice or value judgments about what someone ought or ought not to do.

┌───┐
│ **• Critical Thinking Lapse •**   │
│   │
│ A nineteen-year-old man was hospitalized in Salt Lake   │
│ City after undertaking a personal investigation into   │
│ the eternal question of whether it is possible to fire   │
│ a .22-caliber bullet by placing it inside a straw and   │
│ striking it with a hammer. Answer: Sometimes (including │
│ this time); it went off and hit him in the stomach.[2]   │
└───┘

EXERCISE 2.1

I. Determine whether, in typical contexts, the following sentences are or are not statements. Exercises marked with the icon (○) are answered in the back of the book.

○ 1. Capital punishment is wrong.
    2. Can I get you something to drink?
    3. Ted Williams is the greatest hitter in baseball history.
○ 4. What do you say we stop at the next rest stop?
    5. Abraham Lincoln was the first president of the United States.
    6. Let's party!
○ 7. Great!
    8. Keep off the grass. (sign)
    9. If Sally calls, tell her I'm at the library.
○ 10. I hope Peter likes his new job.
  11. Can't you see that pornography demeans women?
  12. Holy cow!
○ 13. Please print your name legibly.
  14. What will it profit a man, if he gains the whole world and forfeits his life? (Matt. 16:26)
  15. You want mayo on that, right?
○ 16. What a crock!
  17. Give me a call if you have trouble downloading the file.
  18. Blondes are more attractive than brunettes.
○ 19. I'll have a cheeseburger and fries, please. (said to a fast-food restaurant employee)
  20. Give us this day our daily bread. (said in prayer)
  21. Smoke 'em if you've got 'em.
○ 22. Mi casa es su casa.
  23. Don't you realize how silly that hat looks?
  24. What's love but a second-hand emotion? (Tina Turner)
○ 25. Yikes!

II. Determine whether the following passages do or do not contain ought imperatives.

○ 1. Be nice to your kids. They'll choose your nursing home. (bumper sticker)
    2. Toby, never throw a pen at your sister! You could put an eye out! (said by Toby's mother)

3. I'm just a soul whose intentions are good. O, Lord, please don't let me be misunderstood. (Santa Esmeralda song)

4. If you consume three or more alcoholic drinks every day, ask your doctor whether you should take ibuprofen or other pain relievers/fever reducers. Ibuprofen may cause stomach bleeding. (label)

5. Why don't we eat at El Grande Burrito tonight. I feel like Mexican.

6. If you do not get your first meal service choice, please do not be distressed, as all our entrées taste very much the same. (flight attendant)

7. Turn off your engine when waiting to pick up the kids. Idling longer than ten seconds in park uses more gas than restarting the car. (Al Gore)

8. In batting practice you must make a point of leaving the bad pitches alone. You don't want your reflexes to get into bad habits. (Mickey Mantle)

9. Don't bother buying premium gas if your car specifies regular. It won't make your car go faster or operate more efficiently—and it's about 14 percent more expensive. (*Consumer Reports* advertising brochure)

10. Up, sluggard, and waste not life; in the grave will be sleeping enough. (Benjamin Franklin)

11. I never use a whistle in practice. I want the players to get used to reacting to my voice—just like in a real game. (basketball coach Mike Krzyzewski)

12. Associate not with evil men, lest you increase their number. (George Herbert)

13. If you play [poker] enough, accept that from time to time you are going to go bust, because from time to time, everyone, even the best of the best, does. (Doc Holliday)

14. Don't expect people to be friendly. When they're not, you won't be surprised or bothered. If they are, you'll be delighted. (Richard Carlson)

15. O Lord, won't you buy me a Mercedes Benz? My friends all drive Porsches; I must make amends. (Janis Joplin)

16. Borrow money from pessimists—they don't expect it back. (Steven Wright)

IDENTIFYING PREMISES AND CONCLUSIONS

In identifying premises and conclusions, we are often helped by indicator words. **Indicator words** are words or phrases that provide clues that premises or conclusions are being put forward. **Premise indicators** indicate that premises are being offered, and **conclusion indicators** indicate that conclusions are being offered. Here are some common premise indicators:

since	because
for	given that
seeing that	considering that
inasmuch as	as

in view of the fact that   as indicated by

judging from   on account of

The following examples illustrate the use of premise indicators:

Having fun can be the spice of life but not its main course, *because* when it is over, nothing of lasting value remains. (Harold Kushner)

Since effective reasoning requires reliable information, it's important to be able to distinguish good sources and trustworthy experts from less useful ones. (Drew E. Hinderer)

Women are not by any means to blame when they reject the rules of life, which have been introduced into the world, *seeing that* it is men who have made them without their consent. (Michel de Montaigne)

To know that God exists in a general and confused way is implanted in us by nature, *inasmuch as* God is man's beatitude. (Saint Thomas Aquinas)

I think that, *as* life is action and passion, it is required of a man that he should share the passion and action of his time, at peril of being judged not to have lived. (Oliver Wendell Holmes Jr.)

And here are some common conclusion indicators:

therefore   thus

hence   consequently

so   accordingly

it follows that   for this reason

that is why   which shows that

wherefore   this implies that

as a result   this suggests that

this being so   we may infer that

These examples illustrate the use of conclusion indicators:

You want people to be honest with you, *so* be honest with them.

Sorrow is merely a state of mind and may not be warranted by the circumstance. *Hence* whether or not you feel sad over something is all in the mind. (Lie Zi)

Rapid economic improvements represent a life-or-death imperative throughout the Third World. Its people will not be denied that hope, no matter the environmental costs. *As a result,* that choice must not be forced upon them. (Al Gore)

Your life is what your thoughts make it. *That is why* it is important for all of us to guard our minds from unhealthy habits of thinking, habits that hold us back from what we could be accomplishing. (Tom Morris)

As our birth brought us the birth of all things, so will our death bring us the death of all things. *Wherefore* it is as foolish to weep because a hundred years from now we shall not be alive, as to weep because we were not living a hundred years ago. (Michel de Montaigne)

Understanding arguments would be easier if the expressions just listed were used only to signal premises or conclusions. That is not the case, however, as the following examples illustrate:

I haven't seen you *since* high school.

You've had that jacket *for* as long as I've known you.

Thus far everything has been great.

It was *so* cold that even the ski resorts shut down.

I wouldn't mind *seeing that* movie again.

There is water on the floor *because* the sink overflowed.

In none of these examples does the italicized term function as an indicator word. This shows once again why it's so important to consider the context when determining the meaning of an expression.

Many arguments contain no indicator words at all. Here are two examples:

Cats are smarter than dogs. You can't get eight cats to pull a sled through snow. (Jeff Valdez)

I can't be completely responsible for my life. After all, there are many factors outside my control, people and forces that create obstacles and undermine my efforts. And we are subject to pressures and influences from within ourselves: feelings of greed, fear of death, altruistic impulses, sexual compulsions, need for social acceptance, and so on. (John Chaffee, emphasis omitted)

In these passages, there are no indicator words to help us identify the premises and conclusions. Reading carefully, however, we can see that the point of the first passage is to support the claim, "Cats are smarter than dogs," and the point of the second passage is to support the claim, "I can't be completely responsible for my life."

How can we find the conclusion of an argument when the argument contains no indicator words? The following list provides some helpful hints.

Tips on Finding the Conclusion of an Argument

- Find the main issue and ask yourself what position the writer or speaker is taking on that issue.
- Look at the beginning or end of the passage; the conclusion is often (but not always) found in one of those places.
- Ask yourself, "What is the writer or speaker trying to prove?" That will be the conclusion.
- Try putting the word *therefore* before one of the statements. If it fits, that statement is probably the conclusion.
- Try the "because trick." That is, try to find the most appropriate way to fill in the blanks in the following statement: The writer or speaker believes _____ (conclusion) because _____ (premise). The conclusion will naturally come before the word *because*.[3]

The following exercises will give you practice in identifying premises and conclusions.

EXERCISE 2.2

I. Identify the premises and conclusions in the following arguments.

1. Since pain is a state of consciousness, a "mental event," it can never be directly observed. (Peter Singer, "Animal Liberation")

2. You cannot step twice in the same river, for other waters are ever flowing on to you. (Heraclitus)

3. Because so many of the matters of real concern to us center on controversial moral issues, it is important to know how to construct and evaluate moral arguments effectively. (T. Edward Damer, *Attacking Faulty Arguments,* 4th ed.)

4. Business is the art of growth. Growth is the essence of life. And so our answer quickly follows. Business is the art of life. (Tom Morris, *If Aristotle Ran General Motors*)

5. Many just persons are afflicted in this world; which is unjust. Therefore not in every work of God are justice and mercy. (stated but not endorsed in Saint Thomas Aquinas, *Summa Theologica*)

6. There is no definitive way to prove any one set of religious beliefs to the exclusion of all others. For that reason religious freedom is a human right. (Richard Paul and Linda Elder, *The Miniature Guide to Understanding the Foundations of Ethical Reasoning*)

7. Science is based on experiment, on a willingness to challenge old dogma, on an openness to see the universe as it really is. Accordingly, science sometimes requires courage—at the very least the courage to question the conventional wisdom. (Carl Sagan, *Broca's Brain: Reflections on the Romance of Science*)

8. Do not play your sound system loudly as you may not be able to hear warning sirens from emergency vehicles. In addition, hearing damage from loud noise is almost undetectable until it's too late. (car owner's manual)

9. The invention or discovery of symbols is doubtless by far the single greatest event in the history of man. Without them, no intellectual advance is possible; with them, there is no limit set to intellectual development except inherent stupidity. (John Dewey, *The Quest for Certainty*)

10. You know how I know animals have souls? Because on average, the lowest animal is a lot nicer and kinder than most of the human beings that inhabit this Earth. (newspaper call-in column)

11. Democracy has at least one merit, namely, that a member of Parliament cannot be stupider than his constituents, for the more stupid he is, the more stupid they were to elect him. (Bertrand Russell, *Autobiography*)

12. Don't worry about senility. When it hits you, you won't know it. (Bill Cosby, *Time Flies*)

13. There is nothing wrong with burning crude [oil] like crazy—oil isn't helping anyone when it sits in the ground—so long as there's a plan for

energy alternatives when the cheap oil runs out. (Gregg Easterbrook, "Opportunity Costs")

14. There is no doubt that certain events recorded at seances are genuine. Who does not recall the famous incident at Sybil Seretsky's when her goldfish sang "I Got Rhythm"—a favorite tune of her recently deceased nephew? (Woody Allen, *Without Feathers*)

15. So far the states are spending more than 90 percent of the tobacco-settlement money on programs unrelated to smoking, such as building highways. This is good, because we need quality highways to handle the sharp increase in the number of Mercedes automobiles purchased by lawyers enriched by the tobacco settlement. (Dave Barry, "War on Smoking Always Has Room for Another Lawyer")

16. It's part of human nature to be angry at God when bad things happen, but what's the point? If we encourage each other to blame God for injustices, then aren't we giving the evil or dark side a victory by keeping God's precious children—that's all of us—away from His loving arms? (letter to the editor)

17. In great contests each party claims to act in accordance with the will of God. Both may be, and one must be, wrong. God cannot be for and against the same thing at the same time. (Abraham Lincoln, "Meditation on the Divine Will")

18. There seems to be a tacit assumption that if grizzlies survive in Canada and Alaska, that is good enough. It is not good enough for me. The Alaska bears are a distinct species. Relegating grizzlies to Alaska is about like relegating happiness to heaven; one may never get there. (Aldo Leopold, *A Sand County Almanac*)

19. Has it ever occurred to you how lucky you are to be alive? More than 99% of all creatures that have ever lived have died without progeny, but not a single one of your ancestors falls into this group! (Daniel C. Dennett, *Darwin's Dangerous Idea*)

20. Men love the suit so much, we've actually styled our pajamas to look like a tiny suit. Our pajamas have little lapels, little cuffs, simulated breast pockets. Do you need a breast pocket on your pajamas? You put a pen in there, you roll over in the middle of the night, you kill yourself. (Jerry Seinfeld, *SeinLanguage*)

II. Identify the premises and conclusions in the following arguments.

1. When the universe has crushed him man will still be nobler than that which kills him, because he knows that he is dying, and of its victory the universe knows nothing. (Blaise Pascal, *Pensées*)

2. Rights are either God-given or evolve out of the democratic process. Most rights are based on the ability of people to agree on a social contract, the ability to make and keep agreements. Animals cannot possibly reach such an agreement with other creatures. They cannot respect anyone else's rights. Therefore they cannot be said to have rights. (Rush Limbaugh, *The Way Things Ought to Be*)

3. Parenting is about drawing clear moral boundaries and enforcing acceptable limits to produce conscience and compassion in children. To do otherwise is to create kids who think their rights and interests supersede those of others. (Kathleen Parker, "The Sin of Pride Is Killing Our Children")

4. Since moral responsibility presupposes free-will, since this freedom is not compatible with universal causal determinism, and since universal causal determinism appears to be the case, it seems evident that—contrary to what most people believe—human beings are not morally responsible. (stated but not endorsed in William H. Halverson, *A Concise Introduction to Philosophy,* 4th ed. [adapted])

5. Our faith comes in moments; our vice is habitual. Yet there is a depth in those brief moments which constrains us to ascribe more reality to them than to all other experiences. For this reason the argument which is always forthcoming to silence those who conceive extraordinary hopes of man, namely the appeal to experience, is forever invalid and vain. (Ralph Waldo Emerson, "The Over-Soul")

6. The travel rule I will stress here is: Never trust anything you read in travel articles. Travel articles appear in publications that sell large, expensive advertisements to tourism-related industries, and these industries do not wish to see articles with headlines like: "URUGUAY: DON'T BOTHER". So no matter what kind of leech-infested, plumbing-free destination travel writers are writing about, they always stress the positive. (Dave Barry, *Dave Barry's Greatest Hits;* emphasis omitted)

7. How can anyone in his right mind criticize the state police for the speed traps? If you're not speeding, you don't have to worry about them. It could save your life if some other speeder is stopped. (newspaper call-in column)

8. Philosophy is dangerous whenever it is taken seriously. But so is life. Safety is not an option. Our choices, then, are not between risk and security, but between a life lived consciously, fully, humanly in the most complete sense and a life that just happens. (Douglas J. Soccio, *Archetypes of Wisdom,* 3rd ed.)

9. Our nation protests, encourages, and even intervenes in the affairs of other nations on the basis of its relations to corporations. But if this is the case, how can we dissociate ourselves from the plight of people in these countries? (Louis P. Pojman, *Global Environmental Ethics*)

10. If a man say, "I love God," and hateth his brother, he is a liar: for he that loveth not his brother whom he hath seen, how can he love God whom he hath not seen? (I John 4:20)

11. Each of us has an intellectual dimension to his experience. We need ideas as much as we need food, air, or water. Ideas nourish the mind as the latter provide for the body. In light of this, it's clear that we need good ideas as much as we need good food, good air, and good water. (Tom Morris, *If Aristotle Ran General Motors*)

12. What is right in one place may be wrong in another, because the only criterion for distinguishing right from wrong—and so the only ethical

standard for judging an action—is the moral system of the society in which the act occurs. (stated but not endorsed in William H. Shaw, *Business Ethics,* 4th ed.)

13. Whether you like it or not, you'd better accept reality the way it occurs: as highly imperfect and filled with most fallible human beings. Your alternative? Continual anxiety and desperate disappointments. (Albert Ellis and Robert A. Harper, *A New Guide to Rational Living*)

14. We should be emotionally reconciled to the fact of death, rather than fearing it, once we understand that death is necessary for two important, and very positive, things. First, it's necessary for our appreciation of life. The more vivid our sense of the approach of death, the more we relish the small things in life. And secondly, death is necessary for the continued march of evolutionary improvement, an ongoing progress leading to more valuable states of good, to take place on earth. (Tom Morris, *Philosophy for Dummies*)

15. It is a scientific fact that 1974 was the worst year in world history for rock music. And I am NOT saying this because among the top musical acts to emerge that year were Abba AND Barry Manilow. I am saying it because the hit songs included "Kung Fu Fighting," "Seasons in the Sun," "Billy Don't Be a Hero," "The Night Chicago Died" and "(You're) Having My Baby." (Dave Barry, *Dave Barry Turns 50*)

16. Getting in your run early certainly has its advantages. Those who develop the first-thing-in-the-morning routine tend to be more consistent in their training. . . . Morning runs also avoid the heat and peak air pollution. You can enjoy your run without carrying along all the stress that builds up during the day. Early-morning runs . . . save time too by combining your morning and postrun shower. (Bob Glover and Shelly-lynn Florence Glover, *The Competitive Runner's Handbook*)

17. Guys accuse me of constantly singing the praises of Duke [University's men's basketball program]. Well, what is there not to like? You go there and it has everything you dream about in college basketball. Guys play hard. They go to class. They do things the right way. They have discipline. They go out and win. The crowd is behind them. (Dick Vitale, *Campus Chaos*)

18. I wish that someone would give a course in how to live. It can't be taught in the colleges: that's perfectly obvious, for college professors don't know any better than the rest of us. (A. Edward Newton, *The Book-Collecting Game*)

19. Shop at the farmer's market. You'll begin to eat food in season, when they are at the peak of their nutritional value and flavor, and you'll cook, because you won't find anything processed or microwavable. You'll also be supporting farmers in your community, helping defend the countryside from sprawl, saving oil by eating food produced nearby, and teaching your children that a carrot is a root, not a machine-lathed orange bullet that comes in a plastic bag. (Michael Pollan, "Six Reasons for Eating Wisely")

20. The next time you find yourself in an argument, rather than defend your position, see if you can see the other point of view first. . . . When you

• Critical Thinking Lapse •

Larry Walters, a thirty-three-year-old truck driver from North Holly-wood, California, had always dreamed about flying. So, on July 2, 1982, Walters tied forty-two Army surplus weather balloons to an aluminum lawn chair, strapped himself in, and cut himself loose.

Walters expected to float lazily over the housetops. Instead, he shot up to 16,000 feet.

Soon Walters found himself drifting into the main approach corridor of Los Angeles International Airport. Shivering with cold, he managed to get himself down by shooting out some balloons with a pellet gun.

Eventually, Walters crashed into some power lines, briefly blacking out a small area in Long Beach.

When asked why he had done it, Walters simply replied, "A man can't just sit around."[4]

understand other positions and points of view, several wonderful things begin to happen. First, you often learn something new . . . [and] expand your horizons. Second, when the person you are talking to feels listened to, he or she will appreciate and respect you far more than when you habitually jump in with your own position. . . . A side benefit is that the person you are speaking to may even listen to your point of view. (Richard Carlson, *Don't Sweat the Small Stuff . . . And It's All Small Stuff*)

WHAT IS NOT AN ARGUMENT?

We encounter arguments everywhere in daily life—at school, at work, in magazine ads, in newspaper editorials, in political discussions, in television documentaries, and on radio talk shows. Of course, people don't use language only to offer arguments: they also use it to tell jokes, sing songs, recite poetry, express feelings, report events, ask questions, offer explanations, say prayers, give orders, and exchange wedding vows. How then can we distinguish arguments from nonarguments?

The basic test is quite simple. Something counts as an argument when (1) it is a group of two or more statements and (2) one of those statements (the conclusion) is claimed or intended to be supported by the others (the premises). By applying this simple test, we can usually tell whether a given passage is or is not an argument. Now let's look at five types of nonargumentative discourse that are sometimes confused with arguments:

- reports
- unsupported assertions
- conditional statements

- illustrations
- explanations

Reports

The purpose of a **report** is simply to convey information about a subject. Here is an example of a report:

> Sweeping changes occurred in demographics, economics, culture, and society during the last quarter of the 20th century. The nation aged, and more of its people gravitated to the Sunbelt. Sprawling "urban corridors" and "edge cities" challenged older central cities as sites for commercial, as well as residential, development. Rapid technological change fueled the growth of globalized industries, restructuring the labor force to fit a "postindustrial" economy.[5]

In this passage, the authors are simply reporting a series of events; their aim is to narrate and inform, not to offer reasons why one statement should be accepted on the basis of others.

Caution is needed, however, with reports *about* arguments. Here is an example of such a passage:

> Government is legitimate, according to Hobbes, because living under a government is better than living in a state of nature. The advantages of government are so great that it is worth sacrificing some of our freedom in order to bring about these advantages. For this reason, rational people would consent to sign a social contract and subject themselves to the laws and powers of a government.[6]

This is not an argument because the author is merely reporting another person's argument, not endorsing it or putting it forward as his own.

Unsupported Assertions

Unsupported assertions are statements about what a speaker or writer happens to believe. Such statements can be true or false, rational or irrational, but they are parts of arguments only if the speaker or writer claims that they follow from, or support, other claims. Here is an example of a series of unsupported assertions:

> I believe that it is not dying that people are afraid of. Something else, something more unsettling and more tragic than dying frightens us. We are afraid of never having lived, of coming to the end of our days with the sense that we were never really alive, that we never figured out what life was for.[7]

Few may think, yet all have opinions.
—George Berkeley

Because there is no claim that any of these statements follow from, or imply, any other statements, this is not an argument.

Conditional Statements

A conditional statement is an *if-then* statement. Here are several examples:

If it rains, then the picnic will be canceled.
You must speak French if you grew up in Quebec.
If at first you don't succeed, don't try skydiving.

Conditional statements are made up of two basic parts. The first part, the statement(s) following the word *if,* is called the **antecedent.** The second part, the statement(s) following the word *then,* is called the **consequent.**

Conditional statements need not be explicitly in *if-then* form; in fact, in modern usage, *then* is usually dropped. For example, the following statements are conditional statements:

> Should it rain, the picnic will be canceled.
>
> In the event of rain, the picnic will be canceled.
>
> Pete will graduate, provided he passes Critical Thinking.

Conditional statements are not arguments, because there is no claim that any statement *follows* from any part of a conditional statement. Thus, if I say, "If it rains, the picnic will be canceled," I'm not asserting either that it will rain or that the picnic will be canceled. I'm only asserting that *if* the first statement is true, the second statement will also be true. Because there is no claim that any statement follows from, or supports, this conditional statement, no argument has been given.

Although conditional statements are not arguments, some conditional statements do involve a process of reasoning. Thus, if I say, for example,

> If Rhode Island were larger than Ohio, and Ohio were larger than Texas, then Rhode Island would be larger than Texas

it may appear that I have reasoned to a conclusion, and thus offered an argument. In fact, however, no argument has been given. All I have asserted is that *if* the first two statements are true, then the third statement must also be true. I have not claimed that any of these statements *are* true. Thus, I have not put forward any premises or reasoned to any conclusion. In fact, I have asserted only a single claim: that one statement is true *on the condition* that two other statements are true. Certainly, this claim was arrived at by a process of reasoning, but that does not mean that it is an argument. As we have seen, no single claim by itself is ever an argument.

Conditional statements, accordingly, are not arguments. They can, however, be *parts* of arguments. For example:

> If Sturdley fails Critical Thinking, he'll be placed on academic probation.
>
> Sturdley will fail Critical Thinking.
>
> So, Sturdley will be placed on academic probation.

In fact, arguments can be composed entirely of conditional statements:

> If Tech scores on this play, I'll eat my hat.
>
> If I eat my hat, I'll have a bad case of indigestion.
>
> So, if Tech scores on this play, I'll have a bad case of indigestion.

Such arguments are sometimes called **chain arguments** because the antecedent (the *if* part) of the first statement is linked to the consequent (the *then* part) of the last statement by a chain of intervening conditional statements.

Illustrations

Illustrations are intended to provide *examples* of a claim, rather than prove or support the claim. Here is an example:

> Many wildflowers are edible. For example, daisies and day lilies are delicious in salads.

Even though the second statement does provide some evidence for the first, this passage is an illustration rather than an argument. Its purpose is not to provide convincing evidence for a conclusion but merely to provide a few notable or representative examples of a claim.

Distinguishing arguments from illustrations can be tricky for two reasons. First, phrases like *for example* and *for instance* sometimes occur in arguments rather than in illustrations. For example:

> Purists sometimes insist that we should say *between* when two and only two objects are present, *among* if there are more than two. This, however, is an oversimplification. For example, no one would object to *between* in "*The main stumbling block in the present delicate exchanges between Paris, Athens, London and Ankara . . .*"[8]

Second, there is sometimes a fine line between illustrating a claim and providing sufficient evidence for the claim. Consider the following:

> Many of the world's greatest philosophers were bachelors. For instance, Descartes, Locke, Hume, and Kant were all unmarried.

This is a borderline case between an argument and an illustration. Without more information, we cannot tell whether the author's purpose was to provide convincing evidence for a claim or merely to illustrate the claim. Such cases are fairly commonplace and rarely pose any serious difficulty. The general rule here, as with other borderline cases, is simple. Critical thinkers call it the *principle of charity* (see box on page 45).

Applying this simple principle can resolve many otherwise troublesome cases quickly and easily. In the previous example, for instance, it is doubtful whether the four philosophers cited provide sufficient evidence for the claim that "many" of the world's greatest philosophers have been bachelors. It is better, therefore, to treat these as illustrations of the claim rather than as evidence intended to prove the claim.

> *Read not to contradict and confute, nor to believe and take for granted . . . but to weigh and consider.*
>
> —Francis Bacon

Explanations

Consider the following two statements:

> *Titanic* sank because it struck an iceberg.
>
> Capital punishment should be abolished because innocent people may be mistakenly executed.

On the surface, these two statements look very much alike. Both give reasons, and both use the indicator word *because*. There is, however, an important

The Principle of Charity

When interpreting an unclear passage, always give the speaker or writer the benefit of the doubt. Never attribute to an arguer a *weaker* argument when the evidence reasonably permits us to attribute to him or her a *stronger* one. And never interpret a passage as a *bad argument* when the evidence reasonably permits us to interpret it as *not an argument at all*.

difference between the two: The first statement is an explanation and the second is an argument.

An **explanation** tries to show *why* something is the case, not to prove *that* it is the case. In the first example, for instance, it is clear that the speaker isn't trying to argue *that Titanic* sank—everybody already knows that it sank. Instead, he is trying to explain *why* it sank. Of course, you can argue about whether a given explanation is or is not correct. Consider this example:

Dinosaurs became extinct because of the impact of a large asteroid.

Scientists argue vigorously about whether this is the correct explanation of the apparently sudden extinction of the dinosaurs sixty-five million years ago. But the fact that this explanation is controversial (i.e., can be argued about) doesn't mean that it is an argument. The purpose of the passage is not to argue *that* dinosaurs became extinct but to explain *why* they became extinct.

Explanations have two parts. The statement that is explained is the **explanandum.** The statement that does the explaining is the **explanans.** Thus, in the explanation

I fell down because I tripped

the statement "I fell down" is the explanandum, and the statement "I tripped" is the explanans.

In everyday speech, we often use "argument" and "explanation" almost interchangeably. Thus, we might say, for example, that the second speaker above is "explaining" why capital punishment should be abolished. This loose way of speaking no doubt contributes greatly to the confusion many students feel in distinguishing arguments from explanations.

Nevertheless, it is important to be able to distinguish arguments from explanations because the standards for evaluating them are quite different. The fact that Schlomo likes mystery stories may be a more or less satisfactory explanation of *why* he is now reading Sir Arthur Conan Doyle's *The Hound of the Baskervilles,* but plainly it is not a good reason for thinking *that* he is now reading that particular book.

How then does one distinguish arguments from explanations? There are four basic tests.

The Common-Knowledge Test   First, is the statement that the passage seeks to prove or explain a matter of common knowledge? If it is, the passage is probably an explanation rather than an argument. (There's usually little point in trying to prove something that is already a well-known fact.) Thus, the passage

> The North won the American Civil War because it had a larger population and a greater industrial base

is clearly an explanation rather than an argument because it is common knowledge that the North won the Civil War.

The Past-Event Test   Second, is the statement that the passage is seeking to prove or explain an event that occurred in the past? If so, the passage is probably an explanation rather than an argument because it is much more common to try to explain *why* past events have occurred rather than to prove *that* they occurred. Thus, the passage

> Mel flunked out because he never went to class

is best viewed as an explanation because the speaker is referring to a past event, and we usually try to explain such events rather than provide convincing evidence that they have happened.

The Author's Intent Test   Third, is it the speaker's or writer's intent to prove or establish *that* something is the case—that is, *to provide reasons or evidence for accepting a claim as true*? Or is it his intent to explain *why* something is the case—that is, *to offer an account of why some event has occurred or why something is the way it is*? If the former, the passage is an argument; if the latter, the passage is an explanation. Consider this example:

> Kevin is majoring in political science because he wants to go to law school.

Here it is unlikely that the speaker is trying to prove that Kevin is majoring in political science, for the "evidence" offered (the fact that Kevin wants to go to law school) would clearly be insufficient to establish that conclusion. It is therefore more likely that the speaker is offering an explanation rather than an argument.

The Principle of Charity Test   Fourth, the principle of charity, as we have seen, requires that we always interpret unclear passages generously and, in particular, that we never interpret a passage as a bad argument when the evidence reasonably permits us to interpret it as not an argument at all. This test often proves helpful when the other tests yield no clear answer. For example:

> Jeremy won't come to the frat party tonight because he has an important exam tomorrow.

This claim about Jeremy is not common knowledge, nor does it refer to a past event. Thus, neither the common-knowledge test nor the past-event test is applicable to this example. The third test—the author's intent test—also yields no clear answer; the speaker might reasonably be interpreted as offering either an argument or an explanation. If we interpret the passage as an argument, however, the reasoning is bound to strike us as somewhat weak. Our choice therefore (assuming that a choice must be made) is to interpret the passage either as a weak argument or as an apparently satisfactory explanation. In these circumstances the principle of charity dictates that we interpret the passage as an explanation.

It should be noted that none of these four tests is foolproof. Consider this example:

> All men are mortal, and Socrates is a man. Therefore, Socrates is mortal.

Here the concluding statement ("Socrates is mortal") is a matter of common knowledge. Generally, as we have noted, we don't argue for conclusions that are well-known matters of fact; yet, clearly, the passage is an argument.

The past-event test also has exceptions, as this example illustrates:

> No single shooter could have shot as quickly and as accurately as Lee Harvey Oswald is alleged to have done in the Kennedy assassination. Therefore, Oswald was not the lone assassin.

The statement this passage seeks to prove or explain is about an event that occurred in the past, yet clearly the passage is an argument.

Sometimes none of the four tests yields a clear answer. In real life, of course, passages don't come neatly labeled as "argument" or "explanation." And the truth is that sometimes we just can't tell whether a passage is meant to be an argument or an explanation. Consider this quote from former ACLU president Nadine Strossen:

> Because civil libertarians have learned that free speech is an indispensable instrument for the promotion of other rights and freedoms—including racial equality—we fear that the movement to regulate campus expression will undermine equality, as well as free speech.[9]

What is the author's intent here? Is she trying to *explain* why civil libertarians fear that campus speech codes may undermine both freedom and equality? Or is she offering a *reason* why everyone should be concerned about such possible consequences? Or is she perhaps doing both? It is very difficult to say, and none of our four tests yields a clear answer.

Some students find it frustrating that critical thinking doesn't always provide definite, clear-cut answers. In this respect, however, critical thinking simply reflects life. Life is complex and messy, and critical thinking, because it helps us think intelligently about life, naturally reflects this complexity and messiness. Sometimes despite our best efforts we can't be sure whether a passage is an argument or an explanation. When that happens, we shouldn't pretend that a passage is clear. Instead, we should look at the various possibilities and

---

• Critical Thinking Lapse •

A thirty-two-year-old Austrian who admitted to making more than forty thousand obscene phone calls was caught when one of his victims managed to obtain his phone number. The woman, who'd been pestered every day for six months, said she was too busy for an obscene call at that moment but would phone back if he left his number.[10]

---

say, "Well, it's unclear whether this is an argument or an explanation. However, *if* it's an argument, it is a good [bad] argument because _____. And *if* it's an explanation, it is a good [bad] explanation because _____." It is often possible to evaluate a passage in this way, even if we can't be sure how the passage should be understood.

EXERCISE 2.3

Arrange the chairs in the class into a circle. The instructor will give each student a 3 × 5 index card. On one side of the card, write a very brief example of either an argument or an explanation. On the other side of the card, write "argument" or "explanation," whichever is appropriate to your example. When everyone has finished writing, pass your card to the student sitting to your right. Read the card you have received and decide whether it is an argument or an explanation, then check your answer with the answer indicated on the back. Continue passing the cards until each card has been read. The instructor will then collect the cards and discuss the examples with the class.

EXERCISE 2.4

I. Determine which of the following passages contain arguments and which do not.

1. I ate because I was hungry.
2. He must be home. His car's in the driveway.
3. I'm trading in my Ford Explorer for a Toyota Corolla because they're more reliable and get better gas mileage.
4. If Christmas is on a Friday, the day after Christmas must be a Saturday.
5. Dinosaurs became extinct sixty-five million years ago, probably as a result of dramatic global cooling that resulted from the impact of a large asteroid.
6. Dogs make better pets than cats because they're more intelligent and obedient.
7. According to baseball statistician Bill James, Stan Musial was a better all-around baseball player than Ted Williams because Musial was, in addition to being a great hitter, a better fielder and base-runner than Williams was.

8. The rich and famous tend not to be happy, well-adjusted personalities. Look at Michael Jackson.

9. I stayed home from school because I was sick.

10. The Cascades mountain range contains many majestic peaks. Mt. Rainier and Mt. Hood, for instance, are both more than ten thousand feet.

11. The death penalty *costs* too much. Allowing our government to kill citizens compromises the deepest moral values upon which this country was conceived: the inviolable dignity of human persons. (Helen Prejean, CSJ, *Dead Man Walking*)

12. If there were no maldistribution, if everyone shared equally, and if no grain were fed to animals, all of humanity could be adequately nourished today. (Paul Ehrlich and Anne Ehrlich, *Betrayal of Science and Reason*)

13. The British statesman William Gladstone thought that we would all be healthier if we chewed each bite of food precisely 32 times. Why else, he argued, did nature endow us with exactly 32 teeth? (Thomas Gilovich, *How We Know What Isn't So*)

14. Guys are extremely reluctant to make commitments, or even to take any steps that might *lead* to commitments. That is why, when a guy goes out on a date with a woman and finds himself really liking her, he often will demonstrate his affection by avoiding her for the rest of his life. (Dave Barry, *Dave Barry's Complete Guide to Guys*)

15. You can fool all of the people some of the time, and some of the people all the time, but you cannot fool all the people all the time. (Abraham Lincoln)

16. A new study published in the journal *Pediatrics* found that removing a child's tonsils and adenoids can lead to better grades, presumably because the surgery allows for a better night's sleep. (Stacey Burling, "Tonsillectomy Can Hike Grades, New Study Says")

17. Productivity and serving the public and taking care of one's own employees are neither mere means nor an afterthought of business but rather its very essence. Then, as every smart entrepreneur knows well enough, the profits will come as a consequence. (Robert C. Solomon, *Ethics and Excellence: Cooperation and Integrity in Business*)

18. It is clear that there never was a time when nothing existed; otherwise nothing would exist now. (C. S. Lewis, *Miracles*)

19. Children should be taught not to steal because it is wrong. They should not be taught not to steal because there is a rule against stealing. (J. F. Covaleski, "Discipline and Morality: Beyond Rules and Consequences")

20. The wind blows where it wills, and you hear the sound of it, but you do not know whence it comes or whither it goes; so it is with every one who is born of the Spirit. (John 3:8)

21. However "civilized," however much brought up in an artificially contrived environment, we all seem to have an innate longing for primitive simplicity, close to the natural state of living. Hence the city people's pleasure in the summer camping in the woods or traveling in the desert or opening up an unbeaten track. (D. T. Suzuki, *Zen and Japanese Culture*)

22. More than any other time in history, mankind faces a crossroads. One path leads to despair and utter hopelessness, the other, to total extinction. Let us pray that we have the wisdom to choose correctly. (Woody Allen, *Side Effects*)

23. What's right in the corporation is not what is right in a man's home or in his church. What is right in the corporation is what the guy above you wants from you. That's what morality is in the corporation. (Robert Jackal, *Moral Mazes*)

24. Never hit your child. Today health professionals agree that hitting children harms them emotionally as well as physically, fosters rage and self-hate, and often does lasting damage to their self-esteem and sense of worth. (*Dr. Koop's Self-Help Advisor*)

25. Tradition and folklore contain a large number of fallacious beliefs. For example, many widespread and popular beliefs such as "Don't swim for an hour after eating," "You should rub snow on frost bite," "Reading in the dark will ruin your eyes," "You can catch cold from being chilled," and "The more you cut your hair, the faster it will grow" are not true. (I. W. Kelly et al., "The Moon Was Full and Nothing Happened: A Review of Studies on the Moon and Human Behavior and Human Belief")

26. If you don't listen to radio talk shows, you really should, because it gives you a chance to reassure yourself that a great many people out there are much stupider than you are. (Dave Barry, *Dave Barry's Bad Habits*)

27. If a bridge collapses, if a dam breaks, if a wing falls off an airplane and people die, I cannot see that as God's doing. I cannot believe that God wanted all those people to die at that moment, or that He wanted some of them to die and had no choice but to condemn the others along with them. I believe that these calamities are all acts of nature, and that there is no moral reason for those particular victims to be singled out for punishment. (Harold Kushner, *When Bad Things Happen to Good People*)

28. When what is just or unjust is thought to be determined solely by whoever has the power to lay down the law of the land, it unavoidably follows that the law of the land cannot be judged either just or unjust. (Mortimer J. Adler, *Six Great Ideas*)

29. The cause of the Millenium Bug dates back to the 1960s, when computer programmers decided to represent certain types of data in shorthand. Thus 1967 became just "67"; Missouri became just "Mo."; a broiled chicken sandwich with fries and a medium soft drink became just "The No. 4 Combo"; and Charles A. Frecklewanger Jr. became just "Chuck." The programmers did this because, in the 1960s, computer memory was very expensive. Also, back then everybody except Bill Clinton was on drugs. Many of these programmers didn't know what century it was. (Dave Barry, "Come the Millenium, Please Use the Stairs")

30. Your manuscript is both good and original; but the part that is good is not original, and the part that is original is not good. (Samuel Johnson)

31. The human species will one day be extinct. The impact of this realization upon the human psyche is quite jarring, yet science provides evidence for it—99% of all species that have ever lived on earth are now

extinct. (Barbara Forrest, "The Possibility of Meaning in Human Evolution")

32. We owe a lot to Thomas Edison—if it wasn't for him, we'd be watching television by candlelight. (Milton Berle)

33. When you make a mistake, you have to find a way to move on. Otherwise, dwelling on it will just cause you to make another mistake. (Pat Summitt, *Reach for the Summit*)

34. Every day you make decisions that require you to use critical thinking skills. For example, in a drugstore, you need to choose between two bottles of shampoo. One is 6 ounces and costs $2.95. The other is 8 ounces and costs $3.50. Which bottle should you buy? Why? (Angel R. Angel and Stuart R. Porter, *A Survey of Mathematics with Applications*)

35. It's easy to quit smoking. I've done it a hundred times. (Mark Twain)

II. Determine whether the following passages are best understood as arguments or explanations.

1. Neptune is blue because its atmosphere contains methane. (John Fix, *Astronomy: Journey to the Cosmic Frontier*, 2nd ed.)

2. A good schoolmaster is a far more useful citizen than the average bank president, politician, or general, if only because what he transmits is what gives meaning to the life of the banker, the politician, the general. (Clifton Fadiman, *The Lifetime Reading Plan*)

3. My mother, who graduated from high school at sixteen, had no hope of affording college, so she went to work in the local post office for a dollar a day. (Tom Brokaw, *The Greatest Generation*)

4. Since rights claimed against the government should (at least within a democracy) be held equally by all citizens, and since not every citizen could be employed by the government, citizens cannot claim a right to a job from the government. (Joseph DesJardins, *An Introduction to Business Ethics*)

5. Why are there laws of gravity? Because, Einstein revealed, large masses distort space-time, causing objects to move along geodesic paths. (Martin Gardner, "Science and the Unknowable")

6. The Great Lakes area has a concentration of industry because of the availability of water for manufacturing processes, and because water transportation is an efficient way to move raw materials and products. (Eldon E. Enger and Bradley F. Smith, *Environmental Science*, 6th ed.)

7. True success always starts with an inner vision, however incomplete it might be. That's why most of the books on success by famous coaches, business stars, motivational consultants, and psychologists begin with chapters on goal setting. (Tom Morris, *Philosophy for Dummies*)

8. It is a fact of life on our beleaguered little planet that widespread torture, famine, and governmental criminal irresponsibility are much more likely to be found in tyrannous than in democratic governments. Why? Because the rulers of the former are much less likely to be thrown out of office for their misdeeds than the rulers of the latter. (Carl Sagan, *The Demon-Haunted World: Science as a Candle in the Dark*)

9. Men seem to fly around the television more than women. Men get that remote control in their hands, they don't even know what the hell they're not watching. . . . Women don't do this. Women will stop and go, "Well let me see what the show is, before I change the channel. Maybe we can nurture it, work with it, help it grow into something." Men don't do that. Because women nest and men hunt. That's why we watch TV differently. (Jerry Seinfeld, *SeinLanguage*)

10. A bullet has no conscience; neither does a malignant tumor or an automobile gone out of control. This is why good people get sick and get hurt as much as anyone. (Harold Kushner, *When Bad Things Happen to Good People*)

11. We are bound to run into trouble if we seek rational justifications of every principle we use, for one cannot provide a rational argument for rational argument itself without assuming what we are arguing for. (A. F. Chalmers, *What Is This Thing Called Science?* 3rd ed.)

12. Most of us find the ideal of promoting human happiness and well-being an attractive one and, as a result, admire greatly people like Mother Teresa (1910–1997), who devoted her life to working with the poor. (William H. Shaw, *Business Ethics,* 4th ed.)

13. Good hitters have good work habits. They know that practice and lots of it is the surest way to eliminate slumps. And they know that practice is essential to maintaining their edge. Consequently, good hitters are usually always working on something. (Charley Lau, *The Art of Hitting .300*)

14. I always turn to the sports section first. The sports page records people's accomplishments; the front page has nothing but man's failures. (Earl Warren, quoted in Steve Rushin, "The Season of High Heat")

15. Men may live more truly and fully in reading Plato and Shakespeare than at any other time, because then they are participating in essential being and are forgetting their accidental lives. (Allan Bloom, *The Closing of the American Mind*)

16. Because height is inherited, short people bear shorter children than tall people on average. (Wendy Northcutt, *The Darwin Awards*)

17. Many people are concerned that the chemical and biological weapons that Saddam Hussein is supposed to be making could be devastating and deadly. I'm not denying they are, but I don't think whatever he manufactures could have much of an effect on the United States, being that we're already tearing ourselves apart and destroying the very fiber that founded this country. (newspaper call-in column)

18. I wear glasses primarily so I can look for the things that I keep losing. (Bill Cosby, *Time Flies*)

19. [NBA] superstars with dramatic, eye-catching moves are paid vast sums of money, while players who contribute to the team effort in less flamboyant ways often make close to the minimum salary. As a result, few players come to the NBA dreaming of becoming good team players. (Phil Jacksonand Hugh Delehanty, *Sacred Hoops: Spiritual Lessons of a Hardwood Warrior*)

20. When someone dies, it is important that those close to him participate in the process; it will help them in their grief, and will help them face their own death more easily. (Elisabeth Kübler-Ross, *Death: The Final Stage of Growth*)

21. Some people think that arguing is simply stating their prejudices in a new form. This is why many people also think that arguments are unpleasant or pointless. (Antony Weston, *A Rulebook for Arguments*)

22. Good colleges are expensive. This is why you, as a parent, must make every effort to make sure that your child attends a bad college. (Dave Barry, quoted in Mark Henricks, "Funny Money")

23. Who can deny that all individuals have an interest in controlling what happens to their own bodies? Thus, all people should have an enforceable right to refuse sexual intimacy, just as we have a right to refuse medical treatment, and a right not to be beaten. (Patricia Smith, "Four Themes in Feminist Legal Theory")

24. We need to develop the thinking tools and strategies that will enable us to think for ourselves and arrive at intelligent conclusions. We can't simply rely on expert opinions, because those opinions are often in conflict and influenced by the experts' own biases. (John Chaffee, *The Thinker's Way*)

25. I come from the Lower East Side of New York City and from very rough circumstances. As a matter of fact, I came from a family of fourteen children. Fourteen children. It's true. It happened because my mother was hard of hearing. I'll explain this to you. You see, every night when it was time to retire, my father would turn to my mother and say, "Would you like to go to sleep or what?" My mother, who couldn't hear very well would say, "What?" And that's how it happened. (Jackie Mason, *Jackie Mason's America*)

SUMMARY

1. Because critical thinking is concerned primarily with understanding, constructing, and critically evaluating arguments, one of the most basic critical thinking skills is that of recognizing arguments.

2. An *argument,* as that term is used in critical thinking, is a claim defended with reasons. Arguments are composed of one or more premises and a conclusion. *Premises* are statements in an argument offered as evidence or reasons in support of another statement. A *statement* is a sentence that can be viewed as either true or false. A *conclusion* is the statement in an argument that the premises are intended to support or prove.

3. *Indicator words* provide clues that premises or conclusions are being offered. Common indicator words include *therefore, consequently, thus, because,* and *since. Premise indicators* provide clues that premises are being offered, and *conclusion indicators* provide clues that conclusions are being offered. Indicator words,

however, should be approached with caution because not all arguments contain indicator words, and sometimes indicator words are used in passages that are not arguments.

4. It is important to distinguish arguments from various kinds of nonargumentative discourse, such as reports, unsupported assertions, conditional statements, illustrations, and explanations. *Reports* are statements that are intended simply to convey information about a subject. *Unsupported assertions* are statements that indicate what a person believes but don't offer evidence for that belief. *Conditional statements* are *if-then* statements. They claim only that one statement is true *if* another statement is true. *Illustrations* are statements intended to provide examples of a claim, rather than evidence or proof for the claim. *Explanations* are statements intended to explain *why* something is the case, rather than to prove *that* it is the case. None of these types of passages is an argument because none is intended to prove a claim.

CHAPTER 3

Basic Logical Concepts

In the previous chapter, we talked about what arguments are and how we can distinguish them from nonarguments. In this chapter we introduce some basic logical concepts needed to distinguish good arguments from bad ones.

In evaluating any argument, one should always ask two key questions: (1) Are the premises true? and (2) Do the premises provide good reasons to accept the conclusion?

The first question—how to decide whether an argument's premises are true—is discussed in Chapter 8. In this chapter we focus on the second question. What does it mean to say that an argument's premises provide "good reasons" for its conclusion, and how can we know when such reasons are being offered?

DEDUCTION AND INDUCTION

Before we can effectively evaluate an argument, we need to understand clearly what kind of argument is being offered. Traditionally, arguments have been divided into two types: deductive arguments and inductive arguments. Because the standards for evaluating deductive and inductive arguments are quite different, it is important to understand the difference between these two types of arguments.

All arguments claim to provide support—that is, evidence or reasons—for their conclusions. But arguments differ greatly in the amount of support they claim to provide. **Deductive arguments** try to *prove* their conclusions with rigorous, inescapable logic. **Inductive arguments** try to show that their conclusions are *plausible* or *likely* given the premise(s).

Here are some examples of deductive arguments:

All humans are mortal.

Socrates is human.

Therefore, Socrates is mortal.

55

If the president lives in the White House, then he lives in Washington, D.C.

The president does live in the White House.

So, the president lives in Washington, D.C.

Notice how the conclusions of these arguments flow from the premises with a kind of inescapable logic. Each conclusion follows necessarily from the premises; this means that, given the premises, the conclusion could not possibly be false. Arguments are deductive when their premises are intended to provide this kind of rigorous, airtight logical support for their conclusions.

EXERCISE 3.1

I. Deductive reasoning isn't some technical and specialized form of reasoning engaged in only by logicians or mathematicians. It is something we all do easily and naturally. See if you can solve the following mini-mysteries on your own, using your own native reasoning abilities. Then discuss your solutions with a partner.[1]

1. Either Moriarty was the murderer, or Stapleton was the murderer.
    If Stapleton was the murderer, then traces of phosphorus should have been found on the body.
    No traces of phosphorus were found on the body.
    Whodunnit?

2. The murder did not occur in the library.
    If Adler was the murderer, then the weapon was a revolver.
    Either Hope was the murderer, or Adler was the murderer.
    If Hope was the murderer, then the murder took place in the library.
    Whodunnit? With what weapon?

3. The murder was not committed on the moor.
    If Windibank was the murderer, then the weapon was a rope.
    Either Windibank was the murderer, or Calhoun was the murderer.
    If the weapon was a rope, then the murder was committed on the downs.
    If Calhoun was the murderer, then the weapon was a crowbar.
    If the weapon was a crowbar, then the murder was committed on the moor.
    Whodunnit? With what weapon? Where was the murder committed?

II. The following logic problems are slightly more difficult than the ones in the previous exercise. See if you can solve the problems on your own, then discuss your solutions with a partner.

1. At a picnic, Mike went for soft drinks for Amy, Brian, Lisa, and Bill, as well as for himself. He brought back iced tea, grape juice, Diet Coke, Pepsi, and 7-Up.
    Mike doesn't like carbonated drinks.
    Amy would drink either 7-Up or Pepsi.
    Brian likes only sodas.
    Lisa prefers the drink she would put lemon and sugar into.
    Bill likes only clear drinks.
    What drinks did Mike bring for each person?[2]

> We think in logic, as we talk in prose, without aiming at doing so.
>
> —John Henry Newman

> The study of logic appeals to no criterion not already present in the learner's mind.
>
> —C. I. Lewis

2. Seth, Maria, Antoine, and JoBeth are college friends in the United States who plan to spend a semester abroad. They can study in China, Germany, Australia, Japan, England, or Canada. Seth is willing to go anywhere except Asia. Maria prefers not to go to a country south of the Equator. Antoine wants to study in either Europe or Australia. JoBeth doesn't care where they go, as long as it's not England.

   Which is the one country that satisfies all of these various preferences?

3. Five college students, Buck, Jennifer, Li, Ursula, and Tyler, are talking about what they should bring to Patrick's party. Buck says he'll bring chips or mixed nuts unless somebody else wants to bring a salty snack, in which case he'll bring some soda. Jennifer says she's allergic to nuts but would be happy to bring some pretzels if Buck wants to pick up some soda. Li says he'll bring cookies unless somebody else brings a dessert, in which case he'll bring some homemade dip. Ursula says if Li brings a dip, she'll bring chips if nobody else does. Tyler says he'll bring soda if nobody else does; otherwise, he'll bring ice cream.

   If each of these students does what he or she says, what will each bring to the party?

Much that is taught in college classes grows soon out of date, but the skills of correct reasoning never become obsolete.
—Irving M. Copi and Carl Cohen

Deductive arguments claim to provide logically conclusive grounds for their conclusions. That is, they attempt to show that their conclusions *must* be true given the premises asserted. Inductive arguments, on the other hand, simply claim that their conclusions are *likely* or *probable* given the premises offered. Here are some examples of inductive arguments:

Polls show that 75 percent of Republicans favor a school prayer amendment.

Joe is a Republican.

Therefore, Joe probably favors a school prayer amendment.

Every ruby so far discovered has been red.

So, probably all rubies are red.

The bank safe was robbed last night.

Whoever robbed the safe knew the safe's combination.

Only two people know the safe's combination: Lefty and Bugsy.

Bugsy needed money to pay his gambling debts.

Bugsy was seen sneaking around outside the bank last night.

It is reasonable to conclude, therefore, that Bugsy robbed the safe.

It is sometimes said that the basic difference between deduction and induction is that deduction moves from general premises to particular conclusions, whereas induction moves from particular premises to general conclusions.[3] That, however, is a misconception.

Here, for example, is a deductive argument that moves not from general premises to a particular conclusion but from particular premises to a general conclusion:

> Lincoln was president from 1861 to 1865. (particular premise)
>
> So, all persons born during Lincoln's presidency were born in the nineteenth century. (general conclusion)

Here is an example of an inductive argument that moves from general premises to a particular conclusion:

> All of Stephen King's previous novels have been good. (general premise)
>
> Therefore, Stephen King's next novel will probably be good. (particular conclusion)

In fact, it is possible to find examples of *any* possible combination of general or particular premises or conclusions in deductive or inductive arguments. Thus, it is a mistake to regard any particular pattern of general or particular statements as a defining characteristic of deductive or inductive reasoning.

What makes an argument deductive or inductive is not the pattern of particularity or generality in the premises and conclusion. Rather, it is the *type of support* the premises are claimed to provide for the conclusion. The following list summarizes the key differences between deductive and inductive reasoning.

Key Differences between Deductive and Inductive Arguments

Deductive arguments claim that . . .	*Inductive arguments claim that . . .*
If the premises are true, then the conclusion *must* be true.	If the premises are true, then the conclusion is *probably* true.
The conclusion follows *necessarily* from the premises.	The conclusion follows *probably* from the premises.
The premises provide *conclusive* evidence for the truth of the conclusion.	The premises provide *good* (but not conclusive) evidence for the truth of the conclusion.
It is *impossible* for all the premises to be true and the conclusion false.	It is *unlikely* for the premises to be true and the conclusion false.
It is *logically inconsistent* to assert the premises and deny the conclusion, if you accept the premises, you *must* accept the conclusion.	Although it is logically consistent to assert the premises and deny the conclusion, the conclusion is *probably* true if the premises are true.

HOW CAN WE TELL WHETHER AN ARGUMENT IS DEDUCTIVE OR INDUCTIVE?

We have seen that an argument is deductive if its premises are intended to provide conclusive grounds for the truth of its conclusion, and inductive if its premises are intended to provide merely probable grounds for the truth of its conclusion. But it is not always easy to know what a given speaker or writer intends. For that reason it is sometimes difficult to tell whether a particular argument is deductive or inductive.

Fortunately, there are four tests that greatly simplify the task of determining whether an argument should be regarded as deductive or inductive:

- the indicator word test
- the strict necessity test
- the common pattern test
- the principle of charity test

The Indicator Word Test

Just as we use indicator words to signal the assertion of premises or conclusions, we use indicator words to signal when our arguments are deductive or inductive. For example, a phrase like "it necessarily follows that" almost always indicates that an argument is deductive. Here are some other common **deduction indicator words:**

certainly	it logically follows that
definitely	it is logical to conclude that
absolutely	this logically implies that
conclusively	this entails that

These are some common **induction indicator words:**

probably	one would expect that
likely	it is a good bet that
it is plausible to suppose that	chances are that
it is reasonable to assume that	odds are that

The **indicator word test** is often extremely helpful. Nevertheless, two limitations of the test should be noted.

First, many arguments contain no deduction or induction indicator words. Here are two examples:

> Capital punishment should be abolished because innocent persons may be mistakenly executed.

> Pleasure is not the same thing as happiness. The occasional self-destructive behavior of the rich and famous confirms this far too vividly. (Tom Morris)

Neither of these arguments contains any indicator words that would help us decide whether it is deductive or inductive. For arguments such as these, we must rely on one or more of the other tests discussed in this section.

Second, arguers often use indicator words loosely or improperly. For example, it is common to hear speakers use strong phrases like "it must be the case that" and "it is logical to assume that" when the context makes clear that the argument is not intended to be strictly deductive. For these reasons the indicator word test must be used with caution.

The Strict Necessity Test

All deductive arguments claim, explicitly or implicitly, that their conclusions follow necessarily from their premises. Moreover, we know from experience (1) that most arguers don't offer *obviously bad* deductive arguments and (2) that most arguers don't offer logically conclusive arguments unless they *mean* to offer logically conclusive arguments. From these simple facts, we can usually determine whether an argument is meant to be deductive or inductive.

The **strict necessity test** can be stated as follows:

An argument's conclusion either follows with strict logical necessity from its premises or it does not.

If the argument's conclusion *does* follow with strict logical necessity from its premises, the argument should always be treated as deductive.[4]

If the argument's conclusion does *not* follow with strict logical necessity from its premises, the argument should normally be treated as inductive. (The few exceptions to this rule are discussed later in this section.)

Now let's apply this test to a couple of examples. Consider the following arguments:

Alan is a father. Therefore, Alan is a male.

Jill is a six-year-old girl. Therefore, Jill cannot run a mile in one minute flat.

So logical!
—Supertramp

Does the conclusion of the first argument ("Alan is a male") follow with strict necessity from the premise ("Alan is a father")? Could it possibly be true that Alan is a father yet false that he is a male? Clearly not, for by definition all fathers are male. According to the strict necessity test, therefore, the first argument is clearly deductive.

What about the second argument? Could it be true that Jill is a six-year-old girl yet false that she cannot run a mile in one minute flat? Yes. Of course, it's not *physically possible* for a six-year-old girl to run a mile in one minute flat. Six-year-old girls (and human beings in general) just lack the physical equipment to be able to do that. But there is no *logical contradiction* in thinking that there *could* be a six-year-old girl who could run that fast. It is logically possible, therefore, that the premise is true and the conclusion is false. Thus, the conclusion does not follow with strict logical necessity from the premises. Therefore, the argument should be treated as inductive.

The Common Pattern Test

Because deductive and inductive arguments often occur in characteristic, telltale patterns of reasoning, we can apply the **common pattern test** to determine which kind of reasoning we are dealing with.

Consider this argument:

If we're in Paris, then we are in France.

We are in Paris.

Therefore, we are in France.

This argument has a particular pattern or form that occurs frequently in deductive reasoning. The general pattern of the argument is this:

If [*the first statement*] is true, then [*the second statement*] is true.

[*The first statement*] is true.

Therefore, [*the second statement*] is true.

Because it is awkward and wordy to talk about "the first statement," "the second statement," and so on, logicians generally use *letters* to stand for the various parts of an argument. Suppose we let the letter *A* stand for the statement "We are in Paris" and the letter *B* stand for the statement "We are in France." We can then state the general pattern of the argument as follows:

If A then B.

A.

Therefore, B.

This is an argument pattern that logicians call **modus ponens**, a Latin expression that means "affirmative mode." Because it is obvious that this is a logically reliable pattern of reasoning, arguments of this pattern should always be treated as deductive.

Modus ponens is one very common pattern of deductive reasoning. Later in this chapter, we discuss several other common patterns of deductive and inductive reasoning. Once you have learned to recognize such patterns, you will find it easy to identify everyday examples of deductive and inductive reasoning.

The Principle of Charity Test

Suppose you have tried each of the three tests we have discussed and you are still not sure whether a particular argument should be treated as deductive or inductive. In that case, it is time to fall back on the important principle discussed at the end of Chapter 2: the *principle of charity*. Recall what that principle says: When interpreting an unclear argument or passage, always give the speaker or writer the benefit of the doubt. Never attribute to an arguer a weaker argument when the evidence reasonably permits us to attribute to him or her a stronger one. And never interpret a passage as a bad argument when the evidence reasonably permits us to interpret it as not an argument at all.

The principle of charity serves two important goals in critical thinking. First, it fosters goodwill and mutual understanding in argument by demanding that we treat the arguments of others with the same generous and respectful spirit that we would like others to treat our own arguments. Even more important, it promotes the discovery of truth by insisting that we confront arguments that we ourselves admit to be the strongest and most plausible versions of those arguments.

Let's apply the **principle of charity test** to an actual example. Consider the following:

> Andy told me that he ate at Maxine's Restaurant yesterday. But Maxine's was completely destroyed by fire less than a month ago. It is certain, therefore, that Andy is either lying or mistaken.

Should this argument be regarded as deductive or inductive? Let's apply our various tests.

First, are there any deduction or induction indicator words? Yes. We have seen that the phrase "it is certain that" is often used as a deduction indicator. But we have also seen that people often use indicator words—especially deduction indicator words—loosely or improperly. So this first test, though it clearly suggests that the argument is meant to be deductive, shouldn't be treated as conclusive.

Second, does the conclusion follow with strict necessity from the premises? No. Although it seems quite unlikely, it is certainly conceivable that the restaurant has been quickly rebuilt and has reopened for business. This suggests that the argument should be regarded as inductive.

Third, does the argument have a pattern of reasoning that is either characteristically deductive or characteristically inductive? Not really, as we shall see. Thus, the third test doesn't apply in this case.

In short, the first test suggests that the argument is deductive, the second test suggests that the argument is inductive, and the third test doesn't apply. So where does that leave us? Up the proverbial creek without a paddle?

No, because this is where the principle of charity comes to the rescue. According to that principle, we should always interpret a doubtful argument in the way most favorable to the arguer. In this case, we are in doubt as to whether the argument should be treated as deductive or inductive. But consider: If we treat the argument as deductive, it is clearly a bad deductive argument because the conclusion plainly does not follow necessarily from the premises. On the other hand, if we treat the argument as inductive, the argument is a good inductive argument because the premises, if true, do make the conclusion likely. Thus, the most charitable way to interpret the argument is to interpret it as inductive. This is what the principle of charity requires that we do.

A word of caution, however: *The principle of charity should never be used to reinterpret bad arguments as good ones.* The principle of charity is a principle of interpretation, not a principle of argument repair. Its basic purpose, like that of the other three tests, is to help us decide what arguments are actually being offered, not to replace bad arguments with ones we think are better. Thus, the principle should be used only when there is genuine uncertainty about how an argument should be interpreted. It should not be used when it is clear what argument has actually been put forward.

Exceptions to the Strict Necessity Test

We saw earlier that an argument should generally be treated as inductive if its conclusion does not follow necessarily from its premises. There are, however, exceptions to this general rule. Two broad exceptions should be noted.

An argument in which the conclusion does not follow necessarily from the premises should nonetheless be treated as deductive if either

1. the *language or context* makes clear that the arguer *intended* to offer a logically conclusive argument, but the argument, in fact, is not logically conclusive;

or

2. the argument has a *pattern of reasoning* that is characteristically deductive, and nothing else about the argument indicates clearly that the argument is meant to be inductive.

Here is an example of the first exception:

> Magellan's ships sailed around the world. It necessarily follows, therefore, that the earth is a sphere.

Here the phrase "it necessarily follows that" indicates that the argument is meant to be deductive. In this case, however, it is clear that the conclusion does not follow necessarily from the premise, because it would still be possible for a ship to sail around the world if the earth were, say, egg-shaped or cylindrical rather than spherical.

Here is an example of the second exception:

> If I'm Bill Gates, then I'm mortal.
> I'm not Bill Gates.
> Therefore, I'm not mortal.

This is a terrible argument. The premises provide no support whatsoever for the conclusion, much less logically conclusive support. Nevertheless, the argument is rightly regarded as deductive because, as we shall see, it employs a pattern of reasoning that is almost invariably deductive.

This has been a rather complex discussion. The following list is the simplest and clearest way we know to sum up the basic guidelines for distinguishing deductive from inductive arguments.

How to Distinguish Deductive from Inductive Arguments

1. If the conclusion follows necessarily from the premises, the argument should always be treated as deductive.
2. If the conclusion does not follow necessarily from the premises, the argument should be treated as inductive unless (a) the language or context of the argument makes clear that the argument is deductive

---

• Critical Thinking Lapse •

WILKES-BARRE (Pa.)—Jeremy Miller can't remember getting jolted by a train early Monday morning.

Miller, 25, said he and his brother, John, 27, were walking to his brother's home when they stopped at an already-burning fire in the middle of the tracks.

The two fell asleep, and Miller only remembers waking up to "all these people" around him.

The two remained hospitalized Tuesday night. John remained in critical condition with severe internal and head injuries. Jeremy suffered severe injuries to one hand and a gash in the back of his head.

Police said there was ample evidence of beer drinking at the scene.[5]

---

or (b) the argument has a pattern of reasoning that is characteristically deductive.

3. If the argument has a pattern of reasoning that is characteristically deductive, the argument should be treated as deductive unless there is clear evidence that the argument is intended to be inductive.

4. If the argument has a pattern of reasoning that is characteristically inductive, the argument should be treated as inductive unless there is clear evidence that the argument is intended to be deductive.

5. Arguments often contain indicator words—words like *probably, necessarily,* and *certainly*—that provide clues in determining whether an argument is deductive or inductive. Keep in mind, however, that indicator words are often used loosely or improperly.

6. If there is significant doubt about whether an argument is deductive or inductive, always interpret the argument in the way most favorable to the arguer.

COMMON PATTERNS OF DEDUCTIVE REASONING[6]

Often, the quickest way to determine whether an argument is deductive or inductive is to note whether it has a pattern of reasoning that is characteristically deductive or inductive. In this section we discuss five common patterns of deductive reasoning:

- hypothetical syllogism
- categorical syllogism
- argument by elimination
- argument based on mathematics
- argument from definition

Hypothetical Syllogism

A *syllogism* is simply a three-line argument, that is, an argument that consists of exactly two premises and a conclusion. A hypothetical syllogism is a syllogism that contains at least one hypothetical or conditional (i.e., *if-then*) premise.[7]

Here are two examples of hypothetical syllogisms:

> If the Tigers beat the Yankees, then the Tigers will make the playoffs.
>
> The Tigers will beat the Yankees.
>
> So, the Tigers will make the playoffs.

> If I want to keep my financial aid, I'd better study hard.
>
> I do want to keep my financial aid.
>
> Therefore, I'd better study hard.

Notice that these two arguments each have the same logical pattern or form:

> If A then B.
>
> A.
>
> Therefore, B.

This pattern, as we have seen, is called *modus ponens*. Arguments with this pattern consist of one conditional premise, a second premise that asserts as true the antecedent (the *if* part) of the conditional, and a conclusion that asserts as true the consequent (the *then* part) of the conditional. Other common varieties of hypothetical syllogisms include

- chain argument
- *modus tollens* (denying the consequent)
- denying the antecedent
- affirming the consequent

Chain arguments consist of three conditional statements that link together in the following way:

> If A then B.
>
> If B then C.
>
> Therefore, if A then C.

Here is an example of a chain argument:

> If we don't stop for gas soon, then we'll run out of gas.
>
> If we run out of gas, then we'll be late for the wedding.
>
> Therefore, if we don't stop for gas soon, we'll be late for the wedding.

Modus tollens[8] arguments have the following pattern:

> If A then B.
>
> Not B.
>
> Therefore, not A.

Arguments of this pattern are sometimes called "denying the consequent" because they consist of one conditional premise, a second premise that denies (i.e., asserts to be false) the consequent of the conditional, and a conclusion that denies the antecedent of the conditional. Here is an example:

> If we're in Sacramento, then we're in California.
>
> We're not in California.
>
> Therefore, we're not in Sacramento.

Modus ponens, chain argument, and *modus tollens* are all logically reliable patterns of deductive reasoning. That is, any argument that has one of these patterns is absolutely guaranteed to have a true conclusion if the premises are also true. But not all patterns of deductive reasoning are completely reliable in this way. Two patterns that are *not* logically reliable are denying the antecedent and affirming the consequent.

Denying the antecedent arguments have the following pattern:

> If A then B.
>
> Not A.
>
> Therefore, not B.

O most lame and impotent conclusion!
—Shakespeare

Here is an example:

> If Shakespeare wrote *War and Peace,* then he's a great writer.
>
> Shakespeare didn't write *War and Peace.*
>
> Therefore, Shakespeare is not a great writer.

Notice in this example that the premises are true and the conclusion is false. This shows straightaway that the pattern of reasoning of this argument is not logically reliable.

Another faulty pattern of deductive reasoning is **affirming the consequent.** Its pattern is as follows:

> If A then B.
>
> B.
>
> Therefore, A.

Here is an example:

> If we're on Neptune, then we're in the solar system.
>
> We are in the solar system.
>
> Therefore, we're on Neptune.

Given that this argument has true premises and a false conclusion, it is clear that affirming the consequent is not a logically reliable pattern of reasoning.

Because *modus ponens, modus tollens,* and chain argument are logically reliable patterns of reasoning, they should always be treated as deductive. Denying the antecedent and affirming the consequent are not logically reliable patterns of reasoning; nevertheless, they should generally be treated as deductive because they have a pattern of reasoning that is characteristically deductive.

EXERCISE 3.2

For each of the following, indicate which type of hypothetical syllogism it is: *modus ponens, modus tollens,* chain argument, denying the antecedent, or affirming the consequent. In some cases, the argument may need to be rephrased slightly to make the logical pattern explicit.

1. If we're in London, then we're in England. We are not in England. So, we are not in London.
2. If we're in Los Angeles, then we are in the United States. We are in the United States. So, we are in Los Angeles.
3. If we're in the United States, then we are on Earth. We are in the United States. So, we are on Earth.
4. If we're in Paris, then we are in France. If we're in France, then we are in Europe. So, if we are in Paris, then we are in Europe.
5. If we're in Houston, then we are in the United States. We are not in Houston. So, we are not in the United States.
6. If we're in Shanghai, then we are in China. So, we are in China, because we are in Shanghai.
7. We are not in Mexico, because if we are in Mexico City, we are in Mexico, and we are not in Mexico City.
8. Since we're in India, we are in Calcutta, since we are in India if we are in Calcutta.
9. If we're in Toronto, then we are in Canada. So, because if we are in Canada, we are in North America, if we are in Toronto, then we are in North America.
10. We're in Berlin, given that if we are in Berlin, then we are in Germany, and we are in Germany.

Categorical Syllogism

Another common pattern of deductive reasoning is categorical syllogism. For present purposes, a **categorical syllogism** may be defined as a three-line argument in which each statement begins with the word *all, some,* or *no.*[9] Here are two examples:

All oaks are trees.

All trees are plants.

So, all oaks are plants.

Some Democrats are elected officials.

All elected officials are politicians.

Therefore, some Democrats are politicians.

Because categorical reasoning like this is such a familiar form of rigorous logical reasoning, such arguments should nearly always be treated as deductive.

Argument by Elimination

An **argument by elimination** seeks to logically rule out various possibilities until only a single possibility remains. Here are two examples:

Either Joe walked to the library or he drove.

But Joe didn't drive to the library.

Therefore, Joe walked to the library.[10]

Either Dutch committed the murder, or Jack committed the murder, or Celia committed the murder.

If Dutch or Jack committed the murder, then the weapon was a rope.

The weapon was not a rope.

So, neither Dutch nor Jack committed the murder.

Therefore, Celia committed the murder.

Because the aim of such arguments is to logically exclude every possible outcome except one, such arguments are always deductive.

Argument Based on Mathematics

Mathematics is a model of logical, step-by-step reasoning. Mathematicians don't claim that their conclusions are merely likely or probable. They claim to prove their conclusions on the basis of precise mathematical concepts and reasoning. In an **argument based on mathematics,** the conclusion is claimed to depend largely or entirely on some mathematical calculation or measurement (perhaps in conjunction with one or more nonmathematical premises).[11] Here are two examples:

Eight is greater than four.

Four is greater than two.

Therefore, eight is greater than two.

Light travels at a rate of 186,000 miles per second.

The sun is more than 93 million miles distant from the earth.

Therefore, it takes more than eight minutes for the sun's light to reach the earth.

Because mathematical arguments are generally models of precise logical reasoning, arguments based on mathematics are usually best treated as deductive. Arguments based on mathematics *can* be inductive, however, as this example shows:

My blind uncle told me that there were 8 men, 6 women, and 12 kids at the party.

By simple addition, therefore, it follows that there were 26 people at the party.

➤ **Pop Culture Connection** ◄

Logic in Narnia

Fans of C. S. Lewis's best-selling children's book series, *The Chronicles of Narnia,* will readily recall the memorable scene in *The Lion, the Witch, and the Wardrobe* (also featured in the recent Disney/Walden Media film version of the book) in which the Professor uses an argument by elimination to convince Peter and Susan Pevensie that, fantastic as it may seem, their sister, Lucy, is probably telling the truth about a magical realm she calls "Narnia." Lucy claims to have walked through a wardrobe into a wintry world inhabited by witches, fauns, and other strange and mythological creatures. After muttering, "Logic! Why don't they teach logic in these schools?" the Professor reminds Peter and Susan that there are only three possibilities: Lucy is lying, or she's crazy, or she's telling the truth. The children quickly agree that it would be completely out of character for Lucy to lie. They also agree that she has shown no telltale signs of madness. "For the moment, then," the Professor concludes, "and unless any further evidence turns up, we must assume that she is telling the truth."

The Professor's argument by elimination is clearly modeled on "Lewis's trilemma," a famous argument for Christian belief Lewis had put forward in his 1952 book, *Mere Christianity.* The trilemma Lewis offers is that Jesus did not claim to be simply a moral teacher; he claimed to be God. This leaves us only three real viable alternatives: Jesus was lying, or he was crazy, or he was exactly who he claimed to be: God. Based on everything we know about Jesus, it is impossible to believe he was either lying or insane. Thus, we should conclude, Jesus was God.

Is Lewis's trilemma a sound argument by elimination? In particular, are there any other possibilities besides the three Lewis identifies ("Liar, Lunatic, Lord")?

Here, the conclusion clearly does *not* follow from the premise because it is possible for the premise to be true and the conclusion false. (Maybe my blind uncle miscounted, for example.) For that reason, the argument is best treated as inductive.

Argument from Definition

In an **argument from definition,** the conclusion is presented as being "true by definition," that is, as following simply by definition from some key word or phrase used in the argument. Here are two examples:

Janelle is a cardiologist. Therefore, Janelle is a doctor.

Bertha is an aunt. It follows that she is a woman.

Because a statement that follows by definition is necessarily true if the relevant definition is true, arguments from definition are always deductive.

Our discussion of common patterns of deductive reasoning can be summarized as follows:

Arguments by elimination and arguments from definition should always be treated as deductive.

Logically reliable hypothetical syllogisms, categorical syllogisms, and arguments based on mathematics should always be treated as deductive.

Logically unreliable hypothetical syllogisms, categorical syllogisms, and arguments based on mathematics should be treated as deductive unless there is clear evidence that they are intended to be inductive.

COMMON PATTERNS OF INDUCTIVE REASONING

In this section we look at six common patterns of inductive reasoning:

- inductive generalization
- predictive argument
- argument from authority
- causal argument
- statistical argument
- argument from analogy

Inductive Generalization

A **generalization,** as that term is used in critical thinking, is a statement that attributes some characteristic to *all* or *most* members of a given class. Here are some examples of generalizations:

All wild grizzly bears in the United States live west of the Mississippi River.

Most college students work at least part-time.

Men are so unromantic!

An **inductive generalization** is an argument in which a generalization is claimed to be probably true based on information about some members of a particular class. Here are two examples:

> *Life is the art of drawing sufficient conclusions from insufficient premises.*
> —Samuel Butler

All dinosaur bones so far discovered have been more than sixty-five million years old.

Therefore, probably all dinosaur bones are more than sixty-five million years old.

Six months ago I met a farmer from Iowa, and he was friendly.

Four months ago I met an insurance salesman from Iowa, and he was friendly.

Two months ago I met a dentist from Iowa, and she was friendly.

I guess most people from Iowa are friendly.

Because all inductive generalizations claim that their conclusions are probable rather than certain, such arguments are always inductive.

Predictive Argument

A **prediction** is a statement about what may or will happen in the future. In a **predictive argument,** a prediction is defended with reasons. Predictive arguments are among the most common patterns of inductive reasoning. Here are two examples:

> It has rained in Vancouver every February since weather records have been kept.
> Therefore, it will probably rain in Vancouver next February.

> Most U.S. presidents have been tall.
> Therefore, probably the next U.S. president will be tall.

Because nothing in the future (including death and taxes) is absolutely certain, arguments containing predictions are usually inductive. It should be noted, however, that predictions can be argued for deductively. For example:

> If Amy comes to the party, Ted will come to the party.
> Amy will come to the party.
> Therefore, Ted will come to the party.

Even though this argument contains a prediction, it is clearly deductive because the conclusion must be true if the premises are true.

Argument from Authority

An **argument from authority** asserts a claim and then supports that claim by citing some presumed authority or witness who has said that the claim is true. Here are three examples:

> More Americans die of skin cancer each year than die in car accidents. How do I know? My doctor told me.

> The *Encyclopaedia Britannica* says that parts of Virginia are farther west than Detroit. In general, the *Encyclopaedia Britannica* is a highly reliable source of information. Therefore, it's probably true that parts of Virginia are farther west than Detroit.

> There are bears in these woods. My neighbor Frank said he saw one last week.

Because we can never be absolutely certain that a presumed authority or witness is accurate or reliable, arguments from authority should normally be treated as inductive. Arguments from authority are sometimes deductive, however. For example:

> Whatever the Bible teaches is true.
> The Bible teaches that we should love our neighbors.
> Therefore, we should love our neighbors.

Because the conclusion of this argument follows necessarily from the premises, the argument should be regarded as deductive.

Causal Argument

A **causal argument** asserts or denies that something is the cause of something else. Here are three examples:

> I can't log-in. The network must be down.

> Rashid isn't allergic to peanuts. I saw him eat a bag of peanuts on the flight from Dallas.

> Medical care is the number-one cause of sudden rapid aging among middle-aged people. Ask yourself how many times you have heard somebody tell you a story like this: "Ralph was feeling fine, no problems at all, and then he went in for a routine physical checkup, and the next thing we heard he was in critical condition with the majority of his internal organs sitting in a freezer in an entirely different building." [12]

As we shall see in Chapter 11, we can rarely, if ever, be 100 percent certain that one thing causes, or does not cause, something else. For that reason causal arguments are usually best treated as inductive.

It cannot be assumed, however, that causal arguments are *always* inductive. The following causal argument, for example, is clearly deductive:

> Whenever iron is exposed to oxygen, it rusts.

> This iron pipe has been exposed to oxygen.

> Therefore, it will rust.

Statistical Argument

A **statistical argument** rests on statistical evidence—that is, evidence that some percentage of some group or class has some particular characteristic. Here are two examples:

> Eighty-three percent of St. Stephen's students are Episcopalian.

> Beatrice is a St. Stephen's student.

> So, Beatrice is probably Episcopalian.

> *Doctor to patient:* Studies show that condoms have an annual failure rate of 2 to 3 percent, even if they are used consistently and correctly. So, you should not assume that condoms will provide complete protection from the risk of pregnancy or sexually transmitted diseases.

Because statistical evidence is generally used to support claims that are presented as probable rather than certain, statistical arguments are usually inductive. It should be noted, however, that statistical evidence can be used in deductive reasoning. For example:

> If 65 percent of likely voters polled support Senator Beltway, then Senator Beltway will win in a landslide.

Sixty-five percent of likely voters polled do support Senator Beltway.

Therefore, Senator Beltway will win in a landslide.

Argument from Analogy

An **analogy** is a comparison of two or more things that are claimed to be alike in some relevant respect. Here are two examples of analogies:

> Habits are like a cable. We weave a strand of it every day and soon it cannot be broken. (Horace Mann)

> As man casts off worn-out garments and puts on others that are new, similarly the embodied soul, casting off worn-out bodies, enters into others, which are new. (Bhagavad-Gita)

In an **argument from analogy,** the conclusion is claimed to depend on an analogy (i.e., a comparison or similarity) between two or more things.
Here are two examples:

Hershey Park has a thrilling roller-coaster ride.

Dorney Park, like Hershey Park, is a great amusement park.

Therefore, probably Dorney Park also has a thrilling roller-coaster ride.

Bill is a graduate of Central University, and he is bright, energetic, and dependable.

Mary is a graduate of Central University, and she is bright, energetic, and dependable.

Paula is a graduate of Central University.

Therefore, most likely, Paula is bright, energetic, and dependable, too.

Note the basic logical pattern of these arguments:

These things are similar in such-and-such ways.

Therefore, they're probably similar in some further way.

Because the conclusions of arguments of this pattern are claimed to follow only probably from the premises, such arguments are clearly inductive.
Not all analogical arguments are inductive, however. For example:

1. Automobiles cause thousands of deaths each year and produce noxious and offensive fumes.
2. Smoking causes thousands of deaths each year and produces noxious and offensive fumes.
3. Thus, if smoking is heavily regulated, automobiles should also be heavily regulated.
4. But automobiles shouldn't be heavily regulated.
5. Therefore, smoking shouldn't be heavily regulated, either.

This is an analogical argument because the main conclusion, statement 5, is claimed to depend on an analogy between automobiles and smoking.

Nevertheless, the argument is deductive because it would be logically inconsistent to assert all the premises and deny the conclusion.

Our discussion of common patterns of inductive reasoning can be summarized as follows:

Inductive generalizations, by definition, are always inductive.

Predictive arguments, arguments from authority, causal arguments, statistical arguments, and arguments from analogy are generally, but not always, inductive.

It takes practice to be able to recognize the patterns of deductive and inductive reasoning that we have discussed, but it is important to be able to do so because such patterns often provide the best clue available as to whether an argument is deductive or inductive.

EXERCISE 3.3

I. Determine whether the following arguments are deductive or inductive. For each argument, state which test(s) you used in reaching your decision (i.e., the indicator word test, the strict necessity test, the common pattern test, and/or the principle of charity test). If the common pattern test is used, indicate which specific pattern the argument exemplifies (e.g., causal argument, argument from authority, and so on).

1. Because $x = 3$ and $y = 5$, then $x + y = 8$.
2. According to the *New York Public Library Desk Reference,* the pop-up toaster was invented by Charles Strite in 1927. The *New York Public Library Desk Reference* is a highly reliable reference work. Therefore, it's reasonable to believe that Charles Strite did invent the pop-up toaster in 1927.
3. Seventy-three percent of Ft. Gibson residents enjoy fishing. Lonnie is a Ft. Gibson resident. So, it's likely that Lonnie enjoys fishing.
4. Either Elmo will win the election or Schlomo will win the election. But Elmo won't win the election. Therefore, Schlomo will win the election.
5. The burglar is tall and thin. Duncan is short and fat. Obviously, therefore, Duncan isn't the burglar.
6. There are no visible signs of forced entry. It seems certain, therefore, that the burglar had a key.
7. The sign says it is seven miles to Lake Lily. Therefore, it is approximately seven miles to Lake Lily.
8. Joan is an extravert. It follows that she is outgoing.
9. All inductive generalizations are inductive. Some inductive generalizations are unreliable. Therefore, some inductive arguments are unreliable.
10. If it rains, the game will be postponed until next Saturday. According to the National Weather Service, there's a 90 percent chance of rain. Therefore, probably the game will be postponed until next Saturday.

11. If the batter bunts in this situation, he'll move the runner over to second base. But the batter won't bunt in this situation. Therefore, the runner will never be moved over to second base.

12. Hughie is the father of Louie. It follows that Hughie is the grandfather of Dewey because Louie is the father of Dewey.

13. Mandatory school uniforms are a good idea because they keep students' minds focused on their schoolwork rather than on what the kid sitting next to them is wearing.

14. Klaus ingested a large dose of rat poison just before he died. Therefore, the rat poison must have caused Klaus's death.

15. All previously observed polar bears have weighed less than 1,500 pounds. Therefore, all polar bears probably weigh less than 1,500 pounds.

16. Kevin says he can lift 1,000 pounds over his head. A full-grown cow weighs less than 1,000 pounds. So, Kevin can lift a full-grown cow over his head.

17. If my car is out of gas, it won't start. My car won't start. Therefore, it is out of gas.

18. Yale is an Ivy League school, and it has a good library. Harvard is an Ivy League school, and it has a good library. Therefore, because Brown is an Ivy League school, it must have a good library, too.

19. I wouldn't swim in that water if I were you. It might be polluted.

20. This tree is deciduous. It must be the case, therefore, that it periodically sheds its leaves.

21. Whatever the Church teaches as infallible doctrine is true. The Church teaches as infallible doctrine that God is eternal. Therefore, God is eternal.

22. Every argument is either deductive or inductive. Because this argument isn't deductive, it must be inductive.

23. Five alleged eyewitnesses have testified that they saw Frank Lane stab Melissa Jenkins. So, Frank Lane did stab Melissa Jenkins.

24. Tiger Woods is one of the best golfers in the world. Melvin Rumsley has never played golf in his life. It is certain, therefore, that Melvin Rumsley could never beat Tiger Woods in a round of golf.

25. If Steve is 48 years old and Pam is exactly 19 years younger than Steve, it necessarily follows that Pam is 29 years old.

26. Some college students love pizza. Some college students love ice cream. It stands to reason, therefore, that some college students who love pizza are college students who love ice cream.

27. Wexford College won the NCAA Division III national championship in football last year, and eighteen of its twenty-two starting players are returning this year. It's a good bet, therefore, that they will win the national championship again this year.

28. Dogs are put to sleep when they become too old or too sick to enjoy life further. Similarly, human beings should be mercifully put to death when they become too old or too sick to enjoy life further.

29. Studies show that between 35 and 45 percent of marriages end in divorce. Therefore, one should not enter into marriage lightly.

30. On Monday I ate at the Sizzling Wok Restaurant in Toledo, and the food was good. On Tuesday I ate at the Sizzling Wok Restaurant in Detroit, and the food was good. Therefore, if I eat at the Sizzling Wok Restaurant in Chicago today, the food will also be good.

DEDUCTIVE VALIDITY

In this section we introduce the most important concept in deductive logic: the concept of deductive validity.

We have seen that all deductive arguments *claim,* implicitly or explicitly, that their conclusions follow necessarily from their premises. A logically reliable deductive argument is one in which the conclusion *really does* follow necessarily from the premises. In logic, a logically reliable deductive argument is called a *valid* deductive argument.

More formally, a **valid deductive argument** is an argument in which it is impossible for all the premises to be true and the conclusion false. Put another way, a valid deductive argument (or *valid argument* for short) is an argument in which these conditions apply:

> If the premises are true, the conclusion *must* be true.
>
> The conclusion follows *necessarily* from the premises.
>
> The premises provide logically *conclusive* grounds for the truth of the conclusion.
>
> The truth of the premises *guarantees* the truth of the conclusion.
>
> It is logically *inconsistent* to assert all the premises as true and deny the conclusion.

In everyday language, *valid* often means "good" or "true." We say, for instance, that a person makes a "valid point" or offers a "valid suggestion." In logic, however, *valid* never means simply "good" or "true." It is always used in the precise technical sense indicated above.

EXERCISE 3.4

Working individually, see if you can determine which statement follows validly from the statements provided. When you are finished, discuss your answers with a partner.

1. If alpha, then beta.
   Alpha.
   Therefore, _____.

2. Either alpha or beta.
   Not beta.
   Therefore, _____.

3. All alphas are betas.
   Delta is an alpha.
   Therefore, _____.

4. If Delta is an alpha, then Delta is a beta.
   Delta is not a beta.
   Therefore, _____.

5. No alphas are betas.
   Delta is an alpha.
   Therefore, _____.

6. All alphas are betas.
   Delta is not a beta.
   Therefore, _____.

7. If Delta is an alpha, then Delta is a beta.
   If Delta is a beta, then Delta is a theta.
   Therefore, _____.

8. If Delta is an alpha, then Delta is a beta.
   If Delta is a theta, then Delta is a beta.
   Either Delta is an alpha or Delta is a theta.
   Therefore, _____.

9. Either Delta is an alpha or Delta is a beta.
   If Delta is an alpha, then Delta is a theta.
   If Delta is a beta, then Delta is a sigma.
   Therefore, _____.

10. Some alphas are betas.
    All betas are thetas.
    Therefore, _____.

As the preceding exercises make clear, it is not necessary to know whether an argument's premises or conclusion are true to know whether the argument is valid. In fact, some valid arguments have obviously *false premises* and a *false conclusion*. For example:

All squares are circles.

All circles are triangles.

Therefore, all squares are triangles.

Some valid arguments have *false premises* and a *true conclusion*. For example:

All fruits are vegetables.

Spinach is a fruit.

Therefore, spinach is a vegetable.

And some valid arguments have *true premises* and a *true conclusion*. For example:

If you're reading this, you are alive.

You are reading this.

Therefore, you are alive.

There is, however, one combination of truth or falsity that no valid argument can have. *No valid argument can have all true premises and a false conclusion.* This important truth follows from the very definition of a valid argument. Because a valid argument, by definition, is an argument in which the conclusion *must* be true if the premises are true, no valid argument can have all true premises and a false conclusion.

A deductive argument in which the conclusion does *not* follow necessarily from the premises is said to be an **invalid deductive argument.** Here are four examples:

All dogs are animals.

Lassie is an animal.

Therefore, Lassie is a dog.

If I'm a monkey's uncle, then I'm a primate.

I'm not a monkey's uncle.

So, I'm not a primate.

All pears are vegetables.

All fruits are vegetables.

Therefore, all pears are fruits.

All dogs are cats.

All cats are whales.

Therefore, all whales are dogs.

Each of these arguments is invalid. The first argument has true premises and a true conclusion. The second argument has true premises and a false conclusion. The third argument has false premises and a true conclusion. And the fourth argument has false premises and a false conclusion.

To recap: An invalid argument can have any combination of truth or falsity in the premises or conclusion. A valid argument can have any combination except one: No valid argument can have true premises and a false conclusion.

Because an argument's conclusion either does or does not follow necessarily from its premises, it follows that all deductive arguments are either valid or invalid. For the same reason, all deductive arguments are either 100 percent valid or 100 percent invalid. Either a deductive argument provides logically conclusive grounds for its conclusion or it does not. If it does, the argument is valid. If it does not, the argument is invalid. Thus, no deductive argument can be "mostly valid" or "almost valid." Deductive validity doesn't come in degrees.

Probably the most common mistake students make when they are first introduced to the concept of deductive validity is to think that *valid* means "true." Remember: *Valid* does *not* mean "true." *Valid* means that the argument is well reasoned, that the pattern of reasoning is a logically reliable pattern of

Valid deductive arguments are like steel traps. Once a person walks into the trap by accepting the premises, there is no escape; the conclusion follows necessarily.

—Kathleen Dean Moore

reasoning, that the conclusion follows necessarily from the premises. Thus, the basic test of deductive validity is not whether the premises are actually true. Instead, the basic question is this: *If the argument's premises were true, would the conclusion also have to be true?* If the answer is yes, the argument is valid. If the answer is no, the argument is invalid.

Now let's apply this test of validity to a few examples. Here's one:

> The Eiffel Tower is in Paris.
>
> Paris is in France.
>
> Therefore, the Eiffel Tower is in France.

If the premises of this argument were true (as they are, of course), would the conclusion also have to be true? Yes, it would be contradictory to assert that the Eiffel Tower is in Paris and that Paris is in France and yet deny that the Eiffel Tower is in France. Thus, the argument is deductively valid.

Here is a second example:

> All pigs are sheep.
>
> All sheep are goats.
>
> Therefore, all pigs are goats.

Here both the premises and the conclusion are false. Does this mean that the argument is invalid? No, because if the premises were true, the conclusion would also have to be true. Thus, the argument is valid.

Here is a third example:

> Some people like spinach.
>
> Some people like anchovies.
>
> Therefore, some people who like spinach also like anchovies.

Here the premises and the conclusion are all true. Does the conclusion follow necessarily from the premises? No, it is logically possible that the class of people who like spinach doesn't overlap at all with the class of people who like anchovies. Thus, there is no contradiction in asserting the premises and denying the conclusion. Hence, the argument is invalid.

Consider a final example:

> No dogs are cats.
>
> Some dogs are not housebroken.
>
> Therefore, some things that are housebroken are not cats.

Is this argument valid? Does the conclusion follow necessarily from the premises? In this case, the logic of the argument is complex, so it is not easy to say. In fact, the argument is *invalid,* but most of us have trouble seeing that using just our seat-of-the-pants logical intuitions. Fortunately, logicians have discovered several nifty ways of testing whether arguments are valid or invalid. We study two of these techniques (the Venn diagram method and the truth table method) later in this book.

Critical Thinking Lapse

A small-town emergency squad was summoned to a house where smoke was pouring from an upstairs window. The crew broke in and found a man in a smoldering bed. After the man was rescued and the mattress doused, the obvious question was asked: "How did this happen?"

"I don't know," the man replied. "It was on fire when I lay down on it." [13]

Why is the concept of validity so important? Because validity is the basis of all exact, rigorous reasoning directed at the discovery of truth. Much as a leakproof pipe perfectly preserves whatever fluids flow through it, a valid argument perfectly preserves whatever truth is contained in the argument's premises. In short, validity is important because *validity preserves truth.* Only by reasoning validly can we reason rigorously from truth to truth.

Important as the concept of validity is, however, we shouldn't presume that every valid argument is a *good* argument. Consider the following:

All heavenly bodies are made of green cheese.

The moon is a heavenly body.

Therefore, the moon is made of green cheese.

This is a valid argument. It is also clearly a *bad* argument. What examples like this show is that we don't merely want our deductive arguments to be valid; we also want them to have *true premises.* Deductive arguments that combine both of these desirable features—that is, deductive arguments that are both valid and have all true premises—are called **sound deductive arguments.** Deductive arguments that either are invalid or have at least one false premise, or both, are called **unsound deductive arguments.**

INDUCTIVE STRENGTH

Inductive arguments, like deductive arguments, can be well reasoned or poorly reasoned. A well-reasoned inductive argument is called a *strong* inductive argument. More precisely, in a **strong inductive argument,** the conclusion follows probably from the premises. Put otherwise, a strong inductive argument is an argument in which the following conditions apply:

If the premises are true, the conclusion is probably true.

The premises provide probable, but not logically conclusive, grounds for the truth of the conclusion.

The premises, if true, make the conclusion likely.

Here are two examples of strong inductive arguments:

> Most college students own CD players.
>
> Andy is a college student.
>
> So, Andy probably owns a CD player.

> All recent U.S. presidents have been college graduates.
>
> Thus, it is likely that the next U.S. president will be a college graduate.

An inductive argument that is not strong is said to be *weak*. In a **weak inductive argument,** the conclusion does *not* follow probably from the premises. In other words, a weak argument is an inductive argument in which the premises, even if they are assumed to be true, do not make the conclusion probable. Here are two examples of inductively weak arguments:

> All previous popes have been men.
>
> Therefore, probably the next pope will be a woman.

> Fifty-five percent of students at East Laredo State University are Hispanic.
>
> Li Fang Wang, owner of Wang's Chinese Restaurant, is a student at East Laredo State University.
>
> Therefore, Li Fang Wang is probably Hispanic.

Because the conclusions of these arguments are not probably true even if we assume that the premises are true, the arguments are weak.

Like deductively valid arguments, inductively strong arguments can have various combinations of truth or falsity in the premises and conclusion. Some strong arguments have *false premises* and a *probably false conclusion*. For example:

> All previous U.S. vice presidents have been women.
>
> Therefore, it is likely that the next U.S. vice president will be a woman.

Some inductively strong arguments have *false premises* and a *probably true conclusion*. For example:

> Every previous U.S. president has been clean-shaven.
>
> So, the next U.S. president probably will be clean-shaven.

And some inductively strong arguments have *true premises* and a *probably true conclusion*. For example:

> No previous U.S. president has been a native Hawaiian.
>
> So, the next U.S. president probably will not be a native Hawaiian.

As with valid deductive arguments, however, there is one combination of truth or falsity no strong inductive argument can ever have. Because, by definition, a strong inductive argument is an argument in which the conclusion follows probably from the premises, *no strong inductive argument can have true premises and a probably false conclusion.*

Weak inductive arguments, on the other hand, like invalid deductive arguments, can have any combination of truth or falsity in the premises and conclusion. Here are some examples:

Most U.S. presidents have been married.

Therefore, probably the next U.S. president will be a man.

Most U.S. presidents have been over fifty years old.

Therefore, probably the next U.S. president will be single.

Most U.S. presidents have been women.

Therefore, probably the next U.S. president will be married.

Most U.S. presidents have been less than 5 feet tall.

Therefore, probably the next U.S. president will be single.

Each of these inductive arguments is weak. That is, each has a conclusion that does not follow probably from the premise, even if we assume that the premise is true. The first argument has a true premise and a probably true conclusion. The second argument has a true premise and a probably false conclusion. The third argument has a false premise and a probably true conclusion. The fourth argument has a false premise and a probably false conclusion.

As these examples make clear, whether an inductive argument is strong or weak generally does not depend on the actual truth or falsity of the premises and the conclusion. Rather, it depends on whether the conclusion *would probably be* true if the premises *were* true. Thus, the key question we ask about inductive strength is this: *If the argument's premises were true, would the conclusion probably be true?* If the answer is yes, the argument is strong. If the answer is no, the argument is weak.

The concept of inductive strength is similar in many ways to the concept of deductive validity, but there is one important difference: Inductive strength, unlike deductive validity, does come in degrees. Deductive arguments, as we have seen, are either 100 percent valid or 100 percent invalid. Inductive arguments, in contrast, can be more or less strong or weak. Consider the following examples:

According to the National Weather Service, there is a 60 percent chance of rain today.

Therefore, probably it will rain today.

According to the National Weather Service, there is a 90 percent chance of rain today.

Therefore, probably it will rain today.

According to the National Weather Service, there is a 40 percent chance of rain today.

Therefore, probably it will rain today.

According to the National Weather Service, there is a 10 percent chance of rain today.

Therefore, probably it will rain today.

The first and second arguments are both strong inductive arguments because the conclusions are probably true if the premises are true. The second argument, however, is stronger than the first because its premise provides greater support for its conclusion than the premise of the first argument provides for its conclusion. Similarly, the third and fourth arguments are both weak inductive arguments because the conclusions do not follow probably from the premises. The fourth argument, however, is weaker than the third because its premise provides less support for its conclusion than the premise of the third argument provides for its conclusion.

Finally, keep in mind that an inductive argument can be strong and yet still be a bad argument. For example:

> All previous U.S. presidents have worn togas.
> Therefore, probably the next U.S. president will wear a toga.

Although this argument is inductively strong, it is a poor argument because the premise is obviously false. A good inductive argument must both be strong (i.e., inductively well reasoned) and have all true premises. If an argument both is inductively strong and has all true premises, it is said to be a **cogent argument.**[14] If an inductive argument either is weak or has at least one false premise, it is said to be an **uncogent argument.** Consider these examples:

> No U.S. president has been a U.S. skateboarding champ.
> Therefore, probably the next U.S. president will not be a U.S. skateboarding champ.
>
> All previous U.S. presidents have been Democrats.
> Therefore, probably the next U.S. president will be a Democrat.
>
> All previous U.S. presidents have been professional football players.
> Therefore, probably the next U.S. president will be an astronaut.

The first argument is cogent because it meets both conditions of a cogent argument: Its premise is true and the argument is strong. The second argument is uncogent because it fails one of the conditions of a cogent argument: Its premise is false. The third argument is uncogent because it fails both conditions of a cogent argument: Its premise is false and the argument is weak.

In light of the preceding definitions, arguments may be diagrammed as follows:

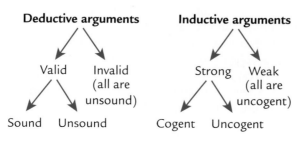

Summary of Key Definitions

Argument: A set of statements in which a claim (called the *conclusion*) is defended with reasons (called the *premises*).

Deductive argument: An argument in which the conclusion is claimed or intended to follow necessarily from the premises.

Inductive argument: An argument in which the conclusion is claimed or intended to follow probably from the premises.

Valid argument: A deductive argument in which the conclusion follows necessarily from the premises—that is, a deductive argument in which it is impossible for the premises to be true and the conclusion false.

Invalid argument: A deductive argument in which the conclusion does not follow necessarily from the premises—that is, a deductive argument in which it is possible for the premises to be true and the conclusion false.

Sound argument: A deductive argument that both is valid and has all true premises.

Unsound argument: A deductive argument that either is invalid or has at least one false premise, or both.

Strong argument: An inductive argument in which the conclusion follows probably from the premises—that is, an inductive argument in which it is unlikely that its conclusion is false if its premises are true.

Weak argument: An inductive argument in which the conclusion does not follow probably from the premises—that is, an inductive argument in which it is unlikely that if its premises are true, its conclusion is also true.

Cogent argument: An inductive argument that both is strong and has all true premises.

Uncogent argument: An inductive argument that either is weak or has at least one false premise, or both.

EXERCISE 3.5

I. The following arguments are deductive. Determine whether the arguments are valid or invalid. Explain your answer in each case.

1. If Flipper is a dolphin, then Flipper is a mammal. Flipper is a dolphin. So, Flipper is a mammal.

2. If anything is a trout, then it's a fish. A dolphin is not a fish. Therefore, a dolphin is not a trout.

3. If we're at the North Pole, then we're on Earth. We are on Earth. Therefore, we're at the North Pole.

4. If Bigfoot is human, then Bigfoot has a heart. Bigfoot is not human. So, Bigfoot doesn't have a heart.

5. Some people like ice cream. Some people like cake. So, some people who like ice cream must also like cake.

6. Simba is a lion. Necessarily, therefore, Simba must have four legs.

7. Your mother can't be a professional race car driver. Only men are professional race car drivers, and your mother, obviously, is not a man.

8. *Science student:* Science is often defined as the organized arrangement of known facts. But that cannot be the correct definition because a

phone book is an organized arrangement of facts, and a phone book is not science.

9. *Bill:* I guess some of the seniors were late to practice this morning.
Diane: How do you know?
Bill: Because the coach said that anyone late to practice this morning would have to do wind sprints, and I just saw some of the seniors doing wind sprints. That'll teach them.

10. *Frank:* I'm going to bring my cell phone with me when I take the logic test tomorrow. Whenever I don't know the answer, I'll just call my roommate, Ted. He aced Logic last semester.
Maria: Are you crazy? Professor Hardy will never allow you to cheat like that!
Frank: Sure he will. I distinctly heard him say, "No notes or books are allowed during the test," and phone calls, my friend, qualify as neither. It's simple logic: No notes or books may be used during the test; phone calls aren't notes or books; so, they are allowed.
Maria: Clearly, you're going to need all the help you can get.

II. The following arguments are deductive. Determine whether the arguments are sound or unsound. Explain your answer in each case.

1. All mosquitoes are insects. All insects are animals. So, all mosquitoes are animals.
2. Either dogs are cats, or dogs are fish. Dogs are not fish. So, dogs are cats.
3. If Rome is in Italy, then Rome is in Europe. Rome is in Italy. So, Rome is in Europe.
4. If Bill Gates is a billionaire, then he's rich. Bill Gates is rich. So, he's a billionaire.
5. No cars are trucks. A Mazda Miata is a car. So, a Mazda Miata is not a truck.
6. California has a larger population than Ohio. Ohio has a larger population than Vermont. So, California has a larger population than Vermont.
7. If the pope plays for the New York Yankees, then he is a professional baseball player. The pope does not play for the New York Yankees. So, the pope is not a professional baseball player.
8. Some apples are red. Some apples are delicious. So, some apples are red and delicious.
9. Los Angeles is west of Chicago. Hence, Atlanta is east of Chicago because Atlanta is east of Los Angeles.
10. Halloween is always on a Friday. Therefore, the day after Halloween is always a Saturday.

III. The following arguments are inductive. Determine whether the arguments are cogent or uncogent. Explain your answer in each case.

1. It tends to be cold in Alaska in January. So, probably it will be cold in Alaska next January.
2. Cigarette smoking causes lung cancer. Therefore, if you have been a heavy cigarette smoker for many years, you will probably die of lung cancer.

3. The vast majority of popes have been Americans. Therefore, the next pope will probably be an American.

4. In poker it's OK to lie and deceive. Business is like poker. Therefore, in business it's OK to lie and deceive.

5. Billions of men around the world shave daily. Therefore, somewhere in the world, someone must be shaving right now.

6. Shakespeare was English, and he was a great poet. Milton was English, and he was a great poet. Wordsworth was English, and he was a great poet. I guess most great poets were English.

7. Harvard University has been a leading American university for many years. Therefore, probably Harvard University will be a leading American university ten years from now.

8. Ninety percent of Americans jog daily. Tom Cruise is an American. So, Tom Cruise probably jogs daily.

9. Very few people in this country are named Obadiah. Therefore, the next person I meet is unlikely to be named Obadiah.

10. John F. Kennedy was a Democratic president, and he cheated on his wife. Bill Clinton was a Democratic president, and he cheated on his wife. I suppose all Democratic presidents have cheated on their wives.

IV. Determine whether the following arguments are deductive or inductive. If the argument is deductive, determine whether it is valid or invalid. If the argument is inductive, determine whether it is strong or weak. Explain your answer in each case.

1. If Boston loses, Cleveland will make the play-offs. If Cleveland makes the play-offs, the first play-off game will be played in Seattle. Therefore, if Boston loses, the first play-off game will be played in Seattle.

2. All birds can fly. Penguins are birds. So, penguins can fly.

3. Most college students sleep late on Sunday mornings. Wes is a college student. So, Wes probably sleeps late on Sunday mornings.

4. Exercise is good for the vast majority of people. Therefore, it would be good for my ninety-five-year-old grandfather to run in next year's Boston Marathon.

5. John's home address is 47 Riverside Drive. It follows that he must live near a river.

6. It is totally dark in here, but I know that the only things in the drawer are socks, ten black, ten white. I had better take out eleven socks to be sure I get a matched pair.[15]

7. According to the *Cambridge Dictionary of Philosophy,* philosopher William James was born in New York City in 1842. So, William James was born in New York City in 1842.

8. If it rained, then the streets are wet. The streets are wet. So, it rained.

9. This bathwater is tepid. It follows that it is neither extremely hot nor extremely cold.

10. States were justified in suing tobacco companies to recover the health-care costs associated with smoking. Similarly, states would be justified in suing McDonald's and Burger King to recover the health-care costs associated with eating fatty foods.

• Critical Thinking Lapse •

Dwayne Carver was a maintenance man at the Cedar Wood Apartments in Virginia Beach, Virginia. He had a good job, his own tools, and a blue uniform that read "Cedar Wood" on the back and "Dwayne" on the front.

Now, if you were going to rob a 7-Eleven store, as Dwayne did, you would probably wear a ski mask, as Dwayne did. But you probably wouldn't wear your work uniform . . . yes, as Dwayne did.

When he approached the clerk, his face was completely covered. He even made his voice sound deeper as he ordered, "Give me all the money." The clerk stared at Dwayne and his name tag and handed over several hundred dollars. Dwayne fled to a carefully concealed rental car that he had rented just for the day so that he couldn't be traced.

The police arrived shortly, and the clerk was asked to give a description of the robber. "All I can tell you is that he was wearing a ski mask and a blue maintenance uniform with 'Cedar Wood' on the back and 'Dwayne' on the front."

The two officers looked at each other. Surely not . . . no, this was too easy. Maybe the thief stole the uniform or purchased it at Goodwill. . . .

But it was Dwayne, all right. When the officers appeared at his apartment, he hadn't even changed clothes. The gun, the ski mask, and the money were all found in his pockets.[16]

11. There are more than fifty students in this class. It must be the case, therefore, that at least one of them is a Capricorn.

12. In a recent Gallup poll, 72 percent of Americans said they favored the death penalty. Therefore, approximately 72 percent of Americans do favor the death penalty.

13. On Monday I drank ten rum-and-Cokes, and the next morning I woke up with a headache. On Wednesday I drank eight gin-and-Cokes, and the next morning I woke up with a headache. On Friday I drank nine bourbon-and-Cokes, and the next morning I woke up with a headache. Obviously, to prevent further headaches, I must give up Coke.[17]

14. Smedley ran 5 miles in 38 minutes. It follows that he must have run at least 1 mile in less than 8 minutes.

15. Some Native Americans are Democrats. Some Democrats are Supreme Court justices. So, some Supreme Court justices must be Native Americans.

16. All but two U.S. presidents (Bill Clinton and George W. Bush) were born before 1925. It stands to reason, therefore, that the next U.S. president will have been born before 1925.

17. The Empire State Building is taller than the Sears Tower. Therefore, because the Eiffel Tower is shorter than the Empire State Building, it follows that the Sears Tower is taller than the Eiffel Tower.

18. Do most Americans like rap music? Apparently not. In a random survey of ten thousand nursing home patients around the country, fewer than 5 percent said they enjoyed listening to rap.

19. Richard Dawkins, the famous scientist, has said that the heavy elements like iron and zinc that compose human bodies were created billions of years ago in the interiors of long-extinct stars. Moreover, virtually all scientists agree with Dawkins on this point. Therefore, it is probably true that the heavy elements like iron and zinc that compose human bodies were created billions of years ago in the interiors of long-extinct stars.

20. Jerry was born on Easter Sunday. It necessarily follows, therefore, that his birthday always falls on a Sunday.

21. Whatever Rush Limbaugh says is true. Rush Limbaugh has said that there are more trees in America now than when Columbus discovered America in 1492. Therefore, it is true that there are more trees in America now than when Columbus discovered America in 1492.

22. Wally weighs 200 pounds. Hence, Joyce weighs 150 pounds because she weighs exactly 25 percent less than Wally does.

23. Most Americans favor a constitutional amendment allowing prayer in public schools. Melvin Bixby, president of the North American Atheist Society, is an American. So, Melvin Bixby presumably favors such an amendment.

24. If the moon is made of green cheese, pigs can fly. The moon is not made of green cheese. So, pigs can fly.

25. If you master if-then reasoning, you will do well in Critical Thinking. You will do well in Critical Thinking. Therefore, you will master if-then reasoning.

SUMMARY

1. All arguments are either deductive or inductive. In a *deductive argument,* the conclusion is claimed to follow necessarily from the premises. In an *inductive argument,* the conclusion is claimed to follow only probably from the premises.

2. In deciding whether an argument is deductive or inductive, one should apply four simple tests. The *indicator word test* asks, Are there any indicator words—words such as *probably, necessarily,* and *likely*—that signal whether the argument is intended to be deductive or inductive? The *strict necessity test* asks, Does the conclusion follow with strict necessity from the premises? The *common pattern test* asks, Does the argument have a pattern that is characteristically deductive or inductive? The *principle of charity test* urges us to treat doubtful arguments in whatever way is most favorable to the arguer.

3. We looked at five common patterns of deductive reasoning. A *hypothetical syllogism* is a three-line argument that contains at least one conditional

(*if-then*) statement. A *categorical syllogism* is a three-line deductive argument in which each line in the argument begins with *all, some,* or *no.* An *argument by elimination* seeks to logically rule out various possibilities until only a single possibility remains. In an *argument based on mathematics,* the conclusion is claimed to depend largely or entirely on some mathematical calculation or measurement (perhaps in conjunction with one or more nonmathematical premises). In an *argument from definition,* the conclusion is presented as being true by definition.

4. We studied six common patterns of inductive reasoning. An *inductive generalization* is an argument in which a generalization is claimed to be likely on the basis of information about some members of a particular class. In a *predictive argument,* a prediction is defended with reasons. An *argument from authority* asserts that a claim is true and then supports that claim by alleging that some presumed authority or witness has said that the claim is true. A *causal argument* asserts or denies that something is the cause of something else. A *statistical argument* rests on statistical evidence—that is, evidence that some percentage of some group has some particular characteristic. In an *argument from analogy,* the conclusion is claimed to depend on an analogy (i.e., a comparison or similarity) between two or more things.

5. Deductive arguments are either valid or invalid. In a *valid deductive argument,* the conclusion follows necessarily from the premises. In other words, it is an argument in which it is impossible for all the premises to be true and the conclusion false. In an *invalid deductive argument,* the conclusion does not follow necessarily from the premises.

6. A *sound deductive argument* both is valid and has all true premises. An *unsound deductive argument* either is invalid or has at least one false premise, or both.

7. Inductive arguments are either strong or weak. In a *strong inductive argument,* the conclusion follows probably from the premises. In other words, it is an inductive argument in which, if the premises are (or were) true, the conclusion would probably be true. In a *weak inductive argument,* the conclusion does not follow probably from the premises.

8. A *cogent argument* is an inductive argument that both is strong and has all true premises. An *uncogent argument* is an inductive argument that either is weak or has at least one false premise, or both.

CHAPTER 4

LANGUAGE

We take our language for granted. Seldom do we think about how much we depend on the ability to use words and put them together in phrases and sentences. With language we plan the day's events, curse the television, exclaim our surprise or frustration ("Damn!"), express pain ("Ouch!"), scribble reminders on scraps of paper, record our thoughts and feelings in diaries and journals, recall past conversations and events, talk to ourselves in anxious moments, pray, wonder, and worry. We could, perhaps, think in other ways—with images, for example—but that would be very limiting.

Thought and language create our world, and so to think critically about the world we must pay careful attention to words—the words we choose and the words others use. In this chapter we focus on the skills of choosing the right word, defining words, and identifying the emotive and slanted messages some words carry.

> *Only where there is language is there world.*
>
> —Adrienne Rich

FINDING THE RIGHT WORDS: THE NEED FOR PRECISION

Failure to be precise in communicating can result in confusion and misunderstanding. What makes perfectly good sense to one person might be confusing to someone else. "My father is a painter," you tell a friend, but does your father paint houses or canvases? A professor writes "vague" in the margins of what you consider your best paper. Whose fault is it that your professor didn't "get it"? (*Hint:* not your professor's.) To communicate clearly, to defend our claims without confusing or misleading anyone, and to assess the truth of premises presented to us in the arguments of others, we must insist that language in the context of argumentation be clear and precise.

> *The slovenliness of our language makes it easier to have foolish thoughts.*
>
> —George Orwell

Say, for example, that as support for the claim that college bookstores should stop selling clothes manufactured in foreign sweatshops, the following were offered as premises:

90

> Sweatshop laborers earn minimal pay working in suffocating conditions in factories owned by American corporations. They claim that economic realities force them to participate in this practice.

To the writer this may be clear, but the reader will question what is meant by "sweatshop" and "minimal pay" and may wonder if "suffocating" is a literal description of the factory (limited fresh air to breathe) or a metaphorical description of the oppressive working conditions. The reader might also wonder if "they" in the second sentence refers to the corporations or to the laborers, both of which could conceivably feel "forced" into such practices. Thinking critically and arguing effectively often depends on recognizing imprecise language—that is, language that is vague, overgeneral, or ambiguous.

Vagueness

One kind of imprecision in language is vagueness. A word (or group of words) is **vague** when its meaning is fuzzy, blurry, or inexact. The phrase *minimal pay* in our example is vague because it does not indicate precisely how much money is paid to laborers. Or consider the word *rich*. It is clear that Bill Gates is rich. It is equally clear that most welfare recipients are not rich. But what about an NBA benchwarmer who earns $400,000 a year? Or a plastic surgeon who earns $1 million a year but has large gambling debts? Are such people rich? It is hard to say because the word *rich* isn't precise enough to provide a clear answer. The term *middle-aged* is also vague. Everyone would agree that President Bush is middle-aged. Everyone would also agree that Lindsay Lohan and former President Carter are not middle-aged. But what about Steffi Graf or Mick Jagger? No definite answer can be given because the word *middle-aged* has no clear and distinct meaning.

As these examples suggest, a vague word divides things into three classes: those things to which the word clearly applies, those things to which it clearly does not apply, and those things to which it may or may not apply. In such borderline cases, it is hard to say whether the word refers to those things or not.

> *I like sharp outlines. I hate misty vagueness.*
> —Bertrand Russell

Nearly all words are vague to some degree. Some words, such as *indecent* and *obscene,* are extremely vague: they create lots of difficult borderline cases. Other words, like *vehicle,* are moderately vague. Ordinary cars and trucks are clearly vehicles, but what about roller skates, baby carriages, snow sleds, and motorized wheelchairs? Still other words, such as *triangle* and *prime number,* have very precise meanings, with little or no vagueness.

Vague language is useful and appropriate in many contexts. It lets us speak with suitable caution when we lack precise information. ("I think I did pretty well on the exam.") It frequently adds richness, subtlety, and complexity to poetry and other literary forms ("a slumber did my spirit seal"). In diplomacy a certain deliberate vagueness may be needed to avoid disclosing important information. ("If you invade, there will be severe consequences.") And vague language is useful—indeed probably indispensable—in formulating suitably broad legal standards ("freedom of speech") in contexts in which it would be unwise to attempt to enact a detailed code of laws.

Generally speaking, however, vagueness should be avoided because it frustrates clear thinking and communication. Imagine, for example, living in a police state in which the following laws were enacted:

> Anyone behaving *immorally* will be severely punished.
>
> Anyone speaking *disloyally* will be shot.

Would you have any clear idea what kinds of conduct were prohibited by such vague laws?

Overgenerality

Vagueness is often confused with overgenerality. There is, however, an important distinction between the two. Words are vague if they have fuzzy or inexact boundaries and hence give rise to unclear borderline cases. In contrast, words are **overgeneral** if the information they provide is too broad and unspecific in a given context.

Consider the following brief dialogues:

> *Teacher:* Johnny, what is seven plus five?
>
> *Johnny:* More than two.

> *Dean of students:* What were you drinking at this keg party?
>
> *Freshman:* A beverage.

> *Mother:* Where are you going?
>
> *Teenager:* Out.
>
> *Mother:* When will you be back?
>
> *Teenager:* Later.

None of these replies is particularly vague in the sense of having blurry boundaries. The phrase "More than two," for example, gives rise to no troublesome borderline cases. The problem with these answers is not vagueness but overgenerality. The answers are not specific enough to count as satisfactory answers in the context indicated.

Whether an expression is overly general usually depends on the context. "He's human" may be a perfectly adequate response to the question "Is your chess opponent human or a computer?" But it is a poor response to the question "What's your new boyfriend like?"

Sometimes, of course, words may be both vague and overgeneral. Thus, if I describe my lost luggage simply as "a large black bag," my description is too vague ("large," "black," and "bag" all have fuzzy, inexact meanings) and too general (the phrase "large black bag" isn't specific enough to distinguish my bag from many others).

Walking Naked—As Promised

He wasn't nude but the mayor of North Platte, Neb., did keep his promise to walk naked down the street.

Mayor Jim Whitaker said he'd "walk naked" if the Paws-itive Partners Humane Society raised $5,000. When the scheme drew national attention—and angry calls—Whitaker revealed that he actually planned to walk a dog named Naked instead of walking in the buff himself.[1]

Ambiguity

Ambiguity refers to a doubtful sense of a word or phrase. Many words have more than one meaning. The word *star,* for example, can mean, among other things, a Hollywood celebrity or a twinkling celestial object. A word or expression is *ambiguous* if it has two or more distinct meanings and the context does not make clear which meaning is intended. Ambiguity is what makes puns and many jokes funny, but used unintentionally it can destroy the effectiveness of an argument.

Ambiguity, like overgenerality, is often confused with vagueness. The basic difference between ambiguity and vagueness is this: A vague word is imprecise because it has blurry boundaries and unclear borderline applications. An ambiguous word is imprecise because it is unclear which of two or more *distinct* meanings (each of which may be quite precise) is the one intended by the author. A handy way to remember the distinction is to keep in mind that *ambi* means "both," as in *ambidextrous:* "able to use both hands with equal skill."

Some expressions are ambiguous because it is not clear to what a single word or phrase in the expression refers:

> Joe went to the bank. ["Bank" in the sense of a financial institution or "bank" in the sense of a slope bordering on a river? Or could it be a sperm bank?]
>
> John called. [John Smith or John Brown?]
>
> Margie sold out. [Did Margie sell her inventory or did she surrender her ideals?]

Ambiguities that result from uncertainty about the meaning of an individual word or phrase are called **semantic ambiguities.**

Other expressions are ambiguous because of a faulty sentence structure:

> As a young girl, her grandfather often told her stories about the Wild West. [Her grandfather was never a young girl.][2]
>
> One morning he shot an elephant in his pajamas. (Groucho Marx) [Those must have been big pajamas!]
>
> On Monday, Professor Kraus will give a lecture on safer-sex in the college auditorium. [Students are having sex in the auditorium?!]

If a man is capable of thinking anything at all, he is also always able to express it in clear, intelligible, unambiguous terms.

—Arthur Schopenhauer

Sometimes words have two meanings.

—Led Zeppelin

Words have a meaning, whether we mean that meaning or not.

—John Henry Newman

Zen and the Art of Writing Litigation-Proof Letters of Recommendations

Recent legal changes have eroded the traditional confidentiality of letters of recommendation. As a result, it is not uncommon for letter writers to be sued by disgruntled job candidates. To avoid such lawsuits, letter writers might wish to consider some strategically ambiguous expressions:

To describe a candidate who is extremely lazy: "In my opinion, you will be very fortunate to get this person to work for you."

To describe a job applicant who is totally inept: "I most enthusiastically recommend this candidate with no qualifications whatsoever."

To describe an ex-colleague who is difficult to get along with: "I am pleased to say that this candidate is a former colleague of mine."

To describe a job applicant who is not worth further consideration: "I would urge you to waste no time in making this candidate an offer of employment."

To describe a person with lackluster credentials: "All in all, I cannot say enough good things about this candidate or recommend him too highly."

A little Internet humor.

Newspaper ad: Dog for sale. Eats anything and is especially fond of children.

Billboard for Planned Parenthood: Come to us for unwanted pregnancies.[3]

Church sign: What is hell? Come to church next Sunday and listen to our new minister.[4]

Newspaper headline: Prostitutes Appeal to Pope.

Headline: Two Sisters Reunited after 18 Years in Checkout Line.

Sign in Laundromat: Customers are required to remove their clothes when the machine stops.[5]

Ambiguities that result from faulty grammar or word order are called **syntactical ambiguities.**

Some phrases that on their own may be ambiguous are clarified in the context of an argument. For instance, "Joe went to the bank" creates no confusion in the sentence "Joe went to the bank to complain to the manager about the increase in ATM fees."

But miscommunication can result when a word has more than one meaning and the intended meaning is not clarified by definition or by context. In some cases, this failure results in what is known as a **verbal dispute,** which occurs when people appear to disagree on an issue but in actuality have simply not resolved the ambiguity of a key term. Suppose two people were asked the same question: "Is the suspect arrested last night *guilty* of the crime?" The first person answers, "No, a person is innocent until proven guilty." The second person disagrees: "I say he is guilty; he confessed when he was picked up." There is really no disagreement here on whether the suspect *committed* the crime; the first person is defining *guilt* in a legal sense (the suspect hasn't been convicted yet), and the second is defining it to mean that the suspect did the crime of which he or she is accused.

A **factual dispute,** on the other hand, occurs when opponents disagree not over the meanings of words but over the relevant facts. Person A might say, "That man did not commit the crime; he has an alibi." Person B might respond, "He did commit the crime; I saw him do it."

In other cases, though, assessing the truth of a claim that hinges on an ambiguous term can be nearly impossible. If someone claims, without further elaboration, that on average "men are more powerful than women," we would have no way of assessing the claim because *powerful* has several meanings; and whereas one of those meanings (physical strength) may be defensible, the others may not be.

> *How many a dispute could have been deflated into a single paragraph if the disputants had dared to define their terms.*
>
> —Aristotle

EXERCISE 4.1

I. Identify problems of vagueness, overgenerality, and ambiguity in the following passages. You'll notice that many of the examples are comical, whether or not the writer intended them to be so. See if you can determine which of the comical passages contain some clever and deliberate use of imprecision and which are unintentionally funny.

1. No cruising on this street.
2. As a member of Parliament, Anglo-Irish playwright Richard Brinsley Sheridan (1751–1816) had been asked to apologize for insulting a fellow member of Parliament. "Mr. Speaker," replied Sheridan, "I said the honorable member was a liar it is true and I am sorry for it. The honorable member may place the punctuation where he pleases."[6]
3. *Headline:* Need Plain Clothes Security: Must Have Shoplifting Experience.[7]
4. *Weather forecast:* Cloudy with a chance of rain.
5. *Headline:* Advice to Teachers and Parents on Drugs.
6. He ate his cheesecake with relish.
7. With her enormous bottom exposed to the sky, Ellen watched *Titanic* slowly sink.
8. On returning from church one day, President Coolidge was asked on what topic the minister had preached. After a moment's thought, he replied, "Sin." "And what did he say about the sin?" his interlocutor asked. "He was against it," Coolidge replied.[8]
9. *Sign:* Dogs must be carried on escalator.

10. Bob told Devlin he was hot.
11. *Headline:* Former Concentration Camp Guard Helps Burn Victims.
12. $3 + 5 \times 3 = ?$
13. *Politician:* We need a tax code that is fair to working families. I intend to introduce appropriate legislation that achieves this end.
14. She cannot bear children.
15. *Headline:* British Left Waffles on Falkland Islands.
16. British Prime Minister Benjamin Disraeli had a standard acknowledgment for people who sent him unsolicited manuscripts for his opinion: "Thank you for the manuscript; I shall lose no time in reading it." [9]
17. Lost: Small brown dog with black collar. Generous reward for return.
18. *Headline:* Teacher Strikes Idle Kids.
19. Jana told her sister she was envious.
20. Never withhold herpes infection from a loved one.
21. *Sign in private restroom:* Flush only when necessary. [10]
22. *From a student paper:* The German Emperor's lower passage was blocked by the French for years and years. [11]
23. *From the U.S. Bill of Rights:* Congress shall make no law respecting an establishment of religion, or prohibiting the free exercise thereof.
24. *Cricket rule (Law 42, Part 9):* It is unfair for any member of the fielding side to waste time.
25. *Headline:* Panda Mating Fails; Veterinarian Takes Over.

II. Determine whether the following disputes are verbal or factual.

1. *Tracy:* Sue is really religious. She reads her Bible and prays every day.
   Mark: Sue isn't religious. She never goes to church.
2. *Paul:* This is a maple tree. I know because it's just like the maple tree in my backyard.
   Amy: Maple tree, my foot! Maple trees don't have acorns!
3. *Mitch:* Professor Tomkins is a great professor. She tells funny stories, gives easy exams, and never assigns any homework.
   David: On the contrary, a good professor challenges his or her students and motivates them to do their best.
4. *Mike:* We better leave now. Coach said the game starts at 1:00.
   Lindo: We have plenty of time. He said it starts at 4:00.
5. *Hal:* Let's take Highway 6. It's shorter. We can save at least 10 miles.
   Yavonna: It's not shorter. Highway 6 is always backed up this time of day. It will take us at least 10 minutes longer.
6. *Prosecutor:* The defendant was neither legally insane nor coerced when he shot Frank Smith, mistaking him for a porcupine. Thus, the defendant acted freely.
   Defense attorney: Your honor, my client shot Frank Smith accidentally, not intentionally. So, my client did not act freely.
7. *Belinda:* Ty Cobb has the highest single-season batting average—.420.
   Ned: Wrong as usual, sportsfan. Rogers Hornsby hit .424 one year.

8. *Professor:* John, it's clear you didn't study hard for this test. This was a very straightforward exam, and you failed every section.
John: But, I did study hard! I spent over an hour last night studying for this exam!

THE IMPORTANCE OF PRECISE DEFINITIONS

A convincing argument often depends on the clear and accurate definition of language. The failure to define terms carefully can result in a messy battle, with some participants struggling to find the truth and others fighting to avoid it. Former president Clinton's entire political career nearly came to a crashing halt because he and investigators looking into an alleged affair disagreed on the definition of the term *sexual relations.* Prosecutors provided a legal definition of the phrase, a definition Clinton believed excluded the specific behavior he had engaged in. He denied the affair on the grounds that the term was inaccurate. While many observers might argue that Clinton, knowing full well the meaning of *sexual relations,* played games with the meaning of the phrase, others might claim that, like any good lawyer, Clinton held the prosecutor's language to the highest standard: It wasn't as precise as it should have been. In some respects Clinton's looking for an escape hatch is understandable. You would be very aware of the need for clarity if, for example, you were arrested and charged with an offense. Our radar for undefined terms seems to kick in quickest when we are on the defensive: "What, exactly," you might ask, "is 'reckless driving'?"

In many discussions, terms may need to be defined before a position can be advanced. Take, for example, the issue of whether Congress should approve an amendment outlawing desecration of the American flag. The attempt to adopt a flag desecration amendment, in June 2006, failed in the Senate by only one vote. Such an amendment would make it a crime to deliberately deface or destroy the flag in certain circumstances. Of course, if such an amendment passes, individual cases of "desecration" will be decided on the basis of courts' definition of the term. Clearly, *desecration* would require defining: Would tying the flag to your bumper and dragging it through the streets be considered desecration? How about sewing an old flag into a T-shirt or a bathing suit? Using it as a tablecloth? Flying it upside down? But the word *flag* would also need defining. What is a "flag"? Is it only the cloth banner that flies or hangs from a pole? What if, after a law against desecration has been passed, someone using a slide projector projects the image of a flag onto a white wall, throws paint or blood against the wall, and shouts obscenities at the "flag"? What if the same person projected the image, not against a white wall, but against a wall with anti-government slogans spray-painted on it?

The difference between the almost right word and the right is really a large matter—'tis the difference between the lightning and the lightning bug.
—Mark Twain

Definitions are the foundation of reason. You can't reason without them.
—Robert M. Pirsig

That depends on what the meaning of the word "is" is.
—Bill Clinton

➤ **Pop Culture Connection** ◄

Language Games in The Simpsons

Imprecise language, especially ambiguity, is the foundation of much of the humor in movie and sitcom dialogue. Consider these examples from *The Simpsons:*

1. In a National Park Service building, Bart encounters a Smokey Bear robot equipped with an electronic quiz:

    Smokey: Only *who* can prevent forest fires?

    Bart examines the two choices, "you" and "me." He selects "you."

    Smokey: You pressed "you," referring to me. That is incorrect. The correct answer is "you." ("Mountain of Madness")

2. According to urban legend in Springfield, Troy McClure, the movie star, has a strange sexual proclivity involving fish. One day, Troy walks into the Department of Motor Vehicles, creating a stir:

    Dr. Hibbert: Troy McClure? I thought he disappeared after that scandal at the aquarium.

    Louie: Hey, I thought you said Troy McClure was dead.

    Tony: No, what I said was, "He sleeps with the fishes." ("A Fish Called Selma")

Clearly, the interpretation of such documents as the Constitution can depend heavily on our definitions of key terms; and whereas an amendment might be deliberately left vague, it is up to the courts to decide on a case-by-case basis whether individual actions fall under the amendment.

In almost any argument, the definition of words can be at the heart of the debate. In fact, whereas some arguments take place over the truth or falseness of a claim ("The death penalty should be abolished"), other arguments center on the meaning of the words used to express the claim. Suppose that your former high school proposes to begin testing students for drug use. Even if you agree that this is a good idea, you need to know what school officials mean by "drug." What specific drugs do they intend to test for? Or suppose that a local PTA petitions the school board to ban violent movies from classrooms. Because many of us disagree on the definition of *violence,* those parents making the suggestion must clearly define what they mean by "violent movie." If the PTA's proposition were accepted without a clear definition, teachers would never know whether a film they intended to show fit the category "violent movie." Driver-education teachers could be charged with violating the rule if, in an effort to encourage safer driving, they were to show driving students films depicting the aftermath of traffic accidents.

If you wish to converse with me, define your terms.

—Voltaire

He who defines the terms wins the argument.

—Chinese proverb

Types of Definitions

To use language correctly in an argument, it is important to remain aware that not everyone reading or listening to your claims has the same background, experience, and values that you do. Your audience, therefore, might not understand completely what you mean by certain terms. In fact, your audience may have very different definitions of the terms you are using. Therefore, you need to present definitions of words that might be misunderstood. There are several types of definitions you can use.

Stipulative Definitions   If you've ever created a new word or used an old word in an entirely new way, you have provided a **stipulative definition,** that is, you tell your readers or listeners what it is *you* mean by the term. Here are two examples:

> "Buddy-dumped" means dropped from a person's Internet Buddy List.
>
> "Lottoholic" means someone who is obsessed with playing the lottery.

A stipulative definition is among the most subjective of definitions because the definition is one you have determined. In other words, a stipulative definition cannot be true or false, though it can, of course, be more or less fitting or appropriate. Writers frequently stipulate definitions when they give labels to cultural trends, political movements, schools of thought, and so forth. Similarly, scientists and technologists often stipulate definitions when they make new discoveries or invent new products. Stipulative definitions rarely create problems unless a writer fails to explain clearly that he or she is coining a new word or using an old word with a new meaning.

Persuasive Definitions   Another kind of subjective definition is a **persuasive definition,** in which an arguer defines a term in an effort to persuade a reader or listener to agree with the arguer's point of view regarding the thing being defined. Persuasive definitions usually contain emotional appeals and slanted terms and are often given in arguments over highly charged political and social topics on which people have firm views. Here are two examples:

> *Capital punishment* means the state-sanctioned, vengeful murder of helpless prisoners.
>
> *Capital punishment* means the infliction of appropriate punishment on vicious cowards who have no regard for life.

Each of these is a slanted, "loaded" definition, whose point is not to provide an objective, neutral definition of *capital punishment* but to persuade the audience to adopt the speaker's particular attitude toward the death penalty.

Although persuasive definitions are often presented as objective and authentic, they are convincing only if they are very well defended. For example, someone claiming that capital punishment is "vengeful murder" would have to provide strong support for that statement.

> "When I use a word," Humpty Dumpty said in a rather scornful tone, "it means just what I choose it to mean— neither more nor less."
>
> —Lewis Carroll

Lexical Definitions   Less personal definitions include lexical definitions and precising definitions. In a *lexical definition,* a word is defined in the way it is standardly used in the language. In other words, the purpose of a **lexical definition** is to state the conventional, dictionary meaning of a word. Here are two examples:

Pastel means a color having a soft, subdued shade.

Rug means a heavy fabric used to cover a floor.

The second definition accurately states how most people in the United States define *rug.* In England, however, *rug* can also mean a type of blanket used to cover the legs while a passenger sits in a car or train. Notice that the definition of *rug* reflects its general usage, not one person's use of the word.

Precising Definitions   A **precising definition** is intended to make a vague word more precise so that the word's meaning is not left to the interpretation of the reader or listener. Here are two examples:

From a class syllabus: "Class participation" means attending class, listening attentively, answering and asking questions, and participating in class discussions.

A "heavy smoker," for purposes of this clinical trial, is anyone who smokes more than twenty-four cigarettes per day.

In general usage, terms like *class participation* and *heavy smoker* are vague. In these examples, they are given comparatively precise meanings to permit clearer understanding and more accurate assessment.

In giving a precising definition, we should be careful to avoid attaching fanciful, biased, or purely personal qualities to the definition. A professor could not, for example, claim that bringing gifts is part of "class participation." Moreover, a precising definition must be appropriate for the particular context. Whereas belting out a rowsing rendition of "YMCA" might be appropriate participation in a talent show, it would not fit the definition of participation in a classroom.

Strategies for Defining

Writers rely on a number of strategies that, though not strictly definitions, may be helpful in clarifying the meanings of certain words. Each of these strategies, while useful in particular contexts, has limitations of which we should be aware.

Ostensive Definitions   Sometimes the simplest way to explain the meaning of a word is to give an **ostensive definition,** which consists in simply pointing to, or demonstrating, the thing being defined. Here are two examples:

Door means *this.* (as you point to one for the benefit of a foreign visitor)

Popping means this! (as you demonstrate your latest dance moves)

Ostensive definitions are often useful (indeed indispensable) in various contexts, but they have obvious limitations. For instance, your foreign visitor might conclude that a door must be made of wood or that anything with hinges is a door (lids can have hinges). You could take your visitor on a tour and point to every type of door you come across (elevator doors, sliding glass doors, car doors, and so forth) to provide a more complete ostensive definition, but such an exercise would obviously be time-consuming, and in the end the visitor still might conclude that *door* means "anything pointed at by my kind and somewhat obsessive host."

Enumerative Definitions   Another simple way to clarify what you mean by a word is to use an **enumerative definition,** that is, to provide specific examples of what the word refers to. For example, to help someone understand the meaning of *baseball player,* you might list some famous baseball players: Babe Ruth, Joe DiMaggio, and Mickey Mantle. To define *river* you could mention the Nile, the Mississippi, the Thames, and so forth. Here are additional examples:

> *Actor* means Tom Cruise, Jack Nicholson, Nicholas Cage, and so on.
> *Bible-belt state* means Texas, Oklahoma, Arkansas, Tennessee, and the like.

The trouble with enumerative definitions is that they tend to be incomplete, and hence may give rise to misunderstandings or convey only a very limited understanding of what the word means. For example, your list of baseball players might give the impression that *baseball player* is synonymous with *Yankee.* Sometimes it is possible to provide a complete list of a word's referents (*Low Countries* means Belgium, Luxembourg, and the Netherlands), but even these may not be very useful if the reader or listener is unfamiliar with the things being enumerated (*Diencephalon* means thalamus, hypothalamus, epithalamus, and ventral thalamus).

Definitions by Subclass   A **definition by subclass** assigns a meaning to a word by listing subclasses of the general class to which the word refers. Two examples:

> *Mammal* means gorilla, horse, lion, whale, and so forth.
> *Poem* means sonnet, limerick, haiku, epic, ode, and the like.

Definitions by subclass are similar to definitions by enumeration in that both attempt to clarify the meaning of a word by illustrating what the word refers to; however, whereas definitions by enumeration list *individual things* signified by a word, definitions by subclass list entire *classes or categories.*

Although often helpful, definitions by subclass suffer from the same shortcomings as definitions by enumeration. They can give rise to misunderstandings (our list of mammals might lead someone to think all mammals are large), and they are helpful only if one is broadly familiar with the classes that are named.

Etymological Definitions   A good dictionary tells what part of speech a word is, how it is commonly pronounced, and whence it came—its ancestry, or **etymology**. *Automobile,* for example, comes from the Greek *autos,* meaning. "self," and the French *mobile* (from the Latin *mobilis*), meaning "move." An automobile is self-moving or self-propelled.

Because the meaning of words can change over time, knowing a word's etymology is not always useful, but it will often help us define the word correctly and use it properly. For example, some people say "ambivalent" when they really mean to say "apathetic" (unconcerned). *Ambivalent* comes from the Latin word for "both" (*ambi-*) and "vigor" (*valentia*); so, to be ambivalent is to feel strongly both ways. *Apathy* comes from the Latin prefix *a,* meaning "not," and from the Greek *pathos,* meaning "suffering" or, more common, "feeling." So, to be apathetic is to lack feeling. You might feel ambivalent about abortion, but you are probably not apathetic about it.

Besides pronunciation and etymology, dictionaries also, obviously, provide definitions. But because they are written in a particular time and place, dictionaries cannot contain all of the meanings for each word in our language. Meanings change over time, and new words are added as they become popular. *Gay,* for example, means something different from what it meant fifty years ago, and *CD burner* is difficult to find in even the most recent dictionaries, including those published for access on a computer. Dictionaries are best considered history books that describe the way words were used when the dictionary was written, rather than prescribe how we should define a word. Furthermore, because dictionaries are written by people, they can show the bias of a particular person or group. A dictionary can also be incomplete, limited in the number of definitions it gives for a word, or just plain incorrect. Considered the best dictionary in English, the *Oxford English Dictionary (OED)* overcomes many of the deficiencies inherent in dictionaries by providing extensive definitions, etymologies, and examples of a word's use throughout history.

Synonymous Definitions   A **synonymous definition** assigns a meaning to a word by offering a synonym—that is, another word that has approximately the same meaning as the word being defined. Two examples:

> *Loquacious* means talkative.
>
> *Deleterious* means harmful.

Synonymous definitions can be helpful in many contexts. The confusion caused by technical jargon, for example, can be lessened if the jargon is accompanied by a synonymous definition. An apprentice carpenter might be puzzled to hear about a chisel's "bezel" until he or she discovers that the bezel is more commonly known as the "bevel" or even more commonly as the "edge," or imprecisely as the "point." Speaking among themselves, teachers might use words like "assessment" or "inventory." When speaking to parents, teachers might refer instead to "tests." It should be noted, however, that there are few true synonyms in the English language, and the subtle differences

Those Who Control the Definitions

Former Defense Secretary Donald Rumsfeld sparred with reporters over his use of the word "slog" in an internal memo that questioned whether the United States is winning the war on terrorism. Alluding to a line in which he said that U.S. forces were in for a "long, hard slog" in Iraq, Rumsfeld asked reporters, "How many people looked up 'slog' in the dictionary?" A reporter shot back: "Quagmire." Rumsfeld insisted on a definition of "to strike hard" rather than to struggle. A reporter said the preferred definition was, "To walk or progress with a slow, heavy pace; plod as in slog across the swamp." Rumsfeld said he's seen that one but "I read the one I liked." (*USA Today*, October 24, 2003)

between words like *rob* and *steal* or *excuse* and *justification* prevent us from substituting one for the other without regard to our real intentions. Robbers threaten or use violence to get what they want; someone could steal from you without your knowing it. And while poverty might be an excuse for robbing someone, it is certainly no justification.

Definition by Genus and Difference   One of the most useful strategies for defining terms is to define by genus and difference, a method that lexicographers (dictionary writers) often use to create definitions. A **definition by genus and difference** assigns a meaning to a word by identifying a general class (genus) to which things named by the word belong and then specifying a differentiating quality (difference) that distinguishes those things from all other things in the class. Two examples:

Buck means male deer.

Calf means young cow.

In the first example, *deer* names the general class (genus) to which bucks belong, and *male* names the differentiating characteristic that distinguishes bucks from all other deer.

The first step in defining by genus and difference is to place the term into an appropriate general class or genus. For example, *automobile* belongs not in the classes of furniture, clothes, or trees, but in the class of vehicles. Now we are left with the much tougher task of listing characteristics—the differences—that distinguish an automobile from other objects in the class of vehicles—trucks, golf carts, motorcycles, and so forth. To distinguish an automobile from a truck, you might say that an automobile is intended for the transportation of passengers. Unlike a motorcycle, an automobile usually has four wheels. An internal-combustion engine separates an automobile from a golf cart. Your definition now looks like this: *An automobile is a passenger vehicle that usually has four wheels and an internal-combustion engine.*

Next, ask if your definition could apply to anything that is not an automobile. In other words, is there anything that *is* a passenger vehicle with four wheels and an internal-combustion engine but is *not* an automobile? You might argue that a gas-powered, four-wheeled car used to transport coal miners (passengers) satisfies the definition, but it is certainly not an automobile. To separate automobiles from coal cars, you could add a distinguishing characteristic to your definition: *An automobile is a passenger vehicle that usually has four wheels and an internal-combustion engine and is used for transportation on streets, roads, and highways.*

Defining by Genus and Difference

Term	Genus	Difference
Automobile	Vehicle [and so are buses, trucks, bicycles, motorcycles, airplanes, golf carts, the space shuttle, and so on]	To transport passengers [distinguishes an automobile from a truck]
		Usually has four wheels [distinguishes an automobile from a bicycle, a bus, and a motorcycle]
		With an internal-combustion engine [further distinguishes an automobile from bicycles and from other four-wheeled vehicles, such as golf carts]
		Used for transportation on streets, roadways, and highways [distinguishes an automobile from such things as cars that run on rails]

It should be noted that one limitation of the genus and difference method is that it can be used to define a word without capturing the true essence of the thing that is defined. One famous example involves Plato's definition of a human being: a human being is an *animal* (excludes all inanimate objects and plants) that *walks on two legs* (excludes all four-legged animals, but birds, such as chickens, walk on two legs) and that *has no feathers*. That definition is a good definition by genus and difference: a human being is in fact the only featherless animal that walks on two legs. But the definition isn't fully adequate because it doesn't really capture the essence of being human—as an ancient wiseacre once proved by plucking a chicken and throwing it over the wall of Plato's school with a sign that read "Plato's man." Besides our upright stature and lack of feathers, what essential attributes separate us from all other animals? The capacity for language? The ability to laugh? Critical thinking skills? How would you define *human being*?

Rules for Constructing Good Lexical Definitions

Some readers may have noticed how difficult it is come up with good, accurate definitions. Every method has its pitfalls. While you may have occasion to stipulate a definition or to indicate precisely what is meant by a vague term such as *participation* or *heavy smoker,* most critical thinking contexts call for lexical definitions. Here are a few simple rules that will help you to construct sound definitions and evaluate those of others.

- **Don't make the definition too broad or too narrow.** A definition is too broad if it includes too much and is too narrow if it includes too little. A good definition applies to *all and only* the things being defined. A definition of *automobile* as "a vehicle with four wheels" would be too broad because it would include golf carts and lawn mowers. A definition of *sibling* as "brother" would be too narrow because it fails to include sisters.

- **Convey the essential meaning of the word being defined.** A good definition should do more than just pick out some uniquely identifying properties of the thing being defined. Defining *horse,* for example, as "the animal ridden by Napoleon during the battle of Waterloo" is clearly a poor definition, even though the defining expression does apply uniquely to horses. The problem with the definition is that it fails to capture the really important and necessary properties that make horses *horses,* rather than, say, cows or sheep. Expressing the essential meaning of a word can be very difficult and often requires specialized knowledge.

- **Provide a context for ambiguous words.** Many words are ambiguous; that is, they have two or more distinct meanings. For example, a "walk" in baseball is different from a "walk" in the park. To prevent confusion, therefore, a good definition should indicate the context in which an ambiguous word is being used. Thus, we might say, " 'Walk' means (in baseball) an award of first base to a batter who receives four pitched balls that are outside the strike zone and are not struck at by the batter."

- **Avoid slanted definitions.** Don't let personal preferences or attitudes interfere with your definition. Avoid slanted definitions—that is, biased or emotionally charged definitions that improperly play on the emotions or attitudes of an audience. Slanted definitions may be OK for a laugh, as in Woodrow Wilson's famous definition of a conservative as "a man who sits and thinks, mostly sits." But don't try to win a debate by a definition that can rightly be won only by an argument.

- **Avoid figurative definitions.** A good definition should express clearly the conventional meaning of a word, not be couched in figurative or metaphorical language. Consider these examples:

  Slot machine means one-armed bandit.
  Advertising means legalized lying.
  Religion means the flight of the alone to the Alone.

> *We had better not follow Humpty Dumpty in making words mean what we please.*
> —C. S. Lewis

"Definitions" such as these may have their place (they may be humorous or clever, for example); but if a straightforward definition is in order, such figurative language should be avoided.

- **Avoid needlessly obscure definitions.** A good definition should clarify the meaning of a word for someone who may be unfamiliar with the term. Thus, a definition should not include a lot of big words or technical jargon that readers aren't likely to understand. For example:

  Mouse means a quadrupedal mammalian of any of the more diminutive species of the genus *Mus* of the order *Rodentia*.

  For people not trained in biology, this definition is likely to be more confusing than helpful.

- **Avoid circular definitions.** A definition is circular if a person would need to know what the defined word means in order to understand the word or words used to define it:

  Entomologist means someone who engages in the science of entomology.

  Gambler means someone who gambles.

  Such definitions are likely to be unhelpful because the defining phrases are just slight variants of the words being defined.

EXERCISE 4.2

I. In groups define eight words from the list below, using any of the methods we have discussed—or a combination of them. The class will compare definitions. What do your definitions have in common? What makes them unique? Could you come to some agreement on a definition for each of the terms? How important is it that you agree as a group on the definition of some of these terms?

chair	sports star	blues
sofa	fan (sports)	horror novel
pencil	fanatic	drunk
coat	poet	democracy
jacket	rock and roll	advertising
actor	grunge	racism
patriotism	knowledge	
justice		

II. As a group read and respond to each situation given below. Your answer will depend on how you define the key word in the question. Group members might debate the definitions and the application of the definition to the given situation. Use any strategy for defining terms, or use a combination of strategies. You may

Types of Definitions and Strategies for Defining

TYPES

Stipulative: A definition that a writer or speaker has assigned to a term or that has been assigned to a term for the first time. *Example:* "The Wild Bunch" means our intramural football team. I call my little sister "the gnat."

Persuasive: A definition given to a term in an effort to persuade the reader or listener to agree with the writer's or speaker's point of view. *Example:* Advertising is the means by which companies convince unsuspecting consumers to buy defective or unnecessary products.

Lexical: A definition in which terms are defined in the way they are generally used in the language. *Example:* Blue jeans are pants made of blue denim.

Precising: A definition in which the writer or speaker assigns a precise meaning to a vague term so that the word's meaning is not left to the interpretation of the reader or listener. *Example:* The newly elected governor wants to raise taxes on the rich, which he defines as anyone making more than $100,000 a year in take-home pay.

STRATEGIES

Ostensive Definition: Provide a concrete example of the term. *Example:* The capital letter a looks like this: A.

Enumerative Definition: List members of the class to which the term refers. *Example:* The term *country* refers to France, England, Iraq, Mexico, and so on.

Definition by Subclass: Indicate what subclasses the word contains. *Example:* Fiction includes short stories, novellas, and novels.

Etymological Definition: Show the history of the term. *Example:* A playwright is not one who writes plays, but one who makes a play the way a wheelwright makes a wheel. The term *wright* comes from an Old English word, *wrytha*, meaning "work."

Synonymous Definition: Use a word that has the same meaning or nearly the same meaning as the term being defined. *Example:* A playwright is a dramatist.

Definition by Genus and Difference: Place the term in a class that helps narrow its meaning and then provide characteristics that distinguish the term from other terms in the same class. *Example:* A fawn is a young deer.

have to consult outside sources in deciding on your definitions, and you may want to agree on some contextual details that are not provided in the question. Some students, for example, might argue that the first question depends on how long the couple has been dating.

1. You just caught your boyfriend or girlfriend carrying on a sexually explicit dialogue with someone in an electronic chat room. Has your mate "cheated" on you?

2. As a "computer genius," you can access the college's computer files anytime you like. You can review your transcript, check your medical records, read what your high school guidance counselor said about you, and so forth. All of this information would be provided to you if you asked, but you don't. Can you be accused of "stealing"?

3. A sign posted outside the auditorium reads, "No food or drink in the auditorium." During a lecture your neighbor is loudly sucking on a lollipop. You remind him that food is not allowed. He tells you he doesn't have "food." Who is right?

4. Jack knows that the college to which he is applying gives preference to minorities. He argues in his application letter that his being a second-generation Irish immigrant distinguishes him from other people applying to the college. Is he a "minority"?

5. Nancy has a paper due tomorrow morning. She has written a very rough, undeveloped draft. Last semester Nancy's roommate, Sharon, wrote a paper on the very same topic. Sharon gives Nancy the paper and tells her to "take as much of it as you want." With Sharon's permission and help, Nancy copies passages from Sharon's paper. Is Nancy guilty of "plagiarizing"?

6. An acquaintance of yours was just seen leaving your room with one of your favorite CDs, which you did not give him permission to take. Can he be charged with "robbery"? With "larceny"?

7. Your professor thinks women are far superior to men in every way—intellectually, morally, emotionally, and so forth. Is your professor a "feminist"?

8. The cheerleaders at your school have petitioned to have cheerleading listed as one of the school's sports teams. Is cheerleading a "sport"?

9. One day, out of frustration, your roommate throws a full plate of mashed potatoes against the wall of the room, where, amazingly, it sticks. You get up to remove the plate and potatoes from the wall. "Leave it," your roommate insists. "It says something. It's art." "It's garbage," you reply. Who is right?

10. One day Professor Smith tells the class a joke he heard on a popular late-night talk show. The joke involves a sexual situation, and the punch line is quite offensive. Several students in the room, including a number of women, are clearly shocked by the joke. Could Smith be accused of "sexual harassment"? Does it make a difference if Smith is male or female?

11. Recently, a third-grader (age eight) told several off-color jokes to a female classmate. Is this an example of "sexual harassment"?

12. A high school football coach in Florida, upset at the behavior of one of his black players, warned the student not to "act like a street nigger." Many of the coaches, players, parents, and community members have accepted the coach's apology and pointed out that the incident is not typical of the coach, but others insist that the coach's remark indicates that he is "racist." What do you think? Does it make a difference if the coach is white or black?

13. After meeting Brad at a party, Sarah accompanies him to his apartment. After several minutes of kissing on his bed, Brad asks Sarah if she'd like to have sex. She says no, but as they continue to kiss and touch, Brad is persistent in his efforts to persuade Sarah, and she finally consents, even though she is not entirely sure she is doing the right thing. Has a "rape" occurred?

14. You are standing in a line of about one hundred people of varying ages, waiting to buy movie tickets at a multiscreen cinema. Your attention is

drawn to a woman who is speaking very loudly to a child of about six who is pleading with the woman to take him to the bathroom. She tells him to "quiet down" several times before slapping him firmly once on the cheek. The force of the slap is equivalent to what you would use to swat a mosquito on your own skin. Has this child been "abused"?

15. In the last three seconds of a professional hockey game, team A is losing by two goals. A member of team A skates up behind a player from team B and swings his stick at the player, hitting him on the side of the head and knocking him unconscious. The player is removed from the rink on a stretcher and taken to the hospital, where doctors find that he has sustained a concussion. His wound requires twenty stitches to close. He is hospitalized for several days. Should the player from team A be charged with "assault"? (You may wish to consult a dictionary of legal terms.)

III. During the writing of the third edition of this textbook, newspapers and magazines were filled with examples of debates over definitions: Under what circumstances can it be claimed that a foreign army is "occupying" a country? What is the definition of "planet," and how many planets orbit the sun in our solar system? What constitutes "victory" in warfare? When do the events in a country amount to a "civil war"? What conditions must exist in a country (the Sudan, for example) to warrant use of the term "genocide"? How should "terrorism" be defined? Can a soft drink containing high-fructose corn syrup be advertised as containing only "natural" ingredients? Why do so few young women today identify themselves as "feminists"? How prevalent is "binge drinking" on college campuses? Read a week's worth of newspapers and magazines and find several examples of debates involving the use of language and the definition of terms. Determine whether the examples you find are instances of verbal or factual disputes. Alternatively, you might wish to respond to some of the debates listed above, some of which may be unsettled even a year or two from now.

IV. Determine whether the following are stipulative definitions, persuasive definitions, lexical definitions, or precising definitions.

1. *Funky two-step* means the funny dance Peppermint Patty does in the Charlie Brown Christmas special.
2. *Oar* means a stout pole, widened and flattened at one end into a blade, used as a lever to propel a boat.
3. *Philosopher* means a deluded dreamer who spends his or her life attempting to answer questions that can't be answered.
4. *Beyond a reasonable doubt* means, for purposes of determining a defendant's guilt or innocence in a court of law, a degree of certainty of 95 percent or higher.
5. *Litter-butt* means a person who throws lighted cigarette butts out car windows.
6. *Affluent* means, for purposes of this sociological study, having an annual family income of $250,000 or greater.
7. *Labyrinth* means an intricate structure of intercommunicating passages, through which it is difficult to find one's way without a clue.

8. *Circler* means someone who spends an inordinate amount of time circling parking lots, looking for the closest possible parking place.

9. *Chronically tardy* means being late to class five or more times in any quarter or three or more times in any two-week period.

○ 10. *Faith* means an illogical belief in occurrence of the improbable. (H. L. Mencken)

11. *Tic-tac-toe* means a mindless game for bored children that almost invariably ends in a tie.

12. *Intoxicated,* for purposes of driving a car in this state, means having a blood alcohol ratio of 0.08 or higher.

○ 13. *Garden* means a plot of ground, usually near a house, where flowers, vegetables, or herbs are cultivated.

14. *Chathead* means a person who stays glued day and night to Internet chat rooms.

15. *Republican Party* means a political organization of patriotic, civic-minded citizens dedicated to preserving the cherished freedoms of all Americans.

○ 16. *Kite* means a toy consisting of a light frame, with paper or other thin material stretched over it, to be flown in a strong wind by means of a string attached and a tail to balance it.

17. By *full employment* economists mean an unemployment rate of 5 percent or lower.

18. *Democracy* means rule by the ignorant masses.

○ 19. *Indolent* means having or showing a disposition to avoid exertion; lazy; slothful.

20. *Normal speech volume,* according to audio engineers, is approximately 70 to 73 decibels in a quiet environment with the talker and listener 6 feet apart.

V. Determine whether the following are ostensive definitions, enumerative definitions, definitions by subclass, etymological definitions, synonymous definitions, or definitions by genus and difference.

○ 1. *Poet* means a person such as John Keats, Walt Whitman, or Emily Dickinson.

2. *Halitosis* means bad breath.

3. *Psychic* is a word that derives from the Greek word *psyche,* which means "mind" or "soul."

○ 4. *Bird* means cardinal, sparrow, robin, starling, and the like.

5. *Bull* means a male cow.

6. *Industrious* means hardworking.

○ 7. *Red* means this, and this, and this (as you point successively to a red fire truck, a red apple, and a red crayon).

8. *Metropolis* means a place like New York City, London, or Paris.

9. *Sagacious* means wise.

○ 10. *Gander* means a male goose.

11. *Optometrist* originates from the Greek word *optos,* meaning "seen" or "visible."

12. *Moon* means *that* (as you point to it).

○ 13. *Beverage* means drinkable liquid.

14. *Clement* means merciful or lenient.
15. *Sport* means baseball, basketball, football, hockey, soccer, and the like.
16. *Faith* derives from the Latin verb *fidere,* meaning "to trust."
17. *Yucky* means *that* (as you point to the sticky, congealed residue at the bottom of a trash can).
18. *Question mark* means this →?
19. *Purloin* means steal.
20. *Amateur,* from the Latin *amator,* or "lover," means a person who plays for the love of the game rather than for compensation.

VI. Each of the following definitions is defective in some way. Determine whether the definition is too broad, too narrow, lacking in context, figurative, slanted, obscure, or circular. If the definition suffers from none of these defects, determine whether it is nevertheless defective because it fails to capture the essential meaning of the word.

1. *Rectangle* means a geometrical figure.
2. *Epistemology* means the systematic study of epistemological issues.
3. *Lawyer* means a scum-sucking scavenger licensed to practice law.
4. *Spade* means a black figure shaped like an inverted heart with a short stem at the cusp opposite the point.
5. *Poem* means a rhymed composition in verse.
6. *Human* means the animal that does crossword puzzles.
7. By *knowledge* we mean information that has been objectively verified and is consistent with existing knowledge.
8. *Deodorant* means any preparation for masking or retarding the malodorous secretions of the apocrine sudoriferous glands.
9. *Conservative* means a person who is enamored of existing evils, as distinguished from a liberal, who wishes to replace them with others. (adapted from Ambrose Bierce)
10. *King* means the chief piece of each color, moved one square at a time in any direction.
11. *Hockey* means a game played on ice between two teams of vicious thugs wearing skates, the object being to beat up the other team and to score goals by shooting a puck into the opponents' net, using a stick with a blade.
12. *Prestidigitator* means a person who practices the art of prestidigitation.
13. *Spouse* means wife.
14. *Architecture* means frozen music.
15. *New York City* means the city in which the Statue of Liberty is located.
16. *Pope* means the infallible vicar of Christ and head of the Roman Catholic Church.
17. *Guard* means either of the two players stationed in the backcourt.
18. *Cello* means a stringed musical instrument.
19. *Evolution* means an integration of matter and concomitant dissipation of motion, during which the matter passes from an indefinite, incoherent homogeneity to a definite, coherent heterogeneity, and during which the retained motion undergoes parallel transformation. (Herbert Spencer)

20. And what, then, is *belief*? It is the demi-cadence which closes a musical phrase in the symphony of our intellectual life. (Charles S. Peirce, emphasis added)

EMOTIVE LANGUAGE: SLANTING THE TRUTH

So far in this chapter, we have seen how language is used to convey information and defend claims in an argument. We have seen that clarity, precision, objectivity, and clear definitions will go a long way toward making our ideas comprehensible and our claims more convincing. But although we may be careful to avoid vague and ambiguous words and to define our terms, we aren't always as cautious as we should be when claims are presented to us, and we sometimes find ourselves falling under the sway of those whose masterful use of language we find hard to resist. Consider the way college brochures are written. What follows is a fictional illustration assembled from the brochures of several colleges and universities; you might recognize some of the language:

> Most people, when visiting our campus, say Wexford feels like a college should feel: warm and welcoming—a community atmosphere. Wexford's faculty and staff form the kind of close relationships with students that challenge them to their full potential. Students appreciate the personal attention in the classroom, the relatively small classes, and the dedicated faculty. Our residence halls provide a sense of family from your first days here. You will find activities to suit your personal style, from the performing arts and competitive sports to volunteer service and student-run organizations.
>
> Students are involved and enjoy being at Wexford. Nearly nine of every ten freshmen return for their sophomore year—well above the national average. Parents and students comment frequently on how friendly and professional the people are at Wexford.
>
> From our innovative freshman orientation program to the ongoing support for planning a career, you will find your four years at Wexford marked by a sincere interest in both your personal and your academic growth.

"Close relationships," "relatively small classes," a "dedicated faculty," a "sense of family," "well above the national average," "innovative"—all these words and phrases were carefully chosen for their intended impact on the reader beyond their literal meaning. The words are selected not so much for the information they convey as for their **emotive force**—the appeal they make to readers' feelings, desires, and needs. Emotive language more overtly reveals a writer's attitude and feelings toward the subject than precise, neutral, and more objective language does; and it is intended to create in the reader the same *attitude and feelings* toward the subject, rather than increase the reader's *knowledge* about it. *Emotive* is the adjective form of *emotion,* which comes from the same Latin word, *movere,* from which we get *motion* and *move.* You have no doubt heard the expressions "moved to tears" or "moved by your kind words." Emotive language in an argument is intended to rile, to *move* readers by agitating, disturbing, angering, or exciting them.

Look again at the college brochure. The phrase "relatively small classes," for example, suggests that such small classes are a desirable thing. Instead of telling us precisely how many students are in an average class, the writer assures us that the classes are "relatively small," which in this case gives us no information whatsoever. Relative to what? The Los Angeles Coliseum? The writer doesn't exactly lie about the college, but merely slants the truth to a degree that makes the college more attractive. The writer could easily have said that "the faculty do the jobs they are paid for" or that "the orientation program was created by the staff," but "dedicated" and "innovative" sound so much better and are almost guaranteed to create a warm feeling in the receptive reader. The danger is that we might believe that information has been conveyed, when in truth we have learned nothing factual.

> *The tongue of man is a twisty thing.*
> —Homer

The Emotive Power of Words

The emotive power of a word can come from the word's **denotation,** or literal meaning. If someone tells you that a child was "punched," you might find yourself moved to disgust or even action at hearing a word that means "hit forcefully with the closed fist." But emotive meaning also comes from the word's **connotation**—the images and feelings that are associated with the word. The word *waterfall,* for example, *denotes* (or means literally) the steep descent of water from a high point, but it also *connotes* (or suggests) power, strength, the beauty of nature, island paradises, and so forth. Connotations of words come from many sources, including people's experiences, the use of the word in the culture (in poems, for instance, or in advertisements), the way the word is used as a symbol or metaphor in various religions, and even from the word's sound.

To see just how language can generate feelings and reactions by connotation and sound, consider the names of any number of motor vehicles currently on the market: Aurora, Blazer, Bravado, Breeze, Camaro, Catera, Concorde, Crown Victoria, Expedition, Explorer, Integra, Intrigue, Mustang, Ranger, Regency, Sebring, Sierra, Sonoma, Taurus, Voyager, Windstar. Several of those names are chosen for what they might suggest. The names Ranger or Explorer or Blazer, for example, let the prospective buyer know what the vehicle can best be used for and suggest a feeling of strength and adventure. Other names suggest wealth and status (Crown Victoria and Regency), speed and privilege (Concorde), wild independence (Mustang), or youthful freedom (Breeze). Other names, though, are chosen entirely for their sound. Because there is no conventional meaning for Sebring or Catera, consumers are simply expected to associate those words with something positive. *Sebring* has a luxurious sound and so might suggest elegance and refinement. What does *Catera* suggest?

Exercise 4.3

I. In groups of three, come up with names for several new cars—a massive luxury sedan, an SUV for the family, an off-road vehicle for the sports-minded, an affordable four-door, and a sleek, sporty coupe. Then choose one of your new cars and write an ad to sell it.

II. You have probably noticed that the builders of shopping malls and housing developments often use emotive language when naming their facilities. It is not uncommon to see such things as Meadowbrook Farms Shopping Plaza and Sunnydale Apartments in the most unlikely places. Even cemeteries get in on the emotive act (Riverview Memorial Gardens). Discuss as a group some of the names you have seen on housing complexes, shopping malls, and cemeteries in your hometown or college area. You might want to discuss the reason for these names and perhaps even the irony involved in their creation—how, for example, a deer hasn't been seen alive in Deer Run Community Acres for more than twenty years.

Let's look now at more-sophisticated examples of the use of words to slant the truth and evoke predictable responses from a reader. Whereas advertisers use words deliberately to get us to buy their products or services, not everyone is so aggressively manipulative. It is up to critical readers to keep their eyes and minds open to the use of connotative language (language that evokes certain images or emotions) in all forums, including supposedly neutral sources such as newspapers, magazines, and encyclopedias. Read the following passages from *Time* magazine and the *Philadelphia Inquirer,* both of which describe the launch of a space shuttle.

Time describes the launch of *Discovery,* the first shuttle to be launched after the *Challenger* disaster in January 1986. The *Inquirer* describes the launch of the former Soviet Union's first shuttle launch.

From *Time*

As the countdown clock flashed out the number of seconds until lift-off, the eyes of an entire nation focused on Launch Pad 39-B and the gleaming white shuttle *Discovery,* flanked by its two solid rocket boosters and clinging to the side of a giant, rust-colored external fuel tank. . . .

Finally, spectators joined in for the last 15 seconds of countdown, the engines ignited and the shuttle rose majestically from the pad, carrying its crew of five veteran astronauts. Over the space center's loud-speakers came the triumphant announcement: "Americans return to space, as Discovery clears the tower." But the cheers were muted as the crowd—many with clenched fists, gritted teeth and teary eyes—nervously watched the spacecraft rise—on its pillar of flame, then begin its roll out over the Atlantic.[12]

From the *Philadelphia Inquirer*

For the 6 a.m. launch, Buran could be seen piggy-backed on the white Energia rocket, towering against the pre-dawn sky at the Baikonur Cosmodrome in the central Asian republic of Kazakhstan. As the countdown neared zero, the rocket was enveloped first in smoke and then in a giant ball of flame as it lumbered off the launch pad and into the dark blue sky.

Three and half hours and two orbits later, the gleaming white Buran with its black underbelly came back into the television camera's view. Buran glided on automatic pilot until it bumped onto the specially built runway stretching across the vast, flat steppes a few miles from Baikonur.[13]

The difference in the language used in these two accounts is obvious. Whereas the American shuttle rises "majestically" on a "pillar of flame," the Soviet shuttle "lumber[s] off the launch pad" in "a giant ball of flame." The American shuttle, "gleaming white," "cling[s]" to its fuel tank; the Soviet shuttle "can be seen piggy-backed" on its white rocket, and we are reminded of the "black underbelly" when it lands. The difference in these two descriptions is truly amazing because the Soviet space shuttle, aside from the national markings it carried and the fact that it was imperceptibly smaller, looked precisely the same as the American space shuttle and lifted off in an identical manner. In other words, if the two shuttles had had no flags and such to indicate their countries of origin, an observer would have seen no difference between them. Why, then, does NASA's shuttle "rise majestically" whereas the Soviets' "lumbers"? Because both of these launches took place during the Cold War, and because *Discovery* marked a return to space after a national tragedy, the shuttle lifting off from Cape Canaveral appeared to an American writer much more thrilling than the liftoff of the shuttle from the Baikonur Cosmodrome.

The test for emotive language is not whether a reader or listener is emotionally moved by the words in an argument. Some words have inescapable connotations, and an audience's reactions are often individual and unpredictable. The word *mother,* for example, which means, simply and precisely, a female parent, will stir up positive images and feelings in many people and may evoke negative reactions in others. But even though these associations are inescapable, a writer who uses the word *mother* in an argument may have no intention of evoking the reader's emotions and may simply mean a female parent—nothing more or less: "Single mothers returning to work have difficulty finding affordable day care."

The test for emotive words is, instead, whether the writer or speaker *appears* to be using the word unfairly to generate predictable feelings in an audience or to manipulate the audience into either agreeing with the argument or overlooking its flaws. Much depends, of course, on the context and the tone of the argument. For example, a young man who says to his girlfriend, "Don't mother me," intends the word in a negative sense and appears to be claiming that his girlfriend's attention diminishes his independence. One way to distinguish between the fair and unfair use of emotive words is to ask whether the use of the word needs to be defended. No one would challenge the use of *mother* in the first example because a woman (whether single or married) with a child is, in fact, a mother. On the other hand, the girlfriend in the second example might say, "How do I 'mother' you?" or "What do you mean by 'mother'?"

The best way to determine whether words are unduly emotive is to ask whether the words could be replaced with neutral words and phrases with no damage to whatever information is being conveyed. Good examples often come from the sports world. A writer will claim that one team "slaughtered" —or "annihilated," "destroyed," "crushed," "embarrassed," and so forth—another team that in a more neutral sentence simply "lost" or was "beaten." A writer who chooses "slaughtered" for "beat" is slanting the statement to evoke the reader's emotions.

> *Language exerts hidden power, like the moon and the tides.*
>
> —Rita Mae Brown

When determining whether language is unduly emotive, it is helpful to ask the following questions:

1. Is the term—even though it may have emotive power—actually an accurate and precise way to describe an event, an idea, a person, and so forth? *Slaughter* is not always manipulative if it is used correctly—to describe events in warfare, for example.
2. Does the writer appear to be manipulating the reader's reactions or attempting to move the reader toward feelings of rage, fear, joy, desire, and so forth? What other evidence in the context of the argument supports the conclusion that the writer's language is unfairly emotive? Be sure to separate your personal reactions to certain words from reactions that the writer appears to be targeting.
3. Should the writer be expected to defend the term? A political candidate who calls his opponent a "fascist" would have to define the term and show how the opponent's words and actions fit that definition.
4. Is there a more neutral way to make the same point?
5. How important to the argument, information, or explanation is the suspected emotive language? We don't usually quibble over the emotive naming of cars or complain about a coach's emotional pep talk. Nor should we deny a writer some leeway in an argument for the expression of feelings and attitudes.

EXERCISE 4.4

I. Look at the italicized words in the sentences below and think of three or four words you could use to describe the action. Then discuss what differences are suggested by the words you have listed. The first is done as an example.

1. Bill used a blunt instrument to *make contact with* Bob. (hit, strike, bash, bludgeon) *Hit* and *strike* suggest less force and aggression; *bash* and *bludgeon* connote a greater impact.

2. She *said*, "I don't love you."
3. "I want ice cream," the child *said*.
4. "Do this, please," she *asked*.
5. "Did you *look at* that woman?"
6. Out of anger, he *damaged* the CD player.
7. He *held on to* her arm.
8. You were *not rational* to do that.
9. I am a *firm believer* in that cause.
10. He is a man *without feeling*.
11. She is a woman of *inaction*.
12. He became *angry*.
13. The boss *approved of* her work.
14. You're *thinking only of yourself*.
15. His actions were *inappropriate*.

II. Identify the emotive language in the following passages. Indicate which emotive terms you feel are manipulative and which you feel are appropriate.

1. *From an ad for a home:* Charming, cozy three-bedroom Cape Cod in an older neighborhood, wall-to-wall carpeting throughout, lower-level recreation room opening onto large deck, modern kitchen, new roof, garage, needs some tender loving care.
2. *From a personal ad:* DWF, mature, petite, attractive, spiritual, intelligent business professional, occasional drinker, enjoys quiet evenings, serious movies, and long novels.
3. Leave it to the People for the Ethical Treatment of Animals (PETA) to try and spoil the party for all of us fishing families.

   The animal rights group traipsed across the country last week in an attempt to disrupt National Fishing Week activities and indoctrinate schoolchildren. Circumventing parents and teachers, PETA members stood outside schoolyards and distributed "Look, Don't Hook" toy binoculars to kids. A 6-foot-tall, anti-fishing mascot, "Gill the Fish," hovered nearby while activists spread the animal rights' gospel. . . .

   Kids, take note: This kind of self-indulgent terrorism by animal rights activists is truly "cruel—not cool." (Michelle Malkin, "PETA, Go Jump in the Lake," *Philadelphia Daily News*)
4. Women, unless they were quite wealthy, have always worked: in the house and out of the house, on the farm, in factories, sometimes caring for other people's kids, often leaving their own with the family herd under grandma's practiced eye. I've read that early in this century, when desperate families flooded into cities seeking work, leaving their rural support systems behind, female factory workers had to bundle their toddlers up on boards and hang them on hooks on the walls. At break time they'd unswaddle the kids and feed them. I like to mention this to anyone who suggests that modern day care is degrading the species. (Barbara Kingsolver, "The Household Zen," *High Tide in Tucson: Essays from Now or Never*)
5. Five years after a world war has been won, men's hearts should anticipate a long peace, and men's minds should be free from the heavy weight that

comes with war. But this is not such a period—for this is not a period of peace. This is a time of the "cold war." This is a time when all the world is split into two vast, increasingly hostile armed camps—a time of a great armaments race. . . .

The reason why we find ourselves in a position of impotency is not because our only powerful potential enemy has sent men to invade our shores, but rather because of the traitorous actions of those who have been treated so well by this Nation. It has not been the less fortunate or members of minority groups who have been selling this Nation out, but rather those who have had all the benefits that the wealthiest nation on earth has had to offer—the finest homes, the finest college education, and the finest jobs in Government we can give.

This is glaringly true in the State Department. There the bright young men who are born with silver spoons in their mouths are the ones who have been the worst. . . . In my opinion the State Department, which is one of the most important government departments, is thoroughly infested with Communists.

I have in my hand 57 cases of individuals who would appear to be either card carrying members or certainly loyal to the Communist Party, but who nevertheless are still helping to shape our foreign policy. . . .

I know that you are saying to yourself, "Well, why doesn't the Congress do something about it?" Actually, ladies and gentlemen, one of the important reasons for the graft, the corruption, the dishonesty, the disloyalty, the treason in high Government positions—one of the most important reasons why this continues is a lack of moral uprising on the part of the 140,000,000 American people. In the light of history, however, this is not hard to explain.

It is the result of an emotional hang-over and a temporary moral lapse which follows every war. It is the apathy to evil which people who have been subjected to the tremendous evils of war feel. As the people of the world see mass murder, the destruction of defenseless and innocent people, and all of the crime and lack of morals which go with war, they become numb and apathetic. It has always been thus after war.

However, the morals of our people have not been destroyed. They still exist. This cloak of numbness and apathy has only needed a spark to rekindle them. Happily, this spark has finally been supplied. . . .

[This] moral uprising . . . will end only when the whole sorry mess of twisted, warped thinkers are swept from the national scene so that we may have a new birth of national honesty and decency in government. (Senator Joseph McCarthy, Remarks, *Congressional Record;* originally "Speech Delivered to the Women's Club of Wheeling, West Virginia")

III. Divide into groups of four. Each group is to select a name from the following list, and each member of the group is to look up the name in an encyclopedia, making sure that no two members of a single group use the same encyclopedia. After the group members have done their research, the group reassembles and compares notes on how the various encyclopedias portrayed their subject. Compare, especially, the language used by the writers of the encyclopedia entries. Some writers may focus on different aspects of the person's life, but does the language reveal anything about the attitude of the writer toward the subject?

John F. Kennedy

John Brown

Malcolm X

Benedict Arnold

Elizabeth Cady Stanton

Martin Luther King Jr.

Now do the same with newspapers. Choose a contemporary issue and read about it in four different newspapers. What differences in language can you find? Many daily papers can be found on the Internet. You can find them by starting at *newslink.org,* an index of thousands of newspapers and magazines on the Internet.

EUPHEMISMS AND POLITICAL CORRECTNESS

Very often in our communications with one another, we avoid language that we feel might offend, upset, or insult our listeners or readers. For example, when consoling a friend who has suffered a death in the family, we might refer to that death as a "passing away" or "passing on": "I'm sorry your uncle has passed on," we say, because saying "I'm sorry your uncle died" seems too blunt or because "died" seems so final, whereas "passing" connotes moving to another place. Whatever our reasons, when we choose a more gentle and less negative word over those we feel would be offensive or too direct, we are speaking in **euphemisms:** mild, comforting, or evasive words that take the place of harsh, blunt, or taboo words.

Many euphemisms exist to describe actions and places associated with bodily functions. *Bodily function* is itself a euphemism, and so are words and phrases such as *the facilities, restroom, ladies' room, powder room,* and so forth. It is no surprise that many everyday euphemisms are used to cover up our most private actions; perhaps we believe we lend some measure of dignity to our lives if we talk about our instincts, drives, and needs in more refined and civilized language.

There is nothing wrong with using euphemisms to make us more comfortable in "polite society," but a critical thinker should be aware that pleasant or vague language is often used to hide reality or avoid facing the truth. For example, knowing that the word *downsizing*—itself a euphemism

One of the discoveries of the twentieth century is the enormous variety of ways of compelling language to lie.

—Jules Henry

for *firing*—can evoke fear and anger from workers or citizens, corporations and the U.S. government often substitute language that, because it is confusing or overly technical, does not immediately generate negative responses. Sometimes the word is a clear synonym for *downsizing*. For example, *rightsizing* has been used by executives in a number of firms to suggest that the number of employees had grown to an excessive number and that trimming that number would return the workforce to its "right size." So although these companies were, in fact, downsizing, they avoided, at least momentarily, the negative results of using that word. Other companies have used even more creative euphemisms. General Motors instituted a "career transition program"; Wal-Mart began a "normal payroll adjustment"; National Semiconductor called its efforts at downsizing "reshaping"; Tandem Computers called it "reducing duplication"; and Procter & Gamble, in perhaps the most pleasant-sounding euphemism, called it "strengthening global effectiveness."[14] In all of these cases, the companies were scaling back their workforces. They were downsizing.

Government employees and politicians are especially notorious for using euphemisms. The military of the United States, for example, has referred to civilian casualties as "collateral damage" and has labeled soldiers "expendable resources." Enemy troops are sometimes called "soft targets." Soldiers who die by "friendly fire" have been accidentally killed by their own forces. The word *retreat* would never be uttered among the military elite, but *strategic redeployment* would be. In some cases the media has helped promote the use of euphemisms. In 2004, a vice president at FOX News asked his reporters to refer to U.S. Marines pictured in Fallujah, Iraq, as "sharpshooters" rather than "snipers," a word with negative connotations. Not every euphemism is used in an effort to bamboozle audiences or hide the truth, and some writers simply use synonyms to avoid repetition. But when euphemisms are used in a deliberate effort to confuse the audience or evade the truth, a critical thinker can call the lie what it is.

Over the past several years, euphemisms for various people and groups have proliferated. It is not unusual to hear that the school has hired several "custodial engineers" or that the local market is looking to hire "meat cutters." It seems that no one wants to be a janitor or a butcher any longer. In many cases, this use of euphemisms has been an attempt to find language more precise than the words commonly used. For example, although someone confined to a wheelchair may face some difficulty getting around, the terms *crippled* and *disabled* strike many people as inaccurate in describing the wheelchair-bound, who are often very resourceful in overcoming common obstacles and who can lead lives as productive as anyone else's provided their needs are considered in the design of buildings and transportation. In other words, "disability" might be more the result of obstacles placed in the way than a quality inherent in those people. For some people, then, the word *challenged* more accurately describes the condition of the wheelchair-bound. Because we often begin to perceive people by the words we use to describe

> The ill and unfit choice of words wonderfully obstructs the understanding.
> —Francis Bacon

> Thanks to words, we have been able to rise above the brutes, and thanks to words, we have often sunk to the level of demons.
> —Aldous Huxley

them, calling someone "challenged" rather than "disabled" can have the positive result of changing our perceptions.

Other attempts have been made to use more-precise language in describing human beings. *Native American* is more accurate than *Indian,* and *firefighter* is more precise than *fireman* if that firefighting human being's name is Barbara. There is little danger in using words such as these, and, in fact, doing so only improves our way of communicating and may even help keep the peace.

But perhaps we have gone too far in some regards. What was once an effort at accuracy has in some aspects become excessive. The term *political correctness* was coined to indicate the almost ridiculous extremes to which some people have gone to avoid using language that might offend or insult. In this case, politically correct language can be euphemistic. Take, for example, the term *urban,* which is used by some contemporary writers in place of *black* or *African American.* Reviews now often refer to "urban" films or "urban" themes rather than say that the film portrays an African American cast of characters confronting racial issues. The use of the term *urban* betrays an effort on the writer's part to remain politically correct. Similarly, writers often refer to the "economically disadvantaged" rather than the "poor," or say that someone is "chemically dependent" rather than a "drug addict." Such use of euphemisms may hide the real tragedy of poverty or addiction. Critical thinkers should strive to remain aware of euphemisms that conceal reality and should make every effort in their own writing to use words that are accurate and precise.

EXERCISE 4.5

In groups of three or more, discuss which word from each of the pairs below you think is more accurate. Which word in the pair would you prefer to use? Which would you prefer to see used by writers and speakers? How would the context of the word influence your answers to the previous questions? How would the context influence your judgment? The words in the right column might be considered euphemisms or politically correct terms.

retarded	mentally challenged
old, elderly	senior citizen
used car	pre-owned car
stewardess	flight attendant
fat	full-figured
deaf	hearing impaired
ghetto	culturally deprived area
divorced	newly single
primitive	preliterate
doorman	access controller
job	career
pimples	blemishes

pornography	adult entertainment
blockaded	quarantined
bombed	pacified
secretary	administrative assistant
freshman	first-year student
obese	overweight

Summary

1. Failing to be precise can lead to miscommunication. *Vague* words have meanings that are fuzzy and inexact and thus have debatable, borderline applications. *Overgenerality* occurs when language is too broad and unspecific. *Ambiguous* words have two or more distinct meanings in a particular context, making it difficult if not impossible for the reader or listener to decide which is intended. Ambiguity can also occur because of faulty sentence structure.

2. Very often, good arguments will depend on the precise definition of words and phrases that opponents in an argument might define differently.

3. Definitions can be *stipulative* (a word's meaning is determined by the writer), *persuasive* (the writer reveals bias or a point of view in the definition), *lexical* (the word is defined in the way it is generally used), or *precising* (a vague word is given a clear, precise meaning). A writer might provide concrete examples of what is meant by a word by pointing to the object being defined (*ostensive definition*), by listing members of the class (*enumerative definition*), or by indicating what subclasses the word contains (*definition by subclass*). *Etymological definitions* give a word's history, whereas *synonymous definitions* provide more-familiar equivalent terms. A *definition by genus and difference* records the characteristics that distinguish one thing from the other things in its class.

4. A good definition should be neither too broad nor too narrow, convey the essential meaning of a word, provide a context where needed, and not be slanted, figurative, obscure, or circular.

5. Good critical thinkers are careful to avoid vague language and to define terms, but they are also aware of the manipulations of language, especially language intended to evoke emotional responses that trick us out of attention and skepticism. Even sources we expect to be objective may contain language that subtly edges us toward a particular, predictable feeling or attitude.

6. *Euphemisms* are mild or evasive words that take the place of harsh, negative words. Some euphemisms are perfectly acceptable. Euphemisms are unacceptable when they are used in an effort to hide the truth. The effort to label people and groups more precisely led to creations such as *Native American* in place of *Indian*. Although this is seen by some people as an example of "political correctness," that term is better applied to efforts to dress up reality with euphemistic language.

LOGICAL FALLACIES—I

We encounter arguments all over the place: in books, advertisements, TV talk shows, political speeches, newspaper editorials, class discussions, and late-night bull sessions with our friends. Some of those arguments are sound and convincing, but many are fallacious. An argument is *fallacious* when it contains one or more logical fallacies. A **logical fallacy**—or *fallacy,* for short—is an argument that contains a mistake in reasoning.[1] In this chapter and the next, we discuss many of the most common logical fallacies.[2] In general, these are fallacies that are both frequently committed and often psychologically persuasive.

There are many common logical fallacies, and they can be classified in various ways. The simplest way—and the one we adopt in this text—is to divide such fallacies into two broad groups: fallacies of relevance and fallacies of insufficient evidence. **Fallacies of relevance** are mistakes in reasoning that occur because the premises are *logically irrelevant* to the conclusion. **Fallacies of insufficient evidence** are mistakes in reasoning that occur because the premises, though logically relevant to the conclusion, *fail to provide sufficient evidence* to support the conclusion. Fallacies of relevance are discussed in this chapter. Fallacies of insufficient evidence are discussed in Chapter 6.

THE CONCEPT OF RELEVANCE

Before we consider the fallacies of relevance, we must first clarify the concept of relevance itself.

To say that one statement is *relevant* to another is to say that *it counts either for or against that other statement.* In other words, a statement is relevant to another statement if it provides at least some evidence or reason for thinking that the second statement is true or false.

There are three ways in which a statement can be relevant or irrelevant to another. A statement can be positively relevant, negatively relevant, or logically irrelevant to another statement.[3]

A statement is *positively relevant* to another statement if it counts in favor of that statement. Here are several examples of **positive relevance:**

First argument: Dogs are cats. Cats are felines. So dogs are felines.

Second argument: All dogs have five legs. Rover is a dog. So Rover has five legs.

Third argument: Most Wexford College students live off-campus. Annie is a Wexford College student. So, probably, Annie lives off-campus.

Fourth argument: Chris is a woman. Therefore, Chris enjoys knitting.

Each of these premises is positively relevant to its conclusion. That is, each provides at least some reason for thinking that the conclusion is true. In the first and second arguments, the premises provide logically conclusive reasons for accepting the conclusion. In the third argument, the premises provide probable reasons for accepting the conclusion.[4] In the fourth argument, the premise ("Chris is a woman") provides neither probable nor conclusive reasons for accepting the conclusion ("Chris enjoys knitting"). The premise does, however, make the conclusion slightly more probable than it would be if the conclusion were considered independent of that premise. Thus, the premise does provide some evidence for the conclusion, and hence is positively relevant to it.

These examples highlight two important lessons about the concept of **relevance:** First, a statement can be relevant to another statement even if the first statement is completely false. Thus, in the first example, the statement "Dogs are cats" is clearly false. Nevertheless, it is relevant to the statement "Dogs are felines" because if it *were* true, the latter statement would have to be true as well.

Second, whether a statement is relevant to another usually depends on the *context* in which the statements are made. Thus, in the second example, the statement "All dogs have five legs" is positively relevant to the statement "Rover has five legs" only because it is conjoined with the statement "Rover is a dog."

Statements that count *against* other statements are said to be *negatively relevant* to those statements. Here are two examples of **negative relevance:**

Marty is a high-school senior. So, Marty likely has a Ph.D.

Althea is two years old. So, Althea probably goes to college.

In both of these examples, the premises are negatively relevant to the conclusion. Each premise, if true, provides at least some reason for thinking that the conclusion is false.

Finally, statements can be logically irrelevant to other statements. A statement is *logically irrelevant* to another statement if it counts neither for nor against that statement. Here are two examples of **logical irrelevance:**

The earth revolves around the sun. Therefore, marijuana should be legalized.

Last night I dreamed that the Yankees will win the pennant. Therefore, the Yankees will win the pennant.

Neither of these two premises provides the slightest reason for thinking that its conclusion is either true or false. Thus, they are logically irrelevant to those conclusions.

My motto is: TO THE POINT.

—Voltaire

History is a catalog of incidents in which a poor argument convinced hordes of people to act badly, or even brutally.

—S. Morris Engel

> ● **Critical Thinking Lapse** ●
>
> Kodak introduced a single-use camera called The Weekender. Customers have called the support line to ask if it's OK to use it during the week.[5]

EXERCISE 5.1

Determine whether the premises in the following arguments are positively relevant, negatively relevant, or logically irrelevant to the conclusion.

1. Carlos recently gave Amy an engagement ring. Therefore, Carlos loves Amy.
2. Marcos lives in Costa Rica. So, Marcos probably speaks German.
3. The sky is blue. Hence, the next president will be a Democrat.
4. Thousands of tobacco farm workers will lose their jobs if cigarette taxes are doubled. Therefore, smoking does not cause cancer.
5. Thousands of tobacco farm workers will lose their jobs if cigarette taxes are doubled. Therefore, cigarette taxes should not be doubled.
6. Emily is CEO of a Fortune 500 company. Thus, it's likely that Emily earns more than $50,000 a year.
7. Mel lives in Pittsburgh. Hence, Mel lives in Ohio.
8. Sue lives in Ohio. So, Sue probably lives in Cleveland.
9. The last three coin tosses have been heads. So, the next coin toss will probably be tails.
10. You should believe in God. You have everything to gain if God does exist, and little to lose if He doesn't.
11. Peter and his wife are both over 6 feet tall. Therefore, their daughter is likely to be over 6 feet tall, too.
12. Hmm, the wiper blades were turned on when I started the engine of this rental car. It must have been raining when the last person returned the car.
13. Martina partied all night last night. However, Martina was valedictorian of her high school class. Therefore, she will do well on her critical thinking test this morning.
14. Xu is a five-year-old child living in China. Therefore, Xu is probably a boy.
15. Most Americans believe that abortion should be legal. Therefore, abortion should be legal.

FALLACIES OF RELEVANCE

A fallacy of relevance occurs when an arguer offers reasons that are logically irrelevant to his or her conclusion. Fallacies of relevance often *seem* to be good arguments but aren't. In this chapter we look at eleven fallacies of relevance.

One Good *Ad Hominem* Deserves Another

In one of his famous debates with Abraham Lincoln, Stephen Douglas spoke disparagingly of Lincoln's humble origins and in particular of Lincoln's brief career as a storekeeper. Lincoln responded: "Many a time I have been on one side of the counter and sold whiskey to Mr. Douglas on the other side. But now there's a difference between us: I've left my side of the counter, but he sticks to his as tenaciously as ever."[6]

Personal Attack (*Ad Hominem*)

We commit the **fallacy of personal attack**[7] when we reject someone's argument or claim by attacking the person rather than the person's argument or claim. Here is an example:

> Hugh Hefner, founder of *Playboy* magazine, has argued against censorship of pornography. But Hefner is an immature, self-indulgent millionaire who never outgrew the adolescent fantasies of his youth. His argument, therefore, is worthless.

Notice what is going on here. The arguer makes no attempt to show why Hefner's arguments against the censorship of pornography are flawed. Instead, he simply attacks Hefner's character. In effect, he argues this way:

1. Hugh Hefner is a bad person.
2. Therefore, Hugh Hefner's argument must be bad.

But the pattern of reasoning is clearly fallacious. Even if it is true that Hefner is a bad person, that doesn't mean he is incapable of offering good arguments on the topic of censorship. The attack on Hefner's character is simply irrelevant to the point at issue, which is the strength of Hefner's case against the censorship of pornography.

It is important to bear in mind, however, that not every personal attack is a fallacy. The fallacy of personal attack occurs only if (1) an arguer rejects another person's argument or claim and (2) the arguer attacks the person who offers the argument or claim, rather than considering the merits of that argument or claim.

Consider some examples of personal attacks that *aren't* fallacies but might easily be mistaken as fallacies. Here is one example:

> Millions of innocent people died in Stalin's ruthless ideological purges. Clearly, Stalin was one of the most brutal dictators of the twentieth century.

It would be a very good thing if every trick could receive some short and obviously appropriate name, so that when a man used this or that particular trick, he could at once be reproved for it.
—Arthur Schopenhauer

This personal attack is not a fallacy, because no *argument* offered by Stalin is rejected on irrelevant personal grounds. There is no fallacious claim that any particular argument of Stalin's must be bad because Stalin himself was a bad person. The argument, in fact, is a good one.

Here is another example:

> Becky Fibber has testified that she saw my client rob the First National Bank. But Ms. Fibber has twice been convicted of perjury. In addition, you've heard Ms. Fibber's own mother testify that she is a pathological liar. Therefore, you should not believe Ms. Fibber's testimony against my client.

Here the issue is whether Ms. Fibber is or is not a believable witness. Because the arguer's personal attack is relevant to this issue, no fallacy is committed.

Attacking the Motive

Closely related to the fallacy of personal attack is the fallacy of attacking the motive. **Attacking the motive** [8] is the error of criticizing a person's motivation for offering a particular argument or claim, rather than examining the worth of the argument or claim itself. Here are two examples:

> Professor Michaelson has argued in favor of academic tenure. But why should we even listen to Professor Michaelson? As a tenured professor, of course he supports tenure.

> Barbara Simmons, president of the American Trial Lawyers Association, has argued that punitive damage awards resulting from tobacco litigation should not be limited. But this is exactly what you would expect her to say. Trial lawyers stand to lose billions if such punitive damage awards are limited. Therefore, we should ignore Ms. Simmons's argument.

Note that these examples share a common pattern:

1. X is biased or has questionable motives.
2. Therefore, X's argument or claim should be rejected.

The pattern of reasoning is fallacious because people with biases or questionable motives do sometimes offer good arguments. You cannot simply assume that because a person has a vested interest in an issue that any position he or she takes on the issue must be false or weakly supported.

It is important to realize, however, that not all attacks on an arguer's motives are fallacious. Here are two examples:

> Burton Wexler, spokesperson for the American Tobacco Growers Association, has argued that there is no credible scientific evidence that cigarette smoking causes cancer. Given Wexler's obvious bias in the matter, his arguments should be taken with a grain of salt.

> "Crusher" Castellano has testified that mafia hit man Sam Milano was at the opera at the time mob informer Piero Roselli was gunned down. But Castellano was paid $30,000 by the mob for his testimony. Therefore, Castellano's testimony should not be believed.

It is a matter of perfect indifference where a thing originated. The only question is: "is it true in and for itself?"

—G. W. F. Hegel

→ **Pop Culture Connection** ←

Monty Python's Argument Clinic

What's the difference between "argument" and "abuse"? Monty Python, the zany British comedy team, offered a classic take on that eternal question in *Monty Python's Flying Circus* (Episode 29, "The Money Programme"). A customer, hoping to hone his argumentative skills, enters an "Argument Clinic," where he finds Mr. Barnard:

Mr. Barnard: What do you want?

Customer: Well, I was just . . .

Mr. Barnard: Don't give me that, you snotty-faced heap of parrot droppings!

Customer: What?

Mr. Barnard: Shut your festering gob, you tit! Your type really make me puke, you vacuous, toffee-nosed, malodorous pervert!!!

Customer: Look, I came here for an *argument*, I'm not going to just stand . . . !!

Mr. Barnard: OH! Oh, I'm sorry, but this is Abuse.

By mistake, the customer had walked into the Argument Clinic's "Abuse Room."

Both of these arguments include attacks on an arguer's motives; neither, however, is fallacious. Both simply reflect the commonsense assumption that arguments put forward by arguers with obvious biases or motivations to lie need to be scrutinized with particular care. Thus, the fallacy of attacking the motive does not consist of simply criticizing another arguer's motives. Instead, it consists of criticizing an arguer's motives rather than offering a rational critique of the argument itself.

> *Some people will take every other kind of trouble in the world, if they are saved the trouble of thinking.*
> —G. K. Chesterton

Look Who's Talking (*Tu Quoque*)

The fallacy of **look who's talking**[9] is committed when an arguer rejects another person's argument or claim because that person fails to practice what he preaches. Here are several examples:

Doctor: You should quit smoking.

Patient: Look who's talking! I'll quit when you do, Dr. Smokestack!

Parent: Honey, I don't want you to skip school on senior skip day. You don't want to jeopardize your chances of being class valedictorian, do you?

Daughter: But Mom, you told me you skipped out on senior skip day! Why do you always get to have all the fun?

> *Presidential candidate Bill Bradley:* When Al [Gore] accuses me of negative campaigning, that reminds me of the story about Richard Nixon, the kind of politician who would chop down a tree, then stand on the stump and give a speech about conservation.[10]

The logical pattern of these arguments is this:

1. X fails to follow his or her own advice.
2. Therefore, X's claim or argument should be rejected.

But this reasoning is clearly fallacious. Arguments are good or bad not because of who offers them but because of their own intrinsic strengths or weaknesses. You cannot refute a person's argument simply by pointing out that he or she fails to practice what he or she preaches.

It should be noted, however, that there is nothing fallacious as such in criticizing a person's hypocritical behavior. For example:

> *Jim:* Our neighbor Joe gave me a hard time again yesterday about washing our car during this drought emergency.
>
> *Patty:* Well, he's right. But I wish that hypocrite would live up to his own advice. Just last week I saw him watering his lawn in the middle of the afternoon.

Here, Patty is simply pointing out, justifiably, that their neighbor is a hypocrite. Because she does not reject any argument or claim offered by the neighbor, however, no fallacy is committed.

Two Wrongs Make a Right

Closely related to the fallacy of look who's talking is the **fallacy of two wrongs make a right,** which occurs when an arguer attempts to justify a wrongful act by claiming that some other act is just as bad or worse. Here are some examples:

> I don't feel guilty about cheating on Dr. Boyer's test. Half the class cheats on his tests.
>
> Why pick on me, officer? Nobody comes to a complete stop at that stop sign.

> *Marge:* Bart, quit hitting your sister.
>
> *Bart:* Well, she pinched me.

We have all offered our share of such excuses. But however tempting such excuses may be, we know that they can never truly justify our misdeeds.

Of course, there are times when an act that would *otherwise* be wrong can be justified by citing the wrongful actions of others. Here are two examples:

> *Police officer:* Why did you spray this man with pepper spray?
>
> *You:* Because he attacked me with a knife. I did it in self-defense.

> *Father:* Why did you go swimming when the pool was closed?
>
> *Son:* Because my friend Joe jumped in and was drowning. I did it to save his life.

How to Distinguish the Look Who's Talking Fallacy from the Two Wrongs Make a Right Fallacy

The look who's talking fallacy always involves a charge of hypocrisy or failing to practice what one preaches; the two wrongs make a right fallacy often does not.

Here is an example of an argument that commits the fallacy of look who's talking but does not commit the fallacy of two wrongs make a right:

> I can't believe our pastor told us that wives should stay home and not work! What a crock! I happen to know that his own wife worked to put him through college.

The two wrongs make a right fallacy always involves an attempt to justify an apparently wrongful act; the look who's talking fallacy often does not.

Here is an example of an argument that commits the two wrongs make a right fallacy but does not commit the fallacy of look who's talking:

> I don't feel any obligation to report all of my waitressing tips to the IRS. I don't know a single waitress who does.

These are clear cases where the justifications offered do, in fact, serve to justify what would otherwise be wrongful behavior. Not all cases, however, are so clear. Here are two cases that are not:

> Jedediah Smith murdered three people in cold blood. Therefore, Jedediah Smith should be put to death.

> *Umpire:* Why did you throw at the opposing pitcher?
> *Pitcher:* Because he threw at three of our players. I have an obligation to protect my teammates if you guys won't.

Do these arguments commit the fallacy of two wrongs make a right? They do only if the justifications offered are insufficient to justify the apparently wrongful behavior. Whether they do or not is, of course, debatable.

The fallacy of two wrongs make a right is often confused with the fallacy of look who's talking. This is understandable, because it is easy to think of examples of arguments that commit *both* fallacies. For example:

> *Mother:* Honey, it's wrong to steal. How would you feel if someone stole your favorite doll?
> *Child:* But you told me you stole your friend's teddy bear when you were a little girl. So stealing isn't *really* wrong.

This argument commits the fallacy of two wrongs make a right because it attempts to justify a wrongful act by citing another wrongful act. It also commits the fallacy of look who's talking because it dismisses an argument based on the arguer's failure to practice what she preaches.

Force or Reason?

Once while giving a speech, Catholic historian Hilaire Belloc was repeatedly heckled by a member of the audience. Belloc, who was built like a boxer, bore these interruptions patiently for some time. Finally, however, he could endure no more. Fixing the heckler with a glare, he said, "I should prefer, sir, to settle this question by physical encounter, but since the rules of this club do not permit that method, I am compelled to attempt the task of teaching you how to think."[11]

The fallacy of two wrongs make a right is, in fact, distinct from the fallacy of look who's talking. The key differences between the two are summarized in the box on page 131.

Scare Tactics

The fear of man brings a snare.
—Proverbs 29:25

Fear is a powerful motivator—so powerful that it often causes us to think and behave irrationally. The **fallacy of scare tactics**[12] is committed when an arguer threatens harm to a reader or listener if he or she does not accept the arguer's conclusion and this threat is irrelevant to the truth of the arguer's conclusion. Here are two examples:

> *Diplomat to diplomat:* I'm sure you'll agree that we are the rightful rulers of the San Marcos Islands. It would be regrettable if we had to send armed forces to demonstrate the validity of our claim.

> *Gun lobbyist to politician:* This gun-control bill is wrong for America, and any politician who supports it will discover how wrong they were at the next election.

No passion so effectively robs the mind of all its power of acting and reasoning as fear.
—Edmund Burke

In both of these examples, the scare tactics employed provide no relevant evidence that supports the stated conclusion. As the second example makes clear, the fallacy of scare tactics need not involve a threat of *physical* force. Any kind of threat can be involved, and the threat may be veiled.

Of course, not all threats involve fallacies. Consider these two examples:

> *Parent to teen:* If you come home late one more time, your allowance will be cut.

> *President John Kennedy to Soviet Premier Nikita Krushchev:* If you don't remove your nuclear missiles from Cuba, we will have no choice but to remove them by force. If we use force to remove the missiles, that may provoke an all-out nuclear war. Neither of us wants a nuclear war. Therefore, you should remove your missiles from Cuba. (paraphrased)

The first example is not a fallacy because it is simply a statement, not an argument. The second example is not a fallacy because the premises are logically relevant to the conclusion.

Appeal to Pity

The **fallacy of appeal to pity**[13] occurs when an arguer inappropriately attempts to evoke feelings of pity or compassion from his listeners or readers. Here are two examples:

> *Student to professor:* I know I missed half your classes and failed all my exams, but I had a really tough semester. First my pet boa constrictor died. Then my girlfriend told me she wants a sex-change operation. With all I went through this semester, I don't think I really deserved an F. Any chance you might cut me some slack and change my grade to a C or a D?

> *Parent to high school football coach:* I admit my son Billy can't run, pass, kick, catch, block, or tackle, but he deserves to make the football team. If he doesn't make the team, he's going to be an emotional wreck, and he may even drop out of school.

These arguments may or may not be effective in arousing our sympathies. Logically, however, the arguments are clearly fallacious because the premises provide no relevant reasons to accept the conclusions.

Are all arguments that contain emotional appeals fallacious? No, as the following examples illustrate:

> *Mother to daughter:* Nana was asking about you the other day. She's so lonely and depressed since Grandpa passed away, and her Alzheimer's seems to get worse every day. She's done so much for you over the years. Don't you think you should pay her a visit?[14]

> *High school softball coach:* Girls, this state championship is the biggest game of your lives. This is what you've been working for all year. Your parents are counting on you, your school is counting on you, and your community is counting on you. Make them proud! Play like the champions you are!

In these examples the appeals to emotion are both appropriate and relevant to the arguers' legitimate purposes. Too often, however, people use emotional appeals to hinder or obscure rational thinking. When emotional appeals are used in this way, the appeals are fallacious.

Bandwagon Argument

We all like to feel loved, admired, appreciated, and accepted by others. **A bandwagon argument** is one that plays on a person's desire to be popular, accepted, or valued, rather than appealing to logically relevant reasons or evidence. Here are three examples:

> All the really cool kids at East Jefferson High School smoke cigarettes. Therefore, you should, too.

Our feelings or emotions about a particular claim have no bearing on the truth or falsity of that claim.

—T. Edward Damer

It is never too late to give up our prejudices. No way of thinking or doing, however ancient, can be trusted without proof.

—Henry David Thoreau

I can't believe you're going to the library on a Friday night! You don't want people to think you're a nerd, do you?

There must be something to astrology. Millions of Americans can't be wrong.

The basic pattern of these arguments is this:

1. Everybody (or a select group of people) believes or does X.
2. Therefore, you should believe or do X, too.

This pattern is fallacious because the fact that a belief or practice is popular usually provides little or no evidence that the belief is true or that the practice is good.

Not all appeals to popular beliefs or practices are fallacious, however, as these examples illustrate:

All the villagers I've talked to say that the water is safe to drink. Therefore, the water probably is safe to drink.

Lots of my friends recommend the Back Street Deli, so it's probably a good place to eat.

These bandwagon appeals are not fallacious because the premises are relevant to the conclusions.

Straw Man

The **straw man fallacy** is committed when an arguer distorts an opponent's argument or claim to make it easier to attack. For example:

Pete has argued that the New York Yankees are a better baseball team than the Atlanta Braves. But the Braves aren't a bad team. They have a great pitching staff, and they consistently finish at or near the top of their division. Obviously, Pete doesn't know what he's talking about.

This argument misrepresents Pete's view. Pete hasn't claimed that the Braves are a *bad* team, merely that the Yankees are a *better* team than the Braves. By mischaracterizing Pete's view—making it seem weaker or less plausible than it really is—the arguer has committed the straw man fallacy.

Straw man fallacies are extremely common in politics. For example:

Senator Biddle has argued that we should outlaw violent pornography. Obvi-ously, the senator favors complete governmental censorship of books, maga-zines, and films. Frankly, I'm shocked that such a view should be expressed on the floor of the U.S. Senate. It runs counter to everything this great nation stands for. No senator should listen seriously to such a proposal.

This argument distorts the senator's view. His claim is that *violent pornography* should be outlawed, not that there should be complete governmental censor-ship of books, magazines, and films. By misrepresenting the senator's position and then attacking the misrepresentation rather than the senator's actual posi-tion, the arguer commits the straw man fallacy.

The logical pattern of straw man arguments is this:

1. X's view is false or unjustified [but where X's view has been unfairly characterized or misrepresented].
2. Therefore, X's view should be rejected.

Clearly, arguments of this pattern provide no logically relevant support for their conclusions.

Red Herring

The **red herring fallacy** is committed when an arguer tries to sidetrack his audience by raising an irrelevant issue and then claims that the original issue has effectively been settled by the irrelevant diversion. The fallacy apparently gets its name from a technique used to train English foxhounds.[15] A sack of red (i.e., smoked) herrings was dragged across the trail of a fox to train the foxhounds to follow the fox's scent rather than the powerful distracting smell of the fish. In a similar way, an arguer commits the red herring fallacy when he seeks to distract his audience by raising an irrelevant issue and then claims or implies that the irrelevant diversion has settled the original point at issue. Here is an example:

> Many people criticize Thomas Jefferson for being an owner of slaves. But Jefferson was one of our greatest presidents, and his Declaration of Independence is one of the most eloquent pleas for freedom and democracy ever written. Clearly, these criticisms are unwarranted.

The issue here is whether Jefferson can rightly be criticized for owning slaves, not whether he was one of America's greatest presidents or whether he deserves credit for writing the Declaration of Independence. By diverting the reader's attention from the original argument and then claiming that the original argument has been refuted by the irrelevant diversion, the arguer commits the red herring fallacy.

Red herring fallacies are also extremely common in politics. For example:

> Critics have accused my administration of doing too little to save the family farm. These critics forget that I grew up on a farm. I know what it's like to get up at the crack of dawn to milk the cows. I know what it's like to work in the field all day in the blazing sun. Family farms are what made this country great, and those who criticize my farm policies simply don't know what they're talking about.

The issue here is whether the speaker's administration is doing enough to save the family farm. The fact that the speaker grew up on a farm is simply a smokescreen used to distract attention from this issue.

It should be noted, however, that it is *not* a fallacy simply to change the subject or evade an issue. For example:

> *Political opponent:* Congressman Crookley, now that you have been convicted of bribery, extortion, and grand theft auto, isn't it high time that you resigned from office?

Intellectual debate is impoverished when one attacks caricatures; soft targets generally only suit weapons of corresponding low firepower.

—William T. Twining

The chief trait of the orderly mind is tenacity, concentration— that undeviating attention which in various sports is enjoined in the precept "Keep your eye on the ball."

—Wilson Follett

How to Distinguish the Straw Man Fallacy from the Red Herring Fallacy

The straw man fallacy always involves misrepresenting another person's argument or claim; the red herring fallacy often does not.

Here's an example of an argument that commits the straw man fallacy but does not commit the red herring fallacy:

> I overheard my friend Hal say that democracy isn't always the best form of government. Funny, I never figured Hal for a communist.

The red herring fallacy always involves changing or evading the issue; the straw man fallacy often does not.

Here's an example of an argument that commits the red herring fallacy but does not commit the straw man fallacy:

> Jessica Wu has argued that immediate steps should be taken to reduce global warming. The most serious environmental problem, however, isn't global warming—it's overpopulation. Unless something is done to reduce population growth in the third world, mass starvation and irreversible environmental damage will result. Frankly, I think Jessica's view is ridiculous.

> *Representative Crookley:* How 'bout those Yankees? A ten-game lead at the All-Star break!

Here the speaker doesn't deny the charge or pretend it is refuted by discussing irrelevant issues; rather, he simply evades the issue. Because there is no mistake in reasoning in the argument, no fallacy is committed.

Equivocation

We saw in Chapter 4 that words often have more than one meaning. The **fallacy of equivocation** is committed when a key word is used in two or more senses in the same argument and the apparent success of the argument depends on the shift in meaning. Here are several examples:

> It is a crime to smoke grass. Kentucky bluegrass is a grass. Therefore, it is a crime to smoke Kentucky bluegrass.

> I distinctly heard Mo say, "Hit me," as he was playing cards in Las Vegas. To hit someone is to slug them. So, Mo must enjoy being slugged.

> Any law can be repealed by the proper legal authority. The law of gravity is a law. Therefore, the law of gravity can be repealed by the proper legal authority.[16]

In each of these arguments, a key word is used ambiguously or *equivocally*—that is, with two or more distinct senses. The first argument equivocates on the word *grass*. In the first premise, it means marijuana; in the second it means ordinary lawn grass. The second argument equivocates on the word *hit*. In the first premise, it means dealing a card; in the second it means being punched or struck. The third argument equivocates on the word *law*. In the first premise, it

---

• Critical Thinking Lapse •

I've been told by a friend of a friend of a great mathematician that this genius cannot remember where he lives, although his house is only a short distance from the campus of the university where he works. The story, sworn to be true, is that this man must count each day the number of streets away from campus, and the number of houses down the street on the right, as he walks home. Three streets down, take a right, twelve houses on the right. One day, I am told, as he was walking home he was deep in thought about a mathematical problem and lost count. Utterly confused and totally lost, he saw a little boy playing at the side of the road. He called out, "Young man, can you tell me where the mathematician lives?" The boy looked up and said, "What's wrong with you, Daddy?" [17]

---

refers to a law regulating human conduct; in the second it refers to an observed uniformity of nature.

Fallacies of equivocation can be difficult to spot because they often *appear* valid, but they aren't. The third example above appears to have the following logical pattern:

1. All A's are B's. [All laws are things that can be repealed by the proper legal authority.]
2. C is an A. [The law of gravity is a law.]
3. Therefore, C is a B. [Therefore, the law of gravity is a thing that can be repealed by the proper legal authority.]

Such a pattern is, of course, valid. Moreover, the premises appear to be true. Nevertheless, the argument is clearly fallacious. Why?

The argument is fallacious because it only *appears* to have a valid argument form. This becomes clear if we make explicit the two different senses in which the word *law* is used in the argument.

1. All A's are B's. [All laws regulating human conduct are things that can be repealed by proper legal authority.]
2. C is a D. [The law of gravity is an observed uniformity of nature.]
3. Therefore, C is a B. [Therefore, the law of gravity is a thing that can be repealed by the proper legal authority.]

When the two senses of the word *law* are distinguished in this way, it is clear that the premises provide no relevant support for the conclusion.

Begging the Question

The **fallacy of begging the question** is committed when an arguer states or assumes as a premise the very thing he or she is trying to prove as a conclusion. There are two common ways to commit this fallacy.

Summary of Fallacies of Relevance

Personal attack: Arguer attacks the character of another arguer.

Attacking the motive: Arguer attacks the motive of another arguer.

Look who's talking: Arguer attacks the hypocrisy of another arguer.

Two wrongs make a right: Arguer tries to justify a wrong by citing another wrong.

Scare tactics: Arguer threatens a reader or listener.

Appeal to pity: Arguer tries to evoke pity from a reader or listener.

Bandwagon argument: Arguer appeals to a reader's or listener's desire to be accepted or valued.

Straw man: Arguer misrepresents an opponent's position.

Red herring: Arguer tries to distract the attention of the audience by raising an irrelevant issue.

Equivocation: Arguer uses a key word in two or more different senses.

Begging the question: Arguer assumes the point to be proven.

The most obvious way is to simply *restate* the conclusion in slightly different words. Here are two examples:

> Bungee-jumping is dangerous because it's unsafe.
>
> Capital punishment is morally wrong because it is ethically impermissible to inflict death as punishment for a crime.

In the first example, the premise basically repeats the conclusion: saying that bungee-jumping is "unsafe" is another way of saying that it is "dangerous." In the second example, the conclusion is begged because saying that it is "ethically impermissible" to inflict death as punishment for a crime is equivalent to saying that capital punishment is "morally wrong."

The second common form of begging the question involves "circular reasoning" or "arguing in a circle." This occurs when an arguer offers a chain of reasons for a conclusion, where the conclusion of the argument is stated or assumed as one of the premises. For example:

> *Kylie:* God wrote the Bible.
>
> *Ned:* How do you know?
>
> *Kylie:* Because it says so in the Bible, and what the Bible says is true.
>
> *Ned:* How do you know what the Bible says is true?
>
> *Kylie:* Because God wrote the Bible.

Note the tight circle of reasoning here: A because B, B because A. In more-complex arguments, the circular reasoning may be more difficult to spot, as in this example:

> Wexford College is a better college than Aggie Tech. Wexford is a better college because it has better students. It has better students because it has better faculty. It has better faculty because it pays higher faculty salaries. It pays higher

faculty salaries because it has a larger endowment. It has a larger endowment because it has more generous and loyal alumni. It has more generous and loyal alumni because it is a better college.

Here the chain of reasoning is so lengthy that it is easy to overlook the fact that the statement "Wexford College is a better college than Aggie Tech" appears both as a premise and as a conclusion in the argument.

EXERCISE 5.2

I. Identify the fallacies of relevance committed by the following arguments. There may be more than one. If no fallacy is committed, write "no fallacy."

1. The new Volkswagon Beetle is the coolest car around. It's selling like hotcakes. You should ask your parents to buy you one.

2. *Jason:* Did you hear Andrew's class presentation on senior-class rights and privileges?
   Kyle: Yeah, but I don't buy any of his arguments. He's just a rich snob who likes to hear himself talk.

3. Bill Baxter deserves to be promoted to vice president. He has three small children, and just last week his wife was diagnosed with breast cancer.

4. School superintendent Kate Duncan has argued that children in public schools should be allowed to participate in a voluntary moment of silence at the beginning of each school day. But it's wrong to allow teachers to indoctrinate children with their own religious views. Duncan's argument must be firmly rejected.

5. My driving instructor, Mr. Peterson, told me that it's dangerous to drive without a seat belt. But why should I listen to him? Last week I saw *him* driving without a seat belt.

6. Jeff and Maribeth slept together on prom night. Sleep is a state of unconscious or semiconscious rest or repose. It follows that Jeff and Maribeth must have spent a very restful night together.

7. Paper is combustible because it burns.

8. Jesse Jackson has argued that last week's police shooting was racially motivated. But this is exactly what you would expect Jackson to say. After all, he's black.

9. *Child to playmate:* Admit it! Admit that *Scooby-Doo* is a better cartoon show than *Pokémon*! If you don't, my big brother is going to beat you up!

10. *Al:* I can't believe it! My bank made a mistake on my account balance. There's an extra $3,000 in my checking account.
    Joe: Are you going to report the mistake?
    Al: Why should I? They've been ripping me off for years with their high ATM fees.

11. Opponents of capital punishment have argued that the death penalty is unfair and discriminatory. But it's ridiculous to suggest that cold-blooded murderers should not have to pay for their crimes. How is that fair to the victims or their families?

12. Malcolm Cox isn't qualified to be a kindergarten teacher. He's lazy and incompetent and has twice been convicted of child abuse.

13. Only man has an immortal soul. No woman is a man. Therefore, no woman has an immortal soul.

14. Surveys show that more than 70 percent of high school seniors believe that *novel* means "book." Therefore, *novel* does mean "book."

15. I almost lost it when I heard the Maharishi condemn Western materialism and consumerism. What a crock! Did you see the Rolls Royce he drove up in?

16. *Dean of students to student:* Mr. Boosely, you've twice been cited for violating the college's alcoholic beverage policy. If you commit a third violation, I'll have no choice but to suspend you from school.

17. You often hear people say that the French are rude, especially to people who don't speak their language. But France is a wonderful country! The wine, the food, the museums! There's no country in Europe I'd rather visit.

18. I wish I could take my four basset hounds with me when I move, but I just can't. I know you have only a small apartment, but won't you consider adopting them? I hate to think of them starving in the street or winding up in the dog pound.

19. Recently, a scientific study found that eating large amounts of chocolate ice cream is actually good for you. We shouldn't be too quick to accept this conclusion, however, because the study was funded entirely by Baskin-Robbins and other leading ice-cream makers.

20. Dear Mr. Ferguson, I'm sure you'll agree that after three years working as head of company security I'm long overdue for a raise. By the way, may I respectfully suggest that you make sure the surveillance cameras are turned off next time you and your secretary need to "catch up on some paperwork"?

21. Convicted murderer Johnny Palko has argued that he did not receive a fair trial. But Palko is a vicious thug who's spent most of his adult life behind bars. Why should we even listen to such a parasite?

22. Rachel Peters has argued that assault weapons should be outlawed. Apparently, Rachel believes that no one has the right to own firearms for purposes of self-protection. But such a view is completely indefensible. It would leave law-abiding citizens defenseless against predatory criminals.

23. Baseball owners have argued that baseball should continue to be exempt from antitrust laws. But the owners stand to lose millions if baseball's antitrust exemption is revoked. No sensible person should be taken in by the owners' obviously self-serving arguments.

24. I see nothing unethical in paying bribes to foreign officials to obtain business favors. That's the way business is done in many parts of the world. Like they say, "When in Rome, do as the Romans do."

25. Karen has argued that the secretaries at Acme Steel will get more respect if they change their title from "secretary" to "office assistant." But everyone knows that Acme Steel has a bottom-line mentality. They'll let you call yourself anything you want, but they won't raise your salary a nickel.

26. Hi, Mrs. Bowman, this is Debbie at Little Tykes Day Care. Sorry to bother you at work. I know you asked us not to give Petey any more candy or desserts at day care, but there's a birthday party today and all the kids are having chocolate cupcakes. Petey feels so left out. He's the only one without a cupcake, and he's just bawling his little eyes out. Wouldn't it be OK if I gave him a dessert just this once?

27. You're home alone. You've just heard on the radio that a homicidal maniac has escaped from the state pen. Suddenly, you hear the sound of breaking glass. What do you do? What *do* you do? Don't let this happen to you! Give your family the peace of mind they deserve. Call Allied Security today!

28. At the global-warming conference in Kyoto, many developing nations argued against setting strict emissions standards, claiming that this would put them at a competitive disadvantage against rich industrialized nations that have already benefited from lax environmental standards. But these developing nations are just jealous of the high standard of living industrialized nations have achieved. Sour grapes, that's all their arguments amount to.

29. Sigrid is an illegal alien. An alien is a creature from outer space. Therefore, Sigrid is a creature from outer space.

30. Wellington's is a classier bar than Jake's. It's a classier bar because it has a more upscale clientele. It has a more upscale clientele because it has a nicer décor. It has a nicer décor because it's a classier bar.

31. Flag-burning is illegal. Just ask anybody.

32. My doctor told me I need to eat right and lose weight. What a laugh! You know where that tub o' lard was when he gave me this great advice? He was a contestant in the banana-split-eating contest at the county fair.

33. I can't believe that these convicted murderers have the gall to claim that their rights have been violated by prison officials. They didn't respect the rights of their victims. Why should we respect theirs?

34. Of course you should have your nose pierced. "Body modification" is all the rage these days.

35. Mr. Martin claims that boys tend to be better at math than girls. What a ridiculous overgeneralization! My friend Alice is the best math student in her class. So, it's clear that boys are not always better at math than girls.

36. Penicillin is a miracle of modern medicine. A miracle is a divinely produced violation of a law of nature. Therefore, penicillin is a divinely produced violation of a law of nature.

37. Dr. Christina Sparks has argued that the morning-after pill is an effective contraceptive. But the morning-after pill simply encourages sexual promiscuity. Sexual promiscuity is the reason why we have such high rates of abortion and out-of-wedlock births in this country. Obviously, Dr. Sparks's argument is flawed.

38. Mrs. Devlin, your right rear tire is practically bald. I recommend that you replace it. I know you do a lot of driving at night on backcountry roads, and I'm sure you wouldn't want to get stranded.

39. Professor Douglas has argued that marijuana should be legalized. But Douglas is a radical ex-hippie whose brains were fried at Woodstock. No sensible person should listen to such a fruitcake.

40. *Al:* Doc Miller told me I've been working too hard. He said I need a vacation.
Deb: He's a fine one to talk! I bet Doc hasn't taken a vacation in forty years. But you know he's probably right. You have been working awfully hard lately.

II. Write an original example of each of the fallacies of relevance discussed in this chapter. Be prepared to share your examples with the class.

III. Find examples of the fallacies discussed in this chapter from everyday life (newspapers, magazines, TV, radio, class discussions, and so on). Collect your examples in a notebook or portfolio. For each example, indicate where you found the fallacy and give a brief explanation why you think it commits the fallacy you claim. Be prepared to share your examples with the class.

Summary

1. A *logical fallacy* is an argument that contains a mistake in reasoning. Fallacies can be divided into two general types: fallacies of relevance and fallacies of insufficient evidence. *Fallacies of relevance* are arguments in which the premises are logically irrelevant to the conclusion. *Fallacies of insufficient evidence* are arguments in which the premises, though logically relevant to the conclusion, fail to provide sufficient evidence for the conclusion. We discussed fallacies of relevance in this chapter. Fallacies of insufficient evidence are discussed in Chapter 6.

2. A statement is *relevant* to another statement if it provides at least some reason for thinking that the second statement is true or false. There are three ways in which a statement can be relevant or irrelevant to another: A statement is *positively relevant* to another statement if it provides at least some reason for thinking that the second statement is true. A statement is *negatively relevant* to another statement if it provides at least some reason for thinking that the second statement is false. A statement is *logically irrelevant* to another statement if it provides no reason for thinking that the second statement is either true or false.

3. This chapter discussed eleven common fallacies of relevance:
a. *Personal attack (ad hominem):* An arguer rejects a person's argument or claim by attacking the person's character rather than the person's argument or claim.

Example

Professor Snodblatt has argued against the theory of evolution. But Snodblatt is a pompous, egotistical windbag and a card-carrying member of the Nazi Bikers Association. I absolutely refuse to listen to him.

b. *Attacking the motive:* An arguer criticizes a person's motivation for offering a particular argument or claim, rather than examining the worth of the argument or claim itself.

Example

Jim Gibson has argued that we need to build a new middle school. But Gibson is the owner of Gibson's Construction Company. He'll make a fortune if his company is picked to build the new school. Obviously, Gibson's argument is a lot of self-serving baloney.

c. *Look who's talking (tu quoque):* An arguer rejects another person's argument or claim because that person is a hypocrite.

Example

My opponent, Bill Peters, has accused me of running a negative political campaign. But Peters has run a much more negative campaign than I have. Just last week he ran television ads falsely accusing me of embezzlement and cruelty to animals. Clearly, Peters's charge that I'm guilty of mudslinging is untrue.

d. *Two wrongs make a right:* An arguer attempts to justify a wrongful act by claiming that some other act is just as bad or worse.

Example

I admit we plied Olympic officials with booze, prostitutes, free ski vacations, and millions of dollars in outright bribes to be selected as the site of the next Winter Olympics. But everybody does it. That's the way the process works. Therefore, paying those bribes wasn't really wrong.

e. *Scare tactics:* An arguer threatens harm to a reader or listener and this threat is irrelevant to the truth of the arguer's conclusion.

Example

You've argued that Coach Bubba should be fired because he's twice been arrested for starting barroom brawls. But Coach Bubba is the winningest football coach we've ever had at Culmbank High. He doesn't deserve to be fired. And if you can't understand that, maybe these boys with baseball bats can change your mind.

f. *Appeal to pity:* An arguer attempts to evoke feelings of pity or compassion, where such feelings, however understandable, are not relevant to the truth of the arguer's conclusion.

Example

Officer, I know I was going 80 miles per hour in a 15-mile-an-hour school zone, but I don't deserve a speeding ticket. I've had a really tough week. Yesterday I got fired from my job, and last Monday my Chihuahua got eaten by a Great Dane.

> *Though in all places of the world men should lay the foundations of their houses on sand, it could not thence be inferred that so it ought to be.*
>
> —Thomas Hobbes

g. *Bandwagon argument:* An arguer appeals to a person's desire to be popular, accepted, or valued, rather than to logically relevant reasons or evidence.

Example

All the popular, cool kids at Westmont Middle School wear Mohawk haircuts. Therefore, you should, too.

h. *Straw man:* An arguer misrepresents another person's position to make it easier to attack.

Example

Professor Davis has argued that the Bible should not be read literally. Obviously, Davis believes that any reading of the Bible is as good as any other. But this would mean that there is no difference between a true interpretation of Scripture and a false interpretation. Such a view is absurd.

i. *Red herring:* An arguer tries to sidetrack her audience by raising an irrelevant issue, and then claims that the original issue has been effectively settled by the irrelevant diversion.

Example

Frank has argued that Volvos are safer cars than Ford Mustang convertibles. But Volvos are clunky, boxlike cars, whereas Mustang convertibles are sleek, powerful, and sexy. Clearly, Frank doesn't know what he's talking about.

j. *Equivocation:* An arguer uses a key word in an argument in two (or more) different senses.

Example

Hanes is advertising "tanks for all occasions." It's illegal for anyone but the military to sell tanks. So, Hanes is breaking the law.

k. *Begging the question:* An arguer states or assumes as a premise the very thing he is seeking to prove as a conclusion.

Example

I am entitled to say whatever I choose because I have a right to say whatever I please.

CHAPTER 6

LOGICAL FALLACIES—II

FALLACIES OF INSUFFICIENT EVIDENCE

In Chapter 5, we looked at fallacies of relevance, mistakes in reasoning that occur when the premises are logically irrelevant to the truth of the conclusion. In this chapter we discuss **fallacies of insufficient evidence**—mistakes in reasoning in which the premises, though relevant to the conclusion, fail to provide sufficient evidence for the conclusion. We discuss nine such fallacies.

Inappropriate Appeal to Authority

All of us depend on things that other people tell us. Children rely on their parents and teachers for basic guidance and instruction. Scientists rely on other scientists to report their findings accurately. Historians depend on primary sources and other historians for reliable information about the past. Indeed, it is hard to see how any stable and cohesive society could exist without a great deal of shared trust in its members' basic honesty and reliability. For that reason, trust in authority has aptly been described as "the very foundation of civilization."[1]

Too often, however, people rely *uncritically* on the authority of others. Throughout history blind faith in authority has bred superstition, intolerance, and dogmatism. Consequently, it is of great importance to be able to distinguish legitimate appeals to authority from those that are fallacious.

The fallacy of **inappropriate appeal to authority** is committed when an arguer cites a witness or authority who, there is good reason to believe, is unreliable. But when, in general, is it reasonable to believe that a witness or an authority is unreliable? Here are some relevant circumstances:

- when the source is not a genuine authority on the subject at issue
- when the source is biased or has some other reason to lie or mislead
- when the accuracy of the source's observations is questionable
- when the source cited (e.g., a media source, a reference work, or an Internet source) is known to be generally unreliable

- when the source has not been cited correctly or the cited claim has been taken out of context
- when the source's claim conflicts with expert opinion
- when the issue is not one that can be settled by expert opinion
- when the claim is highly improbable on its face

Let's look briefly at each of these reasons for questioning the reliability of a source.

Is the Source Not an Authority on the Subject at Issue?   An *authority* is a person who possesses special knowledge, competence, or expertise in a particular field. The most obvious way to commit the fallacy of inappropriate appeal to authority is to appeal to a person who is not a genuine authority on the subject at issue. For example:

> My barber told me that Einstein's general theory of relativity is a lot of hogwash. I guess Einstein wasn't as smart as everybody thinks he was.

Because the arguer's barber presumably is not an authority on Einstein's general theory of relativity, this argument commits the fallacy of inappropriate appeal to authority.

Fallacies of this sort are particularly common in advertising. Consider this example:

> Hi, I'm heavyweight boxing champ Buster Brawler. After a tough night in the ring, my face needs some tender loving care. Lather-X Sensitive Skin Shaving Gel. You can't get a smoother, closer shave.

The arguer may be an expert on knocking out opponents in the boxing ring, but because he is no expert on the comparative virtues of shaving products, the argument is fallacious.

There is nothing so stupid as an educated man, if you get him off the thing he was educated in.

—Will Rogers

Is the Source Biased?   Common sense tells us that we should be cautious about accepting a claim when the person making the claim is biased or has some other obvious motive to lie or mislead. Here are two examples:

> Ned Bumpley has been paid $100,000 by the *Sensational Enquirer* tabloid for his story that he is Bill Gates's illegitimate son. Given Mr. Bumpley's reputation for honesty, I think we should believe him, even though he has produced no corroborating evidence and DNA tests fail to support his claim.

> Mrs. Cox has testified that her son Willie was home with her at the time when Willie is alleged to have shot Steve Wilson. Even though Willie's fingerprints were found on the murder weapon and six witnesses have identified Willie as the assailant, I can't believe that a good woman like Mrs. Cox would lie to protect her son. I think Willy is innocent.

In both of these examples, the testifier has an obvious motive to lie (financial gain in the first example, maternal love in the second). Given these motivations, together with other information contained in the examples, these appeals to authority are fallacious.[2]

Is the Accuracy of the Source's Observations Questionable?   A source may also be unreliable if we have reason to doubt the accuracy of his or her observations or experiences. Here are two examples:

> Jerry [who was playing heavy metal music at full blast on his boom box] claims he heard the victim whisper his name from more than 100 feet away. Jerry has always struck me as a straight shooter. So, I have to believe that Jerry really did hear the victim whisper his name.

> After taking LSD and drinking seven beers, Jill claims she had a conversation with Elvis's ghost in the alley behind McDearmon's Bar. I've never known Jill to lie. So, I think we should believe her.

In these examples there are obvious reasons for doubting the reliability of the witnesses' observations or experiences. Consequently, these appeals to authority are fallacious.

Is the Source Known to Be Generally Unreliable?   Generally speaking, it is reasonable to accept claims made in reputable newspapers, magazines, encyclopedias, radio and television news programs, and Internet Web sites. But we must be cautious about accepting claims found in sources that we have reason to believe are generally unreliable. Here is an example from the *Weekly World News,* a popular supermarket tabloid.

> Scientists' Research Reveals . . . It Takes 3 Million Years for a Human Soul to Reach Heaven . . . And No One from Earth Has Arrived There Yet!
>
> Heaven is a mind-boggling 3 billion light-years from earth, space scientists have recently determined—a distance so vast that not a single person who's died in all of recorded history has yet reached the Pearly Gates! . . .
>
> Startling photos taken by the Hubble Space Telescope and the Mars Pathfinder have pinpointed a shining white city suspended in the blackness of space, roughly 3 billion light-years away.
>
> Those secret NASA photos, leaked by an insider and published in the *Weekly World News,* are widely believed to depict Heaven itself.
>
> And the implication of the great distance is staggering.
>
> "Even a single light-year, the distance light travels in one year, is enormous— 5.8 trillion miles," said [French astrophysicist Antoine] Letelier.
>
> "Presumably, the human soul has zero mass, allowing it to travel at the speed of light—the fastest any natural object can move.
>
> "In fact, let's assume that because of its supernatural nature, a soul can travel 1,000 times faster than light.
>
> "Even at that breakneck rate, the earliest cavemen would just now be arriving at Heaven's gates . . . and if you died today, you wouldn't get there until the year 2998003 A.D."[3]

Would You Believe . . . ?

Here are some more wacky headlines from the *Weekly World News*:

Haunted Toilet Claims Third Plumber in Eight Years!

Hitler's Clone Turns Seven Years Old!

Want Hot Sex with an E. T.? Wear Flowery Hat.

UFOs Are Piloted by Angels and Demons—And They're Planning a Dogfight That Could Destroy Us All!

Your Internet Dream Girl Could Be a CHIMP!

Ghost Pours Ice Water on Couple—Every Time They Have Sex!

Gypsy Curse Turns Entire Supreme Court Bench Liberal.

3,600-lb. Mystery Sphere Is Hairball from Space Alien!

Olympic Broad Jumpers Using Gas Pills to Boost Athletic Performance!

Aliens Are Here for Our Krispy Kremes!

> *Testimony is like an arrow shot from a long bow; the force of it depends on the strength of the hand that draws it. Argument is like an arrow shot from a crossbow, which has equal force though shot by a child.*
>
> —Samuel Johnson

Given the obvious weaknesses of the reported argument and the fact that tabloids like the *Weekly World News* are known to concoct outlandish stories, an argument based on an appeal to the authority of the *Weekly World News* would be fallacious.

Has the Source Been Cited Incorrectly?   The fallacy of inappropriate appeal to authority can also be committed if the arguer has not cited a source correctly. For example:

> It states in the Constitution that there must be a "wall of separation" between church and state. Publicly funded school vouchers clearly violate this wall of separation. Therefore, publicly funded school vouchers are unconstitutional.

Though many people believe that the phrase "wall of separation" is found in the Constitution, it actually appears in a letter Thomas Jefferson wrote to the Danbury, Connecticut, Baptist Association on January 1, 1802. For that reason this appeal to authority is fallacious.

Does the Source's Claim Conflict with Expert Opinion?   Damon Runyon once said, "The race is not always to the swift, nor the battle to the strong, but that's the way to bet."[4] Much the same can be said about expert opinion. Though experts are often wrong (sometimes spectacularly so), it is generally unwise to accept a claim that conflicts with a clear expert consensus. For example:

> Dr. Duane Gish, a biochemist with a Ph.D. from Berkeley and senior vice president of the Institute for Creation Research, has argued that there is no credible evidence supporting the theory of evolution. In view of Dr. Gish's expertise on this subject, we should conclude that evolution is a myth.

Because an overwhelming majority of scientists disagree with this view, it would be fallacious to accept this conclusion simply on the authority of Dr. Gish.

Is the Source's Claim Not One That Can Be Settled by an Appeal to Expert Opinion?   Some issues are so inherently controversial that they cannot be settled by appeals to expert opinion. Here are two examples:

> Dr. Stanford P. Higginbotham, a leading social philosopher, has argued that capital punishment is always morally wrong. Given Dr. Higginbotham's impressive credentials, we should conclude that capital punishment is always morally wrong.

> Swami Krishnamurti Chakrabarti, spiritual leader of the Worldwide Church of Cognitive Enlightenment, has said that the meaning of life lies in achieving mystical unity with the Great I Am. In view of the swami's deep spiritual insight, it is clear that this is indeed the meaning of life.

Topics such as the morality of capital punishment and the meaning of life are issues on which no expert consensus exists or is likely to exist. Consequently, debates on these issues cannot be settled by appeals to authority.

To every Ph.D. there is an equal and opposite Ph.D.
—B. Duggan

In discussion it is not so much weight of authority as force of argument that should be demanded.
—Cicero

Is the Claim Highly Improbable on Its Face?   The more improbable a claim is in itself, the less willing we should be to accept it merely on the say-so of a witness or an authority. If we accept an extraordinary claim on authority and it is more likely that the alleged authority is lying or mistaken than it is that the claim is true, we commit the fallacy of inappropriate appeal to authority. For example:

> Old Doc Perkins says he has an eighty-year-old friend who can run a 100-yard dash in less than ten seconds. Old Doc is one of the most trusted members of this community. So, if Old Doc says he has an eighty-year-old friend who can run a 100-yard dash in less than ten seconds, I, for one, believe him.

This claim, considered independent of Old Doc's report, is so improbable that it should be rejected unless strong additional evidence is provided.

Extraordinary claims require extraordinary evidence.
—Carl Sagan

Appeal to Ignorance

When we lack evidence for or against a claim, it is usually best to suspend judgment—to admit that we just don't know. When an arguer treats a *lack* of evidence as reason to think that a claim is true or false, he or she commits the fallacy of appeal to ignorance. More precisely, the fallacy of **appeal to ignorance** occurs when an arguer asserts that a claim must be true because no one has proven it false or, conversely, that a claim must be false because no one has proven it true. Here are several examples:

> There must be intelligent life on other planets. No one has proven that there isn't.

> There isn't any intelligent life on other planets. No one has proven that there is.

> No one has proven that global warming is occurring. Therefore, we must conclude that it is not occurring.

> No one has proven that global warming is not occurring. Therefore, we must conclude that it is occurring.

Absence of evidence is not evidence of absence.
—Carl Sagan

*Ignorance is igno-
rance; no right to
believe anything
can be derived
from it.*

—Sigmund Freud

Each of these examples suffers from the same basic flaw: it assumes that the lack of evidence for (or against) a claim is good reason to believe that the claim is false (or true). If such reasoning were allowed, we could "prove" almost any conclusion:

> No one has proven that three-eyed, four-armed, polka-dotted gremlins don't exist deep in the interior of the moon. Therefore, it's reasonable to believe that three-eyed, four-armed, polka-dotted gremlins do exist deep in the interior of the moon.

> There is no evidence that it was cloudy in Rome on September 8, AD 643. Therefore, we must conclude that it wasn't.

Is it ever legitimate to treat a lack of evidence for a claim as evidence that the claim is false? In some cases, yes. Two exceptions, in particular, should be noted.

First, sometimes the fact that a search *hasn't* found something is good evidence that the thing isn't there to be found. Here are two examples:

> We've searched this car from top to bottom looking for the stolen jewels, and no trace of them has been found. Therefore, probably the jewels aren't in the car.

> After years of extensive scientific testing, there is no evidence that substance XYZ is toxic to rodents. Therefore, it's reasonable to conclude that substance XYZ is not toxic to rodents.

It is important to keep in mind, however, that this "fruitless search" exception applies only when (1) a careful search has been conducted and (2) it is likely that the search would have found something if there had been anything there to be found.

The second exception applies to cases in which special rules require that a claim be rejected as false unless a certain burden of proof is met. Here is an example:

> In the American legal system, a criminal defendant is legally guilty only if his or her guilt is proved beyond a reasonable doubt. My client has not been proven guilty beyond a reasonable doubt. Therefore, my client is not legally guilty.

In this example, special rules of evidence require that a claim be rejected as false unless it is proven to be true by some elevated standard of proof. Because these special rules justify the inference "not proven, therefore false," no fallacy is committed.

False Alternatives

The fallacy of **false alternatives** is committed when an arguer poses a false either/or choice.[5] Here are two examples:

> Look, the choice is simple. Either you support a pure free-market economy or you support a communist police state. Surely you don't support a communist police state. Therefore, you should support a pure free-market economy.

• Critical Thinking Lapse •

Joseph Pileggi thought he knew the woman he was marrying. But the woman he wed three years ago apparently wasn't eighty-three-year-old Ducile Palermo. It was her sixty-one-year-old daughter, Carli Buchanan. Pileggi, sixty-nine, says he was shocked when he came across the marriage license that Buchanan had signed as the bride and Palermo as a witness. He says he thought he married Palermo, with whom he'd lived since 1992. But the daughter claims Pileggi knew he was marrying her and that they consummated the wedding the same day. "He truly is in a state of disbelief," said Russell Pry, Pileggi's attorney. Pry said much of the confusion may be traced to Palermo's tendency to use her daughter's name. "I'm not sure what names were used in the wedding ceremony. I'm not even sure Joe knows," Pry said.[6]

Either we elect a Republican as president, or crime rates will skyrocket. Obviously, we don't want crime rates to skyrocket. Therefore, we should elect a Republican as president.

In these examples, the arguers claim that there are only two relevant choices when, in fact, there are more than two.[7] The first arguer poses a false choice by ignoring a wide range of political and economic systems that lie somewhere between a pure free-market economy on the one hand and a communist police state on the other. The second arguer poses a false choice by assuming, implausibly, that the only way to avoid rapidly rising crime rates is to elect a Republican as president.

Note that the fallacy of false alternatives need not involve just *two* false choices. For example:

There are just three types of base hits in baseball: a single, a double, and a triple. Slugger got a base hit but didn't get a single or a double. Therefore, Slugger must have gotten a triple.

This argument poses a false choice between three alternatives: single, double, or triple. This is a false choice because it ignores the possibility that Slugger may have hit a home run.

Note also that the fallacy of false alternatives need not be explicitly expressed in *either-or* form. Often, for instance, a false choice is expressed as a conditional (*if-then*) statement, as in this example:

If we don't elect a Democrat as president, then the economy will go down the tubes. Obviously, we don't want the economy to go down the tubes. So, we should elect a Democrat as president.

Here the first sentence is equivalent to saying, "*Either* we elect a Democrat as president *or* the economy will go down the tubes."

> Mankind likes to think in terms of extreme opposites. It is given to formulating its beliefs in terms of Either-Ors.
>
> —John Dewey

Finally, it should be noted that fallacies of false alternatives are often expressed as incomplete arguments. Here are two examples:

> Either buy me some candy, Daddy, or I'll hold my breath until I die.
>
> Dad, I know a new BMW is expensive, but you wouldn't want me riding around in this old rust bucket all winter long, would you?

It is not difficult to fill in the missing parts of these arguments.

Loaded Question

A loaded question is a question that contains an unfair or questionable assumption. For example, "Do you still steal from your boss?" is a loaded question if it presupposes, without justification, that you once did steal from your boss. The **loaded question** fallacy occurs when an arguer asks a question that contains an unfair or unwarranted presupposition. Here is a particularly blatant example:

> *Joe:* Have you stopped cheating on exams?
>
> *Pete:* No!
>
> *Joe:* Oh, so you admit that you still cheat on exams?
>
> *Pete:* No, I meant to say yes!
>
> *Joe:* Oh, so you admit that you used to cheat on exams?
>
> *Pete:* No!

It is easy to spot the trick here. Joe's question, "Have you stopped cheating on exams?" is a loaded question because any direct yes or no answer to it will force Pete to admit something that he does not want to admit. Joe's apparently single question is really two questions rolled into one.

> *Question 1:* Did you cheat on exams in the past?
>
> *Question 2:* If you did cheat on exams in the past, have you stopped now?

By applying Pete's single "yes" or "no" answers to both questions, Joe commits the fallacy of loaded question.

Here is a more realistic example:

> *Honorable Flora MacDonald (Kingston and the Islands)* [speaking in the Canadian House of Commons]: Madam Speaker, my question is also directed to the Minister of Finance. I would like to say to him that his policies are directly responsible for the fact that 1,185 more Canadians are without jobs every single day, 1,185 more Canadians with families to feed and mortgages to pay. How long is the Minister prepared to condemn 1,200 more Canadians every day to job loss and insecurity because he is too stubborn and too uncaring to change his policies?[8]

This question is loaded because it unfairly rolls *three* questions into one.

> *Question 1:* Are the Minister of Finance's policies directly responsible for the fact that 1,185 Canadians lose their jobs every single day?

An answer is contained in your question.

—Plato

Question 2: If so, are these policies allowed to continue because the Minister is too stubborn and uncaring to change his policies?

Question 3: If the Minister is too stubborn and uncaring to change his policies, how much longer will this stubborn and uncaring attitude continue?

To respond to a loaded question effectively, one must distinguish the different questions being asked and respond to each individually.

Are all loaded questions fallacies? No. Strictly speaking, a loaded question is fallacious only if it is used unfairly in an argumentative context. For purposes of this text, however, it can be assumed that all loaded questions are fallacious. Thus, for example, the following questions may be regarded as fallacious:

When are you going to stop acting so immature?

Tell me, how long have you been embezzling money from the firm?

Where did you hide the body?

How long had you planned this bank robbery before you carried it out?

Why do you always act like a total jerk when you're around my ex-boyfriend?

Are you still in favor of this fiscally irresponsible bill?

Did you write this immoral trash?

Questionable Cause

We live in a complex and mysterious world. Often it's hard to know what has caused some event to occur. When an arguer claims, without sufficient evidence, that one thing is the cause of something else, he commits the fallacy of **questionable cause.**

There are three common varieties of the questionable cause fallacy: the post hoc fallacy, the mere correlation fallacy, and the oversimplified cause fallacy.

The **post hoc fallacy** (from the Latin *post hoc ergo propter hoc* ["after this, therefore because of this"]) is committed when an arguer assumes, without adequate evidence, that because one event, A, occurred before another event, B, A is the cause of B. Here are two examples:

How do I know that ginseng tea is a cure for the common cold? Last week I had a bad case of the sniffles. I drank a cup of ginseng tea, and the next morning my sniffles were gone.

Medieval villager: Two days after that old hag Jezebel Taylor moved into the village, my cow died. That witch must have put a hex on my cow!

> *Do not let anyone deceive you with empty arguments.*
> —Ephesians 5:6

In the first example, the arguer assumes that because her sniffles disappeared after she drank ginseng tea, drinking the tea must have caused her sniffles to disappear. This is precisely the kind of post hoc reasoning that underlies almost all quack cures. It is much more reasonable to suppose that the arguer never really had a cold or that the cold simply got better on its own.[9]

The second example illustrates how superstitions often have their origin in post hoc thinking. It is a fallacy to think that because something bad happened to you after a black cat crossed your path, black cats are bad luck.

Another common variety of the false cause fallacy is the **mere correlation fallacy,** which is committed when an arguer assumes, without sufficient evidence, that because A and B regularly occur together, A must be the cause of B or vice versa. Here are two examples:

> On Monday I stayed up all night partying, had eggs for breakfast, and failed my calculus test. On Wednesday I stayed up all night partying, had eggs for breakfast, and failed my biology test. On Thursday I stayed up all night partying, had eggs for breakfast, and failed my history test. Obviously, to do better on tests, I must stop eating eggs for breakfast.[10]

> *Aztec high priest:* Every spring we sacrifice a virgin to the sun god, and every spring the life-giving rains come. Therefore, sacrificing a virgin to the sun god causes the life-giving rains to come.

In these examples the arguers have mistakenly assumed that because two events are regularly correlated (i.e., occur together), there must be a cause-and-effect relationship between them. But correlation does not imply causation. The rooster may crow every morning just before Farmer Jones milks the cows, but that doesn't mean that the rooster's crowing causes Farmer Jones to milk the cows.

Perhaps the most common form of the questionable cause fallacy is the **oversimplified cause fallacy.** This fallacy is committed when we assume, without adequate evidence, that A is the sole cause of B when, in fact, there are several causes of B. Here are two examples:

> Violent crime has declined steadily in recent years. Obviously, tougher imprisonment policies are working.

> SAT scores have fallen sharply since the 1960s. Clearly, students are watching too much TV.[11]

The first argument oversimplifies the situation by ignoring other causes that have likely contributed to falling crimes rates (new policing strategies, changing demographics, reduced use of crack cocaine). In the second argument, the arguer correctly identifies one likely cause of declining SAT scores: kids today do watch too much TV. He fails to mention, however, other important causes that have also contributed to the decline (e.g., the fact that a much larger number of average and below-average students now take the SAT than was true in the past). For those reasons these arguments commit the fallacy of questionable cause.

Hasty Generalization

A *generalization* is a statement that asserts that all or most things of a certain kind have a certain quality or characteristic. Here are some examples of generalizations:

> All emeralds are green.

> Most college students receive financial aid.

> The majority of dogs are not dangerous.

> Plays are boring! [All plays? Most plays?]

We commit the fallacy of **hasty generalization** when we draw a general conclusion from a sample that is biased or too small. Here are two examples:

> Do most Americans still believe in God? To find out, we asked more than ten thousand scientists at colleges and universities throughout America. Less than 40 percent said they believed in God. The conclusion is obvious: Most Americans no longer believe in God.

> *Small-business owner:* I've hired three San Pedrans in the past six months, and all three were lazy and shiftless. I guess most San Pedrans are lazy and shiftless.

The first argument is fallacious because it draws a general conclusion from a sample that is *biased* (i.e., not representative of the target population as a whole). Surveys indicate that scientists tend to be far more skeptical of religious beliefs than average Americans.[12]

The second argument illustrates how hasty generalizations can give rise to harmful stereotypes and prejudices. In this example a general conclusion is drawn from a sample that is too small to support a reliable generalization. It is unfair, as well as illogical, to stigmatize an entire class of people on the basis of the perceived faults of a few.

It should be noted that not every argument that jumps to a conclusion is a hasty generalization. For example:

> That large biker with the swastika tattoo and the brass knuckles looks friendly enough. I bet he wouldn't mind if I introduced myself with a joy buzzer handshake.

This is certainly a hasty conclusion, but it is not a hasty generalization because it is not a generalization at all. The conclusion is a particular statement about one particular biker, not a general statement about bikers in general. A hasty generalization must have a general statement (i.e., a statement about all or most members of a group) as its conclusion. Consequently, this argument does not commit the fallacy of hasty generalization.[13]

Slippery Slope

We often hear arguments of this sort: "We can't allow A, because A will lead to B, and B will lead to C, and we sure as heck don't want C!" Arguments of this sort are called slippery-slope arguments. Often, such arguments are fallacious. We commit the **slippery-slope fallacy** when we claim, without sufficient evidence, that a seemingly harmless action, if taken, will lead to a disastrous outcome. Some examples:

> Senator Walker has argued that we should outlaw terrorist threats on the Internet. This proposal is dangerous and must be strongly resisted. If we allow the government to outlaw terrorist threats on the Internet, next it will want to ban "hate speech" and other allegedly "harmful" speech on the Internet. Next the government will want to censor "harmful" ideas on television, radio, and in newspapers. Eventually, everything you see, hear, or read will be totally controlled by the government.

> Bans on so-called assault weapons must be vigorously opposed. Once the gun-grabbing liberals have outlawed assault weapons, next they'll go after handguns.

Those sweeping judgments which are so common are meaningless. They are like men who salute a whole crowd of people in the mass. Those who really know them salute and take notice of them individually and by name.

—Michel de Montaigne

After that, it will be shotguns and semiautomatic hunting rifles. In the end, law-abiding citizens will be left totally defenseless against predatory criminals and a tyrannical government.

In a recent letter to the editor, Stella Davis argued that we should legalize same-sex marriage. But allowing same-sex marriage would undermine respect for traditional marriage. Traditional marriage is the very foundation of our society. If that foundation is destroyed, our whole society will collapse. Thus, if we want to prevent the complete disintegration of our society, we must oppose the legalization of same-sex marriage.

Notice that each of these arguments has the same basic pattern:

1. The arguer claims that if a certain seemingly harmless action, A, is permitted, A will lead to B, B will lead to C, and so on to D.
2. The arguer holds that D is a terrible thing and therefore should not be permitted.
3. In fact, there is no good reason to believe that A will actually lead to D.[14]

It should be noted that many slippery-slope arguments leave out some or all of the intermediate steps that an arguer believes will occur. Here are two examples:

Dr. Perry has proposed that we legalize physician-assisted suicide. No sensible person should listen to such a proposal. If we allow physician-assisted suicide, eventually there will be no respect for human life.

Socialized medicine really frightens me. Once you start down that road, there's no turning back. A complete socialist dictatorship is the inevitable result.

In general terms it is not difficult to imagine what sorts of intermediate steps these arguers fear will occur.

It is important to note that not all slippery-slope arguments are fallacious. Sometimes there are good reasons for thinking that a very bad outcome may result from a seemingly harmless first step. For example:

Brad, I know you've been shootin' up heroin. Man, don't you know what that stuff can do to you? First you shoot up "just when you need a high." After a while you become addicted to the stuff. You lose your job, your apartment, even rob from your best friend to feed the habit. Eventually, you wind up dead in some alley or strung out in some detox center. Listen to me, I'm your best friend. Think about what you're doing.

In this case, there are perfectly sound reasons for avoiding this all-too-genuine slippery slope.

Weak Analogy

We have all heard the expression "That's like comparing apples and oranges." This saying points to a mistake called the fallacy of **weak analogy,** which occurs when an arguer compares two (or more) things that aren't really comparable in relevant respects. Here are two examples:

Teachers of false religions are like carriers of a deadly plague. Just as we rightly quarantine plague victims to prevent them from infecting others, so we should quarantine teachers of false religions to prevent them from spreading their spiritual poison.

Lettuce is leafy and green and tastes great with a veggie burger. Poison ivy is also leafy and green. Therefore, poison ivy probably tastes great with a veggie burger, too.

In these examples there are obvious and important differences, or "disanalogies," between the things being compared. Because of these differences, the premises don't provide good reasons to accept the conclusion.

Although fallacies of weak analogy occur in many different forms, three patterns are particularly common.

One common pattern is to compare two things that have several identified similarities. For example:

Alan is tall, dark, and handsome and has blue eyes. Bill is also tall, dark, and handsome. Therefore, Bill probably has blue eyes, too.

The basic pattern here is

1. A has characteristics w, x, y, and z.
2. B has characteristics w, x, and y.
3. Therefore, B probably has characteristic z too.

Many arguments with this pattern are perfectly good arguments. For example:

Alice lives in a mansion, drives a Rolls Royce, wears expensive jewelry, and is rich. Beatrice also lives in a mansion, drives a Rolls Royce, and wears expensive jewelry. Therefore, Beatrice probably is rich, too.

This is a good argument from analogy because people who live in a mansion, drive a Rolls Royce, and wear expensive jewelry are usually rich. There is no relevant connection, however, between being tall, dark, and handsome on the one hand and having blue eyes on the other.

Another common pattern of reasoning by analogy is a comparison of several things that have only one or two identified similarities. For example:

Jake is a member of the Wexford College Football Fanatics, and he goes bare-chested to all the home football games. Kyle is a member of the Wexford College Football Fanatics, and he goes bare-chested to all the home football games. Brad is a member of the Wexford College Football Fanatics, and he goes bare-chested to all the home football games. Jennifer is also a member of the Wexford College Football Fanatics. So, she probably goes bare-chested to the home football games, too.

The pattern of this argument is

1. A is an x, and A is a y.
2. B is an x, and B is a y.
3. C is an x, and C is a y.
4. D is an x.
5. Therefore, D is probably a y too.

> *The human mind is an inveterate analogizer.*
> —Richard Dawkins

> *He who would not be found tripping, ought to be very careful in this matter of comparisons, for they are most slippery things.*
> —Plato

This argument is clearly fallacious because it ignores an obvious difference between the things being compared (the fact that Jennifer is a woman). Some arguments with this logical pattern, however, are good arguments. For example:

> Steven Spielberg directed *Jaws,* and that was a good movie. Spielberg directed *Schindler's List,* and that was a good movie. Spielberg directed *Saving Private Ryan,* and that was a good movie. In fact, I've seen all of Spielberg's movies, and almost all of them have been good. Therefore, Spielberg's next movie will probably also be good.

This is a good argument from analogy because there is good reason to think that the things being compared are, in fact, relevantly similar.

A third common pattern of argument by analogy is simply to assert, without further elaboration, that two cases are relevantly similar. For example:

> Why does a family who has no children in a school district have to pay school taxes? This is like paying cigarette taxes even though you don't smoke.[15]

Here the arguer doesn't bother to spell out why he thinks these two cases are analogous. To critically evaluate an argument like this, we need to do three things: (1) list all important similarities between the two cases, (2) list all important dissimilarities between the two cases, and (3) decide whether, on balance, the similarities are strong enough to support the conclusion.

Let's apply this three-step method to the school taxes argument.

1. List important similarities.

How *making families that have no children in a public school system pay school taxes* is like *making people who don't smoke pay cigarette taxes:*

Both are taxes that you are required to pay regardless of whether you or your family derives any immediate benefit from them.

2. List important dissimilarities.

How *making families that have no children in a public school system pay school taxes* is not like *making people who don't smoke pay cigarette taxes:*

Imposing school taxes on all property owners benefits society by promoting equal educational opportunities and helping create an educated and informed citizenry. Imposing cigarette taxes on nonsmokers would harm society by subsidizing an activity that is harmful and addictive.

Imposing school taxes on all property owners provides significant indirect benefits even to families without school-age children because the taxes help create a better-educated workforce and citizenry. Imposing cigarette taxes on nonsmokers would provide few, if any, indirect benefits to people who don't smoke.

It is fair to require cigarette smokers to pay cigarette taxes because smokers impose economic and health costs on the rest of society in the form of higher insurance premiums, increased Medicare costs, lost workdays, health risks of secondhand smoke, and so on. It would *not* be

Sign Language

Signs are sometimes a good source of entertaining inconsistencies. Here are a few examples:

Sign outside a disco: Smarts is the most exclusive disco in town. Everyone welcome.

Sign in a London department store: Bargain basement upstairs

Sign on a repair shop door: We can repair anything. (Please knock hard on the door—the bell doesn't work.)

Sign in the Mammoth Caves in Virginia: Bottomless Pit—175 Feet Deep

Sign at Dicker's Department Store: 47th Annual Once-in-a Lifetime Sale

Sign at Burger King: 10 FREE french fry certificates for only $1.00

Sign on school grounds: No trespassing without permission

Sign on display of "I Love You Only" Valentine cards: Now available in multi-packs

Sign on the wall of a Baltimore estate: Trespassers will be prosecuted to the full extent of the law—Sisters of Mercy

Sign in a church vestry: Will the last person to leave please see that the perpetual light is extinguished.

Sign in social services building: Illiterate? Write for free help today.

fair to require nonsmokers to pay cigarette taxes because this would force nonsmokers to pick up the tab for a costly and unhealthy activity that doesn't benefit them and for which they bear no personal responsibility.

3. Decide whether the similarities or the dissimilarities are more important.

In this case, the relevant differences between the two cases are too great to support the conclusion. For that reason the argument commits the fallacy of weak analogy.[16]

Inconsistency

Two statements are inconsistent when they both can't be true. The fallacy of **inconsistency** occurs when an arguer asserts inconsistent or contradictory claims. Here are several examples:

Moral absolutist: I can't believe that members of the Mabunga tribe still practice child sacrifice. If anything is absolutely and universally wrong, it's child sacrifice.

Moral relativist: Hey, get with the times, man! All value judgments are relative. And that's the absolute truth.

Pearson Q. Legacy: Preferential treatment is unfair and discriminatory. It has no place in college admissions.

Roommate: But didn't you say a minute ago that you got into this college only because your father was a rich alumnus?

Summary of Fallacies of Insufficient Evidence

Inappropriate appeal to authority: Arguer cites an unreliable authority or witness.

Appeal to ignorance: Arguer claims that something is true because no one has proven it false or vice versa.

False alternatives: Arguer poses a false either/or choice.

Loaded question: Arguer asks a question that contains an unfair or unwarranted assumption.

Questionable cause: Arguer claims, without adequate evidence, that one thing is the cause of something else.

Hasty generalization: Arguer draws a general conclusion from a sample that is biased or too small.

Slippery slope: Arguer claims, without adequate evidence, that a seemingly harmless action will lead to a very bad outcome.

Weak analogy: Arguer compares things that aren't truly comparable.

Inconsistency: Arguer asserts inconsistent claims.

Pearson Q. Legacy: Well, yeah. But what's wrong with that?

Roommate: Just checking, man.

Mickey Mantle: Hey, Yogi, what do you say we eat at Toots' tonight?

Yogi Berra: That place is old news. Nobody goes there anymore. It's too crowded.[17]

> *The foolish and the dead alone never change their opinion.*
>
> —James Russell Lowell

In the first example, the arguer asserts a claim ("It's absolutely true that all value judgments are relative") that is self-contradictory; in the second and third examples, the arguers assert inconsistent premises.

Inconsistency is a logical fault that critical thinkers are careful to avoid. We should remember, however, that it is also a mistake to cling stubbornly to an old idea when new information suggests that the idea is false. No real learning takes place without an openness to new ideas.

EXERCISE 6.1

I. Identify the fallacies of insufficient evidence in the following arguments. If no fallacy is committed, write "no fallacy."

1. I'd better eat my Wheaties. Michael Jordan says that it's the breakfast of champions.
2. I can't believe I failed my chemistry test. I knew I should have worn my lucky sweatshirt to take the test.
3. Did you vote for the idiot or the liar in the last presidential election?
4. Podunk State University is a better university than Harvard University. I've been assured of this by Dr. Bigelow Hype, dean of admissions at Podunk State.

5. Skeptics have tried for centuries to prove that reincarnation is a myth, and no one has ever succeeded. Therefore, we must conclude that reincarnation is a fact.

6. I've long been convinced that nothing exists outside my own mind. Indeed, the arguments for this seem so obvious to me that I can't understand why everybody else doesn't believe it, too.[18]

7. Ford cars are lemons. I've owned two, and they gave me nothing but trouble.

8. *Police detective:* Did you get a good look at the bank robber?
   Witness: Yes, I saw his face clearly. It was Willie, the night watchman.
   Detective: And were you also able to recognize his voice?
   Witness: No, I couldn't really hear what he said very well. His voice was muffled by the full ski mask he wore.

9. Either you support preferential treatment for disadvantaged minorities in university admissions, or you're a racist. But surely you're not a racist. Therefore, you support preferential treatment for disadvantaged minorities in university admissions.

10. Old Mr. Ferguson (who resides at the Burnside Home for the Blind) claims he could read the car's license plate from more than 150 feet away. I've never known Mr. Ferguson to be deliberately dishonest. Therefore, we should conclude that Mr. Ferguson really did read the car's license plate from more than 150 feet away.

11. Students have asked that we extend residence hall visitation hours by one hour on Friday and Saturday nights. This request will have to be denied. If we give students an extra visitation hour on weekends, next they'll be asking us to allow their boyfriends and girlfriends to stay over all night. Eventually, we'll have students shacking up in every room.

12. There is no information in Private Baker's service record that indicates that he is not a homosexual. Consequently, I can only assume that he is.

13. A Saint Bernard is large, cuddly, furry, and makes a great house pet. A baby grizzly bear is also large, cuddly, and furry. Therefore, a baby grizzly bear would make a great house pet, too.

14. I've searched my car carefully, and I haven't found my lost car keys there. It's reasonable to conclude, therefore, that my car keys aren't in the car.

15. You're not seriously thinking of voting for that bum, are you? Why don't you wake up and smell the coffee?

16. Most immigrants who enter this country wind up in jail or on welfare. I know this because I read it on a White Power Web site.

17. It would be a much greater wrong to destroy the last remaining copy of Shakespeare's *Macbeth* than it would be to destroy an individual copy of *Macbeth*. Similarly, it is a much greater wrong to cause the extinction of an entire animal species than it is to destroy an individual member of that species.

18. Don't fire that cannon in these snow-packed hills. The cannon could cause an avalanche, and the avalanche could destroy the ski lodge and possibly the village below. Hundreds of people might die.

19. It says in the *Encyclopaedia Britannica* that the Bermejo River is a western tributary of the Paraguay River in south-central South America. This is

probably true because the *Encyclopaedia Britannica* is a highly reliable reference source.

20. The volcano erupted shortly after the king abandoned worship of the ancient tribal spirits. The tribal spirits must be angry.

21. Strong measures must be taken to halt the flood of Mexican immigrants into the United States. If we allow this immigration to continue, soon Spanish will become the official language of California and Texas. Eventually, the entire United States will be just a cultural offshoot of Mexico.

22. On Tuesday I was passed by a reckless woman driver. On Thursday I was passed by a reckless woman driver. On Friday I was passed by a reckless woman driver. It's clear that most reckless drivers today are women.

23. *Coach Phil, giving a pep talk to his soccer team in the film* Kicking and Screaming: You can win and go on to glory, or you can lose and probably face a series of cataclysmic events.

24. Why all the fuss about preserving old-growth redwood forests? Redwood trees are like Motel 6's. Once you've seen one, you've seen them all.[19]

25. My taxicab driver this morning told me he once drove from New York to Los Angeles in less than 18 hours at an average speed of 165 miles per hour. I hate to think how many speeding tickets he must have gotten along the way!

26. If a large asteroid had struck China in AD 1200, it's likely that some historical records of the disaster would have been preserved. But there is absolutely no mention of any such catastrophe in any of the numerous Chinese historical records that survive from that period. Therefore, it's reasonable to conclude that a large asteroid did not strike China in AD 1200.

27. Why do you find it so difficult to be fair and impartial?

28. I'm prejudiced only if I hold irrational biases. But I don't hold any irrational biases. I just think this country's being overrun by Catholics and Jews.

29. Since the 1960s promiscuity, divorce, abortion, teen suicide, and out-of-wedlock births have all risen sharply. Clearly, we need to restore prayer in public schools.

30. Dr. Leonard Vesey, chief of Pediatrics at Boston Children's Hospital, has argued that abortion is always immoral. Given Dr. Vesey's impressive professional credentials, we must conclude that abortion is always immoral.

31. Everything that exists is animal, or vegetable, or mineral. The number 7 obviously isn't an animal or a vegetable. Therefore, the number 7 is a mineral.

32. Rich Kowalski is a young, successful CEO of an Internet start-up company, and his parents come from Poland. Kelly Yablonski is a young, successful CEO of an Internet start-up company, and her parents come from Poland. Matt Golembeski is a young, successful CEO of an Internet start-up company, and his parents come from Poland. Miguel Gonzalez is also a young, successful CEO of an Internet start-up company. So, his parents probably come from Poland, too.

33. A benevolent, all-powerful Creator may exist. On the other hand, a benevolent, all-powerful Creator may not exist. No one knows for certain which

of these claims is true. But one thing is certain: one of these claims must be true.

34. There's nothing wrong with segregating restrooms on the basis of race. After all, we've always had separate restrooms for men and women, and no one seems to complain about that.

35. Which sport is more popular: sailing or snow skiing? To find out we asked more than five hundred people on the streets of Miami, Florida. The result? Americans prefer sailing by a margin of more than 3 to 1.

36. I have no proof that my refrigerator light goes off when I close the refrigerator door. Therefore, it's reasonable to believe that it doesn't.

37. Most women from California believe in astrology. I know because I've dated three women from California, and they all believed in astrology.

38. I don't understand why you have to wear a helmet to play football. Soccer is a dangerous sport, and they don't make soccer players wear helmets.

39. Carl Sagan, the world-famous astronomer, argued that Venus is too hot to support life. Moreover, I've consulted three astronomy textbooks, and they all agree with Dr. Sagan on this point. Therefore, it is reasonable to believe that Venus is too hot to support life.

40. If we don't dramatically increase defense spending, the Chinese will soon surpass us as a military power. And, if the Chinese surpass us as a military power, it's only a matter of time before we'll all be speaking Chinese and eating chop suey.

II. Most of the following passages were taken from letters to the editor and newspaper call-in columns. Identify any fallacies discussed in Chapters 5 and 6 that you find. If no fallacy is committed, write "no fallacy."

1. When will the American people finally realize that the Democrats are leading this country straight into socialism? (newspaper call-in column)

2. Nasrudin was throwing handfuls of crumbs around his house. "What are you doing?" someone asked him. "Keeping the tigers away." "But there are no tigers in these parts." "That's right. Effective, isn't it." (Idries Shah, *The Exploits of the Incomparable Mulla Nasrudin* [slightly adapted])

3. I'd like to make a comment on the boy who wore the KKK outfit to school. I think it was blown way out of proportion. You have other organizations, the KKK is an organization, the Knights of Columbus is an organization, the Shriners are an organization, the Masons are an organization, they all have uniforms. This is a uniform of something that is all over the United States, the KKK. Now, I don't see anything wrong with it. (newspaper call-in column)

4. See it or be un-American! (ad for *The Adventures of Rocky and Bullwinkle* movie)

5. In regard to Thursday's paper: To have a gay lead a Boy Scout troop. Isn't that like putting the fox in the henhouse? What a travesty of common sense. (newspaper call-in column)

6. Television actor and liberal Democratic activist Martin Sheen says that President Bush is a "moron." . . . Before Sheen makes such a childish assertion in the future, maybe he should remember that "it takes one to know one." (James Whittington, letter to the editor, *USA Today*)

7. Party labels don't mean anything anymore. You can draw a line right down the middle. On the one side are the Americans, on the other are the Communists and Socialists. (George Murphy, speech to a Republican fund-raiser)[20]

8. Could we please have a move on to abolish parole in this state, in fact in the country? If you get sentenced for a crime, you should serve the entire time, not just a portion of it. Just like when you take out a mortgage or a car loan, they don't say you paid it nice for the first couple of years and we'll eliminate the next twenty-some years. (newspaper call-in column)

9. The resurrection is a myth because the Bible is myth, and the Bible is a myth because it contains obviously mythical stories like the resurrection. (discussed but not endorsed in Peter Kreeft and Ronald K. Tacelli, *Handbook of Christian Apologetics*)

10. After nine years at Pacific Bell I learned just about everything there was to know about *looking* busy without actually being busy. During that time the stock price of Pacific Bell climbed steadily, so I think I can conclude that my avoidance of work was in the best interest of the company and something to be proud of. (Scott Adams, *The Dilbert Principle*)

11. *U.S. Army Captain Laughlin Waters:* "Well, you were supposed to have 1,500 prisoners. Where are they?"
    Polish captain: "They are dead. We shot them. These are all that are left."
    Captain Waters: "Then why don't you shoot these too?" A pause, then Waters corrected himself: "No, you can't do that."
    Polish captain: "Oh, yes we can. They shot my countrymen."[21]

12. This is about the person who is concerned about McDonald Corporation's treatment of pigs and chickens. What about the poor potatoes? They gouge out their eyes, they rip off their skin, and they throw them in boiling oil. (newspaper call-in column)

13. Dudley said that whenever anything would go wrong at his last job, his boss would always say he was responsible. I guess Dudley must be a very responsible person. I'd better hire him. (adapted from Tom Morris, *True Success*)

14. Miscarriages of justice are rare [in capital sentencing], but they do occur. Over a long enough time they lead to the execution of some innocents. Does this make irrevocable punishments morally wrong? Hardly. Our government employs trucks. They run over innocent bystanders more frequently than courts sentence innocents to death. We do not give up trucks because the benefits they produce outweigh the harm, including the death of innocents. (Ernest Van Den Haag, "The Death Penalty Once More")

15. To the guy who reads five newspapers and is bashing President Bush. Five newspapers a day? Let me guess. You don't have a job. You're probably living off the government. (newspaper call-in column)

16. In regards to the teachers working on the Dallas [Pennsylvania] curriculum. That's a joke. I had two daughters nine years apart in the Dallas Middle School. Both had the same two science teachers, they used the same exact questions and lesson plans nine years later. Come on guys, wake up. Science

changes on a daily basis. Dallas teachers are a joke and an embarrassment. (newspaper call-in column)

17. One of your readers suggested we should ban smoking [in public places] like California does. I'm from New York and New York State tried to do something similar, but think about this. You might be concerned with the filthy smoke that streams over to the nonsmoking section, but realize this: When your state starts to control your actions that's just the beginning, and soon everything else will be controlled. You might want to think about that. If you don't like places that allow smoking, try going somewhere that does not allow it. (newspaper call-in column)

18. I hope that you understand why it would be wrong to allow a club for homosexuals in school. It would only encourage a lifestyle that is destructive and immoral. If you still believe there should be a gay club, then you should insist on there being a club for thieves and robbers and a club for murderers including abortionists. (letter to the editor, *Scranton Times*)

19. Life is divided up into the horrible and the miserable. The horrible would be like terminal cases, blind people, cripples—I don't know how they get through life. It's amazing to me. And the miserable is everyone else. So when you go through life, you should be thankful that you're miserable. (Alvy Singer, in *Annie Hall*)

20. In Lane Filler's opinion, whoever the hell he is, real life resembles a football game. If that were true, Mr. Filler, I think I'd slit my wrists right now. What an awful thing to say . . . you have a fat head and your picture proves it. (from a newspaper call-in column)

21. If a proposed amendment to the Pennsylvania state constitution to grant residents of Pennsylvania the right to hunt is passed, the floodgate will be opened for other groups to follow. What's next? An amendment allowing the right to play golf or go shopping? (letter to the editor, *Wilkes-Barre Times Leader* [slightly adapted])

22. Judges make the decision to return children to an abusive home once the Department of Human Services has investigated a home and have presented their findings to the judge. Unfortunately most judges are incompetent to make a decision. I have watched three cases in which judges in Pawhuska [Oklahoma] have allowed access of their children to abusive parents. (letter to the editor, *Tulsa World*)

23. Yeah, this is for the person who called in and said that he likes enjoying cold weather football and there are sissy teams in the dome and down in Florida. I have one question for this macho man. Was he sitting outside in his yard with his TV and cold beer out in the snow? Or was he in his warm, warm living room? Who's the real sissy, pal? (newspaper call-in column)

24. If angels don't exist, how do you explain the days when you haven't studied for a test, and there is a snow day the next day? Or when you're mean to someone, and the very next day you see someone getting teased and you realize how bad it must feel? (Jack McKenna, age 12, quoted in *Parade* magazine)

25. Methadone, what a crock. Just because you can't get high off of it doesn't mean it's not a narcotic. What all these addicts are doing is trading one narcotic for another. It's like having an alcoholic drink beer instead of whisky. (newspaper call-in column)

26. Amid cries that there is too much violence on TV, members of Congress are moving to censor network programming. Congress should mind its own dang business. . . .

    Rep. Edward Markey, D-Mass., wants to require new TV sets to include a computer chip that will allow parents to block violent programs.

    That's not as harmless as it seems. What's next? A computer chip to block anti-government programs? (editorial, "On TV Censorship," *Charleston (West Virginia) Daily Mail*)

27. The Democratic Party makes victims out of all taxpaying Americans. For 40 years they had control of Congress and the money. The results? We've had an out-of-control illegitimacy rate, out-of-control entitlements for illegal immigrants, a public education system that's broken. There's more people in prison than any other nation. We've had moral decay. It seems that the Democratic Congress' objective was to keep everybody uneducated, overweight, drugged and drunk, and charge responsible taxpayers for the cost. (newspaper call-in column)

28. I don't believe in superstitions. They're bad luck. (New York Mets coach Bobby Valentine, quoted in George F. Will, "2002: Let's Keep Dancing," *Newsweek*)

29. You know who's pushing [the right to abortion]. You saw some of those women out there. I mean those women aren't ever going to have a baby by anybody. I mean, these are primarily lesbians, and lesbians don't have babies. And it's the one thing a mother has—that a lesbian can never have—is this femininity, and they can never achieve that. And so, in order to level the field, they say, "Hey, let you abort your baby so you'll be like us, because we don't have them." (Pat Robertson, statement on *The 700 Club*)[22]

30. People want to take sex education out of the schools. They believe sex education causes promiscuity—if you have the knowledge, [you'll] use it. Hey, I took algebra. I never do math. (Elayne Boosler)

31. ". . . I've always reckoned that looking at the new moon over your left shoulder is one of the carelessest and foolishest things a body can do. Old Hank Bunker done it once, and bragged about it; and in less than two years he got drunk and fell off of the shot tower, and spread himself out so that he was just a kind of layer, as you may say; and they slid him edgeways between two barn doors for a coffin, and buried him so, so they say, but I didn't see it. Pap told me. But anyway it all come of looking at the moon that way, like a fool." (Huck Finn, *The Adventures of Huckleberry Finn*)

32. To give equal time to "Creation Science" whenever cosmology, geology, or biology are at issue in public school classes would be identical to giving equal time to Mother Goose and her goslings whenever the origin of snow is at issue in meteorology classes, or to giving equal time to Jack Frost

when the death of tree leaves in the fall is at issue in botany departments, or giving equal time to magical practices in colleges of engineering. (Delos B. McKown, *The Mythmaker's Magic: Behind the Illusion of "Creation Science"*)

33. "No one is to be let out of the house today. And anyone I catch talking about this young lady will be first beaten to death and then burned alive and after that be kept on bread and water for six weeks." (Lasaraleen, in C. S. Lewis, *A Horse and His Boy*)

34. We shouldn't hastily ban human cloning. Nature clones us—look at identical twins. Shall we ban them? No! Go ahead—send in the clones. (Titus Stauffer, letter to the editor, *Time* magazine)

35. It is a proven scientific fact that video games are . . . corrupting American youth. In a recent experiment, scientific researchers exposed a group of teenaged boys to an arcade game, and found all of them had unclean thoughts. Of course, the researchers got the same result when they exposed the boys to coleslaw, an alpaca sweater, and "The McNeil-Lehrer News Hour" but that is beside the point. The point is that we should all write letters to our elected officials to urge them to ban video games. (Dave Barry, *Dave Barry's Bad Habits*, 1985)

III. Write an off-beat or amusing example of each of the fallacies of insufficient evidence discussed in this chapter. Be prepared to share your examples with the class.

IV. Find examples of the fallacies discussed in this chapter from everyday life (newspapers, magazines, TV, radio, the Internet, and so on). Collect your examples in a notebook or portfolio. For each example indicate where you found the fallacy and give a brief explanation why you think it commits the fallacy you allege. Be prepared to share your examples with the class.

V. Watch the classic 1957 film *12 Angry Men* in class and keep in mind the following questions for class discussion.

1. What evidence initially points to the guilt of the defendant? How was this evidence later undermined or called into question by good critical thinking?

2. What fallacies were committed by individual jurors? (*Hint:* There are lots of them.)

3. In your opinion, was the final verdict correct or incorrect? Defend your answer.

4. What do you see as the basic message of the film?

5. Why aren't there any women on the jury?

6. Does the film lower your confidence in the jury system? Why or why not?

7. How does the film underscore the practical value of critical thinking skills and dispositions?

VI. This exercise is a game we call *Name That Fallacy!* Here's how the game is played: The instructor divides the class into teams of four or five students, then reads an example of a fallacy (or puts it on an overhead). The first team to raise a hand gets a chance to identify the fallacy. Before the instructor reveals the

► Pop Culture Connection ◄

Monty Python and the Logic of Witch Detection

In the film *Monty Python and the Holy Grail* (1975), there's a classic spoof of the kinds of bogus logic that led to the persecution of "witches" in the Middle Ages. A mob of peasants plans to burn a woman whom they claim is a witch. How do they know she's a witch? She looks like one! On the other hand, since the mob admits they dressed her up to look like a witch, this proof is hardly a clincher. The dialogue, slightly abridged, proceeds as follows:

> *Sir Bedivere:* What do you do with witches?
>
> *Mob:* Burn them!
>
> *Sir Bedivere:* And what do you burn apart from witches?
>
> *First Peasant:* Wood!
>
> *Sir Bedivere:* Wood! So why do witches burn?
>
> *First Peasant:* 'Cause they're made of wood.
>
> *Sir Bedivere:* Does wood sink in water?
>
> *Mob:* No, it floats.
>
> *Sir Bedivere:* What also floats in water?
>
> *King Arthur:* A duck.
>
> *Sir Bedivere:* Yes, exactly. So, logically . . . ?
>
> *Mob:* If she weighs the same as a duck . . . she's made of wood!
>
> *Sir Bedivere:* And therefore . . . ?
>
> *Mob:* A witch! Burn her!

Hmmm, seems a little shaky to us. How many fallacies can you detect in this passage?

correct answer, the other teams are given the opportunity to challenge the first team's answer. Scoring is as follows:

Correct answer:	5 points
Incorrect answer:	−5 points
Correct challenge:	5 points
Incorrect challenge:	−5 points

The first team to reach 40 points wins.[23]

SUMMARY

1. In this chapter we studied *fallacies of insufficient evidence*—arguments in which the premises, though logically relevant to the conclusion, fail to provide sufficient evidence to support the conclusion.

2. We looked at nine common fallacies of insufficient evidence:

a. *Inappropriate appeal to authority:* citing a witness or authority that is untrustworthy.

Example

My hairdresser told me that extraterrestrials built the lost city of Atlantis. So, it's reasonable to believe that extraterrestrials did build the lost city of Atlantis.

b. *Appeal to ignorance:* claiming that something is true because no one has proven it false or vice versa.

Example

Bigfoot must exist. No one has proved that it doesn't.

> *You can't convert the absence of information into a conclusion.*
> —Tom Clancy

c. *False alternatives:* posing a false either/or choice.

Example

The choice in this election is clear: either we elect a staunch conservative as our next president, or we watch as our country slides into anarchy and economic depression. Clearly, we don't want our country to slide into anarchy and economic depression. Therefore, we should elect a staunch conservative as our next president.

d. *Loaded question:* posing a question that contains an unfair or unwarranted presupposition.

Example

Al: Are you still dating that total loser Phil?
Mary: Yes.
Al: Well, at least you admit he's a total loser.

e. *Questionable cause:* claiming, without sufficient evidence, that one thing is the cause of something else.

Example

Two days after I drank lemon tea, my head cold cleared up completely. Try it. It works.

f. *Hasty generalization:* drawing a general conclusion from a sample that is biased or too small.

Example

BMWs are a pile of junk. I have two friends who drive BMWs, and both of them have had nothing but trouble from those cars.

> *Facts have sworn eternal enmity to generalizations.*
> —Will and Ariel Durant

g. *Slippery slope:* claiming, without sufficient evidence, that a seemingly harmless action, if taken, will lead to a disastrous outcome.

Example

Immediate steps should be taken to reduce violence in children's television programming. If this violent programming is allowed to continue, this will almost certainly lead to fights and acts of bullying on school playgrounds. This in turn will lead to an increase in juvenile delinquency and gang violence. Eventually, our entire society will become engulfed in an orgy of lawlessness and brutality.

h. *Weak analogy:* comparing things that aren't really comparable.

Example

Nobody would buy a car without first taking it for a test drive. Why then shouldn't two mature high school juniors live together before they decide whether to get married?

i. *Inconsistency:* asserting inconsistent or contradictory claims.

Example

Note found in a Forest Service suggestion box: Park visitors need to know how important it is to keep this wilderness area completely pristine and undisturbed. So why not put up a few signs to remind people of this fact?

> I made up my mind but I made it up both ways.
> —Casey Stengel

CHAPTER 7

ANALYZING ARGUMENTS

To *analyze* an argument means to break it down into its various parts to see clearly what conclusion is defended and on what grounds. Analyzing arguments is an important critical reasoning skill because, to paraphrase Bob Dylan, we can't think critically about what we don't understand. In this chapter we discuss two methods for analyzing arguments, one for short arguments and one for longer arguments.

DIAGRAMMING SHORT ARGUMENTS

Diagramming is a quick and easy way to analyze relatively short arguments (i.e., arguments that are roughly a paragraph in length or shorter). This section explains how the diagramming method works.

First, read through the argument and circle any premise or conclusion indicators you see. For example:

> The death penalty should be abolished (because) it's racially discriminatory, there's no evidence that it's a more effective deterrent than life imprisonment, and innocent people may be executed by mistake.

Second, number the statements consecutively as they appear in the argument:

> ① The death penalty should be abolished (because) ② it's racially discriminatory, ③ there's no evidence that it's a more effective deterrent than life imprisonment, and ④ innocent people may be executed by mistake.

Third, arrange the numbers on a page with premises placed above the conclusions(s) they are claimed to support:

②   ③   ④

①

Fourth, omit any logically irrelevant statements—that is, statements that don't function as either premises or conclusions in the argument. In this particular example, there are no logically irrelevant statements.

Finally, using arrows to mean "is offered as evidence for," create a kind of flowchart that indicates relationships of argumentative support:

In this argument each of the three premises provides *independent support* for the conclusion. A premise provides independent support for a conclusion when it provides a separate, freestanding reason for accepting the conclusion. More precisely, a premise provides **independent support** for a conclusion when the amount of support it provides would *not* be weakened or destroyed by the removal of any other premise in the argument. We symbolize this relationship of independent support by drawing arrows from each of the three premises to the conclusion.

In some arguments the premises work cooperatively, rather than independently, to support the argument's conclusion. For example:

① Every member of the Applewood Association is more than fifty years old.
② Bob is a member of the Applewood Association. So, ③ Bob is more than fifty years old.

Here the argument's premises provide *linked support* for the conclusion. A premise provides linked support when it works conjointly with another premise to support the conclusion. More precisely, a premise provides **linked support** for a conclusion when the amount of support it provides would be weakened or destroyed by the removal of some other premise in the argument.[1] We symbolize relationships of linked support by underlining the linked premises and putting a plus sign (+) between them. Thus, the argument above can be diagrammed as follows:

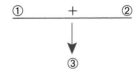

The basic distinction between linked and independent premises isn't hard to understand. Two premises are *linked* if the omission of one of the premises would reduce the amount of support provided by the other. For example:

① No members of the Mill City High School marching band are Yankee fans.
② Allan is a member of the Mill City High School marching band. So, ③ Allan isn't a Yankee fan.

In this example neither premise provides any support for the conclusion without the other. Taken together, however, the **linked premises** validly imply the

How to Decide Whether Premises Are Linked or Independent

Two premises are *linked* when the omission of one of the premises would cancel or reduce the amount of support provided by the other.

Example

No student at Wexford College is a Rhodes Scholar.

Melissa is a Rhodes Scholar.

So, Melissa is not a student at Wexford College.

Two premises are *independent* when neither premise would provide less support for the conclusion if the other premise were omitted.

Example

Nick doesn't own a car.

Nick is legally blind.

So, Nick probably won't drive a car to the game.

---

conclusion. The premises are linked because the amount of support provided by one of the premises would be reduced if the other premise were omitted.

Similarly, two premises are *independent* if neither premise would lose any power to support the conclusion if the other premise were removed. Here are two examples:

> ① Ten witnesses say they saw Blotto rob the bank. ② The stolen bank money was found in Blotto's apartment. ③ Blotto's fingerprints were found on the note the robber handed to the bank teller. Therefore, ④ probably Blotto robbed the bank.

> ① Agatha is a mother. ② Agatha is an aunt. Therefore, ③ Agatha is a female.

In the first example, the premises work independently to build a cumulative case to support the conclusion. In the second example, each of the premises independently provides complete logical support for the conclusion. Both are examples of **independent premises** because the amount of support each provides individually would not be reduced or destroyed even if every other premise in the argument were omitted.

Let's practice this diagramming technique with a few examples:

> If Amy runs marathons, then she's probably very fit. Amy does run marathons. She's also a B student. So, Amy probably is very fit.

First we circle all the premise and conclusion indicators:

> If Amy runs marathons, then she's probably very fit. Amy does run marathons. She's also a B student. (So), Amy probably is very fit.

Next we number the statements in the argument consecutively:

> ① If Amy runs marathons, then she's probably very fit. ② Amy does run marathons. ③ She's also a B student. (So), ④ Amy probably is very fit.

Then we check to see if there are any logically irrelevant statements in the argument. In this case, statement ③ is clearly irrelevant. It is simply an aside that provides no support whatsoever for the conclusion. Thus, we will omit it from our diagram.

Finally, we diagram the argument by arranging the numbers on a page with premises placed above the conclusion(s) they are claimed to support. In this argument the conclusion indicator *so* indicates that ④ is the conclusion. Because ① supports ④ only if it is conjoined with ②, ① and ② provide linked support for ④. Thus, the argument can be diagrammed as follows:

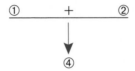

Here is a second example:

Jim is a senior citizen. So, Jim probably doesn't like hip-hop music. So, Jim probably won't be going to the Ashanti concert this weekend.

First we circle the indicator words:

Jim is a senior citizen. (So), Jim probably doesn't like hip-hop music. (So), Jim probably won't be going to the Ashanti concert this weekend.

Next we number the statements in the argument:

① Jim is a senior citizen. (So), ② Jim probably doesn't like hip-hop music. (So), ③ Jim probably won't be going to the Ashanti concert this weekend.

Then we determine whether any of the premises are irrelevant to the argument. In this case, none is.

Finally, we diagram the argument by placing the numbers for the premises above the conclusion(s) they support and adding arrows to indicate relationships of support. In this argument we see that the conclusion indicator *so* is used twice. This tells us that ① is offered as a reason for ②, and ② is offered as a reason for ③. Thus, we diagram the argument as follows:

Here is a third example:

Most Democrats are liberals, and Senator Dumdiddle is a Democrat. Thus, Senator Dumdiddle is probably a liberal. Therefore, Senator Dumdiddle probably supports affirmative action in higher education, because most liberals support affirmative action in higher education.

First we circle all premise and conclusion indicators:

> Most Democrats are liberals, and Senator Dumdiddle is a Democrat. (Thus), Senator Dumdiddle is probably a liberal. (Therefore), Senator Dumdiddle probably supports affirmative action in higher education, (because) most liberals support affirmative action in higher education.

Next we number the statements consecutively:

> ① Most Democrats are liberals, and ② Senator Dumdiddle is a Democrat. (Thus), ③ Senator Dumdiddle is probably a liberal. (Therefore), ④ Senator Dumdiddle probably supports affirmative action in higher education, (because) ⑤ most liberals support affirmative action in higher education.

Then we check to see whether any of the numbered statements is irrelevant to the argument. In this case, none is.

Finally, we diagram the argument by arranging the numbers on a page with premises placed above the conclusion(s) they allegedly support. ① and ② clearly work conjointly to support ③. Thus, they provide linked support for ③. We therefore diagram this part of the argument as follows:

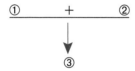

③ and ⑤ likewise provide linked support for ④. Thus, the entire argument can be diagrammed as follows:

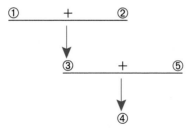

Here is a final example:

> Cheating is wrong for several reasons. First, it will ultimately lower your self-respect because you can never be proud of anything you got by cheating. Second, cheating is a lie because it deceives other people into thinking you know more than you do. Third, cheating violates the teacher's trust that you will do your own work. Fourth, cheating is unfair to all the people who aren't cheating. Finally, if you cheat in school now, you'll find it easier to cheat in other situations later in life—perhaps even in your closest personal relationships.[2]

We must learn to take thinking apart.
—Richard Paul and Linda Elder

First we circle the premise and conclusion indicators:

> Cheating is wrong for several reasons. First, it will ultimately lower your self-respect (because) you can never be proud of anything you got by cheating. Second, cheating is a lie (because) it deceives other people into thinking you know more than you do. Third, cheating violates the teacher's trust that you will

do your own work. Fourth, cheating is unfair to all the people who aren't cheating. Finally, if you cheat in school now, you'll find it easier to cheat in other situations later in life—perhaps even in your closest personal relationships.

Next we number the statements consecutively, as follows:

> ① Cheating is wrong for several reasons. First, ② it will ultimately lower your self-respect (because) ③ you can never be proud of anything you got by cheating. Second, ④ cheating is a lie (because) ⑤ it deceives other people into thinking you know more than you do. Third, ⑥ cheating violates the teacher's trust that you will do your own work. Fourth, ⑦ cheating is unfair to all the people who aren't cheating. Finally, ⑧ if you cheat in school now, you'll find it easier to cheat in other situations later in life—perhaps even in your closest personal relationships.

Then we decide whether any of the numbered statements is logically irrelevant to the argument. In this argument, none is.

Now we diagram the argument. As the premise indicator *because* indicates, ③ is offered as support for ②, and ⑤ is offered as support for ④:

Finally, we note that ②, ④, ⑥, ⑦, and ⑧ all provide independent support for the main conclusion ①. Thus, the complete diagram of the argument is as follows:

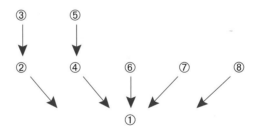

Analysis is a skill you need everywhere in life. Lawyers analyze complex claims and sort out the issues; physicians analyze symptoms; detectives look for patterns in the evidence; business people sort through the parts of an intricate deal; parents try to untangle and get a grip on the issues troubling a family.

—Tom Morris

Tips on Diagramming Arguments

Diagramming arguments is a little like learning to play golf: difficult at first, but challenging and fun once you get the hang of it. This section provides a few tips on how to diagram arguments like a pro:[3]

1. *Find the main conclusion first.* It is easy to get lost if you don't have a clear idea where you are going. For that reason it is often a good idea, especially when diagramming complex arguments, to start by locating the main conclusion and then working back through the passage to see how the argument as a whole works together to support the conclusion. (For help in locating the main conclusion of an argument, review "Tips on Finding the Conclusion of an Argument" on page 36.)

2. *Pay close attention to premise and conclusion indicators.* One common mistake students make in diagramming arguments is to overlook premise and conclusion indicators such as *since, as, so,* and *because.* Pay especially close attention to premise indicators like *since* and *because* that precede independent clauses, as in this example:

> All dogs go to heaven. So, Sparky will go to heaven *because* Sparky is a dog.

In this argument the premise indicator *because* signals that, logically speaking, there are two statements in the second sentence (a premise and a conclusion) rather than one. These two statements must be distinguished for purposes of argument analysis.

3. *Remember that sentences containing the word* and *often contain two or more separate statements.* We have seen that a single sentence frequently expresses two or more distinct statements. Sometimes these statements are separated by the word *and.* For example:

> Never fly Cattle Car Airlines. They're never on time, and the food tastes like warmed-over cardboard.

Here the second sentence is a compound sentence that expresses two logically distinct premises separated by the word *and.* These distinct premises should be diagrammed separately.

4. *Treat conditional statements* (if-then *statements*) *and disjunctive statements* (either-or *statements*) *as single statements.* As we saw in Chapter 2, conditional statements should always be treated as a single logical unit because they assert a single complete thought. For example, the conditional sentence

> If I win the lottery, then I'll move to Tahiti

doesn't assert that I'll win the lottery, nor does it assert that I'll move to Tahiti. Rather, it asserts a single conditional statement: that one event will occur (I'll move to Tahiti) *if* another event occurs (I win the lottery). Because conditional sentences assert only a single statement, they should always be treated as a single logical unit for purposes of argument analysis.

For similar reasons disjunctions (*either-or* statements) should also be diagrammed as single statements. Notice that if I say

> Either Boston will win the pennant or Cleveland will win the pennant

I am not saying that Boston will win the pennant or that Cleveland will win the pennant. Rather, I am asserting a single (disjunctive) statement: that one of two events will occur—*either* Boston will win the pennant *or* Cleveland will win the pennant (but not both). Because disjunctive statements, like conditional statements, express a single complete thought, they should always be diagrammed as single statements.

How to Diagram an Argument

1. Read through the argument carefully, circling any premise or conclusion indicators you see.
2. Number the statements consecutively as they appear in the argument. Don't number any sentences that are not statements.
3. Arrange the numbers on a page with the premises placed above the conclusion(s) they support. Omit any irrelevant or redundant statements.
4. Using arrows to mean "is offered as evidence for," create a kind of flowchart that shows which premises are intended to support which conclusions.
5. Indicate independent premises by drawing arrows directly from the premises to the conclusions they are claimed to support. Indicate linked premises by placing a plus sign between each of the premises, and drawing an arrow from the underlined premises to the conclusions they support.
6. Put the argument's main conclusion at the bottom of the diagram.

5. *Don't number or diagram any sentence that is not a statement.* Arguments, by definition, consist entirely of statements—that is, sentences that it makes sense to regard as either true or false. Consequently, questions, suggestions, exclamations, and other nonstatements should be omitted from argument diagrams.

6. *Don't diagram irrelevant statements.* In real life most lengthy and complex arguments contain logically irrelevant statements—that is, statements that don't support the conclusion in any way. Because the purpose of an argument diagram is simply to map the logical structure of an argument, such statements should be omitted.

7. *Don't diagram redundant statements.* Many arguments contain redundant statements—that is, statements that basically repeat what's already been said. Such statements are often useful for rhetorical purposes, but they should be omitted in argument diagrams because they merely clutter the argument.

> *The essence of thinking is to analyze—that is, to discriminate.*
> —D. T. Suzuki

EXERCISE 7.1

I. Diagram the following arguments using the method presented in the preceding section.

1. Bertie probably isn't home. His car isn't in the driveway, and there are no lights on in his house.
2. No members of the volleyball team like rap music. Andrea is a member of the volleyball team. So, Andrea doesn't like rap music.
3. Don't copy off Sturdley's exam. He's one of the worst students in class. My roommate told me he's bombed every test this semester.

4. Affirmative action in higher education is morally justifiable because it compensates for past discrimination, provides valuable role models for women and minorities, and promotes multicultural understanding.

5. This is either my car or Sandy's car. If it is my car, my key should fit in the lock. But my key doesn't fit in the lock. So, this is Sandy's car.

6. Wexford College is a really great college. The students are friendly. The faculty really care about the students. The campus is beautiful, and the athletic facilities are great.

7. Only three people could have stolen the CD: Danny, Stacy, or Patrick. But Stacy couldn't have stolen the CD because she was out riding her bike. Patrick couldn't have stolen the CD because he was at a friend's house. Therefore, Danny must have stolen the CD.

8. Something is a square only if it is a rectangle. But this isn't a rectangle. Look, it has only three sides, and some of the sides aren't even straight. So, this can't be a square.

9. There are only two ways Sturdley could pass this exam: by cheating or an act of divine inspiration. But Sturdley won't be able to cheat because the instructor is watching him like a hawk. And Sturdley won't be struck by divine inspiration because God performs miracles only for those who believe in Him, and Sturdley is an atheist. Accordingly, Sturdley won't pass this exam. I doubt he'll pass his history test either.

10. Several states have abolished the insanity defense as a defense against criminal responsibility. This may be popular with voters, but it is morally indefensible. Insanity removes moral responsibility, and it is wrong to punish someone who is not morally responsible for his crime. Moreover, it is pointless to punish the insane because punishment has no deterrent effect on a person who cannot appreciate the wrongfulness or criminality of his or her actions.

11. All Republicans are either moderates or conservatives, and Senator Hornswaggle is not a moderate. Because Senator Hornswaggle is a Republican, it follows that he is a conservative. All conservatives oppose socialized medicine. Thus, Senator Hornswaggle opposes socialized medicine.

12. It's foolish to smoke cigarettes. Smoking is expensive, unhealthy, and obnoxious to many nonsmokers. I wouldn't date anyone who smokes cigarettes.

13. If today is Saturday, then tomorrow is Sunday. If tomorrow is Sunday, then we'll be having pasta for dinner. If we'll be having pasta for dinner, then I should pick up some red wine today because in this state wine can be purchased only at liquor stores, and the liquor stores are closed on Sundays. Today is Saturday. Therefore, I should pick up some red wine today.

14. It makes no sense to ask God for things in prayer. The thing you ask for is either good or it is not. If it is good, God will do it anyway. If it is not, he won't. In neither case can your prayer make any difference.[4]

15. If Amy isn't dating Sturdley, she's dating Mel or Steve. Amy isn't dating Sturdley because she doesn't date anyone who uses drugs, and Sturdley

sniffs glue practically every weekend. Thus, Amy is dating Mel or Steve. Amy won't date anyone who isn't a football player, however, nor will she date anyone who isn't good-looking. Both Mel and Steve are good-looking, but Steve isn't a football player. Consequently, Amy is not dating Steve. We can logically deduce, therefore, that Amy is dating Mel.

II. Diagram the following real-life arguments using the method presented in this section. For convenience, the statements have been numbered.

1. Since ① our feelings, desires, and preferences can be either beneficial or harmful, noble or ignoble, praiseworthy or damnable, and since ② they can be either in harmony or in conflict with other people's feelings, desires, and preferences, ③ they are obviously not accurate tools for analysis of moral issues or trustworthy guidelines to action. (Vincent Ryan Ruggiero, *The Moral Imperative*, 2nd ed.)

2. ① Suppose you had one sheep which fell into a ditch on the Sabbath; is there one of you who would not catch hold of it and lift it out? And ② surely a man is worth more than a sheep! ③ It is therefore permitted to do good on the Sabbath (Jesus, Matt. 12:11–12)

3. Since ① the end of individuals and of states is the same, ② the end of the best man and of the best constitution must also be the same; it is therefore evident that ③ there ought to exist in both of them the excellences of leisure, for ④ peace, as has often been repeated, is the end of war, and leisure of toil. (Aristotle, *Politics*)

4. ① School tests should be abolished. ② Tests introduce competition where it does not belong. ③ They deny the individuality of students' talents and interests. ④ They degrade education by encouraging passivity, mindlessness, and triviality. Finally, ⑤ they send the wrong messages about what is valuable in education and in life. (stated but not endorsed in E. D. Hirsch Jr., *The Schools We Need and Why We Don't Have Them*)

5. ① The rule of equal incomes is socially impracticable. ② It would deter the great majority of the more efficient from putting forth their best efforts and turning out their maximum product. As a consequence, ③ the total volume of product would be so diminished as to render the share of the great majority of persons smaller than it would have been under a rational plan of unequal distribution. (John A. Ryan, *Distributive Justice*, 3rd ed.)

6. ① Many that live deserve death. And ② some that die deserve life. ③ Can you give it to them? Then ④ do not be too eager to deal out death in judgment. ⑤ For even the wise cannot see all ends. (Gandalf, in J. R. R. Tolkien, *The Lord of the Rings*)

7. ① Everything eternal is necessary. But ② whatever God wills, He wills from eternity, for ③ otherwise His will would be mutable. Therefore, ④ whatever He wills, He wills necessarily. (stated but not endorsed in Saint Thomas Aquinas, *Summa Theologica*)

8. ① Testing at the national level is indicated; ② we are all aware of the abysmal education of too many young people, especially in certain areas and certain schools. ③ Such people tend to become narrow-minded, ignorant and

hateful, and contribute little to advancing the highest ideals of which we are capable. ④ National testing can help to devote extra attention to such places. (John D. Leith, letter to the editor, *The Key Reporter*)

9. Since ① what is in the past cannot be changed, and since ② God's knowledge of my future actions is in the past, ③ God's knowledge of those actions cannot change. But ④ if God's knowledge of those actions cannot be changed, then those actions cannot be changed. Thus, ⑤ what I will do in the future is unchangeably settled, and I have no power to alter it. ⑥ I am not free with regard to anything I cannot alter, and thus, ⑦ I have no freedom with regard to any of my actions. (Richard Purtill, *C. S. Lewis's Case for the Christian Faith* [adapted])

10. ① Education implies teaching. ② Teaching implies knowledge. ③ Knowledge is truth. ④ The truth is everywhere the same. Hence ⑤ education should be everywhere the same. (Robert Maynard Hutchins, *The Higher Learning in the United States*)

11. ① All humans have equal positive value. ② There is no morally relevant difference between humans and some animals (such as mammals). Therefore, ③ some animals have equal positive worth with humans. ④ Moral rights derive from the possession of value. Since ⑤ humans have rights (to life, not to be harmed, and so forth), ⑥ animals have those same rights. (Louis P. Pojman, *Global Environmental Ethics*)

12. ① True/false and multiple-choice tests have well-known limits. ② No matter how carefully questions are worded, some ambiguities will remain. ③ The format of the questions prohibits in-depth testing of important analytic skills. ④ Students can become so "test savvy" that objective tests measure test-taking skill as much as subject-matter content. (Douglas J. Soccio, *Instructor's Manual for Archetypes of Wisdom*, 3rd ed.)

13. ① Planetary exploration has many virtues. ② It permits us to refine insights derived from such Earth-bound sciences as meteorology, climatology, geology and biology, to broaden their powers and improve their practical applications here on Earth. ③ It provides cautionary tales on the alternative fates of worlds. ④ It is an aperture to future high technologies important for life here on Earth. ⑤ It provides an outlet for the traditional human zest for exploration and discovery, our passion to find out, which has been to a very large degree responsible for our success as a species. And ⑥ it permits us, for the first time in history, to approach with rigor, with a significant chance of finding out the true answers, questions on the origins and destinies of worlds, the beginnings and ends of life, and the possibilities of other beings who live in the skies—questions as basic to the human enterprise as thinking is, as natural as breathing. (Carl Sagan, *Broca's Brain: Reflections on the Romance of Science*)

14. ① Creation has no place in a science class because ② it is not science. Why not? Because ③ creationism cannot offer a scientific hypothesis that is capable of being shown wrong. ④ Creationism cannot describe a single possible experiment that could elucidate the mechanics of creation. ⑤ Creationism cannot point to a single prediction that has turned out to be right, and supports the creationist case. ⑥ Creationism

cannot offer a single instance of research that has followed the normal course of scientific inquiry, namely, independent testing and verification by skeptical researchers. (Douglas J. Futuyma, *Science on Trial: The Case for Evolution*)

15. ① Nonhuman animals lack linguistic capacity, and, for this reason, ② lack a mental or psychological life. Thus, ③ animals are not sentient. ④ If so, of course, they cannot be caused pain, appearances to the contrary. Hence, ⑤ there can be no duty not to cause them pain. (Christine Pierce and Donald VanDeveer, "General Introduction," in Christine Pierce and Donald VanDeveer, eds., *People, Penguins, and Plastic Trees: Basic Issues in Environmental Ethics,* 2nd ed. [slightly paraphrased])[5]

16. ① All students should study a foreign language. ② It improves mastery of English. ③ It helps to avoid cultural provincialism by expanding the cultural experience of students. ④ It is useful for travel and commerce. ⑤ It makes it possible to do advanced work in a foreign language, including the study of the major literary works in that language. Finally, ⑥ the ability to read, speak, and think in a second language is a source of pleasure and satisfaction even if this language is not used for travel and business and even if it does not become a field of further study. (Geraldine Van Doren and Charles Van Doren, "A Foreign Language," in Mortimer J. Adler, ed., *The Paideia Program: An Educational Syllabus* [slightly adapted])

17. ① All change is either change for the better or change for the worse. But ② God is necessarily a greatest possible being. So ③ he cannot change for the better, since ④ if he did, he would not have been the greatest possible being prior to the change. And ⑤ he cannot change for the worse, since ⑥ if he did, he would not be the greatest possible being subsequent to the change. Therefore, ⑦ God cannot change. (Thomas V. Morris, *Our Idea of God*)[6]

18. ① We have ideas of many things. ② These ideas must arise either from ourselves or from things outside us. ③ One of these ideas we have is the idea of God—an infinite, all-perfect being. ④ This idea could not have been caused by ourselves, because ⑤ we know ourselves to be limited and imperfect, and ⑥ no effect can be greater than its cause. Therefore, ⑦ the idea must have been caused by something outside us which has nothing less than the qualities contained in the idea of God. But ⑧ only God himself has those qualities. Therefore, ⑨ God himself must be the cause of the idea we have of him. Therefore, ⑩ God exists. (Peter Kreeft and Ronald K. Tacelli, *Handbook of Christian Apologetics* [slightly adapted])[7]

19. ① Lefty Grove was the greatest pitcher of all time, period. ② The one best indicator of a pitcher's ability is his ERA, and ③ Lefty Grove led leagues in earned run average nine times. ④ No one else even approaches this record. ⑤ The second-best indicator of a pitcher's ability is his winning percentage. Guess what? ⑥ Grove also led the league in that more times than anyone else. (Bill James, *The Bill James Historical Baseball Abstract* [slightly adapted])

• Critical Thinking Lapse •

Police in Fort Smith, Ark., charged James Newsome, 37, with robbing a Gas Well convenience store after the cashier provided a key identifying detail: The robber had entered the store wearing an orange hard hat with the name "James Newsome" printed on it.[8]

> The better off you become at analyzing complex problems, the better off you are for solving them.
>
> —Tom Morris

20. ① Here is a gentleman of a medical type, but with the air of a military man. ② Clearly an army doctor, then. ③ He has just come from the tropics, for ④ his face is dark, and ⑤ that is not the natural tint of his skin, as ⑥ his wrists are fair. ⑦ He has undergone hardship and sickness, as ⑧ his haggard face says clearly. ⑨ His left arm has been injured. ⑩ He holds it in a stiff and unnatural manner. Where in the tropics could an English doctor have seen much hardship and get his arm wounded? ⑪ Clearly in Afghanistan. (Sherlock Holmes, in Sir Arthur Conan Doyle, *A Study in Scarlet*)

SUMMARIZING LONGER ARGUMENTS

Diagramming works well with relatively short arguments, but with longer arguments it quickly becomes tedious and confusing. Consequently, it is usually better to *summarize* lengthy arguments rather than diagram them. In summarizing we don't try to identify every single step in an argument. Instead, the goal of an **argument summary** is to provide a synopsis of the argument that accurately restates the main points in the summarizer's own words. In this section we introduce a method for summarizing longer arguments, called **standardization.**

Summarizing involves two skills of argument analysis that are not generally used in argument diagramming, namely, paraphrasing and finding missing premises and conclusions. Let's look at these two skills before we introduce our technique for summarizing arguments.

> A good arguer or clear speaker is one who excels in analyzing or expressing a process of reasoning.
>
> —John Henry Newman

Paraphrasing

The purpose of an argument summary is to clarify an argument's structure by restating its main points as briefly, clearly, and accurately as possible. Because many arguments are expressed in ways that are needlessly wordy, complex, or obscure, it is often necessary to restate them in ways that are simpler and easier to understand. A **paraphrase** is a detailed restatement of a passage using different words and phrases. A good paraphrase is *accurate, clear, concise,* and *charitable.* Let's look at each of these four qualities.

A Good Paraphrase Is Accurate   The first virtue of a good paraphrase is that it is accurate. An accurate paraphrase is faithful to an author's intended meaning; it reproduces that meaning fairly and without bias or distortion. For example:

Original passage

Europe has a set of primary interests, which to us have none, or a very remote relation.—Hence, she must be engaged in frequent controversies, the causes of which are essentially foreign to our concerns.—Hence, therefore, it must be unwise in us to implicate ourselves, by artificial ties in the ordinary vicissitudes of her politics, or the ordinary combinations and collisions of her friendships or enmities. (George Washington, "Farewell Address," 1796)

Paraphrase 1

Europe's vital interests are totally different from ours. For this reason European nations will often become embroiled in conflicts that don't concern us. Therefore, we shouldn't become involved in Europe's political affairs.

Paraphrase 2

Europe's has a set of vital interests that are of little or no concern to us. For this reason, European nations will often become embroiled in conflicts for reasons that don't concern us. Therefore, we shouldn't form artificial ties that would get us involved in the ordinary ups and downs of European politics.

The first paraphrase clearly distorts Washington's argument, making it easier to attack. Washington does not say, for example, that Europe's vital interests are *totally* different from ours. Nor does he say flatly that we shouldn't become involved in Europe's political affairs. The second paraphrase is more faithful to Washington's intent.

A Good Paraphrase Is Clear   Arguments are often expressed in language that is needlessly wordy or confusing. Because one of the basic aims of an argument summary is to clarify what an argument is saying, it's often necessary to translate (i.e., paraphrase) complex or confusing language into language that's easier to understand. Here are several examples:

Clearness is the first essential.
—Quintilian

Original passage

The patient exhibited symptoms of an edema in the occipital-parietal region and an abrasion on the left patella.

Paraphrase

The patient had a bump on the back of his head and a scrape on his left knee.

Original Passage

High-quality learning environments are a necessary precondition for facilitation and enhancement of the ongoing learning process.

Paraphrase

Children need good schools if they are to learn properly.[9]

Original passage

'Twas the nocturnal segment of the diurnal period preceding the annual Yuletide celebration and throughout our place of residence, kinetic activity was not in evidence among the organic possessors of this potential, including the species of diminutive rodent known as *Mus musculus*.[10]

Paraphrase

'Twas the night before Christmas, when all through the house, not a creature was stirring, not even a mouse.

In short, anytime you can accurately say something more simply and clearly than the author has, by all means do so.

A Good Paraphrase Is Concise   A good summary captures the essence of an argument. It strips away all the irrelevant or unimportant details and puts the key points of the argument in a nutshell. To lay bare the essence of an argument, it is often necessary to paraphrase portions that can be stated more briefly than they are by the author. Here are some examples:

Beware of and eschew pompous prolixity.
—Charles A. Beardsley

Original passage

The office wasn't open at that point in time, owing to the fact that there was no electrical power in the building. (22 words)

Paraphrase

The office was closed then because there was no electricity in the building. (13 words)

Original passage

Macbeth was very ambitious. This led him to wish to become king of Scotland. The witches told him that this wish of his would come true. The king of Scotland at this time was Duncan. Encouraged by his wife, Macbeth murdered Duncan. He was thus enabled to succeed Duncan as king. (51 words)

A fool multiplies words.
—Ecclesiastes

Paraphrase

Encouraged by his wife, Macbeth achieved his ambition and realized the prediction of the witches by murdering Duncan and becoming king of Scotland in his place. (26 words)[11]

Original passage

Look round the world: Contemplate the whole and every part of it: You will find it to be nothing but one great machine, subdivided into an infinite number of lesser machines, which again admit of subdivisions, to a degree beyond what human senses and faculties can trace and explain. All these various machines, and even their most minute parts, are adjusted to each other with an accuracy, which ravishes into admiration all men, who have ever contemplated them. The curious adapting of means to ends, throughout all nature, resembles exactly, though it much exceeds, the productions of human contrivance; of human design, thought, wisdom, and intelligence. Since therefore the effects resemble each other, we are led to infer, by all the rules of analogy, that the causes also resemble; and that the Author of Nature is somewhat similar to the mind of man; though possessed of much larger faculties, proportioned to the grandeur of the work, which he has executed.[12] (160 words)

Paraphrase

The universe is like a giant machine, made up of an infinite number of smaller machines. These machines are similar to human artifacts, though far more complicated and impressive. Since human artifacts are made by intelligent beings, the universe is probably also made by an Intelligent Being, though one far wiser and more powerful than human beings are. (58 words)

As these examples show, a paraphrase can be significantly shorter than the original but still remain faithful to the author's intent.

It should be noted, however, that to be accurate some paraphrases must be longer than the original passage. Suppose, for instance, you are driving down a quiet residential street and see a road sign that says, "Watch Children." What this means is that drivers should watch out for children who may be on or near the road—not that they should watch the children in their own cars or those who might be playing on their front porches. The point is to make the paraphrase as concise as possible, *provided* it remains accurate.

Genius is the ability to reduce the complicated to the simple.

—C. W. Cernan

A Good Paraphrase Is Charitable   It is often possible to interpret a passage in more than one way. In such cases, the principle of charity requires that we interpret the passage as charitably as the evidence reasonably permits.[13] Here are two examples:

Original passage

You know as well as I do that you can't get a good job today unless you have a college degree. So, I hope you'll rethink your decision not to go to college.

First paraphrase

No one can get a good job today unless they have a college degree, so I hope you'll rethink your decision not to go to college.

Second paraphrase

It's very difficult to get a good job today unless one has a college degree, so I hope you'll rethink your decision not to go to college.

Original passage

Cigarette smoking causes lung cancer. Therefore, if you continue to smoke, you are endangering your health.

First paraphrase

Cigarette smoking invariably produces lung cancer. Therefore, if you continue to smoke, you are endangering your health.

Second paraphrase
Cigarette smoking is a positive causal factor that greatly increases the risk of getting lung cancer. Therefore, if you continue to smoke, you are endangering your health.

In these examples, the second paraphrases are better than the first because they clarify the arguer's intent in ways that make the arguments stronger and less easy to attack.

Exercise 7.2

Paraphrase the following passages. Be prepared to share your answers with the class as a whole. (*Note:* You'll probably need a dictionary for this exercise.)

1. Californians are friendly.
2. It's the squeaky wheel that gets the grease.
3. Thou shalt not kill. (Exod. 20:13)
4. Only man is rational.
5. Past cure is past care.
6. No person except a natural born Citizen . . . shall be eligible to the Office of President. (U.S. Constitution, Article 2)
7. Money can't buy happiness.
8. The grass is always greener on the other side.
9. All men are created equal. (Declaration of Independence)
10. A well-regulated Militia, being necessary to the security of a free State, the right of the people to keep and bear Arms, shall not be infringed. (Second Amendment)
11. He jests at scars that never felt a wound. (Shakespeare)
12. With reference to yesterday's electronic-mail communication from you, I would urge you to take into consideration that at this point in time there are no parking facilities within close proximity to the convention center, due to the fact that the Jefferson Street Parking Garage is currently closed for repairs.
13. Prudence, indeed, will dictate that Governments long established should not be changed for light and transient causes; and accordingly all experience hath shown, that mankind are more disposed to suffer, while evils are sufferable, than to right themselves by abolishing the forms to which they are accustomed. But when a long train of abuses and usurpations, pursuing invariably the same Object evinces a design to reduce them under absolute Despotism, it is their right, it is their duty, to throw off such Government and to provide new Guards for their future security. (Declaration of Independence)
14. Not every man should have the knowledge of his duty left to his own judgment; he should have it prescribed to him, and not be allowed to choose at his discretion. Otherwise, seeing the imbecility and infinite variety of our reasons and opinions, we should in the end forge for

ourselves duties that would set us on devouring one another. (Michel de Montaigne)

15. In 1994, Missouri lawmakers passed a law intended, according to a later Missouri Supreme Court interpretation, to outlaw nonconsensual sex. The law read as follows: "A person commits the crime of sexual misconduct in the first degree if he has deviate sexual intercourse with another person of the same sex, or he purposely subjects another person to sexual contact or engages in conduct which would constitute sexual contact except that the touching occurs through the clothing without that person's consent."[14]

What does this law, read literally, actually prohibit? How would you paraphrase it to express more accurately and clearly the lawmakers' intent?

Finding Missing Premises and Conclusions

In real life, people often leave parts of their arguments unstated. Sometimes a premise is left unstated:

Store clerk: I'm sorry, I can't sell you any beer; you're under twenty-one.

Implied here is the premise, "I can't sell beer to anyone under twenty-one." In other cases, a conclusion is left unstated:

Advertisement: The bigger the burger, the better the burger. Burgers are bigger at Burger King.

Implied here is the conclusion, "Burgers are better at Burger King."

There are many reasons why a premise or conclusion might be implied rather than stated. Sometimes the missing statement is something so obvious and familiar that it would be tedious to state it explicitly. For example:

Sally can't drive because she doesn't have a driver's license.

Understood here is the premise, "No one can drive without a driver's license." This is something so widely known that in most contexts it can simply be assumed.

At other times an arguer may leave a premise or conclusion unstated because he wishes to conceal a weak or questionable step in his argument. For example:

She's Cuban, so she's probably hot-tempered.

Here the unstated premise is "Most Cubans are hot-tempered." By leaving this questionable premise unstated, the arguer makes the argument appear stronger than it actually is.

An argument with a missing premise or conclusion is called an **enthymeme.** There are two basic rules in filling in missing steps in enthymemes:[15]

1. *Faithfully interpret the arguer's intentions.* The most important rule in filling in missing premises and conclusions is to be as accurate as possible in

> *One of the familiar tricks of the orator or propagandist is to leave certain things unsaid, things that are highly relevant to the argument, but that might be challenged if they were made explicit.*
>
> —Mortimer Adler and Charles Van Doren

interpreting an arguer's intent. A missing premise or conclusion is a genuine part of an argument only if it was implicitly understood to be part of the argument by the arguer himself. Consequently, we should always try to fill in a missing step in an argument in a way that the arguer himself would recognize as expressing his own thought. One way to determine this is to ask *what else the arguer must assume—that he does not say—to reach his conclusion.* All assumptions you add to the argument must be consistent with everything the arguer says.

2. *Be charitable.* Sometimes it is difficult or impossible to know what unstated premise or conclusion an arguer had implicitly in mind. In such cases, the principle of charity requires that we interpret the argument as generously as possible. In general, this means that we should search for a way of completing the argument that (1) is a plausible way of interpreting the arguer's uncertain intent and (2) makes the argument as good an argument as it can be. Such judgments require practice and skill. But you'll seldom be far off the mark if you remember this simple golden rule: *Be as generous in interpreting other people's incompletely stated arguments as you would like them to be in interpreting your own.*

EXERCISE 7.3

I. Assume that the following arguments are deductive. Identify the missing premises or conclusions that are needed to make the arguments deductively valid.

1. Because this is a Mazda Miata, it's a convertible.
2. All Volkswagens are fuel efficient, and this Beetle is a Volkswagen.
3. Either Blazers are made by Chevy, or Blazers are made by Ford. Therefore, Blazers are made by Chevy.
4. This is a Civic only if it's a Honda. Therefore, this is not a Civic.
5. If this is a Camaro, then it's a Chevy. If this is a Firebird, then it's a Pontiac. Therefore, this is either a Chevy or a Pontiac.
6. Ford Windstars are roomy; after all, Windstars are minivans.
7. If this is a Camry or a Corolla, then it's a Toyota. If this is a Toyota, then it gets good gas mileage. This is a Corolla. Therefore, it gets good gas mileage.
8. If this car gets good gas mileage, it's good for the environment. If this car doesn't get good gas mileage, I don't want it. This car isn't good for the environment. Therefore, I don't want it.
9. Either this is a Contour or it's a Mystique. If this is a Contour, it's a Ford. If this is a Mystique, it's a Mercury.
10. Some Fords are trucks because all Rangers are trucks.

II. Identify the missing premises or conclusions in the following enthymemes. Some of the arguments are deductive and some are inductive.

1. Li Fong is from Singapore, so she probably speaks English.
2. Boxing should be banned because it's dangerous.

3. Angela is blonde, so she's probably dumb.

4. If it's snowing, then it's cold. My car won't start if it's cold. My car will start. If it's not snowing, then Uncle Fred will be coming over for dinner.

5. Kevin graduated from Princeton, so he must be smart. Therefore, he should be able to solve this logic puzzle in the time allotted.

6. If I'm Bill Gates, I'm rich. Hence, I'm not Bill Gates. Hence, I'm not the chairman of Microsoft.

7. If today is Thursday, Zoe is either at work or on the golf course. Therefore, Zoe is at work.

8. Everything in this world will come to an end. So, my life will come to an end, and all the consequences of my life will come to an end. Thus, my life is meaningless, and so is everything else.[16]

9. If Sparky committed the robbery, he was working for Curley. If Sparky was working for Curley, Bugsy drove the getaway car. But Bugsy became totally blind last year. So, I guess we can cross Sparky off our list of suspects.

10. Most Hampton College students are Republicans. Therefore, Jay is probably a Republican. I know he voted the straight Republican ticket in the last election. I also know that he regularly attends meetings of the Young Republicans. Because Jay is probably a Republican, it's likely that he favors a constitutional amendment banning abortion.

Summarizing Extended Arguments

Now that we have learned how to paraphrase passages and fill in missing premises and conclusions, it is time to introduce our method for summarizing longer arguments. The method is called **standardization** because it consists of restating an argument in standard logical form. An argument is said to be in **standard logical form** when each step in the argument is numbered consecutively, premises are stated above the conclusions they are claimed to support, and justifications are provided for each conclusion in the argument.

The following list shows the steps in argument standardization.

How to Standardize an Extended Argument

1. Read through the argument carefully and try to identify its main conclusion (it may be only implied). Once you have identified the main conclusion, go back through the argument to identify major premises and subconclusions offered in support of the main conclusion. Paraphrase as needed to clarify meaning.

2. Omit any unnecessary or irrelevant material. Focus only on the key points in the argument. Omit any statements that provide little or no direct support for the main conclusion.

3. Number the steps in the argument and stack them in correct logical order (i.e., with the premises placed above the conclusions they are intended to support). State the main conclusion last.

Dispense with trifles.
—Shakespeare

4. Fill in any key missing premises or conclusions. Don't worry about filling in all missing steps in the argument. Include only those missing premises or conclusions that are important in understanding and evaluating the central argument. Place brackets around implied statements to indicate that they have been added to the argument.

5. Add parenthetical justifications for each conclusion in the argument. In other words, for each conclusion or subconclusion, indicate in parentheses from which previous lines in the argument the conclusion or subconclusion is claimed to directly follow.

Let's practice this technique for summarizing extended arguments with a few examples. First, a very brief example provides a quick illustration of how the method works:

> [The] desire for perfect happiness is inborn in all of us, it is a universal human longing, it is rooted in human nature. But everything that is in human nature has been put there by God. In His Wisdom and Goodness, he could not have implanted a natural longing that was impossible to fulfill. Therefore, there must exist, somehow, a real perfect happiness which is within the capacity of struggling men to attain.[17]

In this argument there are four statements: three premises and a conclusion (here stated last and indicated by the word *therefore*). To standardize the argument, we first number the statements and list them in logical order:

1. The desire for perfect happiness is a natural longing, inborn in all human beings.
2. Everything that is in human nature has been put there by God.
3. In His Wisdom and Goodness, God could not have implanted a natural longing that was impossible to fulfill.
4. Therefore, it must be possible for human beings to achieve perfect happiness.

Next we check to see whether any of the steps in the argument are unnecessary or irrelevant. In this short argument, none is.

Then we check to see whether there are any crucial premises or conclusions missing in the argument. In this case, no statements need to be added because the argument is deductively valid as it stands.

Finally, we add justifications to indicate which premises are intended to support which conclusions. In this case, there are three premises that support the conclusion. The complete argument summary is as follows:

1. The desire for perfect happiness is a natural longing, inborn in all human beings.
2. Everything that is in human nature has been put there by God.
3. In His Wisdom and Goodness, God could not have implanted a natural longing that was impossible to fulfill.
4. Therefore, it must be possible for human beings to achieve perfect happiness. (from 1–3)

Here's a slightly more complex example:

> We can see something only after it has happened. Future events, however, have not yet happened. So, seeing a future event seems to imply both that it has and has not happened, and that's logically impossible.[18]

Reading this argument carefully, we can see that it contains three stated premises and one stated subconclusion. First, we number the statements and list them in logical order:

1. We can see something only after it has happened.
2. Future events have not yet happened.
3. So, seeing a future event seems to imply both that it has and has not happened.
4. It is logically impossible for an event both to have happened and not to have happened.

Second, we check to see whether the argument contains any unnecessary or irrelevant steps. In this case, none of the statements is unnecessary or irrelevant.

Third, we look to see if there are any important premises or conclusions missing in the argument. Examining the argument, we see at a glance that there is indeed an important step missing: the argument is lacking a main conclusion. Reading closely, we see that what follows logically from the argument is this conclusion:

> It is logically impossible to see a future event.

Thus, we add this conclusion to the argument, using brackets to indicate that it is implied rather than stated. Finally, we add parenthetical justifications to indicate which premises are claimed to support which conclusions. The complete argument summary, then, is this:

1. We can see something only after it has happened.
2. Future events have not yet happened.
3. So, seeing a future event seems to imply both that it has and has not happened. (from 1-2)
4. It is logically impossible for an event both to have happened and not to have happened.
5. [Therefore, it is logically impossible to see a future event.] (from 3-4)

Here is a more complex example:

EBR's Students Need Your Vote

Students in East Baton Rouge Parish schools need your help today. Please vote to extend, for 10 years, a 4.98-mill property tax that helps operate the public school system.

The School Board has been strapped for funds for several years. State aid is stagnant, property tax revenue has grown more slowly than inflation and the board has trimmed considerable fat from its budget.

Losing the $6.7 million a year generated by the tax would force budget cuts that could affect the quality of learning in a school system already struggling to improve academic achievement.

This tax should not be confused with the School Board's past or potential proposals to raise taxes for school improvements. This tax is modest, amounting to less than 3 percent of the system's general revenue. It already is on the books; voting "for" won't raise anyone's taxes, but just keep them from dropping slightly. And the money will keep going to day-to-day operations, not new buildings or programs.

We understand why some people are less than satisfied with the School Board and might be eager to send a message. But a negative vote today will not hurt the board; it will hurt the 56,000 students who rely on the public schools for an education.

Voters probably will have a chance to vote for or against another tax-increase plan this summer. They definitely will have a chance to vote on School Board members when all the board seats come up for election this fall.

Today, vote for the students.[19]

Here is one reader's standardization of the argument:

1. The School Board has been short of money for several years because state aid has not increased, inflation has outstripped increases in property tax revenue, and the board has cut spending.

2. Losing the $6.7 million a year generated by the tax would force budget cuts that could harm the quality of learning at a time when schools are struggling to improve academic achievement.

3. [Voters should not place the quality of learning at risk by depriving the school system of money.]

4. The tax is not a large one, but amounts to less than 3 percent of the school system's general revenue.

5. The tax is already in effect, meaning that taxes will stay as they are now rather than go up.

6. The money will be used to fund the daily operation of the schools, not to build new buildings or add programs.

7. Voting against the tax will hurt the 56,000 students who rely on the public schools.

8. Therefore, voters in East Baton Rouge should vote for the 4.98-mill property tax that funds public school operation. (from 1–7)

This standardization, though somewhat lengthy, is relatively straightforward: little paraphrasing is required, and there are few missing premises or conclusions. Not all arguments, however, can be reconstructed so straightforwardly. Here is an argument that requires more-radical reconstruction:

Editor:

Regarding your editorial (Sept. 7), "Give us better SAT scores," that's the last thing we need! It is common knowledge that many successful entrepreneurs and inventors were not high honor students. In fact, many were high school and college drop-outs, and many did not get outstanding SAT scores.

Professional speaker Jim Rohn states: "Formal education will earn you a living. Self-education will earn you a fortune. You determine how much of a fortune you will earn by how much self-education you decide to get."

So, there must be better predictors of success than grades and standardized tests. As a business owner, I want to hire people who have excellent people skills and positive attitudes and are committed to doing quality work. These skills are a million times more important to me, as well as to other employers in the long run, than perfect SAT scores.

In my opinion, our country is in the shape it's in because of our illiteracy in human relations. Memorization-based education does not teach our children how to find answers, solve problems, deal with difficulties in their personal or professional lives, take responsibility for their actions, or develop their skills and talents. It does encourage people to seek the easy way out. And it destroys our children's ability to use their common sense. The United States has more people in prison, in terms of percentage of population, than any other nation. They're not there because they didn't memorize easily looked-up information.

The political and power structures of the medical community as well as our legal system damage our country with their lack of common sense. Throughout history, mainstream organizations have always resisted change. The most educated people believed the earth was flat. It was the so-called dumbbell who proved them wrong.

If we want high scores, let's get them in kindness. In the words of Theodore Roosevelt, "The most important single ingredient in the formula of success is knowing how to get along with people."

So tell me about the schools where our kids get great grades in kindness and consideration. You can build a life on those traits. We can build bombs and prisons when we focus on the opposite.[20]

This argument is neither as clear nor as well organized as the previous argument we examined. Here is one reader's attempt to summarize the writer's central argument:

1. Memorization-based education does not teach our children how to find answers, solve problems, deal with difficulties in their personal or professional lives, take responsibility for their actions, or develop their skills and talents.

2. Memorization-based education encourages people to take the easy way out and destroys our children's ability to use their common sense.

3. Memorization-based education is largely responsible for the bad shape this country is in today, including the high prison population and the lack of basic common sense in our medical and legal communities.

4. [Thus, memorization-based education is a mistake. (from 1–3)]

5. [The SAT is mainly a test of memorized information.]

6. Many successful entrepreneurs and inventors were high school or college drop-outs who did not get outstanding SAT scores.

7. Good people skills are a million times more important to employers than perfect SAT scores.

8. Thus, success in life depends much more on good people skills than it does on good grades or high SAT scores. (from 6–7)

9. [Therefore, contrary to the September 7 editorial, it is much more important for schools to teach good people skills than it is for them to teach the kinds of memorized information tested on the SAT. (from 4–5, 8)]

This argument is fairly typical of arguments encountered in letters to the editor, radio talk shows, and other popular forums. Key parts of the argument are left unstated (including the main conclusion), some statements appear to have little or no relevance to the main conclusion, and a fair amount of paraphrasing and reading between the lines is needed to clarify the author's apparent intent. The standardization we have offered is an example of the kind of major reconstruction that is sometimes needed to summarize an argument briefly and accurately.

Common Mistakes to Avoid in Standardizing Arguments

It takes practice to become good at standardizing arguments. Here are some common mistakes to watch out for.

1. *Don't write in incomplete sentences.*

   Example 1
   1. Because animals can experience pain and suffering (*incorrect*)
   2. Therefore, it's wrong to kill or mistreat animals. (from 1)

   Line 1 is a sentence fragment, not a complete sentence. Because arguments are composed entirely of statements (i.e., sentences that can sensibly be regarded as true or false), only complete sentences should be included in argument standardizations. In this argument the standardization can be repaired simply by deleting the word *because* in the first line. The correct version is thus

   Example 2
   1. Animals can experience pain and suffering. (*correct*)
   2. Therefore, it's wrong to kill or mistreat animals. (from 1)

2. *Don't include more than one statement per line.*

   Example 3
   1. The president should resign, since he no longer enjoys the confidence of the Board of Trustees. (*incorrect*)

   There are two statements on this line: a premise ("he no longer enjoys the confidence of the Board of Trustees") and a conclusion ("The president should resign"). These two statements should be placed on separate lines as follows:

   Example 4
   1. The president no longer enjoys the confidence of the Board of Trustees.
   2. Therefore, he should resign. (from 1) (*correct*)

3. *Don't include anything that is not a statement.*

Example 5
1. It's all the same whether there's a Democrat or a Republican in the White House.
2. Therefore, why should I care about presidential politics? (from 1) (*incorrect*)

Here the second line is phrased as a rhetorical question rather than as a statement. Because only statements are included in arguments, for the argument to be standardized this question must be rephrased as a statement. This can be done as follows:

Example 6
1. It's all the same whether there's a Democrat or a Republican in the White House.
2. Therefore, I have no reason to care about presidential politics. (from 1) (*correct*)

4. *Don't include anything that is not a premise or a conclusion.*

Example 7
1. Many people today argue that capital punishment is morally wrong. (*incorrect*)
2. But the Good Book says, "an eye for an eye, a tooth for a tooth."
3. What the Good Book says is true.
4. Therefore, capital punishment is not morally wrong. (from 2–3)

Arguments are composed entirely of premises and conclusions. In this argument, the first line is neither a premise nor a conclusion. Therefore, it should be omitted.

The following exercise will give you practice in standardizing arguments.

EXERCISE 7.4

Standardize the following arguments using the method presented in the preceding section.

1. *Professor Jack W. Meiland, offering advice to new college students:* There is one question which you should *not* ask, nor feel any temptation to ask, your instructor. That question is: "Will this be on the exam? This question infuriates many instructors, and rightly so. For this question indicates that your main interest is in getting through the course with a good grade rather than in learning what the instructor has to teach. It is insulting to the teacher who has worked hard to put you in a position to appreciate the material—its intrinsic interest, its subtlety, its complexity.

2. *Douglas J. Futuyma on the limits of science:* [S]cience seeks to explain only objective knowledge, knowledge that can be acquired independently by different investigators if they follow a prescribed course of observation or

experiment. Many human experiences and concerns are not objective and so do not fall within the realm of science. As a result, science has nothing to say about aesthetics or morality. . . . The functioning of human society, then, clearly requires principles that stem from some source other than science.

3. *From Chief Justice Earl Warren's opinion in* Brown v. Board of Education *(1954):* Today, education is perhaps the most important function of state and local governments. Compulsory school attendance laws and the great expenditures for education both demonstrate our recognition of the importance of education to our democratic society. It is required in the performance of our most basic public responsibilities, even service in the armed forces. It is the very foundation of good citizenship. Today it is a principal instrument in awakening the child to cultural values, in preparing him for later professional training, and in helping him to adjust normally to his environment. In these days, it is doubtful that any child may reasonably be expected to succeed in life if he is denied the opportunity of an education. Such an opportunity, where the state has undertaken to provide it, is a right which must be made available to all on equal terms.

4. *Professor Vincent Ryan Ruggiero on teaching critical thinking to students of all ability levels:* Thinking instruction in elementary and secondary education should not be limited to the honors program. Everyone needs thinking skills to meet the demands of career and citizenship. More important, everyone needs such skills to realize his or her potential as a human being. The highest of Abraham Maslow's hierarchy of human needs, self-actualization, is unachievable without the ability to think productively. Thus to deny meaningful instruction in thinking to students below a certain IQ or proficiency level is to deny them an essential part of their humanity. Similarly, the constitutional guarantees of freedom to speak, to choose one's own religion, and so on, lose much of their meaning when only some individuals are trained to evaluate and choose among competing views.

5. *Management Professor James O'Toole on vocational education (slightly adapted):* Consideration should be given to providing all students in the twelfth grade with some kind of work-and-study experience. This would help to overcome age segregation by allowing students to observe adults at work and, in doing so, to learn what it is like to work all day. It would give students the opportunity to overcome stereotypes about people who perform kinds of jobs different from their parents'. The jobs would enhance the meaning of schoolwork, because students would see how education actually contributes to workaday life. Young people would come to know better what they really like to do and what they are good at doing, and thus develop clearer career aspirations. Most important, the work experience could be used to make classroom discussions of social and economic institutions vivid and individually relevant.

6. *From a newspaper call-in column:* My opinion regarding the amount of homework a child receives is basically threefold. I don't believe the children should receive any homework whatsoever. One, because the teacher has seven or

eight hours during the course of the school day to instruct children and do work assignments with them, to review material for tests. They do not need to be sending work home. To me, homework is an excuse for a teacher's lack of ability to do their job properly. Two, there are too many children that come home with either no adult there or no adult with the ability to help them with their homework. That places too many children at a disadvantage compared to other children who have their parents there to help them with their homework. Three, an adult spends eight hours at work, comes home, and has the rest of the day to enjoy themselves. That is a luxury that a child should definitely be afforded. They don't need to spend time after school. Teacher, it is time to wake up.

7. *Theologian Thomas Aquinas, in* Summa Theologica: It is impossible for any sorrow or pain to be man's greatest evil. For all sorrow or pain is either for something that is truly evil, or for something that is apparently evil, but good in reality. Now pain or sorrow for that which is truly evil cannot be the greatest evil: for there is something worse, namely, either not to reckon as evil that which is really evil, or not to reject it. Again, sorrow or pain, for that which is apparently evil, but really good, cannot be the greatest evil, for it would be worse to be altogether separated from that which is truly good. Hence it is impossible for any sorrow or pain to be man's greatest evil.

8. *Educators Ann Flanagan and David Grissmer, on improving lower-performing public schools:* Besides disproportionately low spending and high numbers of disadvantaged students, there are several other reasons that urban, southern, and western school districts should receive the focus of policy attention. First, students in these areas constitute a growing proportion of U.S. students, and future productivity will depend on learning how to provide better education for them. Second, recent research suggests that the achievement scores of minority and disadvantaged students respond to additional well-targeted educational expenditures and that significant score gains could occur. Third, research also suggests that additional educational investment might be recouped through lower future social expenditures and improved economic productivity. Fourth, such policies would reduce the achievement gap between racial or ethnic and income groups—a source of continuing social and political divisions and economic costs in society. Finally, improving the United States' international standing requires lifting the scores of these students.

9. *From a newspaper editorial:* The recent use of mail ballots in Oregon's election of a U.S. senator has led some people to hail this as the wave of the future in our democratic republic.

We do not share that enthusiasm.

The primary advantage of the mail ballot is that it requires little time and effort on the part of the voter. We think that also is a primary shortcoming of this process.

It is worth a little of both our time and our energy to exercise the right to vote, and that personal investment should serve to make us a bit more conscious of the value of that opportunity.

Another negative aspect for the electorate is that a mail election necessarily must take place over a relatively long time frame, rather than a single day that is the culmination of an election campaign process.

That means voters who cast their ballots near the end of the designated voting period might have a larger volume of information, and perhaps more accurate information, than those who vote early in the process.

We also are seriously concerned about the potential for voter fraud in elections conducted by mail. A state with Louisiana's political history would be fertile ground for that.

Finally, we take note of one of the more ironic potential shortcomings of this procedure, and that is the very fact that this process involves using the mail, rather than a voting machine.

Many of us, at one time or another, have sent or received mail that, through no fault of our own, did not arrive on time or was lost altogether.

We would prefer not to risk having that happen to our ballots in any local, federal or state election.

10. *From a guest column by Carmen F. Ambrosino,* Wilkes-Barre Times Leader: I am hoping that you're as fed up as I am with all this pro-legalization of drugs nonsense. It is offensive to those of us who have dedicated our lives to helping the addicted and their families.

Some people might say I have a self-serving reason for writing this article, because I work in the drug treatment and prevention/education field.

Well, consider this: If I was selfish, I'd say legalize drugs because, without doubt, all drug treatment professionals would have an abundance of work. Rather, we treatment professionals are dedicated to significantly reducing and eventually eliminating America's No. 1 health problem.

I would welcome the day when our drug problem will be so insignificant that there would no longer be a need for professional drug and alcohol treatment agencies.

With this said, let me set the record straight, because you won't get the full picture from these pro–legalizing drug advocates.

Fact 1: Legalization advocates always use the argument that legalizing drugs will take the profit motive away from the street or clandestine manufacturers. They never tell you, however, that the economic cost of legal drugs is $2\frac{1}{2}$ times greater than that of illicit drugs.

Additionally, these advocates never use the argument that legalization will reduce hospitalizations, crimes, car accidents, addicted babies, industrial accidents, family breakups, etc. The reason they don't is, if the drugs were legalized, every one of these problems would worsen significantly.

Common sense should tell us when there are fewer controls, there will be more incidents.

For example, between 1972 and 1978, 11 states decriminalized marijuana, and marijuana use escalated to unprecedented levels.

Fact 2: Drug use is not a right and should never be. People who proclaim, "It's my body, and I have a right to do with it what I want," need to re-examine this naïve statement. Drug use not only impacts on the user, but has serious implications for families, community, consumers and others.

Legalizing drugs would open the floodgates of access to these mood-altering chemicals and would send a message that drugs are not harmful.

Think about flying to Disney World and having to depend on a pilot or an air-traffic controller who is high. Or having your child's surgery being performed by a surgeon who has just ingested mood-altering chemicals. Or entrusting your children to school bus drivers who fire up a joint of marijuana before their daily run. . . .

Legalizing drugs is not a solution; in fact, it is a ridiculous option. It's like saying our child abuse laws are not effective because abuse of children is escalating, therefore we should do away with these child protection laws.

Fact 3: If we still don't believe that legalizing drugs will make the problems worse, then I would ask you to examine two of America's favorite legal drugs: alcohol and nicotine. I don't think much more needs to be said about the epidemic use of these two chemicals and the tremendous negative impact they have had on the physiological, social, psychological, economic and spiritual aspects of our lives.

By legalizing illicit drugs that are proven harmful, you'd better be ready to hire thousands of police officers, physicians, counselors and other medical personnel to respond to the human carnage.

Some could argue that I am very emotional when I write or lecture about this topic.

You bet I am.

When legalization proponents have seen 24 years of human misery in the form of suicide, homicides, overdoses, psychiatric institutionalizations, medical emergencies, etc., then you'll qualify to be emotional as well.

I took a pledge in 1973 to use my God-given energies to help people to find the joys that come with living a drug-free life.

I am confident that our public will reject any effort that might be made by a small minority who has, unfortunately, chosen not to get all the facts before they talk.

If you want the facts, talk with recovering addicts and families who have lost their loved ones to a chemical that some want to legalize.

11. *From John Stuart Mill's inaugural address at St. Andrews University (1867):* Of Logic I venture to say . . . that there is no part of intellectual education which is of greater value, or whose place can so ill be supplied by anything else. Its uses, it is true, are chiefly negative: its function is, not so much to teach us to go right, as to keep us from going wrong. But in the operations of the intellect it is so much easier to go wrong than right; it is so utterly impossible for even the most vigorous mind to keep itself in the path but by maintaining a vigilant watch against all deviations, and noting all the byways by which it is possible to go astray—that the chief difference between one reasoner and another consists in their less or greater liability to be misled. Logic points out all the possible ways in which, starting from true premises, we may draw false conclusions. By its analysis of the reasoning

process, and the forms it supplies for stating and setting forth our reasonings, it enables us to guard the points at which a fallacy is in danger of slipping in, or to lay our fingers upon the place where it has slipped in. When I consider how very simple the theory of reasoning is, and how short a time is sufficient for acquiring a thorough knowledge of its principles and rules, and even considerable expertness in applying them, I can find no excuse for omission to study it on the part of anyone who aspires to succeed in any intellectual pursuit. Logic is the great disperser of hazy and confused thinking: it clears up the fogs which hide from us our own ignorance, and make us believe that we understand a subject when we do not. We must not be led away by talk about inarticulate giants who do great deeds without knowing how, and see into the most recondite truths without any of the ordinary helps, and without being able to explain to other people how they reach their conclusions, nor consequently to convince any other people of the truth of them. There may be such men, as there are deaf and dumb persons who do clever things; but for all that, speech and hearing are faculties by no means to be dispensed with. If you want to know whether you are thinking rightly, put your thoughts into words. In the very attempt to do this you will find yourselves, consciously or unconsciously, using logical forms. Logic compels us to throw our meaning into distinct propositions, and our reasonings into distinct steps. It makes us conscious of all the implied assumptions on which we are proceeding, and which, if not true, vitiate the entire process. It makes us aware what extent of doctrine we commit ourselves to by any course of reasoning, and obliges us to look the implied premises in the face, and make up our minds whether we can stand to them. It makes our opinions consistent with themselves and with one another, and forces us to think clearly, even when it cannot make us think correctly.

SUMMARY

1. In this chapter we learned how to analyze arguments. To *analyze* an argument means to break it up into its various parts to see clearly what conclusion is being defended and on what grounds.

2. To analyze short arguments we use a method called *diagramming,* which involves six basic steps:
   a. Read through the argument carefully, circling any premise or conclusion indicators you see.
   b. Number the statements consecutively as they appear in the argument. (Don't number any sentences that are not statements.)
   c. Arrange the numbers spatially on a page with the premises placed above the conclusion(s) they are alleged to support. Omit any irrelevant or redundant statements.

   d. Using arrows to mean "is evidence for," create a kind of flowchart that shows which premises are intended to support which conclusions.

   e. Indicate independent premises by drawing arrows directly from the premises to the conclusions they are claimed to support. Indicate linked premises by placing a plus sign between each of the linked premises, underlining the premises, and drawing an arrow from the underlined premises to the conclusions they are claimed to support. (Two premises are *independent* if neither premise would provide less support for the conclusion if the other premise were removed. Two premises are *linked* if at least one of the premises would provide less support for the conclusion if the other premise were removed.)

   f. Put the argument's main conclusion last.

3. To analyze longer arguments, we use a method called *standardizing*. There are five basic steps in standardizing arguments:

   a. Read through the argument carefully. Identify the main conclusion (it may be only implied) and any major premises and subconclusions. Paraphrase as needed to clarify meaning. (A *paraphrase* is a restatement of a passage using different words and phrases. A good paraphrase is clear, concise, accurate, and charitable.)

   b. Omit any unnecessary or irrelevant material.

   c. Number the steps in the argument and list them in correct logical order (i.e., with the premises placed above the conclusions they are intended to support).

   d. Fill in any key missing premises and conclusions.

   e. Add justifications for each conclusion in the argument. In other words, for each conclusion or subconclusion, indicate in parentheses from which previous lines in the argument the conclusion or subconclusion is claimed to directly follow.

CHAPTER 8

Evaluating Arguments and Truth Claims

In previous chapters we learned to

- appreciate the importance of critical thinking standards such as clarity, precision, accuracy, consistency, and fairness
- distinguish arguments from nonarguments
- identify premises and conclusions
- recognize hidden assumptions and implied premises and conclusions
- distinguish deductive from inductive arguments
- assess the logical validity or strength of arguments
- distinguish relevant from irrelevant reasons
- identify common logical fallacies
- analyze extended arguments to clarify their content and structure

In this chapter we use this tool kit of skills to tackle the $64,000 question: When is an argument a good one? We will also address an issue that is crucial in argument evaluation, namely: When is it reasonable to accept a premise as true? Finally, we will learn some powerful strategies for refuting bad arguments.

When Is an Argument a Good One?

Arguments can be good or bad in various ways. To help us understand what a good argument is from the standpoint of critical thinking, we begin by spelling out a few things that a good argument is *not*.

What "Good Argument" Does Not Mean

"Good Argument" Does Not Mean "Agrees with My Views" One of the most serious mistakes in critical thinking is to confuse "good argument" with "argument whose conclusion I agree with." To suppose that an argument is good only if it agrees with your own preexisting opinions is the epitome of

> The supreme end of education is expert discernment in all things—the power to tell the good from the bad, the genuine from the counterfeit.
>
> —Samuel Johnson

> I realize I can be seriously, dreadfully, fatally wrong, and wrong about what it is enormously important to be right. That is simply the human condition.
>
> —Alvin Plantinga

203

close-mindedness. It reflects the mind-set of someone who thinks, "I have a monopoly on the truth. Anyone who disagrees with me must be wrong." Such an attitude makes it impossible to learn from viewpoints that differ from one's own and is completely opposed to the spirit of critical thinking.

"Good Argument" Does Not Mean "Persuasive Argument"   A good archery shot hits the bull's-eye. A good putt goes in the hole. A good pair of scissors cuts the paper efficiently. In many contexts a thing is said to be good if it does successfully what it was intended to do.[1] Does this hold true of arguments as well? Is a good argument a *persuasive* argument—that is, an argument that actually succeeds in convincing an audience to accept a conclusion? Not necessarily—for two reasons.

> *A man is not reck-oned wise because he speaks skilfully.*
> —Chuang-tzu

First, not all arguments are meant to persuade. Sometimes the arguer is just "playing devil's advocate," or "preaching to the choir," or "going through the motions," or "thinking out loud," or giving examples without any intention of persuading anybody. Second, bad arguments often persuade, whereas good arguments often fall on deaf ears. In the years leading up to World War II, for example, Hitler's demagogic ravings convinced millions, whereas Churchill's well-founded warnings were largely ignored. Yet no critical thinker would suggest that Hitler's arguments were, therefore, "better" than Churchill's.

> *Demeanor, face, voice, attitude, and the gown may set off a speech, which in itself is mere twaddle.*
> —Michel de Montaigne

"Good Argument" Does Not Mean "Well-Written or Well-Spoken Argument"   We sometimes praise arguments for their literary or rhetorical merit—their clarity, eloquence, organization, imaginativeness, and the like. Does it follow that a good argument is, or must be, a well-written or well-spoken argument? No, because some obviously bad arguments possess literary merit, whereas some obviously good ones do not. A subtly deceptive political speech may be a masterpiece of rhetorical skill and still be seriously flawed from the standpoint of critical reasoning. By the same token, an argument in, say, science or mathematics may be a perfectly good argument but possess little or no literary merit.

What "Good Argument" *Does* Mean

What, then, *is* a good argument from the standpoint of critical thinking? To answer this question, we need to review some things we learned in previous chapters.

In Chapter 3 we learned that a good argument is basically an argument in which two conditions are met: All the premises are true,[2] and the premises provide good reasons to accept the conclusion.

We also learned in Chapter 3 that a set of premises provides good reasons to accept a conclusion when the argument is either deductively valid or inductively strong. (*Remember:* An argument is *deductively valid* if the conclusion *must* be true if the premises are true. An argument is *inductively strong* if the conclusion is *probably* true if the premises are true.) Arguments that are both deductively valid and have all true premises are said to be deductively *sound*. Arguments that are both inductively strong and have all true premises are said to be inductively *cogent*. Thus, *a good argument, fundamentally, is an argument that is either deductively sound or inductively cogent.*

That definition, however, is not fully adequate. As we saw in Chapter 1, there are certain basic critical thinking standards that all good thinking and argumentation must meet. Among the most important of these standards are clarity, precision, accuracy, relevance, consistency, logical correctness, completeness, and fairness. An argument that is deeply obscure, full of irrelevant statements, and grossly incomplete in its examination of the relevant evidence doesn't count as a "good" argument, even if it is deductively sound.

Imagine, for example, that you're the dean of students at Wexford College, and you write the following letter to the parents of a student, Binger Boosely, explaining why their son has been expelled from college:

> Dear Mr. and Mrs. Boosely,
>
> This letter is to inform you that your son, Binger Boosely, has been expelled from Wexford College. I deemed this action to be necessary for the following reasons:
>
> 1. Paris is the capital of France.
> 2. The capital of France is Paris.
> 3. Binger deserved to be expelled.
> 4. Binger earned F's in all his classes and was continuously drunk from the first day of classes to the last day of final exams.
> 5. Any student who earns F's in all his classes and is continuously drunk from the first day of classes to the last day of final exams deserves to be expelled.
> 6. Therefore, Binger deserved to be expelled.

This, obviously, is an atrocious argument. Premise 1 is completely irrelevant to the conclusion. Premise 2 is redundant; it merely repeats premise 1 in slightly different words. Premise 3 is simply a restatement of the conclusion, causing the argument to commit the fallacy of begging the question. Only premises 4 and 5 provide any support at all for the conclusion.

Despite these obvious defects, however, the argument is deductively sound (assuming that the premises are true, which we can stipulate is the case). Premises 4 and 5 do validly imply the conclusion; and, because deductively valid arguments remain valid no matter what other premises are added to them,[3] the argument as a whole is deductively valid, despite the obvious defects of premises 1–3.

Hence, it is not enough for an argument to be deductively sound or inductively cogent. It must also satisfy (at least up to a certain threshold) the key critical thinking standards discussed in Chapter 1.

Now that we have combined these insights from Chapters 1 and 3, we are ready to answer the question, "When is an argument a good one?"

Validity is not the only aspect of an argument that concerns us. In many contexts, it is not even our chief concern.

—Robert J. Fogelin and Walter Sinnott-Armstrong

A good argument, from the standpoint of critical thinking, is an argument that *satisfies the relevant critical thinking standards that apply in a particular context.* The most important of these standards are accuracy (Are all the premises true?) and logical correctness (Is the reasoning correct? Is the argument deductively valid or inductively strong?). But other critical thinking standards must also be taken into account, including clarity, precision, relevance, consistency,[4] completeness, and fairness.

Given this general definition of "good argument," we can offer the following general guidelines on evaluating arguments.

Evaluating Arguments: Some General Guidelines

- Are the premises true?
- Is the reasoning correct? Is the argument deductively valid or inductively strong?
- Does the arguer commit any logical fallacies?
- Does the arguer express his or her points clearly and precisely?
- Are the premises relevant to the conclusion?
- Are the arguer's claims logically consistent? Do any of the arguer's claims contradict other claims made in the argument?
- Is the argument complete? Is all relevant evidence taken into account (given understandable limitations of time, space, context, and so on)?
- Is the argument fair? Is the arguer fair in his or her presentation of the evidence and treatment of opposing arguments and views?[5]

WHEN IS IT REASONABLE TO ACCEPT A PREMISE?

> *The possession of truth is the ultimate good of the human mind.*
>
> —Mortimer Adler

All good arguments, as we have seen, have true premises. But when is it *reasonable* to accept a premise as true? This is a complex issue, and only a few general suggestions can be offered here. A more detailed discussion of some of these issues is presented in later chapters.

Let's suppose that somebody asserts a claim—for example, that *women are more superstitious than men* or that *I saw Elvis at a Dunkin' Donuts in Lubbock.* For simplicity, let's suppose that the claim is unsupported (i.e., no argument is given for it) and that for some reason it is either impossible or not worthwhile to try to verify the claim for ourselves. Under what conditions is it reasonable to accept such a claim?

The most general principle can be summed up in the following **principle of rational acceptance:** generally speaking, it is reasonable to accept a claim if (1) the claim does not conflict with personal experiences that we have no good reason to doubt, (2) the claim does not conflict with background beliefs that we have no good reason to doubt, and (3) the claim comes from a credible source.[6]

Let's briefly discuss these three conditions.

How Many *F*'s?

Here's a quick observation exercise. Reading at normal speed, count the number of times the letter *f* appears in the following sentence:

These functional fuses have been developed after years of scientific investigation of electric phenomena, combined with the fruit of long experience on the part of the two investigators who have come forward with them for our meeting today.

How many *f*'s did you count? Check endnote 7 to see if your answer is correct.[7]

Does the Claim Conflict with Our Personal Experiences?   Sometimes people assert claims that conflict with our own personal observations and experiences. When this happens it is usually best to trust our own experiences. Thus, if your neighbor's Doberman pinscher is snarling, foaming at the mouth, and chewing on the tattered remnants of a mail carrier's bag, it is probably a good idea to trust your own eyes rather than your neighbor's assurance that his dog is "as gentle as a kitten."

The problem is that people often place *too much* trust in their own observations and experiences. As Brooke Moore and Richard Parker point out, we often overestimate the reliability of our observations by failing to take into account such factors as poor physical conditions for making observations (e.g., bad lighting, excessive noise, frequent distractions); sensory impairment (e.g., poor vision or hearing); poor physical condition of the observer (e.g., fatigue, stress, intoxication); unreliable measuring instruments; and failures of memory.[8] Indeed, studies show that even under good observational conditions, people are often much less accurate in their observations than they generally assume.[9]

Critical thinkers also recognize that their beliefs, hopes, fears, expectations, and biases can affect their observations. Children, for example, "see" monsters in the closet. Sports fans perceive referees as partial to the other team. Coffee drinkers who unwittingly drink decaffeinated coffee typically feel more alert. Teachers who expect improvement from their students often "perceive" better performance even when none exists. And love, as the adage says, is blind.

In short, personal experiences are often less reliable than we think. We need to be aware that often "believing is seeing" and that things are not always as they appear.

Does the Claim Conflict with Our Background Beliefs?   Sometimes a claim doesn't conflict with any of our personal observations or experiences but does conflict with certain background beliefs we hold. By "background beliefs" we mean that vast network of conscious and unconscious convictions we use as a framework to assess the credibility of claims that can't be verified

> Who you gonna believe—me or your own eyes?
> —Chico Marx

> Our very eyes are sometimes, like our judgments, blind.
> —Shakespeare

> Loving eyes can never see.
> —Percy Sledge

• Hyper-Critical Thinking? •

Tom Morris, author of *Philosophy for Dummies,* tells the following anecdote about the demand for evidence: "An old friend of mine, a professor of philosophical theology at Yale, once received an unexpected phone call from his little son's Sunday school teacher. The teacher said, 'Professor, every time I say anything new in Sunday school class, your little boy blurts out "Prove it!" Could you please have a talk with him and explain that no one can prove everything?' "[10]

Critical thinkers, certainly, are sticklers for evidence and proof. But not all of our beliefs can be supported by evidence because this would lead to an infinite regress. So when *do* beliefs need to be supported by evidence? What do you think?

Fix reason firmly in her seat and call to her tribunal every fact, every opinion.

—Thomas Jefferson

In doubt a man of worth will trust to his own wisdom.

—Hama, in
J. R. R. Tolkien's
The Lord of the Rings

A healthy garden of beliefs requires well-nourished roots and tireless pruning.

—W. V. O. Quine
and J. S. Ullian

directly. In general, if a claim fits well with our background beliefs, it is reasonable for us to accept it. For example, the claim, "It was hot in Las Vegas last Fourth of July," is quite believable given background information most of us share about midsummer weather conditions in the Nevada desert. The claim, "It snowed in Las Vegas last Fourth of July," however, would rightly be rejected out of hand unless it was accompanied by strong supporting evidence.

The problem is that most of us place too much confidence in the accuracy of our background beliefs. A chain is only as strong as its weakest link. Consequently, if our backgrounds beliefs are unreliable, any beliefs based on them will also be unreliable. Suppose, for example, I believe that

George W. Bush is a cleverly disguised Martian robot.

And suppose I believe this based entirely on my background belief that

All politicians are cleverly disguised Martian robots.

Clearly, it would be unreasonable for me to believe the first statement if the only reason I have for believing the second statement is that I read it in a supermarket tabloid.

Because critical thinkers know how important it is to have accurate and well-grounded background beliefs, they think very carefully about the beliefs they accept. *Never to believe without sufficient evidence* and *Never to believe more strongly than the evidence warrants* are the watchwords of the wise.

EXERCISE 8.1

For each of the claims in this exercise, indicate whether you think the claim is

Completely believable ("I know this is the case.")
Somewhat believable ("I am somewhat confident that this is the case.")
Somewhat unbelievable (I am somewhat confident that this is not the case.")
Completely unbelievable ("I know this is not the case.")

Then, for each claim, list some background beliefs that led you to assign the claim the degree of confidence you did. Be prepared to discuss your responses in small groups.

1. Your astrological sign determines some of your basic personality.
2. The biblical story of Noah's Ark is literally true.
3. The Loch Ness monster really exists.
4. After people die, their souls are reincarnated in other human bodies.
5. Extraterrestrials have visited the earth in some form.[11]

Does the Claim Come from a Credible Source?   Much of what we believe about the world is based on testimony or authority. All of us believe, for example, that George Washington was the first president of the United States, that the earth revolves around the sun, that there is such a place as the Sahara Desert, and that it is cold at the North Pole in January. Yet few of us have personally verified any of this information for ourselves. Thus, a crucial question for critical thinkers is When is it reasonable or justifiable to accept a claim based simply on the testimony or authority of another?

This complex topic is discussed in Chapter 6 and is examined further in Chapter 12. Here we'll just recap some of the highlights of Chapter 6.

Generally speaking, we should accept a claim on authority if it comes from a credible source that we have no good reason to doubt. Good reasons to doubt the credibility of a source may include the following:

- The source is not a genuine expert or authority.

- The source is speaking outside his or her area of expertise.

- The source is biased or has some other motive to lie or mislead.

- The accuracy of the source's personal observations or experiences is questionable.

- The source is contained in a source (e.g., a supermarket tabloid or sensationalistic Web site) that is generally unreliable.

- The source has not been cited correctly or has been quoted out of context.

- The issue is one that cannot be settled by expert opinion.

- The claim made by the source is highly improbable on its face.

Finally, it is important to remember that the principle of rational acceptance applies only to claims that are unsupported by arguments and that are either impossible or not worthwhile to verify for ourselves. If the claim *is* supported by reasons, then of course we must consider the strength of those reasons in deciding whether we should accept the claim. Specifically, we must ask, "Are all the premises true?" and "Do the premises provide good reasons to accept the conclusion?"

> To . . . accept anything without questioning is to be somebody else's puppet, a second-hand person.
> —Daniel Kolak and Raymond Martin

> Trust in a witness in all matters in which neither his self-interest, his passions, his prejudices, nor the love of the marvelous is strongly concerned.
> —Thomas Henry Huxley

• Critical Thinking Lapse •

A Houston man learned a succinct lesson in gun safety when he played Russian roulette with a .45-caliber semiautomatic pistol. The nineteen-year-old man was visiting friends when he announced his intention to play the deadly game. He apparently did not realize that a semiautomatic pistol, unlike a revolver, automatically inserts a cartridge into the firing chamber when the gun is cocked. His chance of winning a round of Russian roulette was zero, as he quickly discovered.[12]

Moreover, if the claim is an important one, and one that we can reasonably investigate for ourselves, we have an intellectual responsibility to do so. Indeed, a willingness to seek out evidence and then to proportion one's belief to that evidence lies at the very heart of what it means to be a critical thinker.

EXERCISE 8.2

I. How good are your powers of observation and recollection? Answer the following questions outside of class, then bring your answers to class and be prepared to compare your responses with those of your classmates.

Remember the last time the class met? Answer the following questions about your instructor.

a. Was he/she wearing a jacket? _____
b. If so, what color? _____
c. Was he/she wearing slacks? Jeans? A skirt? _____
d. If so, what color? _____
e. Was he/she wearing a tie or scarf? _____
f. If so, what color? _____
g. Was he/she wearing a ring? _____
h. Was he/she wearing a watch? _____
i. Was he/she carrying a briefcase or backpack? _____ If so, describe it.
j. Did the instructor end class early? _____[13]

II. For each of the following unsupported claims, indicate whether or not it would be reasonable to accept the claim. Also state the criteria you use in reaching your decision.

1. Tigers live in Africa.
2. There are wolves in Yellowstone National Park.
3. Black cats bring bad luck.
4. Ninety-eight percent of statistics are just made up.
5. Dunleavy Ford: *Nobody* sells for less. (heard on the radio)

6. The closest star to the earth, other than the sun, is Proxima Centauri. (said by your astronomy instructor)

7. I fought in World War II. (said by a man who appears to be about forty-five years old)

8. There is no hard scientific evidence that smoking is addictive. (said by a tobacco company executive)

9. Parts of Alaska are farther west than Hawaii. (overheard on the bus)

10. Parts of Alaska are farther west than Hawaii. (said by your geography instructor)

11. Analgex brand aspirin: Nothing works stronger or faster on your tough headaches. (said by a paid sports celebrity)

12. I read the entire *Encyclopaedia Britannica* last summer. (said by a stranger at a party)

13. Most hate crimes in this country are not committed against African Americans or Jews. They are committed against evangelical Christians. (said by TV evangelist Jerry Falwell)

14. Did you know that gun control laws *actually increase* the violent crime rate? (statement on anti–gun control Web page)

15. A Space Alien Tried to Mate with My Harley! (tabloid headline)[14]

REFUTING ARGUMENTS

To refute an argument isn't merely to challenge, rebut, or criticize it. It is to *defeat* it, to show that the premises do not provide convincing reasons to accept the conclusion. Arguments can be criticized in various ways (e.g., as obscure, wordy, or repetitious). But there are only two ways in which an argument can be refuted:

1. Show that a premise—or a critical group of premises—is false or dubious.

2. Show that the conclusion does not follow from the premises.

Let's look at these two refutation strategies in turn.

Strategy One: Show That a Premise—or a Critical Group of Premises— Is False or Dubious   Sometimes it is possible to defeat an argument by showing that a single premise is false. Consider this example:

1. All presidents live in the White House.

2. Paris Hilton is president.

3. So, Paris Hilton lives in the White House.

Here, simply noting that the second premise is false is enough to refute the argument. Because this premise is false, the argument fails to provide good reason to accept the conclusion.

Some arguments, however, cannot be refuted simply by showing that one of their premises is false. Here are two examples:

1. Children who have unsupervised access to the Internet may be exposed to pornographic and violent images.
2. Some sexual predators use the Internet to find and communicate with children.
3. Children have no ability to use a keyboard or mouse correctly.
4. So, children should not be allowed unsupervised access to the Internet.

1. All circles are squares.
2. All squares are rectangles.
3. All rectangles are geometrical figures.
4. So, all squares are geometrical figures.

In the first example, the third premise is false (many children do know how to use a keyboard and mouse correctly). However, showing that the premise is false is not sufficient to refute the argument, for premises 1 and 2 are adequate to support the conclusion even without premise 3. In the second example, the first premise ("All circles are squares") is obviously false. As we have seen, however, an argument can be valid even if it contains some false or irrelevant premises. Since premises 2 and 3 are true and the conclusion follows validly from those premises, the premises do provide good reason to accept the conclusion. The argument cannot be refuted simply by noting that the first premise is false.

However, arguments like this *can* be refuted by showing that one or more of their *critical* premises is false. All well-reasoned arguments have some premise or group of premises that are necessary to support the argument's conclusion. These are the argument's **critical premises,** its essential supports. Consider these two examples:

1. I ran 5 miles on Saturday.
2. I ran 10 miles on Sunday.
3. So, I ran 15 miles this weekend.

1. Bob, who was drunk at the time and doesn't see very well, claims he saw Buster rob the bank.
2. Bank surveillance tapes show Buster in the act of robbing the bank.
3. So, Buster robbed the bank

In the first example, both premises are critical to the success of the argument. If either was shown to be false, the conclusion would be unsupported. In the second example, only the second premise is critical. The argument can't be refuted merely by showing that the first premise is false. But it can be refuted by proving that the second premise is false.

As these examples suggest, some arguments can be refuted by means of *selective targeting:* Pick out those premises that are essential to the argument's success, and refute as many as you need to knock out the conclusion's support. Some arguments are built like a house of cards; remove one or two vital cards and the entire structure collapses.

Here are two examples that will illustrate this notion of selective targeting:

1. TJ is a bachelor.

2. TJ is an uncle.

3. So, TJ is a male.

1. Bob, who was drunk and doesn't see very well, claims he saw Buster rob the bank.

2. Bank surveillance tapes show Buster in the act of robbing the bank.

3. DNA tests on the robbery note and stolen loot show that there is a high probability that Buster is the robber.

4. So, Buster robbed the bank.

In the first example, neither premise is critical to the conclusion, but each is individually sufficient. (The conclusion follows validly from either premise.) To refute the argument, therefore, it is necessary to reject both premises. In the second example, none of the premises is individually necessary to support the conclusion. In this case, however, it is not necessary to reject *all* the premises in order to refute the argument. Since the first premise, even if it is true, fails to support the conclusion, it suffices to reject premises 2 and 3. These are the premises that must be selectively targeted to refute the argument.

For simplicity, we have spoken so far only of refuting *false* premises. In fact, however, arguments can often be defeated simply by showing that one or more of their premises are *dubious,* that is, open to significant doubt. Consider this example:

1. The last surviving dinosaur was a Triceratops.

2. Triceratops had horns.

3. So, the last surviving dinosaur had horns.

The weak point of this argument is clearly the first premise—the claim that the last surviving dinosaur was a Triceratops. Even though it would be difficult or impossible to show that the premise is false, that isn't necessary to refute the argument. Nobody has a clue whether the last surviving dinosaur was a Triceratops, a T-Rex, or some other species of dinosaur that existed just before the Great Extinction. That fact alone is enough to show that the premises do not provide good reason to accept the conclusion.

There are, of course, a wide variety of ways to demonstrate that a premise is false or dubious. You could, for instance:

- appeal to personal experience ("What do you mean there are no bears in New Jersey! I've seen several.")

- appeal to common knowledge ("Everybody knows Germany lost the Second World War.")

- appeal to a reputable reference source ("Wrong again, sports fan. It says in *The Sports Encyclopedia: Baseball* that Mickey Mantle was the American League MVP in 1957.")

- note that the premise is self-contradictory or otherwise false or dubious on its face ("How can Adam Sandler be an aunt?! Only women can be aunts!")

- point out that the premise conflicts with some other premise in the argument ("You say it's wrong to eat animals, yet you say it's OK to eat fish. But aren't fish animals?")

- show that the premise is based on an unwarranted assumption or stereotype ("How can you say that most illegal immigrants don't want to learn English?")

- personally demonstrate that the claim is false or dubious ("You're wrong! Snow-cones *can* give you a brain freeze. Here, take a big bite of mine.")

In addition to these general refutation strategies, there are two specific techniques that are often useful in refuting false or dubious premises: reducing to the absurd and refutation by counterexample.

Reducing to the absurd (*reductio ad adsurdum,* in the traditional Latin) is attempting to show that a statement is false by proving that it logically implies something that is clearly false or absurd. Suppose your roommate says that "absolutely all killing is wrong." You could reduce this claim to the absurd—and hence refute it—by pointing out that this implies that it is wrong to eat any plants or animals (since this necessarily involves killing) or even to breathe or brush my teeth (since these acts kill microorganisms). The claim, taken literally, has absurd implications and so is false.

Another effective refutation strategy is *refutation by counterexample*. A *counterexample,* in this context, is an example that proves that a general claim (i.e., a claim of the form "All A's are B's" or "Most A's are B's") is false. Suppose you say, "All twentieth-century U.S. presidents have been rich." I could refute your universal claim by means of a single counterexample ("Wait a minute. Harry Truman wasn't rich by any stretch of the word."). Or suppose I say, "Nearly all post–World War II presidents have been Republicans." You could refute my claim by noting that Truman, Kennedy, Johnson, Carter, and Clinton were all Democrats.

To sum up: You can refute an argument by showing that a key premise (or critical group of premises) of the argument is false or dubious. And two useful strategies in proving that a premise is false are reducing to the absurd and refutation by counterexample.

Strategy Two: Show That the Conclusion Does Not Follow from the Premises   The second way to refute an argument is by showing that the reasoning is faulty—that the conclusion does *not* follow properly from the premises. You can show that an argument is poorly reasoned by showing that it is either (a) *deductively invalid* (the conclusion does not follow with strict necessity from the premises) or (b) *inductively weak* (the conclusion does not follow probably from the premises).

In previous chapters we looked at a variety of methods for determining whether arguments are deductively invalid or inductively weak. (Additional methods will be explored in later chapters.) As we have seen, the most important questions to ask in assessing the logic of an argument are

- If the argument is deductive, does the conclusion follow *necessarily* from the premises? (Do the premises, if true, absolutely *guarantee* the truth of the conclusion? Or could the premises conceivably be true and the conclusion false?)

- Are the premises *relevant* to the conclusion? (Does the argument, for example, commit the fallacy of straw man, personal attack, or some other fallacy of relevance?)

- Are the premises *sufficient* to support the conclusion? (Even if we assume all the premises are true, do they provide enough support to justify the conclusion?)

In evaluating the sufficiency of an argument's supporting premises, it is often important to ask a more specific question: *Does the argument omit any crucial countervailing evidence?*

In real life, as we've seen, it is relatively uncommon for arguments to be posed in explicit deductive or inductive form. What *is* very common is for people to offer a series of reasons for a claim that they believe *on balance* provide adequate support for the claim. Here are two examples:

> Get high-speed Internet access by satellite. It's fast, reliable, and won't tie up your phone lines.

> All mothers should stay home with their young kids. It would promote closer family ties, and studies show that children with stay-at-home moms do better in school, have higher self-esteem, and are less likely to get involved with drugs or commit crimes.

In evaluating arguments of this sort, the important question to keep in mind is Do the premises provide *enough* evidence for the conclusion? In many cases, the answer will be "No," because the arguer has *omitted important evidence* that points to a contrary conclusion. For instance, the ad for high-speed Internet access fails to mention any costs associated with purchasing high-speed service (a hefty installation fee plus high monthly payments) or the long-term contractual commitments that are typically required. And the second argument ignores the facts that many mothers *have* to work to make ends meet and that the economic and social costs of removing working mothers from the workforce would be enormous.

In sum: Even if you agree that all the premises in an argument are true and relevant, you can still refute the argument if you can show that the premises do not provide adequate support for the conclusion. Often this can be done by citing evidence, not mentioned by the arguer, that points to a different conclusion.

EXERCISE 8.3

I. In small groups, reduce the following claims to absurdity. Be prepared to share your answers with the class.

1. No statements are true.
2. All generalizations are false.
3. Some brothers are nieces.
4. No beliefs are justified; we should be absolute and total skeptics.
5. This ball is both red all over and blue all over.
6. I was kissed by an angel, a disembodied spirit.
7. Lake Wobegon: Where all the children are above average.
8. Joseph went back in time and accidentally killed his own grandfather.

II. In small groups, refute the following statements by citing one or more counterexamples. Be prepared to share your answers with the class.

1. No large mammals live in the Arctic.
2. It's always wrong to break a promise.
3. No student should ever have his or her cell phone on in class.
4. America has produced no truly great writers.
5. The great majority of supermarket fruits are red.
6. The United States consistently favors democratic rule and has never supported corrupt authoritarian regimes.
7. Except for Iowa, there are no U.S. states with names that have fewer than five letters.

III. In small groups, *refute,* if possible, the following arguments by citing omitted countervailing evidence. If you think the argument is strong and can't be refuted, cite omitted countervailing evidence that *weakens* the argument. Be prepared to share your answers with the class.

1. Why should I go to college? It costs a fortune, it's boring, and I can get a high-paying job in trucking or construction without a college education.
2. My buddy keeps telling me I should save for retirement, but I tell him, "Look: I'm overweight. I smoke. Neither of my parents lived past sixty-five. Honestly, I'd rather enjoy my money now than save it for a nursing home that I'll never need."
3. This whole business about "equal pay" between men and women is a crock. Sure, forty years ago there was job discrimination against women, but that's ancient history. Today there's only one reason men make more money than women. It's called personal choice. A lot of women *choose* to work as low-paid teachers, librarians, or secretaries or *choose* to drop out of the workforce or to work only part-time to raise a family. Where's the "inequity" in that?
4. Bans on owning AK-47's and other assault weapons should be repealed. The Constitution guarantees the right to bear arms, and if there's ever a foreign

invasion or a breakdown of society, I, for one, want to be able to protect my family.

5. Tanning booths are great. They're available day or night and at any season of the year. You don't have to worry about getting burned, and you can get a great, even tan *quick*.

6. All able-bodied applicants for U.S. citizenship should be required to join the armed forces for three years before being eligible for citizenship. It would help them learn English, strengthen our national defense, inculcate patriotic values, and serve as a deterrent to potential immigrants who care only about what America can do for them and nothing at all about what they can do for America.

7. Drugs like LSD and cocaine should be legal. Let's face it, the "war on drugs" has failed. Legalizing drugs would drastically reduce drug-related crime, alleviate prison overcrowding, unclog the courts, and allow police to concentrate on catching robbers and rapists, instead of petty dealers or substance abusers. Plus, we could tax these legalized drugs and use the money for more productive purposes.

8. Don't marry career women. Research shows that women tend to be happier when their husband is the primary breadwinner. It also shows that career women are more likely to cheat, more likely to get divorced, less likely to have kids, and more likely to be unhappy if they do have kids.

9. Come for the sun, the wide, sandy beaches, the nightlife, the history. Beirut: the perfect vacation spot for the entire family.

IV. **Writing a Critical Essay** A *critical essay* is one in which you analyze and critically evaluate another person's argument. Write an 800- to 1,000-word critical essay on one of the selections on pages 218–227 or on a topic approved by your instructor. Your essay should include the following four elements.

Introduction: Identify the title, author, and context of the essay you are critically evaluating. Summarize very briefly the writer's basic position and state in general terms your overall evaluation of the argument.

Argument summary: Standardize the writer's argument using the five-step method presented in Chapter 7 (or, if your instructor prefers, summarize the argument in paragraph form).

Critical evaluation: Evaluate the argument; that is, say whether you think the argument is a good, convincing argument and give reasons to support your view. You may find it helpful to keep in mind the following general guidelines on evaluating arguments, discussed earlier in this chapter:

- Are the premises true? (*Note:* You may need to do some research to make an informed judgment on this issue.)
- Is the reasoning good? Is the argument deductively valid or inductively strong?
- Does the arguer commit any logical fallacies?
- Does the writer express his or her points clearly and precisely?
- Are the arguer's claims logically consistent?

- Is the argument complete? Is all relevant evidence taken into account?
- Is the argument fair? Is the arguer fair in his or her presentation of the evidence and treatment of opposing arguments and views?

Conclusion: Briefly restate the key points of your critical response to reinforce them in the reader's mind. If possible, end with a strong concluding line (e.g., an apt quotation) that nicely sums up your response or puts the issue in a larger context.

A sample critical essay is included in an appendix to this chapter.

Helmet Laws Discriminate against Bikers

Stan Daniels

Freedom is a most valued and cherished possession. People are willing to fight, and even die, for it.

Isn't it great to live in the United States of America where we can choose to live the sort of life we care to live, choose any religion, decide which schools to attend, and choose our own livelihood?

As an avid motorcyclist, I wonder why the governments of some states, including Pennsylvania, target me and other riders with discriminatory legislation such as mandatory helmet laws.

There is no discernible difference in motorcycle injuries or fatalities among those states where helmet use is voluntary.

Motorcycles represent just 2 percent of total vehicles in the United States and account for less than 1 percent of all vehicle accidents. Trucks and buses account for 28 percent of accidents, and pedestrians account for 15 percent of total vehicle fatalities. Maybe they, too, should have been required to wear helmets, although I believe it wouldn't have mattered.

For me, this is an issue of personal freedom.

Mandatory helmet laws are annoying and unnecessary to an extremely small minority of citizens who would prefer to make their own decision on an issue which has no effect on anyone else.

To the average citizen who does not share an affection for motorcycles, this may not seem important. But what if the government decided to discriminate against your small group?

Would golfers enjoy a sunny afternoon on the greens sporting helmets to protect them from a stray golf ball, or would hunters care to wear bullet-proof vests in the woods?

Recently, a local television station conducted a telephone poll asking if the state should repeal its current mandatory helmet law. The results were 82 percent in favor of repealing the existing law.

I believe that the time has come for the government to allow responsible citizens to choose what safety measures best suit their particular needs.[15]

Don't Use God's Law to Beat Up on Gays

Leonard Pitts

This is for those who hated my recent column about Ellen DeGeneres and Jerry Falwell—the lesbian comic and the preacher who finds her disgusting. It's for the ones who pointed me to the Bible, specifically Leviticus 20:13, which calls homosexuality an "abomination" worthy of death. . . .

Let me begin by saying that I have no answer.

When it comes to reconciling the words in the ancient book with the conundrums of modern life, such is often the case.

The same chapter of Leviticus, for instance, also mandates death for cursing your parents (Leviticus 20:9) or committing adultery (Leviticus 20:10).

Why aren't those who quote Leviticus as literal law rushing to obey this injunction? Why aren't the streets running red with the blood of sluttish spouses and spoiled brats?

I have no answer.

It is emphatically not my intention to ridicule God's Book. However, I do mean to challenge those who seem to take their faith as an excuse for spurning two of His greatest gifts. Meaning a heart that knows compassion and a mind that entertains questions.

They claim there's nothing personal in their persecution of gays. They are, they say, just following God's law.

But we seldom hear of anyone getting this hot and bothered over faithless spouses or ill-mannered children, both worthy of capital punishment according to the Bible.

For that matter, you seldom hear rage over men with long hair (I Corinthians 11:14) or women who speak out in church (I Corinthians 11:34–35)—both also scorned by the Bible. And so, if these people are honest with themselves, they must admit that their antipathy toward gays has less to do with God's law than with human aversion—the visceral shudder of revulsion many feel at the thought of all things homosexual. . . .

What's this say about us that so many are willing to interpret the Bible only to the limits of their own narrow-mindedness and bigotry? That so many are inclined to ignore passages that say men ought not to judge? Or that so many seem to disregard what happened when the scribes and Pharisees brought before Jesus a woman caught in the act of adultery and demanded that she be stoned in accordance with God's law. Instead, Jesus faced them and said the one who was without sin should cast the first stone.

Why is it so few ever take that literally?

I have no answer.

Is homosexuality an abomination?

No answer for that, either, except that if I was given heart and mind, the giver must have wanted me to use them. No answer except that my heart and mind find it difficult to justify loathing or impeding people who have done me no harm. No answer except to note that God is mercy. And, of course, He is love.

So it doesn't bother me to have no answers.

But I fear the man who has no questions.[16]

We're Spendthrift "Environmentalists"

Constance Hilliard

Eight out of 10 Americans regard themselves as environmentalists. Yet while we Americans comprise a mere 5% of the world's population, we consume an estimated 30% of its non-replenishable resources. So much of what we call "environmentalism" in this country, from recycling soda cans to petitioning Congress for wetlands preservation, represents little more than a clamorous sideshow to the far more painful issues at hand.

We may be quick to take sides in political debates over environmental issues, but upon closer inspection we often are all on the same side in the larger ecological debate. Our voracious patterns of consumption engulf gadgetry-addicted, fossil-fuel guzzling environmentalists and anti-environmentalists alike.

The more single-mindedly we grab for that elusive, nirvana-like American Dream, the more inexorable the slippage in our quality of life. We suffer more stress-related illnesses now than ever before, while neglecting family and intimate relationships in our time-consuming struggles to surpass the Joneses.

America's most pressing ecological crisis stems from our societal addiction to consumerism. Our patterns of overconsumption reflect a dependency, a need for constantly whispering promises of untold bliss that mere goods simply cannot keep. This unbridled consumerism, editor Roger Rosenblatt notes in the book *Consuming Desires,* is "threatening the ecological balance of our entire globe."

In this holiday season of frenzied shop-'til-you-drop spending, those of us who call ourselves environmentalists might just wish to take time out to re-evaluate our personal patterns of consumption. What emotional or spiritual wounds do we really think that new item will heal? More to the point, what are the unspoken costs to the fragile, unreplenishable resources of this planet of our endless material acquisitions?

And we Americans call ourselves environmentalists.[17]

Campus Rules Overreach

USA Today

Our view: Students have a right to express views that offend some others.

Following the September 11, 2001, attacks, several students at Shippensburg (Pa.) University put up posters in their dorms depicting Osma bin Laden in a rifle's crosshairs. But school officials ordered the posters removed. The students said they were told the signs might offend other dorm residents.

In response to that bit of political correctness run amok, a group representing the students sued the university, claiming its code of student conduct limits free speech. A federal judge agreed. Last week, the school revised its code, which had banned "any unwanted conduct which annoys, demeans or alarms."

The case illustrates how colleges' efforts to promote campus harmony can violate constitutional rights to free expression by squelching all but the most bland and conformist comments. While some views may be offensive, the best way to confront them is by encouraging open dialogue, not giving veto power to those most easily offended.

Yet, many colleges still prohibit provocative speech protected by the First Amendment, according to the Foundation for Individual Rights in Education (FIRE), which sued Shippensburg and other colleges that attempted to censor debate.

Examples of campus restrictions the group has challenged:

- Officials at the College of William and Mary in Virginia, University of Colorado and the University of California at Irvine prevented some students from holding bake sales with discount prices for minority students as satirical protests of affirmative-action policies. They relented after FIRE threatened to sue.
- Last year, Gonzaga University in Spokane, Wash., took disciplinary action against a student group that posted fliers about a speech by the author of the book *Why the Left Hates America*. Offended students and

administrators have complained that the title could be considered a form of hate speech. Gonzaga reversed itself after FIRE protested.
- A writing instructor at Forsyth Technical Community College in Winston-Salem, N.C., claims she was let go last year after criticizing the Iraq war during a class. FIRE is working to have her reinstated.

Some universities argue that speech codes are needed to comply with federal rules that ban sexual or racial harassment. But the head of the U.S. Department of Education's Office of Civil Rights says the regulations don't "impair the exercise of rights protected under the First Amendment." The rules are intended to protect students from discrimination, not regulate speech, he said.

Encouraging students to show sensitivity to others is laudable, but it's better achieved through persuasion than coercion of those who express disagreeable views. After all, a free exchange of ideas is supposed to be an integral part of the college experience.

Universities can support civility without tearing down posters or limiting speech. Free expression will make some uncomfortable, but that's not sufficient reason to block it within the ivy-covered walls of academia.[18]

Hate Cannot Be Tolerated

Richard Delgado

Opposing view: Limits on the most offensive forms of speech are reasonable.

Anonymous vandals scrawl hate-filled graffiti outside a Jewish student center. Black students at a law school find unsigned fliers stuffed inside their lockers screaming that they do not belong there. At a third campus, a group of toughs hurls epithets at a young Latino student walking home late at night.

In response to a rising tide of such incidents, some colleges have enacted hate-speech codes or applied existing rules against individuals whose conduct interferes with the educational opportunities of others. Federal courts have extended "hostile environment" case law to schools that tolerate a climate of hate for women and students of color.

Despite the alarm these measures sometimes elicit, nothing is wrong with them. In each case, the usual and preferred response—"more speech"—is unavailable to the victim. With anonymous hate speech such as the flier or graffiti, the victim cannot talk back, for the hate speaker delivers his message in a cowardly fashion. And talking back to aggressors is rarely an option. Indeed, many hate crimes began just this way: The victim talked back—and paid with his life.

Hate speech is rarely an invitation to a conversation. More like a slap in the face, it reviles and silences. College counselors report that campuses where highly publicized incidents of hate speech have taken place show a decline in minority enrollment as students of color instead choose to attend school where the environment is healthier.

A few federal courts have declared overly broad hate-speech codes unconstitutional, as well they should. Nothing is gained by a rule so broad it could be construed as forbidding the discussion of controversial subjects such as evolution or affirmative action.

But this is not what most people mean by hate speech, nor are colleges barred from drafting narrow rules that hone in on the conduct they wish to control. And when they do, courts are very likely to find in their favor. Recent

Supreme Court rulings striking down laws that ban sodomy, upholding affirmative action, and approving punishment for cross-burning show that the court is not unaware of current trends. Society is becoming more diverse. Reasonable rules aimed at accommodating that diversity and regulating the conduct of bullies and bigots are to be applauded—not feared.[19]

Drop Out of the College

New York Times

The Electoral College is an antidemocratic relic. Everyone who remembers 2000 knows that it can lead to the election of the candidate who loses the popular vote as president. But the Electoral College's other serious flaws are perhaps even more debilitating for a democracy. It focuses presidential elections on just a handful of battleground states, and pushes the rest of the nation's voters to the sidelines.

There is an innovative new proposal for states to take the lead in undoing the Electoral College. Legislatures across the country should get behind it.

Both parties should have reason to fear the college's perverse effects. In 2000, the Democrats lost out. But in 2004, a shift of 60,000 votes in Ohio would have elected John Kerry, even though he lost the national popular vote decisively.

Just as serious is the way the Electoral College distorts presidential campaigns. Candidates have no incentive to campaign in, or address the concerns of, states that reliably vote for a particular party. In recent years, the battleground in presidential elections has shrunk drastically. In 1960, 24 states, with 327 electoral votes, were battleground states, according to estimates by the National Popular Vote, the bipartisan coalition making the new proposal. In 2004, only 13 states, with 159 electoral votes, were. As a result, campaigns and national priorities are stacked in favor of a few strategic states. Ethanol fuel, a pet issue of Iowa farmers, is discussed a lot. But issues of equal concern to states like Alabama, California, New York and Indiana are not.

The Electoral College discourages turnout because voters in two-thirds of the nation know well before Election Day who will win their states. It also discriminates among voters by weighing presidential votes unequally. A Wyoming voter has about four times as much impact on selecting that state's electors as a California voter on selecting that state's.

The answer to all of these problems is direct election of the president. Past attempts to abolish the Electoral College by amending the Constitution have run into difficulty. But National Popular Vote, which includes several former members of Congress, is offering an ingenious solution that would not require a constitutional amendment. It proposes that states commit to casting their electoral votes for the winner of the national popular vote. These promises would become binding only when states representing a majority of the Electoral College signed on. Then any candidate who won the popular vote would be sure to win the White House.

The coalition is starting out by trying to have laws passed in Illinois and a few other states. Americans are rightly cautious about tinkering with mechanisms established by the Constitution. But throughout the nation's history, there have been a series of reforms affecting how elections are conducted, like the ones that gave blacks and women the vote and provided for the direct election of United States senators. Sidestepping the Electoral College would be in this worthy tradition of making American democracy more democratic.[20]

The Case for Profiling

Charles Krauthammer

The latest airport-security scandal is the groping of female flight attendants and passengers during patdowns. Not to worry. The Transportation Security Administration chief is right on it. "We're going to fix that right away," he said recently, announcing the appointment of an ombudsman.

A nice bureaucratic Band-Aid. No one, however, asks the obvious question: Why are we patting down flight attendants in the first place? Why, for that matter, are we conducting body searches of any female passengers?

Random passenger checks at airports are completely useless. We've all been there in the waiting lounge, rolling our eyes in disbelief as the 80-year-old Irish nun, the Hispanic mother of two, the Japanese-American businessman, the House committee chairman with the titanium hip are randomly chosen and subjected to head-to-toe searching for . . . what?

Not for security—these people are hardly candidates for suicide terrorism—but for political correctness. We are engaged in a daily and ostentatious rehearsal of the officially sanctioned proposition that suicide terrorists come from anywhere, without regard to gender, ethnicity, age or religious affiliation.

That is not true, and we know it. Random searches are a ridiculous charade, a charade that not only gives a false sense of security but, in fact, diminishes security because it wastes so much time and effort on people who are obviously no threat. . . .

Imagine that Timothy McVeigh and Terry Nichols had not been acting alone but had instead been part of a vast right-wing, antigovernment, terrorist militia with an ideology, a network and a commitment to carrying out attacks throughout America. Would there have been any objection to singling out young white men for special scrutiny at airports and other public places? Of course not. And if instead, in response to the threat posed by the McVeigh Underground, airport security began pulling young black men or elderly Asian women out of airport lines for full-body searches, would we not all loudly say that this is an outrage and an absurdity?

As it happens, the suicide bombers who attacked us on Sept. 11 were not McVeigh Underground. They were al-Qaeda: young, Islamic, Arab and male. That is not a stereotype. That is a fact. And there is no hiding from it, as there is no hiding from the next al-Qaeda suicide bomber. He has to be found and stopped. And you don't find him by strip-searching female flight attendants or 80-year-old Irish nuns.

This is not to say your plane could not be brought down by a suicide bomber of another sort. It could. It could also be brought down by a meteorite. Or by a Stinger missile fired by Vermont dairymen in armed rebellion. These are all possible. But because they are rather improbable, we do not alter our daily lives to defend against the possibility.

True, shoe bomber Richard Reid, while young and Islamic and male, was not Arab. No system will catch everyone. But our current system is designed to catch no one because we are spending 90% of our time scrutinizing people everyone knows are no threat. Jesse Jackson once famously lamented how he felt when he would "walk down the street and hear footsteps and start thinking

about robbery—then look around and see somebody white and feel relieved."
Jackson is no racist. He was not passing judgment on his own ethnicity. He
was simply reacting to probabilities. He would rather not. We all would rather
not make any calculations based on ethnicity, religion, gender or physical
characteristics—except that on airplanes our lives are at stake.

The pool of suicide bombers is not large. To pretend that it is universal
is absurd. Airport security is not permitted to "racially" profile, but every
passenger—white or black, male or female, Muslim or Christian—does. We
scan the waiting room, scrutinizing other passengers not just for nervousness
and shiftiness but also for the demographic characteristics of al-Qaeda. We do
it privately. We do it quietly. But we do it. Airport officials, however, may not.
This is crazy. So crazy that it is only a matter of time before the public finally
demands that our first priority be real security, not political appearances—and
puts an end to this charade.[21]

On Campus, a Good Man Is Hard to Find

John Tierney

When a boy opens his acceptance letter from college, he now has to wonder
what most impressed the admissions officers. Did they want him for his mind,
or just his body?

The admissions director at Kenyon College, Jennifer Delahunty Britz, published an Op-Ed article this week revealing an awkward truth about her job:
affirmative action for boys. As the share of the boys in the applicant pool keeps
shrinking—it will soon be down to 40 percent nationally—colleges are admitting
less-qualified boys in order to keep the gender ratio balanced on campus.

This week's revelation did not please Kim Gandy, the president of the National
Organization for Women, who told me that she might challenge the legality of
affirmative action for male applicants. She and I are not normally ideological
soulmates, but I have some sympathy with her on this policy.

It's not fair to the girls who are rejected despite having higher grades and
test scores than the boys who get fat envelopes. It's not fair to the boys, either,
if they're not ready to keep up with their classmates.

After consulting with the federal Education Department, I can confidently
report that this discrimination may violate the law—or then again, it may not.
Either way, I agree with Gandy that public colleges shouldn't practice it, because
the government shouldn't favor one group over another. Gandy's also wary of
allowing private schools like Kenyon to discriminate, and she's skeptical of their
justification: that they need a fairly even male-female ratio on campus to attract
the best applicants of either sex. I'm not sure if that's true, but I trust the colleges to know better than me or Gandy or federal lawyers. As long as a school is
private, let it favor whomever it wants—men, women, alumni children, Latinos,
African-Americans—without any interference from the Education Department.

What the department should be doing is figuring out how to help boys
reach college. The gender gap has been getting worse for two decades, but the
Education Department still isn't focusing on it. Instead, it has an "educational
equity" program aimed at helping girls and women.

The department is paying to encourage African and Slavic girls and women
in Oregon to pursue careers in science. There's a grant to help women in West
Virginia overcome "traditional, outdated 19th-century attitudes" by pursuing
jobs in blue-collar trades. Another grant aims to motivate women at the Medgar
Evers College in Brooklyn, N.Y., to study math.

These are all noble goals. I'd be glad to see the women of Brooklyn take up advanced calculus. But the chief "equity" issue at their college is the shortage of men, who make up barely a fifth of the student body. What happened to the boys who didn't make it?

Boys are, on average, as smart as girls, but they are much less fond of school. They consistently receive lower grades, have more discipline problems, and are more likely to be held back for a year or placed in special education classes. The Harvard economist Brian Jacobs attributes these problems to boys' lack of "noncognitive skills," like their difficulties with paying attention in class, their disorganization, and their reluctance to seek help from others.

Those are serious handicaps, but they could be mitigated if schools became more boy-friendly. A few educators have suggested reforms: more outdoor exercise, more male teachers, more experiments with single-sex schools. But those ideas have gotten little attention or money. Schools have been too busy trying to close the gender gap in the few areas where boys are ahead, like sports and science.

No matter what changes are made to help boys, they'll probably still be less likely than girls to go on to college, simply because girls' skills and interests are better suited to the types of white-collar jobs that now require college degrees. Boys will remain more inclined to skip college in favor of relatively well-paying jobs in fields like construction and manufacturing.

There's no reason to expect a 50-50 ratio on campus—and certainly no reason to mandate it. Boys don't need that kind of affirmative action. What they could use, long before college, is equal attention.[22]

Don't Blame the Burgers

USA Today

Our view: "Fat" lawsuits won't fix the obesity epidemic. Personal responsibility will.

People who overeat used to be called gluttons. Now, they're victims. Two overweight Bronx, N.Y., teens who scarfed down McDonald's burgers and fries several times a week blame the company for their health problems. Their attorneys assert they are victims of corporate malfeasance because the chain deceives customers about its products.

The "McDonald's-made-me-fat" lawsuit leaps to mind whenever the subject of frivolous litigation comes up. Nine of 10 Americans say it's wrong to hold food companies liable for obesity-related health problems, a 2003 Gallup Poll found. A federal judge who dismissed the case that year agreed, noting, "Nobody is forced to eat at McDonald's."

A federal appeals court reinstated the lawsuit last week, saying the teens should be allowed to collect more evidence before trial. So the case that became a meal ticket for comedians and inspired an Oscar-nominated documentary, Super Size Me, about a man who ate nothing but McDonald's food for 30 days, can again clog the arteries of American jurisprudence. Fourteen states have passed "cheeseburger" bills to protect chains from lawsuits about their customers' girth.

The McDonald's lawsuit is no joke to the attorneys who see food as their next cash cow. The lawyers acknowledge that their goal is to use class-action suits to hold food firms liable for a lucrative portion of the $117 billion in annual public health costs related to obesity. Of at least eight "fat" lawsuits filed so far, five have been partially successful in pushing companies to provide better nutritional information. The trial lawyers hope that securing documents from food chains will yield the kind of incriminating memos they found with Big Tobacco.

It's a stretch to suggest that McNuggets are as addictive or dangerous as nicotine. Although two-thirds of Americans are overweight, lawsuits and government edicts are no way to trim the nation's midsection. Market forces and public education work better.

Food companies are responding to health findings and consumer demand. McDonald's has phased out its Super Size program. Mascot Ronald McDonald will visit elementary schools to promote fitness, not burgers. More nutritional information is displayed on the restaurants' Web sites.

Most fast-food chains have cut fat content and offer salads and low-carb meals. All 1,500 Applebee's restaurants, for example, offer Weight Watchers meals. People who choose Hardie's 1,418-calorie Monster Thickburger have only themselves to blame.

Advice to avoid such foods is hard to miss. The government's new dietary guidelines, issued earlier this month, counsel people to exercise more, eat more fruits, vegetables and whole grains, and cut their intake of trans fats in processed foods. The Food and Drug Administration will soon grade food-health claims, and the Centers for Disease Control and Prevention is studying the effects of food marketing on children's diets.

Ultimately, good eating habits are a matter of personal and parental responsibility. As the trial judge in the McDonald's case put it: "If a person knows or should know that eating copious orders of supersized McDonald's products is unhealthy and may result in weight gain, it is not the place of the law to protect them from their own excesses."[23]

End the Death Penalty; Use Life without Parole

USA Today

The evidence is in: the verdict is beyond dispute. The death penalty is a failure as a tool of law, justice or public safety. . . .

You need not be a legal scholar to see the death penalty's many flaws. Nor do you need to be "soft on crime." Other punishments are more meaningful and just as satisfying. Indeed, the death penalty actually makes our society more violent and our persons less secure.

Capital punishment has a "brutalizing effect" that actually seems to incite killers. The phenomenon has been documented as far back as the 1850s, both here and in Europe. One famous study found that in New York between 1907 and 1963, the murder rate increased, on average, by two in every month following a public execution.

There's a simpler way to prove the death penalty doesn't work: Look at the crime stats. In 1992, the average murder rate in death-penalty states was 7.8 per 100,000 people. In states without: 4.9 per 100,000. Where do you want to live? . . .

Capital punishment satisfies a natural urge for revenge that is complete and final. And, certainly, the courts should impose lasting punishments that truly punish.

But the death penalty dooms the innocent along with the guilty. Since 1900, as many as 23 people have been put to death for crimes they did not commit. Even now, death-row inmates scheduled for execution are regularly reprieved. In 1993 alone, five death-row inmates were found to be completely innocent.

• Critical Thinking Lapse •

Wayne, 38, of Pittston, Pennsylvania, was bitten by a cobra belonging to his friend, Roger, after playfully reaching into the tank and picking up the snake. Wayne subsequently refused to go to a hospital, telling Roger, "I'm a man, I can handle it." Falser words have seldom been spoken. Instead of a hospital, Wayne reported to a bar. He had three drinks and enjoyed bragging that he had just been bitten by a cobra. Cobra venom is a slow-acting central nervous system toxin. He died within a few hours, in Jenkins Township, Pennsylvania.[24]

The risk of error has a companion: The taint of racism.

On the federal level, 75% of those convicted under the Drug Kingpin Act have been white, but 90% of those who face capital prosecutions under the same statute are minorities. In the states, only one white in 18 years has been executed for killing a black. A black murderer is twice as likely to be executed if his victim was white than if his victim was a minority.

Make no mistake. Opposition to capital punishment is not opposition to swift and certain punishment. An alternative that meets both standards is available: Life in prison with no possibility of parole, now available in at least 33 states.

This sentence means what it says. A convict will not get out in seven years, or 12 years or 15 years. *There is no parole.*

Many jurors, like most Americans, think there's no such thing as a life sentence. They fear a killer will get out and kill again. But in California, for instance, not one person sentenced to life without parole has been freed. This is life in a cage—forever.

The only problem is that this sentence isn't more common. Life without parole:

- Is easier to win than the death penalty, and cheaper by one-third or one-half. . . .
- Is indisputably constitutional.
- And may actually deter crime, especially for those in communities where the prospect of death may be more tolerable than the prospect of life in a cage.

The death penalty offers no certainty of justice. It is arbitrary. It wastes money. It makes us less safe. It cannot be reconciled with the Constitution. It bogs down the courts. It encourages legalistic manipulation, and it erodes the system's integrity.

So why bother with it? Life in prison without any possibility of parole will put the bad guys where it hurts the most and improve our judicial system at the same time. . . . Abolish the death penalty.[25]

SUMMARY

1. In critical thinking a *good argument* is an argument that satisfies the relevant critical thinking standards that apply in a particular context. The most important critical thinking standards are *accuracy* (Are the premises

true?) and *logical correctness* (Do the premises, if true, provide good reasons to accept the conclusion?). There are, however, other critical thinking standards that should also be considered in evaluating arguments. Among these are clarity, precision, relevance, consistency, completeness, and fairness.

2. In general, it is reasonable to accept an unsupported claim as true when (1) the claim does not conflict with personal experiences that we have no good reason to doubt, (2) the claim does not conflict with background beliefs that we have no good reason to doubt, and (3) the claim comes from a credible source.

3. To refute an argument is to defeat it—to show that the premises do not provide good reasons to accept the conclusion. There are two ways to refute an argument: (1) show that a premise—or a critical group of premises—is false or dubious, or (2) show that the reasoning is bad—that the premises do not provide adequate logical support for the conclusion. Two often-effective strategies for showing that a premise is false are *reducing to the absurd (reductio ad absurdum)* and *refutation by counterexample.* Reducing to the absurd seeks to refute a claim by showing that the claim implies something that is obviously false or absurd. Refutation by counterexample attempts to show that a general claim (i.e., a claim of the form "All A's are B's" or "Most A's are B's") is false by producing one or more counterexamples—that is, examples or exceptions that demonstrate that the claim is false.

    The second way to refute an argument is to show that its reasoning is bad—that the premises, even if they are conceded to be true, fail to provide sufficient logical support for the conclusion. Many real-life arguments can be refuted by showing that the argument *omits crucial countervailing evidence*—that is, evidence or information not mentioned by the arguer that points to a different or contrary conclusion.

4. Key questions we should ask in evaluating arguments include the following:

    • Are the premises true?

    • Is the reasoning correct? Is the argument deductively valid or inductively strong?

    • Does the arguer commit any logical fallacies?

    • Does the arguer express his or her points clearly and precisely?

    • Are the premises relevant to the conclusion?

    • Are the arguer's claims logically consistent? Do any of the arguer's claims contradict other claims made in the argument?

    • Is the argument complete? Is all relevant evidence taken into account (given understandable limitations of time, space, context, and so on)?

- Is the argument fair? Is the arguer fair in his or her presentation of the evidence and treatment of opposing arguments and views?

Appendix: Sample Critical Essay

Below is a sample critical essay, written by us (Jamie Kendall is a pseudonym). The essay is a critical analysis of a guest editorial by Jack Pytleski that appeared in the *Wilkes-Barre Times Leader* on July 10, 1997. First an edited and abridged version of Pytleski's editorial is given, followed by the critical essay.

Defending My Right to Claim My "Steak" in the Animal Kingdom
[A recent caller to a newspaper call-in column] opined that the "healthiest way to prepare and eat meat is not to eat it at all."
  Who cares!
  I love a good steak. . . . But I'm not about to start carrying a sign that promotes a carnivorous diet. Your health is your business, not mine. If you wish to clog your arteries with cholesterol, saturated fat and other toxins, go right ahead. Just make sure you've made plenty of room at your table for me. And pass the butter for that ear of roast corn while you're at it, OK?
  Let's quickly examine two of the three popular reasons for vegetarianism, the health aspect and the animal rights point of view. . . . The third reason, the use of edible grain and arable land for animal feed, is worth an entire column at another time.
  I freely admit that excessive consumption of meat is probably not the best thing for your body. I contend, however, that gastronomic preference is a highly personal choice, and claim refuge under my "constitutional right to privacy" (feminists, take note) and the privilege of doing whatever I please with my body.
  Once you're born, death is inevitable. Since I'll die no matter what I eat, I plan to enjoy every minute of my alloted time on earth, including consuming my favorite foods. Am I killing myself? Possibly, but I'm as good as dead anyway, aren't I?
  Now some of you might say that eating meat shortens my natural life span. Maybe. But given the choice of sitting around drooling all over myself in something euphemistically called a "personal care home" and punching out earlier with a massive thrombosis, guess which deal I'll take, Monty? You've got it—the one behind Door Number Two. . . .
  Pass the sour cream, please. . . .
  There are just some things I take on faith. One of those is that some animals, like it or not, have another purpose besides wandering around doing animal-like things in the weeds. This includes everything from guide and companion duties to gracing the body on the table. Unfortunately for most herbivores and some carnivores, . . . they haven't yet become accepted as caregivers or companions. So we eat 'em or wear 'em. At least I do. What you do is your business. . . .

Don't misunderstand. I'm on the side of a certain degree of animal rights. I believe that all animals deserve humane treatment. . . . Companion animals should be spayed or neutered and properly fed, loved and sheltered.

Some animals shouldn't be kept as companions, and even animals used for food or clothing ought to be kept in clean and compassionate surroundings—until that final two hundred and thirty grains catches them between the running lights.

As I stated at the outset, what you eat is your business. What I eat is mine. But whoever you are, if you feel you have the right to dictate something so fundamental as my diet I reserve the privilege to answer accordingly.

Stick that in your Brussels sprouts! And pass the bacon.

Sample Critical Essay

Jamie Kendall   Kendall 1

Critical Thinking 101

Professor Lewis

March 25, 2007

              Animal Rights and Human Health

For a variety of reasons, more and more people today are choosing to become vegetarians. Two of the most common reasons given for adopting a vegetarian diet are that it is healthier than a meat-based diet and that eating animals is wrong because it inflicts suffering on sentient creatures without good reason. In a column titled "Defending My Right to Claim My 'Steak' in the Animal Kingdom" that appeared in the *Wilkes-Barre Times Leader* on July 10, 1997, Jack Pytleski argues that neither of these two popular arguments for vegetarianism is convincing. In this essay I will argue that Pytleski's argument for this conclusion is weak.

Pytleski's basic argument can be summarized as follows:

1. I'm going to die no matter what I eat.

2. I want to enjoy every minute of my allotted time on earth.

Kendall 2

3. If given a choice between sitting around drooling in a "personal care center" or checking out earlier from a massive heart attack, I would choose the latter.

4. I have a right to do as I please with my own body.

5. I have a constitutional right of privacy that gives me the right to eat the kinds of foods I enjoy.

6. [Thus, contrary to one popular argument for vegetarianism, the fact that eating a balanced vegetarian diet tends to be healthier than a meat-based diet is not a good reason for me to switch to a vegetarian diet. (from 1-5)]

7. I believe on faith that animals were put on earth to provide food, clothing, and other benefits to humans.

8. [Thus, contrary to a second popular argument for vegetarianism, animals have no right not to be killed and eaten by humans. (from 7)]

9. [Therefore, two popular arguments for vegetarianism—the health benefits argument and the animal rights argument—do not provide good reasons for adopting a vegetarian diet. (from 6 and 8)]

Pytleski's essay, while it raises some interesting issues, is flawed for a number of reasons.

First, much of Pytleski's argument in lines 1-6 misses the point of what his opponents are arguing. In this part of his argument, Pytleski seems to be arguing for two things: first, that people have both a moral and a constitutional right to eat unhealthy foods and, second, that it is reasonable, given certain personal

Kendall 3

preferences, to prefer a less healthy meat-based diet to a more healthy vegetarian diet. But both of these claims rest on a misunderstanding of what the health benefits argument asserts. As it is typically formulated, all that the health benefits argument asserts is that it is *prudent* to eat a balanced vegetarian diet *if* one wants to live a long, healthy life (Stephens 294-95). Nothing in Pytleski's argument shows that this claim is false. At best what Pytleski shows is that he personally is unmoved by the health benefits argument because he prefers eating foods he enjoys rather than living a long, healthy life.

Some of Pytleski's arguments are shaky on other grounds as well. Let's examine two of these arguments: the "drooling" argument in lines 3 and 6 and the animal rights argument in lines 7 and 8.

Pytleski says that he'd rather die earlier of a massive heart attack than sit around drooling in a personal care center. This argument is weak because it falsely assumes that there are only two relevant possibilities: dying of a sudden massive heart attack or vegetating in a personal care center. This overlooks the fact that there are many adverse health effects other than heart disease that are linked to diets high in animal fat, including kidney disease, osteoporosis, diverticulitis, food poisoning, hypertension, and, most significant, stroke and many kinds of cancer. The possibility of stroke is particularly relevant in this context because many of the 570,000 stroke victims in the United States each year do suffer from precisely the kind of severe long-term mental impairment that Pytleski fears.

Kendall 4

Furthermore, Pytleski's response to the animal rights argument is also very weak. Boiled down to essentials, the animal rights argument is this:

1. Practices that inflict suffering on sentient beings without good reason are morally wrong.

2. Thus, sentient beings have a right not to be made to suffer without good reason. (from 1)

3. For humans to kill and eat sentient animals inflicts suffering on them without good reason.

4. Therefore, sentient animals have a right not to be killed and eaten by humans. (from 2-3)

Pytleski's response to this argument is simply to state that he believes "on faith" that animals exist for the purpose of providing food and other benefits to humans. But of course this is precisely what animal rights supporters deny. So this isn't so much an argument against the animal rights view as it is simply a denial of that view.

Finally, it should be noted that Pytleski's argument is unclear at key points. In fact, as the argument summary reveals, Pytleski leaves it to his readers to formulate every major conclusion in the argument.

In sum, Pytleski offers a very weak argument for his conclusion. Several of his arguments against the health benefits argument misfire because they are based on a misunderstanding of what that argument claims. His "drooling" argument is faulty because it poses a false either/or choice between dying early from a massive heart attack and sitting around drooling in a personal care center. His "argument" against the animal rights view basically boils down to just a denial of that

Kendall 5

view. And Pytleski's argument as a whole is neither as clear nor as explicit as it should be.

Albert Einstein once said, "Our task must be to free ourselves . . . by widening our circle of compassion to embrace all living creatures and the whole of nature and its beauty." It may be that a strong case can be made against widening this circle of moral concern, but Pytleski's argument against doing so is unconvincing.

Kendall 6

Works Cited

Stephens, William O. "Five Arguments for Vegetarianism," *Philosophy and the Contemporary World* 1 (Winter 1994): 25–39. Rpt. in *Environmental Ethics: Concepts, Policy, Theory*. Ed. Joseph DesJardins. Mountain View, CA: Mayfield, 1999: 288–301.

CHAPTER 9

A LITTLE
CATEGORICAL LOGIC

To help us make sense of our experience, humans constantly group things into classes or categories. These classifications are reflected in our everyday language. For instance, we often encounter statements like these:

> All donuts are fattening.
>
> No minors are permitted in the store.
>
> Some mushrooms are poisonous.
>
> Some Republicans are not conservatives.

The first statement says that anything included in the class of donuts is also included in the class of things that are fattening. The second statement says that no member of the class of minors is included in the class of persons permitted in the store. The third statement says that some members of the class of mushrooms are also members of the class of things that are poisonous. And the fourth statement says that some members of the class of Republicans are not members of the class of conservatives.

These are examples of what logicians call *categorical statements*. In this chapter we introduce a simple yet powerful technique for testing the validity of simple arguments made up of categorical statements.

> *One of the most fundamental and pervasive of all human psychological activities is the propensity to categorize.*
>
> —David A. Levy

CATEGORICAL STATEMENTS

A **categorical statement** makes a claim about the relationship between two or more categories or classes of things. In this chapter we focus on what are called **standard-form categorical statements,** which have one of the following four forms:

> All *S* are *P*. (*Example:* All Democrats are liberals.)
>
> No *S* are *P*. (*Example:* No Democrats are liberals.)
>
> Some *S* are *P*. (*Example:* Some Democrats are liberals.)
>
> Some *S* are not *P*. (*Example:* Some Democrats are not liberals.)

Logicians have discovered a number of techniques to test the validity of simple categorical arguments. The easiest method involves drawing a series of overlapping circles and associated markings called **Venn diagrams.**[1] Let's start with a few simple examples to see how the method works.

Suppose we wish to draw a Venn diagram of the statement "All Democrats are liberals." We start by drawing a circle to stand for the class of Democrats:

Democrats

Then we draw a circle to stand for the class of liberals:

Liberals

The first circle includes anyone who is a Democrat; the second circle includes anyone who is a liberal.

Next we need to connect the two circles to indicate that the two classes are being related to each other in the statement. We do this by drawing the circles so that they partially overlap:

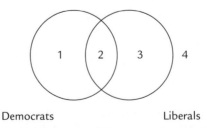

Democrats   Liberals

Anything in area 1 is a Democrat but not a liberal. Anything in area 2 is both a Democrat and a liberal. Anything in area 3 is a liberal but not a Democrat. And anything in area 4, the area outside the two circles, is neither a Democrat nor a liberal.[2]

Finally, we need some way to represent the asserted relationship between these two classes, namely, that all members of the class of Democrats are also members of the class of liberals. To do this we shade that part of the Democrats circle that does not overlap with the Liberals circle:

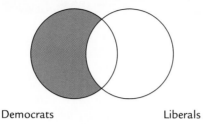

Democrats   Liberals

The shading means that that part of the Democrats circle that does not over-lap with the liberals circle is *empty;* that is, it contains no members.[3] The dia-gram thus asserts that there are *no* Democrats who are not liberals. This is what we mean when we say that all Democrats are liberals.

Next let's diagram the statement "No Democrats are liberals." Once again we start by drawing two overlapping circles, one to represent Democrats and the other to represent liberals:

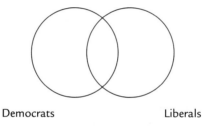

Democrats   Liberals

To say that no Democrats are liberals is to say that no members of the class of Democrats are members of the class of liberals—that is, that there is *no overlap* between the two classes. To represent this claim, we shade that portion of the two circles that overlaps:

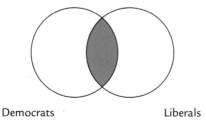

Democrats   Liberals

The diagram now tells us that anyone who is a Democrat is *not* a liberal—that is, that the class of people who are both Democrats and liberals is empty. And that is what it means to say that no Democrats are liberals.

Categorical statements that begin with *some* must be treated differently from categorical statements that begin with *all* or *no*. *Some* is often ambiguous in ordinary usage. Does it mean "a few," "at least a few," "at least one but not

Two Important Things to Remember about *Some* Statements

1. In categorical logic, *some* always means "at least one."
2. *Some* statements are understood to assert that something actually exists. Thus, "Some mammals are cats" asserts that at least one mammal exists and that that mammal is a cat. In contrast, *all* or *no* statements are not interpreted as asserting the existence of anything. Instead, they are treated as purely conditional statements. Thus, "All trespassers will be prosecuted" asserts that *if* anyone is a trespasser, he or she will be prosecuted, not that there *are* trespassers and that all of them will be prosecuted.

all," "at least one and maybe all," "at least a few but not all," "lots," "many"? To avoid such confusions, logicians always use *some* with the same consistent meaning. In logic *some* always means "at least one." For example,

Some dogs are animals

means "At least one dog is an animal" (which is true), not "At least one dog is an animal, but not all" (which is false).

There is another important difference between *some* statements and *all* or *no* statements. In modern logic, *all* or *no* statements are treated as purely *conditional* ("if-then") statements. Thus, the statement "All Hobbits are mushroom-lovers" doesn't say that there *are* any Hobbits. Rather, it says that *if* anything is a Hobbit, *then* it is a mushroom-lover. In contrast, the statement "Some Hobbits are mushroom-lovers" *does* assert that something exists. Specifically, it asserts that at least one Hobbit exists and that that Hobbit is a mushroom-lover. This difference between the two kinds of quantifiers isn't very intuitive, but it causes few problems as long as the special meanings assigned to these expressions are kept firmly in mind.

In logic, accordingly, the statement "Some Democrats are liberals" means "There exists at least one Democrat and that Democrat is a liberal." To diagram this statement, we place an *X* in that part of the Democrats circle that overlaps with the Liberals circle:

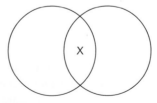

Democrats   Liberals

The *X* here stands for that at-least-one-Democrat who is definitely asserted to be a liberal.

A similar strategy is used with statements of the form "Some *S* are not *P*." In logic the statement "Some Democrats are not liberals" means "At least one Democrat is not a liberal." To diagram this statement, we place an *X* in that part of the Democrats circle that lies outside the Liberals circle:

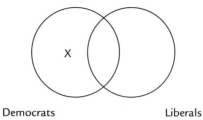

Democrats   Liberals

The diagram now asserts that at least one member of the class of Democrats is not a member of the class of liberals. And that is what it means, in logic, to say that some Democrats are not liberals.

In summary, the four kinds of standard-form categorical statements are diagrammed as follows:

All *S* are *P*.

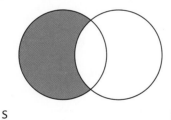

S   P

No *S* are *P*.

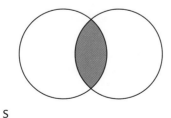

S   P

Some *S* are *P*.

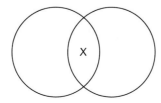

S   P

Some *S* are not *P*.

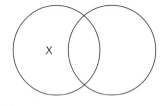

S   P

EXERCISE 9.1

Draw Venn diagrams of the following statements. In some cases, you may need to rephrase the statements slightly to put them in one of the four standard forms (i.e., All *S* are *P*, No *S* are *P*, Some *S* are *P*, or Some *S* are not *P*).

1. No artichokes are fruits.
2. Some rectangles are squares.
3. All architects are professionals.
4. Some skateboarders are jazz fans.
5. Some tattoo artists are not archbishops.
6. All persons born in the United States are U.S. citizens.
7. No women are persons who have been U.S. presidents or vice presidents.
8. Many dwarves are bachelors.
9. Not a single chess master is a rock star.
10. Some of the world's greatest soccer players are South Americans.

The main practical value of logic to one who wants to distinguish between straight and crooked thinking is that it introduces him to the device of reducing arguments to their skeleton form as a means of judging whether or not they give sound support to their conclusions.

—Robert H. Thouless

TRANSLATING INTO STANDARD CATEGORICAL FORM

Although relatively few of our everyday statements are explicitly in standard categorical form, a surprisingly large number of those statements can be *translated* into standard categorical form. That is why Venn diagrams are so useful in testing everyday arguments.

Before we discuss ways to translate ordinary English sentences into standard-form categorical statements, let's take a closer look at what such statements involve.

Standard-form categorical statements have a very simple logical structure. Here, once again, are the four standard categorical forms:

All *S* are *P*.

No *S* are *P*.

Some *S* are *P*.

Some *S* are not *P*.

⎯ • **Critical Thinking Lapse** • ⎯

TACOMA, Wash.—Kerry Bingham had been drinking with several friends when one of them said they knew a person who had bungee-jumped from the Tacoma Narrows Bridge in the middle of traffic. The conversation grew heated, and at least 10 men trooped along the walkway of the bridge at 4:30 A.M. Upon arrival at the midpoint of the bridge, they discovered that no one had brought bungee rope. Bingham, who had continued drinking, volunteered and pointed out that a coil of lineman's cable lay nearby. One end of the cable was secured around Bingham's leg and the other end was tied to the bridge. His fall lasted 40 feet before the cable tightened and tore his foot off at the ankle. He miraculously survived his fall into the icy river water and was rescued by two nearby fisherman. "All I can say," said Bingham, "is that God was watching out for me on that night. There's just no other explanation for it." Bingham's foot was never located.[4]

Notice that each of these statement forms has four basic parts:

1. They all begin with the word *all, no,* or *some.* These words are called **quantifiers** because they are used to express a quantity or a number.
2. They all have a **subject term**—a word or phrase that names a class and that serves as the grammatical subject of the sentence. In these statement forms, the subject term is represented by *S.*
3. They all have a **predicate term**—a word or phrase that names a class and that serves as the subject complement of the sentence. In these statement forms, the predicate term is represented by *P.*
4. They all have a **copula,** or linking verb, which is some form of the verb *to be.* The copula serves to link, or join, the subject term with the predicate term.

With this helpful terminology in mind, we can now offer the following tips on how to translate ordinary English sentences into standard categorical form.

Tip 1: Rephrase all nonstandard subject and predicate terms so that they refer to classes.

Many everyday English sentences have adjectives as their grammatical predicates. Because adjectives name attributes rather than classes, they must be rewritten as nouns, pronouns, or noun phrases that refer to classes. Here are two examples:

All actors are vain.	All actors are vain *people.*
Some roses are white.	Some roses are white *flowers.*

Tip 2: Rephrase all nonstandard verbs.

For the sake of consistency, only two linking verbs (copulas) are allowed in standard-form categorical statements: *are* and *are not*. Sentences that contain linking verbs other than *are* or *are not* must be rewritten in standard form. Here are two examples:

Some students walk to school.	Some students *are persons who* walk to school.
All the northern counties were flooded.	All the northern counties *are places that* were flooded.

Tip 3: Fill in any unexpressed quantifiers.

Often categorical statements have no stated quantifier. In such cases, the unexpressed quantifier must be added. Here are two examples:

Koalas are marsupials.	*All* koalas are marsupials.
Californians are health nuts.	*Some* Californians are health nuts.

Sometimes it is hard to know what quantifier a speaker or writer may have had implicitly in mind. In such cases, we should interpret the speaker's or writer's intent as charitably as possible. Here are two examples:

Bankers are conservatives.	*Some* bankers are conservatives. (*Not: All* bankers are conservatives.)
Texans are friendly.	*Some* Texans are friendly people. (*Not: All* Texans are friendly people.)[5]

Tip 4: Translate singular statements as *all* or *no* statements.

A *singular statement* makes a claim about a particular person, place, or thing. Often, with a little ingenuity, such statements can be translated into *all* or *no* statements. Here are several examples:

Caesar crossed the Rubicon.	*All persons identical with* Caesar *are persons who* crossed the Rubicon.
Joe wasn't born in Kansas.	*No persons identical with* Joe *are persons who were* born in Kansas.
Paris is the capital of France.	*All places identical with* Paris *are places that are* the capital of France.
This flower is blooming.	*All things identical with* this flower *are things that are* blooming.

Such translations, however artificial, are useful because they greatly increase the number of everyday arguments that can be tested by means of Venn diagrams.

Tip 5: Translate stylistic variants into the appropriate categorical form.

Each of the four standard categorical forms has numerous *stylistic variants*—that is, different ways of saying essentially the same thing.[6] For instance, the statement

Mary is loved by John

is a stylistic variant of the statement

John loves Mary.

Following is a list of some of the most common stylistic variants of statements of the form "All *S* are *P*."

Common Stylistic Variants of "All S are P"

Every *S* is a *P*.	*Example:* Every dog is an animal.
Whoever is an *S* is a *P*.	*Example:* Whoever is a bachelor is a male.
Whatever is an *S* is a *P*.	*Example:* Whatever is a lemon is a fruit.
If anything is an *S*, then it is a *P*.	*Example:* If anything is a lizard, then it is a reptile.
If something is not a *P*, then it is not an *S*.	*Example:* If something is not a bird, then it is not a sparrow.
Any *S* is a *P*.	*Example:* Any triangle is a geometrical figure.
Each *S* is a *P*.	*Example:* Each monkey is a primate.
S are all *P*.	*Example:* Senators are all politicians.
S are always *P*.	*Example:* Racists are always bigots.
Only *P* are *S*.	*Example:* Only Catholics are popes.
Only if something is a *P* is it an *S*.	*Example:* Only if something is a fish is it a salmon.
The only *S* are *P*.	*Example:* The only seats available are seats in the upper deck.
Something is an *S* only if it is a *P*.	*Example:* Something is an elm only if it is a tree.

Pay special attention to the phrases containing the word *only* in that list. *Only* is one of the trickiest words in the English language. Note, in particular, that as a rule the subject and predicate terms must be *reversed* if the statement begins with the words *only* or *only if*. Thus, "Only citizens are voters" must be rewritten as "All voters are citizens," not "All citizens are voters." Similarly, "Only if a thing is an insect is it a bee" must be rewritten as "All bees are insects," *not* "All insects are bees." Subject and predicate terms in sentences that contain the phrase *the only*, however, generally should *not* be reversed. Thus, "The only seats available are seats in the upper deck" means "All seats that are available are seats in the upper deck," *not* "All seats in the upper deck are available seats."

EXERCISE 9.2

Translate the following *only* sentences into standard categorical form.

1. Only doctors are psychiatrists.
2. Only fools rush in. (Elvis).

3. Something is a blue jay only if it's a bird.
4. Only if something is a Ford is it a Mustang.
5. *Sign:* Employees' restroom only.
6. The only persons eligible for the honor society are persons with a 3.8 GPA or higher.
7. Pitchers and catchers are the only players due to report on Monday.
8. No one is allowed in the hall without a pass.
9. None except senior citizens are eligible for the discount.
10. Teachers alone may use the Teacher's Lounge.
11. Fire is the devil's only friend. (Don McClean)
12. Only a lunatic would dance when sober. (Cicero)
13. God loveth none but him that dwelleth in wisdom. (Wisdom 7:28)
14. Man . . . is wholly human only when he plays. (Friedrich von Schiller)
15. I loathe none but executioners. (Albert Camus)
16. The wise man seeks only that which is useful. (Saint Thomas Aquinas)
17. We have nothing to fear but fear itself. (Franklin Roosevelt)
18. Man alone of all animals hath understanding to know his God. (George Berkeley)
19. No one is free who is not master of himself. (Epictetus)
20. "Cain't nobody tend to a man's private business but himself." (Senator Snopes, in Faulkner's *Sanctuary*)

Following is a list of some of the most common stylistic variants of statements of the form "No *S* are *P*."

Common Stylistic Variants of "No S are P"

No *P* are *S*.	*Example:* No vegetables are fruits.
S are not *P*.	*Example:* Oaks are not conifers.
Nothing that is an *S* is a *P*.	*Example:* Nothing that is a known fact is a mere opinion.
No one who is an *S* is a *P*.	*Example:* No one who is a Democrat is a Republican.
None of the *S* is a *P*.	*Example:* None of the students is a registered Independent.
Not a single *S* is *P*.	*Example:* Not a single U.S. president is a woman.
If anything is an *S*, then it is not a *P*.	*Example:* If anything is a plant, then it is not a mineral.
All *S* are non-*P*.	*Example:* All robots are nonhumans.

Following is a list of some common stylistic variants of statements of the form "Some *S* are *P*."

Common Stylistic Variants of "Some S are P"

Some *P* are *S*.	*Example:* Some Democrats are women.
A few *S* are *P*.	*Example:* A few mathematicians are poets.
There are *S* that are *P*.	*Example:* There are monkeys that are carnivores.
Several *S* are *P*.	*Example:* Several planets in the solar system are gas giants.
Many *S* are *P*.	*Example:* Many billionaires are Internet tycoons.
Most *S* are *P*.	*Example:* Most high school principals are men.
Nearly all *S* are *P*.	*Example:* Nearly all Hollywood producers are liberals.[7]

Following is a list of some common stylistic variants of statements of the form "Some *S* are not *P*."

Common Stylistic Variants of "Some S are not P"

Not all *S* are *P*.	*Example:* Not all mammals are quadrupeds.
Not everyone who is an *S* is a *P*.	*Example:* Not everyone who is a used-car dealer is a crook.
S are not always *P*.	*Example:* Sailors are not always swimmers.
Some *S* are non-*P*.	*Example:* Some theologians are nonbelievers.
There are *S* that are not *P*.	*Example:* There are bears that are not carnivores.
A few *S* are not *P*.	*Example:* A few logicians are not eccentrics.
Several *S* are not *P*.	*Example:* Several of the world's most famous sports celebrities are not good role models.
Most *S* are not *P*.	*Example:* Most students are not binge drinkers.
Nearly all *S* are not *P*.	*Example:* Nearly all physicists are not sharp dressers.

It should be emphasized that these translation tips are not intended as hard-and-fast rules. Language is far too subtle an instrument ever to be reduced to any mechanical set of do's and don'ts. The best general advice we can give is this: *Always try to restate the speaker's or writer's intended meaning as accurately as possible.* Don't assume that because two sentences look alike they can be translated alike. In the final analysis, as William Halverson remarks, there is no safe route to accurate categorical translation except "through the brain of an alert restater."[8]

EXERCISE 9.3

I. Translate the following sentences into standard-form categorical statements.

1. Maples are trees.
2. Roses are red.
3. Some bats are nocturnal.
4. Each insect is an animal.
5. Not all desserts are fattening.
6. If anything is an igloo, then it is made of ice.
7. All that glitters is not gold.
8. Cheaters never prosper.
9. Every cloud has a silver lining.
10. You have to swing the bat to hit the ball.
11. World War II began in 1939.
12. If something is not a vehicle, then it is not a car.
13. There are birds that cannot fly.
14. Almost all Wexford College students graduate in four years.
15. Not every sheep is white.
16. The grass is always greener on the other side.
17. Some persons are nonhumans.
18. Nothing is a mammal unless it is not a reptile.
19. Polar bears live in Canada.
20. Every man prefers belief to the exercise of judgment. (Seneca)
21. Success has ruined many a man. (Benjamin Franklin)
22. Show me a liar, and I will show thee a thief. (George Herbert)
23. Only the educated are free. (Epictetus)
24. Anybody who goes to see a psychiatrist ought to have his head examined. (Samuel Goldwyn)
25. The mass of men lead lives of quiet desperation. (Henry David Thoreau)
26. There is no place more delightful than home. (Cicero)
27. What's not worth doing is not worth doing well. (Don Hebb)
28. Only the fool perseveres in error. (Cicero)
29. The unexamined life is not worth living. (Socrates)
30. Faithless is he who says farewell when the road darkens. (J. R. R. Tolkien)
31. The only certainty is that nothing is certain. (Pliny the Elder)
32. Whoso would be a man must be a nonconformist. (Ralph Waldo Emerson)
33. He who has a why to live can bear with almost any how. (Friedrich Nietzsche)
34. There's ne'er a villain dwelling in all Denmark but he's an arrant knave. (Shakespeare)
35. Ignorance of the law excuses no man. (John Selden)
36. All ladies are far from alike (E. M. Forster)
37. You should never fret about trifles. (Jane Austen)
38. Nothing ventured, nothing gained. (proverb)
39. Freedom is not the answer to everything. (Albert Camus)
40. Men are all rogues, pretty nigh. (Anthony Trollope)

• Critical Thinking Lapse •

Paul Stiller, 47, was hospitalized in Andover Township, N.J., and his wife, Bonnie, was also injured, when a quarter-stick of dynamite that blew up in their car. While driving around at 2 A.M., the bored couple lit the dynamite and tried to toss it out the window to see what would happen, but they apparently failed to notice that the window was closed.[9]

---

41. Without faith it is impossible to please God. (Hebrews 11:6)
42. I can resist everything except temptation. (Oscar Wilde)
43. A law that is not just is no law. (St. Augustine)
44. Wherever you are, you should always be contented. (Jane Austen)
45. Dogs do ever bark at those they know not. (Sir Walter Raleigh)

II. Arrange the chairs in the class into a circle. Your instructor will give each student a 3-by-5-inch index card. On one side of the card, write your own original example of a stylistic variant of a standard-form categorical statement. On the other side of the card, write the correct standard-form translation of your example. (For example, you might write "Only men are uncles" on one side and the correct translation—"All uncles are men"—on the other. Check the lists of stylistic variants for ideas.) When everyone has finished, pass your card to the student sitting to your right. Read the card you have received and decide what you think is the correct translation. Then check your answer with the answer indicated on the back of the card. If your answer was wrong, place a checkmark on the back of the card. Continue passing the cards until each card has been read. The instructor will then collect the cards and go over the examples that students found difficult.

CATEGORICAL SYLLOGISMS

A **syllogism** is simply a three-line deductive argument—that is, a deductive argument that consists of two premises and a conclusion. In a **categorical syllogism,** all the statements in the argument are categorical statements. Here are several examples of categorical syllogisms:

> No doctors are professional wrestlers.
>
> All cardiologists are doctors.
>
> So, no cardiologists are professional wrestlers.

> All snakes are reptiles.
>
> All reptiles are cold-blooded animals.
>
> So, all snakes are cold-blooded animals.

> Some Baptists are coffee-lovers.
>
> All Baptists are Protestants.
>
> So, some Protestants are coffee-lovers.

I consider the invention of the form of syllogisms one of the most beautiful, and also one of the most important, made by the human mind.

—Gottfried Leibniz

◦ Critical Thinking Lapse ◦

OSLO—A drunken Norwegian who pulled a pair of underpants over his face and robbed a post office was awakened by police two days later to find he had tipped them off about his identity.

The 47-year-old drunk charged into the post office and handed over a note saying "This is a robbery," the local newspaper *Bergensavisen* reported.

But his wife's name and personal details were on the demand note, the newspaper said.

The man told a court he did not remember the robbery, but admitted he had a suspicion of having been up to no good when he woke up and saw a picture of the beknickered robber in the newspaper and found a large wad of money in his living room.[10]

No Democrats are Republicans.

Some lifeguards are Republicans.

So, some lifeguards are not Democrats.

In this section we see how Venn diagrams can be used to test the validity of categorical syllogisms.

Let's start with the first preceding example:

No doctors are professional wrestlers.

All cardiologists are doctors.

So, no cardiologists are professional wrestlers.

Because this argument, like all standard-form categorical syllogisms, has three category terms (in this case, "cardiologists," "professional wrestlers," and "doctors"), we need three interlocking circles rather than two to represent the three categories. By convention the two circles for the conclusion are placed at the bottom. Thus, the diagram for our example is as follows:

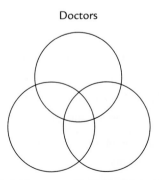

Doctors

Cardiologists   Professional wrestlers

The first premise states that no doctors are professional wrestlers. To represent this claim, we shade that part of the Doctors circle that overlaps with the Professional wrestlers circle:

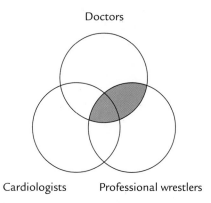

The second premise states that all cardiologists are doctors. To represent this claim, we shade that part of the Cardiologists circle that does not overlap with the Doctors circle:

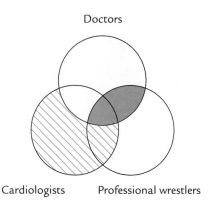

We now have all the information we need to see whether the argument is valid. The conclusion tells us that no cardiologists are professional wrestlers. This means that the area where the Cardiologists and Professional wrestlers circles overlap is shaded, that is, empty. We look at the diagram to see if this area is shaded, and we see that it is indeed shaded. That means that the conclusion is implicitly "contained in" (i.e., follows logically from) the premises. Thus, the argument is shown to be valid.

Now, let's look at the second example:

All snakes are reptiles.
All reptiles are cold-blooded animals.
So, all snakes are cold-blooded animals.

First we draw and label the three circles, placing the circles for the conclusion at the bottom:

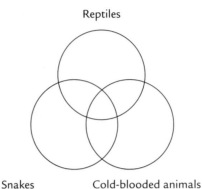

Next we diagram the first premise, which states that all snakes are reptiles. We represent this information by shading the area of the Snakes circle that does not overlap with the Reptiles circle:

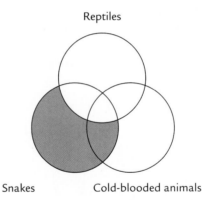

Next we diagram the second premise, which states that all reptiles are cold-blooded animals. We represent this claim by shading that part of the Reptiles circle that does not overlap with the Cold-blooded animals circle:

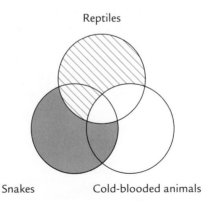

Finally, we look to see if the information contained in the conclusion is depicted in the diagram. The conclusion tells us that all snakes are cold-blooded animals. This means that the part of the Snakes circle that does not overlap with the Cold-blooded animals circle should be completely shaded. Inspection of the diagram shows that this is indeed the case. So, the argument is valid.

Let's turn to the third example:

Some Baptists are coffee-lovers.

All Baptists are Protestants.

So, some Protestants are coffee-lovers.

Notice that this example includes two *some* statements. Diagramming *some* statements is a little trickier than diagramming *all* or *no* statements. As we have seen, *some* statements are diagrammed by placing X's rather than by shading. Most mistakes in Venn diagramming involve incorrect placement of an X.

To avoid such mistakes, remember these three rules:

1. If the argument contains one *all* or *no* statement, this statement should be diagrammed first. In other words, *always do any necessary shading before placing an* X. If the argument contains two *all* or *no* statements, either statement can be done first.

2. When placing an X in an area, if one part of the area has been shaded, place the X in the unshaded part. *Examples:*

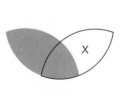
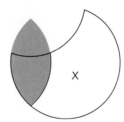

3. When placing an X in an area, if neither part of the area has been shaded, place the X precisely on the line separating the two parts. *Examples:*

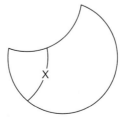

The rationales for these rules are explained in the following discussion.
Now, let's return to the third example:

Some Baptists are coffee-lovers.

All Baptists are Protestants.

So, some Protestants are coffee-lovers.

First we draw and label the three circles:

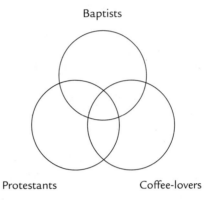

Next we need to decide which premise to diagram first. Should it be the *some* premise or the *all* premise? Suppose we start with the *some* premise. Right away we see that we have a problem: Where exactly in the overlap between the Baptists and Coffee-lovers circles do we put the *X*? Any choice at this point would be a sheer guess (and a guess that might later be shown to be wrong by additional information contained in the argument). To avoid this problem, *always diagram an* all *or a* no *premise before diagramming a* some *premise.*

So we begin by diagramming the second premise. That premise states that all Baptists are Protestants. This means that the class of Baptists that are not Protestants is empty. To represent this claim, we shade that area of the Baptists circle that does not overlap with the Protestants circle:

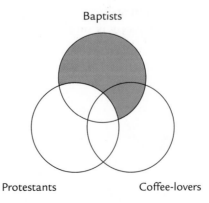

Now we can diagram the first premise, which states that some Baptists are coffee-lovers. To represent this claim, we place an *X* in the area of the Baptists circle that overlaps with the Coffee-lovers circle. Part of this area, however, is shaded. This means that there is nothing in that area. For that reason we place the *X* in the unshaded portion of the Baptists circle that overlaps with the Coffee-lovers circle:

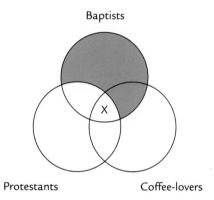

Baptists

Protestants   Coffee-lovers

Finally, we inspect the completed diagram to see if the information contained in the conclusion is represented in the diagram. The conclusion states that some Protestants are coffee-lovers. This means that there should be an *X* in the area of the Protestants circle that overlaps with the Coffee-lovers circle. A glance at the diagram shows that there is an *X* in this area. Thus, the argument is valid.

Let's turn to the fourth example:

No Democrats are Republicans.

Some lifeguards are Republicans.

So, some lifeguards are not Democrats.

First we draw and label the three circles:

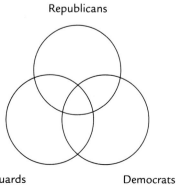

Republicans

Lifeguards   Democrats

Because one premise begins with *no* and one begins with *some,* we start by diagramming the premise that begins with *no.* That premise states that no Democrats are Republicans. To represent this information, we shade that part of the Democrats circle that overlaps with the Republicans circle:

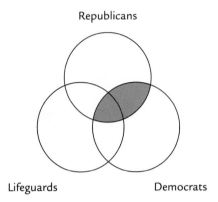

The second premise states that some lifeguards are Republicans. To diagram this claim, we place an *X* in the area of the Lifeguards circle that overlaps with the Republicans circle. Because part of this area is shaded, we place the *X* in that part of the area that is not shaded:

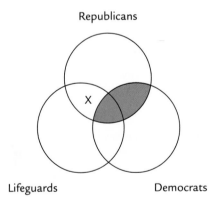

Finally, we look at the completed diagram to see if the claim made in the conclusion is represented in the diagram. The conclusion states that some lifeguards are not Democrats. This means that there should be an *X* in that part of the Lifeguards circle that does not intersect with the Democrats circle. Inspection of the diagram shows that there is an *X* in this area. Thus, the argument is shown to be valid.

So far, all the categorical syllogisms we have looked at have been valid. But Venn diagrams can also show when a categorical syllogism is invalid.

Here is one example:

All painters are artists.

Some magicians are artists.

So, some magicians are painters.

First we draw and label the three circles:

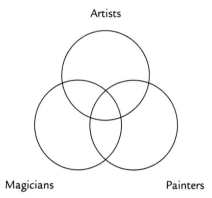

Because the first premise begins with *all* and the second premise begins with *some,* we diagram the first premise first. The first premise states that all painters are artists. To depict this claim, we shade that part of the Painters circle that does not overlap with the Artists circle:

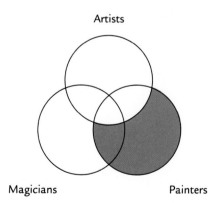

Next we enter the information of the second premise, the claim that some magicians are artists. To represent this claim, we place an X in that portion of the Magicians circle that overlaps with the Artists circle. That area, however, is divided into two parts (the areas marked "1" and "2"), and we have no information that warrants placing the X in one of these areas rather than the other. In such cases, we place the X *precisely on the line* between the two sections:

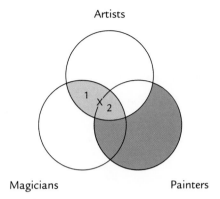

The *X* on the line means that we have no way of knowing from the information given whether the magician-who-is-an-artist is also a magician-who-is-a-painter.

The conclusion states that some magicians are painters. This means that there should be an *X* that is definitely in the area where the Magicians and Painters circles overlap. There is an *X* in the Magicians circle, but it dangles on the line between the Artists circle and the Painters circle. We don't know whether it is inside or outside the Painters circle. Consequently, the argument is invalid.

Let's look at a final example:

No scientists are toddlers.

All physicists are scientists.

So, some physicists are not toddlers.

First, we draw and label the circles:

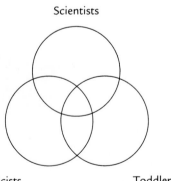

Because both of the premises are *all* or *no* statements, it doesn't matter which premise we diagram first. Let's start with the first. That premise states that no scientists are toddlers. To diagram this information, we shade that portion of the Scientists circle that intersects with the Toddlers circle:

Scientists

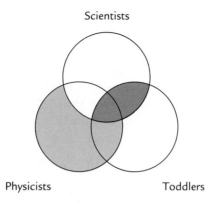

Physicists   Toddlers

Next we diagram the second premise, the claim that all physicists are scientists. To represent this claim, we shade that part of the Physicists circle that does not overlap with the Scientists circle:

Scientists

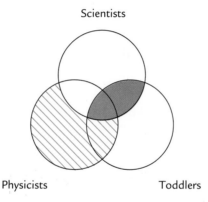

Physicists   Toddlers

Finally, we look at the diagram to see if the information contained in the conclusion is represented in the diagram. The conclusion states that some physicists are not toddlers. This means that there should be an X in the part of the Physicists circle that does not overlap with the Toddlers circle. Inspection of the diagram shows that there are no Xs at all in the diagram. Hence, the argument is invalid.

The following list summarizes the basic steps to be followed in Venn diagramming.

Using Venn Diagrams to Test the Validity of Categorical Syllogisms

Step 1: Translate all statements in the argument (if necessary) into standard-form categorical statements.

Step 2: Draw and label three overlapping circles, one for each term (class name) in the argument, with the two circles for the conclusion at the bottom.

Step 3: Use shading to represent the information in *all* or *no* statements. To diagram statements of the form "All *S* are *P*," shade that portion of

A familiarity with logical principles tends very much (as all feel, who are really well acquainted with them) to beget a habit of clear and sound reasoning.
—Richard Whately

the *S* circle that does not overlap with the *P* circle. To diagram statements of the form "No *S* are *P*," shade that portion of the *S* circle that overlaps with the *P* circle.

Use *X*'s to represent the information in *some* statements. To diagram statements of the form "Some *S* are *P*," place an *X* in that portion of the *S* circle that overlaps with the *P* circle. To diagram statements of the form "Some *S* are not *P*," place an *X* in that portion of the *S* circle that does not overlap with the *P* circle.

Step 4: Diagram the two premises. (No marks should be entered for the conclusion.) If the argument contains one *all* or *no* premise and one *some* premise, diagram the *all* or *no* premise first. Otherwise, diagram either premise first.

Step 5: When placing an *X* in a two-part area, if one part of the area has been shaded, place the *X* in the unshaded part. If neither part of the area has been shaded, place the *X* precisely on the line separating the two parts.

Step 6: Look to see if the diagram contains all the information presented in the conclusion. If it does, the argument is valid. If it doesn't, the argument is invalid.

It takes practice to become skilled at Venn diagramming. Once you get the hang of it, however, you'll find that it is a neat way to check the validity of a surprisingly wide range of everyday arguments.

EXERCISE 9.4

I. Use Venn diagrams to test the validity of the following arguments.

1. No sharks are pets, since no barracuda are pets, and no sharks are barracuda.
2. No farmers are city dwellers. Hence, since all city dwellers are urbanites, no urbanites are farmers.
3. All curmudgeons are pessimists. All pessimists are cynics. So, some cynics are curmudgeons.
4. Some bankers are vegetarians. No anarchists are bankers. So, some anarchists are not vegetarians.
5. No beach bums are workaholics. Some beach bums are rollerbladers. So, some rollerbladers are not workaholics.
6. All violinists are musicians. Therefore, since some bookworms are violinists, some bookworms are musicians.
7. No poker players are early risers. Some firefighters are early risers. So, some firefighters are not poker players.
8. Some dot-com millionaires are philanthropists. All philanthropists are altruists. Hence, some altruists are dot-com millionaires.
9. Some telemarketers are Methodists. Some Methodists are Democrats. So, some Democrats are telemarketers.

10. No Fords are Pontiacs. All Escorts are Fords. So, some Escorts are not Pontiacs.

11. No mockingbirds are cardinals. Some cardinals are songbirds. So, some songbirds are not mockingbirds.

12. All ecologists are environmentalists. Hence, because all ecologists are wilderness-lovers, all wilderness-lovers are environmentalists.

13. No landlubbers are sailors. Some sailors are not pirates. So, some pirates are not landlubbers.

14. All cats are carnivores. All tigers are cats. So, all tigers are carnivores.

15. All sound arguments are valid arguments. Therefore, because some sound arguments are mathematical arguments, some mathematical arguments are not valid arguments.

16. No fish are reptiles. All trout are fish. So, some trout are not reptiles.

17. Some dreamers are not romantics, because some idealists are not romantics, and all idealists are dreamers.

18. Some stockbrokers are couch potatoes. Hence, because all stockbrokers are e-traders, some e-traders are couch potatoes.

19. Some butchers are not bakers. No butchers are candlestick makers. Therefore, some candlestick makers are not bakers.

20. All meteorologists are forecasters. Hence, because some forecasters are psychics, some psychics are meteorologists.

II. Translate the following into standard categorical form. Then use Venn diagrams to test the arguments for validity.

1. No one who is a Nobel Prize winner is a rock star. A number of astrophysicists are Nobel Prize winners. Therefore, a number of astrophysicists are not rock stars.

2. Many philosophers are determinists. Anyone who is a fatalist is a determinist. So, many fatalists are philosophers.

3. If anything is a maple, then it's a tree. Hence, because nothing that is a bush is a tree, nothing that is a bush is a maple.

4. Everybody who is a liberal is a big spender. Therefore, because Senator Crumley is a big spender, Senator Crumley is a liberal.

5. Many tarot-readers are lottery players. Every tarot-reader is a fraud. So, many frauds are not lottery players.

6. Only poems are sonnets. No mathematical treatise is a poem. Therefore, no mathematical treatise is a sonnet.

7. At least one lawyer is not a golfer. Only persons who have attended law school are lawyers. So, at least one person who has attended law school is not a golfer.

8. No one who is a cardsharp is a psychic. Someone is a cardsharp only if he is a poker player. Therefore, some poker players are not psychics.

9. Whatever is a fish is a nonmammal. Each pickerel is a fish. So, no pickerel is a mammal.

10. Only social scientists are political scientists. Many political scientists are persons who favor campaign finance reform. Accordingly, many persons who favor campaign finance reform are social scientists.

11. Egoists are not humanitarians. Not a single humanitarian is a sweatshop owner. So, not a single sweatshop owner is an egoist.

12. There are e-mail messages that are not spell-checked. There are interoffice memos that are e-mail messages. Therefore, there are interoffice memos that are not spell-checked.

13. Every tax evader is a lawbreaker. Hence, because no one who is a lawbreaker is a model citizen, no one who is a model citizen is a tax evader.

14. If anything is a truck, then it is not a car. There are Mazdas that are trucks. It follows that there are Mazdas that are not cars.

15. Any dog is furry. Lassie is a dog. So, Lassie is furry.

16. Not every lie is immoral, for no harmless acts are immoral and some lies are harmless.

17. Mystics are always religious. At least one religious person is not greedy. Consequently, at least one mystic is not greedy.

18. Every person who drinks and drives is an irresponsible person. Not every person who talks on a car phone is an irresponsible person. Hence, not every person who talks on a car phone is a person who drinks and drives.

19. Anyone who eats pizza every night is at risk for heart disease. Some people who are at risk for heart disease are cab drivers. So, some cab drivers are people who eat pizza every night.

20. Joey is in kindergarten. Only children in kindergarten fingerpaint in school. So, Joey fingerpaints in school.

SUMMARY

1. A *categorical statement* makes a claim about the relationship between two or more classes or categories of things. In this chapter we focused mainly on *standard-form categorical statements,* which have one of the following four forms: All *S* are *P,* No *S* are *P,* Some *S* are *P,* or Some *S* are not *P.*

2. Standard-form categorical statements have four basic parts:

   • They all begin with the word *all, no,* or *some.* These words are called *quantifiers* because they are used to express a quantity or a number.

   • They all have a *subject term*—a word or phrase that names a class and that serves as the grammatical subject of the sentence. In the four statement forms listed above, the subject term is represented by *S.*

   • They all have a *predicate term*—a word or phrase that names a class and that serves as the subject complement of the sentence. In the statement forms listed above, the predicate term is represented by *P.*

   • They all have a *copula,* or linking verb, which is either *are* or *are not.* The copula serves to link, or join, the subject term with the predicate term.

3. With a little ingenuity, many ordinary English sentences can be translated into standard-form categorical statements. When translating into standard categorical form, keep in mind the following tips:

   Tip 1: Rephrase all nonstandard subject and predicate terms so that they refer to classes.

   Tip 2: Rephrase all nonstandard verbs so that the statement includes the linking verb *are* or *are not.*

   Tip 3: Fill in any unexpressed quantifiers.

   Tip 4: Translate singular statements as *all* or *no* statements.

   Tip 5: Translate stylistic variants into the appropriate categorical form.

4. A *categorical syllogism* is a three-line deductive argument in which all three statements in the argument are categorical statements. A simple way to test the validity of categorical syllogisms is to use *Venn diagrams,* in which overlapping circles represent relationships among classes. The Venn diagram technique for checking the validity of categorical syllogisms involves six basic steps:

   Step 1: Translate all statements in the argument (if necessary) into standard-form categorical statements.

   Step 2: Draw and label three overlapping circles, one for each term (class name) in the argument, with the two circles for the conclusion at the bottom.

   Step 3: Use shading to represent the information in *all* or *no* statements. To diagram statements of the form "All *S* are *P,*" shade that portion of the *S* circle that does not overlap with the *P* circle. To diagram statements of the form "No *S* are *P,*" shade that portion of the *S* circle that overlaps with the *P* circle.

   Use *X*'s to represent the information in *some* statements. To diagram statements of the form "Some *S* are *P,*" place an *X* in that portion of the *S* circle that overlaps with the *P* circle. To diagram statements of the form "Some *S* are not *P,*" place an *X* in that portion of the *S* circle that does not overlap with the *P* circle.

   Step 4: Diagram the two premises. (No marks should be entered for the conclusion.) If the argument contains one *all* or *no* premise and one *some* premise, diagram the *all* or *no* premise first. If the argument contains two *some* or two *all* or *no* premises, diagram either premise first.

   Step 5: When placing an *X* in a two-part area, if one part of the area has been shaded, place the *X* in the unshaded part. If neither part of the area has been shaded, place the *X* on the line separating the two parts.

   Step 6: Look to see if the completed diagram contains all the information presented in the conclusion. If it does, the argument is valid. If it does not, the argument is invalid.

CHAPTER 10

A LITTLE
PROPOSITIONAL LOGIC

It is often difficult to determine whether a long and complex argument is valid or invalid just by reading it. Consider the following example:

> If the Democrat loses the Senate race, the Republicans will have a majority in the Senate.
>
> If the Republicans have a majority in the Senate, the Senate will vote down the new bill.
>
> It is not the case that the Senate will vote down the new bill or the Democrat will lose the Senate race.
>
> So, it is not the case that if the Democrat does not lose, the Senate will not vote down the new bill.

Can you tell whether that argument is valid or invalid? Most people can't. In this chapter we learn the basics of **propositional logic,** a way to symbolize the parts of arguments so that we can analyze whole arguments for validity. By the end of the chapter, difficult examples, such as the one above, will be easy to analyze.

The method we present for analyzing arguments for validity involves assigning variables to the different parts of the argument, much as we do in algebra. For example, if $a = 3$ and $b = 7$, then $a + b = 10$. With the same variables, we can solve for an unknown: $a + c = b$, so $3 + c = 7$. We know that c must equal 4. We won't be solving equations or crunching numbers in this chapter, but we will be using variables to consider arguments in a more abstract and more manageable way. In algebra we start with variables whose values we know and solve for variables whose values we don't know. Similarly, in propositional logic we start by assigning variables to the parts of the argument that are given and "solve for" what we don't know, namely, whether the argument is valid or invalid.

Propositional logic is nothing to be afraid of. In fact, some students consider it the most enjoyable and interesting part of their critical thinking course. With some practice anyone can become a master of propositional logic. This

The object of reasoning is to find out, from the consideration of what we already know, something else which we do not know.

—Charles S. Peirce

chapter is full of exercises, so you'll get all the practice you need. We start with simple arguments and gradually build up to more-complex arguments.

CONJUNCTION

As we learned in Chapter 2, arguments are composed of statements. A **statement** is a sentence that can sensibly be regarded as either true or false. A **simple statement** consists of just one sentence that sensibly can be regarded as either true or false—for example, "Tina is tall." A **compound statement** consists of two or more statements, each of which can separately be considered either true or false—for example, "Tina is tall, and Sarah is tall."

Sometimes the premise or the conclusion of an argument is a simple statement, such as "Tina is tall." We can easily symbolize a simple statement by assigning it a variable. Let's assign "Tina is tall" the variable p. If the argument contains a second simple statement—for example, "Sarah is tall"—we can symbolize it by assigning it a different variable. Let's assign "Sarah is tall" the variable q.

Let's assume that we do not know whether our premises are true or false. In that case, each of the variables has two possible **truth values;** that is, each variable could be true or it could be false. With that in mind, we can now set up a truth table for each variable. A **truth table** is just a list of all possible truth values.

The truth table for p is

$$p$$
$$\overline{}$$
$$T$$
$$F$$

The truth table displays the information that p is either true or false.

We can do the same now for our second variable, q:

$$q$$
$$\overline{}$$
$$T$$
$$F$$

This displays the information that q is either true or false.

Let's consider the compound statement "Tina is tall, and Sarah is tall." This compound statement consists of two simple statements joined by the word *and*. In grammar the word *and* is a conjunction; that is, it "conjoins," or joins together, two elements. In propositional logic a **conjunction** is a compound statement. Notice that the conjunction "Tina is tall, and Sarah is tall" consists of two simple statements to which we have already assigned variables, p and q, joined by the word *and*. In propositional logic we symbolize the word *and* with the ampersand, *&*. Thus, we symbolize the conjunction "Tina is tall, and Sarah is tall" as p & q.

Now we are ready to determine the truth values for *p* & *q*. The compound statement *p* & *q* is true only when both of its variables stand for true simple statements. Put another way, only when *p* is true and *q* is true is the statement *p* & *q* true. If either *p* or *q* is false, the statement *p* & *q* is false. If both *p* and *q* are false, the whole statement *p* & *q* is false. To set up the truth table for *p* & *q*, we need to account for all four possible combinations of *p* & *q*. We do this as follows:

p	*q*	*p* & *q*
T	T	T
T	F	F
F	T	F
F	F	F

In a truth table that includes two variables, the first two columns will follow the pattern of the two columns in the truth table shown above. The first variable is true in the first and second lines and false in the third and fourth. The second variable alternates between true and false. Although all four possible combinations of the two variables can be obtained in other ways, this is the conventional way of setting up a truth table with two variables and is the easiest to remember.

We used *p* & *q* to stand for "Tina is tall, and Sarah is tall," but *p* & *q* can be used to stand for other compound statements as well. The compound statement "Winter is cold, and summer is warm" could also be represented by *p* & *q*, where *p* stands for "winter is cold" and *q* stands for "summer is warm." In fact, *p* & *q* is a propositional form that can stand for an infinite number of compound statements: "The train is late, and the bus is on time"; "The sky is blue, and the grass is green"; and so on.

A word of caution: Not every use of the word *and* indicates a compound statement that can be represented by *p* & *q*. That makes sense, given the fact that the word *and* does not always join two simple statements. Sometimes *and* joins two things within the same simple statement—for example, "The Knicks and the Bulls are playing each other tonight." This is one simple statement, not two, and is properly symbolized by a single variable, say, *p*.

To determine whether a statement is simple or compound, we must ask ourselves what the statement means. Our example does not consist of two simple statements: "The Knicks are playing each other tonight" and "The Bulls are playing each other tonight." Rather, it is one simple statement: "The Knicks and the Bulls are playing each other tonight." Take another example: "Peanut butter and jelly is my favorite lunch." This too is a single simple statement and is properly symbolized by a single variable, say, *q*. To see the contrast, consider a compound statement: "I like peanut butter, and she likes jelly." This compound statement consists of two simple statements joined by the word *and*. Thus, it is properly symbolized by the conjunction of two variables, say, *r* & *s*. If we are ever unsure whether a statement is simple or compound, we should ask ourselves, "What does the statement mean?" Does the statement consist of two simple statements? If it does, it is compound. If it doesn't, it is simple.

Don't feel that you always have to use the variables p, q, r, and s. Any letters will do. Be careful, however, that you don't repeat variables when you symbolize an argument. Once a variable has been used to represent one statement, it cannot be used again to represent a different statement in the same argument. We'll discuss this more when we get deeper into analyzing argument forms for validity.

Propositional logic has many advantages when it comes to dealing with arguments, but it also has one important disadvantage: it does not capture the richness of everyday language. For example, there may be a big difference in emphasis between "He likes Fords, and she likes Chevys" and "He likes Fords, *but* she likes Chevys." The first statement may simply be pointing out the likes of two different people, whereas the second may be contrasting their different likes. The fact is that each of the two compound statements is true only when both of its simple statements are true—that is, when it is true that he likes Fords and it is true that she likes Chevys. In every other case, it is false. Because in propositional logic there is no difference in logical significance between the words *but* and *and,* they are interchangeable for the purposes of determining truth value. So, both of the compound statements fit the propositional form p & q, and both can be analyzed by the following truth table:

p	q	p & q
T	T	T
T	F	F
F	T	F
F	F	F

In propositional logic any word that conjoins two simple statements is symbolized by the ampersand, &. For the purposes of propositional logic, then, all these words are equivalent and can be symbolized by the ampersand: *and, but, yet, while, whereas, although, though,* and *however.* The following compound statements are all correctly symbolized as p & q:

Tony had steak, *and* Theresa had chicken.

Tony had steak, *but* Theresa had chicken.

Tony had steak, *yet* Theresa had chicken.

Tony had steak, *while* Theresa had chicken.

Tony had steak, *whereas* Theresa had chicken.

Tony had steak, *although* Theresa had chicken.

Tony had steak, *though* Theresa had chicken.

Tony had steak; *however* Theresa had chicken.

Each of these compound statements has a slightly different emphasis, but each is true only when it is true that Tony had steak and it is also true that Theresa had chicken.

EXERCISE 10.1

I. Put the following statements in symbolic form.

1. Ken hit a home run.
2. Hank went fishing, and Dirk went hunting.
3. Hank and Dirk went fishing.
4. Hank went fishing, but Dirk went hunting.
5. The train was late, and the bus was on time.
6. The train was late, though the bus was on time.
7. France is in Europe, and China is in Asia.
8. France is in Europe, but China is in Asia.
9. France and Germany are in Europe.
10. Sally ate a peanut butter and jelly sandwich, whereas Nancy ate a salad.

II. Let the following variables stand for the following statements:

a = December is cold. x = February is sunny.
b = June is warm. y = July is cold.
c = March is windy. z = August is snowy.

Assume that a, b, and c are true and x, y, and z are false. Determine whether each of the following is true or false.

1. $a \,\&\, b$ 6. $c \,\&\, a$
2. $b \,\&\, z$ 7. $c \,\&\, z$
3. $z \,\&\, y$ 8. $x \,\&\, y$
4. $c \,\&\, b$ 9. $a \,\&\, c$
5. $x \,\&\, z$ 10. $y \,\&\, a$

III. Without knowing what they stand for, assume for the sake of this exercise that p, q, and r are true and w, x, and y are false. Determine whether each of the following is true or false.

1. $p \,\&\, q$ 6. $y \,\&\, w$
2. $p \,\&\, w$ 7. $x \,\&\, w$
3. $x \,\&\, y$ 8. $q \,\&\, r$
4. $r \,\&\, q$ 9. $p \,\&\, y$
5. $r \,\&\, y$ 10. $r \,\&\, p$

CONJUNCTION AND VALIDITY

Now we are ready to symbolize arguments and analyze them for validity. We already know enough to deal with some very basic arguments. Consider this one:

Tina is tall.

Sarah is tall.

So, Tina is tall, and Sarah is tall.

We can symbolize the argument as follows (in propositional logic the symbol ∴ simply indicates that the conclusion follows):

p

q

∴ *p* & *q*

It should be clear to you just by reading it that this argument is valid, but it is a handy example for illustrating the truth table method for establishing validity. In the previous section, we learned how to set up truth tables for statements; now we'll see how truth tables can be used to determine the validity or invalidity of arguments.

First we must set up the truth table:

p	*q*	*p* & *q*
T	T	T
T	F	F
F	T	F
F	F	F

The truth table above starts with columns for the basic building blocks, the two variables *p* and *q*, and ends with a column for their conjunction, *p* & *q*. In this case, the three columns represent the two premises of the argument and the conclusion. To analyze the truth table for validity or invalidity, we have to recall one very important piece of information about validity: *In a valid argument, it is impossible for all the premises to be true and the conclusion false. So, in examining the truth table, we look for instances in which all the premises are true. If any instance of all true premises is followed by a false conclusion—an F under the conclusion column—the argument is invalid.* It doesn't matter if there are instances in the truth table in which all the premises are true and the conclusion is true, too. If it is even possible for an argument's conclusion to be false while all the premises are true, the argument is invalid.

Let's reconsider the truth table for the argument form we have been examining:

p	*q*	*p* & *q*
T	T	T
T	F	F
F	T	F
F	F	F

> *The greatest progress men have made lies in their learning how to draw correct inferences.*
>
> —Friedrich Nietzsche

There is only one case, the first line across, in which both of the premises are true. And in this case, the conclusion is true as well. This tells us that the argument form for "Tina is tall. Sarah is tall. Therefore, Tina is tall, and Sarah is tall" is valid. That is, the argument form

p

q

$\therefore p \,\&\, q$

is valid. Any two arguments that share the same argument form are either both valid or both invalid. When we know that an argument form is valid, we know that any argument that fits that form is valid.

Thus, we know, for example, that the argument

The sky is blue.

The grass is green.

Therefore, the sky is blue, and the grass is green.

is valid because it fits the valid argument form

p

q

$\therefore p \,\&\, q$

Consider another argument:

Grass is green.

So, grass is green, and the sky is blue.

We hope it is obvious to you that this argument is invalid. Its conclusion may be true, but it doesn't follow from its premise. We can symbolize this argument in the following way:

p

$\therefore p \,\&\, q$

The truth table set up for the argument is familiar to us by now:

p	q	$p \,\&\, q$
T	T	T
T	F	F
F	T	F
F	F	F

We now must examine the truth table to see if there are any cases in which all the premises are true (this argument has only one premise) and the conclusion is false. In other words, are there any cases in which we get a T under the p column and an F under the $p \,\&\, q$ column?

Examining truth tables for validity takes a careful eye. In this book we will mark premises with an asterisk, *, and conclusions with a capital C. This method isn't pretty, but it helps us remember with which columns we are concerned. Because you don't have to be a graphic designer to make an asterisk or a capital C, you can do the same in making your own truth tables for homework exercises. (It isn't *necessary* to use the asterisk and capital C, but it may help you to avoid careless mistakes at first.) In our examples the line across that ultimately allows us to determine validity or invalidity will be circled. Circles are easy to draw and are helpful in focusing attention on lines that are crucial for determining validity.

Here is our truth table appropriately marked:

p^*	q	$p \, \& \, q$ C
T	T	T
(T)	F	(F)
F	T	F
F	F	F

There are two relevant lines across, two cases in which the premise is true. In the first line, the premise is true and the conclusion is true as well. But in the second line, the premise is true and the conclusion is false. This second line allows us to determine that the argument form is invalid. Our examination of the truth table has established that the argument "Grass is green. So, grass is green, and the sky is blue" is invalid. Even more important, it has established that any argument that has the form

p

$\therefore p \, \& \, q$

is invalid.

Consider one more argument:

Franklin is short and stout.

So, Franklin is short.

We must recognize that the first statement is a compound statement. It is an abbreviated way of saying "Franklin is short, and Franklin is stout." Clearly, we can symbolize the argument as follows:

$p \, \& \, q$

$\therefore p$

In setting up the truth table for analyzing this argument form, we start with the basics:

p	q	$p \, \& \, q$
T	T	T
T	F	F
F	T	F
F	F	F

All the information we need to determine the validity or invalidity of the argument form is in the truth table as it stands. To make it easier to examine, though, we can mark the premise and the conclusion:

p C	q	p & q*
T	T	T
T	F	F
F	T	F
F	F	F

To make it even easier and to minimize the chances of making a careless mistake in looking at the argument, we can treat the first two columns as "guide columns" and line up our premises and conclusion from left to right. It isn't necessary to do this, but it is never wrong to repeat information in a truth table, especially if it helps you see the columns and analyze for validity.

p	q	p & q*	p C
T	T	T	T
T	F	F	T
F	T	F	F
F	F	F	F

As the truth table shows, in the only case in which the single premise is true the conclusion is true as well. So, the argument form is valid.

EXERCISE 10.2

I. Determine the validity of the following argument forms using truth tables.

1. *p*
   q
   ∴ *p & q*
2. *p & q*
   ∴ *q*
3. *r*
   ∴ *r & s*
4. *r*
   ∴ *s*
5. *r & s*
   ∴ *r*

II. Put the following arguments in symbolic form and then test them for validity using a truth table.

1. The train was on time. The bus was late. So, the train was on time, and the bus was late.
2. The train was on time. So, the train was on time, but the bus was late.
3. The train was on time. So, the bus was late.

NEGATION

The next element of propositional logic we need to learn is **negation,** which is simply the use of the word *not* (or an equivalent word or phrase) to deny a statement. Let's return to the simple statement "Tina is tall." The negation of this simple statement would be "Tina is *not* tall." If we symbolize "Tina is tall" by assigning it the variable p, we need a convenient way of symbolizing the negation of p, "not p." The conventional symbol for negation is the tilde, ~. So, we can symbolize "Tina is not tall" with ~p.

As you might expect, the truth values for the negation of a statement are the opposite of those for the original statement. When p is true, ~p is false. This makes sense when you consider that when "Tina is tall" is true, "Tina is not tall" must be false. The following, then, are the truth tables for p and ~p:

p	~p
T	F
F	T

It is impossible for anything at the same time to be and not to be . . . this is the most indisputable of all principles.

—Aristotle

The same pattern holds true for all other variables. If we assign "Sarah is tall" the variable q, we symbolize "Sarah is *not* tall" with ~q:

q	~q
T	F
F	T

Now let's use negation and conjunction together. Consider the statement "Tina is tall, and Sarah is not tall." We can symbolize this as p & ~q. To get the truth table for this statement, we first set up the four possible combinations of p's and q's:

p	q
T	T
T	F
F	T
F	F

Next we add the column for ~q, determining the truth value for ~q in each case by taking the opposite of the corresponding truth value for q:

p	q	~q
T	T	F
T	F	T
F	T	F
F	F	T

Finally, we add the column for p & $\sim q$. We determine the truth values for p & $\sim q$ by examining the p column and the $\sim q$ column. *Remember:* A conjunction is true only when both of its statements are true. So, in this case, p & $\sim q$ will be true only when there is a T in the p column and a T in the $\sim q$ column for the same line across:

p	q	$\sim q$	p & $\sim q$
T	T	F	F
T	F	T	T
F	T	F	F
F	F	T	F

Now we are ready to examine an argument that involves both negation and conjunction: "Tina is not tall, but Sarah is tall. So, Tina is not tall." The symbolic form for the argument is

$\sim p$ & q

$\therefore \sim p$

Let's set up the truth table for the argument:

p	q	$\sim p$	$\sim p$ & q^*	$\sim p$ C
T	T	F	F	F
T	F	F	F	F
F	T	T	T	T
F	F	T	F	T

Our argument has one premise and a conclusion. We have set up the premise and the conclusion so that they read from left to right and have marked them accordingly, to keep our attention focused and prevent careless mistakes. Now we must see if there are any cases in which all the premises are true (this argument has only one premise, $\sim p$ & q) and the conclusion is false. We find that our premise is true under only one condition, represented in the third line of the column. And we find that in that third line the conclusion is also true. There are no cases in which all the premises are true and the conclusion is false, so we know that the argument form is valid.

Consider another argument:

Frank does not drive a truck.

So, Frank does not drive a truck, and Vinny does not drive a minivan.

The symbolic form for the argument is

$\sim p$

$\therefore \sim p$ & $\sim q$

Let's set up the truth table for the argument:

p	q	$\~p$	$\~q$	$\~p$*	$\~p$ & $\~q$ C
T	T	F	F	F	F
T	F	F	T	F	F
F	T	T	F	T	F
F	F	T	T	T	T

The first two columns are "guide columns," which lay out the truth values for the four possible occurrences of p and q. The third column lays out the truth values for $\~p$, and the fourth column lays out the truth values for $\~q$. ($\~q$ isn't an independent statement in the argument, but we need it as a building block in forming $\~p$ & $\~q$.) The final column lays out the truth values for $\~p$ & $\~q$. Remember that this conjunction is true only when there is a T in the $\~p$ column and a T in the $\~q$ column. This occurs once, in the fourth line across.

To determine whether the argument is valid or invalid, we examine the truth table to see if there are any cases in which the premise is true and the conclusion is false. In the third line across, the premise is true and the conclusion is false. This alone tells us that the argument form is invalid. In the fourth line across, the premise is true and so is the conclusion, but that doesn't matter. We already know from the third line that the argument form is invalid.

Be careful in dealing with negation. Sometimes a negation applies only to a single simple statement, as in "Lisa does not drive a Jeep," symbolized as $\~p$. Sometimes there are two negations applying to both elements of a compound statement, as in "Lisa does not drive a Jeep, and Jennifer does not drive a Jeep," symbolized as $\~p$ & $\~q$. At other times, one negation applies to a whole compound statement. For example, "It is not the case that Lisa drives a Jeep and Jennifer drives a Jeep," symbolized as $\~(p$ & $q)$. We need to be clear about what this statement means to symbolize it properly. When we consider it carefully, we realize that this statement isn't necessarily saying that Lisa does *not* drive a Jeep *and* Jennifer does *not* drive a Jeep. Rather, it is claiming that it is *not true* that *both* of them drive a Jeep. One of them may drive a Jeep, or neither of them may drive a Jeep. It is just claiming that it isn't the case that both of them drive a Jeep.

To symbolize the statement "It is not the case that Lisa drives a Jeep and Jennifer drives a Jeep," we need a way of showing that the negation applies to the whole statement rather than to just a specific part. To make this distinction, we use parentheses. So, we symbolize "It is not the case that Lisa drives a Jeep and Jennifer drives a Jeep" as $\~(p$ & $q)$. As in mathematics we do the work inside the parentheses first. If there is more than one set of parentheses, we start with the innermost set and work outward. So, first we determine if p & q is true or false, then we negate our answer. So, for example, if p & q is true, we know that $\~(p$ & $q)$ is false. Thus, in forming the truth table for $\~(p$ & $q)$, we first list the truth values for p & q, then we assign the opposite truth values to $\~(p$ & $q)$.

p	q	$p \& q$	$\sim(p \& q)$
T	T	T	F
T	F	F	T
F	T	F	T
F	F	F	T

Accuracy in the placement of the negation is not an insignificant detail. It affects the meaning of a statement. Consider this argument:

> It is not the case that Tina is tall and Sarah is tall.
>
> So, Tina is not tall, and Sarah is not tall.

Is the argument valid? If the premise and the conclusion really mean the same thing, the argument would have to be valid.

The symbolic form of the argument is

$\sim(p \& q)$

$\therefore \sim p \& \sim q$

Now let's look at the truth table for the argument:

p	q	$p \& q$	$\sim p$	$\sim q$	$\sim(p \& q)^*$	$\sim p \& \sim q$ C
T	T	T	F	F	F	F
T	F	F	F	T	T	F
F	T	F	T	F	T	F
F	F	F	T	T	T	T

By examining the truth table, we can easily see that the argument form is not valid. In the second line, the premise is true and the conclusion is false. On that basis alone, we know that the argument form is invalid. This should make it clear that placement of the negation makes a big difference to what a statement means and to whether the argument it is a part of is valid or invalid.

EXERCISE 10.3

I. Assume that a, b, and c are true and x, y, and z are false, then determine whether each of the following is true or false.

1. $\sim a \& b$
2. $\sim x \& \sim y$
3. $\sim(x \& y)$
4. $\sim(a \& b)$
5. $\sim z \& \sim c$
6. $c \& \sim z$
7. $\sim(c \& \sim z)$
8. $y \& x$
9. $\sim(y \& x)$
10. $\sim x \& \sim z$

II. Translate each of the symbolic statements in Exercise I into a statement in English.

III. Put the following statements in symbolic form.

1. The bus was on time, but the train was not.
2. The bus was not on time, and the train was not on time.
3. It's not the case that the bus and the train were on time.
4. Lemons are not sweet, but sugar is.
5. It's not the case that lemons and sugar are sweet.
6. Her friends don't care, and her parents don't, either.
7. Her friends care, but her parents don't.
8. It's not the case that her friends and her parents care.
9. Intentions don't matter, though actions do.
10. It's not the case that intentions and actions matter.

IV. Determine the validity of the following arguments using truth tables.

1. ~p
   q
   ∴ ~p & q
2. ~p
   ~q
   ∴ ~(p & q)
3. ~p & ~q
   ∴ ~(p & q)
4. ~(p & q)
   p
   ∴ ~q
5. ~(p & q)
   ~p
   ∴ ~q

V. Put the following arguments in symbolic form, then test them for validity using a truth table.

1. Vegas Jack didn't commit the crime, and the Weasel didn't commit the crime. So, it is not the case that Vegas Jack and the Weasel committed the crime.
2. It's not the case that Vegas Jack and the Weasel committed the crime. So, the Weasel didn't commit the crime.
3. It's not the case that John failed Calculus and Chemistry. John didn't fail Calculus. So, he didn't fail Chemistry.
4. It's not the case that John failed Calculus and Chemistry. John failed Calculus. So, he didn't fail Chemistry.
5. It's not the case that John failed Calculus and Chemistry. So, John didn't fail Calculus and didn't fail Chemistry.

DEEPER ANALYSIS OF NEGATION AND CONJUNCTION

In learning propositional logic, we need to start with simple building blocks and gradually erect a more complex structure. So far all the arguments we have examined have had only two variables, but now we are ready to work with arguments that have three variables.[1] Everything we have learned so far holds true. The process just gets a little lengthier and more involved.

Consider this example:

Tina is tall.

Sarah is not tall, but Missy is tall.

So, Tina is tall, and Missy is tall.

Let p = "Tina is tall," q = "Sarah is tall," and r = "Missy is tall." The symbolic form of the argument is

p

$\sim q \& r$

$\therefore p \& r$

Before analyzing the argument, let's see how to set up our three guide columns for the three basic variables. With two variables there are only four possible combinations of truth values; with three variables there are eight. The conventional way to set up the truth table for three variables is as follows: The first column contains four "trues" followed by four "falses." The second column contains alternating pairs of true and false. The third column contains alternating trues and falses.

	p	q	r
1.	T	T	T
2.	T	T	F
3.	T	F	T
4.	T	F	F
5.	F	T	T
6.	F	T	F
7.	F	F	T
8.	F	F	F

When working with three variables, we can keep things in order by numbering the lines 1 through 8. Once we have the three guide columns set up, everything else follows naturally. All the rules we have learned so far apply. For a conjunction to be true, both of its variables must be true. The truth value of a negation is the opposite of the truth value of the statement it negates.

Now let's form the truth table for the argument form

p

$\sim q \& r$

$\therefore p \& r$

	p	q	r	~q	p*	~q & r*	p & r C
1.	T	T	T	F	T	F	T
2.	T	T	F	F	T	F	F
3.	T	F	T	T	T	T	T
4.	T	F	F	T	T	F	F
5.	F	T	T	F	F	F	F
6.	F	T	F	F	F	F	F
7.	F	F	T	T	F	T	F
8.	F	F	F	T	F	F	F

The columns for p, q, and r are set up in the conventional way. The truth values in the ~q column are the opposite of the corresponding truth values in the q column. The truth values for the ~q & r column are determined by consulting the ~q column and the r column. Only in lines 3 and 7 is there a T in both columns, so only lines 3 and 7 are true under the ~q & r column. All other lines under ~q & r are false. The truth values for the p & r column are determined by consulting the p column and the r column. Only in lines 1 and 3 are both premises true, so only in lines 1 and 3 is p & r true.

The validity of an argument with three variables is determined in the same way as the validity of an argument with two variables. There simply are eight lines to check instead of four. *If there is any line in which all the premises are true and the conclusion is false, we know the argument is invalid. If there is no such line, we know the argument is valid.* Look at the table again.

	p	q	r	~q	p*	~q & r*	p & r C
1.	T	T	T	F	T	F	T
2.	T	T	F	F	T	F	F
3.	T	F	T	T	T	T	T
4.	T	F	F	T	T	F	F
5.	F	T	T	F	F	F	F
6.	F	T	F	F	F	F	F
7.	F	F	T	T	F	T	F
8.	F	F	F	T	F	F	F

Only in line 3 are both premises true, and in line 3 the conclusion is true as well. There are no cases in which both premises are true and the conclusion is false. So, the argument is valid.

Consider another three-variable example:

~(p & q)

~q & r

∴ ~p

First we set up the truth table, starting with the three basic variables and building from there. Then we examine the table to determine validity.

	p	q	r	$\sim q$	p & q	$\sim(p$ & $q)$*	$\sim q$ & r*	$\sim p$ C
1.	T	T	T	F	T	F	F	F
2.	T	T	F	F	T	F	F	F
3.	T	F	T	T	F	T	T	F
4.	T	F	F	T	F	T	F	F
5.	F	T	T	F	F	T	F	T
6.	F	T	F	F	F	T	F	T
7.	F	F	T	T	F	T	T	T
8.	F	F	F	T	F	T	F	T

To set up the truth table, we follow the familiar pattern. We derive the truth values for the first premise, $\sim(p$ & $q)$, by constructing a column for p & q and then taking the negation of each line's corresponding truth value. We assign truth values to $\sim q$ & r by consulting the column for $\sim q$ and the column for r. We derive the truth values for the conclusion, $\sim p$, by taking the negation of the truth values in the p column.

To determine the validity of the argument, we look for any cases in which both of the premises are true and the conclusion is false. In line 3 both of the premises are true and the conclusion is false. From this line alone we know that the argument is invalid. It does not matter that in line 7 both of the premises are true and the conclusion is true.

Sometimes it makes things easier to assign a variable to a statement that will help us remember what the variable stands for. Consider the following argument:

> The train was on time, but the bus was not on time.
>
> The plane was on time.
>
> ∴ It's not the case that the bus and the plane were on time.

To symbolize the argument, let t = "The train was on time," b = "The bus was on time," and p = "The plane was on time." So, the argument form is

t & $\sim b$

p

∴ $\sim(b$ & $p)$

Now let's set up the truth table:

	t	b	p	$\sim b$	b & p	t & $\sim b$*	p*	$\sim(b$ & $p)$ C
1.	T	T	T	F	T	F	T	F
2.	T	T	F	F	F	F	F	T
3.	T	F	T	T	F	T	T	T
4.	T	F	F	T	F	T	F	T
5.	F	T	T	F	T	F	T	F
6.	F	T	F	F	F	F	F	T
7.	F	F	T	T	F	F	T	T
8.	F	F	F	T	F	F	F	T

We set up the truth table just as we would if the variables were p, q, and r. All the rules for determining the truth values assigned to the columns for the various statements remain the same. And we set up the premises and conclusion so that they read from left to right, marking them accordingly.

Now let's examine the truth table to determine the validity of the argument. Are there any cases in which all the premises are true and the conclusion is false?

	t	b	p	~b	b & p	t & ~b*	p*	~(b & p) C
1.	T	T	T	F	T	F	T	F
2.	T	T	F	F	F	F	F	T
3.	T	F	T	T	F	T	T	T
4.	T	F	F	T	F	T	F	T
5.	F	T	T	F	T	F	T	F
6.	F	T	F	F	F	F	F	T
7.	F	F	T	T	F	F	T	T
8.	F	F	F	T	F	F	F	T

There is only one case in which the premises are both true, and in this case the conclusion is true as well. So, we know that the argument is valid.

Consider this argument:

Bill Clinton didn't serve two terms in office, but Jimmy Carter did.

George H. W. Bush served two terms in office.

So, it is not the case that both Carter and Bush did not serve two terms in office.

You may notice that all the statements in the argument are false, but remember that an argument's validity does not necessarily depend on the truth of its statements.

To symbolize this argument, let b = "Bill Clinton served two terms in office"; let j = "Jimmy Carter served two terms in office"; and let g = "George H. W. Bush served two terms in office." We can symbolize our argument in the following way:

~b & j

g

∴ ~(~j & ~g)

Let's set up the truth table:

	b	j	g	~b	~j	~g	~j & ~g	~b & j*	g*	~(~j & ~g) C
1.	T	T	T	F	F	F	F	F	T	T
2.	T	T	F	F	F	T	F	F	F	T
3.	T	F	T	F	T	F	F	F	T	T
4.	T	F	F	F	T	T	T	F	F	F
5.	F	T	T	T	F	F	F	T	T	T
6.	F	T	F	T	F	T	F	T	F	T
7.	F	F	T	T	T	F	F	F	T	T
8.	F	F	F	T	T	T	T	F	F	F

We use *b*, *j*, and *g* as our guide variables and assign their truth values in the conventional way, just as we would if we were using *p*, *q*, and *r*. Next we build up gradually, assembling the parts we need to state the truth values of the premises and conclusion. Finally, we line up the premises and conclusion from left to right, marking them accordingly.

Now let's examine the truth table to determine the validity of the argument. Are there any cases in which all the premises are true and the conclusion is false?

	b	*j*	*g*	~*b*	~*j*	~*g*	~*j* & ~*g*	~*b* & *j**	*g**	~(~*j* & ~*g*) C
1.	T	T	T	F	F	F	F	F	T	T
2.	T	T	F	F	F	T	F	F	F	T
3.	T	F	T	F	T	F	F	F	T	T
4.	T	F	F	F	T	T	T	F	F	F
5.	F	T	T	T	F	F	F	T	T	T
6.	F	T	F	T	F	T	F	T	F	T
7.	F	F	T	T	T	F	F	F	T	T
8.	F	F	F	T	T	T	T	F	F	F

There is only one case in which the premises are both true, and in this case the conclusion is true as well. So, we know that the argument is valid, even though we know that the premises are false. Remember that an argument can have all false premises and a false conclusion and still be valid. Such an argument is not sound, however.

Exercise 10.4

I. Assume that *a*, *b*, and *c* are true, and *x*, *y*, and *z* are false, then determine whether each of the following is true or false. Remember to start with the innermost parentheses.

1. *a* & *b* & *c*
2. ~(*a* & *b*) & *c*
3. (*a* & *b*) & ~*c*
4. (*b* & *x*) & *a*
5. *b* & ~(*x* & *y*)

6. ~*z* & ~(*a* & *c*)
7. ~*x* & ~(~*b* & ~*c*)
8. ~*y* & ~(*a* & ~*c*)
9. ~[~*y* & ~(*a* & ~*c*)]
10. ~[~(~*a* & ~*b*) & (*x* & ~*a*)]

II. Translate each of the symbolic statements in Exercise I into a statement in English.

III. Put the following statements in symbolic form.

1. Cats and dogs are mammals, but kangaroos are not mammals.
2. Cats, dogs, and humans are mammals.
3. It's not the case that cats, dogs, and humans are mammals.
4. Tuna and bass are fish, but whales are not.
5. It's not the case that tuna and bass are fish but whales are not.

IV. Determine the validity of the following arguments using truth tables.

1. *p* & *q*
   ~(*q* & *r*)
   ∴ ~*r*
2. ~(*a* & *x*)
   ~*y*
   ∴ ~*x* & ~*y*
3. ~(~*b* & *f*)
   g
   ∴ *g* & *f*
4. *b* & ~*t*
   ~(*m* & *b*)
   ∴ ~*m* & ~*t*
5. ~(~*k* & ~*h*)
   z
   ∴ ~(~*z* & *h*)

V. Put the following arguments in symbolic form, then test them for validity using a truth table.

1. Frogs hop, and toads hop. Snakes don't hop. So, it is not the case that frogs and snakes hop.
2. Freshmen take required core courses, and so do sophomores. Seniors do not take required core courses. So, it's not the case that sophomores and seniors take required core courses.
3. It's not the case that fish is fattening and beef is fattening. Vegetables are not fattening. So, fish and vegetables are not fattening.
4. Students can raise their grades by studying hard, but not by doing extra-credit work. It's not the case that students can raise their grades by doing extra-credit work and getting a tutor. So, students can raise their grades by studying hard and by getting a tutor.
5. It's not the case that France and Japan are in Europe. China is not in Europe. So, Japan is not in Europe, and China is not in Europe.

DISJUNCTION

We have seen how to symbolize conjunctions, two statements joined together. Now we are ready to discuss **disjunctions,** two or more statements set apart, usually by the word *or.* For example, "Frank is angry *or* Hank is tired." The symbol for disjunction is the lowercase *v,* also called the **wedge.** So, we can symbolize "Frank is angry or Hank is tired" in the following way: *p* v *q*.

It is important to note that the word *or* has two possible senses. In its **exclusive sense,** the word *or* eliminates or excludes one of the possibilities. For example, if a waiter tells you, "You can have the soup *or* the salad," he usually means that you can have *either* soup or salad *but not both*. In its **nonexclusive sense,** the word *or* does not exclude either possibility. For example, your advisor may inform you, "To fulfill the science requirement, you can take Biology *or* Chemistry." In all likelihood what your advisor means is that you can take Biology, *or* Chemistry, *or both*.

In which sense are we supposed to understand the word *or* for the purposes of propositional logic? The convention is to take the word *or* in its non-exclusive sense. This is the safest way to proceed. (Of course, outside our use of propositional logic, we should use the principle of charity to interpret an *or* statement to the best of our ability in accord with the intention of the speaker or writer.)

A disjunction, such as "Frank is angry or Hank is tired," is true if either Frank is angry or Hank is tired, or both. We can symbolize the disjunction as *p* v *q*, and the truth table for the disjunction is as follows:

p	*q*	*p* v *q*
T	T	T
T	F	T
F	T	T
F	F	F

The truth table shows that the only case in which *p* v *q* is false is the final line, in which both *p* is false and *q* is false.

Consider a simple argument that includes a disjunction:

Frank is angry or Hank is tired.

So, Frank is angry.

Let's put our argument in symbolic form:

p v *q*

∴ *p*

Now we set up the truth table for the argument:

p	*q*	*p* v *q**	*p* C
T	T	T	T
T	F	T	T
F	T	T	F
F	F	F	F

Examining the truth table to determine validity, we notice that there are three cases in which the single premise is true. In the first two cases, the conclusion is true as well, but in the third case the conclusion is false. On that basis we know that the argument is invalid because one instance of all true premises and a false conclusion establishes that an argument is invalid, no matter what else we may find.

Just as conjunctions can involve negations, so too can disjunctions. And as with conjunctions, we must be careful to note what is being negated.

Consider the following disjunctions. Each has the same subject matter, but each has a different truth table resulting from the differences in what is negated:

Frank is not angry or Hank is tired.

p	q	$\sim p$	$\sim p \vee q$
T	T	F	T
T	F	F	F
F	T	T	T
F	F	T	T

Frank is not angry or Hank is not tired.

p	q	$\sim p$	$\sim q$	$\sim p \vee \sim q$
T	T	F	F	F
T	F	F	T	T
F	T	T	F	T
F	F	T	T	T

It's not the case that Frank is angry or Hank is tired.

p	q	$p \vee q$	$\sim(p \vee q)$
T	T	T	F
T	F	T	F
F	T	T	F
F	F	F	T

Now consider a simple argument that involves disjunction, negation, and conjunction:

It's not the case that Frank is angry or Hank is tired.

So, Frank is not angry and Hank is not tired.

The argument form is

$\sim(p \vee q)$

$\therefore \sim p \mathbin{\&} \sim q$

The truth table looks like this:

p	q	$\sim p$	$\sim q$	$p \vee q$	$\sim(p \vee q)$*	$\sim p \mathbin{\&} \sim q$ C
T	T	F	F	T	F	F
T	F	F	T	T	F	F
F	T	T	F	T	F	F
F	F	T	T	F	T	T

Examining the truth table to determine validity, we find that only in the final line is the premise true. And in that line the conclusion is true as well. On that basis we know that the argument is valid.

Consider an argument with three variables that involves disjunction, negation, and conjunction:

Frank is angry or Hank is tired.

It's not the case that Hank is tired and Larry is lonely.

So, Hank is tired.

The argument form is

$p \vee q$

$\sim(q \& r)$

$\therefore q$

Here is the truth table:

	p	q	r	$q \& r$	$p \vee q$*	$\sim(q \& r)$*	q C
1.	T	T	T	T	T	F	T
2.	T	T	F	F	T	T	T
3.	T	F	T	F	T	T	F
4.	T	F	F	F	T	T	F
5.	F	T	T	T	T	F	T
6.	F	T	F	F	T	T	T
7.	F	F	T	F	F	T	F
8.	F	F	F	F	F	T	F

The only thing new to us in the truth table is the disjunction, $p \vee q$, with eight lines rather than four. There is nothing surprising about the truth values in this column, however. The disjunction is true in every case except lines 7 and 8, in which p and q are both false. Examining the truth table to determine validity, we find that both our premises are true in lines 2, 3, 4, and 6. In addition, however, we find that the conclusion is false in line 3; thus, we know that the argument is invalid.

EXERCISE 10.5

I. Assume that a, b, and c are true, and x, y, and z are false, then determine whether each of the following is true or false.

1. $a \vee x$
2. $\sim a \vee \sim x$
3. $\sim(a \vee x)$
4. $(x \vee \sim y) \& a$
5. $(x \vee y) \vee b$

6. $\sim(x \vee y) \vee z$
7. $(y \vee z) \vee (a \vee b)$
8. $\sim(y \vee z) \vee \sim(a \vee b)$
9. $(c \vee z) \& (b \vee \sim x)$
10. $\sim(\sim c \vee \sim z) \& (\sim b \vee x)$

II. Translate each of the symbolic statements in Exercise I into a statement in English.

III. Put the following statements in symbolic form.

1. The Democrat or the Republican won the election.
2. The Democrat or the Republican won the election, but not the Socialist.
3. It's not the case that the Democrat or the Republican won the election.
4. A whale is a mammal or a dolphin is a fish.
5. A whale is a mammal or a dolphin is not a fish.
6. A whale is a mammal or a dolphin is not a fish, but a dog is not a marsupial.
7. Lance passed the exam or he failed the course.
8. It's not the case that Lance passed the exam or he failed the course.
9. Sheila is a soprano or an alto, but she is not both.
10. It's not the case that Tim is a handyman or Al is a tailor, but Wilson is a neighbor.

IV. Determine the validity of the following arguments using truth tables.

1. $p \lor q$
   $\sim p$
   $\therefore q$
2. $\sim(p \lor q)$
   q
   $\therefore \sim p$
3. $\sim(t \lor a)$
   w
   $\therefore \sim a \ \& \ w$
4. $\sim(t \ \& \ a)$
   $a \lor w$
   $\therefore \sim t \ \& \ a$
5. $\sim[(j \lor m) \ \& \ z]$
   $z \lor m$
   $\therefore \sim(j \ \& \ z)$

V. Put the following arguments in symbolic form, then test them for validity using a truth table.

1. The Democrat or the Republican won the election. The Republican did not win. So the Democrat did win.
2. The Democrat or the Republican won the election, but not the Socialist. So, it's not the case that the Socialist or the Democrat won.
3. It's not the case that Lance passed the exam or he failed the course. Lance failed the course. So, Lance did not pass the exam.
4. Sheila is a soprano or an alto. Sheila is not both a soprano and an alto. Sheila is an alto. So, Sheila is a soprano.
5. It's not the case that Tim is a handyman or Al is a tailor. Al is a tailor or Wilson is a neighbor. So, Tim is not a handyman.

CONDITIONAL STATEMENTS

The final element of propositional logic that we need to consider is the conditional statement. We discussed conditional statements in Chapter 2. As you recall, a **conditional statement** is an *if-then* statement consisting of two parts. The first part of the statement, which follows *if* and precedes *then,* is called the **antecedent.** The second part of the statement, which follows *then,* is called the **consequent.**

In the conditional statement "If it rained, then the ground is wet," *it rained* is the antecedent and *the ground is wet* is the consequent. In symbolizing the conditional, we assign one variable to the antecedent and another variable to the consequent. For example, we can let p = "it rained" and q = "the ground is wet." The symbol for the implication involved in an *if-then* statement is the arrow, $\rightarrow$.[2] We therefore symbolize "If it rained, then the ground is wet" as $p \rightarrow q$.

The truth table for conditional statements can be a little tricky. The only time a conditional is false is when the antecedent is true and the conclusion is false.[3] So, the truth table for $p \rightarrow q$ is as follows:

	p	q	$p \rightarrow q$
1.	T	T	T
2.	T	F	F
3.	F	T	T
4.	F	F	T

Clearly, the conditional should be assumed to be true in line 1. If the antecedent is true and the consequent is true, the conditional is true. Even more clear, the conditional must be false in line 2, where the antecedent is true and the conditional is false. Line 3 might seem strange at first: a false antecedent and a true consequent give us a true conditional. It might seem even stranger, in line 4, that a false antecedent and a false consequent give us a true conditional. We can make sense of these peculiarities if we consider each of the four possibilities for the original example, "If it rained, then the ground is wet."

1. If it is true that "it rained" and it is true that "the ground is wet," we have no reason to think that the conditional is false. So, the truth value for the conditional is assumed true.
2. If it is true that "it rained" but it is false that "the ground is wet," we know that the conditional is false. Our information clearly demonstrates it.
3. If it is false that "it rained" but true that "the ground is wet," we have no reason to think that the conditional is false. It didn't rain, but the ground is wet. The conditional doesn't suggest that the ground can become wet *only* as a result of rain. It is perfectly possible that someone wet the ground while washing a car or watering a lawn. So, the conditional is assumed to be true.

4. If it is false that "it rained" and false that "the ground is wet," we have no reason to think that the conditional is false. It didn't rain and the ground isn't wet. This information doesn't contradict the conditional in any way. Without any reason to think that the conditional is false, we assume it is true.

It may be helpful to think of the truth table for conditional statements in terms of the guiding legal principle that a person is presumed innocent until proven guilty. In a similar way, a conditional is presumed true until proven false. The only thing that can definitively show that a conditional is false is a true antecedent followed by a false consequent.

Let's consider a basic argument using a conditional statement:

If it rained, then the ground is wet.

It rained.

So, the ground is wet.

We can symbolize this argument form, known as *modus ponens,* in the following way:

$p \rightarrow q$

p

$\therefore q$

Now let's set up the truth table:

	p	q	$p \rightarrow q$*	p*	q C
1.	T	T	T	T	T
2.	T	F	F	T	F
3.	F	T	T	F	T
4.	F	F	T	F	F

We encounter no surprises in setting up the truth table. We begin with the columns for p, q, and $p \rightarrow q$. Then we move left to right, adding the second premise, p, and the conclusion, q. Examining the table to determine validity, we discover that only in line 1 are both of the premises true. In line 1 the conclusion is also true, so we know that the argument is valid.

Let's consider another basic argument using a conditional statement:

If it rained, then the ground is wet.

The ground is not wet.

So, it did not rain.

We can symbolize this argument form, known as *modus tollens,* in the following way:

$p \rightarrow q$

$\tilde{}q$

$\therefore \tilde{}p$

Few persons care to study logic, because everybody conceives himself to be proficient enough in the art of reasoning already. But I observe that this satisfaction is limited to one's own ratiocination, and does not extend to that of other men.

—Charles S. Peirce

Now let's set up the truth table:

	p	q	$p \rightarrow q$*	$\sim q$*	$\sim p$ C
1.	T	T	T	F	F
2.	T	F	F	T	F
3.	F	T	T	F	T
4.	F	F	T	T	T

Again, we encounter no surprises in setting up the truth table. We begin with the columns for p, q, and $p \rightarrow q$. Then we move left to right, adding the second premise, $\sim q$, and the conclusion, $\sim p$. Examining the table to determine validity, we discover that only in line 4 are both of the premises true. In line 4 the conclusion is also true, so we know that the argument is valid.

As in symbolizing conjunction and disjunction, we must be careful in placing the negation sign in symbolizing a conditional statement. The place of the negation makes a big difference in the setup of the truth table. To illustrate that point, let's look at three different possibilities.

Consider the first conditional:

If it did *not* rain, then the game was played.

$\sim p \rightarrow q$

	p	q	$\sim p$	$\sim p \rightarrow q$
1.	T	T	F	T
2.	T	F	F	T
3.	F	T	T	T
4.	F	F	T	F

To determine the truth values for $\sim p \rightarrow q$, we set up the truth table as you would expect. Keep in mind here that $\sim p$ is the antecedent and q is the consequent. So, to determine the truth values for the conditional, we must look from right to left, and we can remind ourselves of that by drawing an arrow from the $\sim p$ column to the q column. The truth table shows that the only case in which the truth value for the conditional is false is in the fourth line, where $\sim p$ is true and q is false.

Now consider the second conditional:

If it did *not* rain, then the game was *not* played.

$\sim p \rightarrow \sim q$

	p	q	$\sim p$	$\sim q$	$\sim p \rightarrow \sim q$
1.	T	T	F	F	T
2.	T	F	F	T	T
3.	F	T	T	F	F
4.	F	F	T	T	T

To determine the truth values for $\sim p \rightarrow \sim q$, we set up the truth table as you would expect. We use the $\sim p$ column and the $\sim q$ column to determine the truth values. The only case in which the truth value for the conditional is false is in the third line, where the antecedent, $\sim p$, is true and the consequent, $\sim q$, is false.

Finally, consider this conditional:

It is not the case that if it rained then the game was played.

$\sim(p \rightarrow q)$

	p	q	$p \rightarrow q$	$\sim(p \rightarrow q)$
1.	T	T	T	F
2.	T	F	F	T
3.	F	T	T	F
4.	F	F	T	F

To determine the truth values for $\sim(p \rightarrow q)$, we set up the truth table as you would expect. We build up to $p \rightarrow q$ and derive the truth values for $\sim(p \rightarrow q)$ by simply taking the opposite of what is in the $p \rightarrow q$ column for each corresponding line. The only time the conditional is true is when its opposite, $p \rightarrow q$, is false.

To analyze a three-variable argument involving a conditional, we simply follow what we have learned so far. We build the truth table by setting up the first three columns in the conventional way and representing the premises and the conclusion of the argument accordingly. With three variables, there will be two cases in which the antecedent is true and the conclusion is false, and thus the conditional will be false in two cases.

Consider this example:

$p \rightarrow q$

$p \, \& \, r$

$\therefore q$

	p	q	r	$p \rightarrow q^*$	$p \, \& \, r^*$	q C
1.	T	T	T	T	T	T
2.	T	T	F	T	F	T
3.	T	F	T	F	T	F
4.	T	F	F	F	F	F
5.	F	T	T	T	F	T
6.	F	T	F	T	F	T
7.	F	F	T	T	F	F
8.	F	F	F	T	F	F

Having set up the columns for the three variables, we set up the column for the first premise, $p \rightarrow q$. There are two cases, lines 3 and 4, in which the antecedent, p, is true and the consequent, q, is false. In those cases, $p \rightarrow q$ is false. We set up the column for $p \, \& \, q$ by consulting the p column and the q column; and to facilitate reading the table, we repeat the q column for the conclusion. Scanning the table, we see that only in line 1 are both of the premises true. The conclusion is also true in line 1, so we know that the argument is valid.

Let's consider a slightly more complicated argument:

$\sim(p \rightarrow q)$

$q \vee r$

$\therefore q \rightarrow p$

	p	q	r	$p \rightarrow q$	$\sim(p \rightarrow q)$*	$q \vee r$*	$q \rightarrow p$ C
1.	T	T	T	T	F	T	T
2.	T	T	F	T	F	T	T
3.	T	F	T	F	T	T	T
4.	T	F	F	F	T	F	T
5.	F	T	T	T	F	T	F
6.	F	T	F	T	F	T	F
7.	F	F	T	T	F	T	T
8.	F	F	F	T	F	F	T

Having set up the columns for the three variables, we build up to the first premise, $\sim(p \rightarrow q)$. To set up the column for $\sim(p \rightarrow q)$, we set up the column for $p \rightarrow q$ and take the negation of it. We set up the column for $q \vee r$ simply by consulting the q column and the r column. Finally, we set up the column for the conclusion, $q \rightarrow p$, by looking from right to left at the first two columns. Only in lines 5 and 6 is the antecedent, q, true and the consequent, p, false, so only in lines 5 and 6 is $q \rightarrow p$ false. Now, looking at the table to determine validity, we see that only in line 3 are both of the premises true. In line 3 the conclusion is also true, so we know that the argument is valid.

Consider the following argument:

If the Democrat wins the election, then she will raise taxes.

If taxes are raised, then individual savings will decrease.

So, if the Democrat wins, individual savings will decrease.

Is this argument valid? Let's symbolize it and test it for validity using a truth table.

$d \rightarrow t$

$t \rightarrow s$

$\therefore d \rightarrow s$

	d	t	s	$d \rightarrow t$*	$t \rightarrow s$*	$d \rightarrow s$ C
1.	T	T	T	T	T	T
2.	T	T	F	T	F	F
3.	T	F	T	F	T	T
4.	T	F	F	F	T	F
5.	F	T	T	T	T	T
6.	F	T	F	T	F	T
7.	F	F	T	T	T	T
8.	F	F	F	T	T	T

In lines 1, 5, 7, and 8, both of the premises are true. In each of these lines, the conclusion is true as well, so we know that the argument is valid. In fact, of course, this means that any argument fitting this pattern, known as the chain argument, is valid.

Finally, recall the following argument from earlier in this chapter:

If the Democrat loses the Senate race, the Republicans will have a majority in the Senate.

If the Republicans have a majority in the Senate, the Senate will vote down the new bill.

It is not the case that the Senate will vote down the new bill or the Democrat will lose the Senate race.

So, it is not the case that if the Democrat does not lose, the Senate will not vote down the new bill.

Let's test it for validity, symbolizing the argument and checking the truth table:

$d \rightarrow r$

$r \rightarrow s$

$\sim(s \vee d)$

$\therefore \sim(\sim d \rightarrow \sim s)$

	d	r	s	$\sim d$	$\sim s$	$\sim d \rightarrow \sim s$	$s \vee d$	$d \rightarrow r$*	$r \rightarrow s$*	$\sim(s \vee d)$*	$\sim(\sim d \rightarrow \sim s)$C
1.	T	T	T	F	F	T	T	T	T	F	F
2.	T	T	F	F	T	T	T	T	F	F	F
3.	T	F	T	F	F	T	T	F	T	F	F
4.	T	F	F	F	T	T	T	F	T	F	F
5.	F	T	T	T	F	F	T	T	T	F	T
6.	F	T	F	T	T	T	F	T	F	T	F
7.	F	F	T	T	F	F	T	T	T	F	T
8.	F	F	F	T	T	T	F	T	T	T	F

Line 8 is the only line in which all three premises are true. In line 8 the conclusion is false, so the argument is invalid.

EXERCISE 10.6

I. Assume that a, b, and c are true, and x, y, and z are false, then determine whether each of the following is true or false.

1. $a \rightarrow y$
2. $y \rightarrow a$
3. $\sim(x \rightarrow y)$
4. $(z \rightarrow b) \vee \sim c$
5. $(z \rightarrow \sim x) \vee y$

6. $(c \rightarrow a) \vee (z \rightarrow c)$
7. $\sim(b \rightarrow c) \& (\sim x \rightarrow \sim a)$
8. $(a \rightarrow y) \rightarrow y$
9. $(\sim z \rightarrow x) \rightarrow (\sim a \rightarrow \sim c)$
10. $\sim(\sim c \rightarrow y) \rightarrow \sim(\sim b \rightarrow \sim z)$

II. Translate each of the symbolic statements in Exercise I into a statement in English.

III. Put the following statements in symbolic form.

1. If Bert is taking a bath, then Ernie is taking a bath.
2. It's not the case that if Hank is taking a bath, then Tiffany is taking a bath.
3. If Bert is not taking a bath, then Ernie is not taking a bath.
4. If there is helium in the balloon, then it can float.
5. If the balloon can't float, then there is no helium in the balloon.
6. If Lisa passed the final exam, then she passed the course.
7. If Lisa did not pass the course, then she did not pass the final exam.
8. If the groundhog doesn't see his shadow, then spring is not coming in six weeks.
9. It's not the case that if the groundhog doesn't see his shadow, then spring is not coming in six weeks.
10. If it is the case that if the sun shines then the game is on, then if the storm doesn't hit, I'll be at the park.

IV. Determine the validity of the following arguments using truth tables.

1. $p \rightarrow q$
    $\sim p$
    $\therefore \sim q$
2. $\sim(p \rightarrow q)$
    q
    $\therefore \sim p$
3. $\sim p \rightarrow q$
    $\sim p \ \& \ r$
    $\therefore q \ \& \ r$
4. $p \rightarrow q$
    $\sim q \lor r$
    $\therefore \sim p \ \& \ r$
5. $\sim p \rightarrow q$
    $\sim r \lor \sim p$
    $\therefore r \rightarrow q$

V. Put the following arguments in symbolic form, then test them for validity using a truth table.

1. If Bert is taking a bath, then Ernie is taking a bath. Ernie is not taking a bath. So, Bert is not taking a bath.
2. If the balloon can't float, then there is no helium in the balloon. The balloon can float. So, there is helium in the balloon.
3. If Lisa passed the final exam, then she passed the course. Lisa did not pass the final exam. So, she did not pass the course.
4. If the groundhog sees his shadow, then spring is coming in six weeks. So, if the groundhog doesn't see his shadow, then spring isn't coming in six weeks.
5. The game is on if the sun shines. The game is on and the team is excited. So, the sun must be shining.

SUMMARY

1. In propositional logic, the word *conjunction* refers to a compound statement. A compound statement, such as "This chapter was stimulating, and I learned a lot," is symbolized by two variables joined by the ampersand, & (for example, *p* & *q*).

2. If in any case we are unsure whether a statement is *simple* or *compound*, we must ask, "What does the statement mean?" Does the statement consist of two simple statements? If it does, it is compound. If it doesn't, it is simple.

3. *Truth values* for a variable are indicated as true, T, or false, F. A *truth table* is a list of all possible truth values for the variables in an argument form.

4. For the purposes of propositional logic, the following words are all equivalent and can be symbolized by the ampersand: *and, but, yet, while, whereas, although, though,* and *however.*

5. In a *valid* argument, it is impossible for all of the premises to be true and the conclusion false. So, in examining the truth table, we look for instances in which all the premises are true. If there is any instance of all true premises followed by a false conclusion (an F in the conclusion column), the argument is *invalid*. It doesn't matter if there are other instances in the truth table where all the premises are true and the conclusion is true, too.

6. Any two arguments that share the same argument form are either both valid or both invalid. When we know that an argument form is valid, we know that any argument that fits that form is valid.

7. *Negation* is the use of the word *not* (or an equivalent word or phrase) to deny a statement. The conventional symbol for negation is the tilde, ~. So, we can symbolize "Shaq is not short" with ~*p*.

8. Sometimes a negation applies only to a single simple statement—for example, "Sam is not a shortstop," symbolized as ~*p*. Sometimes two negations apply to both elements of a compound statement—for example, "Sam is not a shortstop, and Diane is not an intellectual," symbolized as ~*p* & ~*q*. At other times one negation applies to a whole compound statement—for example, "It's not the case that Sam is a bartender and Woody is a mailman," symbolized as ~(*p* & *q*).

9. The setup and analysis for three variables is lengthier and more complex, but all the same rules apply.

10. A *disjunction* is an *or* statement—that is, a statement that consists of two (or more) statements set apart, usually by the word *or*. For example, "Norm is an accountant or Norm is unemployed." The symbol for

disjunction is the lowercase *v*, also called the *wedge*. We can symbolize the previous disjunction as *p* v *q*.

11. The word *or* has two possible senses. The *exclusive sense* eliminates one of the possibilities. For example, a flight attendant may tell you, "For dinner you may have chicken or fish." The *nonexclusive sense* does not exclude either possibility. For example, a coach may advise you that "when you're feeling dehydrated, you should drink water or Gatorade." It is true when either of the two statements is true, and it is also true when both statements are true. For the purposes of propositional logic, it is conventional to take the word *or* in its nonexclusive sense.

12. A *conditional statement* is an *if-then* statement consisting of two parts. The first part of the statement, which follows *if* and precedes *then,* is called the *antecedent*. The second part of the statement, which follows *then,* is called the *consequent*. The symbol for the implication involved in an *if-then* statement is the arrow, →. We therefore symbolize "If he loves me, then he will call" as, *p* → *q*.

13. The only time a conditional is false is when the antecedent is true and the consequent is false. It may be helpful to think of the truth table for conditional statements in terms of the guiding legal principle that a person is presumed innocent until proven guilty. In a similar way, a conditional is presumed true until proven false. The only thing that can definitively show that a conditional is false is a true antecedent followed by a false consequent.

CHAPTER 11

INDUCTIVE REASONING

INTRODUCTION TO INDUCTION

The topic of inductive reasoning is familiar to us from the discussion of deductive and inductive arguments in Chapter 3. Now it's time to take a closer look at inductive arguments. An **inductive argument** is one in which the premises are intended to provide support, but not conclusive evidence, for the conclusion. Because inductive arguments do not guarantee that their conclusions are true, we evaluate them according to the strength of the support they provide for their conclusions. An inductive argument is *strong* when its premises provide evidence that its conclusion is more likely true than false. An inductive argument is *weak* when its premises do *not* provide evidence that its conclusion is more likely true than false. As we shall see, arguments have varying degrees of strength and weakness.

As we saw in Chapter 3, not all inductive arguments move from specific premises to a general conclusion. Here is an example of an inductive argument that moves from a general premise to a more specific conclusion:

> Most critical thinking students improve greatly in their ability to analyze arguments.
>
> So, *you* will probably improve greatly in your ability to analyze arguments.

This is an inductive argument that has a single premise dealing with a general group, "most students," and a conclusion about a single specific student, "you." Notice that it is inductive because the premise provides support for the conclusion, but the premise is not intended to guarantee the conclusion. Recall from Chapter 3 the *strict necessity test:* Either an argument's conclusion follows with strict necessity from its premises or it does not. If the argument's conclusion *does* follow with strict logical necessity from its premises, the argument should always be treated as deductive. If the argument's conclusion does not follow with strict logical necessity from its premises, the argument should normally be treated as inductive. Clearly, in the preceding example, the conclusion is not meant to follow, and does not follow, with strict necessity from its premises. The argument is inductive.

Another important clue that this is an inductive argument is the word *probably*. In Chapter 3 we called such words induction **indicator words.** Among the important indicator words and phrases for inductive arguments are *likely, probably, it's plausible to suppose that, it's reasonable to believe that, one would expect that, it's a good bet that, chances are that,* and *odds are that*. Notice that most of these phrases can be, and often are, used in making predictions. When an argument makes a prediction, that is a good, but not foolproof, indication that the argument is inductive. Of course, the presence of one or more of these indicator words in an argument does not guarantee that the argument is inductive, but chances are that it is.

Another way to identify inductive arguments is to look for their common patterns. Four of these are *inductive generalizations, statistical arguments, arguments from analogy,* and *causal arguments.*[1] This chapter looks at each of these inductive argument forms in turn.

INDUCTIVE GENERALIZATIONS

A **generalization** is a statement made about all or most members of a group. Inductive generalization is one of the most important kinds of inductive arguments. An **inductive generalization** is an argument that relies on characteristics of a sample population to make a claim about the population as a whole. In other words, it is an argument that uses evidence about a limited number of people or things of a certain type, the **sample population,** to make a claim about a larger group of people or things of that type, the **population as a whole.**

Let's consider an example:

> All the bass Hank has caught in the Susquehanna River have weighed less than one pound.
>
> So, most of the bass in the Susquehanna River weigh less than one pound.

The sample population is the bass Hank has caught in the Susquehanna River. The population as a whole is all the bass in the Susquehanna River. Inductive generalizations, such as our example, fit the stereotype of induction. The argument moves from a specific premise to a more general conclusion. But remember that the important thing about inductive arguments is that the truth of their premises is not intended to guarantee the truth of their conclusions. At best the premises provide strong support for the conclusion.

A good inductive argument should reach a conclusion that is appropriate to the evidence offered by its premises. The conclusion should not claim more than its premises can support. In the preceding example, the conclusion claims that most of the bass in the Susquehanna River weigh less than one pound. The degree of support that the premise lends will depend in part on how much fishing Hank has done and how many bass Hank has caught, but it is unlikely that this will be enough support to make this a strong argument. We could make the argument stronger by making the conclusion less *sweeping;* that is, the conclusion could cover less ground. For example, if we concluded that *many* of the bass in the Susquehanna River weigh less than one pound, the argument would be stronger. Given the premise, the conclusion is more likely to be true if its claim is more limited, restricting itself to *many* rather than *most* bass. If we concluded that *all* the bass in the Susquehanna River weigh less than one pound, the argument would be far weaker. Other phrases that could soften the conclusion are *possibly, probably,* and *likely.* If we soften the conclusion by saying, "So, it is *possible* (or *probable,* or *likely*) that most of the bass in the Susquehanna River weigh less than one pound," the argument is stronger because its conclusion is less forcefully asserted.

Inductive generalizations should not overstate their conclusions. For example:

> No rabbit Alan has come across has tried to attack him.
>
> So, most rabbits are not inclined to attack human beings.

This is a strong inductive generalization. Given its premise it seems very likely that its conclusion is true. Let's assume that Alan has come across thousands of rabbits and has yet to be attacked by one. The sample population, then, is the rabbits Alan has come across. The conclusion is about the population of rabbits as a whole. Notice that the conclusion is modest. It doesn't go too far by claiming that all rabbits are not inclined to attack human beings. It recognizes that there could be an exception to the rule.

Here is another example:

> None of the medical doctors Jen has ever met smoked cigarettes while examining her.
>
> So, no doctor smokes cigarettes while examining patients.

Let's assume that Jen has been examined by six medical doctors over the course of her life. We know that cigarette smoking causes cancer and that doctors in general have been outspoken about the dangers of smoking. This common knowledge aids the argument. However, the conclusion is so sweeping that the argument is not strong. After all, if there is just one doctor somewhere who smokes cigarettes while examining his or her patients, the conclusion is false. To play it safe, then, we might conclude instead that "very few, if any, doctors smoke cigarettes while examining patients." This is still a sweeping conclusion, but it allows for the possibility of the occasional exception. Given the revised premise, it is likely that the conclusion is true, and thus the argument is strong.

Here is a third example:

> Tom has visited Cocoa Beach, Florida, in October several times, and the weather was always great—sunny skies and temperatures in the 80s. So, there's a good chance that Cocoa Beach usually has great weather in October.

The sample population is Tom's experience of the weather in Cocoa Beach in October, based on several visits. The population as a whole is the weather in Cocoa Beach in October, in general. Tom's several visits do not guarantee the conclusion about the weather in general, but they do lend it some support. The conclusion reflects the fact that the evidence is limited. The conclusion does not say that the weather is always great, but only that it *usually* is. Given the premise it is likely that the conclusion is true, and thus the argument is strong.

EXERCISE 11.1

In each case, decide if the example is a strong inductive generalization or a weak inductive generalization. Be ready to explain and justify your answers.

1. All the hunters Ted knows eat the meat from the animals they kill. So, it is possible that many hunters eat the animals they kill.
2. All the blond men Sarah knows are exceedingly intelligent. So, it must be that all blond men are exceedingly intelligent.
3. Some students sell back this textbook at the end of the semester. So, it is likely that all students sell back most of their textbooks at the end of the semester.
4. The fifteen winters Eric spent in New York City were cold. So, it may be that most winters in New York City are cold.
5. Many of the children in Ms. Santuzzi's first-grade class can read. So, most children in the first grade can read.
6. Many of the unemployed steelworkers who hang out at the Dew Drop Inn are actively looking for work. So, it must be that many unemployed steelworkers are actively looking for work.
7. All the unemployed steelworkers who hang out at the Dew Drop Inn are not looking for work. So, it could be that most unemployed steelworkers are not looking for work.
8. None of the many students Lisa knows at State College are majoring in anthropology. So, it may be that not many students at State are majoring in anthropology.
9. Many of the women on the swim team are majoring in women's studies. So, it is possible that some of the women on the swim team consider themselves feminists.
10. None of the players on the New York Knicks is Serbian. So, there must not be any Serbian players in the NBA.

Evaluating Inductive Generalizations

So far we have been relying on our innate logical abilities and common sense to determine whether an inductive generalization is strong or weak. To a great extent, that is what we will continue to do. Although there are standard tests for determining whether a deductive argument is valid or invalid, there is no standard test for determining whether an inductive argument is strong or weak. Still, we are not totally lost when it comes to evaluating inductive generalizations. There are three questions we must ask of each inductive generalization we examine:

- Are the premises true?
- Is the sample large enough?
- Is the sample representative?

Are the Premises True?   One thing that inductive arguments have in common with deductive arguments is the need for true premises. "Garbage in, garbage out" applies just as well to inductive generalizations as it does to deductive arguments. As you know, a deductive argument that is valid and has all true premises leading to a true conclusion is called a **sound argument.** A deductive argument can have good—that is, valid—argumentation and still be unsound if the premises are not all true. In the same way, the premises of an inductive generalization can provide strong support for its conclusion, but if the premises are not all true, it is not a cogent inductive argument. A **cogent argument** has all true premises and supplies strong support for its conclusion. One or more false premises makes an inductive argument *uncogent,* even if its argumentation, its support for the conclusion, is strong.

Consider this example:

Most CEOs of Fortune 500 companies are women.

So, the CEOs of most big businesses are probably women.

The premise in this argument provides strong support for the conclusion. After all, if most of the CEOs of the most financially successful big businesses are women, it would seem likely that the CEOs of most big businesses are women. The premise is false, however (most CEOs are men), so it cannot legitimately be used to support the conclusion. The argument is not cogent.

Is the Sample Large Enough?   Common sense prompts us to ask that obvious question about an inductive generalization. The size of the sample population must be sufficient to justify the conclusion about the population as a whole. A sample is "large enough" when it is clear that we have not rushed to judgment, that we have not formed a **hasty generalization.** Admittedly, this business of specifying what we mean by "enough" is not easy. For the moment, we shall rely on common sense to determine whether the sample is large enough. In the next section of this chapter, we'll take a look at the mathematical determination of sample size.

Let's begin with a familiar example:

None of the thousands of rabbits Alan has come across has tried to attack him.

So, most rabbits are not inclined to attack human beings.

Thousands of encounters with rabbits seems like a large enough sample size to support the modest conclusion that *most* rabbits are not inclined to attack human beings. No inductive argument can guarantee the truth of its conclusion, but you don't have to be an expert in statistics to see that this one is a pretty good bet.

On the other hand, consider this example:

> Brooke taught three students with purple hair last semester, and all of them were A students.
>
> So, all students with purple hair must be A students.

Considering the thousands of students with purple hair, three students is clearly not a large enough sample on which to base this conclusion. The conclusion may or may not be true; but given the small sample, the premise is not strong enough support for it.

Consider this example:

> Two nuclear bombs were dropped on Japan, and today Japan has one of the strongest economies in the world.
>
> So, all the concern about nuclear warfare and the end of humankind is a bunch of nonsense.

The two nuclear bombs dropped on Japan devastated that country, but the Japanese have recovered well. The use of two nuclear bombs, however, is not enough to tell us what would result from the use of more nuclear bombs; they are not a large enough sample. Beyond that, those two nuclear bombs may not be like other nuclear bombs that could be used, which leads us to the third question.

Is the Sample Representative?   An inductive generalization is weak if the sample population it draws on is not enough like the population as a whole about which it makes its claims. In technical terms, we want the sample population to be *representative*. A **representative sample** is like the population as a whole in all relevant ways. It should be a miniversion of the population as a whole.

Let's examine the previous example:

> Two nuclear bombs were dropped on Japan, and today Japan has one of the strongest economies in the world.
>
> So, all the concern about nuclear warfare and the end of humankind is a bunch of nonsense.

The sample population is the two nuclear bombs dropped on Japan. Not only is this sample too small, but it is also not representative. The two bombs dropped on Japan were not nearly as powerful as the nuclear bombs of today. Japan's ability to recover after the bombing cannot be generalized correctly to humankind's ability to survive and recover from the devastation that would be caused by the current generation of nuclear bombs.

Terminology Recap

A *strong inductive argument* has premises that provide evidence that its conclusion is more likely true than false.

A *weak inductive argument* has premises that do not provide evidence that its conclusion is more likely true than false.

A *cogent inductive argument* has all true premises and supplies strong support for its conclusion.

An *uncogent inductive argument* has one or more false premises or weak support for its conclusion.

Recall the first inductive generalization we considered:

All the bass Hank has caught in the Susquehanna River have weighed less than one pound.

So, most of the bass in the Susquehanna River weigh less than one pound.

Let's assume for the sake of argument that Hank has caught hundreds of bass in the Susquehanna River and that they all weighed less than one pound. That would seem to be a large enough sample, but the argument could still be weak. How? It could be that the hundreds of bass Hank caught were not truly representative of the population of bass in the Susquehanna River as a whole. Why? There are many possible reasons. Perhaps Hank has fished only a short stretch of the river, and there are actually much larger bass 20 miles north. Perhaps Hank has fished only with artificial lures, but if he used live bait he could catch three-pound bass right under the Market Street Bridge, where he usually fishes. Can you think of other reasons?

Often the size of the sample is closely connected to how representative it is. But, as we just saw, a large sample is no guarantee of a representative sample. It is also possible, though less common, for a sample to be representative but not large enough. If, for example, Hank has fished every mile of the mighty Susquehanna with both artificial lures and live bait but has caught only a dozen bass—all under one pound—the sample might be representative, in a sense. After all, he varied methods and locations. Still, a dozen bass would not be a large enough sample on which to base the conclusion that most of the bass in the Susquehanna River weigh less than one pound. Maybe there are many three-pounders, but Hank is just a poor fisherman.

EXERCISE 11.2

I. Determine whether the following inductive generalizations are strong or weak. For the sake of this exercise, assume that all the information given is true. In each case, answer these questions: Is the sample large enough? Is the sample representative?

1. All the millions of rubies gemologists have gathered from around the world are red. So, the chances are good that most of the rubies in the world are red.
2. All the guys who live in Jim's dorm room on the first floor and Fred's dorm room on the third floor heard the fire alarm ring last night. So, it is plausible that many of the guys in the three-story dormitory heard it.
3. Most guys who watch the Super Bowl at Wexford College are unprepared for class the next day. So, most students who watch the Super Bowl are probably unprepared for class the next day.
4. Based on a survey of one hundred thousand American high school students, approximately half go on to attend college. So, it is probably the case that about half the people in the world have attended college.
5. There has been at least some snowfall in New York City every January for the past one hundred years. So, the chances are good that there will be at least some snowfall in New York City every January for the next two hundred years.

II. Consider each of the following weak inductive generalizations. Each is flawed in at least one way. For the sake of this exercise, assume that all the information given is true. In each case, answer these questions: Is the sample large enough? Is the sample representative? Explain and defend your answers.

1. Chicago, Los Angeles, and Houston are all big cities with big crime problems. So, all big cities must have big crime problems.
2. All former presidents of the United States have either died in office or died within fifty years of leaving office. So, it is likely that all future presidents will either die in office or die within fifty years of leaving office.
3. All one thousand of the frogs in Springfield Pond, next to the nuclear plant, have only three legs. So, it is reasonable to believe that many other ponds in Springfield have at least some three-legged frogs as well.
4. All four of the biology professors at Wexford College who were considered for tenure over the past twelve years received tenure. So, it is likely that almost all professors at Wexford who are considered for tenure receive tenure.
5. All one hundred children who saw the advance screening of the latest Disney movie said it was great. So, chances are that nearly everyone who sees the movie will think it is great.

Opinion Polls and Inductive Generalizations

Opinion polls are an excellent source of inductive generalizations. In recent years polling has become an increasingly large part of the political process. Gallup and Harris polls are often very accurate in predicting the outcomes of national elections, for example. The aim of a poll is to determine what a large population thinks or believes about a certain issue. To make that determination, it is not necessary to ask every member of that population. Rather, the preferred method is to ask a question of a sample of the population that is both large enough and representative of the population as a whole.

In the case of a presidential election, the population would be those who are eligible to vote and intend to vote in the election in question. Obviously, this is a very large population, consisting of more than one hundred million people. Do we need to survey a million people or more to have a large enough sample? Your inclination might be to answer yes, but in actuality the number of people in the sample population does not have to be nearly that large.

No sample, no matter how large, will ever guarantee that poll results will be accurate. Still, we can use polls to arrive at a level of 95 percent[2] certainty that a sample population will mirror the population as a whole within a small margin of error. The margin of error is usually indicated by a combination of the plus and minus signs, ±. This means that the results will be within a range of plus or minus the amount indicated. For example, let's say that the latest poll shows Sacamano leading Lomez by a margin of 60 to 40 with a margin of error of ±3. This suggests that there is a 95 percent chance that if the population as a whole voted, the result would be somewhere between 63 and 37 percent and between 57 and 43 percent in favor of Sacamano. Not bad. So how large does the sample have to be to yield these kinds of results? The following table gives the breakdown.[3]

Number Polled	Margin of Error
4,000	±2
1,500	±3
1,000	±4
750	±4
600	±5
400	±6
200	±8
100	±11

As you can see, it doesn't take a huge sample to yield a reasonable margin of error. With a sample of just 1,500, the margin of error is ±3. We can add 2,500 more people to the sample, and the margin of error decreases only slightly to ±2. So, we can produce a fairly accurate poll on a presidential election with millions of voters with a sample population of only 1,500 voters, but there's a catch: *The sample must be representative too.* The millions of voters represent a great diversity of people, and somehow the sample must be representative of this larger group. To get an idea of what kinds of things can cause a sample to fail in its attempt to be representative, let's consider a classic case.

A well-respected periodical, the *Literary Digest,* conducted a telephone poll to predict the winner of the 1936 presidential election. The pollsters for the magazine understood that the sample had to be large enough. In fact, they went overboard, gathering more than two million responses. They also understood that the sample had to be representative, so they randomly picked names from phone books all over the country. Having gathered and tabulated all the

Wisdom should reckon on the unforeseen.
—Edgar Allan Poe

responses, the *Literary Digest* predicted a landslide victory for Alf Landon over Franklin Delano Roosevelt. As it turned out, Roosevelt won by an even greater landslide. Although the sample was more than large enough, it was not representative, despite the effort to select the sample population randomly.

Why was the sample not representative? Because in 1936 many people did not have, and could not afford, a telephone in their home, and the people without telephones were mostly members of the lower and middle classes, who voted in droves for Roosevelt. Despite their efforts, the pollsters at the *Literary Digest* failed to draw upon a representative sample. They thought they had selected participants in the survey randomly, but in reality they had allowed a bias in favor of wealthier voters to creep into their sample population. To have a truly representative sample, we must select subjects at random from within the appropriate pool. This means that nothing is done at the outset of the selection process that would automatically eliminate any segment of the population. The selection is random only if each member of the population has an equal chance of being selected as a member of the sample population. As we shall see, many things can prevent random selection.

Some polls do not even attempt to utilize a truly random sample. Instead, they use *self-selecting samples*. Television talk shows and news broadcasts that invite you to call a certain phone number to cast your vote and register your opinion are prime examples of self-selecting samples. The question of the day might be, for example, "Should flag burning be protected under the First Amendment?" Although this is a controversial issue, it would not be surprising to find a large majority of votes against the protection and legality of flag burning. Why? There could be many reasons. Perhaps the show during which this issue was raised has an overwhelming and nonrepresentative percentage of conservative viewers. Perhaps those against flag burning are just more vocal and outspoken about their position and so are more inclined to call in to register their opinion.

Such call-in polls face another problem: they have a significant percentage of *nonresponses*. The nonresponses leave us with the problem of a sample population that is not likely to be representative of the population as a whole. The bias introduced by nonresponses will be even greater if the polling is done using an Internet Web site for people to register their votes. Those who respond to an Internet poll will likely be, on average, younger, better educated, and wealthier than the population as a whole. In fact, most people realize that such call-in polls and Internet surveys are not reliable. The shows responsible for them usually make clear that the results are not the product of a "scientific poll." In other words, aside from the entertainment aspect, they have little value at all.

What might seem random often isn't. Choosing names out of a phone book will not necessarily produce a representative sample, but what about approaching people on the street? This could work, but there are potential pitfalls here too. The pollster, the person taking the poll, might introduce bias into the sample because of a tendency to approach certain kinds of people and not others. Perhaps the pollster is not even aware that he is doing it. For example, he

Calvin and Hobbes   by Bill Watterson

YOUR NEW POLLS ARE IN, DAD.

MM.

A VAST MAJORITY OF HOUSEHOLD SIX-YEAR-OLDS SAY YOU'RE NOT LIVING UP TO THEIR EXPECTATIONS OF FATHERHOOD.

WHAT WERE THEIR EXPECTATIONS?

THAT YOU'D BE MORE LIKE AN AUTOMATIC TELLER MACHINE.

WHERE DO YOU POLLSTERS FIND THESE RESPONDENTS?

might have a tendency to approach only people who look "friendly." This may mean that he is more inclined to approach a well-dressed businesswoman and much less inclined to approach a disheveled man. This may introduce a gender bias and a socioeconomic bias into the sample population, automatically eliminating a significant portion of the population, namely, lower-class males. Perhaps the problem could be solved by randomly selecting the people on the street to be approached. For example, the pollster could be given instructions to approach every tenth person who walks down the block. This would certainly be a better strategy than simply allowing the pollster to approach the people he chooses on the basis of his own whims. Still, there can be problems. For example, if the New York Yankees wanted to know what the reaction would be to tearing down their stadium in the Bronx and building a new one in New Jersey, they would find strong opposition to this plan if they did all their polling in the Bronx. People in the Bronx take pride in their borough as the home of Yankee Stadium, and many residents depend on the stadium, directly or indirectly, for their livelihood. In the same way, if you asked every tenth high school student who walked down the street in Scarsdale, New York, if he or she was planning to go to college, you would get some uncharacteristic results. Perhaps 90 percent of the high school students in this wealthy suburb would indicate that they were planning to go to college, whereas the national average is closer to 60 percent.

Still another factor that may affect the reliability of polls is *dishonesty*. We all like to give the "right answer" to a question, even when the question does not have a right answer but is simply a matter of opinion or an attempt to collect information. The result is that some people lie in response to anonymous polls. For example, in response to the question, "Do you consider yourself racially prejudiced?" we can expect more people to respond no than is actually the case. People think that the "right answer" is no, so some will answer no even if they do indeed consider themselves racially prejudiced. Polling agencies often take advantage of this tendency of people to try to give the right answer by asking slanted questions. That is to say, polling agencies may not be interested in gathering objective data and so ask questions that clearly point toward one response as the right answer. For example, depending on the answer that a polling agency wants respondents to consider the right answer, they might ask two very different questions. On the subject of whether the United States should decrease the size of its nuclear arsenal, a polling agency might ask, "Are you in favor of peaceful multilateral nuclear disarmament?" Or, alternatively, "Are you against the weakening of the ability of the United States of America to offer a sufficient nuclear deterrent against foreign attack?" There is not much need to wonder what the right answer is in each case. Polling is big business, and those who hire polling agencies often have a vested interest in getting results that confirm their own position on an issue.

Another potential pitfall of objective polling is the person who is doing the poll. Even without intending to, he or she may provide a clue as to what the right answer is, or respondents may answer differently depending on the pollster. A white male is much less likely to admit that he considers himself racially prejudiced if he is polled in person by a black male. A woman is much less likely to admit that she has had a venereal disease when polled by a man rather than by a woman. If the polling question is "Do you believe in God?" we would expect a higher number of yes responses if the pollster is dressed in the garb of a priest or minister. What is the solution? Polling should be *double-blind;* that is, the person taking the poll and the person responding should have no information about each other, or at least as little as possible. And neither the pollster nor the respondent should have any indication of the "right answer."

EXERCISE 11.3

Put together your own plans for a campus poll on the death penalty. What questions will you ask? How will you phrase them to avoid pointing to a "right answer"? How will you gather responses? How many people will you include in the sample population? How will you ensure that the sample is representative? Be prepared to present your plans and defend them against possible objections.

There are three kinds of lies: lies, damned lies, and statistics.

—Benjamin Disraeli

STATISTICAL ARGUMENTS

Closely related to inductive generalization is another type of inductive argument. A **statistical argument** argues from premises regarding a percentage of a population to a conclusion about an individual member of that population or some part of that population.[4] For example:

> Ninety percent of college students are in favor of not having a cumulative final exam in their critical thinking class.
>
> Vera Peterson is a college student.
>
> So, Vera Peterson is in favor of not having a cumulative final exam in her critical thinking class.

Like other inductive arguments, statistical arguments are evaluated along a continuum of strong to weak. A statistical argument is strong when it provides evidence that its conclusion is more likely true than false—that is, when the chances that the conclusion is true are greater than 50 percent. A statistical argument is weak when it provides evidence that its conclusion is more likely false than true—that is, when the chances that the conclusion is true are less than 50 percent. The preceding example is thus a strong argument, providing evidence that there is a 90 percent chance its conclusion is true. The evidence does not logically guarantee that the conclusion is true, but the evidence in inductive arguments never does.

Let's look at another example:

> Only 3 percent of Wexford College students are against building the new gymnasium.
>
> Johnny Z is a Wexford College student.
>
> So, Johnny Z is not against building the new gymnasium.

Again, this is a strong argument, offering evidence that there is a 97 percent chance that the conclusion is true. The argument could be made even stronger by softening the conclusion so that the argument would say instead

> Only 3 percent of Wexford College students are against building the new gymnasium.
>
> Johnny Z is a Wexford College student.
>
> So, Johnny Z is *probably* not against building the new gymnasium.

The word *probably* safeguards this conclusion by claiming less than the conclusion in the original formulation did. Although there might be some doubt about the conclusion as originally stated, "So, Johnny Z is not against building the new gymnasium," it would be tough to deny the softened version of the conclusion, "So, Johnny Z is *probably* not against building the new gymnasium." Given the evidence, Johnny Z "probably" is not against building the new gymnasium. Even if 49 percent of Wexford College students were against building the new gymnasium, it would still follow that "Johnny Z is *probably* not against building the new gymnasium."

Let's consider a different version of the argument:

> Only 3 percent of Wexford College students are against building the new gymnasium.
>
> Johnny Z is a Wexford College student.
>
> So, Johnny Z is against building the new gymnasium.

The evidence that this argument provides makes it unlikely that the conclusion is true. In fact, there is a 97 percent chance it is false. The argument, then, is weak. What if we soften the conclusion with the word *probably*?

> Only 3 percent of Wexford College students are against building the new gymnasium.
>
> Johnny Z is a Wexford College student.
>
> So, Johnny Z is *probably* against building the new gymnasium.

The argument is still weak because the evidence overwhelmingly suggests that Johnny Z is probably *not* against building the new gymnasium.

Statistical arguments that approach 50 percent and offer evidence that their conclusion is more likely true than false are strong but *unreliable*. There is no specific percentage point at which a statistical argument is judged unreliable. The best way to determine reliability is to be practical. Ask yourself, "Would a reasonable person act or bet on it?" If the answer is yes, the argument is reliable. If the answer is no, the argument is unreliable. For example:

> Fifty-five percent of Wexford students voted for Watkins as "Teacher of the Year."
>
> Eileen is a Wexford student.
>
> So, Eileen voted for Watkins.

Although it is true that a majority of students voted for Watkins, it would be going out on a limb to say Eileen voted for Watkins. A reasonable person certainly wouldn't bet on it. It would be safer to say that "Eileen *probably* voted for Watkins," but even that would be relatively unreliable. After all, there is a 45 percent chance that she *didn't* vote for Watkins.

Consider another example:

> Just 42 percent of Wexford students come from out of state.
>
> Gloria is a Wexford student.
>
> So, Gloria doesn't come from out of state.

A wise man proportions his belief to the evidence.

—David Hume

This too is a relatively unreliable argument. The fact that only 42 percent of Wexford students come from out of state doesn't make it very likely that Gloria doesn't come from out of state.

Of course, we can have statistical arguments that are stronger than those in the 50 percent range but not as strong as those that approach the extreme of 100 percent. Their strength and reliability depend, in part, on how much the conclusion claims. Consider this example:

> Seventy-six percent of new businesses in this state go out of business within the first year.
>
> Dan the Man's Hot Dog Stand is a new business in this state.
>
> So, Dan the Man's Hot Dog Stand will go out of business within the first year.

→ Pop Culture Connection ←

The Hot Hand in Basketball

Basketball players often speak of having a "hot hand"—of being "in the zone" and feeling that they just can't miss. In recent years, however, a number of well-known scientists and statisticians (among them Stephen J. Gould and Thomas Gilovich) have argued that the hot hand is an illusion (similar to the illusion of being "hot" in poker or roulette). Studies of long-term shooting patterns, they claim, show that shooters are actually slightly *less likely* to make a shot if they have made their previous shot. Thus, contrary to what many players and fans believe, success does not breed success in basketball, and the hot hand is myth.

Suppose, as these studies suggest, there is a slight negative correlation between making a basket and hitting the next shot. Does that show that the hot hand is an illusion? Why or why not?

This argument is strong but not very reliable. In fact, the numbers tell us that there is a 24 percent chance its conclusion is false.

Let's consider a slightly different version of the argument:

> Seventy-six percent of new businesses in this state go out of business within the first year.
>
> Dan the Man's Hot Dog Stand is a new business in this state.
>
> So, Dan the Man's Hot Dog Stand will *probably* go out of business within the first year.

This argument makes use of the same information as the previous one, but the word *probably* softens the conclusion, thus increasing the strength of the argument.

Statistics are the lantern by which we light our way through the dense darkness of the future.

—Daniel Sommer Robinson

Reference Class

In examining opinion polls, we saw that the sample on which the conclusion is based must be representative. Similarly, in statistical arguments the subject of the premise should be as much like the subject of the conclusion as possible. Let's return to our first example:

> Ninety percent of college students are in favor of not having a cumulative final exam in their critical thinking class.
>
> Vera Peterson is a college student.
>
> So, Vera Peterson is in favor of not having a cumulative final exam in her critical thinking class.

All we know about Vera Peterson is that she is a college student, but surely there is more to know about her than that. And who are the students who want the cumulative final? Suppose we discovered that 85 percent of students

Terminology Recap

A *strong argument* has premises that provide evidence that its conclusion is more likely true than false.

A *strong and reliable argument* has premises that provide evidence that its conclusion is more likely true than false, *and* it is an argument that a reasonable person *would* act or bet on.

A *strong but unreliable argument* has premises that provide evidence that its conclusion is more likely true than false, *but* it is an argument that a reasonable person *would not* act or bet on.

who like writing essays want a cumulative final because there will be an essay on the cumulative final—and that Vera is a student who likes writing essays. That would change things. Now our argument is as follows:

> Eighty-five percent of college students who like writing essays want the cumulative final because it will have an essay.
>
> Vera Peterson is a college student who likes writing essays.
>
> So, Vera Peterson probably wants the cumulative final.

Now we have a strong argument that contradicts the conclusion of the original version of the argument. With the added information, we have changed the reference class. The **reference class** is the group to which statistics apply. As a rule, the more specific the reference class is, the better the argument is. In changing the reference class from "college students" to "college students who like writing essays," we found that the conclusion about Vera changed. Adding new information to an inductive argument can change its strength. In this case, changing reference classes called for a different conclusion.

Let's return to another familiar example:

> Fifty-five percent of Wexford students voted for Watkins as "Teacher of the Year."
>
> Eileen is a Wexford student.
>
> So, Eileen probably voted for Watkins.

Now let's add more information to arrive at a different argument:

> Eighty-nine percent of Wexford students who took Watkins's critical thinking course voted for Watkins as "Teacher of the Year."
>
> Eileen took Watkins's critical thinking course.
>
> So, Eileen probably voted for Watkins as "Teacher of the Year."

We have changed the reference class, becoming more specific in the second argument. Now we are no longer talking simply about "Wexford students" but about "Wexford students who took Watkins's critical thinking course." The change in reference class in this case changes the argument (though the conclusion remains the same) from a moderately strong but unreliable one to a stronger and more reliable one.

We should also note that a statistical argument can be used to support a conclusion about a group rather than an individual. For example:

> Ninety percent of college students are in favor of not having a cumulative final exam in their critical thinking class.
>
> So, ninety percent of Wexford College students are in favor of not having a cumulative final exam in their critical thinking class.

Notice that the conclusion does not necessarily follow from the premise. The premise concerns all college students, whereas the conclusion concerns a limited group of college students—those who attend Wexford. Wexford students in general could be very much like the population of college students as a whole, or they could be quite different in significant ways. As in other inductive arguments, the argument could be strengthened by softening the conclusion with the word *probably.* The argument is strong, but it might be stronger if the reference class were more specific.

Statistics are like a bikini. What they reveal is suggestive, but what they conceal is vital.

—Aaron Levenstein

EXERCISE 11.4

I. Decide whether each of the following statistical arguments is (a) weak, (b) strong but unreliable, or (c) strong and reliable. Then rewrite each argument, changing the reference class to make weak arguments strong and strong arguments weak.

1. Only 5 percent of registered Republicans voted for the Democratic candidate in the previous presidential election.
   Larry is a registered Republican.
   So, Larry probably did not vote for the Democratic candidate in the previous presidential election.

2. Fifty-two percent of independent voters voted for the Republican candidate in the previous presidential election.
   Shane is an independent voter.
   So, Shane probably voted for the Republican candidate in the previous presidential election.

3. Thirty percent of senior biology majors at Wexford College applied to medical school last year.
   Catherine was a senior biology major at Wexford College last year.
   So, Catherine probably applied to medical school.

4. Ninety-five percent of people who lose weight on a diet gain most or all of it back within three years.
   Ray lost fifty pounds on a diet five years ago.
   So, Ray has probably gained most or all of the weight back by now.

5. Only 5 percent of the students in Watkins's critical thinking course received a grade of D or F.

Sheila was a student in Watkins's critical thinking course.

So, Sheila probably received a D.

6. Forty-eight percent of graduating seniors at Wexford College have a grade point average of 2.9 or higher.

Dean is a graduating senior at Wexford.

So, Dean probably does not have a grade point average of 2.9 or higher.

7. Eighty-eight percent of freshmen at Wexford College return for their sophomore year.

Lindsey was a freshman at Wexford last year.

So, chances are that Lindsey is back for her sophomore year.

8. Only 5 percent of the population of Springfield is unemployed.

Barney lives in Springfield.

So, Barney is probably unemployed.

9. Forty-nine percent of marriages end in divorce.

Beth and Keith just got married.

So, Beth and Keith will probably end up getting divorced.

10. Less than 1 percent of female high school students try out for their high school football team.

Patty is a female high school student.

So, Patty probably did not try out for her high school football team.

II. Construct your own statistical arguments according to the following directions.

1. Give your own example of a strong statistical argument.
2. Give your own example of a strong but unreliable statistical argument.
3. Give your own example of a strong but unreliable statistical argument, then change the reference class and give a stronger version of the argument.
4. Give your own example of a weak statistical argument, then change the reference class and give a strong version of the argument.
5. Give your own example of a strong but unreliable statistical argument with a conclusion dealing with a group rather than an individual; then change the reference class and give a stronger version of the argument.

INDUCTION AND ANALOGY
What Is an Analogy?

Up is to down as right is to?

Understanding analogies and arguments that use analogies is essential to critical thinking. Analogies are not just the stuff of nightmares and entrance exams; they have a useful purpose. As you probably knew right away, the word *left* is the correct answer to the analogy question above. Why? Because the relationship is one of opposites. Up is the opposite of down, and right is the opposite of left.

An **analogy** is a comparison of things based on similarities those things share. Analogies, then, depend on what is similar or the same in two or more cases. Analogies are everywhere: on exams, in arguments, in newspapers, in poems, and in songs. In literature in general, and poetry in particular, analogies are common. *Similes,* which are comparisons using *like* or *as,* are actually a type of analogy. In literature, similes can be quite moving even though they might not stand up well to critical analysis. For example, when a poet says, "My love is like the sun," the comparison is a limited one. The poet may simply want to stress the beauty, warmth, and centrality of his beloved by comparing her to something else that is beautiful, warm, and central. The analogy stops there, however. The poet's love does not dwell in the sky, give off radiation, and so on. Most often poets intend these analogies to make us look at things differently, not to pass muster in a critical thinking textbook.

How Can We Argue by Analogy?

Although analogies are interesting and important for many reasons, including their use in poetry, we focus on one: their importance in constructing inductive arguments. An argument from analogy depends on an analogy or a similarity between two or more things. Analogies compare two or more things; arguments from analogy go one step further. They often claim that another similarity exists, given the similarities already recognized. Whereas an analogy simply points out a similarity, an **argument from analogy** claims that certain similarities are evidence that there is *another* similarity (or other similarities).[5]

Let's look at an example:

The Post Office is a government agency.
The Department of Motor Vehicles is a government agency.

> The Post Office is closed for Martin Luther King Jr. Day.
>
> So, the Department of Motor Vehicles must be closed for Martin Luther King Jr. Day.

The example first notes a similarity between the Post Office and the Department of Motor Vehicles. Then it states something additional about the Post Office. Last, it claims that the same thing is true of the Department of Motor Vehicles.

This example is, in fact, a general form of an argument from analogy. Rather than speak about specific examples, we can give the general form of arguments from analogy by using letters as symbols.

> A has characteristic X.
>
> B has characteristic X.
>
> A has characteristic Y.
>
> Therefore, B has characteristic Y.

That is the basic form, though we can expand it to include even more details. For example:

> The Post Office and the Department of Motor Vehicles are both government agencies, and both were closed on Veterans Day.
>
> The Post Office is closed for Martin Luther King Jr. Day.
>
> So, the Department of Motor Vehicles must be closed for Martin Luther King Jr. Day.

This is also an argument from analogy, but this version of the argument includes one additional detail: that both the Post Office and the Department of Motor Vehicles were closed on Veterans Day. Now the form reflects the additional detail:

> A has characteristics X and Y.
>
> B has characteristics X and Y.
>
> A has characteristic Z.
>
> Therefore, B has characteristic Z.

We could continue to add details represented by variables, but the basic form of the arguments from analogy would remain the same.

Evaluating Arguments from Analogy

Critical thinking involves more than just recognizing arguments from analogy; it also involves evaluating those arguments. All analogies break down . . . eventually. They wouldn't be analogies otherwise because we make analogies only between things that are similar but not the same. If you claim, "A squirrel is just like a squirrel!" people will look at you funny. On the other hand, people may disagree, but they will want to know more if you claim, "Squirrels, which are like suburban rats, should be exterminated."

In other words, there are good and bad analogies, and there are also good and bad arguments from analogy. Sometimes the points of similarity warrant a certain conclusion and sometimes they don't. Most arguments from analogy are inductive arguments, so they are neither valid nor invalid. Rather, they are either strong or weak. Whereas there are cut-and-dried ways to test whether a deductive argument is valid or invalid, there are no such direct methods for determining whether inductive arguments are strong or weak. There are, however, some good questions to ask to help determine whether a particular argument from analogy is a strong or weak inductive argument. Consider the statement "Squirrels, which are like suburban rats, should be exterminated." There must be some reason that you claimed this. Let's suppose that it is the conclusion of the following argument:

> Squirrels and rats are rodents of similar size and appearance.
>
> Rats cause problems in the city, and squirrels cause problems in the suburbs.
>
> Rats should be exterminated.
>
> So, squirrels should be exterminated.

Is this a good argument?

Exercise 11.5

Before we go further in discussing how to determine whether an argument from analogy is a good one, test your logical instincts. Decide whether you think the preceding argument is a good argument by deciding whether the analogy is a good one. Don't focus on whether you agree with the conclusion, just on how well or how poorly the premises support the conclusion.

Evaluating arguments from analogy is not totally new to you. Probably, you have done it for years without realizing it. In Chapter 6 you looked at arguments from analogy in a more formal way in the discussion of logical fallacies. Remember the *fallacy of weak analogy*? It's the fallacy that results from comparing two (or more) things that aren't really comparable. It is a matter of claiming that two things share a certain similarity on the basis of other similarities while overlooking important dissimilarities. For example:

> Tiffany and Heather are both tall and play basketball.
>
> Tiffany also plays volleyball.
>
> So, Heather must also play volleyball.

Not necessarily, right? Clearly, we have come to recognize this kind of argument as a fallacy, but where exactly does the reasoning go wrong? Let's return to this example after we look at what to consider in evaluating an argument from analogy.

The first thing we want in an argument from analogy is what we want in all arguments, whether they are inductive or deductive: *true premises.* (*Remember:* Garbage in, garbage out!) In the example, if Tiffany and Heather are not both tall or don't both play basketball, the argument is doomed from the start. So, we must always ask if the premises are true. Assuming that the premises are true, at least as far as we can tell, we must move on to consider other things.

The second thing we must consider is the *relevance of the similarities.* In the case of Heather and Tiffany, the similarities are relevant because they make a difference as to whether the conclusion is likely to be true. Both women are tall, and height is an advantage in volleyball. They both play basketball, and this shows that they each have some interest in an athletic activity in which height is an advantage. Still, the similarities are not overwhelming. Some other similarities would not be relevant at all. For example, they are both women and have seven letters in their names. These similarities are irrelevant, meaning that they make no difference to whether the conclusion is true. There is no causal or statistical connection between one's sex or the number of letters in one's name and one's athletic ability or interest. In contrast, a truly relevant similarity might be that they both play basketball for a coach who insists that his players also play volleyball. Another might be that they are best friends who rarely do anything without each other; or that they are sisters whose mother insists that they play every sport they possibly can.

The third thing to consider is the *number of relevant similarities.* In the example, there are only two relevant similarities between Tiffany and Heather: they are tall and they play basketball. If additional relevant similarities could be noted, the strength of the argument would increase. For example, if it were noted that they are best friends, rarely do anything apart, have a coach who insists that his basketball players also play volleyball, and attend a college that gives scholarships only to athletes who play more than one sport, the argument would certainly be stronger because these similarities are directly related to Heather's being a volleyball player.

A potential pitfall for all inductive arguments, including arguments from analogy, is "the unknown." No information—no premise—can ever be added to a valid deductive argument to make it invalid. However, information—premises—can be added to a strong inductive argument to make it weak. With regard to arguments from analogy, one important unknown, or neglected area of information, can be relevant differences or dissimilarities. We need to consider both the *relevance* and the *number of dissimilarities.*

Not all differences or dissimilarities are important or relevant. For example, Tiffany may have blonde hair, and Heather may have black hair; Tiffany may be studying philosophy, and Heather may be studying accounting; Tiffany may be left-handed, and Heather may be right-handed. None of these dissimilarities is relevant in arguing that Heather, like Tiffany, plays volleyball. There are, however, possible dissimilarities that would weaken the argument. For example, Heather may have to work at a part-time job, whereas Tiffany may not; Heather may have a medical condition that limits her physical activity, and

When men observe two things to be in some respect similar, they are wont to ascribe to each what they have found to be true of the other to the neglect of that in which they differ.

—René Descartes

Tiffany may not; or Heather may not like volleyball, whereas Tiffany thinks it's great. All of these dissimilarities are relevant to the argument, some perhaps more than others. If any of these dissimilarities were actually true, the argument would be weaker. If more than one were true, it would be even weaker; if all were true, it would be weaker still.

In the example we have been discussing, there is a sample of only two, Tiffany and Heather. A larger sample would strengthen the argument, just as increasing the number of similarities increases the strength of the argument. Consider the following increase in the size of the sample in the original argument:

> Tiffany, Heather, Amber, and Krissy are all tall and play basketball.
>
> Tiffany, Amber, and Krissy also play volleyball.
>
> So, Heather must also play volleyball.

This argument, with its increased sample size, is stronger than the original.

Still, there is another potential pitfall resulting from the unknown. This pitfall has to do with *diversity* in the sample. In the original argument, we were concerned with the similarities between just two people, Tiffany and Heather. What happens when we increase the size of the sample? *With increased sample size, diversity becomes a mark of strength.* If Tiffany, Amber, and Krissy were a diverse group in many ways, the argument would be strengthened. If these three had nothing much in common aside from being tall and playing both basketball and volleyball, there would be greater support for the conclusion that Heather must also play volleyball. If these three were very much alike in other ways—for example, all being A students and coming from the same high school, whereas Heather is a C student who comes from a different high school—the argument would be weakened.

Let's look at another example to highlight the importance of diversity with increased sample size:

> Jason's German car was a lemon and so was Fred's.
>
> So, Dirk's German car is probably a lemon, too.

If Fred and Jason both owned Volkswagens and Dirk owned a BMW, the argument is very weak. If Jason owned a Volkswagen and Fred owned a BMW, the argument is stronger (though still weak) because we have a slightly better case and more evidence for our claim about Dirk's German car.

If we increase the sample size, the importance of diversity becomes all the more apparent:

> Jason's German car was a lemon and so was Fred's, Joe's, Roy's, and Bob's.
>
> So, Dirk's German car is probably a lemon, too.

If they all owned Volkswagens, the argument is very weak. If Jason owned a Volkswagen, Fred owned a BMW, Roy owned a Mercedes, and Bob owned a Porsche, the argument would be stronger (though still perhaps weak because the number of individual cars is still small). The argument would be stronger because the diversity of German cars in the sample makes the claim about a particular German car more likely.

A final consideration in evaluating the strength of an argument from analogy is the *specificity of the conclusion relative to the premises;* that is, we don't want to claim too much. The broader and less specific the conclusion is, the stronger the argument is. In the volleyball example, the conclusion, "Heather must also play volleyball," is narrow and specific, particularly considering the evidence offered by the premises. We could increase the strength of the argument by instead concluding, "Heather must have played a game of volleyball at some time," or "Heather may also play volleyball," or, even better, "Heather may have played a game of volleyball at some time."

To sum up, consider these things in evaluating the strength of an argument from analogy:

- the truth of the premises
- the relevance of the similarities
- the number of relevant similarities
- the relevance of dissimilarities
- the number of relevant dissimilarities
- the diversity of the sample, especially with increased sample size
- the specificity of the conclusion relative to the premises

EXERCISE 11.6

Consider each of the following arguments from analogy. For the purposes of this exercise, assume that all the information is true. In each case, rank the argument along a continuum from weak to strong. Use numbers from 1 to 10 for your ranking, with 1 being extremely weak and 10 being extremely strong. Be prepared to justify your rankings.

1. If you can learn to hit a baseball, you can learn to speak a foreign language fluently. They both take practice.
2. Life is just like chess. It's a complicated game, but you can win if you learn the rules and cheat a little.
3. Taking care of your body is like taking care of your car. Preventive maintenance and a yearly inspection are required.
4. My father did an excellent job of balancing the family budget, so they should let him try to balance the city budget.
5. My brother changed the oil in my Chevy, so he can probably change the oil in your Ford.
6. My brother changed the oil in my Chevy, so he can probably change the brakes on your BMW.
7. Michael Jordan is a gifted athlete and a great basketball player who is interested in tennis. So, with a lot of practice, he could probably play tennis fairly well.

8. You like lobster and other seafood, and king crab legs taste like lobster. So, you would probably like king crab legs.

9. When car dealers charge a lot of money for an automobile, people often assume it must be of higher quality than less expensive models. So, if Wexford College raises its tuition, people will think it's a better school.

10. In "real life," Jerry Seinfeld must be just like the character Jerry Seinfeld on the show *Seinfeld*. After all, the character is based on the person, and they have the same name. (Think carefully about this one.)

EXERCISE 11.7

1. Read Judith Jarvis Thomson's article "A Defense of Abortion" in *Philosophy and Public Affairs* 1 (1971), pp. 47–66. Evaluate the argument from analogy that she offers. Is it weak, strong, or somewhere in between? Be prepared to give reasons in support of your evaluation.

2. The First Amendment to the U.S. Constitution says, "Congress shall make no law respecting an establishment of religion, or prohibiting the free exercise thereof; or abridging the freedom of speech, or of the press; or the right of the people peaceably to assemble, and to petition the Government for a redress of grievances." Construct an argument from analogy either for or against free speech in cyberspace on the basis of the First Amendment. Does your argument apply to pornography? Does it apply to "hate speech"?

3. Construct your own argument from analogy for or against the death penalty.

EXERCISE 11.8

I. Consider the following arguments from analogy. In each case, decide whether the argument is weak or strong. If the argument is weak, what makes it weak? Are there any ways to add to, or otherwise change, the argument to make it stronger?

1. An umpire won't give you first base for swinging hard in baseball. So, a teacher shouldn't give you a passing grade just for trying hard.

2. Animals are like human beings. They feel pain and pleasure and are part of the same chain of evolution. It is wrong to eat human beings, so it must be wrong to eat animals.

3. Flag burning is, or can be, a form of political protest. Verbal political protest is protected and allowed as free speech. Free speech can be nonverbal, as is the case with dance. So, flag burning, as a nonverbal form of political protest, should be allowed and protected as free speech.

4. A man who carries a fat wallet in his back pocket while strolling through a tough neighborhood at night should not be surprised if he is robbed. So, a woman who wears tight and revealing clothes in a bar filled with men should not be surprised if she is raped.

II. Read each of the following arguments from analogy. Each is followed by four additional pieces of information. In each case, decide which of the individual

Common Areas of Argument from Analogy

Arguments from analogy are found in many areas of study and have numerous practical applications. Let's briefly consider two: law and ethics.

American law has its roots in English common law, so legal decisions are often made on the basis of precedent. That is to say, a judge may often support a current decision by appealing to a decision made in a similar case at an earlier date. For example, in deciding whether the free speech guaranteed by the First Amendment applies to cyberspace communications, a judge would be expected to appeal to earlier and analogous free-speech cases. Of course, in deciding whether an earlier case is truly analogous, we apply our criteria for evaluation. Are there a good number of relevant similarities? Are there few, if any, relevant dissimilarities? Is the conclusion of the judicial ruling properly specific?

Arguments from analogy are particularly effective in matters of ethics. On the most basic level, the Golden Rule instructs, "Do unto others as you would have others do unto you." In a sense the message is that you should treat others in a way analogous to the way you would like to be treated. A more involved strategy in moral reasoning is to argue that a controversial issue is analogous to one that is not controversial. Capital punishment is certainly a controversial moral issue. Someone who is against capital punishment might argue that it is about as moral, and about as effective, to put murderers to death as it is to beat a child who hits his sister. In her article "A Defense of Abortion," Judith Jarvis Thomson argues from analogy in favor of the morality of abortion. Using a creative scenario, Thomson argues that a person would have no moral obligation to stay connected to a famous violinist who was linked to her kidneys without her knowledge or consent. She then argues by analogy that a woman similarly has no moral duty to carry her pregnancy to term. There are some similarities here. Neither the pregnant woman nor the woman hooked to the violinist may have wanted to be in their respective situations. In fact, they may have done everything to prevent it. Both have someone of great potential dependent on them. There are also dissimilarities. The question is How relevant are they? Does the analogy work? If we accept that the woman involuntarily linked to the violinist has no moral obligation to continue that way, does it follow by analogy that a pregnant woman has no moral obligation to continue her pregnancy?

pieces of information would strengthen the argument if added and which would weaken the argument if added.

1. Luke and Frank are both students at Jefferson High School in a rural area of Indiana. Each lives on his family's farm. Luke plans to work full-time on the farm after graduation and has no plans to go to college. So, Frank probably has no plans to go to college, either.

   Consider whether each of the following would strengthen or weaken the argument:
   a. Both Luke and Frank have no close relatives who have gone to college.
   b. Neither Luke nor Frank has ever traveled outside his home state.
   c. Luke is a C student, but Frank is an A student.
   d. Luke does not like farming, but Frank does.

2. Lisa and Lauren are identical twins who were separated at birth. Lisa has been in trouble with the law for most of her life. So, it's a good bet that Lauren has been in trouble with the law for most of her life.

   Consider whether each of the following would strengthen or weaken the argument:

   a. Lisa and Lauren were both shuffled from one foster home to another for the first eighteen years of their lives.
   b. Lisa was adopted and raised by a family in which the parents later divorced. Lauren was adopted and raised by a distant relative whose family unit stayed together.
   c. Lisa and Lauren have each sought help for substance abuse.
   d. Lisa went to elite private schools, whereas Lauren went to public schools.

3. Spartansville and Loyalton are both small cities in the northeastern part of the United States with populations under one hundred thousand people. Spartansville has a museum. So, there's a good chance that Loyalton has a museum.

   Consider whether each of the following would strengthen or weaken the argument:

   a. Spartansville is home to a major university, whereas Loyalton is not.
   b. Both cities have a symphony orchestra.
   c. Loyalton is having difficulty obtaining funding for its libraries.
   d. Spartansville and Loyalton compete for tourists.

4. Al and Dave are both unemployed steelworkers. Al has given up looking for work. So, Dave has probably given up looking for work.

   Consider whether each of the following would strengthen or weaken the argument:

   a. Al and Dave are the same age.
   b. Al has no family to support, whereas Dave has a sick wife and three children.
   c. Al recently won the lottery.
   d. Al and Dave are both union members.

5. Capital City and Metropolis are both cities of two million people located in the southern United States. Capital City has a terrible crime problem. So, it's a good bet that Metropolis has a terrible crime problem, too.

   Consider whether each of the following would strengthen or weaken the argument:

   a. Both cities have high rates of unemployment.
   b. Capital City is known as the center of the drug trade in the South.
   c. Metropolis has a tough police commissioner and a well-respected police force.
   d. Neither city has affordable public housing.

_____

Arguing by Analogy

So far we have been looking at how to evaluate arguments from analogy, but we should also consider how to construct arguments from analogy. As you might expect, the criteria for constructing a good argument from analogy

We can hardly think without analogies, comparisons, and metaphors.
—R. S. Jones

are the same as those for evaluating an argument from analogy. A strong argument from analogy can be very effective. People like comparisons, particularly when the comparison relates something difficult or foreign to something they consider easy or familiar. Still, not every position can be defended by an argument from analogy. Offering a weak argument from analogy will do more harm than good.

Here's an example: If Parker wanted to explain to a group of students why they should study critical thinking, he might argue his point by using an analogy to karate. There are many ways in which learning karate and learning critical thinking are similar. They both require patience and discipline but result in greater confidence and increased self-esteem. They are both used for defense and offense. With karate you can defend yourself against attack, and you can attack others (though you should do so only when appropriate). With critical thinking you can defend your positions against the attacks of those who hold other positions, and you can attack the positions of others (though you should do so only when appropriate) or put forward a new position. Learning karate builds on your native abilities but is hard work. You may not always understand the reasons for everything involved in the training, even though it pays off in the end. In a similar way, learning critical thinking builds on your native abilities but is hard work. You may not always understand the reasons for everything involved in the training—the concepts, the terminology, the exercises, and so on. Most serious students of karate agree that there is much to gain and that your effort will be rewarded if you study karate. Therefore, if you are serious about studying critical thinking, you will find that there is much to gain and that your effort will be rewarded.

Here is the argument in more standard form:

> There are important similarities between learning karate and learning critical thinking. They both require patience and discipline and result in increased confidence and self-esteem. They both build on native abilities but involve hard work, of which you may not always immediately see the point. They are both of use for offense and defense.

> Most serious students of karate agree that there is much to gain and that your effort will be rewarded if you study karate.

> Therefore, if you are serious about studying critical thinking, you will find that there is much to gain and that your effort will be rewarded.

Is this a good argument from analogy? Let's see if it meets the criteria we have established. Are the premises true? Yes. Are the similarities relevant? Yes. Just consider the difficulties involved in learning the skills of both critical thinking and karate and the parallels in the way they are used for defense and offense. There are also a good number of similarities, not merely one or two. How about dissimilarities? Well, karate is a physical activity used for physical defense and offense, whereas critical thinking is an intellectual activity. That is a big difference, but it is not relevant to the point we are making. Another difference is that learning karate can actually be good for your cardiovascular system, whereas we cannot say the same thing about learning critical thinking. What about the specificity of the conclusion with regard to the premises? Does it claim too much? "If you are serious about studying critical thinking, you will find that there is much to gain and that your effort will be rewarded." The conclusion is not overly specific, nor does it claim too much. In fact, it is somewhat vague, though not to the point of being a fault. It claims only that *if* you are *serious* about studying critical thinking, your effort will be *rewarded*. In other words, if you expend a good deal of effort in studying critical thinking, you will find that there is some payback. This is, then, a good argument from analogy.

EXERCISE 11.9

Construct your own argument from analogy for each of the following. Decide and explain whether it is a good or a bad argument.

1. Argue that Barbara would be a good mayor of her small town because she is a good employer.
2. Argue that Mr. Sanders would be a good health-science teacher because he is a good football coach.
3. Argue that Jezebel would be a good actress because she lives a life based on lies and deceit.
4. Argue that Warren Beatty would be a good president because he is a good actor.
5. Argue that Sam would be a bad police officer because he was a bad marine.

INDUCTION AND CAUSAL ARGUMENTS

Humans are a curious life form. Our very nature drives us to search for knowledge. One of the most basic, most common, and most important kinds of knowledge we seek is knowledge of **cause and effect.** Why didn't my alarm clock go off when it was supposed to? Why is there no hot water left for my shower? We tend to look for causal connections when we are surprised (pleasantly or unpleasantly) by what occurs. We want to know the cause of what happened. In the absence of a good account, we will often accept a bad one—as in the case of superstition and mythology. In contrast, cats don't care about cause and effect. If a ball rolls by a cat, she'll chase after it if she's in the mood, but she'll never look to see where it came from. On the other hand, if a ball unexpectedly rolled by you, you'd first look to see whence it came.[6]

Roughly speaking, a *cause* is that which brings about a change, that which produces an effect. The relationship of cause and effect, however, doesn't come into play only when we're surprised by something. We count on it all the time without realizing it. For example, you may rarely think much about the law of

gravity, the law that tells us there is a cause-and-effect relationship making heavy objects fall to the ground. Something might have to unexpectedly float upward to get you thinking about gravity. You may count on your car starting every morning. But how often do you think about all the cause-and-effect relationships involved in that occurring?

Our focus here is on inductive arguments that try to identify a cause-and-effect relationship. This kind of argument is notoriously difficult. When we search for the cause of a certain effect, we are looking to identify a certain relationship between two things or events. What *is* that relationship? Certainly, the cause has to come before the effect, but, as we learned in Chapter 6 with the fallacy of questionable cause, not every event that *precedes* another *causes* the other. To a certain extent, that is just common sense, yet it is surprising how prone we are to commit the fallacy anyway. One piece of supporting evidence for a cause-and-effect relationship between two things or events is that one thing regularly comes before the other. For example, every time you let go of your coffee mug, the coffee mug falls to the floor. So, you assume there is a cause-and-effect relationship at work between the release of the heavy object and its falling to the ground. To take another example, one that philosopher David Hume was fond of, every time you have seen one billiard ball strike another, it has caused the other to move. So, you assume that there is a cause-and-effect relationship there. You have witnessed the same pairing of events over and over again—it is no mere coincidence. But, Hume asks us, when you think about it, what have you really witnessed? Just the pairing of two events, one billiard ball striking the other and then the other billiard ball moving. You have witnessed what Hume called "constant conjunction." The two events always happen one before the other—they are "constantly conjoined." You never really see any separate things that you could call "cause" and "effect." You never see "necessary connection" or "causal power."

We don't have to fully agree with Hume to get his point; it is tough to be certain about the cause-and-effect relationships we take for granted. They could simply be the result of coincidence. To make this same point, philosopher Bertrand Russell asks you to consider yourself in the position of a chicken on a farm. Every day that you can remember, the farmer's wife has approached you and then fed you. You have come to associate the two in terms of cause and effect (even though chickens don't really think this way). But then comes the day when the farmer's wife approaches you and doesn't feed you. Instead, she wrings your neck. The moral of the story is that we need to be careful in assuming a cause-and-effect relationship between two things.

As we saw, Hume introduced the issue of trying to understand the relationship of cause and effect. That's a tough issue to settle and, thankfully, is not our concern here. Instead, we want to look at arguments about particular relationships of cause and effect and learn how to evaluate them. As it turns out, it is easier to show that something *couldn't be* the cause of a certain effect than it is to prove what *is* the cause.

Nor is it reasonable to conclude, merely because one event, in one instance, precedes another, that one is the cause, the other the effect.
—David Hume

Let's take a look at arguments of cause and effect. We should note that not all causal arguments contain the word *cause*. Other causal terms include *produce, is responsible for, affects, makes, changes,* and *contributes to.* Such arguments come in two broad types: (1) arguments about the cause of a single instance and (2) arguments about a general relationship.

Here's an example of an argument about a single instance:

Megan's car wouldn't start this morning, and she hasn't replaced the battery since she bought the car six years ago.

So, it is probably a dead battery that caused the car not to start.

Here's an example of an argument about a general relationship:

The Surgeon General has found that there is a strong link between smoking cigarettes and getting lung cancer.

So, smoking cigarettes causes lung cancer.

In each case, it should be clear that the argument is inductive. The premises provide evidence (strong evidence) for the conclusion. The conclusion does not follow with strict necessity from the premises. It is always at least possible that the premises are true and the conclusion is false. Given what the argument says, it is at least possible that the car's alternator is shot and the battery is fine. Of course, there would be ways to investigate the matter further, but the argument, as it stands, does not do so. Given only what the second argument says, there is no guarantee that smoking is the cause of lung cancer. Two things can be linked without one causing the other.

There is a very practical reason why most causal arguments are inductive. It is very difficult to take every conceivable possibility into account when attempting to form an argument concerning cause and effect. Still, some causal arguments are intended to be deductive. Here is one that we mentioned in Chapter 3:

Whenever iron is exposed to oxygen, it rusts.

This iron pipe has been exposed to oxygen.

Therefore, it will rust.

Certain relationships of cause and effect have been well established. Not only has iron exposed to oxygen rusted repeatedly, but there is also sound scientific understanding of why this occurs. Aside from Hume's skeptical concerns about observing cause and effect, this is a very well-established causal relationship.

Let's consider arguments about general causal relationships. When speaking about causality in a population, we usually mean that X causes a higher rate of Y in the population. We do not usually mean that every individual who uses X will get Y. Consider, for example, the argument that smoking cigarettes causes cancer. This does not mean, or intend to claim, that everyone who smokes will get cancer. Rather, it means that smoking cigarettes results in a higher rate of cancer in people who smoke as opposed to people who don't smoke. Some people who do not smoke do get cancer. And some rare individuals may smoke cigarettes every day until they die at one hundred years old without ever getting cancer.

As is the case with all arguments, deductive and inductive, we need true premises for our causal arguments to be of any value. In arguing for a cause-and-effect relationship, we should base our premises on careful observation. *Selective attention and memory* can be problems here. That is, focusing attention on, or recalling from memory, only certain examples distorts the sample. Consider the following example:

Every time we have a full moon, people behave strangely.

So, the full moon must cause the strange behavior.

How might a person be mistaken in this conclusion as a result of selective attention or memory? It could be that he is very alert for any signs of strange behavior every time the moon is full and is quick to interpret behavior as "strange" at those times. But if he thought about it more carefully, he would recall that there were many times that the moon was full and yet he observed no one behaving strangely. Thinking about it some more, he may realize that he has witnessed just as much strange behavior on nights when the moon was not full.

Another danger in forming premises for causal arguments is relying on anecdotal evidence—that is, what others tell us. As we just saw, sometimes we cannot trust our own observations as a result of selective attention or memory. This is all the more true when it comes to the observations of others. Others are also subject to misreporting observations on the basis of their own selective attention or memory. Others may also have reasons to distort the truth. They may have something to gain by deceiving us. As a general rule, we need to be careful and critical when basing causal arguments on the anecdotal evidence of others.

Of course, we must admit that we cannot observe everything for ourselves. Thankfully, there are experts who investigate the causal connections between things the rest of us do not have the time, money, or expertise to explore. Scientists, for example, make use of experimental and control groups for determining causality. To see if chemical X prevents disease Y, a scientist gives chemical X to group one—the *experimental group*—and does not give chemical X to group two—the *control group*. By keeping all conditions except the intake of chemical X the same for the two groups, the scientist can isolate the effects caused by chemical X. It is common for such experiments to initially be done on laboratory animals. Human subjects complicate the matter because a human subject who believes that the drug she is given will prevent or cure her disease will actually have a better chance of prevention or cure. This is known as the **placebo effect.** A **placebo** is a pill that does not contain any drug (or active ingredient). Often it is just a sugar pill. With human subjects, then, the experimental group is given the drug and the control group is given a placebo. To ensure that the results are not compromised, the study should be double-blind. In a **double-blind study,** neither the subjects nor the experimenters know who is receiving the treatment and who is receiving the placebo until the experiment is finished.

Correlation and Cause

Sometimes two things or events are clearly associated or linked: where you find X, you will often find Y. A relationship such as this, in which two things are frequently, or even constantly, found together, is called a **correlation.** In a correlation two things share a mutual relationship; where one is found, the other is often, or always, found. In contrast, in the relationship of causation, one thing *produces* or brings about the other. Sometimes a correlation is an indicator of a cause-and-effect relationship. For example, the high rate of lung cancer deaths among smokers led to the investigation and discovery of a causal link between them. We must be careful, though. Most correlations do not indicate a causal relationship between the two things or events correlated. For example, there is a strong correlation between shoe size and average ability in math among children. The larger the shoe size, the greater the average ability in math. For example, on average, children who wear a size 8 shoe score higher on the same exam than those who wear a size 6 shoe. Does this imply that having large feet causes an increase in mathematical ability? Or does it suggest that mathematical ability causes feet to grow? Of course not. There is an underlying explanation for this phenomenon. A child's age is correlated with both shoe size and mathematical ability. As a child grows older, both shoe size and mathematical ability tend to increase, but neither one causes the other.

Maybe the previous example was obvious, but there are correlations that are more easily and more convincingly mistaken as cause and effect. In fact,

Summary of Key Points on Cause and Correlation

1. It is easier to show that something couldn't be the cause of a certain effect than it is to prove what is the cause.
2. Not all causal arguments contain the word *cause.*
3. When speaking about causality in an entire population, we usually mean that X results in a higher rate of Y in the population, not that every individual who uses X will get Y.
4. When we are speaking of a cause, we do not always mean to suggest that it is a necessary or a sufficient condition for bringing about the effect.
5. Sometimes two things or events are clearly associated or linked. Where you find X, you will often or always find Y. A mutual relationship such as this, in which two things are frequently or invariably found together, is called a *correlation.*

6. Sometimes, but not always, a correlation is a sign of a cause-and-effect relationship.
7. The correlation of two things or events, their mutual presence or absence, can be positive or negative. If they are found together to exactly the same extent as they are found apart, there is no correlation.
8. *Is the correlation significant?* The answer depends, in part, on the size of the sample.
9. Correlation can always be a result of mere coincidence, and most of the time it is.

one of the biggest problems with popular news reports is their tendency to make a new study sound as if it proves a cause-and-effect relationship between two things, when all the study actually does is report a significant correlation. To critically evaluate such reports, we must grasp the nature of correlation.

The correlation of two things or events, their mutual presence or absence, can be positive or negative. If the two things are found together to exactly the same extent as they are found apart, there is no correlation. A *positive correlation,* one that indicates two things are found together more than 50 percent of the time, *may* indicate a causal connection between one thing and the other. A *negative correlation,* one that indicates two things are found together less than 50 percent of the time, *may* indicate that one thing prevents the other. The important question is this: Is the correlation significant? The answer depends, in part, on the size of the sample.

The sample must be large enough to put our observations within an acceptable margin of error. For example, suppose we notice that of three people we know who took vitamin C all winter long, two never became sick. That is a strong correlation—nearly 67 percent—between taking vitamin C and remaining healthy through the winter. But the sample of just three people is much too small for the correlation to be significant. If we did a controlled study using two thousand subjects and found that 67 percent of those who took vitamin C remained healthy through the winter, we might have a significant correlation. We would have to compare it with the correlation between *not* taking vitamin C and remaining healthy through the winter. If we found that 66 percent of those who did not take vitamin C remained healthy through the winter, our correlation would no longer be useful as evidence for establishing cause and effect. Nearly the same percentage of people remained healthy without vitamin C.

Let's suppose, however, that our study revealed that only 52 percent of those who did not take vitamin C remained healthy through the winter. Then the correlation of 67 percent would be good evidence to support the claim that vitamin C prevents illness. If the study were not properly controlled, this would not in itself, no matter how large and representative the sample, be conclusive evidence of a cause-and-effect relationship. Why? Because something else might be independently correlated with both the vitamin C intake and the good health. For example, the correlation between health and vitamin C intake could be the result of each being further correlated with proper rest. Perhaps proper rest promotes health and prevents illness, and people who get proper rest tend to do other things they think might promote health and prevent illness, such as taking vitamin C.

We must always be on our guard against arguments that base their conclusions about cause and effect on correlations. Correlation can always be a result of mere coincidence, and most of the time it is. When a correlation is not absolute, neither 0 percent nor 100 percent, we should be suspicious. The discovery of a significant correlation can be the beginning of an investigation, but it should never be the end of one, particularly when arguing about cause and effect.

EXERCISE 11.10

I. Examine the following claims. In each case, decide whether what is being reported is good or bad evidence for a cause-and-effect relationship.

1. Most people who are over the age of seventy do not feel comfortable with computers.
2. All ten of the people who ate the fish at the buffet were sick the next day.
3. Most National Hockey League Players are Caucasians.
4. Eighty percent of students who studied more than ten hours for the exam earned a grade of B or higher, whereas only 5 percent of students who studied less than ten hours for the exam earned a grade of B or higher.
5. Most people who quit smoking report at least some weight gain.
6. All fifty-two Republicans in the Senate voted for the new bill.
7. Ninety-three out of one hundred people who cut down their calorie intake and exercised more lost weight.
8. All twelve of the students who went on the camping trip came back with a cold.
9. All fourteen players on the basketball team are over six feet tall.
10. None of the twenty experimental subjects who took the new flu shot caught the flu all season.

II. For each example, decide what questions you would ask and what additional information, if any, you would need to tell if there is a cause-and-effect relationship, a correlation, or no relationship.

1. Gomez became violently ill after eating the fish he caught under the Pierce Street Bridge.
2. Whenever the space shuttle is launched in Florida, we have nasty weather in Pennsylvania.
3. Chewing tobacco causes mouth cancer.
4. Silicone breast implants cause connective tissue disease.
5. People who drink vegetable juice every day never seem to get sick.
6. More acts of violence are committed by children who watch professional wrestling than by children who do not watch professional wrestling.
7. Students who sit in the front row tend to get higher-than-average grades.
8. Minimizing salt in your diet can bring down high blood pressure.
9. Dioxin in the soil leads to cancer in the population.
10. Drinking two glasses of red wine per day will give you a healthier heart.

A FEW WORDS ABOUT PROBABILITY

Why discuss probability in a chapter on inductive reasoning? The answer is that there is an important connection between probability and induction. All inductive arguments are a matter of probability because they are not certain. They do not guarantee the truth of their conclusions, but only offer evidence that the conclusion is probably true.

We need to clarify what we mean by *probability* because there are several different senses of the word. Consider these three examples:

There is a pretty high probability that I'll go to the beach sometime this summer.

There is a 90 percent probability that the operation will be successful.

There is a 50 percent probability of getting tails on a fair coin toss.

The first example, "There is a pretty high probability that I'll go to the beach sometime this summer," illustrates **epistemic probability,** which expresses how likely we think an event is given other things we believe. This is the kind of probability we assign to statements we believe but to which we cannot assign a probability on any truly mathematical basis. Knowing that I want to go to the beach sometime this summer and believing with good reason that I'll have time to do so, I can rationally assert that there is a high probability that I will indeed go to the beach. Along the same lines, we can also assign low probabilities to certain events. For example, "Considering the way Sid and Nancy were arguing last night, I'd say there's a pretty low probability that they will get married."

The second example, "There is a 90 percent probability that the operation will be successful," illustrates **relative frequency probability,** which takes information about a group as a whole and applies it to an individual case. The

Could You Predict the Weather?

Some weather forecasters give a "5-degree guarantee." They will "guarantee" that they can predict tomorrow's high temperature within 5 degrees. This sounds impressive until you consider that this means within a range of eleven. If the weatherperson predicts 51 degrees, she is right if the high temperature falls anywhere within the range of 46 to 56 degrees. You don't have to be a weather forecaster to make that kind of prediction most days.

application is based on accumulated data, derived from what has already been observed in the group. In this sense it is related to the statistical arguments discussed earlier in this chapter. For example, a surgeon may inform her patient that ninety out of one hundred of her patients who had this surgery found it improved their condition. Of course, it is always possible to improve the accuracy of a prediction based on relative frequency probability by increasing the size of the sample or by being more specific about the group to which it applies. Perhaps the surgery has a 90 percent success rate with patients in general, but a 98 percent success rate for patients under thirty-five and only an 81 percent success rate for patients over eighty. What is the probability of an infant's surviving the first year of life? More than 99 percent in the United States in general, but less than that in some inner-city areas. It is greater than 99 percent for infants with no apparent problems at birth, and far less than 99 percent for infants with certain kinds of congenital birth defects.

The third example, "There is a 50 percent probability of getting tails on a fair coin toss," illustrates **a priori probability**—statements that have odds that can be calculated prior to, and independent of, sensory observation. Even if I have never seen a coin before, you can explain the nature of the coin toss, and I will be able to tell you that the probability of the coin coming up tails is 50 percent and the probability of its coming up heads is likewise 50 percent. The same would be true of a deck of cards. Even if I have never seen one, you can explain to me that there is a total of fifty-two cards with thirteen different values and four different suits. I can then tell you that the chance of any one particular card's being drawn is 1 in 52, or 1.92 percent. The chances of an ace's being drawn are 4 in 52, or 1 in 13, or 7.7 percent.

Probabilities direct the conduct of the wise man.
—Cicero

EXERCISE 11.11

Decide whether each of the following is an example of epistemic probability, relative frequency probability, or a priori probability.

1. The probability of a random student passing the next exam without studying.
2. Your chances of picking the winning number in the state lottery.

3. The probability of a hurricane hitting the Northeast in October.
4. The probability of your mother going to a Marilyn Manson concert.
5. The odds of the horse you bet on winning the Kentucky Derby.
6. The probability of being dealt a royal flush in poker.
7. The chances of a random student getting an A in this course.
8. The likelihood of your getting a perfect score in bowling.
9. The odds of your favorite team winning the Super Bowl.
10. The chances of rolling a 6 with two standard dice.

A Closer Look at a Priori Probability

The rules of probable inference are the most difficult part of logic, but also the most useful.

—Bertrand Russell

Sometimes we want to know the probability of a situation involving two events. For example, let's say you need to draw *either* a 7 *or* a king from a full deck of fifty-two cards. What are the chances? The probability of either of two events occurring is the sum of their probabilities. In other words, add them: The odds of drawing a 7 are 1 in 13, or 7.7 percent, and the odds of drawing a king are also 1 in 13, or 7.7 percent. So, the chances of drawing either a 7 or a king are $\frac{1}{13} + \frac{1}{13} = \frac{2}{13}$, or 15.4 percent. The probability of *both* of two independent events occurring is substantially less, however. Let's say that this time you have to draw a 7 from a deck of fifty-two cards and then draw a king from another deck of fifty-two cards. What are the odds? The probability of both of two events occurring is the product of their probabilities. In other words, multiply them: The odds of drawing the 7 are 1 in 13, and the chances of drawing the king are also 1 in 13. So, the chances of drawing the 7 from one deck and then drawing the king from the other deck are $\frac{1}{13} \times \frac{1}{13} = \frac{1}{169}$, or 0.59 percent—less than 1 percent.

What are the chances of drawing a 7 from a deck of fifty-two if you have just drawn a 7 from the deck and randomly put it back? As we saw, the odds of drawing the 7 in the first case were 1 in 13, or 7.7 percent; but you may be surprised to find that the odds of randomly drawing the 7 again are also 1 in 13, or 7.7 percent. If you thought the odds were much worse, you committed the **gambler's fallacy**—the mistaken belief that a past event has an impact on a current random event. In this example, the past event was the first draw of the 7 and the current random event was the second draw. The question wasn't What are the odds of getting a 7 on two successive draws of the cards? The question was only What are the odds of getting a 7 on the second draw of the cards? Assuming the 7 card was returned to the deck, the past draw has no causal effect on the present one. The cards are dumb. They don't know which one was drawn last.

Chance favors the prepared mind.

—Louis Pasteur

Consider the case of betting on a roulette wheel. On a standard roulette wheel, there are thirty-eight spaces; eighteen of the spaces numbered 1–36 are black, and eighteen are red. There are also two green spaces numbered 0 and 00. The chances of red coming in are 47.37 percent, and the chances are the same for black, 47.37 percent. If you observe that red has come in twice in a row, should you then put your money on black for the next spin of the wheel?

Ya Say It's Your Birthday . . .

Surprising odds: If you are sitting in a classroom with twenty-three other people, what are the odds that two people share the same birthday (excluding year)? Believe it or not, the odds are greater than 1 in 2. Try it out.

No, there is no good reason to because there is no causal connection between one spin and another. The odds are not, as you might think, in your favor. There is still only a 47.37 percent chance of black coming in. Each spin of the wheel is a random event, unaffected by previous events—including previous spins of the wheel. What if you wanted to bet on your lucky number, say 15, but the wheel just came in 15 on the spin before you could get your bet down? Does that mean there is a good reason not to bet on 15 this time? Aside from the nonexistence of lucky numbers and the terrible odds of any one particular number coming in (only 2.63 percent), there is no reason not to bet on 15. The chances of 15 coming in are the same for every spin of the wheel—2.63 percent—even when the number just came in.

"But what about the law of averages?" you might object! Don't things even out over the long run? Yes, they tend to do that. You might be surprised just how long the long run is, though. With thirty-eight different numbers, we're talking about a very large number of spins of the roulette wheel before we are likely to see an even distribution of the numbers that come in. It will be easier to grasp this if we stick with a simple example that has only two possible outcomes—for example, a coin toss. The toss of a fair coin will result in 50 percent heads and 50 percent tails over the long run. No one would be shocked to see 60 percent heads if we tossed the coin five times—that would mean three heads and two tails. We wouldn't be too surprised even if it were ten tosses—six heads and four tails—or twenty tosses—twelve heads and eight tails. It would be more surprising to toss the coin one hundred times and get sixty heads and forty tails, but this is not impossible or unheard of, even with a fair coin. The point is, according to the **law of large numbers,** the proximity of theoretically predicted and actual percentages tends to increase as the sample grows. In other words, the bigger the sample, the closer the actual results are likely to be to the predicted results. If we tossed the coin ten thousand times, it would be surprising if we didn't have something very close to a 50-50 split. But it would also be surprising if we did have exactly that. An exact match between actual and theoretically predicted percentages is more likely with a smaller sample. This is easy to see, in that there is a better chance of having a 50-50 split after two coin tosses (there is a 50 percent chance of this) than there is after ten tosses. The same reasoning can be applied to spins of the roulette wheel. The chance of black coming in is just under 50 percent, at

---

• Critical Thinking Lapse •

Out for some Italian food one night, Yogi Berra was asked if he wanted his pizza cut into four slices or eight slices. His response: "Better make it four. I don't think I could eat eight."[7]

47.37 percent, but strange things do happen. In 1918 in Monte Carlo, black came up twenty-six consecutive times on the roulette wheel.

There are different ways to assess the value of making a bet, ranging from the objective to the subjective. **Expected value** is essentially the payoff or loss you can expect from making a bet. Without getting heavily into the mathematics of it, we can fairly easily eyeball the expected value of a particular bet to see if it is positive, negative, or neutral. For example, if five hundred $1 chances are being sold for a raffle in which the first and only prize is a bicycle worth $200, buying a raffle ticket is a pretty bad bet in terms of expected value. In fact, it has a negative expected value. How can you tell? Consider what would happen if you could somehow manage to buy all the raffle tickets. The good news is that you would be guaranteed to win. The bad news is that you would have spent $500 to win a $200 bicycle. If there were only two hundred $1 tickets sold for the raffle, the bet would have a neutral expected value of 0. If you bought all two hundred tickets, you would win a $200 bicycle. If there were only one hundred $1 tickets sold for the raffle, this would be a good bet with a positive expected value. If you could manage to buy all the tickets, you would have spent only $100 and be guaranteed to win a $200 bicycle. Unfortunately, bets with positive or even neutral expected values are rare. Most bets have a negative expected value. This gives "the house" the edge, making it profitable for it to offer the bet. That is no big secret. Most people know the odds are against them when they make a bet or buy a raffle ticket. But they do it anyway! Why?

Wise venturing is the most commendable part of human prudence.

—Marquis of Halifax

They do it because it's fun and the bets are worth it to the people making them, even when they know that it is not a sound investment of their money. Perhaps they get some thrill out of the possibility of turning their $1 into a $200 bicycle. Maybe the profits from the sale of the raffle tickets go to support a good cause, and that alone makes it worthwhile. What we see illustrated here is **relative value**—the value a bet has in relation to an individual's own needs, preferences, and resources. If spending $1 on a raffle ticket is not going to damage your personal finances and if you find it fun and worthwhile to have the chance of winning, it may make perfect sense for you to buy the ticket. The ticket represents a chance to win and has a high relative value. A second ticket, however, is not likely to have a relative value that is quite as high. The tenth ticket will likely have even less relative value. The more money you spend on tickets, the less relative value the tickets have. You had a chance to win with the purchase of the first ticket, and buying ten tickets hasn't increased your odds enough to warrant their purchase. The relative value of the first

The Prisoners' Dilemma

Two thieves are taken into custody and held in separate areas. They are given the following options:

1. Confess and implicate your partner. If he does not confess, you go free and he will get ten years. If you confess and he also confesses, you will each get two years.
2. Don't confess. If neither one of you confesses, you will get six months because we have enough evidence to tie you both to a different crime. If you don't confess and your partner does and implicates you, you will get ten years.

What is the more rational strategy for a prisoner in this situation to adopt? What would you do?

---

ticket was enough to override the negative expected value; but with each ticket you purchase, the ability for relative value to override expected value gets less and less. This is a phenomenon known as **diminishing marginal value:** as quantity increases, relative value tends to decrease.

Diminishing marginal value (sometimes called *diminishing marginal utility*) is a basic economic concept, which your own experience will confirm. If you are hungry, one slice of pizza will have a very high relative value, probably making its cost worthwhile. But consider what happens as the number of slices you buy increases. The relative value tends to go down, doesn't it? The second slice and maybe the third will also have a moderately high relative value, but likely less than the first one, which calmed your rumbling stomach. If you get to a fifth, sixth, or seventh slice, not only will you be a glutton, but you will also find that each slice has less and less value to you—less and less relative value.

Let's consider how these value concepts apply to the lottery. Multistate lotteries, such as Powerball, have become increasingly popular in recent years. It costs one dollar to play one game of Powerball. To win you need to pick five numbers in any order and then pick one number exactly, the Powerball. The lottery officials tell us that the chances of winning are 1 in 146,107,962. The implication is that there are just that many possible number combinations, given the rules of the game. So, does playing Powerball have a positive or a negative expected value? That depends both on what the jackpot is and on how many tickets are sold. Let's say the jackpot reaches $100 million. That sounds pretty good, but there is a negative expected value because you would have to spend more than $146 million to play all possible combinations and guarantee a win.[8]

If the jackpot hits $150 million, the expected value could actually be positive. You could spend a little over $146 million and be guaranteed to hit the jackpot. Still, the expected value could be negative, depending on how many tickets are sold. If you are the only person allowed to buy tickets for this particular drawing (something not likely to happen), you will be guaranteed to win and the expected value will be positive—it is a good bet. If others are playing, too (as you can be sure they will), the expected value will go down in proportion to the number of tickets sold. For example, if 300 million tickets are sold, there is a fair chance that there will be two winners who share the jackpot, that is, split it. D'oh! The bad news is that even if you alone hit the jackpot, you will have to split the prize money with the taxman. What was $150 million will soon be $75 million or less; and according to the rules of most lotteries, if you want it all at once rather than over a period of twenty years, you will get yet less.

It looks like any way you slice it, Powerball is a bad bet in terms of expected value. Most people know this. Still, even many of those who know it's a bad bet will buy a ticket. Why? Because the relative value of one ticket is probably enough to override the negative expected value. For one dollar you can dream of winning a huge jackpot, telling off the boss, quitting your job, and dumping your husband for an Ashton Kutcher look-alike. Still, people don't generally buy tons of Powerball tickets because the relative value goes down with each ticket purchased. Diminishing marginal value, remember? Unfortunately, not everyone gets the point. Many people travel for hours to a state where Powerball tickets are on sale and then proceed to buy hundreds or even thousands of tickets. The negative expected value tells us that with every ticket they purchase, they are in effect throwing money out the window. For some people it is an obsession, even an addiction. One Powerball ticket should be enough for anyone.

EXERCISE 11.12

I. Decide whether each of the following has a positive, a negative, or a neutral expected value.

1. Any 50-50 lottery, one in which first prize is half the amount collected from ticket sales.
2. An even-money $100 bet on a single fair coin toss.
3. Buying one ticket for a raffle in which there are ten tickets in total, each costing $1,000. The prize is a brand-new Mercedes.
4. A $10 bet on red coming in on the next spin of the roulette wheel.
5. Buying ten tickets for a raffle in which there are five hundred tickets in total, each costing $1. The prize is two tickets to a Broadway show.

II. Give your own evaluation of the relative value of the bets in Exercise I.

III. Give your own detailed example of a case of diminishing marginal value.

SUMMARY

1. This chapter focused on forming and critically evaluating *inductive arguments*—arguments whose premises are intended to provide support, but not conclusive evidence, for the conclusion. In particular, we examined

four common types: *inductive generalizations, arguments from analogy, causal arguments,* and *statistical arguments.*

2. Inductive arguments do not guarantee their conclusions. We evaluate them according to the strength of the support they provide for their conclusions. An inductive argument is strong when its premises provide evidence that its conclusion is more likely true than false. An inductive argument is weak when its premises do *not* provide evidence that its conclusion is more likely true than false.

3. Among the important indicator words and phrases for inductive arguments are *likely, probably, it's plausible to suppose that, it's reasonable to believe that, one would expect that, it's a good bet that, chances are that,* and *odds are that.*

4. An *inductive generalization* is an argument that relies on characteristics of a sample population to make a claim about the population as a whole. In other words, it is an argument that uses evidence about a limited number of people or things of a certain type (the *sample population*) to make a claim about a larger group of people or things of that type (the *population as a whole*).

5. Ask these questions in evaluating an inductive generalization:

    *   Are the premises true?
    *   Is the sample large enough? (The size of the sample population must be sufficient to justify the conclusion about the population as a whole.)
    *   Is the sample representative? (A *representative sample* is like the population as a whole in all relevant ways. It should be a mini-version of the population as a whole.)

6. A *strong inductive argument* has premises that provide evidence that its conclusion is more likely true than false. A *cogent inductive argument* has all true premises and supplies strong support for its conclusion. A *strong and reliable argument* has premises that provide evidence that its conclusion is more likely true than false *and* it is an argument that a reasonable person *would* act or bet on. A *strong but unreliable argument* has premises that provide evidence that its conclusion is more likely true than false, *but* it is an argument that a reasonable person *would not* act or bet on.

7. Polling should be *double-blind;* that is, the person taking the poll and the person responding should have no information about each other, or at least as little as possible. And neither the pollster nor the respondent should have any indication of the "right answer."

8. A *statistical argument* argues from premises regarding a percentage of a population to a conclusion about an individual member of that population or some part of that population.

9. Like other inductive arguments, statistical arguments are evaluated along a continuum of strong to weak.

10. Statistical arguments that approach 50 percent may be strong but are to be considered relatively unreliable.

11. The *reference class* is the group to which statistics apply. As a rule, the more specific the reference class is, the better the argument is.

12. An *analogy* is a comparison of things based on similarities those things share. Whereas analogies simply point out a similarity, *arguments from analogy* claim that certain similarities are evidence that there is *another* similarity (or other similarities).

13. Things to consider in evaluating the strength of an argument from analogy include the *truth of the premises;* the *relevance of the similarities;* the *number of relevant similarities;* the *relevance of dissimilarities;* the *number of relevant dissimilarities;* the *diversity of the sample* (especially with increased sample size); and the *specificity of the conclusion relative to the premises.*

14. Not all causal arguments contain the word *cause.* Other causal terms include *produce, is responsible for,* and *affects.* Such arguments come in two broad types: arguments about the cause of a single instance and arguments about a general relationship.

15. Sometimes, two things or events are clearly associated or linked: where you find X, you will often find Y. A relationship such as this, in which two things are frequently found together, is called a *correlation.* Sometimes a correlation is an indicator of a cause-and-effect relationship. A *positive correlation,* one that indicates two things are found together more than 50 percent of the time, may indicate a causal connection between one thing and the other. A *negative correlation,* one that indicates two things are found together less than 50 percent of the time, may indicate that one thing prevents the other. The important question is this: Is the correlation significant? The answer depends, in part, on the size of the sample.

16. *Epistemic probability* is the kind of probability we assign to things we have good reason to believe but to which we cannot assign a probability on any truly mathematical basis.

17. *Relative frequency probability* is the kind of probability that takes information about a group as a whole and applies it to an individual case, based on accumulated data derived from what has already been observed in the group.

18. Statements of *a priori probability* have odds that can be calculated prior to, and independent of, sensory observation.

19. The *gambler's fallacy* is the mistaken belief that a past event has an impact on a current random event.

20. According to the *law of large numbers,* the proximity of theoretically predicted and actual percentages tends to increase as the sample grows. In other words, the bigger the sample, the closer the actual results are likely to be to the predicted results.

21. *Expected value* is essentially the payoff or loss you can expect from making a bet.

22. *Relative value* is the value a bet has in relation to an individual's own needs, preferences, and resources.

23. *Diminishing marginal value* is the principle that as quantity increases, relative value tends to decrease.

CHAPTER 12

FINDING, EVALUATING, AND USING SOURCES

Other than "oral presentation required," perhaps no phrase on a syllabus throws students into more consternation than "research paper required." Few students look forward to the long, sometimes grueling, often frustrating process of finding information and incorporating it into a paper. In this chapter we show you that research does not have to be an intimidating academic exercise. Arguments are stronger and more credible when bolstered by support. And for a critical thinker—one committed to truth, fairness, and precision—research also develops the ability to find information, set the record straight, and advance the conversation.

It may be best to begin with some idea of *why* research work is assigned in colleges and universities. Obviously, in researching a topic, you discover data and opinions that you can use as evidence to support the claims in your argument. But conducting research well has implications beyond the immediate success of a single assignment, especially for someone studying critical thinking. Doing research lets you practice the skills of finding, evaluating, summarizing, and using information—skills necessary in just about every profession that requires a college degree. Accountants, physicians, lawyers, managers, computer experts, teachers—all must keep up with trends in the field, find causes and solutions, analyze precedent, collect data, and so forth. The good research habits developed in college will show up again in your nonprofessional life as well. Successfully running for local office, hiring a contractor or a lawyer, investing in the stock market, voting, and even deciding what movie to go to often depend on your ability to find and evaluate information. In fact, it is no exaggeration to say that many of the major decisions in our lives, and even some of the minor ones, would be more rewarding if we arrived at them only after investigation and study rather than on impulse and whim.

Good research can also help you set the record straight and avoid accepting at face value what you hear and read. A politician may convincingly argue that her commitment to the environment is above reproach, but simple research into her voting record on bills affecting clean water and air may suggest otherwise.

Research is formalized curiosity. It is poking and prying with a purpose.

—Zora Neale Hurston

340

Often in the search for truth, you need to go directly to the primary sources. If you want to know what the Constitution says about possessing firearms, it might be wise to read the Constitution and not just what has been written *about* it. Some secondhand sources are highly reliable, fair, and trustworthy, but others are sloppy, biased, or even unethical in their quoting, paraphrasing, and summarizing and, as a result, may relay distorted and inaccurate information. Reading the primary sources lets you set the record straight.

Just as returning to the primary source can help you see more clearly, research can help you correct your own misconceptions and shatter some long-cherished assumptions. Often what people have firmly accepted as true and unassailable has, upon further investigation, been shown to be baseless. What you believe, on just about any topic—welfare, culture, crime, religion, politics, education—might or might not hold up to objective and thorough investigation. Research can help clarify fuzzy, vague notions you may have about certain topics and can help you analyze a complex issue, including what positions are held by others and what evidence is generally provided in support or rebuttal of claims. Research allows you to become something of an expert on a small issue and to speak with some authority as you attempt to correct misunderstanding, speak the truth, and provide accurate information.

EXERCISE 12.1

In groups of four, complete the following test. Be sure to discuss each question or statement as a group and record only one answer on which members of the group agree.

A. Decide whether each of the following is true or false.

1. The first battle between ironclad ships took place between the *Monitor* and the *Merrimack*.
2. "Yankee Doodle" was written as a patriotic song of the American Revolution.
3. "The Star-Spangled Banner" was written during the American Revolution and has been our national anthem for almost two hundred years.
4. Ferdinand Magellan was the first person to circumnavigate the globe.
5. Charles Lindbergh was the first person to fly across the Atlantic.
6. The Declaration of Independence was signed on July 4, 1776.
7. You should never end a sentence with a preposition or start one with *and* or *but*.
8. The United States has never fought a war with China.
9. A teacher with tenure can never be fired.
10. A Catholic priest can never be married.
11. Frankenstein was a monster.
12. Abbreviating Christmas to *Xmas* began as a way to insult Christians.
13. The Emancipation Proclamation freed the slaves.
14. Robert Fulton invented the steamboat, which he named the *Clermont*.

15. A number of women accused of being witches were burned in Salem, Massachusetts.
16. Benjamin Franklin discovered electricity.
17. The Immaculate Conception refers to Christ's having been born of a virgin.
18. Lightning never strikes the same place twice.

B. Answer the following questions.

1. Bagpipes were invented in what country?
2. What is "circumstantial evidence"?
3. Why is Los Angeles's baseball team called the Dodgers?
4. Who invented the sewing machine?
5. *Mr.* is an abbreviation for *Mister.* What is *Mrs.* an abbreviation for?
6. What was President Harry Truman's middle name?
7. What did Henry Ford invent?
8. Who invented the lightbulb?
9. Who invented the telephone?
10. What does the distress signal "SOS" stand for?
11. "Fourscore and seven years ago, our forefathers brought forth upon this continent a new nation" is the opening line of what famous document? Is the line quoted accurately?
12. In Nova Scotia the sun rises in the _____, but on the west coast of Brazil, it rises in the _____.

After you have finished the test, divide up the thirty items among your group members. Each member of the group should research his or her items to determine if the group's responses were correct.

Aside from teaching you how to find information and unveil the truth, researching a topic allows you to enter the debate on an issue, perhaps extending the conversation into new areas. Don't think of research *merely* as gathering and repeating everything you can find on a given topic. Gathering information is certainly part of the task, but well-researched arguments are not simply repetitions of previous arguments or collections of published data. Look carefully, respectfully, and skeptically at what others have said about the research topic. Pore over the data collected by other researchers; read the reactions and conclusions of other thinkers; accept, reject, or modify the claims of essayists, editorialists, and analysts; and ultimately add your own, perhaps innovative, thinking to the mix. Research provides the opportunity to discover and learn, but also to infer and create, to go beyond what has already been said. In fact, if we thought of research as a chance not only to bolster our ideas but also to combine old ideas into new ones and to propel us toward original thoughts, research would be less a boring chore and more an opportunity to increase our knowledge and to add something to the discourse. The great scientist and mathematician Sir Isaac Newton wrote in a letter to Robert Hooke, "If I have seen further, it is by standing on the shoulders of giants." Few of us will

Calvin and Hobbes   by Bill Watterson

I'VE GOT TO WRITE A REPORT FOR SCHOOL.

WHAT'S YOUR TOPIC?

BATS. CAN YOU IMAGINE ANYTHING MORE STUPID?

HECK, *I* DON'T KNOW ANYTHING ABOUT BATS.' HOW AM I SUPPOSED TO WRITE A REPORT ON A SUBJECT I KNOW NOTHING ABOUT ?! IT'S IMPOSSIBLE!

I SUPPOSE RESEARCH IS OUT OF THE QUESTION.

OH, LIKE I'M GOING TO LEARN ABOUT BATS AND *THEN* WRITE A REPORT ?! GIVE ME A BREAK!

be Isaac Newtons, but our ability to see farther than our predecessors depends entirely on our ability to find and to look carefully at what they have already seen.

All too often, especially at the undergraduate level, students conducting research become frustrated by the overwhelming amount of information available and select for their arguments whatever they discover first, assuming perhaps that *any* support is *good* support. That is understandable, given how time-consuming research can be: We are all reluctant to throw out the fruits of our labor, even what is sour and rotten. But an effective research project is based on reliable, accurate sources. When you use sources to support your own conclusions, you are saying to your readers, "Here is someone who agrees with what I am saying," or "Here is information that confirms what I have been claiming." It is vital to the success of the argument that those sources be good ones. The rest of this chapter shows you how to find sources, how to evaluate the sources you find so that only the most accurate and reliable information makes it into your arguments, and how to place those sources into an argumentative essay.

> *I will search far and wide to support my conclusions.*
> —Job 36:3

FINDING SOURCES

Years ago, students doing research in their college libraries might have complained that the library didn't have the necessary resources to permit a thorough investigation of a topic. Today, the opposite seems to be true: you can easily feel overwhelmed by the amount of information available in a modern library and online. To conquer the modern world of research, you need assistance. This section offers some basic instruction for locating sources of print and electronic information when researching an argumentative essay; but trying to provide an exhaustive research guidebook in a few pages would be like attempting to draw a map of New York City on a postage stamp. In fact, the closest thing to an exhaustive guide, the *Guide to Reference Books,* a list of general reference materials (encyclopedias, dictionaries, indexes, and the like), includes more than sixteen thousand entries in more than two thousand pages. The following advice is provided for the critical thinker preparing an argument, but anyone using a library today is strongly encouraged to seek the help of a reference librarian.

Refining Your Search

> *A problem properly stated is partly solved.*
> —Henry Hazlitt

Most researchers approach the library with two types of questions in mind. The first is a simple, single question that requires the retrieval of specific data:

What are the names of Jupiter's moons?

When did Babe Ruth play for the Boston Red Sox?

What does a hellgrammite look like?

Why is the sky blue?

Who said, "Freedom of the press belongs to those who own one?"

The second type of question requires a more complicated and intensive search:

What started the Vietnam War?

How dangerous is moshing?

Was there a conspiracy to assassinate President Kennedy?

What led to the nuclear arms race?

How widespread is identity theft in the United States?

Sometimes the second type of question can indicate an extraordinary amount of research. Researching the nuclear arms race, for example, could lead you down many different paths as you collect information and interpretations from political figures, historians, scholars, and, perhaps, depending on your purpose, even novelists and poets.

Before you begin searching for information, decide what specific questions you need to answer and what general questions you have concerning areas you need to learn more about. For example, in researching workplace safety, you might list the following simple questions: How many workers are injured or killed each year on the job? How many in a specific industry, such as truck driving? What agencies oversee the trucking industry? What are the regulations governing truck transportation? What union representation do truck drivers have? What causes most accidents involving trucks? How many trucks were involved in accidents last year? More-complicated questions might focus on recent improvements in truck safety, or attempts to lower the number of accidents, or the recommendations proposed by state police, the AAA, state departments of transportation, OSHA, or the Federal Highway Administration.

Often these types of questions will occur to you if you have written a draft of an argument based only on your opinions and observations. At other times you may be tackling issues you know too little about to write a draft of more than a few sentences. As a way to guide your research, try writing down your questions and using them to direct but not restrict your search; you might find information you never thought to ask for. And remember that as you research and write, new questions will occur to you, requiring additional research for answers. The purpose of recording questions is to help guide your search and prevent you from approaching your research with ill-defined needs and a sense of hopelessness.

Once you have determined what you are looking for, you can begin your search. Two kinds of source material will be most helpful: material that will *provide* the information you are looking for, and material that will *direct* you toward the material you are looking for. Informational material includes encyclopedias, newspapers, journals, magazines, dictionaries, books, government documents, and Web sites. Directional materials include indexes, bibliographies, card catalogs, guides to reference sources, and online databases. Almost every student is familiar with *The Readers' Guide to Periodical Literature*, a print index that directs researchers toward information contained in magazines and journals.

> *Knowledge is of two kinds. We know a subject ourselves, or we know where we can find information upon it.*
> —Samuel Johnson

Directional Information

The following are among the most popular and accessible reference works and search engines for pointing you in the direction of information located in books and periodicals and on the Internet. To make the best use of these materials, consult the Library of Congress Subject Headings to determine how your topic is classified in reference works; otherwise, you might search in vain for books and articles on "free speech" and "religious tolerance" when your topics are listed in bibliographies and indexes under "freedom of speech" and "freedom of religion." On the other hand, online databases may permit keyword searches that will result in a number of hits whether you use your own terminology or the Library of Congress headings.

Bibliographies   Generally speaking, a *bibliography* is a list of books that provides for each book the name of the author, the title, the place and date of publication, the name of the publisher, and, in some cases, the price of the book. Bibliographies can also include recordings, films, photographs, and computer software programs. The most familiar bibliography to student researchers is the catalog, available in every library in either print or electronic form and listing all the books held by the library and stored on the shelves (often called "stacks") or in special collections areas. Other bibliographies, less well known but available in most libraries in print or in electronic format, include the Library of Congress's *National Union Catalog,* which lists books published in the United States, and the *British National Bibliography,* which lists every work published in Great Britain since 1950. *Books in Print* lists all books currently available from publishers. Other bibliographies, more generally defined as "lists of publications," catalog pamphlets, newspapers, and other periodicals. Such references as *Urlich's International Periodical Directory, Gale Directory of Publications and Broadcast Media, Gale Directory of Databases,* and the *Vertical File Index* (for pamphlets) may be helpful in locating book titles, periodicals, and places of publication for a wide range of sources. Keep in mind that these bibliographies will usually provide only lists of what is available, with little additional information about the publication. One notable exception is *Magazines for Libraries,* which describes periodicals in some detail.

Indexes and Databases   If you're looking for something published before the late 1980s, you may have to consult a print index such as *The Readers' Guide to Periodical Literature* or *Poole's Index to Periodical Literature.* Almost everything published after 1990 (and some older works) can be accessed through the electronic databases available through your library. Some databases are subject- or discipline-specific. Depending on your topic, you could search, for instance, *Business Source Premier, Communications and Mass Media Complete, Philosopher's Index,* or *ERIC,* which indexes articles and documents in education. General databases, such as *LexisNexis,* search a wider variety of sources in, for example, business, law, and communications. Some databases provide only the information needed to locate a source (author's name, title of the article, and so on), whereas others provide the full text of selected articles. Some databases are extremely expensive and are therefore not available in every library. For help in using these services, consult a reference librarian.

Internet Search Engines, Guides, and Directories   Nothing is more emblematic of the information age than the Internet, which has made millions of pages of text and illustrations available with only a few taps on the keyboard and a click of the mouse. But the blessing is also a curse: how do you sort through those millions upon millions of pages? Internet search engines (*google.com, ask.com, alltheweb.com,* to name a few) and metasearch engines (*metacrawler.com, dogpile.com, infogrid.com,* for example) will help provide some direction when you are looking for information, but entering a keyword can result in thousands of "hits," many of which are only marginally related to your interests. Most search engines have indexes for subject areas such as travel, games, movies, sports, and jokes, and these indexes do help reduce the number of pages you need to surf through; however, they are generally limited to popular interests. You may prefer to search the sports pages, but you are not likely to find much support there for a paper on religion and medicine.

If you have only a broad topic and want to find what you can about that subject, try one of the more helpful directories, such as Yahoo! or About.com, which organize Web resources by categories such as "science," "culture," and "education." You can find links to useful sites by working your way through the subdirectories. For example, at Yahoo! the path "Social Science → Political Science → Public Policy → Institutes" will lead you to an annotated list of links to a great many of the various think tanks and policy research institutes that maintain Web sites.

Through the Internet you also can access information in discussion newsgroups and in listservs, discussion groups that operate by e-mail and to which you must subscribe. There are newsgroups and listservs on just about every subject imaginable (and some that are beyond what most of us can imagine). An earnest researcher may find helpful sources of information in some of the more academic and serious groups. Your search engine (*http://groups.google.com* is among the best) and your Web browser will help you locate discussion groups and listservs.

Bibliographies, indexes, and Internet search engines and guides will help point you in the right direction, though they will not provide the actual information you are seeking, whether your inquiry is simple or complex. What follows are some of the informational sources you will find in libraries and the kinds of informational sites you will find on the Internet.

Informational Sources

The directional resources listed in the preceding section will guide you toward the books, articles, and Web sites that you are seeking. But you can find information in places other than the books in the stacks, the periodicals, and the Internet. When looking for information, consider the following reference materials and sources. Some of these sources can provide quick answers to simple questions or get you started in your attempt to familiarize yourself with a topic. Other sources will provide more in-depth analysis and information.

Encyclopedias   General encyclopedias such as *Encyclopaedia Britannica, Collier's, Encyclopedia Americana, Compton's,* and *Grolier* are excellent starting points for finding information about a topic, whether you are seeking specific answers or overviews and historical perspectives. Several of these encyclopedias are available online (see if your school's library subscribes to any of them), or you can consult a widely used, free online encyclopedia, Wikipedia (*wikipedia .org*). Because Wikipedia can be edited by anyone using the site, content does not pass though a review process before it appears on the page. Although well-educated and objective users are quick to remove false, overly subjective, or slanderous content, students using this site are cautioned to read with a critical eye and to be aware that their professor may forbid use of the site for research.

Although encyclopedias don't always get the respect they deserve in colleges and universities, they can be helpful first steps toward understanding the basic concepts behind difficult subjects in disciplines such as psychology, philosophy, theology, science, and literature. In fact, many encyclopedia entries conclude with a short bibliography of reliable sources for further study. For more-concentrated information about disciplines, you can consult subject encyclopedias, which contain information pertinent to specific topics: *Encyclopedia* of *Psychology, Encyclopedia of Philosophy, Encyclopedia of Religion,* the *McGraw-Hill Multimedia Encyclopedia of Science and Technology,* and *Benet's Reader's Encyclopedia* are just a few of the many subject encyclopedias available in most libraries. Additionally, the *Oxford Companion* series (*Oxford Companion to English Literature, Oxford Companion to Chess,* and so forth) provides an excellent starting place for researchers looking for basic information.

Almanacs, Yearbooks, Fact Books, Directories, Handbooks, Manuals, and Atlases   These are the volumes you will most often consult when you need factual answers to uncomplicated questions such as "How many Americans are on Social Security?" or "Where is Mozambique?" or "Who said, 'Neither a borrower nor a lender be'?" As we noted earlier, people frequently assume that their basic knowledge is accurate only to discover that they have been wrong all along. Ready-reference materials such as almanacs and fact books can help researchers find solid evidence to affirm or correct their assumptions and support their claims.

Some of the more popular sources of factual information include *The New York Public Library Desk Reference, The Guinness Book of World Records, Information Please Almanac, World Almanac and Book of Facts, Statistical Abstracts of the United States, Facts on File* (a weekly publication), *The New International World Atlas, Emily Post's Etiquette,* and *Bartlett's Familiar Quotations.* These and other books of factual information can usually be located in one area of the library, most often close to the reference desk, and many are available online. Two excellent starting places for a search of the Web's resources are the Virtual Reference Shelf (*www.loc.gov/rr/askalib/virtualref.html*), maintained by the Library of Congress, and the Internet Public Library (*www.ipl.org*). Additionally, many college libraries maintain a site dedicated to online research. Visit your library's Web site or ask a librarian.

Biographical Sources   When you need to find out who someone is or was, you can turn to a host of biographical sources, some of which are highly reliable sources of information about a person's life, accomplishments, contributions, publications, and even misdeeds or crimes. The well-regarded *Who's Who* series (*Who's Who of American Women, Who's Who among Black Americans, Who's Who in the World,* and so forth) is complemented by other sources, such as *Current Biography, The New York Times Biographical Service,* the *Dictionary of National Biography* (usually referred to as the *DNB* and devoted solely to British and Irish notables), the *Dictionary of American Biography (DAB), World Authors,* and *Contemporary Authors.* All of these sources provide sketches of political figures, authors, scholars, dignitaries, executives, celebrities, socialites, and others whose contributions to their fields, to society, or to the culture have been noteworthy.

Dictionaries   When most students think of a dictionary, they think, sensibly, of a book that provides definitions of words, and there are plenty of such books in most college libraries. The best dictionaries for college use are unabridged, meaning that few English words have been excluded from the book no matter how colloquial, vulgar, esoteric, or obsolescent. *The Oxford English Dictionary* contains a half-million words. *Webster's Third New International Dictionary* contains slightly fewer (roughly 475,000), and the *Random House Unabridged Electronic Dictionary* fewer still (about 315,000). These are available in most libraries, but for general use in college smaller dictionaries, including *Merriam-Webster's Collegiate Dictionary,* the *American Heritage Dictionary of the English Language,* and *Webster's New World Dictionary,* will serve.

But there are plenty of other dictionaries available, including dictionaries of slang, legal terms, rhyming words, symbols, clichés, sign language, saints, theater, math, philosophy, film, names, music, ethics, archeology, politics, and myth. Many of these provide definitions for the terminology unique to the field, but others contain short, introductory passages and, in some cases, bibliographies. These dictionaries are a great place to start in your search for the kind of basic information necessary for a deeper understanding of an issue.

Several Internet dictionaries are convenient and reliable. Start with One-Look Dictionaries (*www.onelook.com*), which indexes more than six hundred general and specialized online dictionary Web sites. Because OneLook is so thorough, further searches are often unnecessary; but, if you like, you can visit Merriam-Webster's home site (*www.m-w.com*) and the Oxford English Dictionary if your school subscribes to it.

Government Documents Many libraries have access to government documents through databases and online services, and a few libraries (at least one in every state) are depositories for government documents, meaning that hard copies are kept on hand. Government documents include everything published by the U.S. government, though, obviously, only unclassified documents are available to the public. Topics range from biographical information about members of Congress to advice on repairing a home. In collecting research for an argument, you might wish to look at government-supplied information such as census reports, labor statistics, or budget information. In looking on the Internet for government documents, start with FirstGov (*http://firstgov.gov*), a large database of government Web sites.

Human Sources Often overlooked in our dependence on the written word are human beings who could easily supply needed information. In looking for library sources, you would be wise to consult a librarian. Although most librarians have advanced degrees and have had extensive, concentrated training in locating information, for some reason students will wander around for hours in a library before asking for help. Perhaps it's because we don't like to admit our shortcomings, and asking for someone's assistance is like asking for directions: we have to admit we're lost.

People besides librarians can be great sources of information, expert advice, and opinion, offering firsthand observations or even directing you toward resources you hadn't thought of. You might have a simple question that someone can answer quickly, or you might want to conduct an extended interview to collect an expert's thoughts on your topic. First consider the human sources close at hand—faculty members, local experts, government officials, members of the business and legal community, even other students who might have extensive experience or training in a particular area. Most faculty members and local authorities are willing to grant students interviews. Look too at the names that have appeared in your research. With e-mail you might be able to contact an author or an editor for clarity on an issue or for additional information. Otherwise, of course, you can write or phone.

Before you interview someone (whether in person, by phone, or in writing), prepare a list of questions you would like the interviewee to answer. Divide your queries into simple, fact-based questions ("How much revenue does the city take in each year in taxes?") and questions that allow the interviewee to expand on an issue or to think out loud ("Should the city lower the tax rate?" or "What benefits do citizens enjoy because of taxes?"). Avoid vague questions or loaded ones ("What do you think of taxes?" or "Don't you think taxes are an unfair burden on the elderly?"). And don't let your questions restrict you; as long as the interviewee stays on track and doesn't digress into irrelevant areas, you might discover information and opinions that you hadn't anticipated.

Remember to be courteous in requesting and conducting an interview. Arrive promptly, finish the interview in a reasonable amount of time, and follow up with a thank-you by e-mail or letter.

EVALUATING SOURCES

It is no exaggeration to say that we live in an information age: more than sixty-eight thousand book titles are published each year (that's almost two hundred a day);[1] by some accounts the Internet grows by three million pages a year; every day in the United States, more than fifteen hundred newspapers are published; and more than ten thousand radio stations broadcast programming around the country.[2] Information is so abundant that one edition of the *New York Times* contains more information than most of us could read in a week, let alone one day. But with all this information comes the difficulty of separating the truth from the lies, the useful and reliable information that helps advance our understanding of the world from the efforts to manipulate our thinking or control our spending. In evaluating all this information, we need to ask several questions about the *content,* the *author* and the *publisher* of the information, and the intended *audience.*

Content: Facts and Everything Else

The research you use to support your claims will generally come from books, articles, interviews with experts, the Internet, and other sources in which writers and compilers inform or attempt to persuade their readers. Occasionally, you may also use creative literature—poems and stories—as references or sources of allusions and quotes, but nonliterary works will provide your primary supply of evidence and expert testimony. As you read and listen to your sources, keep in mind that you are seeking both factual answers and nonfactual, subjective opinions, judgments, interpretations, and so forth. Although both groups are important—facts and nonfacts—you must distinguish between them.

A *fact* is an item of information that is objective and true. The sun is about ninety-three million miles from the earth. That is a fact, whether you knew it or not, believe it or not, live in North or South America, and so forth. The claim is verifiable: you could measure the distance using instruments well calibrated to gauge so great a measurement, and any scientist using such instruments would come to the same conclusion.

Sometimes facts cannot be authenticated. Say, for example, that while golfing alone you hit a hole-in-one. You know that you did, in fact, hit a hole-in-one, but you can't verify or document the occurrence because no one else saw you and no cameras were rolling. In other words, some facts cannot be verified although they are *matters of fact*. You really did, cross your heart and hope to die, hit a hole-in-one; you just can't prove it. Or take as another example the statement "In my opinion, there is life on other planets." Whether or not extraterrestrial life exists is a matter of fact: either it does or it does not. If we had the means to verify existence in outer space, we could once and for all show this writer's statement to be either true or false. So, although this writer's contention that life exists on other planets has not yet been verified, it would be wrong of us to claim that extraterrestrial life is not a fact. A writer's failure to verify a fact does not mean that his or her statement is nonfactual. And, obviously, some "facts" can never be verified. Is it a fact that Abraham Lincoln thought of his wife moments before he died? Who knows? So, for the purposes of using sources to support your own arguments, it is best to separate *verified* and *documented* facts from everything else that a writer offers, including matters of fact that have yet to be verified.

Facts can be verified through eyewitness testimony, measurement, agreement among several sources, and documentation. If you tell a professor that you missed class because of illness, the professor might ask for a doctor's note, a document that helps verify your illness. If you tried to argue that a UFO appeared above your cornfield last night, you might want to prove it with a video or a snapshot. A driver's license proves your age. This isn't to say that apparent verifiability and documentation *always* prove a fact; documents can be altered or forged, and eyewitnesses lie. But the United States Golf Association will *record* your hole-in-one as "fact" only if at least one other person saw you do it.

To summarize, when looking for evidence to support your own claims, be careful to separate objective and verified facts from unverified facts, and all facts from everything else. When reading sources it is essential that you separate facts in your source from the opinions, interpretations, and so forth

offered by the writer. What makes this a difficult task is the manner, sometimes subtle, in which nonfacts are presented as fact. Consider the following
sentences:

> The fact that women must be regarded as having little sense of justice is no
> doubt related to the predominance of envy in their mental life; for the demand
> for justice is a modification of envy and lays down the condition subject to
> which one can put envy aside. We also regard women as weaker in their social
> interests and as having less capacity for sublimating their instincts than men.[3]

Not everyone reading Freud's assessment of women's moral character will
agree with these "facts"; and despite Freud's promise that his lecture contained
"nothing but observed facts, almost without speculative additions," some critics have taken him to task for the excess of speculation and assumption. What
Freud claimed to be "fact" simply is not.

Another problem can occur even when information is presented as fact
and appears to be well documented and verified. The problem occurs most
often in the reporting of the results of surveys. For example, you might read in
an article that "75 percent of college students prefer to live in coed residence
halls," a claim that is backed up in the article by a recent survey of students.
Could you use such a statistic in your own argument? Is it a fact that 75 percent of college students prefer to live in coed dorms, or was the survey conducted in such a way that the results are not a reliable indicator of student
opinion? It is not an easy call. When using such information in defense of your
own claims, always inform your reader of the source of the "fact" and provide
as much context as possible. You might write:

> According to a recent survey of one thousand college students conducted for
> *Campus Harbinger* magazine, "75 percent of college students prefer to live in coed
> residence halls." The survey included students from all four classes in six colleges
> across the country.

In providing the context, you are saying to the reader, "The facts are that a
survey was conducted and that the survey showed *X*." It is clear to the reader
that you are presuming that the facts are true but that you are not stating with
absolute certainty that they are.

Occasionally, the task of separating fact from opinion is simple: almanacs,
indexes, and statistical abstracts provide bare-bones information, usually given
numerically (the population of Rhode Island or the number of reported AIDS
cases, for instance). But in reading essays, arguments, and articles from *any*
source—even the most seemingly objective, such as encyclopedias, dictionaries, and government documents—you must be vigilant. Be sure that any facts
you collect are objective and verifiable and that they could be documented.
Find out what the writer's sources are. Remember that the facts presented by
a writer may not tell the whole story. It is probably safe to assume that few
writers blatantly lie in their essays and arguments, but some writers tell half-
truths or "cherry-pick" evidence, selecting only those facts that support their
claim and conveniently overlooking anything that contradicts it.

Also remember that a writer's choice of words may reveal his or her attitude toward the topic and that you are free to disagree with a writer's interpretation of the facts. If Senator Smith did not serve in the military, is it a *fact* as one reporter might claim, that the senator "avoided" military service, or "evaded" the draft? An objective evaluation of the facts might lead you to a conclusion very different from the one proposed by the writer. You may have to further research Senator Smith's past to get at the truth.

Finally, be certain that the facts are relevant to your purpose. Don't, for instance, assume that you can use facts about the popularity of jazz music in New York City to prove your contention that jazz has national appeal. Similarly, be certain that the facts are up-to-date. Innovations and new discoveries, especially in technology, medicine, and business, can quickly make facts obsolete. Check the dates of your sources and try to find the most recent information.

When you have separated the facts from the nonfacts, you will be in a better position to judge the value of an author's ideas. You can determine whether the opinions, judgments, interpretations, and so forth are backed by objective fact and, if so, whether those facts are presented in the essay or merely assumed. You can also evaluate the ideas on the basis of the writer's authority to speak on the issues.

> *Truth or certainty is obtained only from facts. Every day of my life makes me feel more and more how seldom a fact is accurately stated; how almost invariably when a story has passed through the mind of a third person it becomes, so far as regards the impression it makes in further repetitions, little better than a falsehood.*
>
> —Nathaniel Hawthorne

EXERCISE 12.2

I. Pay careful attention to what you read, watch, and hear in the next twenty-four hours and list between fifteen and twenty facts from your observations. Be sure that the facts are indeed factual. Then list between five and ten opinions that you have heard or read in the same time period.

II. In groups of four, read the following passages and individually list the verified facts and the matters of fact that appear in each passage. Remember to list only information that can be stated objectively and that has been verified or that is at least verifiable. When you are finished, compare your work. Do you and your group members agree on what is fact and what is not? What accounts for any differences you have?

1. The decline of broadcast journalism began in the late '60s when I worked for NBC News. The advertising department, which had been mostly kept out of the news division during the tenure of NBC President Robert Kintner and his predecessor, Sylvester "Pat" Weaver, was allowed in. Ratings for news started to matter, as they did for entertainment. Stories were increasingly selected for the type of audience they would bring, especially women. The ratings declined anyway, along with the respect most people once had for the journalism profession. Add to story imbalance what many correctly perceive to be an ideological tilt to the left and you know why increasing numbers of people are looking elsewhere for real news. (Cal Thomas, "The Television People Kill Broadcast Journalism," *Jewish World Review,* July 28, 1999. Available online at *www.jewishworldreview.com/cols/thomas 072899.asp.*)

2. It is a truism that good books make bad films, and vice versa. By that reckoning, [*The*] *Da Vinci* [*Code*] ought to be an excellent film, since the prose is awful and the plot is tremendous. But something has gone badly wrong. For all the prestige production values and A-list stars, *The Da Vinci Code* is practically catatonic. It just lies there on the screen like a $100 million mattress. The script is bad. The acting is bad. [Audrey] Tautou is very, very bad, and clearly uncomfortable. Hanks looks and performs like a lump of dough in a wig. . . . Director Ron Howard relentlessly patronises his audience with CGI flashbacks to *The World of Ancient History,* and the whole thing goes on for hours and hours. (Paul Arendt, *BBC, co.uk,* May 19, 2006. Available online at *www .bbc.co.uk/films/2006/05/18/the_da_vinci_code_2006_review.shtml.*)

Tom Hanks, Audrey Tautou and Jean Reno do a good job of not overplaying their roles. . . . Yes, the plot is absurd, but then most movie plots are absurd. That's what we pay to see. What Ron Howard brings to the material is tone and style, and an aura of mystery that is undeniable. . . . The movie works; it's involving, intriguing and constantly seems on the edge of startling revelations. (Roger Ebert, *rogerebert.com,* May 18, 2006. Available online at http://rogerebert.suntimes.com/apps/pbcs.dll/article?AID=/20060518/ REVIEWS/60419009/1023.)

3. *Amy Goodman:* Professor Churchill, do you think that the World Trade Center was an acceptable target on September 11? Do you think it was a legitimate target?

Ward Churchill: Do I personally think it was a legitimate target or should have been a legitimate target? Absolutely not. And that's said on the basis of all but absolute rejection of and opposition to U.S. policy. But what you have to understand, and what the listeners have to understand, is that under U.S. rules, it was an acceptable target. And the reason it was an acceptable target, if none other, was that because the C.I.A., the Defense Department, and other parts of the U.S. military intelligence infrastructure, had situated offices within it, and you'll recall that that is precisely the justification advanced by the Donald Rumsfelds of the world, the Norman Schwarzkopfs, and the Colin Powells of the world, to explain why civilian targets had been bombed in Baghdad. Because that nefarious Saddam Hussein had situated elements of his command and control infrastructure within otherwise civilian occupied facilities. They said that, in itself, justified their bombing of the civilian facilities in order to eliminate the parts of the command and control infrastructure that were situated there. And of course, that then became Saddam Hussein's fault. Well, if it was Saddam Hussein's fault, sacrificing his own people, by encapsulating strategic targets within civilian facilities, the same rule would apply to the United States. So, if you've got a complaint out there with regard to the people who hit the World Trade Center, you should actually take it to the government of the United States, which, by the rubric they apply elsewhere in the world, everywhere else in the world ultimately, they converted them from civilian targets into legitimate military targets. Now, that logic is there, and it's unassailable. It's not something that I embrace. It's something that I just spell out. ("The Justice of Roosting

Chickens: Ward Churchill Speaks" [transcript], *DemocracyNow!,* February 18, 2005. Available online at *www.democracynow.org/article.pl?sid*=05/02/18/157211.)

4. The grande dame [of colleges and universities in the Greater Boston area], of course, is Harvard University, the country's oldest institution of higher learning. Harvard grads are an impressive bunch: Among them are 33 Nobel Prize winners, 30 Pulitzer Prize winners and six U.S. presidents. While living in a Cambridge dormitory, Bill Gates developed the programming language BASIC for the first microcomputer. Gates eventually dropped out of Harvard to found Microsoft, the world's leading provider of software for personal computers.

   On the other side of Cambridge Common from the Harvard campus is Radcliffe College, founded in 1879 as a prestigious school for women. Co-ed since 1973, Radcliffe is indistinguishable from Harvard in terms of degrees and admission standards, and students share housing, classes and facilities. The former sister school does, however, function as an independent corporation and has its own president.

   Sprawled along the Charles River in Cambridge is MIT, generally acknowledged to be the nation's top school for science and engineering. The demanding curriculum ensures a student body of "eggheads" who nevertheless are expanding the boundaries of the information age. Across the river in Boston itself is Boston University, founded in 1839. Nearly 26,000 graduates and undergraduates attend its various schools (Martin Luther King Jr. obtained his doctorate in theology there). BU was the first university in the nation to make all of its programs available to women and minorities, and the first to offer a school of music. (Automobile Association of America. *Boston Destination Guide,* 1999.)

5. Every sentient, literate adult knows that the current spike in gas prices is 90 percent due to forces completely beyond the control of Congress, the White House or even "Big Oil" itself. The laws of supply and demand determine gas prices the same way those laws determine the price of eggs, acid-washed blue jeans and Kanye West downloads.

   What determines the price of college tuition? It certainly isn't the quality of the product—as copiously demonstrated in David Horowitz's new book, *The Professors: The 101 Most Dangerous Academics in America.*

   The two big topics on CNN last week were (1) high gas prices and (2) the high cost of college tuition. . . .

   CNN reports that college tuition has risen an astonishing 40 percent since 2000. But the proposed solutions to the exact same problem—high prices for gasoline and tuition, respectively—were diametrically opposed.

   The only solution to high gas prices considered on CNN was to pay oil company executives less, perhaps by order of the president. But somehow, no one ever suggested that the solution to the high price of college—far outpacing inflation—was to pay professors less. In that case, the solution is for the government to subsidize college professors' salaries even more than it already does. . . .

Liberals think hardworking taxpayers who can't afford gas should pay more in taxes because it is vitally important that young people be taught that America is the worst country on Earth and that the American bond traders who were murdered on 9/11 deserved it.

Maybe with a little less subsidized tuition, colleges couldn't afford luxuries like non-Indian Indian studies professor Ward Churchill. He makes $120,000 a year as a department head at the University of Colorado, in addition to many speaking fees paid to him by other institutions of higher learning—all heavily subsidized by taxpayers. . . .

His list of academic achievements consists of his majoring in communications and graphic arts. That's the only part of his resume that has not already been proved false, probably because no one would make that up. . . . (Ann Coulter, "Tuition Soars Due to Knowledge Shortfall," *anncoulter.com,* May 3, 2006. Available online at *www.anncoulter.com/cgi-local/article.cgi? article=111.*)

The Author and the Publisher

Our best guide to truth is free and rational inquiry; we should therefore not be bound by the dictates of arbitrary authority, comfortable superstition, stifling tradition, or suffocating orthodoxy.

—"Statement of Purpose," *Free Inquiry Magazine*

Since we were young, we have been taught to rely on people more experienced, better educated, wiser, and stronger than we are to guide, protect, and nurture us. These authority figures—parents, guardians, grandparents, teachers, ministers, and police officers, to name a few—have usually acted in our best interest, communicating the habits necessary for survival and the rules for success in a civil society. We have learned to trust authority figures and to respect their opinions and decisions. We would be lost without them.

But as critical thinkers, we must question and challenge the authorities we rely on for information and support. Not that we should become belligerent and suspicious—constantly challenging the directives or recommendations of every authority becomes wearisome and could even be dangerous if we refused to accept the authority of, say, a crossing guard. But when looking to make our arguments more convincing, we should scrutinize our authoritative sources as carefully as we would an opponent's arguments. After all, our opponents will be scrutinizing us.

When it comes to gathering information, many of us do not question authority as often as we should. If you completed Exercise 12.1, ask yourself how you regarded "authorities" in the group. Were you more likely to agree with someone who *seemed* to know what he or she was talking about? If someone in the group aggressively insisted that an item was true or false, were you more likely to agree because of the aggressive stance? Did you accept the authority of the group, accept answers that were generally agreed upon?

Let's analyze the notion of an authority. The word *authority* contains, obviously, the word *author,* and, sure enough, the two words derive from the same Latin word, *auctor,* which means "creator." An author creates, and an authority holds the power over that which he or she has created as parents have authority over their children. Because of the similarity between the two words, it may seem safe to assume that authors (creators) are also authorities, and, in fact, that is often the case; many authors have spent countless years studying their subjects down to the finest detail and can speak with great expertise to even the most learned audiences. But not always. One does not have to be an expert to become an author. In fact, some authors speak with very little authority. Something's having been *written*—and written with all the appearances of objective truth—does not necessarily make it true. And although legitimate publishers of books, journals, and newspapers usually make every effort to ensure that their writers are knowledgeable and honest, publications often convey inaccurate and misleading information.

When you read or listen to someone, ask the following questions:

- What is the author's background?
- What are the author's bias and purpose?
- What are the author's sources?
- Who is the publisher or sponsor?

> No statement should be believed merely because it has been made by an authority.
>
> —Hans Reichenbach

What Is the Author's Background?   What credentials does he or she have? What education and at what level? How much research went into the writer's own work? How much experience does the author have? Is the writer an expert in the topic at issue? Is the author recognized by others as an authority in the field? For information on authors, you can consult several biographical resources, including the *Who's Who* series and such works as the *Dictionary of American Biography*. When evaluating the background of an author, don't base your assessment on only one criterion. Don't assume, for instance, that the most highly educated writers speak with the greatest authority or that an uneducated person is ignorant. Be careful not to assume that only recognized authorities can speak knowledgeably on a subject. Fiction writers, for example, often exhaustively research their stories and seem to know as much about their topics as any recognized expert would. It is possible, too, that someone speaking outside his or her field may present a strikingly new and powerful idea. And the number of years that have gone into studying an issue can sometimes have relatively little to do with the writer's expertise. Albert Einstein was only in his midtwenties when he published some of his most influential work. But overall you should look for credible authors who have earned their right through careful study and sound analysis to speak on an issue. You may be tempted to argue that all opinions are equal because they are merely opinions, but some opinions are dangerous or ridiculous and some are valuable, sensible, and well defended. Find authors who express opinions that have been carefully arrived at through intelligent inquiry. In fact, even those authors who represent the *opposing* side of the argument you intend to present should be the best representatives of that side.

> The wise lend a very academic faith to every report which favors the passion of the reporter.
>
> —David Hume

What Are the Author's Bias and Purpose?   Writers and speakers may have a personal or professional interest in the information they are presenting.

And although they may not lie outright (some might), they may hide contradictory information or carefully select language in which to present information most favorably. Perhaps the author is speaking for a company, a special-interest group, an institute, a foundation, a think tank, or a political party. He or she might be getting paid for an endorsement or opinion. When a writer has no special or personal interest in the topic, nothing to gain or lose by the audience's favorable or negative reaction to the topic, we say that the author is "disinterested," impartial, objective. That does not mean that the information provided by "interested" authors is to be discounted. Surely, even advertisers can occasionally present trustworthy information. But knowing what stake an author has in our reactions can be useful in our attempt to evaluate the information that has been filtered through that author's perspectives.

In the case of surveys or studies, the author may have worded the questions in such a way as to ensure the sought-after response. A corporation that sets out to prove that its product is better than everyone else's is likely to devise a method that will not produce disappointing results. And an industry trying to defend its product will most certainly put the best spin on its information. Take, for example, the following paragraph:

> Measurements of atmospheric cigarette smoke taken under realistic conditions indicate that the contribution of tobacco smoke to the air we breathe is minimal. One study at Harvard found only very small amounts of nicotine in the atmosphere of cocktail lounges, restaurants, bus stations and airline terminals. Based on those measurements of a substance specific to tobacco smoke, one astute reader of the literature estimated that a nonsmoker would have to spend 100 hours straight in the smokiest bar to inhale the equivalent of a single filter-tip cigarette.[4]

There may be truth in this statement, but because it is found in a pamphlet published by the Tobacco Institute we should be highly skeptical. Although we should be careful to evaluate all the information we find, the fact that this information on secondhand smoke comes from an industry that profits from the sale of cigarettes should make us even more cautious of what we have read. When was the study done at Harvard? Was that the Harvard University in Cambridge, Massachusetts? What does "very small amounts" mean? "Small" by what standard? At what time of day were the tests done in the restaurants and lounges? Who is this mysterious "astute reader"? If we were preparing an argument on, say, suspending antismoking laws in restaurants, we would be well advised to look elsewhere for support.

In attempting to uncover an author's point of view, try to determine the author's purpose in writing. If the writer is making a claim or trying to persuade the reader toward a particular belief or action, look at how he or she has dealt with opposing points of view or evidence. Does the writer seem fair and evenhanded, or does he or she dismiss opposing points of view without regard to their possible value? Does the writer commit the straw man fallacy, misrepresenting opposing views to more easily mow them down? Does the writer use slanted language or commit personal attacks? Does the writer make sweeping generalizations or demonstrate an either/or approach to complicated issues, thereby revealing a strong bias toward one side? Be wary, too, of writers who claim only to inform or who pretend to objectivity. The writer may be stacking the deck in an effort to subtly direct the reader toward some unstated goal. *Remember:* Biases and hidden agendas don't disqualify the source. You might find plenty of useful information—but useful only after a careful reading.

Treat sources fairly when judging their bias and purpose. Perhaps the writer intended simply to amuse the reader or to comment casually on some inconsequential topic. If a writer intends to be ironic or satirical, if he or she is clearly exaggerating for effect, or if the writer admits to guesswork and speculation, be sure to fairly represent those intentions and admissions.

What Are the Author's Sources?   Writers seldom write in a vacuum. Most writers, as Isaac Newton suggested, respond to those who have preceded them, contributing in some sense to a long, ongoing conversation among thinkers. When you read someone's work, chances are that that writer has depended on other sources for information, ideas, and inspiration. The original sources that a writer cites are "primary sources." It may be important for the success of your work to consider how reliable the primary sources are and to uncover those sources if necessary to ensure that they have not been misquoted or misrepresented. For example, in researching Thomas Jefferson's attitudes toward slavery, you might look at several books on the subject. In those "secondary sources," the authors will most likely cite Jefferson's own writings, his papers, letters, notebooks, and so forth—all of which are primary sources. Returning to the primary sources is especially necessary when an author uses statistical information in defending a claim because statistics, like literature, can be interpreted in various, often contradictory, ways. You might want to see the numbers for yourself. As we noted before, although many authors are honest and trustworthy, not *all* writers are careful or ethical in their use of information, and others (careful *and* ethical) may simply be offering a subjective interpretation of the information. When in doubt, look up the original source of information.

Be wary of unnamed, undocumented, or completely unreliable sources in a writer's essay or argument. As we shall see in Chapter 14, writers often attempt to give legitimacy to their work by referring to a well-known political figure or celebrity as the source of information. Others allude to "an anonymous source" or "sources at the Pentagon" as the originators of important information. Other allusions include such phrases as "surveys have shown" or "according to recent studies." What surveys? What studies? The wise critical thinker is always wary of unnamed sources or those whose reliability cannot be checked.

Who Is the Publisher or Sponsor?   Most students know that not all publications are equal, which is why you don't usually find students using the

National Inquirer or the *Weekly World News* or even *People* magazine as a source of factual evidence. If we want to know whether or not Elvis is dead and, if so, when he died, we usually turn instead to the archives of the *New York Times* or *U.S. News and World Report.* In fact, most national publications employ respected editors whose reputations and job security depend on the quality and the veracity of the writing they publish. Mistakes can happen, and unverified facts occasionally sneak by vigilant editors, but the information that appears in major newspapers and daily, weekly, and monthly magazines is *generally* reliable, although a critical reader, as always, would be wise to question even the most seemingly objective reports. Commercial interests often dictate editorial policy, and there have been several interesting cases of exceptional periodicals being the victims of hoaxes and sabotage, resulting in embarrassing retractions and even, in one famous case, the return of a Pulitzer Prize.[5]

Published opinions are another matter. Many periodicals have an editorial bias that governs not only the topics chosen but the perspective and slant of the writing as well. Although there is nothing wrong with a periodical's having a political slant, the careful reader should know what that slant is. *In These Times* and *Mother Jones,* for example, publish articles and arguments from a working-class perspective, whereas *Commentary* usually takes a conservative stance on labor issues. Scanning the table of contents and looking at the advertisements and any editorials will give you a good sense of the political and cultural biases of the periodical. A reference book called *Magazines for Libraries* provides brief descriptions, including the political dispositions, of periodicals available in libraries.

Publishers of academic books and journals are usually extremely careful to publish work of high quality, which is ensured by a rigorous system of peer review. Submissions to scholarly presses and journals (Oxford University Press or the *New England Journal of Medicine,* for example) are commonly sent to leading scholars familiar with the topic, who recommend the submission for publication, suggest revisions, or recommend that the submission be rejected. Ideally, the process helps guarantee that what gets published is trustworthy, although even the most scrutinizing journals can get fooled by an unscrupulous contributor or a writer perpetrating a hoax. Still, while you should carefully evaluate everything you read, you can usually trust the content of scholarly publications. The box on pages 362–363 will help you distinguish between scholarly and nonscholarly periodicals.

In short, it is important to discover whatever you can, not only about the author of the piece, but about the publisher as well. Many publishers protect their well-deserved reputations by attempting to verify every statement they print. Some information makes it into print, however, without ever having passed through an exacting review process. Some presses (university presses, for example) publish only books of the highest caliber; others publish what they know will sell. Books can be published through vanity presses, in which the author pays all costs associated with publication—printing, marketing, distributing, and so forth. Pamphlets and many newsletters are published without editing or review by disinterested parties. Some newspapers publish op-ed pieces that contain misinformation and distortions. In an effort to antagonize their listeners, radio commentators often say blatantly false things. Certainly, *published* (literally, "made public") is not synonymous with *truthful*.

Where does the Internet fit into all of this? Honestly, it's a mess. Whereas most information in most traditional print sources (periodicals, books, newspapers) has passed through some sort of quality control to ensure its accuracy and value, anyone with a computer and access to a server can publish absolutely anything on the Internet. Surfing the Internet for information is like shopping blindfolded in the world's largest grocery store. You might come away with exquisite gourmet delicacies, spices you had no idea existed, and nutritious fruits and vegetables; or you might find sweets that taste good but are harmful to your health, bland cereals, or even deadly poisons for cleaning bathrooms or killing rats. Because of the excess of poison available, some students and their professors refuse to use the World Wide Web as a source of scholarly information; that is unfortunate given the riches a careful shopper can find there. When you shop around on the Internet, it is vital to your intellectual survival that you take off the blindfold.

Evaluating electronic sources is similar to evaluating print sources: ask a great many questions about the content and the author. When evaluating the site itself, give preference to those maintained by recognized and respected organizations and institutions such as universities (the Cornell University Library or Purdue University's Online Writing Lab, for example), government agencies (the Library of Congress or the Smithsonian Institution), and non-commercial, service-oriented sites (the American Cancer Society). Often the URL, the address of the site, will provide some information about the site's sponsor. Internet addresses with *.edu* (short for *education*) usually originate at colleges and universities. Other current URL suffixes include the following:

.com or *.cc* (commercial site)

.gov (government agencies)

.info (information sites)

.mil (military sites)

.net (networks and service providers)

.org (nonprofit organizations)

Because the Web is growing so fast, new suffixes will most likely be added soon, including, possibly, *.kids* (sites safe for children). A tilde (~) in the address usually indicates that the page is maintained by an individual who may be working independent of the school, organization, or agency that provides the Web address.

At a helpful Web site called Whois (*www.networksolutions.com/whois/index.jsp*), you can find limited information about a site, including contact information for the person who registered the domain name. Whois won't tell

Distinguishing Scholarly from Nonscholarly Periodicals

There is no surefire method for distinguishing scholarly journals from other periodicals, but the characteristics listed below will offer some guidance. Generally speaking, scholarly journals are trustworthy because the information they contain has undergone rigorous review by experts and scholars. But that in no way suggests that nonscholarly journals cannot be trusted or that scholarly journals are infallible. The following guidelines will help you categorize a journal, but you will still have to determine whether the information you collect is credible.

SCHOLARLY JOURNALS

- Have a serious and professional look; generally contain few visuals except for graphs and charts; carry very few advertisements, which are usually limited to announcements of upcoming conferences and recently published books and calls for papers.
- Contain articles based on research and experimentation, written by scholars who cite their sources in footnotes and bibliographies.
- Are written for other scholars, practitioners, and students who have some familiarity with the topic and the language used in the discipline.
- Are often, but not always, published by colleges and universities, professional and scientific societies, organizations, and associations.

Examples: *Journal of the American Medical Association; New England Journal of Medicine; Philological Quarterly; American Journal of Sociology; Reading Teacher; Journal of Accountancy; Harvard Business Review; and College English.*

NONSCHOLARLY PERIODICALS

Nonscholarly periodicals include journals of opinion, news and general-interest magazines, popular magazines, trade publications, and sensational publications.

Journals of Opinion
(also called policy journals)

- Appearance can range from a sober format to a glossier look; sometimes have the appearance of a newspaper; include few pictures, sometimes none; often contain political cartoons; contain limited and selective advertisements.
- Usually have a professed or easily inferred editorial policy that falls somewhere along the political spectrum, although some journals of opinion collect viewpoints from across the spectrum. The writers are often well-respected and educated experts, commentators, and journalists who write frequently on political and social topics. Political figures occasionally write for journals of opinion. Content is usually well researched; notes and bibliographies may appear with articles. Often contain book and movie reviews and sometimes include original poetry.
- Are aimed at a broad, educated audience familiar with and interested in current social, political, economic, and cultural events. Tone and style are usually serious but not as academic as that found in scholarly journals.
- Published by think tanks, private organizations, political parties, policy institutions, and other groups that hope to foster a particular opinion.

Examples: *Dissent; Mother Jones; Nation; Utne Reader; New Republic; American Spectator; Insight; Human Events; Commentary; National Review; Public Interest; Policy Review; Progressive; Z Magazine; Reason; Weekly Standard; Christian Century; In These Times.*

News and General-Interest Magazines

- Glossy, attractive appearance; illustrated with colorful photographs, charts, and graphs; wide range of advertisements.
- Wide range of authors from freelance journalists, staff writers, scholars, editors, invited guests, and so forth. Sometimes contain articles and essays reprinted from other sources. Language is nontechnical. Topics covered range widely—from current events and social trends to politics, the economy, and art. Coverage also ranges from short and superficial to extensive and thoughtful. Most periodicals in this category contain movie and book reviews; some general-interest magazines contain original art, such as poetry and fiction.
- Audience is educated and interested in current news and issues but does not necessarily have extensive knowledge of the topics covered.
- Published almost entirely by for-profit corporations.

Examples: News: *Time; Maclean's* (Canada); *Newsweek; U.S. News & World Report.* General interest: *New Yorker; Harper's; Atlantic Monthly; Scientific American; National Geographic.*

Popular Magazines

- Glossy, attractive, colorful appearance with plenty of illustrations and advertisements geared toward specific groups.
- Written by staff and freelance writers. Some writers may know a great deal about their topics; others may simply be reporting what they have discovered. Topics are usually selected for specific consumer groups and often include such things as recipes and "how-to" essays. Ads are also geared toward specific groups.
- Audience is interested in topic of the magazine (sports, health, home decorating, and so forth); minimal reading skills necessary.
- Published for profit.

Examples: *People; Sports Illustrated; Rolling Stone; Ebony; Vanity Fair; Modern Maturity; Redbook; Southern Living; This Old House;* and most health, fitness, and fashion magazines.

Trade Publications

- Similar in appearance to news and general-interest magazines: glossy appearance, many pictures and other illustrations, such as easy-to-read graphs and charts. Advertisements for a wide range of products and services and many specialized ads aimed at practitioners in a particular field.
- Articles are usually written by practitioners and educators, often in technical jargon common to the profession or industry. Focus on current trends and practical applications. Often include job announcements and personality profiles.
- Written for practitioners and students in a particular field.
- Usually published through professional organizations but also by corporations.

Examples: *Industry Week; Advertising Age; Hotel and Motel Management; Bookbag; Forbes; Fortune; Business Week; Publisher's Weekly; Broadcasting and Cable; Variety.*

Sensational Publications

- Often look like tabloid newspapers; often contain shocking or attention-grabbing photographs and equally astonishing advertisements promoting products of questionable value.
- Articles are written by staff and freelance writers to hold reader's interest. Sources are seldom cited. Language is simple. Headlines often make outlandish claims.
- Audience is usually gullible and superstitious, interested in pseudoscience and the paranormal.
- Published for profit.

Examples: *National Enquirer; Globe; National Examiner; Weekly World News; Star.*

you whether the site is trustworthy, but it can get you started on finding more information about a site.

Appearance can sometimes help distinguish scholarly sites from the more commercial ones: Scholarly sites are often the least flashy, looking more like electronic versions of typed pages—no banners, few pictures, dull graphics. But appearances, of course, can be deceiving, and some highly reliable sites are very attractive and user-friendly. All in all it is difficult to make any general statements about Web sites, the designers of which are clever indeed. If there were a clear indicator of a trustworthy site, Web masters at less legitimate sites would turn it to their advantage. In fact, some sites have managed to secure an *.edu* suffix even though the sites are not legitimate schools. In an effort to assist readers, some organizations—the Librarians' Internet Index (*www.lii.org*), for example— evaluate Web content, filter out unreliable sites, and arrange links to trustworthy sites under headings such as "Arts and Humanities," "Business," and "Media." Such filtering organizations can be useful at times, but relying on them will do little to sharpen our critical thinking skills.

To determine whether to believe that facts you find on a site are reliable and whether the opinions expressed on the site are trustworthy, try the following:

- See if you can find out more about the author or the sponsoring site. Are there links on the site that will lead you to a résumé or biography of the author? Use a search engine to see what others have written about the author or the organization. Perhaps current news articles will provide helpful information or even warnings.

- If an organization sponsors the site, see if you can find out more about the organization by following links to the home page, by clicking on any links labeled "About Us" or "Who We Are," or by looking at the part of the URL before the first slash.

- What does your common sense tell you about the site? Does the author seem to have a pronounced bias? Are opposing views ridiculed or misrepresented? Is the author attempting to sell you something or solicit a donation? Is the site littered with banner advertisements?

- Consider how you found the site. Did you link to it from another, reliable site, or did you find it through a search engine?

- Follow the author's links to other sites. Do the linked sites reveal the same bias as that of the original site? Are the linked sites reliable and objective sources of information?

Assessing Web sites is a notoriously difficult task. It is probably no exaggeration to say that only researchers already well informed about a topic can know for certain whether the information on a site is reliable. Besides keeping your eyes open, the best method to determine whether a site is a legitimate source of information is to use some of the guides mentioned in the second section of this chapter and to count on professors and librarians who can point

→ Pop Culture Connection ←

Colbert on "Truthiness"

We've been encouraging you in this chapter to back up your arguments with information from reliable sources, a practice that, if you ask Stephen Colbert, seems to be unpopular today. In the first episode of *The Colbert Report,* in October of 2005, Colbert introduced his audience to the word "truthiness," a word he invented to describe the tendency among some people to trust their instincts and their "guts" no matter what the facts or logic might suggest. People who demonstrate "truthiness" offer little evidence for their claims other than their opinions and perceptions. Here's Colbert:

I will speak to you in plain, simple English. And that brings us to tonight's word: "truthiness." Now I'm sure some of the "word police," the "wordinistas" over at *Webster's,* are going to say, "Hey, that's not a word." Well, anyone who knows me knows I'm no fan of dictionaries or reference books. They're elitist, constantly telling us what is or isn't true, or what did or didn't happen. Who's *Britannica* to tell me the Panama Canal was finished in 1914? If I want to say it happened in 1941, that's my right.

I don't trust books. They're all fact, no heart. And that's exactly what's pulling our country apart today. 'Cause face it, folks, we are a divided nation. Not between Democrats and Republicans, or conservatives and liberals, or tops and bottoms. No, we are divided between those who *think* with their head, and those who *know* with their heart. Consider Harriet Miers [President Bush's first nomination to replace retiring Supreme Court Justice Sandra Day O'Connor]. If you *think* about Harriet Miers, of course her nomination's absurd. But the president didn't say he "thought" about his selection. He said this: (shows video clip of President Bush saying "I know her heart"). Notice how he said nothing about her brain? He didn't have to. He "feels" the truth about Harriet Miers. And what about Iraq? If you *think* about it, maybe there are a few missing pieces to the rationale for war. But doesn't taking Saddam out *feel* like the right thing—right here, right here in the gut? (video available at *www.comedycentral.com*)

you in the direction of trustworthy sites. If you have any doubts about what you find on the Internet, do your best to verify the information through other sources. Do not make the mistake of thinking that what you have found is any good just because you found it and it fits your purpose.

The Audience

Besides examining the content of sources and asking a great many questions about the author and the publisher, inquiring about the intended audience and studying reader reactions can provide insight into the quality of a source.

Who Is the Intended Audience?   Knowing something about the author's intended audience can help you evaluate the information. In some cases, journals and books are aimed at readers far better versed than you are in the topic under study.[6] To familiarize yourself more completely with an issue, you may have to research a topic even more deeply than you first expected. On the other hand, writing intended for younger audiences, though accurate, may not contain the complete picture. Certain encyclopedias—those published on CD or DVD for use in a computer, for example—are often written at levels that make them unreliable for research at the college level. They may be helpful in getting started, especially if you are completely unversed in a topic, but good research at the collegiate level must go beyond such sources. To help you determine the intended audience of an encyclopedia, consult Kenneth F. Kister's *Kister's Best Encyclopedias* (2nd ed., Oryx Press, 1994), which evaluates the reliability and objectivity of more than eight hundred encyclopedias.

Some authors write strictly for an audience that is predisposed to agree with the author's point of view. Newsletters published by radio-talk-show hosts and many pages published on the Internet, for example, are intended to provide data and opinions to readers who are merely looking to support long-held convictions. Pages devoted to "proving" that one race is superior to another, that one political viewpoint is uniquely correct, that religious beliefs are dangerous, that conspirators are stealing our freedoms, and so forth should be treated with suspicion. It is possible that these sites and sources contain some accurate or useful information, but the obviousness of the writer's objectives— to speak to like-minded readers, to "preach to the choir," as the cliché goes— can in some cases make the information nearly useless to a critical thinker. Knowing the intended audience, however, should not lead you to conclude automatically that the information is tainted. Several journals of opinion (the *Nation, Commentary,* and the *National Review,* to name a few) have the highest editorial standards. Still, no critical thinker reads them with a closed mind.

How Has the Audience Responded?   Another part of the context of research is what has been written in *response* to the information you intend to use in your argument. Usually, after the publication of a scholarly book, for example, reviews written by other scholars will appear in journals and on Web sites. These reviews, although sometimes petty and personal (some reviewers are settling old scores or pushing their own agendas), can be helpful in alerting readers to the presence of misinformation or shoddy research. In doing research on a political, historical, or literary figure, for example, you might consult reviews to determine if the biography you intend to quote from is considered by scholars to be accurate and fair to the subject. (Start with *Book Review Digest,* or the online database *Book Review Digest Plus* if your library subscribes to it.) If it turns out that the biographer based the book on rumor and speculation, you are better off not using it. The methodology used in surveys and studies might be challenged in subsequent issues of a scholarly journal or even in the popular press. And the "letters" or "corrections" section of journals and magazines can rectify, or provide alternative interpretations of, information that appeared in previous issues. Even if you don't have access to comments made about a specific work, it can help to consider the writer's reputation in the community for which she or he writes. Authors who are often cited by other writers or who show up often in bibliographies are usually considered experts in their fields.

EXERCISE 12.3

Suppose you want to use the following passages in an argument. How reliable do you judge them to be? Evaluate each passage according to the criteria outlined in this chapter: (1) author's background, (2) author's bias and purpose, (3) publisher or sponsor, and (4) intended audience. (The author's sources will be unavailable as a criterion in these exercises.) In several cases, you may have to conduct a little research to determine something about the speaker, the author, or the organization.

1. Liberals tell kids in school all over America that the best way to protect themselves from AIDS is to wear condoms while engaging in sexual intercourse. It's a lie. They are imposing a death sentence on kids. The failure rate of condoms is around 17 percent. They're teaching kids to play Russian roulette. (Rush Limbaugh, *See, I Told You So,* 1993)

2. Awful. Avoid at all costs. Basically failed me to prove a point. Does not respect anyone standing up for themselves. Horrible "teaching" methodology. Turns a three-hour class into a five-hour torture session. Don't dare disagree with him, even with scientific proof and hard numbers or you'll be his next example. (Comment on Professor X, published on *ratemyprofessor.com*)

3. The average breakage rate of all condoms is 5.6 percent. The average slippage rate of all condoms is 3.67 percent. The total failure rate of all condoms is 9.13 percent. (Summary of Table 16-3 in Robert A. Hatcher et al., *Contraceptive Technology,* 17th ed., 1998)

4. "Over 80% of Americans support very little or no immigration. Is anyone listening to us?" "Tired of sitting in traffic? Every day, another 6,000 immigrants arrive. Every day!" (Billboards in Queens and Brooklyn, New York, sponsored by Craig Nelson, founder of ProjectUSA, *www.projectusa.org*)

5. Did you know that you can use a condom and still get pregnant? A variety of studies have found that condoms have an "annual failure rate" of 10% to 36% when it comes to preventing pregnancy. . . . One of the studies found that among teenagers, the condom failure rate regarding pregnancy was 36%! On average, that means that one out of every three teenage couples using condoms will become pregnant each year. (Pro-Life America, *www.prolife.com,* accessed July 2006)

6. Emerson and Thoreau both learned from their experience as reformers that withdrawal of the good simply abandons the field to the evil. Both were involved with the Underground Railroad, and when John Brown came to Concord in 1856, seeking money to buy rifles for his Kansas partisans, they gave generously. (Len Gougeon, professor of American literature, letter to the editor, *Harper's Magazine,* August 2006).

7. Sixty-seven percent of people would prefer that the races be separated. That's what a poll of my listeners is showing. (Mike Gallagher, radio-talk-show host)

8. There's no such thing as a bad Picasso. (Pablo Picasso)

9. PLANET-DISSOLVING DUST CLOUD IS HEADED TOWARD EARTH! It was spewed from a black hole 28,000 light-years from Earth and is vaporizing everything in its path, astronomers say! (headline in *Weekly World News*)

10. More than 11,000 trendsetters, tastemakers, movers, and shakers gathered in Brooklyn's Williamsburg neighborhood Monday to declare a strike against the broad segment of the American population that they say routinely copies their fashions, musical tastes, and sensibilities. Should the strike persist, experts said, it could bring the pop-cultural life of the nation to a standstill. ("U.S. Trendsetters Go On Strike: Nation's 'Hip' Seek Recognition, Royalties," *The Onion, www.theonion.com,* July 18, 2006)

11. In 1994, faced with a national crime crisis, Congress passed the *Violent Crime Control and Law Enforcement Act* (Crime Bill), which provided federal funds to allow state and local law enforcement to hire additional police officers. The results were dramatic: between 1994 and 2001, violent crime dropped by 29 percent, the most sustained decline in 40 years.

    Since 2001, however, the President and the Republican-controlled Congress have cut more than $2 billion in funding for state and local law enforcement. And the results have been equally dramatic: violent crime is on the rise again. In 2005, violent crime increased at the fastest rate in fifteen years. These statistics foreshadow what could be a troubling trend, a backsliding into the "bad old days" of the 1980s and early 1990s when we were losing the war on crime. ("Bush Republicans Cut Law Enforcement Funding, Crime Rate Increases at the Fastest Rate in Fifteen Years," Democratic Policy Committee, *www.democrats.senate.gov,* July 10, 2006)

12. The scary claims about heat waves and droughts are based on computer models. But computer models are lousy at predicting climate because water vapor and cloud effects cause changes that computers fail to predict. They were unable to anticipate the massive amounts of heat energy that escaped the tropics over the past 15 years, forcing modelers back to the drawing board. In the mid-1970s, computer models told us we should prepare for global cooling.

    The fundamentalist doom-mongers ignore scientists who say the effects of global warming may be benign. Harvard astrophysicist Sallie Baliunas says added carbon dioxide in the atmosphere may actually benefit the world because more CO_2 helps plants grow. Warmer winters would give farmers a longer harvest season. (Tracy, blogger, posted on Anti-Strib, *http://anti-strib .blogspot.com,* July 10, 2006)

13. When the Founders sat down to create this new civil order, they had two central truths in mind. One, representative democracy would be the most stable and lasting form of government. Two, when the Constitutional Convention wrapped up, they were all going to be out of work. The latter led to the formulation of what historians would come to know as the "Madison Hypothesis." "What if," opined the diminutive Virginian, "we created a national legislature copious enough in membership, and curious enough in

structure, as to provide the whole of us a gig for life?" (Jon Stewart, Ben Karlin, David Javerbaum, *America (The Book),* 2004)

14. In 2003, 791 Hispanic workers were fatally injured while at work, down 12 percent from a high of 895 in 2001. Hispanic worker fatalities accounted for 14 percent of the 5,559 total fatal work injuries that occurred in the U.S. in 2003. The rate of 4.5 fatalities per 100,000 workers recorded for Hispanic workers was a 13 percent higher rate than the rate of 4.0 fatalities per 100,000 employed recorded for all workers. (U.S. Bureau of Labor Statistics)

15. The little park originally had been the city's Potter's Field, the final resting place of its unclaimed dead, but in the nineteenth century Washington Square became the city's most fashionable area. By 1911 the old town houses stood as a rear guard of an aristocratic past facing the invasions of industry from Broadway to the east, low-income groups from the crowded streets to the south, and the first infiltration of artists and writers into Greenwich Village to the west. (Leon Stein, *The Triangle Fire* [1962], reprinted in 2001 by Cornell University Press)

TAKING NOTES

When reading, some college students, perhaps overwhelmed by the amount of new information they discover in college, tend to highlight an excessive number of sentences and paragraphs in their textbooks, waste hundreds of dimes at the photocopier, and attempt to write down every word a professor utters. That is an understandable reaction, especially since success on tests and projects often depends on the ability to recount what was read or heard. But the truth is that it is impossible to remember every detail, and trying to note every idea sinks the most important content in a sea of yellow highlighting and ink. Taking notes on what you have read, especially when researching a topic, means *carefully* selecting what is important and useful as you try to faithfully represent the opposing argument and support your own claims.

There are probably as many ways to take notes as there are writers, ranging from simple notations in a notebook to elaborate computer files, but the easiest and most effective method of note-taking is still the 3-by-5-inch or 4-by-6-inch index card. The process of recording information on cards is not difficult, and the use of cards can make the initial drafting of an essay much easier than using notes recorded in a notebook or even on a computer because the cards can be arranged and rearranged as you see fit. Arranging the cards is easier if you record only a small amount of information on each card. And be sure to number the cards; you'll know why after you drop them all the first time. If you decide not to use note cards, be sure to devise a system that you can keep control over and that will serve you well when you begin to draft your essay. Some students prefer to photocopy or print out their sources on sheets of paper and then to highlight the important information or even cut and paste the quotes to their draft. Whatever system you use, your notes will be of two kinds: bibliographical and content. Although some of the following advice assumes that you will use note cards, you can modify the advice to fit whatever system you prefer.

Bibliographical Information

Use one card to record the publication information for each work you will cite in your paper. Later in this chapter, you will see what publication information (author, title, place of publication, date, page numbers, and so forth) is needed in a list of works cited or a bibliography. Be sure to devote one card to this information for each source, and remember to record everything you will need. There is nothing more frustrating than scrambling around the night before a paper is due, looking for bibliographical information. (You're not the only person to have just thought to yourself, "I'll just make it up." Don't forget, your professors know the tricks and are usually on the lookout for them!)

Content Notes: Quotes, Summaries, and Paraphrases

Most of your cards will contain summaries, paraphrases, and quotations from sources. You can decide how you want your cards to look, but be consistent in whatever format you choose. One possibility is to record a shortened form of the source (perhaps the author's last name), the page number of the source, and the note-card number at the top of the card. Then record your note.

> *Quoting: the act of repeating erroneously the words of another.*
> —Ambrose Bierce

Quotations   Obviously, the easiest note to record is a quotation. Select quotations carefully; as you will see shortly, it is far better for both you and your reader to paraphrase when possible. But when you do record a quotation, be very careful to place quotation marks around the material and to transcribe the quotation accurately. It is best not to omit anything if you copy a quotation, but if you do, replace the omission with ellipsis points (three dots). If you add anything to the quotation, place the addition in brackets so that you don't later forget that it was not part of the original. Keep in mind that you will not have the original passage before you when you write your essay, so it is vitally important that you indicate clearly in your notes all the information you'll need to accurately cite the quotation. Finally, if you use index cards, be sure to organize them in a uniform manner. For example, you might give a shortened form of the author's name and the page number at the top of the card along with the number of the card. Below is a passage from an essay by William Carlos Williams, followed by several examples of cards with quotations.

> Hamilton had hounded him for years. At length he openly called Burr "politically dangerous." What did he mean? Burr wrote demanding an explanation. To the party in power, yes, dangerous he may have been, but to the country—How? Hamilton refused to answer. Then let it be pinned down. Either it must be one or the other. Burr was not angry. If any one feared it was not he. His head was clear, he slept well, he was refreshed and went to the place of the duel. Hamilton was fifty-seven. Burr somewhat younger.

Hamilton fired first, the bullet clipping a twig above Burr's head. His hand was trembling. Did he fire wild, as his seconds say he did, on purpose? Burr's seconds said no, and stuck to it; the bullet came too close to their man's head to have been anything but a plain miss due to a shaking hand. Then Burr fired. He shot coolly, seriously and with conviction. He killed his man, logically and as he meant to do and knew he must. For a moment, as he saw his adversary fall, he was overcome with compassion, then he turned away. Hamilton, before he died, dictated his astonishing testament, in which he says—imagine the flimsy nature of his lifelong enmity toward the man—that, regarding Burr, he "might have been misinformed of his intentions." Good God, what an answer! Work till you are fifty-seven to ruin a man, insult him, malign him and then say, dying: I may have been misinformed.[7]

Williams, page 201   12

"He [Burr] shot coolly, seriously and with conviction. He killed his man, logically and as he meant to do and knew he must. For a moment, as he saw his adversary fall, he was overcome with compassion, then he turned away."

QUOTATION

Williams, page 201   13

   "Hamilton, before he died, dictated his astonishing testament, in which he says—imagine the flimsy nature of his lifelong enmity toward the man—that, regarding Burr, he, 'might have been misinformed of his intentions.' Good God, what an answer! Work till you are fifty-seven to ruin a man, insult him, malign him and then say, dying: I may have been misinformed."

QUOTATION

Summaries   In Chapter 7 we looked at methods for summarizing and paraphrasing arguments, and some of what we discuss here will refresh your memory. But in using sources, you will often find that you need to summarize and paraphrase not just arguments but also essays, reports, explanations, and other materials that will aid in the defense of your own claim. A *summary* of an argument, essay, or article contains only the main idea (the thesis) or the claim and, depending on the purpose of the summary, the main premises or supporting points. A summary of an essay might contain the thesis sentence and the topic idea from each body paragraph. How much you summarize depends on how much of the original work you will need to remember and how much you intend to use. If you're simply going to refer to the article or argument or highlight its main idea, you can limit yourself to a sentence or two, perhaps to an outline; but if you hope to recall some of the author's evidence, you should record that evidence in your summary, as well.

To write a summary, read the original several times, underlining (if the book or periodical is your property) the main idea and subpoints on the second or third reading. Much of what you learned in Chapter 7 about analyzing arguments will come in handy here. Then try to write the summary without looking at the source. You can start with a sentence like "The author is saying that . . ." or "The author is arguing that . . ." or "The author is trying to prove that . . . ." If you are using cards, you can write this sentence on one card. Then try to recall the main developmental points, writing each on a separate card. After you have given the recall method your best shot, go back to the source to see how closely you captured the author's ideas. Revise your cards if necessary, being careful to use your own words whenever possible and to put quotation marks around any key words and phrases that appear in the original. At this point you can also enter additional information under the main points. Sloppy cards full of crossouts and revisions should be rewritten to make the task of drafting your essay easier.

The following essay is summarized on cards at the end of the essay.

Raised on Rock-and-Roll

Anna Quindlen

Mister Ed is back on television, indicating that, as most middle-of-the-road antique shops suggest, Americans cannot discriminate between things worth saving and things that simply exist. *The Donna Reed Show* is on, too, and *My Three Sons,* and those dopey folks from *Gilligan's Island.* There's *Leave It to Beaver* and *The Beverly Hillbillies* and even *Lassie,* whose plaintive theme song leaves my husband all mushy around the edges.

Social historians say these images, and those of Howdy Doody and Pinky Lee and Lamb Chop and Annette have forever shaped my consciousness. But I have memories far stronger than that. I remember sitting cross-legged in front of the tube, one of the console sets with the ersatz lamé netting over the speakers, but I was not watching puppets or pratfalls. I was born in Philadelphia, a city where if you can't dance you might as well stay home, and I was raised on rock-and-roll. My earliest television memory is of *American Bandstand,* and the central question of my childhood was: Can you dance to it?

When I was fifteen and a wild devotee of Mitch Ryder and the Detroit Wheels, it sometimes crossed my mind that when I was thirty-four years old, decrepit, wrinkled as a prune and near death, I would have moved on to some nameless kind of dreadful show music, something akin to Muzak. I did not think about the fact that my parents were still listening to the music that had been popular when they were kids; I only thought that they played "Pennsylvania 6-5000" to torment me and keep my friends away from the house.

But I know I'm never going to stop loving rock-and-roll, all kinds of rock-and-roll: the Beatles, the Rolling Stones, Hall and Oates, Talking Heads, the

Doors, the Supremes, Tina Turner, Elvis Costello, Elvis Presley. I even like bad rock-and-roll, although I guess that's where my age shows; I don't have the tolerance for Bon Jovi that I once had for the Raspberries.

We have friends who, when their son was a baby, used to put a record on and say, "Drop your butt, Phillip." And Phillip did. That's what I love: drop-your-butt music. It's one of the few things left in my life that makes me feel good without even thinking about it. I can walk into any bookstore and find dozens of books about motherhood and love and human relations and so many other things that we once did through a combination of intuition and emotion. I even heard recently that some school is giving a course on kissing, which makes me wonder if I'm missing something. But rock-and-roll flows through my veins, not my brain. There's nothing else that feels the same to me as, say, the faint sound of the opening dum-doo-doo-doo-doo-doo of "My Girl" coming from a radio on a summer day. I feel the way I felt when I first heard it. I feel good, as James Brown says.

There are lots of people who don't feel this way about rock-and-roll. Some of them don't understand it, like the Senate wives who said that records should have rating stickers on them so that you would know whether the lyrics were dirty. The kids who hang out at Mr. Big's sub shop in my neighborhood thought this would make record shopping a lot easier, because you could choose albums by how bad the rating was. Most of the people who love rock-and-roll just thought the labeling idea was dumb. Lyrics, after all, are not the point of rock-and-roll, despite how beautifully people like Bruce Springsteen and Joni Mitchell write. Lyrics are the point only in the case of "Louie, Louie"; the words have never been deciphered, but it is widely understood that they are about sex. That's understandable, because rock-and-roll is a lot like sex: If you talk seriously about it, it takes a lot of the feeling away—and feeling is the point.

Some people over-analyze rock-and-roll, just as they over-analyze everything else. They say things like "Bruce Springsteen is the poet laureate of the American dream gone sour," when all I need to know about Bruce Springsteen is that the saxophone bridge on "Jungleland" makes the back of my neck feel exactly the way I felt the first time a boy kissed me, only over and over and over again. People write about Prince's "psychedelic masturbatory fantasies," but when I think about Prince, I don't really think, I just feel—feel the moment when, driving to the beach, I first heard "Kiss" on the radio and started bopping up and down in my seat like a seventeen-year-old on a day trip.

I've got precious few things in my life anymore that just make me feel, that make me jump up and dance, that make me forget the schedule and the job and the mortgage payments and just let me thrash around inside my skin. I've got precious few things I haven't studied and considered and reconsidered and studied some more. I don't know a chord change from a snare drum, but I know what I like, and I like feeling this way sometimes. I love rock-and-roll because in a time of talk, talk, talk, it's about action.

Here's a test: Get hold of a two-year-old, a person who has never read a single word about how heavy-metal musicians should be put in jail or about Tina Turner's "throaty alto range." Put "I Heard It Through the Grapevine" on the stereo. Stand the two-year-old in front of the stereo. The two-year-old will begin to dance. The two-year-old will drop his butt. Enough said.[8]

Here is a one-card summary, highlighting only the main idea:

Quindlen   1

Rock and roll appeals to our feelings, not to our reason or understanding.

SUMMARY OF MAIN IDEA

Here is an additional card summarizing the main points of the article:

Quindlen   2

    My consciousness was shaped not by television, but by rock-
and-roll, and I'll never stop loving it. Rock-and-roll has an effect
on me; it makes me feel good. I don't have to think about the
music or analyze its deeper meaning the way some people have
over-analyzed so much of what used to come naturally to us. I've
studied and analyzed things too, but not rock-and-roll. For me,
rock music lets me forget the pressures of life. I respond to rock-
and-roll the way babies do: I just feel it.

SUMMARY

Here is a card summarizing the central claim in Quindlen's argument
and her supporting premises:

Quindlen   3

It's a dumb idea to put rating stickers on rock-and-roll albums.
    1. It would have the opposite effect. Kids could choose
albums that got the lowest rating.
    2. The lyrics aren't the point of rock-and-roll. Rock music
appeals to our feelings not our reasoning.

SUMMARY

Notice how card 2 summarizes the essay, whereas card 3 summarizes
Quindlen's argument. How you intend to use Quindlen's remarks will dictate
how you summarize her work. Keep in mind that if you intend to summarize

an argument completely, including missing premises, you'll need to look again at Chapter 7.

Paraphrasing   Whereas a summary condenses an entire argument or article, a paraphrase restates a passage in different words. Just as explaining a complex process to someone else helps you better learn the process, recasting an idea into your own words helps you take possession of the idea. You still have to acknowledge your source, but you will be better able to use the idea for your own purposes if you have stated it in a manner that you understand. Consider, for example, the following passage, written by Francis Bacon in the seventeenth century:

> Studies serve for delight, for ornament, and for ability. Their chief use for delight is in privateness and retiring; for ornament, is in discourse; and for ability, is in judgment and disposition of business. For expert men can execute and perhaps judge of particulars, one by one; but the general counsels, and the plots and marshaling of affairs, come best from those that are learned. To spend too much time in studies is sloth; to use them too much for ornament is affectation; to make judgment wholly by their rules is the humor of a scholler.[9]

Some modern readers, faced with this passage, might give up a few sentences into it. The expression appears alien to us; some words even seem to have been misspelled. But a close examination of the passage allows us to rephrase Bacon's Renaissance style and language and to take from the passage an interesting idea.

For the sake of comparison, the original passage is given on the left:

Studies serve for delight, for ornament, and for ability. Their chief use for delight is in privateness and retiring; for ornament, is in discourse; and for ability, is in judgment and disposition of business.	Reading and pursuing knowledge ("study") allows us to do three things: entertain ("delight") ourselves in private, adorn or embellish ("ornament") our speech ("discourse"), and increase our abilities to, for example, make better decisions ("judgment and disposition") in conducting our business.
For expert men can execute and perhaps judge of particulars, one by one; but the general counsels, and the plots and marshaling of affairs, come best from those that are learned.	Experts, those who excel at or specialize in one thing, are good at handling particular problems within their area of expertise, but the larger issues of life ("the general counsels," etc.) are handled best by those who have studied more widely, who are more "learned."
To spend too much time in studies is sloth; to use them	Of course, spending too much time reading is laziness ("sloth"); referring

| too much for ornament is affectation; to make judgment wholly by their rules is the humor of a scholler. | too much to our reading, dropping quotes in everywhere, for example, is just showing off ("affectation"); and reacting to life according to the rules we've read is the characteristic ("humor" in the old sense) of a scholar, someone who spends too much time in school, someone who doesn't get out much into the real world. |

You will notice that paraphrasing means more than just substituting synonyms for original words. Paraphrasing is almost like translating—looking up words to discover their meanings (*sloth* means "laziness"), using language you are more comfortable with, condensing phrases into words, turning words into phrases, and adding details to help clarify the point. If necessary, you can break up sentences and rearrange the parts as long as you don't lose the original meaning. You don't have to replace every word of the original, struggling to find your own words for common expressions ("too much time" appears in both the original and the paraphrase). Nor do you have to "translate" every word, especially those that you believe are essential (our paraphrase retains the word *learned*). The goal of a good paraphrase is to capture the essence of the original passage and to repeat the original in your own voice, proving to the reader that you have full *possession* of the idea, even though you had to borrow it.

In other words, paraphrasing is not easy, primarily because it requires that you know what you are doing. You must actively, energetically engage the text you are reading, think about it, and understand it. Your instinct may be to give up, to say to yourself, "What?! I don't get it!" and to move on, or fall asleep, or order a pizza. Paraphrasing is harder than quoting because it requires greater understanding of the original so that the author's meaning is not misrepresented or distorted. When paraphrasing, imagine the original author looking over your shoulder, reading every word that you write. If he or she gives you a funny look or says, "Hey, I didn't mean that!" you must start again. If while recording your notes you run out of energy trying to paraphrase, copy down the entire quotation (be sure to mark it as a quotation); you can always work on the paraphrase when you get to your draft.

EXERCISE 12.4

Split into groups of three or four and, working individually, paraphrase each of the following passages on an index card. (The passages get progressively more difficult.) Then compare your paraphrases. Are there any differences between individual cards? If so, what accounts for those differences: a misreading of the original, an ill-chosen synonym, a detail not warranted in the original?

1. College students dream of the clean sheets, good food and private bathroom that are home. Many schools have a long weekend break in October, and

frosh who live nearby often come home for the first time then. They may bring along new friends, or arrive with only their dirty laundry and new ideas. Many other students don't make it home until Thanksgiving. Still others, who attend distant schools, first return at Christmas. That four-week or four-month absence feels like an eon, and the distance from school to home—even if it's only an hour—seems like travel from outer space to Earth or the other way around. (Linda Polland Puner, *Starting Out Suburban: A Frosh Year Survival Guide*)

2. America is also the inventor of that most mythic individual hero, the cowboy, who again and again saves a society he can never completely fit into. The cowboy has a special talent—he can shoot straighter and faster than other men—and a special sense of justice. But these characteristics make him so unique that he can never fully belong to society. His destiny is to defend society without ever really joining it. He rides off alone into the sunset like Shane, or like the Lone Ranger moves on accompanied only by his Indian companion. But the cowboy's importance is not that he is isolated or anti-social. Rather, his significance lies in his unique, individual virtue and special skill, and it is because of those qualities that society needs and welcomes him. (Robert N. Bellah et al., *Habits of the Heart: Individualism and Commitment in American Life*)

3. The photograph—to narrow it down—reduces us to two dimensions and it makes us small enough to be represented on a piece of paper or a frame of film. We have been trained by the camera to see the external world. We look *at* and not *into*, as one philosopher has put it. We do not allow ourselves to be *drawn* into what we see. We have been trained to go by the externals. The camera shows us only those, and it is we who do the rest. What we do this *with* is the imagination. What photographs have to show us is the external appearance of objects or beings in the real world, and this is only a portion of their reality. It is after all a convention. (Saul Bellow, "Graven Images")

4. One of many insights that individuals must gain along the path to literacy is phonemic awareness. Research has shown that phonemic awareness is a more potent predictor of success in reading than IQ or measures of vocabulary and listening comprehension and that if it is lacking, emergent readers are unlikely to gain mastery over print. However, teachers can provide activities that facilitate the acquisition of phonemic awareness. With an assessment device readily available, practitioners can quickly identify those children who may benefit most from phonemic awareness activities and reduce the role that one factor—phonemic awareness—plays in inhibiting their success in reading and spelling. (Hallie Kay Yopp, "A Test for Assessing Phonemic Awareness in Young Children")

5. Hip-hop culture is quickly becoming American culture.

Children as young as five years old are singing hip-hop lyrics, not knowing what they mean.

Unfortunately, more and more messages of sexism and misogyny are being taught through lyrics and music videos. As these ideas and thoughts continue to cultivate in mainstream hip-hop, narrow-mindedness floods the brains of listeners of all races.

As this new "lifestyle" gains more popularity, the influence on society becomes apparent. Women are no longer seen as human beings, but sex objects, more or less fashion accessories. These feelings and ideas then force themselves into conventional thinking. Directly or indirectly, listeners are supporting an environment that consents to sexism. . . .

. . . [W]ith the rise in rap and hip-hop popularity, there seems to be a rise in violence against women, too. Coincidentally, violence against women is rising steadily with females being more and more sexualized in mainstream media. Not only that, but there is also a steady increase in the imprisonment of minority youths alongside the glamorization of rap music. . . . (Shandra Liyanarchi, "Hip-Hop Culture Degrades Women," *The Kentucky Kernel,* February 16, 2005. Available online at *www.kykernel.com/media/storage/paper305/news/2005/02/16/Opinions/HipHop.Culture.Degrades.Women-865462.shtml?norewrite200608011132&sourcedomain=www.kykernel.com.*)

If summarizing and paraphrasing are so difficult, why not just quote? For one thing, it can be very confusing for the reader to see so many quotations stitched together in a paper. Because you write, whether you know it or not, in a particular style and voice, the reader gets accustomed to that voice, which is interrupted by a different voice each time you drop in a quotation. Many inexperienced writers quote too often, creating a harsh blend of dissonant sounds and producing a paper that suggests the writer is uncomfortable with his or her own voice and ideas. But more important, quoting should be saved for words that are truly worth quoting. If it is the writer's *idea* you want to use, there is no reason to use the words; but if you want to analyze the writer's language, or if the words are particularly significant, quoting is warranted. The last sentences of *The Communist Manifesto,* for instance, would lose their impact if translated into a paraphrase:

> *Quotation:* At the end of their manifesto, Marx and Engels must have terrified many of Europe's capitalists: "Let the ruling classes tremble at a communist revolution. The proletarians have nothing to lose but their chains. They have a world to win. Working men of all countries, unite!"

> *Paraphrase:* Marx and Engels must have terrified many of Europe's capitalists when they mentioned revolution in the last lines of their manifesto. They called on the world's workers to join together. After all, the workers had little to sacrifice and much to gain.

I hate quotations. Tell me what you know.

—Ralph Waldo Emerson

Although the paraphrase doesn't misrepresent the intent of the original, it washes it clean of any power or significance. In a case like this, it might be best to let the writers speak for themselves.

EXERCISE 12.5

Below are quotations from various sources. If you were using these sources in a paper, would you quote, summarize, or paraphrase? Explain your decision.

1. A player loses the point if in playing the ball he deliberately carries or catches it on his racket or deliberately touches it with his racket more than once. (United States Tennis Association, rule 20d)

2. I am in awe of them, and I feel privileged to have been a witness to their lives and their sacrifices. There were so many other people whose stories could have been in this book, who embodied the standards of greatness in the everyday that the people in this book represent, and that give this generation its special quality and distinction. As I came to know many of them, and their stories, I became more convinced of my judgment on that day marking the fiftieth anniversary of D-Day. This is the greatest generation any society has produced. (Tom Brokaw, *The Greatest Generation;* Brokaw's book is about American men and women who came of age during the Great Depression and World War II.)

3. Gym class was another brush with fascism. You line up in your squads, and you better be wearing your little gym suits. If you are not wearing the gym suit, you are not taking gym class. "Remember kids, exercise has no effect unless you're wearing these special suits." (Jerry Seinfeld, *SeinLanguage*)

4. American athletes tend to be an obsessed bunch, but the trend toward endurance extremes has sounded alarms in the medical community. In the short term, common consequences of prolonged, strenuous exercise include tendonitis, stress fractures and chronic fatigue syndrome. But research is beginning to show that by racing ever farther and longer, athletes may also be putting themselves at risk for a host of chronic diseases, even cancer. (Andrew Tabor, "Using Up Too Much Too Soon: Pushing the Body to Athletic Extremes May Be Harmful to Your Health," *Salon,* July 26, 1999. Available online at *www.salon.com/health/feature/1999/07/26/ultrathletics/index.html.*)

5. We hold these truths to be self-evident, that all men are created equal, that they are endowed by their Creator with certain unalienable rights, that among these are life, liberty and the pursuit of happiness. That to secure these rights, governments are instituted among men, deriving their just powers from the consent of the governed. That whenever any form of government becomes destructive to these ends, it is the right of the people to alter or to abolish it, and to institute new government, laying its foundation on such principles and organizing its powers in such form, as to them shall seem most likely to effect their safety and happiness. (Thomas Jefferson, *Declaration of Independence*)

A final word about taking notes: As you read—quoting, summarizing, and paraphrasing on your note cards or in your notebook—you will inevitably have ideas of your own, reactions to what you have read or thoughts about where to place quotations and paraphrases in your final paper. If you are actively engaged with what you read, you will be shocked or upset to discover evidence contrary to your claims, thrilled to find supporting evidence, disturbed at the tone of a writer, incredulous at some author's outrageous assertions, and puzzled over another's implausible conclusions. As we said earlier in this chapter, you will also be inspired toward your own inferences, and you will see connections previously unknown. Whenever these thoughts and reactions occur to you, write them down! We all know the frustration of being unable to recall the insights that pop like a soap bubble in our heads and are gone forever. When you record these reactions and thoughts, be sure to indicate clearly that they are yours. If using cards, use a different color of card or give the card a distinguishing heading. But whatever you do, write it down.

USING SOURCES

So now you have a stack of note cards and a head full of ideas. In Chapter 13, we address the process of drafting and revising essays, advice that is applicable to this chapter as well if you are going to assemble your thoughts and notes into an effective paper, so you might want to read Chapter 13 before you begin writing. Keep in mind that it is *your* paper that is being written—don't turn your essay over to your sources, allowing them to carry the weight or speak for you. Think of your paper as a conversation between you, the reader, and the various outsiders you have brought in to help you defend your viewpoint or represent your opponent. Your quotations, summaries, and paraphrases should flow naturally with your own writing, creating an almost seamless presentation from start to finish. What follows are recommendations on incorporating outside sources into your essay.

Acknowledging Sources

Plagiarism. It would be almost impossible to find a college student who hasn't heard that ugly word, and, honestly, it might be just as difficult to find one who hasn't committed some small act of plagiarism somewhere in his or her academic life—the lifted passages from the *World Book Encyclopedia* in fourth grade, the middle-school essay that a parent contributed more than a few sentences to, the fabricated bibliography entry in a high school research project. Although these actions may have been disregarded or gone unnoticed, plagiarism, especially in college, is considered one of the most severe forms of academic dishonesty. Punishments for those who are caught range from failure on the specific paper to expulsion from school. Even those who get away with it suffer, primarily because the failure to develop research skills inevitably shows up at some point in the future.

There are probably as many reasons for cheating as there are cheaters. Students may panic because they have waited too long to begin a paper or because they can't find the best words to express their ideas. Some students lack the confidence to trust their own thoughts, or they argue to themselves, frustrated and defeated, that someone else has already expressed those thoughts in better language.

There may be students who simply feel overwhelmed by the course material—in over their heads to the point where it seems better to hand in

---

• Critical Thinking Lapse •

A student at Texas Tech University submitted a paper to a professor who immediately recognized the work. The professor himself had written the paper years earlier while a student at the same university. It had apparently ended up in a fraternity's files.

---

someone else's paper than to submit a sure failure of one's own. Some students claim that cheating is a common practice and necessary to get ahead in the world, and others seem to believe that the goal of higher education is to receive a degree, not to learn skills or develop the dispositions and habits of an educated person. Whatever the reason, plagiarism is wrong. Period. It is theft: It violates the principles of academic integrity; it provides an unfair advantage over students who work hard at their own writing; it shows great disrespect for the original author and contempt for the reader; it wastes tuition dollars; it cheapens the institution the student attends; it leaves the thief with no skills other than deception; and it can be discovered, even years later, with dire consequences. And because most students know that plagiarism is wrong, it seems to us that *real* plagiarists—the ones who buy papers on the Internet or copy whole passages from obscure journals—are rare. Most plagiarism, we contend, occurs because students are not sure exactly what plagiarism is and how to avoid it.

Plagiarism comes from the Latin *plagium,* meaning "kidnapping." A plagiarist, in other words, is a kidnapper. Not only does the origin of the word show how serious the crime is considered to be, it also gives some idea of how authors feel when their words are stolen. To plagiarize means to kidnap, or, to be more modern about it, to take, the creations—thoughts, words, writings, inventions, charts, or tables—of another person, whether those creations have been published or not, and to pass them off as one's own creations. And even if you take those creations and dress them up a bit differently, using synonyms or rearranging the sentences, you are still guilty of plagiarism if you fail to tell your readers or listeners who the original creator is. Although most students haven't yet published their ideas, many of us know the feeling of having our creations stolen. Have you ever, in a moment of inspiration, produced a snappy one-liner, sending your friends into hysterical laughter, only to hear your line repeated later by someone else who fails to acknowledge you? Or have you ever proposed a truly insightful solution to a problem, only to have the solution repeated to you days later as if you had never heard it before? If so, you know the feeling of having your creations plagiarized.

When plagiarism appears in a scholarly work, it usually takes one of three forms:

- Material from an outside source is presented *word-for-word* or detail-for-detail as the student's original work with no acknowledgment whatsoever of the source. In this type of plagiarism, a student is taking credit for an author's words and ideas.

Better thine own work is, though done with fault, than doing others' work, even excellently.

—Bhagavad-Gita

- Material from an outside source is *paraphrased* with no acknowledgment of the source. In this type of plagiarism, the student is taking credit for an author's idea.

- Material from an outside source is incorporated into a student's work and a weak effort is made to acknowledge the source. Usually, the student fails to use the conventional means of acknowledgment: introductions to quotations, quotation marks where necessary, parenthetical mention of page numbers, indentation of longer quotes, internal references ("the author goes on to argue . . ."), footnotes, and so forth. This kind of plagiarism is usually the result of indifference, uncertainty, carelessness, or ignorance.

It is this last sort of plagiarism—cheating from ignorance—that shows up most often in student papers. So let's assume that no student wants to plagiarize. No student wants to deliberately take credit for ideas that are not his or her own. How is plagiarism to be avoided?

First, know what *does not* have to be acknowledged. All writers owe a great debt to the millions of writers who have preceded them. Many of the ideas that we hold are the result of years of reading and thinking about what others have taught us. Much of what we know and think does not have to be credited. Any generally known fact, facts available in a wide variety of sources, and indisputable facts—Hemingway wrote *A Farewell to Arms;* the Great Depression began in 1929; Canada has ten provinces; George W. Bush was born in 1946—need not be footnoted. Even if you are discovering the fact for the first time, it might not have to be cited. For example, in doing research for an argument on capital punishment, you might discover that capital punishment was suspended for several years in this country, from 1972 to 1976. Although that fact is new to you, it is one that many people are aware of or one that can be verified in many sources, so it need not be cited.

Some phrases and quotations do not have to be cited, but these are rare and usually amount to proverbs, clichés, and recognized literary quotations. If you started a paper with, for example, "The Lord is my shepherd," or "To err is human," or "To be or not to be," you would not necessarily have to mention the Bible, Alexander Pope, or Shakespeare. You could if you liked, but without acknowledgment the reader would know that the saying is not your creation.

You *do* have to acknowledge the following and provide documentation:

- Direct quotations.
- Statistics and results of surveys. If you find in a paragraph, a table, or a chart, for example, that Americans watch an average of five hours of television a day, you must tell your reader who provided that information.
- Facts not currently widely known, especially new discoveries. If, for example, a writer uncovered the truth about a historical event or person, you must give the writer credit. Eventually, the discovery

may become extensively known, but until it does, acknowledge the source.

- Facts that have not yet gained acceptance, that are still considered controversial, or that you feel your reader might find hard to believe.

- Descriptions of events and any plans, graphics, drawings, tables, charts, or other visual items that you reproduce in a paper.

- Unusual verbal illustrations. If a writer clarifies a point by providing an illustration that is unique, unusual, very creative, and so forth, give the writer credit if you borrow the illustration.

- Any ideas not your own. The judgments, opinions, interpretations, explanations, definitions, and claims made by other thinkers, including writers, speakers, and professors, must be cited.

Use your best judgment in deciding when to cite sources. It can be very discouraging to discover that our best thoughts have been expressed elsewhere. Many students who fail to give credit to their sources do so because they feel that if they attribute their ideas to someone else, the reader will think them ignorant for coming up with nothing new. There are ways to incorporate the ideas of other writers without turning your essay over to those writers. We address these methods in the following section.

EXERCISE 12.6

In groups of four, individually examine the following facts, all of which are true. Which of these facts do you feel should be documented? Which do you feel could be used in an essay without reference to a source? After you have decided, share your answers as a group. What differences do you note? Discuss those differences and try to reach agreement on what should be documented and what can appear without citation.

1. With the Gulf of Tonkin Resolution, the U.S. Congress authorized increased military action in Vietnam.
2. In 1764, Wolfgang Amadeus Mozart composed a symphony. He was eight years old.
3. In one Amish community in Pennsylvania, roughly three-quarters of all suicides that occurred in a one-hundred-year period were in just four families.
4. The best-selling album of all time is The Eagles' *Their Greatest Hits.*
5. Alabama imports rocks from other states for prison chain gangs to crush.
6. Johnny Rotten, lead singer of the Sex Pistols, was born John Lydon.
7. Audrey Hepburn, not Julie Andrews, starred in the 1964 movie version of *My Fair Lady.*
8. The two most prevalent judicial systems in the world are the inquisitorial system and the adversarial system. The United States uses the latter.
9. The Bill of Rights originally applied only to the federal government, not to the states.

10. Charles Dickens's childhood experiences of humiliation, including his father's imprisonment for debt and Dickens's subsequent work in a shoe-polish factory, influenced his work as a novelist.

11. Hoping to become an artist, Adolf Hitler applied to the Vienna Academy of Fine Arts in October 1907 but was rejected. Later, penniless and unwilling to work, he ended up in a homeless shelter.

12. Because digital circuits operate in the binary number system, all circuit variables are either 1 or 0. Information in digital systems is processed through the use of Boolean algebra, which is based on the idea that logical propositions are either true or false. "True" corresponds to the digital value of 1; "false" corresponds to 0.

13. There is water on Mars.

14. Barry Bonds holds the record for home runs in a season: 73.

15. The rings of Jupiter are made up of dust created when Jupiter's four innermost moons collide with comets, asteroids, and other material.

Incorporating Sources

A researched argument should be more than a collection of source material. The argument you write should present your conclusion, your point of view, your opinion, backed up by the evidence and arguments that you have collected. One method for ensuring that your paper is your own is to write the argument first without sources and then to plug in your sources where needed. If you use this method, be careful not to "accidentally" borrow some ideas that you fail to credit.

When you write, remember that the paper is yours: your name is on it; you will receive a grade for the work, including the quality of the writing, the strength of the argument, the caliber of your sources, and the appropriate use of those sources. Because it is your paper, let your sources serve you rather than the other way around. Present your case and use your sources to bolster your argument. In other words, as you write, think, "This is my argument and so-and-so agrees with me," or "This is my argument and here's the evidence I found to prove it." Don't think, "This is what everyone else said, and I agree with them."

The trick to using quoted material is to make the quotation fit gracefully and logically into your own writing. Even with quotations added, your sentences must make grammatical sense, and your paragraphs must be coherent. The quoted material cannot interrupt the flow of your prose. Following is some advice on incorporating sources into your writing. All documentation in this section accords with guidelines established by the Modern Language Association (the MLA). These guidelines are generally used by writers of research papers in the humanities (philosophy, literature, foreign languages, and so forth). Not all disciplines use MLA style; some use, for example, the guidelines of the American Psychological Association (APA). Your professor will tell you which he or she prefers.

Quoting Words and Phrases   Often the passage you find useful will amount to no more than a word or a phrase. Even such short passages must be quoted if the word or phrase is unique to the writer or if it clearly indicates the writer's point of view or opinion. If you use a quoted word within a paraphrase, be sure to use quotation marks around the word:

> So great was essayist William Cobbett's hatred for cities and upper-class government officials that he often referred to London as "The Wen," which means pimple, and to Parliament as "The Thing."

> One especially poor customer saved a few pennies for "luxury" items, a packet of Kool-Aid and a small angel food cake for his children (Fetterman 117).

Notice how the quoted words fit neatly into each sentence. The same smooth effect can be accomplished when quoting longer passages.

Quoting and Paraphrasing Longer Passages   In quoting a sentence or two (usually under fifty words) from the original, provide an introduction to the sentence that establishes its context and helps the reader understand its meaning and relevance to your point. Your introduction can include the author of the quote and, if necessary and applicable, the printed source of the quote. The following are examples of a quoted sentence that follows from the introduction and the same quotation introduced with the author's name.

> Before the new student union is constructed, we should gather items to place in the foundation, in much the same way ancient builders "buried under cornerstones and posts and thresholds and inside walls and chimney piles these among other items: food, gems, coins, pottery, plants, statues, arrowheads, bottles of wine, carcasses of cattle and sheep, horses' heads and hoofs, and, as many legends have it, living human beings" (Kidder 304).

> Before the new student union is constructed, we should gather items to place in the foundation, in much the same way ancient builders, as Tracey Kidder reminds us, "buried under cornerstones and posts . . ." (304).

You can introduce your quotation in a variety of ways. Use dialogue tags at the beginning of the sentence or within it, or use an introductory phrase and the word *that,* or use an introductory phrase and a colon or a comma:

> As Tracey Kidder points out, ". . ."

> As Albert Camus once noted, ". . ."

> According to Julia Kristeva, ". . ."

> From this evidence, concludes Caute, ". . ."

> In a recent lecture on John Donne's later poems, Professor Marian Williams pointed out that ". . ."

> One look at the transcript of the trial reminds us that ". . ."

> Churchill decided quickly: ". . ."

> Darrow's argument seemed irrefutable: ". . ."

Occasionally, an introductory comment or phrase can be omitted, as when, for example, you want to start your essay with a quotation or when you want to segue into a quotation without announcing it. The transition between your words and the quoted passage must be smooth so as not to jar the reader, and the connection between your words and the quotation must be apparent. Notice how in the following paragraph John Kenneth Galbraith leads his reader gracefully to the quotation:

> Economics, not entirely by accident, became a subject of serious study at an important turning point in the history of western man. This was when the wealth of national communities began, for the first time, to show a steady and persistent improvement. This change, which in advanced countries like England and Holland came some time in the eighteenth century, must be counted one of the momentous events in the history of the world. "From the earliest times of which we have record—back, say, to two thousand years before Christ—down to the beginning of the eighteenth century, there was no very great change in the standard of living of the average man living in the civilized centers of the earth. Ups and downs certainly. Visitations of plague, famine and war. Golden intervals. But no progressive violent change." [10]

If you want to include a paraphrase in your paper, you must be sure to credit the source of the idea, which means you must be a bit more careful about your introduction because there are no quotation marks to tell the reader where the borrowed idea begins. Compare, for example, the following two paragraphs:

> If we hope to cure some of the ills plaguing our system of education in America, we might do well to look to China, where the education system has produced children steeped in the basics and often capable of great accomplishments. China cannot solve all of our educational problems, but the fact that its children generally grow up happy may indicate something about the success of education there (Gardner 317–318).

> If we hope to cure some of the ills plaguing our system of education in America, we might take Howard Gardner's advice and look to China, where the education system has produced children steeped in the basics and often capable of great accomplishments. China cannot solve all of our educational problems, Gardner concedes, but the fact that its children generally grow up happy may indicate something about the success of education there (Gardner 317–318).

In the first paragraph, it is impossible to tell where Gardner's contribution begins and ends. The reader might assume that only the last sentence or even the last phrase has come from Gardner's book. In paraphrasing, be careful to provide a clear introduction and reminders along the way. Phrases like "Gardner continues," "He further notes that," "In a later passage, Gardner retracts his comments," and so forth will make your writing clear and keep you free from charges of plagiarism.

If you are following one quotation or paraphrase with another, be sure to let the reader know how the two passages relate to each other. Is the second a refutation, a clarification, a confirmation, or what? A simple transition might do the trick:

> Shelley responded emphatically, ". . ."

Or you might need a somewhat more elaborate transition:

> Refusing to accept Peacock's definition of poetry, Shelley offered his own: ". . ."

Block Quotations   If a quotation amounts to more than four or five lines of type in your text (generally fifty or more words), you should block the quotation, maintaining the double spacing, omitting quotation marks, and indenting the left margin five spaces.

> It's difficult not to be moved by Lincoln's testament to the fallen soldiers at Gettysburg:
>
>> The world will little note nor long remember what we say here, but it can never forget what they did here. It is for us the living rather to be dedicated here to the unfinished work which they who fought here have thus far so nobly advanced. It is rather for us to be here dedicated to the great task remaining before us—that from these honored dead we take increased devotion to that cause for which they gave the last full measure of devotion—that we here highly resolve that these dead shall not have died in vain, that this nation under God shall have a new birth of freedom, and that government of the people, by the people, for the people shall not perish from the earth.

Because of the indentation, readers know where the quotation begins and ends, which is why quotation marks are unnecessary, as are reminders or dialogue tags.

Conducting research, reading carefully and critically, taking notes, and coherently and accurately incorporating what you have found into your own work is not easy, but if you remember that it is your argument you are defending with the help of outside sources, not someone else's argument that you are repeating or copying, and if you approach research with the right attitude—that we can all learn a great deal from the giants on whose shoulders we stand—your work as a researcher and writer will be gratifying and rewarding. You can quote us on that.

SUMMARY

1. Research does not have to be an intimidating task. Besides helping you to write more-solid arguments, research can assist you in your effort as a critical thinker to correct misunderstandings, discover the truth, and set the record straight. If you approach research with the right attitude, treating it less as a chore and more as an opportunity, you will find yourself amply rewarded, not only with the skills necessary to speak more intelligently, convincingly, and truthfully on your topics, but also with the skills you will need to succeed in your career.

2. Modern libraries are astonishing and often confusing places. With the help of a reference librarian and the many directional sources available, you can find a wealth of information without ever leaving campus. Focus your search so that you don't waste time and effort chasing too much information.

Consult bibliographies, indexes, and abstracting services to help locate information in the library and in databases. Use Internet search engines and guides to sort out the best information available on the Internet.

3. When searching for information on your topic, use periodicals and the books in the stacks, but also consult encyclopedias, almanacs, yearbooks, fact books, directories, handbooks, manuals, atlases, biographies, dictionaries, and government documents both to get started and to provide in some cases advanced and specialized knowledge about a subject. Human sources of information—faculty members, businesspeople, local experts, and so forth—are often overlooked but can provide quick answers to simple questions and the kind of in-depth knowledge that comes from experience.

4. Evaluating sources means asking a great many questions about the information you uncover, including questions about the content, the author, the publisher, and the audience. Be sure to separate facts from opinions in a writer's work. Don't repeat a writer's opinions as if they were factual, and don't repeat a writer's facts without being certain that they are indeed true. Be sure that the facts are complete and up-to-date.

5. When evaluating an author and a publisher, ask the following questions: What is the author's background? What is the author's bias and purpose? What are the author's sources? Who is the publisher or sponsor?

6. Ask the following questions about the audience: Who is the intended audience? How has the audience responded?

7. Good research depends on good note-taking skills. Be sure to copy down all the bibliographical information you will need to cite your sources and document your research. When recording quotations, be accurate and careful. When summarizing an essay or argument for use in your own paper, decide how extensive your summary should be. When paraphrasing, be faithful to the intent of the original. Choose to paraphrase more than to quote. Be sure to separate your own impressions and reactions from the quotations, summaries, and paraphrases that you record. Whatever system you use for note-keeping, be consistent and remember that the extra effort put forth while taking notes will pay off when drafting your essay.

8. Be exceptionally careful when incorporating sources into your argument. Plagiarism is among the most serious of academic offenses and can result in severe consequences. Learn well what does and does not have to be acknowledged. Always err on the side of giving credit.

9. Make your researched material fit gracefully into your own writing. Keep the reader in mind as you write: introduce your quotes rather than just drop them into your paragraphs. Cite your sources in the text and provide an accurate list of references.

CHAPTER 13

WRITING ARGUMENTATIVE ESSAYS

We have all been there: The Fight. The heart-pounding, teeth-clenching, name-calling, blood-boiling battle of words, from our first "*You* are!" "No, *you* are!" and "Did *not*," "Did *too*!" to the more memorable and emotionally charged moments of our lives—

> "Give me one reason why I should let you go to the ball game."
>
> "Is that my sweater you're wearing?"
>
> "It's my house, and while you're living in it . . ."
>
> "You spend too much time with your friends and not enough with me."
>
> "Can't you see why we're meant to be together?"

—and a thousand other familiar lines that have been the catalyst for our most heated arguments with one another.

Of course, at this point in your reading of this text, you should be saying, "Wait a minute! An argument is not a quarrel or a fight; it's a _____," and you should fill in the blank without batting an eye. If we are honest, though, we all have to admit that even when we know we're supposed to coolly, rationally present evidence to support our claims, we often resort to the kinds of argument we are most familiar with: the kinds of no-holds-barred matches that take place between us and our families and friends. The "flaming" that goes on in some newsgroups and chat rooms is one example of the nasty combats we allow ourselves to engage in, so much so that many newsgroups have established "Netiquette" rules to help cool down the scorching rhetoric that participants throw at one another.

The first rule of argument should be to consider logical discourse less as a battle for supremacy and more as an attempt to work as a community that *communicates* in an effort to arrive at the truth or at least, when it comes to practical matters and decision making, to arrive at compromises that make life easier and more enjoyable. As we have mentioned several times throughout this book, thinking critically often depends on applying the *principle of charity,* which means

> *In all disputes, so much as there is of passion, so much is there nothing to the purpose.*
> —Sir Thomas Browne

> *When you disagree, do so reasonably, and not disputatiously or contentiously.*
> —Mortimer Adler and Charles Van Doren

that unless there is evidence to the contrary, you should assume that your opponents are rational people and that their arguments are sound and cogent. In other words, thinking critically does not mean intellectually beating people up or using your thinking skills to take advantage of others. Arguing, as opposed to fighting, means that you respect your opponents, accurately and fairly represent their points of view, and support your conclusions with true premises and sound reasoning. Writers who construct arguments merely to "win," who go for the jugular or manufacture evidence or appeal unfairly to the emotions of their readers, do little to advance knowledge or understanding.

You should always strive to present a solid argument; if you convert others to your way of thinking, great. But if you have presented a powerful and sensible case, you have done your job, even if someone says, "I don't agree with your position, and I'm still voting Democrat" (or voting Republican, or supporting capital punishment, or getting married, or quitting my job, or whatever). Think of it this way: when you write an argument, make it your goal to be heard and listened to, to have your ideas considered and measured, to be regarded as an intelligent, rational, and sensitive person. If you win the argument in the process, congratulations; but the true measure of your success lies in what you have said or written and how you have said or written it, not in who agrees with you.

> Reason must be our last judge and guide in everything.
>
> —John Locke

EXERCISE 13.1

We have been maintaining that your objective in writing an argument should be to present a rational, well-evidenced, solid defense of your claim. Blatant emotional appeals are, we claim, inappropriate in a good argument. What do you think? Is it always the case that you should choose a well-reasoned approach over an emotional approach? Can you think of any occasions (real or imagined) when it would be appropriate to appeal to emotions to win your point?

WRITING A SUCCESSFUL ARGUMENT

Writing takes place in three very broad stages: what you do before you begin the first draft, what you do during the writing of the first draft, and what you do after you have completed the first draft. This chapter shows you how to prepare and write an argument, but you should keep one important point in mind as you read: although the advice and information is arranged in a step-by-step fashion, writing an argumentative essay is *not* a linear process. You can't write a paper the way you follow a recipe, carefully adding one ingredient after the other until the dish is prepared. Writing a paper is more like decorating a room. You start with a vision of what you want the room to look like, but halfway through the process you might change your mind and move the desk to another location or tack your favorite poster to a different wall. You try to move the bookcase, but it won't fit in the new spot, so you return it to its original spot. Or you throw it out and buy one that does fit. Maybe you give up, buy all new furniture and decorations, and start again. Like decorating a room, writing a paper means thinking and rethinking, backing up, adding and subtracting, rearranging ideas, throwing out what doesn't fit, and bringing in new ideas to achieve the look you want. In the process of writing, you may discover an idea that changes the entire focus and point of your paper. You may throw everything out and start again.

The following outline will help you keep track of the steps in the process of writing an argument.

Before You Write

Know yourself

Know your audience

Choose and narrow your topic

Write a sentence that expresses your claim

Gather ideas: brainstorm and research

Organize your ideas

Writing the First Draft

Provide an interesting opening

Include a thesis statement

Develop your body paragraphs

Provide a satisfying conclusion

After the First Draft

Read what you have written and revise

Consider what you have not written and revise

Show your work

Edit your work

Hand it in

BEFORE YOU WRITE

You should spend a great deal of time just preparing to write your first draft; in fact, the more time you spend preparing to write, the less frustrating the writing will be. Taking the time to think before you write will help prevent the panic that comes from plunging into a paper without any clear idea of how cold or deep the water is and then thrashing about without any idea of where you are going or how to get out. Before you write, take some time to think about how well you know your topic and who will be reading your argument. Decide what claim you would like to defend, and gather and organize your ideas for defending that claim.

Know Yourself

Make it thy business to know thyself, which is the most difficult lesson in the world.

—Cervantes

To write a good argument, you first must *want* to write a good argument and you must be willing to inventory your critical thinking dispositions: Are you prepared to be precise and accurate, to offer only premises you believe to be true, to fairly represent opposing points of view, to credit your sources, and so forth? If you want only to win the fight, you can resort to sucker punches and taunting; but to present a good argument, you must be willing to work hard at constructing a fair and honest case.

A healthy approach to writing arguments for a college class is to ask yourself *why* you are writing an argument. Of course, you are writing an argument because your professor wants you to; you are required to write an argument. That's true, but you will be in college for only a small fraction of your life. In the "real world," you may be called on to voice a claim and defend it on many occasions—at work, at the PTA meeting, as a member of the school board, in letters to editors or clients or constituents. Learning to argue well in writing allows you to use your talents for good purposes, to defend someone or some group that you feel is being maligned, to oppose what you believe to be an unethical or immoral act, to bring an end to a dangerous situation, or to prevent a disaster. It may sound trite or flattering, but you do have something to say, and you should be willing to take the time to say it well.

You must also be willing to ask yourself how well you know the issue you are going to address. We all have opinions, but we don't often stop to ask why we hold those opinions or how we arrived at them. If you have had a long-standing opinion on an issue, ask yourself where that opinion may have come from. It is possible that you can find many reasons to *explain* where a belief came from (perhaps from your parents, your church, or your studies), but if you are going to *argue* in support of your beliefs, you will have to provide justification and support that goes beyond explaining their origin. In other words, you may know how you *feel* about something, but what your readers want to know is what you *think*.

If you want to write about a topic you don't know very well, take the time to learn as much as you can about it. If you feel strongly about an issue, you should be willing to defend it intelligently and rationally. That doesn't mean, of course, that you must know all there is to know about an issue before you begin to formulate your opinion and take your stand or that you must present your case in an absolute or exhaustive manner. Few of us can maintain that we know all there is to know about *any* issue, or that we are absolutely, certifiably correct about our point of view, or that new evidence won't be discovered to prove us wrong, or that the opposing side is wholly without merit. It is no crime, when warranted, to use words such as "could be" and "possibly," to modify generalizations with "many" and "some," or to temper advice by saying, "I suggest" or "I recommend." We don't have to be overly humble, but we should be willing to grant our opponent his or her good points and to defend our own gracefully and considerately.

Know Your Audience

Some writers present arguments as if the reader were either an archenemy or a devoted fan. Neither is usually the case, but let's suppose for a moment that one or the other is true. Take the first hypothetical reader, our enemy. If our purpose is to be understood and to present a well-reasoned argument in support of our claim, does it make sense to antagonize the person we hope will judge us fairly? And if we actually do hope to "win" the argument, forget it! Jabbing at someone, taunting him, or hurling insults will almost always result in retaliation.

The second hypothetical reader—our loving champion—may agree with everything we say and, at the end of our presentation, tell us that we have presented a beautiful argument, full of truth and well structured, but there is very little to be gained from being evaluated by someone who is predisposed to compliment us. And what purpose is served, what progress is made, if our arguments are aimed at those who are ready to agree with everything we say? Certainly, we can find examples all around us of "arguments" presented to these two audiences. Listen, for instance, to any number of talk-show hosts on the radio, most of whom speak to an audience who is divided among the true believers and those who despise the host but listen, almost masochistically, because they "can't believe what I'm hearing." Radio hosts know that their audiences are divided this way; few people listen to popular talk radio for a keen analysis of complicated issues. For the sake of the show's sponsors, a radio host must

> *Turn your eyes inward, look into your own depths, learn first to know yourself!*
> —Sigmund Freud

> *Doubt and ignorance are sanctified when based on a firm resolve to believe nothing but truth.*
> —William Irvine

→ Pop Culture Connection ←

Blog Etiquette

If you want your argument to be taken seriously by your readers, it's a good idea not to insult them. This simple truth doesn't seem to apply to Internet bloggers. Consider these excerpts from a blog entry, entitled "Put on your bras, shave your armpits and quit your bitching," ostensibly directed at feminist readers. (The passage is quoted verbatim.)

Why the hell do women get offended when they're called *chicks*? I don't see how that word can be remotely offensive in anyway. But, some women think it's derogatory and belittling. Some women are so petty, that they resent any male implication in the english language. Who cares? What if guys suddenly felt like bitching and wanted to eradicate all the derogatory male phrases from the language? *Buster, Pal, Buddy, Stud, Hunk.* Oooh, don't call me a buster, I'll be offended. . . .

I can usually pick out a feminist in a croud of women. She'll usually have short hair, regular pants, a regular shirt, and an unbathed look; she'll look very much like a stereotypical guy. I think why a feminist might appear like this is to make a statement that "if men can do it and be accepted, then women should be able to". How bold, to go around and look like a stereotypical guy as opposed to a stereotypical girl. Who cares? Either way, you're an ass for thinking anybody cares about the statement you're making. (*http://setharius.spaces.live.com/Blog/cns!DC9D22BCF284F905!148.entry*)

Does this writer really hope to convince feminists to see things his way? Or does blogging come with a whole new set of rules? What do you think? Should arguments in blogs follow the same rules outlined in your textbook? Who is the intended audience? What are the benefits of blogs? What are the dangers?

keep the listeners tuned in, so he or she targets two audiences—the committed fans and those who vehemently disagree.

Perhaps we shouldn't fault the talk-show hosts for targeting their audience; that's what they are supposed to do. In fact, the first rule of all communication is to know who your audience is and adjust your style (though not necessarily your point) accordingly. If you were to write a letter to your grandmother, telling her about your romantic weekend, you would most likely use language and a tone different from what you would use in an e-mail to your best friend. If you were asked to prepare a speech on the difficulties of being a first-year college student, how would that speech be different if you were speaking to seniors in high school, business leaders from the community, elementary students, parents with children in college, and so forth? When preparing an argument, you should try whenever possible to know who your audience is: Are you writing for the citizens of your community, students of your age and background, professionals in the field, political figures, administrators in the school? Knowing who will be reading your argument will help you decide what tone to use, how sophisticated your word choices can be, how much background you must provide, and how much detail you need to go into. In the business world, even your position in a company or firm can dictate how you write your argument or proposal. Are your readers highly skeptical, or are they open to even the riskiest proposals? Do they hate to spend a dime on new ideas, or do they enjoy taking a gamble on costly innovations? Are you in a position of some authority so that your readers must implement your suggestions, or do you have to work hard at proving your case?

Anticipate Your Readers' Reactions   On the basis of what you know about your topic and your audience, try to determine how your audience might react to your claim and its defense. Perhaps your topic is appealing and your audience will receive your argument graciously. Say, for example, that you are writing to your classmates urging them to oppose 7:00 A.M. classes. Some of your classmates—those who start work at 8:00 A.M.—might actually want early-morning classes, but it's a safe bet that most will agree with your proposal. You will probably be facing an audience inclined to agree with your claim. If you were to present the same claim to the administration, on the other hand, you could probably assume that their reaction would differ from that of your classmates and that they would offer all sorts of reasons why 7:00 A.M. classes are a good idea. The administration would not necessarily act with hostility toward you or your ideas, but you might assume that they would not leap to embrace your idea without a very solid defense. You might find a more neutral audience in a group of people unaffiliated with the college. We often face neutral audiences when we address topics that our readers or listeners have little knowledge about or issues about which they are undecided. You might find a largely neutral audience if, for example, you argued that life existed on other planets or that Pete Rose should be allowed into the Baseball Hall of Fame.

When you consider how your audience will react to your claim, you almost automatically begin thinking about their reasons for reacting that way. You begin considering their points of view, their claims, their counterarguments. Predicting what an audience might say in response to your claim will help you to create a stronger argument. You should argue courageously and never change your point of view to placate your audience; on the contrary, you will be better able to defend your claim if you are prepared for the reactions you will encounter. Anticipating some of the administration's primary reasons for beginning the class day at 7:00 A.M. will help you head off some of those reasons when you present your case.

Often you can predict your audience's reactions by considering how *you* would feel as a reader. For example, people generally don't like to be told that they are wrong about something; so, instead of telling your readers that they are wrong, try to discover what values you and they have in common and show that your approach is based on those values, not detrimental to them. If you want to correct what you believe to be dangerous behavior, point out what you see to be the terrible consequences to your readers of continuing to act as they are. If you hope to change their thinking on moral or ethical grounds, don't insult them or write in a haughty or superior tone. Showing an audience that you share their concerns, that you respect them, and that you believe there is merit in both your view and theirs can go a long way toward getting your viewpoint heard.

In the absence of information about your readers, or when writing for a general readership, there are a few things you can assume. First, assume that your readers are slightly skeptical, that they do not necessarily agree with everything you say, but that they are open-minded and fair. Believing that they are impartial and objective will prevent you from overstating your case. Assume that your readers are intelligent, rational, and humane. You don't necessarily have to prove that accepting your claim will benefit each reader individually, but you should try to show, when the topic warrants it, that your argument takes into consideration the lives of people other than yourself. Surely, you wouldn't argue that speed limits should be raised because you enjoy driving fast. How would you argue that claim to a slightly skeptical, open-minded, intelligent, rational, humane person? Always assume the best about your audience, but keep in mind that, even if a close-minded, prejudicial audience refuses to listen to you, if you have defended your claim with solid evidence and clear reasoning, you have done your job.

EXERCISE 13.2

Look at the following letter, written to the editor of a newspaper. The paper had recently reported that Pennsylvania teachers were among the best paid in the country. Summarize the key points of the argument in a few sentences. Look for fallacies and examples of vague or slanted language. Then consider the overall effect of the argument. Determine as specifically as you can the writer's purpose. Does he seem to be writing to an audience inclined to agree with him, or is he trying to convince neutral readers and members of the opposition that he is correct in his thinking? How do you think the newspaper's readers would respond to this letter? How would a student of critical thinking evaluate this letter?

> Editor:
>   Once again, the taxpayers of the Wyoming Area School District are being ordered to "open wide" and not for the purpose of checking for cavities. The dentist in this case is the Wyoming Area School Board and the order to open wide is directed to our wallets. With the passage of the 1998 budget, Wyoming Area has the dubious honor of joining the 200 and Above Club. The new budget includes a 15-mill tax hike, putting Wyoming Area's millage at 200.

When property owners are writing the check to pay that bill, they should remember that the largest part of that check, by far, is going into the pockets of members of the Wyoming Area "Education" Association. The current average cost per teacher to the taxpayers of Wyoming Area is $53 per hour.

To make matters worse, our school board is currently negotiating with the teachers union for a new contract. Unless we act now and let our board members know we will no longer accept big give-away contracts for the sake of peace, we will continue to pay for our silence and complacency with more big tax hikes in the future.

A mere 2 percent pay raise for one year for the $53-per-hour people will cost the taxpayers of Wyoming Area an additional $125,000, or 3.5 mills.

The teachers union is able to extort this money from the taxpayers of Pennsylvania; through their forced union dues, they are able to pour huge sums of money into the campaigns of their lap-dog political candidates. Under the guise of "doing it for the children," these teacher-union lackeys pass laws which make it very easy for the teachers union to get what it wants.

With the upcoming elections in November, taxpayers should know two things:

According to figures I have seen, approximately 40 percent of the delegates at the last Democratic National Convention were members of the teachers union. They apparently have plenty of time on their hands to corrupt our nation's political system.

Secondly, about 90 percent of all teacher union PAC money goes to Democratic candidates. They apparently have plenty of extra money with which they can corrupt our nation's political system. With figures like this, can there be any doubt about who controls the Democratic Party?

In my opinion, the teachers union is the taxpayers' greatest enemy, and a vote for a Democrat, generally speaking, is a vote for the enemy. Had it not been for a Republican governor and a Republican-controlled state House and Senate, we would never have had tenure reform, sabbatical leave reform, charter school legislation, or this meager but promising attempt at tax reform in Pennsylvania.

On the national level, the Democrats and President Clinton have stopped every single attempt made by Republicans to improve education in our country. As the cost of public education continues to sky-rocket with no corresponding improvement in results, the teachers union monopoly must not go on unchallenged.

As bad as things seem, they would be worse without the existence of taxpayer groups. Taxpayer groups are organized all around the state and every taxpayer who cares about fiscal responsibility in government functions should join and support their local group. We do make a difference.

> George R. Race
> President
> Wyoming Area Taxpayers Association
> Wyoming, Pennsylvania

Choose and Narrow Your Topic

If your professor has not assigned a topic to be investigated but has, instead, given you freedom to choose, decide on a topic that is both controversial and interesting to you. It does not have to be one you are familiar with; in fact, you might want to select one that you have always been curious about or one that you have always wanted to learn more about so that you can argue your case more convincingly. Also, pick a topic that you can manage to cover completely in the space allowed for your paper. Often the first question students ask is how long the essay should be. It's a fair question. If you are to write a 500- or 750-word essay, you are going to choose a different topic from the one you would select for a 10,000-word essay.

Say the required length is 750 words, or three double-spaced pages, and say you are interested in the topic of work or labor. List some of the controversial topics that fall under the heading "Work":

- Are families harmed when both parents work?
- Do company perks such as on-site gyms and day care hurt employees more than help them?
- Should the minimum wage be increased?
- Should welfare recipients be required to work?
- Should employers be required to give advance notice to employees who are about to be laid off?
- How necessary (useful, outdated, relevant) are labor unions?
- Should child labor laws be relaxed?
- Should your college bookstore sell clothes made in sweatshops?
- Does the U.S. government interfere too much in overseeing workplace safety?
- How serious a problem is sexual harassment in the workplace?
- How far can companies go in "invading the privacy" of workers?
- Should the U.S. institute a four-day workweek?
- Should a law be passed mandating equal pay to both sexes for comparable work?
- Should companies offer benefits to same-sex partners?

Your list of controversial topics could go on for pages if you knew enough about the subject of work. Certainly, because you couldn't write about all these topics in a short argument, you would have to limit yourself to one. But you could also continue to narrow your focus by limiting one of the subtopics listed above. Take the invasion-of-privacy issue, which is narrower than the issue of work, but which could be further narrowed to something more manageable:

- How far can employers go in using surveillance cameras in the workplace?

- Does an employer have the right to know what an employee does in his or her off-hours?

- How far can an employer go in conducting background checks on a potential employee?

- What questions should and should not be asked in a job interview?

- If an employee receives e-mail from outside the company, does the employer have a right to read it?

- Should an employer have unlimited access to an employee's desk, computer, and file cabinets?

- Should any employer be allowed to randomly test for drugs?

- Does an employer have the right to know an employee's sexual orientation?

Any one of these topics could serve for a short essay, but you could actually narrow the topic even further. The first three topics in the list above, for example, might become

- Should airlines install surveillance cameras in the cockpits of commercial airliners?

- Can an employer with a no-smoking policy fire employees who smoke after business hours and off company property?

- In deciding whether to hire a prospective employee, should an employer consider the applicant's profile on an online social network such as MySpace and FaceBook?

You may initially feel that if you narrow the topic down you won't have enough to say, but it is better to work at developing a focused topic than to leave a large issue undeveloped. And as you improve your writing and arguing skills, you will usually find that you have too much to say even about the most slender of topics.

> *Out of clutter, find simplicity.*
> —Albert Einstein

Finally, keep in mind that the best arguments are often those that present an unusual point of view or a claim few people have considered. When deciding what to write about, don't hesitate to take a risk and choose a topic that is controversial or uncommon. Several of the topics in our first list—"Do company perks such as on-site gyms and day care hurt employees more than help them?" "Should child labor laws be relaxed?"—may strike you as unusual or absurd, but on second thought or after researching the topic, you might see some reason to answer yes to both.

EXERCISE 13.3

I. Choose one of the broad topics below and narrow the topic to one that could be addressed in a three-page (750-word) argument. Start by listing as many controversial issues as you can; then narrow even further until you have a workable topic.

the environment	birth control	television
AIDS	domestic violence	professional athletics
alcoholism	free trade	NCAA
gambling	Cuba	genetic testing
HMOs	smoking	9/11 prisons
child abuse	cloning	hip hop

II. The following list of questions provides topics that can be used to practice the skills we discuss in this chapter. In groups of three or individually, choose a question from the list and use it to arrive at a narrow topic that you could address in a three- to four-page argument. As you proceed through the chapter, apply what you are learning to the topic you have selected.

1. Should the government be responsible for the unemployed?
2. Are minorities discriminated against in the media?
3. Should physician-assisted suicide be permitted?
4. Should the United States provide foreign aid to developing nations?
5. Is community service an appropriate punishment for criminals?
6. Isn't police brutality sometimes the only proper response to some situations?
7. Are beauty pageants harmful to those who participate in them?
8. Is feminism an outdated ideology?
9. Have historians been guilty recently of revising history?
10. Have environmentalists gone too far in their efforts to stop global warming?
11. Is there a date-rape crisis in society? On your campus?
12. Has racism diminished at all over the past fifty years in America?
13. Is the mainstream media liberal?
14. Do we need a return to family values?
15. Which does more damage, street crime or white-collar crime?
16. Should pornography be outlawed?
17. Can a businessperson be both successful and ethical?
18. Should Congress continue to propose an amendment outlawing desecration of the American flag?
19. Should taxpayers receive vouchers to send their children to private schools?
20. Do you think marine mammals should be held in tanks and used in shows?

Write a Sentence That Expresses Your Claim

Once you have decided what you want to write about, formulate a single sentence that presents the central claim of your argument and write it on a blank sheet of paper: "I think . . . ," "People should . . . ," "We must . . . ," "It's time for . . . ," "It is true that . . . ," and so forth. State your claim as forthrightly as you can and be sure that your claim is debatable, something with which someone could disagree. You might write, for instance, "An employer has no right to read an employee's private e-mail messages," or "Lee Harvey Oswald was the lone assassin of JFK," or "The college should eliminate the football program." At this point you are only focusing your argument, so don't worry about how clumsy or awkward your claim sounds. You can always revise it as your paper gets going.

Gather Ideas: Brainstorm and Research

Writers generally get their ideas from two sources: their own heads and the heads of other people, usually other writers. As with the larger process of writing, the gathering of ideas does not proceed strictly step-by-step. Some writers do a great deal of reading and research before formulating ideas and approaches for a paper; others record their own thoughts first and then look for additional ideas and support; still others combine the two approaches in a variety of ways. The approach you take will depend on your own habits, your familiarity with the topic, and your need for facts and expert opinion to back you up.

Brainstorming is a method for generating ideas for a paper. Like any other kind of storm, brainstorming is spontaneous and wild, but many writers make the mistake of trying to channel their creative thinking into grammatical sentences and coherent paragraphs. When you brainstorm, allow your ideas to flow freely. Write down whatever occurs to you, and don't censor any ideas as irrelevant or uninteresting. Don't worry about being incorrect or even sounding foolish. No one will judge your argument on your brainstorming. It is like a dialogue with yourself. You can always cut ideas after you have listed them.

You can brainstorm in several ways. Some writers like to freewrite, which entails writing for a measure of time, usually fifteen minutes, without stopping. Other writers favor the technique "mapping," in which the writer freely associates ideas, writes them down, and connects them in a weblike fashion. The method we recommend here is slightly more structured than traditional methods of brainstorming, but it will better help you generate ideas for supporting an argument.

List Supporting Premises   First, when brainstorming for an argument, list as many reasons as you can to support the claim. For the claim that an employer should not read private e-mail, you might list the following premises:

> E-mail is like regular mail, and it's illegal to open someone else's regular mail, so it should be illegal to open someone's e-mail.

> Even if it weren't illegal to read e-mail, it's unfair to the recipient of the e-mail, who might be discussing personal matters, such as medical or family problems.

> If people know that their private correspondence might be read by someone else, they might be reluctant to speak freely, which would limit their ideas and perhaps encourage them to be dishonest.

> If an employee knows that his e-mail might be read by the boss, he could take advantage of the situation by telling his friends to send him e-mail about how great the boss is.

Some of these premises might not sound too convincing, and after consideration you might eliminate one or two. That last premise, for example, sounds especially weak and may be impossible to defend.

> One thing will grow plain when compared to another.
>
> —Lucretius

If you find that you can't think of more than one or two premises, you may want to change your topic. But the inability to come up with premises is not always a sign that you should abandon your topic. If you believe in your claim but cannot think of support for it, you might have to seek help through research. In fact, reading more about your topic and examining the arguments made by other writers can bring on a storm of ideas that otherwise would not have arisen.

List Opposing Premises   Second, write down as many premises as you can think of to *oppose* your claim. What would someone who disagreed with you say?

> Employers have paid for the computer, the lines, and the service provider and therefore have a right to see how e-mail is being used.
>
> Employees waste time writing and reading personal e-mail.
>
> E-mail coming into the company or going out might contain sensitive material that the company needs to keep under wraps.

Like your own premises, some of these might be eliminated, and you might have to research your topic to determine if you have overlooked any opposing arguments. Sometimes it helps to get another mind involved at this point. Ask a friend, a family member, or a professor to play devil's advocate and tell you how someone might disagree with you.

Think Critically about Your Claim   Are you overgeneralizing in any way? Are there any exceptions to your claim? Maybe, for example, some employers (e.g., the Defense Department) must read all incoming e-mail. Are you creating a false alternative? Is there some middle ground you have overlooked? Are there solutions you have ignored? Has someone else already solved the problem or proposed a viable solution? Do you need to modify your claim to allow room for uncertainty? Don't hesitate to get into an argument with yourself at this point. Remember, your reader is a critical thinker.

Think on Paper   Now write down what you know or think you know about your topic. In this part of brainstorming, you are simply trying to create and gather ideas from your own mind; in other words, you are thinking on paper. Some of the ideas you come up with will serve as additional premises to support your central claim; others will serve to clarify, illustrate, and defend the central premises. You may find that in thinking on paper, you begin to conceive a structure for your argument, a structure that includes both central premises and subarguments.

If you have trouble coming up with ideas, ask yourself some questions: "Why did I choose this topic?" "Why does it bother me so much?" "What do

I want my readers or listeners to do, to believe, to think?" "What are my experiences with this issue?"

Methods of Development   A very productive method for generating ideas is to think about the ways we usually develop and detail our communication with one another: we tell stories, describe people and places, compare and contrast events or things, give examples, define our words, and so on. These methods of development can be very useful both in discovering material to flesh out a paper and in prompting new thoughts in support of your claims.

Narration   A narration tells a *story in chronological order.* Are there any stories associated with your topic? Do you know of anyone whose experiences would be worth recounting? For example, perhaps you or someone you know has a story about working in a place where private e-mail is filtered or read by managers.

Description   A description gives *concrete details to paint a verbal picture* of a person, place, or thing. There may be in your topic something that can be described.

Cause   Causes are *reasons* for the occurrence of an event, a decision, an action, and so forth. Look at your topic and ask, "Why did this happen?" "What caused this?" Ask why some companies began the practice of intercepting and opening private e-mail. Do employees, in fact, dislike the practice? If so, what reasons do they give? Be careful not to commit any of the fallacies that can result from arguing for causes where none may exist.

Effect   Effects are the *results* of an event, a decision, an action, and so forth. What effects are associated with your topic? Ask yourself, "What will happen if . . . ?" and "What has happened?" "What has the outcome been?" Ask what effect intercepting e-mail has had on companies. Has white-collar crime decreased? Have employees worked harder? Have employees revolted? Has production improved? What was the intended effect in the first place? What might happen if the practice continues? Be careful not to commit a slippery-slope fallacy.

Classification and Division   When we classify, we take a large group and *break it down* into smaller, more manageable, groups. All the students in a college can be grouped by class (freshman, sophomore, junior), major, living status, and so forth. When we divide we take one thing (a car) and break it down into its various parts, such as systems (electrical, fuel, cooling) or individual items (seats, battery, rear bumper). Look at your topic to see if classification and division lead to any ideas. Perhaps you are grouping all private e-mail together, when, in fact, you could classify it by sender or where it comes from. Perhaps you could divide messages into header and text, leading to a compromise in your argument: managers could see from whom e-mail was coming but could not read the message. (*Remember:* you're just thinking on paper here; some of this—all of it, even—could end up on the cutting-room floor, as they say in the movie industry.)

Contrast   When we contrast two things, we show them to be *dissimilar* in important ways. Could you develop your topic through contrasts? Perhaps two companies have widely differing approaches to improving employee work habits, and one of those companies does it without opening e-mail.

Comparison   When we compare two things, we discuss the *similarities* between them. Is there anything in your topic that calls for a comparison? Can you defend your claim by comparing the situation under study to something similar? If you were arguing that your workplace should not intercept e-mail, you might be able to point to other companies that have eliminated the practice without harmful consequences.

As you saw in Chapter 11, a comparison used to support a claim is called an *analogy,* a useful but tricky device when used in an argument. In fact, analogies must be used so carefully that it is sometimes wiser to avoid them. Any major weak spots in a comparison, and the analogy—and the argument—falls apart. For example, if you tried to claim that students should always follow their teacher's advice and offered as support the fact that soldiers must always follow their leaders' orders and salespeople must always follow their managers' instructions, some reader is going to point out all the differences between students, soldiers, and salespeople and between teachers, generals, and managers. You can see why some analogies don't work.

Illustration   When we illustrate, we provide *examples* to help clarify a point and defend a general comment. If, for example, you said to someone, "My classmates are very bright," you might follow with, "Take Dawn, for example; she's double-majoring in neuroscience and English." To illustrate the claim that "that movie was terribly frightening," you might say, "In this scene . . . ."

Examples can be very helpful as you begin to build support for your conclusion, but keep in mind that examples have to be carefully chosen. They can come from personal experience or history, or they can be created, depending on your purpose and the topic. If you were trying to support the claim that noise in the dorms sometimes continues past the quiet hour, you might cite some examples of particular nights in the past month on which parties, music, fights, and so forth awakened you in the early hours of the morning. If you were trying to support the claim that U.S. presidents have often had extramarital affairs, you could refer to them by name. Both of those claims could be supported by real examples. Be cautious when you use either personal or historical examples: your experiences may be unique, and you may be unable to generalize from your historical examples. Be sure that your examples are representative and that you have chosen as many as you need to establish your conclusion. Rarely are only a few examples sufficient. The best arguments from example usually combine examples with other support, such as expert opinion.

A hypothetical example is used to support a claim for which there may be no readily available real-life examples or for which a hypothetical example works just as well or better. Say the argument is over whether we are obligated to help someone who is in danger. If you were to argue that we are not, you might begin your defense with "Well, suppose, for example, . . . " You are about to give a hypothetical example. The word *suppose* shows that the illustration is one you are creating, although it will serve your point: "Well, suppose, for example, that someone is drowning and I can't swim. Am I obligated to jump into the water anyway?" Someone might respond that you are obligated to throw a flotation device or run for help, but your example has helped clarify the issue and your position. As you continue the discussion, you can further clarify both, perhaps reaching a more discerning position on when we are and are not obligated to help one another.

Definition   When we define a word, we tell our readers or listeners exactly *what we mean* by a word or a concept. In daily discourse with one another, we often use definitions to, for example, clarify our use of specific words ("He's not very *romantic;* he never brings me flowers") or to persuade ("I wouldn't call her a friend; a 'friend' is someone who never judges you"). While brainstorming for ideas, look at your claim and your premises and ask if there are any words that should be defined for the reader. In the example on e-mail privacy, perhaps *private* could be defined, or even the larger concept of privacy: What exactly is *private* in the context of the workplace?

Look Over Your Brainstorming   Look over the results of your brainstorming and ask yourself the following questions:

- Should I refine my claim? Your brainstorming may lead you to re-evaluate your claim. Decide if you need to modify what you intend to prove. For instance, you may want to limit the scope of your argument or qualify your generalizations: "With a few rare exceptions, employers should not have the right to intercept and read the private e-mails received by employees."

- Are there any additional premises in my rough collection of thoughts and ideas? Did my unstructured thinking on paper produce any additional reasons to support my claim? At this point you should be able to revise your original list of premises.

- What do I still need to find out? Of your premises ask, "Is that really true?" "Do I know that for a fact?" "Where did I hear that?" "Who told me that?" "When did I learn that or hear that?" "What evidence do I have that I'm right?" (I'm not exactly sure, for example, that it's illegal to open someone else's regular mail. I would need to find out.) Ask yourself what more you will need to do or to find out to make your premises acceptable to a reader. At this point, think long and hard about your audience. What questions might a reader have for you? What evidence might a reader challenge? You may have to conduct research at this point to fill in the gaps, supply more support for your argument, and so forth.

- What can I use, and what do I need to exclude? Often, if you are lucky, your brainstorming will lead to more ideas than you can use in your argument. Your brainstorming may have led you off the track, or you may have gotten into areas (causes, for example) that are not immediately relevant to your claim. If you want to argue that plagiarism is a problem on campus that needs to be stopped, the causes of plagiarism may not be relevant to your argument. You, of course, have to decide. Use caution and be selective when deciding what will end up in your argument: more is not always better. It is also a good idea to file away the ideas you don't use; what doesn't make it into this argument could be useful in another.

EXERCISE 13.4

As a group, write out a claim and brainstorm ideas for an argument on the topic you chose in Exercise 13.3, part II. When brainstorming, one member of the group should act as secretary while all members of the group provide premises, raise opposing premises, ask critical questions, "think on paper," and look over the ideas that have emerged.

Do Some Research   If you haven't already done so, you may at this point need to do research to support your claim and your premises. The support you seek will generally fall into two broad categories—facts and opinions. You can draw from a wide variety of reliable sources, including experts in the field, statistical abstracts, textbooks, encyclopedias, journals, and reliable Internet sites. Because Chapter 12 provided extensive advice for conducting research, we will just recap some key points here.

Facts   Certainly, facts are very useful for supporting an argument, but determining what is and is not a "fact" can be tricky; what appears to be certain and indisputable may not be true at all or may actually be a matter of opinion. Loosely defined, a *fact* is something that has objective reality; it is not a matter of perception or opinion. Usually, a fact can be known with some measure of certainty and can be verified with data. Facts include statistical data, reports of observations, and examples of actual occurrences and events.

> *The word "fact" is vital to us. Without it we would be virtually speechless if asked to describe the kind of knowledge we prize.*
>
> —Parker J. Palmer

When using facts to support your argument, keep a few things in mind:

- You may be mistaken about what you believe to be fact. Don't always rely on your memory, on "conventional wisdom," or on what you have always assumed to be true. Spend the extra time to verify your facts.
- For the most part, use facts that have been verified by reliable sources. If you have any doubt about the truth of information, consult more than one source.

- Ask yourself how widely known your facts are. Some facts are generally agreed upon, but some are not. If you are using factual information that your audience is unfamiliar with or that they will have a hard time believing, you should give the source of your information.

Opinions   Yes, we are all entitled to our opinions, but that doesn't mean that we are rationally entitled to believe them or that all opinions are true. Unlike facts, opinions can be so subjective that they are sometimes based on nothing more than prejudice or wishful thinking. Or they can be based on a thorough examination of the facts, formed in a sensitive and reasonable mind and backed by years of experience, study, and research. Clearly, you should choose to support your claims in the second way.

In seeking expert opinion to support your argument, look for opinions from experts who prove that they have the knowledge, fair-mindedness, and clear thinking skills necessary to offer informed opinions. Try to rely on disinterested authorities; and if your readers may be unfamiliar with your authority, be sure to tell who your expert is, providing the person's background to make your citation more persuasive.

Do not find fault before examining the evidence; think first, and criticize afterwards.
—Ecclesiasticus 11:7

Finally, don't discount the authority of creative writers such as poets and novelists. You may be able to find some appropriate and useful thoughts from great writers who, although they may not have "studied" the topic you are addressing, may nonetheless have written eloquently and powerfully in defense of your claim. You may be able to use the insights of a writer to help support your argument—Henry James on privacy or Joyce Carol Oates on boxing, for example—or your own thinking might be sparked by those insights.

Organize Your Ideas

Of all the difficulties faced by writers, organizing ideas seems to be the one that presents the most trouble. But the "block" that can occur from trying to organize ideas is actually a good sign that the writer is trying to communicate effectively with the reader. If we weren't worried about the reader, we could just blabber on in any way we liked. In setting up your organization, use your intuitive "audience-sense" to your advantage by looking at organization not so much from your point of view as from your reader's. Given the claim you are making, how would a reader want to see your evidence and defense presented? What would be the most logical or natural way to present the case? What would be the least confusing way to set up the presentation? You should endeavor not to bore your reader, but there is no need to get too creative or to impress the reader, either. Just present a good, solid, well-reasoned argument.

Once again, remember that the process of writing is nonlinear. New ideas may occur to you as you decide how to organize your essay. You may even change your entire approach. Be prepared to keep thinking and creating. There are many ways to organize an argument. We'll focus on several in this section.

Organize by Premises   In deciding how to organize your argument, keep in mind that each paragraph in the body of the argument will be related somehow to your central claim. In most cases, the body paragraph will present a topic idea that is a premise for the claim made in the thesis. For example, if you were defending the claim that your hometown council should approve the placement of a traffic light at an intersection that currently has a four-way stop, you might organize your argument in the following manner:

Claim: Council should approve a traffic light for several reasons.

First body ¶: An average of six thousand cars pass through the intersection each day. Other equally busy intersections in the city have traffic lights.

Second body ¶: There has been a relatively high number of accidents at that intersection. Traffic lights have been shown to reduce the number of accidents at an intersection.

Third body ¶: A busy elementary school and a popular restaurant are located at the intersection.

Each paragraph helps support the claim being made. You might decide to divide some ideas into two separate paragraphs. For example, the two ideas given in the second body paragraph—the number of accidents at the intersection and the study showing how lights reduce the number of accidents—could be divided into two paragraphs:

Claim: Council should approve a traffic light for several reasons.

First body ¶: An average of six thousand cars pass through the intersection each day. Other equally busy intersections in the city have traffic lights.

Second body ¶: There has been a relatively high number of accidents at that intersection. [The paragraph would give the number of accidents, perhaps collected from a study of police reports, and would compare that number with the number of accidents at other intersections in the city. The paragraph could also include a description of representative accidents that have occurred at that intersection.]

Third body ¶: Traffic lights have been shown to reduce the number of accidents at an intersection. [The paragraph would include statistics to show how many accidents occurred at intersections before and after a traffic light was installed. Examples might be provided for a number of representative intersections.]

Fourth body ¶: A busy elementary school and a popular restaurant are located at the intersection.

If you had a long list of facts and expert opinion to present in support of your claim, you could devote a paragraph to each fact and opinion. For example, if you were arguing that someone is guilty of a crime, you could organize in the following manner:

Claim: Colonel Mustard is guilty.

First body ¶: He was in the billiard room when the murder took place.

Second body ¶: His fingerprints are on the murder weapon, the lead pipe.

Third body ¶: He confessed to the police.

Fourth body ¶: All other suspects have been cleared.

Fifth body ¶: Experts from the Parker Brothers Crime Lab have all testified that only he could have committed the murder.

Sixth body ¶: The psychologist Professor Plum claims that Mustard is just crazy enough to do something like this.

Seventh body ¶: Ms. Scarlet saw him do it.

Eighth body ¶: Professor Plum heard him do it.

Well, you get the picture. Each premise could be developed in its own paragraph so that, for example, you would prove in the first body paragraph that Colonel Mustard was in the billiard room when the murder took place. You couldn't just assert it; you would have to prove it.

If you have too many short paragraphs, you may be able to combine several of them. For example, paragraphs seven (eyewitness) and eight (ear-witness) could be combined into one with a topic sentence about witnesses to the crime. Paragraphs five and six could be combined as well.

Organize by Methods of Development   When organizing by premises, be sure to determine whether your claim is supported by any unstated premises or assumptions that may need to be defended. Suppose, for instance, that you wanted to argue that the sale of radar detectors should be outlawed in all states because radar detectors are designed for no purpose other than to break the law. Your argument would look like this:

Premise: Radar detectors are designed for no purpose other than to break the law.

Claim: The sale of radar detectors should be outlawed.

The missing premise in this argument is that *It is illegal to sell any device designed solely to break the law.* Your organized essay would look like this (rearranged with the claim stated first):

Claim: The sale of radar detectors should be outlawed.

Premise: Radar detectors are designed for no purpose other than to break the law. (Here you would show that radar detectors are intended to alert speeding drivers to the presence of radar, allowing the speeding driver to slow down and avoid a ticket. You would show that radar detectors have no other use, despite some creative advertising claims that radar detectors can be used for lawful purposes.)

Premise: It is illegal to sell a device designed solely to break the law. (Here you would show that nothing can be sold in the United States if the product's sole purpose is to allow citizens to break the law. For example, no one can legally sell a "marijuana pipe." You would be careful in this paragraph to show that you are not suggesting that any device that *can be used* illegally should be outlawed; baseball bats can be used by vandals, but they shouldn't be outlawed. You are showing only that any device created *solely* to facilitate illegal activity is itself illegal and cannot be sold.

In the writing of an argument, all the methods of development (as discussed on pages 403–405) can come into play. Say, for example, you made the claim that citizens of the United States hate warfare. You could support your claim through **illustration,** calling on history to provide examples of how Americans have hesitated to go to war or have protested involvement in war. Of course, your generalization would need to be modified as you found examples showing that some Americans have supported the country's involvement in war. If you wanted to look at two possible **causes** for an event, you might organize your argument along the lines of a **contrast** or **comparison** essay, looking at one cause, then the other. You could argue that some decision or action would lead to several **effects.** For example, a group of citizens in a town in New Jersey argued before their city council that anyone using a laser pointer to "target" other people should be penalized. Such an argument would most likely be built on an analysis of the harmful effects of such devices, perhaps combining causal analysis with illustrations of the damage that has been done by people misusing laser pointers.

Finally, if your claim were intended to show that a particular action or event does or does not fit the **definition** of a term, you could provide the definition in the first half of your argument and then discuss the event in the second half:

Claim: Buying a paper from an Internet supplier is plagiarism.

First body ¶: Definition of plagiarism: passing off the work of others as your own.

Second body ¶: How buying a paper fits the definition of plagiarism.

If the definition were complicated, you could devote a paragraph to showing how each component of the definition applies to the event:

Claim: Despite what some people claim, stock car racing is a sport.

First body ¶: A sport is competitive; stock car racing is competitive.

Second body ¶: A sport involves physical activity; stock car racing involves physical activity.

Third body ¶: A sport is governed by rules; stock car racing . . .

Use the Problem-Solution Pattern   If you were proposing to solve a difficult problem, you might choose this pattern, which has three options:

1. State the problem and give the solution:

   Claim: Binge drinking could be reduced if the school provided more nonalcohol weekend events.

   First body ¶: The presence of binge drinking on campus (illustrations, perhaps).

   Second body ¶: How nonalcohol events could reduce binge drinking.

2. State the solution and then look at the problem that motivated you to discover a solution:

   Claim: The campus needs more security guards in the evening.

   First body ¶: Why more security is needed (to escort people to their dorms, to prevent uninvited visitors from getting into campus buildings, to stop drivers who speed through the campus, and so forth; of course, each premise could receive its own paragraph).

   Second body ¶: More security would prevent some of the problems we have seen in the past few months.

3. State the problem and consider alternative solutions before arguing for your own:

   Claim: Computer access on campus must be improved.

   First body ¶: We could give all students laptops (too expensive).

   Second body ¶: We could leave the computer labs open all night (not secure enough).

   Third body ¶: We could wire every room in the residence halls (cheaper, and security is not an issue).

Use the Evaluative Pattern   This pattern works best when you are trying to determine the worth of something according to certain established criteria. For example, if a professor were to judge the value of a paper you had written, he or she might start by defining what a good paper is, laying out all the criteria for making a judgment: interesting topic and approach, clear organization, coherent paragraphs, and so forth. Then the professor would show how your essay does or does not meet those criteria. You will notice that this pattern makes use of definition in that "good essay" is defined before the question of whether your essay fits the definition is asked.

Respond to Your Opponent's Arguments   Before you decide exactly how to organize your argument, consider what your opponent will say. If you have brainstormed ahead of time, you have given some consideration to your opponent's argument, and you may have even prepared some rebuttal comments. On the other hand, you may have realized that your opponent has some

Hear the other side.
—Saint Augustine

points you simply cannot refute. Either way, you should work those opposing arguments into your paper somehow.

There are at least three ways to do so:

1. Start the paper with the opposing viewpoints and then organize your argument around a refutation of each point. This approach works well if you are proposing a claim that your readers might find upsetting. You can soften the ground a bit if you show your readers up front that you are familiar with their objections. You may, in fact, show that you share your audience's concerns and values.

2. Mention the opposition within each of your premise paragraphs. Some might argue that it is not a good idea to interrupt a paragraph with the opposing view, but most readers will not be disturbed by the interruption and would prefer that the opposition be dealt with on individual points rather than at the end.

3. Save the opposition for the end, showing that your opponent will raise some objections to your argument.

In any case, you have to decide how to deal with opposing views when you do raise them. If you have a stronger case, present it. If your opponent has a good point, don't overlook it. Your reader will consider you more intelligent and fair-minded if you acknowledge and even concede your opponent's strongest points or at least show that you and your adversary have something in common, perhaps a similar ethical code or a similar desire to do good.

Combine Patterns   Often, the most effective method for organizing an argument is to combine some of the patterns given above. An argument about the connection between eating disorders and advertisers' portrayal of beauty might be organized in the following manner:

Claim: The advertising industry's exclusive use of slender models has contributed to the increase in eating disorders among young women.

First body ¶: Illustrations of advertising's use of slender women; *descriptions* of some ads. (Be careful not to overgeneralize.)

Second body ¶: Facts about the prevalence of eating disorders among young women; *comparison* with previous years; some *definition* of "eating disorder."

Third body ¶: Argument to show that advertisements have some *causal* connection to the presence of eating disorders. (Be careful to avoid a questionable cause argument.)

Fourth body ¶: Opposing argument (there is no causal connection); response to opposing argument.

Fifth body ¶: Possible *effects* if current advertising trends continue. (Be sure to avoid a slippery-slope argument.)

When you have decided how you want to proceed in your argument, draw up an outline to keep you on track. Your outline does not have to be elaborate; a few phrases and sentences should do the trick.

EXERCISE 13.5

Working individually, examine the brainstorming and research your topic has generated and produce an outline for the first draft of your argument. Your outline should indicate what you intend to do in each of the body paragraphs and what support (facts, examples, comparisons, expert opinion, and so forth) you will include in each paragraph. Do not write out long paragraphs; in other words, don't write a draft—just outline one.

After you have completed your outline, compare it with the outlines of the others from your group. Discuss with one another why you chose the pattern you did. As a group, can you decide that any one pattern is better than the others? You should realize from doing this exercise that arguments can be organized in any number of ways. It is also true, however, that one pattern may occur more naturally given the topic, your purpose, and your audience.

WRITING THE FIRST DRAFT

The fact that you are more than three-quarters of the way through this chapter should indicate the importance of the activities that lead to the writing of an argument. If you have narrowed your topic, gathered your support, and organized your ideas, you will find writing the first draft of your argument to be much easier and more rewarding than if you had begun your paper with little idea of what you wanted to say, where you wanted to start, or where you wanted to go.

Now it is time to write the first draft. You do not have to follow the advice chronologically. Depending on your own methods for writing papers, you might, for example, write your body paragraphs before you begin your introduction. But your readers will expect your finished product to look like a standard essay, and most successful essays (and arguments) have the following elements: an interesting and relevant opening, a clear thesis, a definition of key terms, well-organized ideas in coherent paragraphs, solidly defended topic ideas within those paragraphs, and a satisfying conclusion.

One more word of advice before you start: writing the draft of an argument can lead you to more ideas than you discovered in your brainstorming, researching, and organizing. In fact, the act of writing can inspire such creativity that you may be surprised at the ideas you are coming up with. Don't slavishly adhere to your outline if you find yourself discovering new and better support or if your writing takes you in new directions. Finally, remember that you are writing a draft; you can—and will!—revise it.

Provide an Interesting Opening

You don't have to begin with your claim, but you can if it is startling, very controversial, or attention-grabbing. Otherwise, start with some background on your topic or show why the issue is an important one. Start with some surprising statistics, an apt quote, a little-known fact, or an interesting story relevant to the topic. A personal account of an event can make a good opening. If you are writing to oppose an argument, you might begin with the point that you intend to oppose or with some mention of the values and ideals you hold in common with the opposing side.

Here are some examples for an argument claiming that boxing should be outlawed.

- STOP THE FIGHT! For good. The start of the twenty-first century is the perfect time to end one of the most brutal, deadliest sports on earth: boxing. [Opening with catchy sentence, followed immediately by the claim]

- In May 1995 a young man named Jimmy Garcia was beaten to death in Las Vegas. Although such a violent act is not uncommon on American streets, this beating took place in front of thousands of people—during a boxing match at Caesar's Palace, the site of another boxing fatality thirteen years earlier, when Korean boxer Duk Koo Kim died in a match with Ray Mancini. Unfortunately, Kim and Garcia are not alone. In the hundred years since boxing has been a sport, nearly five hundred athletes have died as a result of injuries sustained in the ring. [Opening with facts and statistics]

- "Boxing is just show business with blood," claimed Frank Bruno, the famed British boxer and sometime-actor. But, of course, actors don't often get killed on the job. [Opening with quote]

- Boxing is still among the most popular sports in the world. In fact, perhaps the most recognizable athlete in any country is Muhammad Ali, who, although he now suffers from a form of Parkinson's disease that may have been caused by a career of fighting, still draws huge crowds of fans wherever he goes and who had the honor of lighting the Olympic torch in the Atlanta games of 1996. For many people, Ali might represent what is best about boxing, a sport in which the smarter, more adroit, better-conditioned athlete prevails. Because it is in many ways a beautiful sport to watch—a dance in which the point is to avoid contact as much as to make it—it's hard to convince the sport's greatest fans that boxing should be banned. [Opening with concessions to the opposing argument]

Include a Thesis Statement

If you haven't already done so in the opening sentence or two, give a clear, carefully worded statement of your claim (sometimes called a *thesis statement*) somewhere in the opening paragraph. Not all writers place their thesis statement in the first paragraph, and some only imply their thesis. But it is always a good idea to state the claim early in the essay so that your readers know exactly what your point is and can therefore assess the relevance of your claims as they read your argument.

What form your thesis statement takes is up to you. You can give your statement in its own sentence or include it as part of a larger sentence: "Given the popularity of raves and the fact that few problems have been reported in the press, the citizens of Springfield may not realize just how *dangerous these dances can be.*" In the thesis statement of this long sentence, the writer is telling readers that this is the claim that will be defended.

Be sure to limit your thesis statement to the claim you are trying to defend. Say, for example, that you wanted to argue that public schools should not eliminate art and music courses from their curricula, but through brainstorming and research you narrowed your topic to public *elementary* schools and only *music* programs. You might have narrowed it even further to a particular school. Your thesis statement, then, would be "Kingston Elementary should not eliminate music courses from the curriculum."

Your thesis statement can also give some idea of how you plan to defend your claim or some idea of how your paper is organized. The following thesis sentence tells the reader what premises will be offered:

> Because music allows children to express their emotions, helps keep them calm and relaxed, and teaches them to cooperate with one another, Kingston Elementary should not eliminate its music program.

In such a thesis statement, you are announcing your premises and your organization because you will deal with your premises in the order you have presented them.

The following thesis statement also hints at the organization of the argument but does not give away the premises:

> Although music programs are expensive and often hard to staff, Kingston Elementary should retain its program for the benefits it brings to our community's children.

This thesis statement tells the readers that you intend to look at the reasons why the program is being eliminated and then to counter that argument with your own, better, reasons to retain the program.

Of course, you are not required to mention either your reasons or the opposition in your thesis; however, your argument should never contradict the thesis statement or digress into areas for which you haven't prepared. If your thesis concerns music programs at Kingston Elementary, you shouldn't start talking about art classes in high school.

Develop Your Body Paragraphs

Start each body paragraph with a topic sentence and develop the paragraph with details that support your topic sentence. Help your readers to better follow your line of thinking by organizing your ideas in a logical, fluid manner and, when necessary, by providing transitional words and phrases that link ideas in a coherent flow.

The following paragraphs, both from Neil Postman's *Amusing Ourselves to Death,* are well developed, organized, and coherent. The first paragraph provides many examples, organized chronologically, to illustrate the idea given in the topic sentence. Coherency—or flow—is achieved through the use of parallel sentence structures. In the second paragraph, Postman lists several reasons for the popularity of *Sesame Street* among parents. In that paragraph Postman uses several transitional words and phrases, which we have italicized.

It is difficult to say exactly when politicians began to put themselves forward, intentionally, as sources of amusement. In the 1950's, Senator Everett Dirksen appeared as a guest on "What's My Line?" When he was running for office, John F. Kennedy allowed the television cameras of Ed Murrow's "Person to Person" to invade his home. When he was not running for office, Richard Nixon appeared for a few seconds on "Laugh-In," an hour-long comedy show based on the format of a television commercial. By the 1970's, the public had started to become accustomed to the notion that political figures were to be taken as part of the world of show business. In the 1980's came the deluge. Vice-presidential candidate William Miller did a commercial for American Express. So did the star of the Watergate Hearings, Senator Sam Ervin. Former President Gerald Ford joined with former Secretary of State Henry Kissinger for brief roles on "Dynasty." Massachusetts Governor Mike Dukakis appeared on "St. Elsewhere." Speaker of the House Tip O'Neill did a stint on "Cheers." Consumer advocate Ralph Nader, George McGovern and Mayor Edward Koch hosted "Saturday Night Live." Koch also played the role of a fight manager in a made-for-television movie starring James Cagney. Mrs. Nancy Reagan appeared on "Diff'-rent Strokes." Would anyone be surprised if Gary Hart turned up on "Hill Street Blues"? Or if Geraldine Ferraro played a small role as a Queens housewife in a Francis Coppola film? (pp. 132–33)

Parents embraced "Sesame Street" for several reasons, *among them* that it assuaged their guilt over the fact that they could not or would not restrict their children's access to television. "Sesame Street" appeared to justify allowing a four- or five-year-old to sit transfixed in front of a television screen for unnatural periods of time. Parents were eager to hope that television could teach their children something other than which breakfast cereal has the most crackle. *At the same time,* "Sesame Street" relieved them of the responsibility of teaching their pre-school children how to read—no small matter in a culture where children are apt to be considered a nuisance. They could *also* plainly see that in spite of its faults, "Sesame Street" was entirely consonant with the prevailing spirit of America. Its use of cute puppets, celebrities, catchy tunes, and rapid-fire editing was certain to give pleasure to the children and would *therefore* serve as adequate preparation for their entry into a fun-loving culture. (p. 142)

Just as your paragraphs should flow smoothly, so should the entire essay. Make sure that your reader can follow you from paragraph to paragraph. If the connection between topics is not immediately clear, give the reader some help with phrases such as "Another reason . . . ," "In contrast to [the reason just stated] . . . ," and "Finally . . . ." Don't force transitional words to do the job that the content should do: Your argument should move smoothly through paragraphs that are held together by a clear thesis sentence. But if a transitional tag will help, by all means use one.

Provide a Satisfying Conclusion

Almost every example of human communication has a beginning, a middle, and an end. Even a simple phone call begins with "hello" and ends with "good-bye." If one of those elements is missing, we are uncomfortable and we usually aren't sure what to do. If a phone call ends abruptly, we might feel we had been hung up on or that the line had been disconnected.

The same is true in writing an essay. You do not want your readers to feel that you have hung up without saying good-bye, which is the purpose of a conclusion. It lets your readers know that the essay is complete, that there are no missing pages, and that you have said what you intended to say. How you say good-bye will depend on your thesis statement, your organization, your details, and even the length of your argument. If, for example, you have written a short piece—say, an editorial for your campus newspaper—there may be no reason to repeat what you said in your thesis statement or your central premises. After all, most readers can remember the claim and the topic ideas in a short piece, so repeating them may look like an attempt to take up space. If, on the other hand, you write a lengthier or more complicated argument, you might find it necessary to summarize your main ideas. Whatever you do, don't attach a cookie-cutter ending to everything you write. Each essay or argument that you write is unique; try writing conclusions that fit the essay.

Try one of the following ways to conclude your argument:

- *Return to the opening.* Your readers might find your essay more satisfying if it comes full circle to its opening. Suppose you began with a quotation or a story; you might find a way to return to the quotation, providing a new interpretation or reminding your readers of its aptness, or to return to the story, telling the readers what happened next or simply referring to some of the details.

- *Make a prediction.* Tell your readers that things might get worse or better or that new problems might arise. Be careful not to make an unfair appeal to your readers' emotions. They may feel that you have taken a cheap shot to end your argument.

- *Ask a question.* Let your readers know that your argument raises some questions that still must be answered.

- *Call for action.* Very often a good argument will leave readers wondering what they can do. Encourage your readers, if appropriate, to take action in support of your claim: spread the word, avoid certain behaviors, write letters, join a campaign, and so forth. Be careful not to preach at your readers.

- *End with a story different from the one you started with.* If returning to your original opening is not an option, a new story may help close your argument. If you do opt to tell a story, be sure it is a true one. Making something up will only anger readers who know or suspect that the story is fabricated.

- *Emphasize the importance of your claim.* This strategy works very well if you feel your readers might not see the significance of your argument. For example, in the paper about 7:00 A.M. classes, your readers might say that with all the important issues on campus, this one doesn't deserve the attention you have lavished upon it. The conclusion might provide an opportunity to say that it does indeed.

Whatever method you choose to conclude your essay, keep in mind that your purpose is to end the essay, to say good-bye. Try to do so in a manner that is pleasing and satisfying to the readers and that fits your purpose and your point.

EXERCISE 13.6

Write an argument. Although the exercises throughout this chapter have been designed to help you create a group paper, your professor may prefer that you write your argument individually.

If you are to work as a group, keep in mind that collaborating on the writing is somewhat more difficult than working as a group to gather and organize ideas. There are several ways to collaborate on a paper: One member can write the entire draft and hand it to the next group member for revisions, who revises it and hands it to the third. Or group members could sit in a circle and, like a three-headed writer, draft the argument. Or each member could take a certain section or number of paragraphs. Although any method will work, the last works best for longer papers such as business reports. For a short paper, the first or the second works well. The first method (one draft writer at a time) is a good option if your group will be writing more than one argument during the semester because each member can have his or her turn at the first draft. If your professor has no preference, your group will have to choose which method to employ as you write the first draft of your collective argument.

After the First Draft

Once you have organized and defended your argument, you will have a draft of your essay. Most writers like to set their work aside for a short time before they begin revising or editing. Doing so helps those writers get some distance from their own words, which, as you probably know, seem too familiar if you read them too soon after writing them. It is easy to miss errors if our minds are filling in what we meant instead of what actually appears on the page.

When you return to your first draft, you must be willing to see it as a rough sketch of what your final draft will look like. Few writers are entirely happy with the first words that flow from their pens or appear on the screen. Can you imagine what life would be like if in conversations with one another we had no opportunity to correct what we said or take back a comment or clarify our meaning? Take advantage of the opportunity to correct and clarify your first draft, and take as many drafts as you need to get the argument as you want it.

Read What You Have Written and Revise

After you have written a draft of your essay and given your brain time to cool, return to your essay and read it again with a critical eye. Don't look only for clumsy expressions, grammatical problems, meaningless or repetitive sentences, and the like. Look for the large issues and evaluate your argument from the point of view of someone who disagrees with you. Be honest with yourself; question your evidence. Ask yourself if you are simply repeating what you have heard or what you assume to be true. Check your logic. Put your essay through the same rigorous test you have put other arguments through. Revise your draft to correct any problems.

Consider What You Have Not Written and Revise

Most important, consider what you have *not* said. Very often we are so committed to our viewpoints that we fail to examine the ideas and assumptions upon which those views are based. When you look critically at your essay, try to disagree with what you have written by finding a way to reject each of the premises you have offered as support. It may sound like you're being awfully rough on yourself, but it will help reveal areas where connections are left unexplored or where unexamined assumptions are guiding your thinking. You don't have to abandon what you have written; you may simply have to defend it better. Suppose the topic were salaries and someone had suggested that salaries in the United States should be capped at, say, $250,000. You are asked for your argument on the issue, and you write, "Capping salaries is not a good idea because it would reduce competition."

You might write a brilliant paragraph showing that capping salaries would indeed reduce competition. You might provide historical examples and the testimony of experts to back you up. But you need to ask, "So what?" So what if competition is reduced? What's so great about competition anyway? It may be great, but you need to *show* that it is. Your readers may not have the same values that you have. In a case such as this, it is best not to leave anything to chance. If you discover that you have taken too much for granted or that you need to better defend your assertions, revise your essay.

Show Your Work

Show your draft to someone—a friend, a family member, a professor, a tutor in the writing lab—someone who will do you the favor of critically reviewing your essay. Don't let a friend tell you what you want to hear: "It's great. Hand it in." Ask if anything is confusing or undeveloped. Ask your reader to show you where the argument may be weak or unconvincing. Ask if the organization is clear and effective, if the opening paragraph is interesting, and if the conclusion is satisfying. Never hesitate to get advice from a reader. It is not a sign of weakness or insecurity but of strength and intelligence to ask for a critique on a draft. Not even a professional writer considers a piece finished until it has been reviewed by one or more people who can offer advice for improving the writing.

Edit Your Work

When you have revised your argument several times and are happy with the content and organization, look over your sentences very carefully one last time for grammatical mistakes, misused or missing punctuation, misspellings, and typographical errors. And, again, there is no shame in seeking help if you are unsure about things such as comma usage and sentence fragments. Finally, try reading your paper out loud to hear how it sounds. Doing so can sometimes help reveal awkward phrases or repetitive sentence structures.

Hand It In

Someone once said that good writing is never finished, it's just published or, in this case, handed in. You can probably rest assured that your reader—your professor—is the intelligent, impartial, sensitive reader that you have been advised to write for and that your argument will be evaluated on its strength, its form and content, its support, and so forth. If you have done your work well, you will at least get a fair hearing.

Sample Argumentative Essay

Evans 1

Samantha Evans

Professor Gaughran

Humanities 101: Critical Thinking

December 5, 2007

No Public Prayer in Public Schools

Not long after the Columbine massacre in the spring of 1999, a Gallup poll showed what could be considered a very understandable reaction to the killings: more than two-thirds of Americans favor returning organized prayer to our public schools (Gillespie). Undoubtedly, daily prayer is important in the lives of many Americans, and we are all entitled to offer private, silent prayers whenever and wherever we wish and even to shout our prayers in our backyards or on street corners. And some prayer must be permitted even in public schools; no one would deny Muslim students, for example, the right to gather to pray at prescribed times during the school day. But such prayers should be conducted in areas removed from the student body, not publicly in classrooms or assemblies where non-Muslim students are gathered. As tragic as the Columbine killings were, public prayer on public school grounds, whether organized by school officials or by groups within the student body, must be prohibited. While prayer is permitted in exclusively religious schools, private schools or colleges, organized public prayer in public schools not only violates the First Amendment, it discourages students

Interesting opening.

Offers a balanced view: doesn't try to argue in either/or terms; shows good sense of audience.

Defines *prayer* in a specific context.

Thesis provides some idea of how paper will proceed.

_____

This essay is published with the kind permission of the author.

Evans 2

First premise: Public
school prayer violates
First Amendment.

Quotes First Amend-
ment because some
readers might be
unfamiliar with the
exact language.

Uses illustrations to
explain "personal
freedoms."

Divides the First
Amendment state-
ment on religious
freedom into two
parts, the establish-
ment clause and the
free exercise clause,
and defines each.

Shows how school
prayer violates
the establishment
clause.

from expressing minority views for fear of appearing
to go against the majority. Furthermore, allowing
prayers in school interferes with parents' rights to
raise their children as they see fit.

   First, prayer in public schools violates the First
Amendment: "Congress shall make no law respecting an
establishment of religion, or prohibiting the free
exercise thereof, or abridging the freedom of speech,
or of the press; or the right of the people peaceably
to assemble, and to petition the government for a
redress of grievances." The rights guaranteed by
the First Amendment of the Constitution are familiar
to most Americans, and the amendment's underlying
principle--personal freedom--plays a part in our daily
lives: we may, without government interference, choose
our spouse, job, place of residence, college, and
so on. That same freedom also applies to religion,
a concept that is explicitly protected by two
constitutional provisions, namely the establishment
and free exercise clauses. Briefly, the establishment
clause, in the most basic sense, prohibits the
government (interpreted by the Supreme Court to mean
both national and state governments) from promoting
or assisting a specific religion or from interfering in
one. The second provision--the free exercise clause--
allows an individual to practice whatever religion
he or she chooses. We take advantage of that simple
freedom when we worship at a church or synagogue, or
when we choose not to worship at all.

   School-sponsored prayer violates the establishment
clause, since a public school is funded by tax
money and acts as an agent of the state. Just as the

Evans 3

government couldn't lead us in a prayer before our driver's test at the Department of Motor Vehicles, it cannot conduct prayer in its schools. As decided in a 1963 case questioning a school's required reading of ten Bible passages per day and in a 2000 case involving the constitutionality of displaying the motto "In God We Trust" in Colorado classrooms, schools cannot perpetuate established religions associated with the Bible and God (Epstein 201–2; Janofsky A9). This fact holds true regardless of how many people believe in and practice that religion. Even if the school did not require but merely supervised organized prayer on school grounds, the school would be in violation of the establishment clause since it would appear to promote or assist in religion.

    If a school did require its students to pray, it would also, obviously, violate the second provision, the free exercise clause, which allows us to choose *not* to worship if that's what we desire. But, some might ask, doesn't the free exercise clause also give us the right to freely express our religious views? In other words, shouldn't the students themselves be free to assemble to pray in the cafeteria, in the school yard or parking lot, or in the locker room, for example? This very position was recently taken by a school district in Sante Fe, Texas, where a student was chosen by her classmates, and therefore not a school official, to recite "an invocation and/or message" over the loudspeaker during home football games. The school was obviously aware that this practice was occurring and claimed that it was allowable considering the students' right to free exercise (Richey). Unfortunately, the

Supports claim with an analogy.

Provides illustrations.

Shows how school prayer violates the free exercise clause.

Considers opposing point of view: Shouldn't free exercise clause permit us to freely exercise our religious beliefs?

Evans 4

Responds to opposing argument: First, prayer is still taking place on school grounds in violation of establishment clause.

argument is flawed in two areas. Primarily, the activity of prayer itself continues to occur on school grounds, and regardless of whether or not a school official chose the speaker, simply allowing prayer on school property in this context could be interpreted as promoting the religion advocated by the student representative. Put more plainly, the school is not remaining neutral on issues of religion.

Further response to opposing argument: Two clauses create a tension that can be resolved only by giving precedence to the establishment clause, not to the free exercise clause.

Second, such an argument overlooks the tension inherent in the establishment and free exercise provisions, a tension so strong that it may seem to be a contradiction: On the one hand, if the government *permits* us to pray on public property, it promotes a religion; if the government *prohibits* prayer, it is denying our freedom to exercise our religious beliefs. Since tension unquestionably exists, one clause must take precedence over the other in certain public locations such as schools. In a public school setting, the precedence of the establishment clause preserves the school's neutrality. Simultaneously, such a choice still allows for and encourages the free exercise of religion to occur elsewhere, namely in the privacy of one's home (or anywhere else not linked to a public

Considers one opposing argument—that if one clause should take precedence, it should be the free exercise clause.

school). Those who argue that the free exercise clause should prevail sometimes resort to emotional appeals, as does Armstrong William in "Supreme Court Quivers over Prayer Possibility." Mr. William suggests, in the wake of recent Supreme Court decisions regarding school prayer, that the Supreme Court will eventually abolish Christmas and similar religious holidays. By overstating

Responds to the opposing argument.

the case and playing on the fear of the public, he makes it seem as if all religious values are being

Evans 5

questioned and that we are on the slippery slope
toward a completely secular society. What the Court
correctly questioned, however, was a school's *position*
in perpetuating religious values. Upholding the
establishment clause ensures that schools do not
promote a single religion while allowing personal
religious practices to continue without restriction.

What if a school's officials, however, are unaware
of and therefore unable to stop attempts to pray
collectively and publicly on school grounds? Couldn't
we simply ignore the small prayer groups formed,
sometimes spontaneously, by students who pray aloud in
hallways and during assemblies? Couldn't we somehow get
around the First Amendment and let students who want to
pray gather with one another the way some NFL players
do on the field after a game? After all, what harm is
done?

Actually, the potential exists for much harm. All
of us have felt in grade school and high school (and,
yes, even in college) pressure to conform to the wishes
of the group around us. It's often better to laugh at
a friend's unfunny joke simply to be accepted by that
friend. The same can and does hold true for young
adults who practice a religion other than that of
their classmates. If public prayer is allowed, we are
creating an extremely tense and stressful situation
for students who might fear that their choice of a
"different" religion could divide them from classmates
and friends, resulting, possibly, in their being
ostracized or ridiculed. And their fear is warranted.
Recently, in a school located in Maryland, one young
man, refusing to participate in a spontaneous prayer

Introduces second
premise with
questions . . .

. . . and with an
analogy.

Second premise:
One effect of school
prayer is that it
creates a stressful
situation for some
students.

Premise supported
through illustrations.

Evans 6

begun by audience members at commencement, left the
auditorium as a way of expressing his disapproval of
the intended religious message. Security guards refused
to allow the student back into the proceedings, and
school officials subsequently barred him from a school
party occurring on the same evening (Chavez). In the
Sante Fe, Texas, case, Debbie Mason, a mother of four
children attending a public school, testified that the
school's promotion of one religion (through prayer)
pitted students of conflicting faiths against one
another, "If a child was Jewish in this community,
the child was made fun of by other students who were
Christians" (Alford 19). Or, as a final example of what
can happen when an individual refuses to participate
in a majority prayer, consider the case of Greg Thomas.
A former teacher in Hamilton High School, Thomas
suddenly lost the support of his once-friendly
neighbors after complaining about the predominance of
Christian teachings in the schools. Fellow teachers,
previous supporters of the community art program,
stopped bringing their students to plays produced
by Thomas, leading eventually to the cutting of the
program and loss of Thomas' job. The consensus seemed
to be that the community feared Thomas' attempts at
turning the Christian school into "the Jewish league"
(Reeves). Without a doubt, if adults are willing to
treat fellow adults with such disdain over a difference
of religion, it sends the message to students of
minority faiths to keep quiet. We should not be placing
children, or even young adults, in a situation where
they must choose between their faith and their friends.
Students are learning that choosing the former may

Evans 7

result in ridicule, while choosing the latter is a
denial of oneself. Simply keeping public, collective
prayer out of school eliminates any such dilemma.

A final reason to reject school prayer is to prevent
influencing individuals whose religious beliefs have not
been completely forged. Schools that permit or ignore
even spontaneous prayer are in effect robbing parents
of the right to instruct their children on religious
matters if their children are hearing beliefs in school
contrary to those being taught at home.

Some proponents of school prayer argue that morality
must be injected into our classrooms. In the case
involving the use of "In God We Trust," advocates for
prayer feared a replay of the tragic events at Columbine,
contending that such a phrase might help "reinforce
the precepts of moral rectitude" throughout our schools
(Janofsky). Although no one denies the hideous nature
of the events at Columbine, it is conceivable that
some parents do not define "morality" on the basis
of any established religious teachings and may wish to
inculcate moral values through a process that does not
involve religion. Religion must remain a private family
issue. This is not a question of shared responsibility
among parents, community and schools. Realistically,
that type of cooperation is beneficial when used to
encourage student involvement in school sports teams,
clubs or community programs. We can identify a unified
goal for this type of cooperation, such as helping
children make friends. On the contrary, it is nearly
impossible to find one religious absolute that would
cover all students in a school. And not only do
we hold beliefs different from those held in another

Third premise:
School prayer inter-
feres with parents'
right to instruct
children on religious
matters.

Considers opposing
view that morality
must be injected into
schools.

Responds to oppos-
ing argument: Par-
ents will not all agree
on how morality
should be taught.

Development
through contrasts:
Some shared goals,
such as helping stu-
dents make friends,
can be achieved, but
we do not all share
the same religious
beliefs.

Evans 8

denomination, but even within our own faith what we accept and do not accept may vary widely among members of the same church or synagogue. Therefore, worrying about what should be and should not be included when designing a prayer is an overwhelmingly difficult task. The task is much easier when religion is not addressed in public schools at all, but remains a subject dealt with at home.

For many of us, prayer is a vital part of our lives; it can help us cope with and understand our earthly existence. No doubt a bit more religion in our lives could help curb our violent tendencies. But prayer does not belong in schools. Schools should teach subjects that are beneficial to all students, while refraining from getting involved in subjects certain to increase tension between classmates and within individual students. Surely much could be done in our schools to decrease the overwhelming tension that already exists between factions or to provide a more secure and safe environment. But while we might pray at home for providential guidance for ourselves, our teachers and our classmates, praying together in school can only cause more harm than good.

Satisfying conclusion: Shows sensitivity to audience and . . .

. . . comes back to issues addressed in the opening paragraph.

Evans 9

Works Cited

Alford, Deann. "Pregame Prayer Barred." *Christianity Today* 7 Aug. 2000: 19-20.

Chavez, Linda. "Most Americans Want to Return to a Tradition of Public Prayer." *Salt Lake City Enterprise* 7 June 1999: 24.

Evans 10

Epstein, Lee, and Thomas G. Walker. *Constitutional Law for a Changing America: Rights, Liberties, and Justice,* 3rd ed. Washington, D.C.: Congressional Quarterly Inc., 1998.

Gillespie, Mark. "Most Americans Support Prayer in Public Schools." Poll released July 9, 1999. The Gallup Organization. <http://www.gallup.com/poll/releases/pr990709.asp>

Janofsky, Michael. "Colorado Asks: Is 'In God We Trust' a Religious Statement?" *New York Times* 3 July 2000, natl. ed.: A9.

Reeves, Jay. "Alabama Man Crusades against School Prayer." *Community College Week* 10 July 2000: 32.

Richey, Warren. "Can Students Mix Prayer and Football?" *Christian Science Monitor* 29 March 2000: 1.

William, Armstrong. "Supreme Court Quivers over Prayer Possibility." *New York Amsterdam News* 29 June 2000: 8.

SUMMARY

1. An argument is not a fight. Although your objective might be to win, your success in an argument should be measured by how well you defend your claim and how fair, accurate, and honest you are in presenting your case. Whether your opponent agrees or disagrees with you in the end, you should strive to put forward the most rational and evenhanded presentation you can muster.

2. Before writing an argument, know yourself, your audience, and your topic. Present yourself as a humane and generous person. Don't try to write an argument on an issue you know nothing about even though you might have strong opinions concerning it. Know your topic well, even if you have to conduct research. Speak to your audience; don't lecture, antagonize, or bully them. Expect your readers to be fair but skeptical. Try to foresee your readers' reactions and objections.

3. To get started, focus your topic so that you can cover the issue in the number of pages assigned. Brainstorm for ideas and organize your thoughts.

4. When writing the argument, provide a single statement of your central claim and organize your material in a manner that will allow your readers to easily recognize your premises. You can organize your argument in any number of ways. Try organizing according to your premises, both stated and unstated, or around any of the standard developmental patterns for writing essays (illustration, comparison/contrast, cause-and-effect, classification, definition). Depending on the topic, a problem-solution or evaluative pattern might work well. You might use your opponent's claims to help organize your own argument. Give your argument a conclusion that your readers will find satisfying.

5. Defend your central claim with factual evidence, expert opinion, examples, and, when appropriate, analogies. Don't hesitate to research your topic to provide the best support possible.

6. After you have written your argument, read what you have written. Be certain that you have defended your premises and any assumptions on which your argument is based. Before you write your final, edited draft, seek the advice of your professor, a tutor, or a peer who might alert you to any shortcomings in the argument you may have failed to notice.

CHAPTER 14

THINKING CRITICALLY
ABOUT THE MEDIA

We live today in the "information age" and work in a "knowledge-based economy." Throughout the day we are bombarded with information from radio, television, computers, newspapers, books, magazines, phones, faxes, pagers, message boards, signs, and billboards. This daily barrage of information can be so overwhelming that it's easy to allow our intellectual filters to shut down and to fall into the habit of passively absorbing whatever is thrown at us. This chapter will help you develop methods for applying your critical thinking skills to the evaluation of information you encounter in your daily life.

THE MASS MEDIA

Much of what you hear and read comes to you through what is called the *mass media*. Some people mistakenly believe that the word *mass* in this context refers to the size of the organization that delivers news and entertainment, and, certainly, most mass media organizations such as ABC and the New York Times Company are quite large. But the mass media are defined not so much by the size of the organizations as by the size of the audiences they reach through such devices as televisions, radios, computers, cameras, printing presses, copy machines, and so forth. The **mass media** include all print or electronic media intended to inform, entertain, or persuade large audiences and include news broadcasts, sitcoms, talk shows, soap operas, music videos, movies, magazines, newspapers, radio shows, CDs, posters, fliers, advertisements, comic books, novels, and textbooks. The term *media* is also used to indicate the producers of, and contributors to, media creations; thus, we refer to journalists, news anchors, camera operators, performers, and so forth as "the media."

The media in America face an enormous challenge in their efforts to reach very large and diverse audiences. In some cases, the prospective audience is narrowed by the content of the particular production. *Sporting News, Field and Stream, Popular Science, Cosmopolitan, Harper's,* and many other specialized publications are aimed at audiences whose interests or needs distinguish them from other groups. Other publications and productions, such as the *New York Times,* the *Washington Post,* the *Wall Street Journal,* and *All Things Considered* (on National Public Radio), are aimed at educated audiences interested in more-extensive coverage and analysis of national and international events. Another branch of the media narrows its audience through editorial policies that openly declare a political point of view. Often referred to as *journals of opinion,* partisan publications such as the *Nation, Commentary,* the *New Republic,* and *National Review* occasionally report the news but more frequently comment on current events from one side of the political spectrum or the other. A reader has a slightly easier task of evaluating materials from these sources because the editorial policies are stated forthrightly.[1]

But the majority of media productions in the United States profess to maintain an objective political stance and are aimed at audiences whose diversity makes it difficult to assume any common ground, political or otherwise. Local and national daily papers and radio programs; the local and national nightly news on ABC, NBC, and CBS; programming on CNN, MSNBC, and Fox; and the popular newsmagazines (*Time, Newsweek,* and *U.S. News and World Report*)—all reach audiences whose political viewpoints run the spectrum from the most liberal to the most conservative. Although these productions may target particular groups of people defined by age and literacy, they all reach a larger audience than specialized publications. The magazine *Mother Jones* is aimed at progressives, or liberals, who are interested in its investigative reporting and coverage of issues regarding labor, political, and environmental issues. But the managing editor of *World News Tonight,* the editor of your local paper, and the writers for *Time* magazine must assume that their audiences have widely varied interests and viewpoints. A perceived or stated bias on the part of the network, newspaper, or magazine would speak to one segment of the audience and alienate others.

Clearly, the media constitute a large and complex institution. Because a thorough discussion of critical thinking and the media would be impossible in a single chapter, we limit ourselves to two related institutions that we encounter every day: news and advertising.

THE NEWS MEDIA
The Importance of Context

The word *media* is the plural form of *medium,* a word derived from the Latin *medius,* from which we get many words—*mediate, medieval, mediocre, median,* and others—with a common meaning: they all refer to something "in the middle." A mediator tries to resolve conflicts by working with both sides, a median strip separates lanes of traffic, and so on. Similarly, the news media act as middle-agents, a bridge between us and the world of events occurring all around us. Since we cannot be in Iraq or South Africa or on the other side of town this afternoon to see for ourselves the events taking place there, the media will bring those events to us.

When we watch or read the news, we cannot say for certain that we *know* what happened in the world today—we know only what a complex web of journalists, editors, camera operators, technicians, engineers, news anchors, and so forth have shown and told us about the world's events. The news media act as a sort of wire mesh through which the day's events have been sifted and delivered to a massive audience. What gets through the mesh is only a small fraction of what is really going on.

Because of space limitations and because the audience is so large and diverse, most popular news media are forced to exclude any broad discussion of contexts that would give more meaning to the small bits of information we do receive or make them more useful to us. Important, even vital, stories get sifted down to pebbles of information. One example with which many readers will be familiar is the "sound bite." The broadcast media often snip very small segments of a speaker's comments from a longer, more complex, discourse. Although the media may try to clip the most important passages for broadcast, ones that, for example, summarize a political candidate's position on an issue, the practice of using sound bites extracts a comment from its context, which means that a listener has no way of knowing *precisely* what may have been intended by a comment or how to interpret it. Knowing the media's penchant for using sound bites, political advisors and speechwriters often attempt to stay a step ahead of the media by including succinct, snappy lines that will make the nightly news as sound bites. Although politicians can use the sound bite phenomenon to their advantage, the practice does little to help viewers and readers understand intentions and meanings because the surrounding introductions, explanations, qualifiers, and so forth are missing. In fact, in the worst examples of the practice, a speaker is quoted out of context and the audience is given a false impression of the speaker's intentions.

The practice of using sound bites illustrates what amounts to a minor problem given the larger, more consequential, effect of stripping information from its context. In many cases, rather than offer a thorough examination of an issue in all its complexity, the media actually distort meaning in their presentation of the news. In place of complexity, which would require an audience's active, intelligent participation, the media usually employ attention-grabbing techniques that do little to increase our knowledge of a topic. Although some media productions, most notably national newspapers such as the *New York Times* and the *Washington Post,* do undertake extensive investigations and attempt to provide extended analysis, most news outlets provide little, if any, insight into events and issues. Ironically, some network news organizations label segments of the news "In-depth" or "A Closer Look," even though these segments are only a minute or two longer than other segments of the news. The titles do little more than call attention to the usual lack of depth and close analysis.

> *Without context, there is no truth.*
> —Thomas P. Kasulis

Yet another illustration of how lack of context can make information meaningless can be found in the clipped stories that take up much space and time in the media. In an effort to pack as many stories as possible into a broadcast or a newspaper, managers and editors may devote a few moments of time or a few inches of newsprint to the selected national and international events in a segment usually titled something like "The World in a Minute," "Around the Nation," or "Nationline." Newsmagazines are especially fond of presenting pages full of abbreviated news, statistics, quotes, snapshots, and so forth. These brief segments and scraps of information are usually so far removed from their contexts as to be not only useless but sometimes dangerously misleading as well.

In a typical broadcast fragment, an announcer might declare that a foreign government official has stepped down and that a celebrity has filed a protection-from-abuse order, giving the impression that these events are of equal importance and leaving us with no idea why the foreign leader resigned or what will happen next. A brief segment on health issues, such as the introduction of new medications or the latest research findings on nutrition, can be especially hazardous to audiences who fail to realize that the whole story is far more complicated than the segment suggests. Even more useless and potentially detrimental are popular reports of scientific findings, which are often misrepresented by science writers working under deadlines and with limited scientific knowledge. Without sufficient training in the practice of interpreting results and measuring the value of evidence, science writers, unlike scientists who write, often overstate the significance of scientific news, predicting, for example, that cures for deadly diseases are close at hand.

When distant and unfamiliar and complex things are communicated to great masses of people, the truth suffers a considerable and often radical distortion. The complex is made over into the simple, the hypothetical into the dogmatic, and the relative into the absolute.

—Walter Lippmann

Online news sources such as *CNN.com* and *usatoday.com* help readers fill in contextual information by providing links to related stories and videos and to off-site sources such as maps, transcripts, and other documents. But the traditional media are limited in how much information they can provide in a small amount of time and space. Even with the slightly more extended coverage and analysis found in such shows as *Nightline, 60 Minutes, 20/20,* and *Dateline,* there inevitably remains in every story cultural, political, and social implications that the media fail to examine. Very few news organizations make the effort to help us understand isolated events by examining them in larger social or political contexts. To put the matter in personal terms, imagine a decision you made in your life that took a great deal of thought (choosing to live with one parent or the other, breaking up with a girlfriend, quitting a job, selecting a college); then imagine that you have two minutes to tell your entire story to the world so that listeners or readers fully understand your motives, feelings, attitudes, regrets, and so on. Would five minutes be enough? Ten?

But let's suppose you had all of thirty minutes to tell your story, and, to make the task still more challenging, suppose you were only one of several people with a story to tell and your audience could get up and walk out on you at any point in your tale. You might first find yourself inventing more ways to hold your audience's attention than ways to persuade them of your innocence or convince them of your regret. In a similar manner, the news media is motivated less by the desire to educate or inform than it is by the need to get and hold the attention of the largest possible audience.

EXERCISE 14.1

I. Form groups of three and, for the next class, get a copy of *USA Today*, another newspaper with national distribution (the *New York Times*, the *Washington Post*, the *Wall Street Journal*), and a local paper. Each member of the group can be responsible for one paper; be sure to decide in advance and to get papers issued on the same day.

Working as a group in the next class, look through all three papers until you find a story that is covered by all three. Read the longest of the articles first, then the second longest, then the shortest. As a group, compare the coverage, paying close attention to the following questions:

- Which paper covers the story in the greatest depth? List some specific differences in the details that are included and excluded. Be careful not to assume that the longer piece is the more developed because it may simply be repetitive.
- Do any of the papers attempt to discuss the event in a broader context— looking, for example, at historical episodes that may have led to the current event; discussing the impact or possible consequences of the event; comparing the event with similar occurrences; or discussing it in terms of larger political, social, or economic issues? You don't have to know a lot about these broader issues; just ascertain which paper attempts to set the events in a larger context.
- Looking at the difference in how the three papers cover the same story, try to determine how readers might react to each paper. If one paper has excluded some important contextual information, what is the effect on the reader? What kinds of questions might an interested reader have?
- Compare the headlines for similar stories. What does each headline emphasize? How might the headline affect the reader's conception of the story?

When you have finished discussing these questions in your group, report your findings to the class.

II. Find and compare two articles about the same subject. Choose one article from a newspaper and the other from a newsmagazine. Read the newspaper article first and then the one from the newsmagazine. List the aspects of the magazine story not covered in the newspaper story, and answer this question: How is your understanding of the subject changed by the inclusion of additional information in the magazine?

GETTING US TO PAY ATTENTION:
WHAT REALLY DRIVES THE MEDIA

The press owes to society a truthful, comprehensive and intelligent account of the day's events in a context that gives them meaning.

—Freedom of the Press Commission, 1947

So why do the news media go to all this trouble to attract and hold the attention of a large audience? After all, if the purpose is to deliver news into our homes, what does it matter how many of us are reading or watching? The mainstream news media do not exist solely to deliver the news, however, just as sitcoms and dramas are not intended only to entertain us. Although the news media certainly hope to inform us of daily events, they are constrained by the need to achieve an additional objective: to promote and sell commercial products and services to a large audience. The sitcoms and newscasts, radio talk shows and newspaper headlines are intended first to grab our attention so that we will stay tuned for the commercials or read the ads.

This revelation might not startle those of us who have grown accustomed to full-page newspaper ads, annoying radio jingles, banner ads on nearly every Web page, and the constant interruption of television commercials. Sometimes, in fact, it seems as if the show is interrupting the advertisements. But surely the news is exempt from such commercialism; surely the news operates on a higher plane. Unfortunately, no. Whereas we might hope in a perfect world to tune into a half-hour of uninterrupted news every night or to buy a paper that devoted all of its space to detailed reporting and analysis, the news media could not survive without advertisements because it is not the consumers but the sponsors who pay for the production of the news. Take one large network as an example. Although many viewers receive CBS from their local cable provider, CBS is a free, "commercial" network. Anyone with a television set and an antenna can receive CBS, provided the viewer lives close enough to a transmitter. Radio may be a better example: no one gets a bill each month for listening to AM or FM radio. And the fifty cents or so that you pay for your daily paper is just a drop in the bucket of the costs of producing it.

How can these media afford to provide services at little or no charge to consumers? By selling advertising. A sponsor, say, Ford Motor Company, buys commercial time on CBS, which uses the money to produce the news. If viewers stay tuned to the news and the ad is successful, Ford will sell cars and buy more time on CBS. Ford and other corporations keep a close eye on CBS's nightly news ratings to see how many people are watching the broadcasts. If the ratings are too low, meaning that a relatively small number of people are watching the news on CBS, Ford might go to another network, one with higher ratings and a greater share of the news-watching audience. Without sponsorship to pay the bills, the mainstream media would simply collapse.

Some exceptions to commercial media should be noted. In the case of *public* television and radio (Public Broadcast System, National Public Radio, Public Radio International), survival depends on contributions from private corporations, contributing members, and government grants. Church-affiliated radio and television stations survive with contributions from listeners and

● Critical Thinking Lapse ●

Charles D. McKinley, 25, was homesick and looking for a cheap way to get home. So he had himself shipped from New York to Dallas in an airline shipping crate.

Packed into the 42 × 36 × 15-inch crate, McKinley traveled by truck from New York's Kennedy Airport to Newark, New Jersey. The box was then loaded onto a pressurized, heated cargo plane and flown to Niagara Falls, New York; then to Fort Wayne, Indiana; and on to Dallas. The crate was then delivered by truck by Pilot Air Freight to McKinley's parents' home in suburban Desoto.

McKinley startled his parents—and a deliveryman—when he broke out of the box outside his parents' home. The delivery driver called police, and McKinley was arrested.

McKinley took no food or water on the 15-hour journey, just a cell phone, which did not work.

McKinley was lucky, said Richard G. Phillips, chief executive of Pilot Air Freight. His box was carried in the pressurized, heated cabins, but it could just as easily have been placed in the lower, unpressurized holds.

"He could easily have died," Phillips said.

Incidentally, the freight cost was $550. At that rate, said Phillips, "he could have flown first-class." [2]

---

viewers and, of course, with church sponsorship. And the U.S. government, funded by tax money, produces many informative documents. But for almost everyone else in the media, survival depends on advertising revenue. This, obviously, presents a problem—a clash of values represented on the one hand by an audience's need for information and on the other by the media's need to survive. Put bluntly, the mass media in America are businesses, powerfully motivated by the need to sustain themselves and, in the case of privately owned corporations, to make a profit. Certainly, making money is no crime; and because most of us like to be informed, the mass media should have no trouble garnering audiences large enough to sustain the individual companies that supply the information. But it's not that simple.

Simply presenting information—often complicated, detailed, and dense—won't usually do the trick of holding your attention and coaxing you back to the same newspaper or television network again and again. Let's be brutally honest with ourselves here: many Americans, unfortunately, don't enjoy reading long and complicated articles or watching detailed and serious analyses concerning issues unconnected to their everyday lives. And to be fair, a large number of American adults (estimates go as high as 50 percent) cannot read complicated material or follow intricate and demanding analysis. Because the media know this (and may in fact be partly responsible for it), they surround the advertisements with stories and reports that will not tax our intelligence

"Are you a businessman or a newsman?"

—Lowell Bergman (Al Pacino) in *The Insider*

and that will instead attract and keep our interest. With competition from so many contenders for our attention (the Internet, video games, movies, other media sources, family obligations, work, relationships), with the remote control providing a means to silence a news reporter in midsentence, and with the growing lack of interest in reading the printed word, the mass media in America have found themselves with the challenge of delivering information in a manner that keeps the interest of a large, busy, and easily distracted audience. They meet this challenge daily so that we'll keep buying Fords, laxatives, allergy medicines, or whatever else is being sold on the nightly news.

EXERCISE 14.2

Compare the ads in a local newspaper, a national newsmagazine such as *Time* or *Newsweek,* and a more upscale news commentary magazine such as the *New Republic* or *National Review.* How do the ads reflect differences in the readership of the newspaper and magazines you have selected? Consider such characteristics as the education, interests, hobbies, economic class, political views, and social status of the intended readers.

KEEPING OUR INTEREST: THE NEWS AS ENTERTAINMENT

If lust and hate is the candy, if blood and love taste so sweet, then we give 'em what they want.

—Natalie Merchant, 10,000 Maniacs

Operating on the premise that our interest is held best by what we find entertaining, the media direct almost all their efforts, even those involved in the production of news, toward keeping us entertained by making the delivery of information more fun, enjoyable, and amusing—which isn't easy to do when the news involves earthquakes and plane crashes.

We should admit quickly that for most of us, this is perfectly all right. After all, who doesn't like to be entertained? Many people, of course, enjoy intellectual pursuits and are entertained by working out complex ideas, but many of us find that complicated information is more palatable when it has been made enjoyable to consume. The book you are reading is one example. It has been our purpose throughout to provide information useful in your effort to become a better thinker, but how successful would we be if you found the text dull and boring? Information presented in an entertaining or amusing manner is perfectly acceptable; so long as it has not been compromised, no harm is done.

But in their effort to hold our attention, the mass media often *do* compromise information by subordinating depth, substance, and complexity to entertainment and human interest. The goal is to keep us in front of the set or holding on to the newspaper so that we will absorb (even subconsciously) the messages of the advertisers and buy the products that keep the money coming in so that the media operations will survive.

How the Media Entertain Us

We all know just how hard critical thinking can be. Critical thinking requires self-knowledge, concentration, mental discipline, respect for others, awareness of fallacious reasoning, sensitivity to language, and, above all, a willingness to look carefully at arguments and to base evaluations on standards and criteria.

The news media take advantage of our unwillingness to think too rigorously and deliver the news in a noncontextual, entertaining manner that has the added result of tricking us out of critical analysis. In some respects the news media do precisely the opposite of what the authors of this textbook have been encouraging you to do. In place of information that can clarify our thinking and help us make decisions is what F. Scott Fitzgerald called, in *This Side of Paradise,* "predigested food"—the "politics, prejudices, and philosophy" appetizingly served up by the media for our consumption. Rather than provide a thorough look at the world's events, the media carefully select events, exaggerate them or play them down, and present them without helpful analysis. The result is an entertaining array of facts and opinions intended to satisfy our less critical faculties. In the sections that follow, we look at some of the ways in which the media dole out what amounts to a sort of intellectual candy—fun to eat, but ultimately unsatisfying and unhealthy.

> *Cinema, radio, television, magazines are a school of inattention: people look without seeing, listen in without hearing.*
>
> —Robert Bresson

Selecting Events and Details   In a world of nearly seven billion people, enough events are taking place at this very moment that recording even a small fraction of them would take thousands of hours and millions of pages. But to find out what happened during the time you have been reading your critical thinking textbook, you can scan the twenty or so links on a news-gathering Web site, tune in this evening to one of the three main television networks and watch, subtracting commercials, about twenty minutes of world news, or buy tomorrow's paper and "read all about it" in a few dozen pages. The entire world in twenty links? Twenty minutes? Twenty pages?

Obviously, not everything makes the papers or the news broadcast. In selecting some events and excluding others, the media determine what is and is not important for us to know; and because thoroughly examining an event is virtually impossible given time and space limitations, the media select from each newsworthy occurrence a relatively small sliver of the event itself, ignoring, as we showed earlier, much of the larger context that might make the event more meaningful to us. Some selectivity is inescapable. A reporter working under a deadline and allocated only a few inches of space or a few minutes of time in which to file a report inevitably selects what he or she believes to be essential or interesting moments, comments, or facts. But where a reporter decides to set his or her focus can reveal much about the reporter's attentiveness, worldview, and attitudes. In some cases, a journalist's deliberate or unwitting failure to see certain key facts can call the accuracy of the report into question. How can we be sure that we have been told everything? And how can we be sure, without all relevant information, that we aren't being manipulated by carefully chosen facts to see the event in the way the reporter wants us to? Think back to your own story for a moment. If you had only a few moments to tell your story, you'd most likely decide what effect you wanted to produce in your audience—approval or sympathy, for example—and then cautiously select some details and ignore others in an effort to create the desired effect and avoid negative responses. The effect, of course, can be far different from the one at which your readers or listeners might have arrived with *all* the facts in their possession. Like a funhouse mirror, a reporter's selectivity distorts reality so that the original event and our perception of the event diverge greatly.

News editors and managers must be selective when deciding which of the thousands of stories that are collected every day will make the papers or the nightly news. Traditionally, editors and managers have insisted that "newsworthiness" is determined solely on two criteria: a story must be true and it must serve the "public interest," meaning that it must somehow benefit the audience. Although the great majority of mass media news outlets do not lie to their audiences, news organizations often select stories of questionable benefit to the public. In fact, most stories are chosen not because they *serve* the public interest, but because they reflect the entertainment preferences of viewers or readers.

If you want to take your mind off the troubles of the real world, you should watch local TV news shows. I know of no better way to escape reality, except perhaps heavy drinking.

—Dave Barry

What Makes the News   With daily events too plentiful and complicated for the space available, what makes the cut? Judging from what gets selected, we would have to conclude that newsworthy events are those which a reader or viewer will find entertaining, that is, exciting, titillating, shocking, disturbing, frightening, unusual, heartwarming, or easy to comprehend and identify with— "all sex, scandal, brutal crime, sports, children with incurable diseases, and lost puppies," as Diana Christensen describes the nightly news in the film *Network*. This is not to suggest that "hard news" stories have been excluded from the mainstream press; indeed, significant issues of national and global impact often lead the news. But in an effort to hold the attention of a large and diverse audience, the news media often appeal to the lowest common interests among us—sex, gossip, scandal, violence, death, and crime—and to our common emotions—fear for our safety, joy over rescues, anger at injustice, and sympathy for victims. The news media's view of its audience is hinted at in the recent increase in stories intended to alert us to all of the potential dangers in our homes, on the road, in the air, at work, on the athletic field, and so forth. Are we really in such grave danger, or is it simply hard to turn off the television when, "coming up next," we'll be told just how our mattresses might be killing us in our sleep?

The public have an insatiable curiosity to know everything, except what is worth knowing.

—Oscar Wilde

And, of course, if there is video or a photo of some disturbing or violent event, it's almost guaranteed to make the news. Many local news stations air videotape of such events as parachute failures and police chases even though neither event may be of significance to a large audience. Without a context the medium itself becomes context: the importance of the event is determined merely by its being "caught on tape." In fact, for the broadcast media an

All the Entertainment That's Fit to Broadcast

As Americans' appetite for hard news seems to wane, it is becoming ever more difficult to distinguish television news broadcasts from some of the entertainment and celebrity gossip programs that flood the airwaves. For example, six weeks after the September 11 terrorist attacks, these are the lead stories that topped the news on KCAL 9, a major Los Angeles television station, on one of its nightly news broadcasts:

1. A Britney Spears concert in Anaheim.
2. A local Jennifer Lopez concert.
3. A story about a strip club, in which a strip club lawyer complained that Americans want Afghan women to come out from under the veil, but at the same time want American women to cover up.
4. A story about shopping for lingerie.
5. A story about Operation Playmate, in which Playboy bunnies entertain the troops.[3]

event's newsworthiness is often determined not by its true importance but by its visual impact. In a particularly gruesome example, a major network affiliate in the area where this book is being written aired video of a man drowning. A state trooper in a distant state, the man had gone into a raging river to save someone and had become trapped between rocks. The video showed his desperate, futile attempts to free himself. According to the news anchor, "no additional information" was available. His name, his age, his history, his relationship, if any, to the local area, the reasons for showing his awful death—none of those points was ever made. The video was selected for broadcast apparently because it was attention-grabbing and available for broadcast.

> *If it bleeds, it leads.*
> —Television news maxim

To hold our attention, much of the news is presented with all the drama and excitement of literature, complete with suspense, intriguing characters, surprise endings, and, especially, conflict between opposing parties. Because court trials contain all those elements, the media seldom miss a chance to provide extensive coverage of criminal cases, but other favorites in the media include battles between neighbors, political candidates and parties, school boards and teachers, and the government and constituents. The fixation on conflict has spilled over into the coverage itself as reporters and analysts (often called, sarcastically, "pundits") take up sides and shout each other down or one-up each other on political talk shows such as *Meet the Press, This Week with George Stephanopoulos, Crossfire,* and *Hardball with Chris Matthews.* Lost in all this focus on conflict and controversy are the important political issues that affect our lives.

What Doesn't Make the News   What doesn't usually make the newspapers and the nightly news broadcasts are stories too complicated for quick and painless consumption and stories too critical of American corporations, powerful nonprofit organizations, the government, and the news media itself. Each year for the past quarter-century, Project Censored, a media-watch organization at Sonoma State University in California, has endeavored, according to its Web site,

> to explore and publicize the extent of censorship in our society by locating stories about significant issues of which the public should be aware, but is not, for one reason or another. The essential issue raised by the project is the failure of the mass media to provide the people with all the information they need to make informed decisions concerning their own lives and in the voting booth. (*www.projectcensored.org/about.htm*)

According to Project Censored, among the topics largely ignored by the mass media in recent years were the collaboration between multinational corporations and governments suspected of "significant human rights violations," the custom among pharmaceutical companies to devote their resources to the development of profit-making drugs rather than much-needed cures for deadly diseases, the apparent misdirection of revenue within the "increasingly wealthy" American Cancer Society, and the Department of Defense's contract with an American "sweatshop" manufacturer of uniforms. All of these stories appeared somewhere in the media, but primarily in journals of opinion (the *Nation, Mother Jones*), not in the mainstream press. Some might accuse the news media of having an agenda in excluding certain topics; and because news organizations are increasingly under the control of corporate parent companies (NBC is owned by General Electric, ABC by Disney, CBS by Viacom, *Time* and CNN by Time Warner, and so on), news organizations may, indeed, be reluctant or forbidden to investigate their owners and subsidiaries. So, the accusation that the news media have an agenda has some grounding, but in many instances complicated and discouraging stories about the Defense Department or the American Cancer Society are omitted merely to make room for stories presumably more interesting to a mass audience. Whatever the reason, it is clear from a study of the mainstream press that certain topics get very little coverage.

Of course, some media sources are more guilty than others of pandering to their audiences, and, conversely, some publications take great pains to publish more than just the scurrilous and sensational, to publish, in the motto of the *New York Times,* "all the news that's fit to print." But even the *Times* has to make choices, and although the bar for determining what's fit to print might be set higher in national papers, all media, from the most venerable on down, must decide what to select and what to exclude. Even online news aggregators such as *news.google.com, yahoo.com,* and *inform.com,* which retrieve content from a wide variety of news sources, are limited by what those sources have decided to write about.

"News" does not really happen; events are not news until they are selected and labeled as such by the media. The effect of all this cannot be overstated. Because we tend to talk around the dinner table or at work or in the classroom about "the day's news," what is selected becomes part of the social

The most important service rendered by the press and the magazines is that of educating people to approach printed matter with distrust.

—Samuel Butler

dialogue; what doesn't make the news, obviously, draws little attention from us. The news media, as the saying goes, "set the agenda," determining what's important enough to warrant our concern and perhaps our involvement. Unfortunately, when time and space that might be better spent unraveling complicated issues of race relations, public education, labor, poverty, pollution, and so forth are sacrificed to stories of sex scandals and animal rescues, the public receives little education in issues that really matter in our lives.

EXERCISE 14.3

I. List all of the stories covered in one edition of your local nightly news and on one of the major networks. How many of those stories center on a conflict? What are the two sides that are apparently pitted against one another? Does the news seem to be creating a battle where one does not exist, exaggerating a battle that does exist but that could easily be resolved, or justly calling attention to a serious conflict? Are there broader, more important, issues being ignored in favor of the conflict, or is the controversy a serious one that you feel should be examined? What use will you make of what you learned about the conflict?

II. Watch the local and national news broadcasts for one evening in your town and make a list of the stories carried in the broadcast. You can ignore the sports and weather. Do the same for one edition of a local paper. When your list is complete, answer the following: How many stories are apparently intended to appeal to our emotions and our sympathies? Which stories seem to have been intended to grab our attention by appealing to our curiosity or love of scandal? Which seem to have been selected for their entertainment value? How many stories seem intended to make us fearful for our safety or grateful for our security?

III. This exercise requires a partner and a stopwatch (or a watch with a second hand). Pair off with someone in your class and designate yourselves person A and person B. Now spend twenty minutes talking to one another. Each of you tell about your hometowns, your families, your high schools, your greatest accomplishments, your proudest moments, your major, your plans, your living situation, your sport teams, and so forth. Take notes as you listen to each other, but don't merely transcribe each other's comments. Your objective here is to see what you can find out about each other.

After your conversation, each of you write an introduction of the other that you can read aloud to the class in only *ten* seconds at a normal, natural pace. Although our speaking patterns differ, you should be able to read aloud between twenty-five and forty words in ten seconds. Your job is to tell the class something about your partner in the allotted time. After everyone in the class has written a ten-second introduction, everyone takes a turn reading to the class. So that no one exceeds the limit, have someone with a stopwatch keep time.

After you have read your ten-second presentation, write an additional ten seconds' worth of material. And then another. You should now have three 10-second segments. Your instructor may or may not choose to have you read these additions.

When the exercise is complete, consider the following questions and be prepared to discuss them in class:

1. In your first ten-second spot, what facts did you select and which did you omit? When you chose details for the first ten seconds, you were probably trying to capture the essence of the stories or the person you listened to. Explain how you selected the details that found their way into your first report.

2. What frustrations, if any, did you feel at trying to select ten seconds' worth of material? Did you at any point get the feeling that you were pulling facts out of context and that your listeners would fail to understand what you were trying to get at?

3. Look carefully at your selections. Does what you chose to include say anything about you? Are you more impressed with education, accomplishments in sports, work history, personal achievements, family background, where a person comes from, their current status (sophomore English major), plans (wants to be a doctor)? Your selections are not wrong; no one can say you should have chosen differently. But what you selected *may* reveal something about your values.

4. When you chose details for the first ten seconds, were you trying to achieve a particular effect in the students who would be listening to your words? Did you want to evoke their interest, sympathy, or curiosity about your partner?

5. Now look at your twenty- and thirty-second reports. How are they different from the first list? Is there a pattern to your selections? Did you, for example, start with what you thought was most important and add details of decreasing importance? Did you add any direct quotes from your partner?

6. When *your* story was being told in ten seconds, how did you feel about the events that were chosen? Do you think the narrator caught the essential elements of your life? Were you surprised at what was selected?

7. Write a paragraph in which you reflect on this exercise. What you have done here is played the role of a news writer or reporter. Of course, in the real world you would have a little more time to collect your facts, but, interestingly, many stories on television and radio broadcasts are no longer than ten to thirty seconds. What has this exercise shown you about the nature of news gathering?

Arranging and Organizing Stories   Along with selecting or ignoring stories depending on their appeal to audiences, the media employ other techniques for attracting our attention and challenging our critical thinking skills—namely, arranging stories and organizing their content to make some events appear more or less significant than they are. The print media use a variety of techniques to achieve this. A newspaper can highlight a story by placing it on the front page or diminish a story's worth by burying it deep inside, where it is likely to be overlooked. Editors of traditional papers (nontabloid style) must decide what front-page stories to prominently display "above the fold" to attract the attention of potential readers as they pass the newsstand or coin-operated dispensers. The paper can further heighten the sense of importance of a story by including a dramatic photo, placing the event in the top headline, using large font sizes, or allotting more space. Details can be arranged to slant a story in one direction or the other: the paragraph telling you that an arrested suspect has an iron-clad alibi might appear so late in a story that you'll quit reading before you get to it, thereby emphasizing the crime over the suspect's apparent innocence. Mass media magazines can elevate a story to grand status by featuring it on the cover. This isn't to say that a story covered in this manner by newspapers and magazines isn't significant, but we have become so accustomed to seeing screaming headlines on page 1 that whatever we see there takes on an aura of great importance simply by virtue of its location and the attention given the story by media editors.

Similarly, television and radio news editors can determine the worth of a story in several ways. Stories deemed most important will "lead" the broadcast or receive extended coverage, whereas less important stories are quickly covered later in the broadcast. Extensive, wall-to-wall broadcast coverage is rare and predictable: plane crashes, dead celebrities, military actions, and grand-scale violence will almost always set off round-the-clock reporting complete, when carried by the networks, with an attention-grabbing tagline: "Crisis in the Middle East," "Death of a Princess," "War in the Gulf." This kind of endless attention is reserved for the "big event," such as the 1999 crash of John F. Kennedy Jr.'s plane, which the major networks and CNN covered from the first word of the plane's disappearance through the search for and burial of the bodies of Kennedy, his wife, and her sister.

In these extensive-coverage episodes (the Iraq War, the 9/11 terrorist attacks, the Clinton impeachment, the Scott Peterson trial, the death of Terri Schiavo, the Columbine massacre), additional effort is given to providing context as analysts and commentators examine the event from a variety of angles and fill airtime and column inches with some exploration of causes and implications, but the result is usually the same: we are left with far more questions than answers. In some cases, the exaggerated coverage distorts the truth. The saturation coverage of the Columbine shootings, for example, while powerful and moving in many respects, might have left us with the impression that young people are hyperviolent or that only single, isolated cases of extreme violence against youth are worth investigating.

News organizations could, but usually don't, devote their extensive resources to exploring persistent trends, perennial issues, or the root causes and possible solutions of common, everyday problems such as poverty, pollution, or HIV/AIDS. When war breaks out in what we regard as a "remote" part of the world, we are finally informed about the conflict even though tensions may have been present for decades. Likewise, what was once presented as vital and urgent will disappear from the spotlight when the topic has worn thin. We are told of widespread starvation in Ethiopia, but after the story has run its course it disappears from the headlines, leaving us to wonder if the situation has been rectified or if mass starvation has simply become boring.

Newspapers are unable, seemingly, to discriminate between a bicycle accident and the collapse of civilization.

—George Bernard Shaw

Ironically, the media often exhaust issues that mean nothing to us in the long run. The broadcast "newsmagazines" such as *20/20* and *Dateline* will take a long, dramatic, sensationalized look at a single rescue, crime, or police investigation and tell us all there is to know about these relatively inconsequential matters. One reason for the media's reluctance to investigate and report on trends and enduring issues is that long-term investigations cost money, whereas sending a camera crew and reporters to the scene of an accident or the front lawn of the White House takes far fewer resources and less work. But, perhaps more significant, the media are merely giving us what we apparently want—conflict, titillation, mystery, death, and violence—and the big stories have it all.

EXERCISE 14.4[4]

This exercise asks you to select and arrange information in the manner of a news reporter.

The following is the chronology of Daria Jones, a fictitious person. Suppose you were going to write about her for your local paper. Write one short biography (about one hundred words) to make your readers like her and a second short biography to make your readers dislike her. Select and omit details as you wish, but don't make anything up. Try not to reveal your opinion overtly. Use language that will evoke the response you're seeking. (*Remember:* Don't falsify any of the information.)

- She was born in October 1966.
- Her father worked as a printer for a newspaper; her mother was a nurse.
- She was one of five children.
- She attended a Catholic grade school, where she played basketball and earned A's in 65 percent of her classes and B's in the other 35 percent.
- She attended a preparatory high school, where she played basketball for a team that never lost a game in the four years she was there.
- When she was sixteen, her ten-year-old brother died suddenly of a misdiagnosed illness.
- Her GPA in high school was 3.05. She finished 109th in a class of 220.
- She attended Barre College, a Division III school, and played in the national title game in basketball in her freshman year. The team lost.
- She transferred to a Division I school, Maine State University, on a full athletic scholarship, but a knee injury in the first season ended her career. She continued on the scholarship and graduated.
- She switched majors from accounting to communications and earned a GPA of 2.99 over three years.
- In her senior year, she interned at a recognized public relations firm in New York City and met many of the day's most famous athletes, including Muhammad Ali, Mike Schmidt, Michael Jordan, and Martina Navratilova.
- Her job for the PR firm was to drive the athletes from the airport to the company's headquarters.

- After college she worked in a day-care center for a year, then as a fitness trainer for children, then again at a day-care center, then as an office assistant at the paper where her father worked. She earned less than $8,000 a year in each position.
- In 1988 she married an executive in an advertising firm.
- In 1988 she returned to school for a degree in elementary education.
- She divorced in 1993.
- After several years of teaching, she received two master's degrees and published several articles on teaching methods.
- She remarried in 1996.
- She received her first teaching job in 1997 and has taught in three different school districts since then.
- She has no children.

Slanting the News

Mainstream news organizations select and arrange stories in the most entertaining fashion to capture and keep our attention, but that doesn't mean that individual journalists are unconcerned about the quality of their reporting. In fact, it is probably safe to assume that nearly all journalists, if asked, would claim to follow a code of ethics that prohibits deliberately lying or distorting the truth. With rare exception, journalists attempt to relay information accurately, avoid error, and achieve some level of objectivity, which we might define as the ability to describe an event or a situation without being overly influenced by personal attitudes, values, emotions, beliefs, and so forth. Earlier in this book, however, we proposed the notion that total objectivity is almost impossible. We may be able to report a simple event without bias ("The cat is on the kitchen table again"), but *how* we report even that simple event—in this case, the tone of our voice—can reveal whether we are amazed, amused, or angered at the cat's disregard for authority. Obviously, more-complicated events are even more difficult to report without allowing our point of view to intrude: we ignore certain facts and focus on others, choose language that evokes emotional or prejudicial responses in our audiences, reveal our attitudes through tone and organization, and so forth.

Many journalists, well aware that personal values can influence perception and communication, strive to remain conscious of bias and to eliminate it from their work by investigating all sides of a story and by remaining neutral when reporting on controversial issues. In this approach, however, the media often fall into the trap of simply delivering information that has been gathered. The result is a mishmash of information that a journalist has collected without sorting out what's reliable, useful, and meaningful. Often the media will publish unedited, unverified press releases, which public relations directors routinely submit, or provide uncritical coverage of staged events such as award ceremonies and press conferences. One famous example comes from the 1990 Gulf War. Reporters stationed at the Pentagon acted more as intermediaries, some might

> *The greatest felony in the news business today is to be behind or miss a big story. So speed and quantity substitute for thoroughness and quality, for accuracy and context. The pressure to compete, the fear somebody else will make the splash first, creates a frenzied environment in which a blizzard of information is presented and serious questions may not be raised.*
>
> —Carl Bernstein

say, "agents," of the military, dutifully reporting whatever information the military presented and asking few questions that challenged official claims. Military accounts regarding the accuracy of "smart bombs" and the success of Patriot missiles were channeled through reporters into American homes with little investigation of the truth of the military's claims. Several prominent journalists, including CNN's Christiane Amanpour, have argued that leading American news organizations similarly failed to ask tough questions about the Bush administration's justifications for the Iraq War.

The danger in this kind of "objectivity" is apparent. We are left knowing only what someone has said, but not the truth of what was said, and news becomes indistinguishable from rumor. During Hurricane Katrina and the flooding of New Orleans in 2005, many journalists passed along unsubstantiated reports of near anarchy among survivors, including stories of rape and murder in the Superdome, where nearly 20,000 evacuees were sheltered. The reports turned out to be based on little more than rumor. Rather than investigating the rumor, finding it baseless, and dismissing it, news outlets across the country, most likely fearful of missing out on a possible big story, reported the story as factual. In 2004, Dan Rather informed viewers of *60 Minutes* that CBS News had uncovered documents calling into question George W. Bush's service in the National Guard. Although the documents have never been proved to be either genuine or forged, an investigation into CBS's handling of the documents showed that the news agency had done nothing to authenticate them before sharing them with the viewing public. In this case, as in all others involving "sources" of information, readers would be better served by a reporter's willingness to test the reliability of the source and not just repeat suppositions. Unfortunately, many journalists today are, in the most limited sense of the word, "reporters," merely reporting what they have been told by sources.

It's easy to see why the mass media in the United States might choose the path of complete neutrality. With such a large and diverse audience, with bloggers on all sides watching a newsperson's every move, and with high journalistic standards to uphold, it might be safer to simply pass along in its original form whatever information has been collected. Because such an approach sometimes leads to the behavior cited above, and convinced that objectivity is impossible anyway, some media consumers look not to the mainstream media for news, but to the alternative press and its practice of **advocacy journalism,** a form of reporting that, though fact-based, allows writers and editors to promote a point of view on important social, political or economic issues. Alternative news sources such as the *Progressive* and the *New Republic* openly declare their position, for example, on the Enron scandal or the Iraq War or advocate for better treatment of the homeless or lower taxes. Opposing points of view do not have to be represented, but journalists working for the alternative press are expected to follow the canon of journalistic ethics requiring accuracy, truthfulness, and so on. Proponents of advocacy journalism believe that readers and viewers are better served by a media that admits to the impossibility of pure objectivity and declares more openly its moral, philosophical, and political stand on issues. Whether such an approach to news gathering could or should replace the traditional, objective, approach taken by the mainstream media is a matter of debate.

EXERCISE 14.5

Do you believe that absolute objectivity is possible? Can a reporter describe an event without revealing his or her cultural and political biases? Is objectivity always desirable? Should mainstream news organizations in the United States declare a position on the controversial issues of the day and shape the news to match that position? What would be lost if the mass media no longer attempted to achieve objectivity when reporting major events? Defend your answers.

Perceived Bias: Is There a Liberal Press?   A central claim in our discussion of the mass media has been that news organizations select and arrange stories in an effort to entertain a large audience. Some critics of the media, however, argue that selection and arrangement are decided not on entertainment value but on the political biases of either the reporter or the organization. When CBS News failed to authenticate the memos discrediting President Bush's National Guard service, some commentators charged that Dan Rather had allowed his supposed liberal bias and dislike for the President to influence his reporting. Some analysts pointed to the event as evidence that the news media in the United States already practice a form of advocacy journalism with a pronounced liberal slant. A 1997 survey of 1,037 journalists conducted by the American Society of Newspaper Editors might appear to support this contention. The survey revealed that a large majority of journalists place themselves left of center on the political spectrum, as the following table shows.[5]

Political Orientation	Percentage of Respondents to 1997 Survey	Percentage of Respondents to 1988 Survey
Democrat or liberal	36	34
Republican or conservative	8	11
Lean to Democrat/liberal	25	28
Lean to Republican/ conservative	7	11
Independent	24	17

Similarly, a 1995 Roper Center and Freedom Foundation Survey found that 89 percent of journalists voted for Bill Clinton in the 1992 presidential election, whereas only 7 percent of journalists voted for George H. W. Bush.[6]

Of course, the fact that an individual journalist may be liberal, or conservative, does not mean that her or his news coverage reflects personal attitudes. The survey shows only the reported political leanings of journalists, not the effect of their political views on their coverage of the news. In fact, it is closer

Thoughtfully written analysis is out. . . . Do powder-puff, not probing, interviews. Stay away from controversial subjects. Kiss ass, move with the mass, and for heaven's and the ratings' sake don't make anybody mad. . . . Make nice, not news.

—Dan Rather

to the truth to suggest that even though the political orientation of many journalists seems clear, and though editorial writers often take a stand on political issues, it is not likely that a mainstream newspaper, network, or newsmagazine has a pronounced political bias because doing so would alienate too many potential audience members. An analysis of the overall coverage by a mainstream news organization will show that, although an individual reporter may put a liberal or conservative slant on an issue, the great majority of articles are going to fit into a narrow band of ideology that hovers around the center of the political spectrum, where most Americans locate themselves.

In fact, the products of the mainstream press are often interchangeable. An article in *Time* could easily appear in *Newsweek* (in fact, the covers are often similar), and the nightly news on CBS, ABC, and NBC are hardly distinguishable from one another. Local newscasts and newspapers may lean toward one side of the political spectrum depending on the voter registration in a particular area, and many newspapers adhere to the tradition of endorsing a political candidate during campaigns, a practice recalling the fact that many newspapers in America were founded by political parties. And some newspapers—the *Washington Times,* for one—*do* have an advertised political slant. But the goal of reaching a large and diverse audience is more easily achieved by avoiding controversy and appearing to strike a political balance in the reporting of news. The news sells better when the media dodge stories involving hallowed subjects (corporate sponsors) and boring or unpopular topics (welfare, pollution) and avoid swimming against the current of prevailing public opinion. It is much safer and more lucrative to simply float benignly on the surface.

Nonetheless, the media will often give the impression of favoring or opposing, depending on your political point of view, one political perspective over another. Conservatives charge that the media is soft on Democrats and sympathetic to liberal causes such as gay rights, environmental protection, entitlement programs, and abortion. Liberals claim that corporate ownership and sponsorship of the mainstream press preclude covering events embarrassing to big business or examining issues from the perspective of the poor and disenfranchised. Several organizations are committed to watching for bias in the media whether from the right or the left. Groups like FAIR (Fairness and Accuracy in Reporting, *www.fair.org*) and NewsWatch (*www.newswatch.org*) root out inaccuracies and incidents of perceived bias in the mainstream press. FAIR provides an additional service to media watchers by alerting readers to the lack of context in some national newspaper articles and flagging articles that are especially good in providing context.

The corporate grip on opinion in the United States is one of the wonders of the Western World. No First World country has ever managed to eliminate so entirely from its media all objectivity—much less dissent.

—Gore Vidal

Opinion in the Media   While most journalists strive for fairness and detachment, and while most mainstream news organizations go to great lengths to appear evenhanded and politically neutral, a study of the entire spectrum of contemporary media suggests that, on the whole, there has been an explosion of opinion in print, on the airwaves, and online. Traditionally, argumentative viewpoints could be located in the editorial and letters-to-the-editor sections of newspapers and journals. These sections were, and still are, clearly labeled—"editorial," "commentary," "opinion," "letters"—to differentiate them from the more objective, fact-based, reports. More and more, however, the mass media are filled with opinion, much of it unsupported and prejudicial. Reporters routinely speculate about causes of events and support their conjecture with the opinions of "experts" who may have no familiarity with the topic at issue. Radio-talk-show hosts fill hours with nothing but personal attacks and unsubstantiated claims, mainly in an effort to keep both fans and detractors tuned in to the show (sponsors don't care if the listeners love or hate the host). Networks have introduced editorial programs done in the style of news broadcasts: on programs such as *Countdown with Keith Olbermann* and *The O'Reilly Factor* (and parodies such as *The Colbert Report*), the more outrageous the opinion, the more entertained we are. Callers to radio talk shows and television "talkback" lines are invited to briefly air their views on complicated issues. Some newspapers have taken the almost ludicrous step of publishing anonymous phone calls to the paper. And there is never a shortage of opinion among the millions of bloggers working every day online. Surely we are all "entitled to an opinion," and, admittedly, the more insightful and well-reasoned opinions that we encounter in print, on television, and online can help us formulate our own point of view on significant issues. But the proliferation of published and broadcast opinions that are too often undefended underscores our need to stay alert and think critically when reading and watching media productions.

We have focused in this chapter on only some of the methods that news producers use to entertain us in an effort to keep and hold our attention and to influence our reactions. There are, of course, many other techniques, such as using music during newsmagazine shows to heighten dramatic effects, editing film to juxtapose events that may not have occurred near one another in real time, using steep camera angles to distort a subject's size, cropping photos to eliminate context, doctoring photos to suggest relationships or to achieve desired effects, and on and on. All of these techniques work toward keeping us interested, even if truth might be sacrificed. Because the "facts" in a news story are often subordinated to efforts to entertain an audience, today's consumer of news needs a high degree of media literacy.

EXERCISE 14.6

One of the best sources for an examination of the news media is your own college newspaper. Pick up a copy of your campus paper and examine it for the qualities we've discussed in this chapter. Look especially for how events are selected for inclusion in the paper, the emphasis that's placed on some stories, the appearance of objectivity (are sources quoted without analysis and comment?), and evidence of slanting on the part of individual writers.

MEDIA LITERACY

It is easy to trash the media, to blame them for everything from violence in the schools to the dumbing down of higher education. Occasionally the media are demonized by politicians and ideologues looking to blame the messenger for the shortcomings of an administration or a political party. Ironically, the movie industry, part of the mass media, has reveled in pointing out the shallowness, deceptiveness, and even cowardice of television news broadcasts in such movies as *Network, Broadcast News, Wag the Dog,* and *The Insider.* And television occasionally pokes fun at its own news industry in such shows as *Saturday Night Live* and *The Daily Show.* Flaws notwithstanding, the media have contributed greatly to our understanding and acceptance of other cultures, alerted us to the pain and suffering endured by victims of natural and human-created disasters, shown us the surface of the moon and the faces of refugees, warned us about fraud and consumer rip-offs, and uncovered political corruption. In short, the news media have done much good, and our lives would be greatly diminished without them.

Although we admit that the media are not the villains they are sometimes portrayed to be, we can also admit that their need to survive has forced the industry to provide a service more entertaining than informative. And they've done it very successfully, artfully blurring the line between news, entertainment, and advertising.

For a critical thinker faced with a mass media that have substituted entertainment for context, the task is more daunting than ever. The relationship between news, entertainment, and advertising has become so sophisticated and seamless that it is difficult to tell them apart. A growing percentage of airtime in nightly news broadcasts is dedicated to promoting upcoming stories and other news shows. Gossip shows about the lives of celebrities and the making of movies, shows like *Entertainment Tonight,* which are intended primarily to promote the entertainment industry, are presented in the format of a news broadcast. News organizations routinely reenact events using actors and stage sets, which further blurs the distinction between what is real and what is not. Advertisers have been very creative in that regard. Many products, for example, are advertised through "infomercials," usually thirty-minute commercials that take the form of documentaries, talk shows, or news broadcasts. We may be fooled momentarily into thinking that the expert or eyewitness commentary in support of beauty products, exercise equipment, and hair-replacement procedures is unscripted and objective.

Other examples of the increasingly blurry line between news and advertisement are plentiful. Many radio stations across the country carry a syndicated show called *News and Comment,* by noted radio newsman Paul Harvey. A listener to the show is hard-pressed to tell where the news, comment, and advertisements begin and end, since opinions are blended into factual reports, and advertisements are read in the same tone as the news, complete with quotes from sources. It was revealed in 2005 that Armstrong Williams, host of a syndicated television talk show, had been paid $240,000 to promote the No Child Left Behind Act, essentially turning his program into an advertisement for the Bush administration. In perhaps the most egregious example of blurring the line between information and propaganda, some local broadcast news organizations air short, prepackaged video news releases supplied by corporations or the U.S. government. Such videos, which have all the appearances of a news report, might promote a new product or service or tout a government agency's successes. The unwary television viewer has no idea that he or she is watching a form of advertising. Critical thinkers struggling to separate fact from opinion in today's media have their work cut out for them.

To counter the mind-numbing effects of news media devoted primarily to entertaining us, we need to develop **media literacy**—"the ability to effectively and efficiently comprehend and utilize mass communication."[7] Below are some questions that should be asked about any news item, whether on television or the radio, in the papers or newsmagazines. Many of these questions call upon critical thinking skills that we have discussed throughout this book:

1. What message is being sent? What specific, factual information is being delivered? Am I willing to regard the information as accurate? Or should I investigate other sources to be certain that the source has the facts straight?

2. Can I separate the information from how the information is delivered? How much of a reporter's involvement can I detect in the information? Does the reporter, news anchor, or writer subtly or blatantly offer opinion and speculation? Does the report appear to be slanted in any direction? Is the reporter's language emotionally charged, euphemistic, vague, or ambiguous?

3. What is the larger context from which the information has been selected? What do I need to know about what happened before this event took place? What questions do I have about the history leading up to this event? What more would I need to know about this event and its history before I could make use of this information?

4. What can I do with what I have heard, read, or seen? Is the information I've just received giving me nothing more than a cat's-eye view of the world, or can I use it to change my plans, take some action, or solve a problem? Or is the information essentially useless, nothing more than trivia?

5. What methods did the medium use to attract my attention to this piece of information and to hold my interest? In the selection of both the story and the elements in it, what appeals were made to the audience's interest in glamour, gossip, conflict, violence, and tragedy? What appeals were made to the audience's emotions?

6. Who appears to be best served by the way in which the story is told? Is there a clear tie-in with a manufacturer, corporation, or service provider?

ADVERTISING

As we have seen, the media have a great influence on our beliefs and values. Television, newspaper, radio, billboards, and the Internet inject their influence into every aspect of our lives; and advertising, using these media, is a pervasive, powerful force shaping attitudes and behavior in today's world. Advertising is very big business. Advertisers in the United States spend over $260 billion annually marketing their products and services to U.S. consumers.[8] The average American sees 3,000 commercial messages a day and more than 2 million of them by the time he or she is age 25.[9] Today, ads are encountered not only in traditional venues (magazines, billboards, television, etc.), but in movie theaters, cell phones, video games, subways, classrooms, even the bottom of golf cups. As advertisers try to break through the ever-increasing "clutter" of commercial messages, they rely less on rational appeals ("Here's why this is the best buy for your money") and more on sophisticated psychological ploys that appeal to consumers' often subconscious desires and emotions (Here's why you need this). Studying advertising—and its standard gimmicks—can help us become more critical and insightful consumers.

What Ads Do

Advertising campaigns are not sources of product information. They are exercises in behavior modification.

—Jack Solomon

Advertisements have two basic functions: to inform and to motivate. Sometimes these two functions support each another, but often they do not. A good ad is truthful, informative, and persuasive. If it is humorous, thought-provoking, or entertaining, that's all the better.

Some advertisements seek to motivate without providing any information at all. Slogans and jingles, such as "J. C. Penney. It's all inside," "Pepsi. It's the Cola," and "Nike. Just Do It" are examples of ads that seek to sell on the basis of brand recognition alone. No informative claims are made; only snappy phrases or catchy jingles are used.

Some advertisements make a mockery of the function of informing by making false or misleading claims. Listerine mouthwash was long advertised as preventing colds and sore throats or lessening their severity. The Federal Trade Commission (FTC) eventually required the manufacturer to drop the ads and issue corrective advertisements to inform consumers that using Listerine does not in fact have these effects.

The superior man understands what is right; the inferior man understands what will sell.

—Confucius

Do ads create society's values or merely reflect them? Without question, advertising does mirror society's values to a considerable degree. But, as a multibillion-dollar commercial enterprise, advertising does more than passively reflect the attitudes and values of its culture—it contributes to their creation. It does this by selecting certain values and ignoring others. Subtly or not so subtly, ads suggest that consumers should pursue wealth, status, popularity, and prestige. What ads largely ignore are the values of being your own person and thinking for yourself; of focusing on quality of life rather than on mere material affluence; and of being good stewards of the environment.

The fact that advertisers selectively emphasize certain values rather than others gives the lie to the notion that advertising does no more than simply reflect existing values. Television, which has been the dominant medium for the past fifty-five years, best illustrates the point. Given the enormous financial resources that TV programs require, corporate advertisers like Procter & Gamble, General Motors, and RJR Nabisco largely determine what we see and how we see it. Television is much more than a mere medium. It is also an industry and an institution that has as great an influence on people's lives as the institutions of family and government. George Gerbner, former dean of the University of Pennsylvania's Annenberg School of Communications, calls television the "contemporary mythmaker," much in the way that the church was in the Middle Ages. A *myth,* as Gerbner uses the term, is a story that teaches, explains, and justifies the practices and institutions of a given society to the people in that society. Myths deal with our deepest hopes and fears and have a profound influence on the way we see the world and ourselves. They are found in television's dramas, sitcoms, sports programs—and in its advertisements.[10]

Moreover, corporate advertisers do not want just any audience. They seek the largest possible audience that is receptive to the advertiser's message. That is why advertisers target certain groups of people according to their age, race, gender, or economic status to more effectively deliver their message. Given this selectivity, advertisers inevitably present a somewhat distorted view of society's real features, values, and needs.

> *It is in the interests of commercial enterprises to skew the hierarchy of our needs, to promote a material vision of the good and downplay the unsaleable one.*
> —Alain de Botton

> *You can tell the ideals of a nation by its advertisements.*
> —Norman Douglas

EXERCISE 14.7

I. Get a copy of a local daily paper, a national paper, and a national newsmagazine and bring each to class. Rather than look at the articles, focus on the advertisements. You can ignore the "supplements" that often come with the paper. Take a guess at what the ratio of ads to articles is, then count the number of ads in the first section of each newspaper or an entire newsmagazine and compare it to the number of news articles. Look at the sizes of ads and their content. Take note of the ads that appear in particular sections, such as Sports or Business. What can you conclude about the kind of audience toward which the ads are directed? Are there any obvious or subtle connections between any of the advertisements and the stories in the paper? Do any of the stories have the quality of an ad—announcing the opening of a new store, for example? Are there any ads that have the quality of a news story—making claims about a new weight-reducing pill, for example? Are the ads clearly labeled as advertisements or distinguished from the news in other ways, such as being enclosed in a border?

II. Divide the four major television networks—ABC, CBS, NBC, and Fox—among your group members, watch the nightly news on your assigned network, and do the same with the evening news that you did with the print media. Take careful notes of how many ads appear, when they appear, and what they are

> *Advertising may be described as the science of arresting the human intelligence long enough to get money from it.*
> —Stephen Leacock

for. If possible, use a watch to estimate how much of the half hour is taken up with ads. What audience is indicated in the ads? Is there any connection between ads and news? Also, within the news itself, take note of the promotions for upcoming news shows and tie-ins with Internet sites and other broadcast stations. Finally, note the "teasers" that are intended to keep your finger off the remote control—phrases like "When we return . . ." and "Coming up later in our broadcast. . . ." What sorts of appeals do these self-advertisements make?

Defenses of Advertising

Defenders of advertising claim that it provides many benefits. In addition to employing a large number of talented writers and producers, it informs consumers about available products and services. Some ads promote the public interest by informing consumers about health and safety issues. Volvos, for example, were among the first vehicles to provide side-door air bags, a definite safety advantage.

Defenders of advertising also argue that by giving media the financial backing it requires, advertisements allow "free" non-government-regulated programming, thus promoting greater freedom of expression. The survival of many media outlets, such as television and radio stations, depends on advertising revenue. Finally, proponents of advertising claim that it stimulates competition and fuels our mass-consumption economy, raising the standard of living for everyone by making possible what economists call the "economy of large-scale production." Mass production reduces the cost of manufacturing a product, thus making it less expensive to buy; but mass production requires mass consumption, and mass consumption of a product cannot occur unless consumers know that the product exists and where it can be bought. So, advertising is required if we are to reap the benefits of large-scale production.

Criticisms of Advertising

Despite these benefits, numerous criticisms have been leveled at advertising. First, some critics argue, advertising is intrusive. It interferes with almost everything we do (reading, driving, watching TV, lying on the beach) to deliver a generally unwanted message and therefore constitutes an invasion of privacy. Second, critics say, advertising demeans and corrupts culture, making citizens materialistic, preoccupied with things and with possessing more and more. Of course, there is nothing wrong with improving one's standard of living, but by encouraging consumers to measure their worth solely by what they *have,* rather than by who they *are,* advertising weakens social bonds, harms the environment, and contributes to a shallow, materialistic culture. Third, advertising exploits children by targeting dubious messages (sugary cereals are good, parents and teachers are clueless, cool kids wear brand-name clothing) at an audience that is too young and therefore unsophisticated to rationally evaluate their content. Fourth, advertising reinforces harmful sexist and other stereotypes (only women do the laundry, only boys play with trucks). Fifth, critics charge, many ads are manipulative or deceptive.

This last criticism of advertising—that it manipulates and deceives us with sophisticated psychological ploys and other strategies—is the one we are least likely to believe. We don't like to think of ourselves as mere pawns of advertising geniuses, buying products we neither want nor need. Young people, including college students, generally claim that advertising does not influence them. They insist that they simply buy what they want and need. Ad makers know better. Sales figures and market studies reveal that a well-designed ad campaign can greatly increase a product's market share.

Why do we find it so difficult to realize how powerfully advertising influences us? Max Sutherland, author of *Advertising and the Mind of the Consumer,* says that it is because we ask the wrong questions, make the wrong assumptions, and look for major effects rather than minor ones.[11] Too often we look for the ability of a *particular* ad to persuade us. To appreciate the persuasive power of an ad, one has to understand its minor, cumulative effects. Few people notice the effects of the calories from that second helping of food or that second bottle of beer. Determining how much weight you put on in twenty-four hours is like evaluating the effect of being exposed to a single commercial. In both cases, the changes are too small to notice. But even the small effects of advertising can influence which brands we choose—especially when all other factors are equal and one brand is much the same as another.

The majority of the things we buy—toothpaste, shampoo, or soft drinks, for example—involve what Sutherland calls "low-involvement buying." These are purchases to which we give little thought. High-involvement buying involves high-priced items, such as cars and homes. When people are spending a good deal of their hard-earned money to buy a TV, a car, or a home, they do not take the decision lightly. Before buying such items, they talk with friends, read *Consumer Reports,* and generally get as much information as they can about the item. At this level of cost, there are also usually significant differences between one brand and another. Low-involvement buying, on the other hand, because it involves low-cost items, is no big deal. We have more important things to think about, and we are not going to agonize over which brand to buy every time we need a box of facial tissue. This is the way low-involvement buying works. It is like a scale on which each brand weighs the same, and with one brand on each side, the scale is balanced. It takes only a feather added to one side of the balance, however, to tip it in favor of the brand on that side.

Exercise 14.8

Group discussion: For a week or more before you answer the following questions, consider how many times during the week you have thought about the things you really need as opposed to the things you would like to have. Where did these needs and desires come from? Does our culture put too much emphasis on material things? If so, give some examples. Are ads primarily responsible for persuading us that we cannot be happy without the latest fad clothing or gadget? If so, give some examples of how ads do this.

Common Advertising Ploys

There are a number of standard gimmicks that advertisers use to short-circuit rational decision making and con the unwary. These include humor, catchy slogans and jingles, anxiety ads, emotive language, weasel words, fine-print disclaimers, puffery, sex appeals, feel-good ads, image ads, and celebrity endorsements.

Humor   The use of humor in ads can be very effective in grabbing our attention—and in closing down our critical defenses. The purpose of humor in advertising is to create in the viewer or listener a pleasant and memorable association with the product. The top-ranked ad on *USA Today's* Ad Meter for the 2006 Super Bowl commercials involved a secret fridge stocked with Bud Light. The fridge's owner, as a way of keeping his stock of Bud Light secure, has it disappear via a revolving wall into the adjoining apartment. For the guys next door it was a fridge that miraculously filled itself and so was the "magic fridge"—an idol to be worshiped.

Let no one deceive you with empty words.

—Ephesians 5:6

Catchy Slogans and Jingles   Although the strategies used in advertisements are often subtle and difficult to categorize, most ads use some variety of the fallacies we have already studied. An example of a strategy difficult to categorize is the use of endlessly repeated slogans and jingles. Over time, through the process of repetition, such slogans as "There are some things money can't buy. For everything else there's MasterCard." and catchy jingles such as "VISA. It's everywhere you want to be" can, by small increments, produce major perceived differences between brands. But we are rarely aware that this process is taking place. Often the first brand remembered is the one most likely to be purchased. A simple way of gaining easy retrieval from memory is the use of repetition. As simple as it sounds, it's the tried-and-true way of getting an ad remembered.

EXERCISE 14.9

See how well you can match a jingle or slogan from column A with a product or company from column B. Like most of us, you will probably do well on this quiz. What does that tell you about the effectiveness of advertisements?

Column A
— 1. They're great!
— 2. Can you hear me now?
— 3. Grab life by the horns.
— 4. Just do it!

Column B
a. Home Depot
b. Bounty paper towels
c. Capital One
d. Taco Bell

— 5. You can do it, we can help.   e. L'Oréal
— 6. Snap, crackle and pop.   f. Kellogg's Frosted Flakes
— 7. The quicker picker-upper.   g. Cingular Wireless
— 8. They keep going and   h. Volkswagen
     going and going.
— 9. We try harder.   i. Kellogg's Rice Krispies
— 10. Think outside the bun.   j. Dodge
— 11. Like a rock.   k. Chevy trucks
— 12. What's inside your wallet?   l. Avis rental cars
— 13. Eat fresh.   m. Nike
— 14. Zoom zoom.   n. Subway
— 15. Drivers wanted.   o. Energizer batteries
— 16. Finger-lickin' good.   p. Rolaids
— 17. Raising the bar.   q. KFC
— 18. Melts in your mouth,   r. Verizon Wireless
      not in your hand.
— 19. M'm, m'm good.   s. Lay's potato chips
— 20. Because I'm worth it.   t. U.S. Army
— 21. How do you spell relief?   u. BMW
— 22. The happiest place on earth.   v. Olive Garden restaurants
— 23. Don't leave home without it.   w. Mazda
— 24. The ultimate driving machine.   x. Campbell's soup
— 25. When you're here, you're family. y. M&M's candy
— 26. Breakfast of champions.   z. Walt Disney World
— 27. Betcha can't eat just one.   aa. American Express
— 28. Taste the rainbow.   bb. U.S. Marines
— 29. Be all that you can be.   cc. Skittles candy
— 30. We're looking for a few good men. dd. Wheaties cereal

Anxiety Ads   Anxiety ads play on our fears, anxieties, and insecurities. Most of us strive for what psychologists call cognitive balance. Simply put, we are most comfortable when all of our beliefs, actions, attitudes, and relationships are harmoniously balanced. Advertisers attempt to upset this balance by making us worry that we are not as attractive as we may believe. An ad might suggest that you have dandruff or bad breath; this loss of balance will, of course, be restored by the use of the advertised hair treatment or breath mint.

There are plenty of ads that play on people's fears and anxieties. If you are a young man, you may fear losing your hair; of course, there's an advertisement for a product that's guaranteed to get your hair growing again. If you are a young woman, you may fear that your bosom is too small. Again, of course, there's an ad for a bra that will give you the look you desire. Worries about having body odor, being overweight, or having teeth that aren't white enough can all upset your cognitive balance, your self-confidence. You can be certain there is an ad that will promise to allay your fears and restore your confidence. Sometimes these products really do live up to their claims. In many cases, however, the

> *One of the first duties of man is not to be duped.*
> —Carl Becker

results are disappointing, and then you are off searching for another product that will restore your lost self-esteem.

Emotive Language   As we saw in Chapter 4, words often have an emotional impact that goes beyond their purely cognitive or informational meanings. For example, *passed on, died,* and *croaked* all have approximately the same cognitive meaning (the ending of a life), but they differ radically in their *emotive* meaning— their power to express or evoke feelings. Advertisers are well aware of the emotive power of language. As Naomi Klein notes in her best-selling book *No Logo,*[12] advertising today is increasingly focused on creating cultlike "brand loyalty" rooted in emotion rather than reason. Often, use of the correct word can instill an enticing mood and attitude. Think of what is implied, for example, by *joystick,* a control handle used with some computer games, or a computer game itself called PlayStation2. When you go fishing, you do not just want bait, an ad proclaims, you want "Power Bait." *Power* is a positive and dynamic emotive word, useful in selling many things. On the other hand, think of the unfortunate connotations of a restaurant named for a family called Hare, Foote, or Mudd.

Advertisers choose words that evoke positive feelings about their product. Among the most common of these words are *pleasure, fresh, clean,* and *natural.* An ad for Newport cigarettes claims they are "Alive with pleasure." An ad for Winston cigarettes claims "It's only natural." (Is there such a thing as an artificial tobacco?) Kool cigarettes aren't just Kool, they're Kool Natural Lights. That's because, as the copy in the advertisement reads, "they are a blend of tobaccos and natural menthol with other natural flavors for a smooth, fresh taste." To drive the point home, this one ad uses the word *natural* three times.

Weasel Words   *Weasel words* are used to water down or qualify a claim so that it ends up being practically meaningless. The term is appropriately taken from the egg-eating habits of weasels, who suck out the inside of an egg, giving the appearance to the casual observer that the egg is still whole. Claims couched in weasel words practically evaporate on closer examination.

Common weasel words include *helps, may, can be, fights, as low as, as much as,* and *up to.* Countless ads claim that their product "helps fight_____ [fill in the blank] with regular use." Marketing research shows that many consumers mistakenly assume that *helps* means "cures," when in fact it means only "provides some positive benefit." An ad for Hollywood's 48-hour Miracle Diet claims that you can "lose up to 10 pounds this weekend," failing to note, however, that such results are far from typical. When a sign in a sporting goods store says "Running shoes as low as $19," you can be sure that only a few shoes will be priced that low and that most likely they are returns that have been drooled on by somebody's Doberman pinscher.

Fine-Print Disclaimers   How many times have you seen an ad in a newspaper in big, bold letters claiming "Sale 50% off" at one of your favorite stores, only to notice at the bottom of the page, in very small, easy-to-overlook, type

> *Promise, large promise, is the soul of advertising.*
> —Samuel Johnson

> *A dollar spent on brainwashing is more cost-effective than a dollar spent on product improvement.*
> —Scott Adams

Fictitious Fine-Print Disclaimer from Humorist Dave Barry

Warning: Use of this product may cause nausea, insomnia, euphoria, déjà vu, menopause, tax audits, demonic possession, lung flukes, eyeball worms, decapitation, and mudslides. We would not even dare to sell this product if we did not have a huge, carnivorous legal department that could squash you in court like a baby mouse under a sledgehammer. We frankly can't believe that you were so stupid as to purchase this product. Your only hope is to set this product down very gently, back slowly away from it, then turn and sprint for your home, never to return.

---

that the price cut is only on certain marked items? These are called *fine-print disclaimers.* Perhaps the most blatant use of fine-print disclaimers is in sweepstakes advertisements, which often use big, blaring headlines like this: "YOU, MELVIN SCHLOCK, OF 16 WOODSIDE LANE, ARE DEFINITELY OUR GRAND PRIZE WINNER AND WILL RECEIVE $10,000,000.00 CASH! Only when you read the fine print do you discover that the prize is yours *if* you return the winning number and that the chances of winning are smaller than the odds of being trampled by a herd of rampaging caribou.

Puffery   "Prices so hot the fire department comes by to hose off the store every half hour." That's a Radio Shack ad and a good example of what is called puffery in advertising.

One of the biggest problems the Federal Trade Commission (FTC) faces in regulating advertising is drawing a line between false or deceptive advertising and *puffery*—an exaggerated claim that skirts the literal truth but does so in a way that does not deceive most audiences. Most of us know that, although hair dyes will hide the gray, they are not going to make us look as great as the models in their commercials. A run-down, roach-infested restaurant in the Florida Keys claims it serves "the best Mexican food north of the border"; a car dealer claims that "nobody sells for less"; a radio announcer for KOW 98.5 reminds listeners of the new livestock stud service that "everyone is talking about." Few rational consumers would be taken it by such obvious exaggerations, but, as advertisers know all too well, not everybody is rational.

> We live today in a world of hype, exaggeration, and hyperbole. Illusions rule the world.
>
> —Tom Morris

Sex Appeals   There is hardly a brand of soap, car, cigarette, beer, or jeans that has not used sex appeals in its ads. In recent years such appeals have become increasingly blatant, as in Pony shoes' 2003 ads featuring porn star Jenna Jameson or Miller Lite's notorious "Catfight" commercial in which two women rip off each others' clothes and wrestle in cement.

Is there a connection between shampooing your hair and sexual pleasure and excitement? Ads for Herbal Essence shampoo would like you to believe there is. One of their commercials shows a woman stepping into a shower to

> Sex never fails as an attention-getter.
>
> —Jack Solomon

wash her hair. She's using Herbal Essence shampoo. As she lathers up, she cries loudly three times, "Yes, yes, yes!" and then there's an "ooh" and an "ah." It clearly suggests that using this shampoo will send you into a state of orgasmic sexual abandon.

Another magazine advertisement shows a smiling, young, beautiful woman with copy that reads, "Amber O'Brien, 25, is having the time of her life. Recently, she decided it was time to have breast augmentation." The suggestion being made by this advertisement is obvious: if you want a happy sex life, you should have your breasts augmented. It's clear: sex sells.

Feel-Good Ads   Like humorous ads, feel-good ads work by creating positive emotional associations. They link the good feelings elicited by the ad with the brand. Take a closer look at the next new car commercial you see. They almost always show a car on a quiet rained-soaked road, and *there's no traffic.* There's never any traffic in car commercials, even when they film these ads in the middle of major cities. All you see is a traffic-free street or a wide-open highway with no other cars in sight. The camera zooms in on the driver behind the wheel, the music picks up, and the car takes off, purring smoothly as it gracefully zips out of sight down the road into a beautiful sunset. Who wouldn't like to be in a shiny new car on a scenic deserted highway?

Cigarette advertisements targeted at women, such as those for Virginia Slims, typically show a young, attractive, very slim woman at a table in a fashionable restaurant, with a handsome young man staring into her eyes, or the same woman walking along a beautiful, sunlit beach, again with a handsome young man at her side. The message is clear: if you want to be in similar surroundings, looking slim and attractive and pursued by guys who look like *Playgirl* centerfold models, smoke Virginia Slims.

Image Ads   Image ads are used to appeal to certain images people have of themselves—for example, as competent, cool, rugged, responsible, sophisticated, or discriminating.

Many image ads seek to butter up consumers or play on their image of themselves as being better than the average person is. Virginia Slims says, "You've come a long way, baby." Hallmark claims, "When you care enough to send the very best." Piaget watches have "exceptional character," and Saks Fifth Avenue's clothes are "defining style."

Lots of people think that if a product is the most expensive in its class, it's got to be the best. Many advertisements play on this belief, including ads for Mont Blanc pens, Saks Fifth Avenue, and Infiniti cars. Talbot's clothing touts, "A look that says you've arrived." A young newlywed wants to impress her mother-in-law, who is coming to her house for Thanksgiving for the first time. If she buys a cheaper brand of turkey, the turkey may be too dry, and the hapless bride is sure to be seen as a failure in her mother-in-law's eyes. An ad for Butterball, well known to be more expensive than most frozen turkeys, assures her that her Thanksgiving turkey will be moist and sure to impress.

Males are predictable creatures. That makes it easy to craft a marketing message that appeals to them. All successful advertising campaigns that target men include one of two messages:

1. *This product will help you get dates with bikini models.*
2. *This product will save you time and money, which you'll need if you want to date bikini models.*

—Scott Adams

Celebrity Endorsements   We all tend to identify with people we envy and admire for their celebrity status. Advertisers play on this tendency by featuring sports stars, famous actors, or other celebrities. Maybe you will never play ball like a Michael Jordan, but you can feel a little more like him if you wear the same brand of basketball shoes he does. Such ads don't sell just a product; they also sell a lifestyle that people identify with. Often such ads don't even bother to give reasons for purchasing the product; it is enough in the consumer's mind that some celebrity endorses the product. The successful "Got milk?" ads do no more than show a famous celebrity with a milk-mustache. Apparently, that's enough to get some consumers to buy more milk.

> Advertisements aim to make us suspend critical judgment and accept biased testimony at face value.
>
> —Vincent Ruggiero

EXERCISE 14.10

I. Read the advertisements in current newspapers and magazines and find five that are based on mere emotional appeals, slogans, or jingles and that give no reasons for buying their product. Check the criteria given early in this chapter for a good ad and then find five ads that meet these criteria.

II. Choose an ad from a current magazine or newspaper, then analyze it in the following manner:

- Identify the strategy or ploy the ad uses to reach its audience.
- Determine if the ad is using a fallacious appeal and, if so, explain what it is.

> Consumers no longer buy products but rather lifestyles and the stories, experiences, and emotions products convey.
>
> —Revco Group

III. Here are examples of ads taken from various sources. Evaluate each ad for its informational and motivational aspects; then explain which, if any, of the following advertising gimmicks are used: humor, catchy slogan or jingle, anxiety, emotive language, weasel words, fine-print disclaimer, puffery, sex appeal, feel-good ad, image ad, or celebrity endorsement. (Keep in mind that more than one gimmick may be used.)

1. Listerine mouthwash ad: "Listerine fights bad breath."
2. Financial-services ad depicting three attractive young sisters sitting on a couch: "Three car payments. Three private colleges. Three weddings. I think I am having chest pains. How are we going to pay for all this? Invest? Invest in what? The market is more unpredictable than our daughters." The ad copy continues: "Emotional times require sound, unemotional financial advice. Morgan Stanley. One client at a time."
3. VISA credit card commercial: With lively background music and scenes of people bowling, eating, playing basketball, dancing, getting married, skydiving, the voiceover says, "Life takes ambition. Life takes luck. It takes determination. It takes confidence, respect, and talent. Life takes joy and spontaneity. It also takes a little help. That's where we come in. So go on, live life and remember no matter what it takes, life takes VISA."
4. Gatorade ad: "Is it in you?"
5. Typical car dealer ad, listing cars at remarkably low prices: "1/2 price sale.*" (In small print the ad notes, "*The price you see is half the price you pay.")

6. Lysol disinfectant ad: "Life requires Lysol. That's a fact."

7. IBC root beer commercial, featuring a hung-over man who wakes up in a zoo cage with a chimpanzee eyeing and petting him affectionately: "Sometimes the best beer is a root beer."

8. A 1980's commercial: "I am stuck on Band-Aid brand, 'cause Band-Aids stuck on me."

9. Ad for Dodge Stratus: "With a trunk so deep you need lifeguards to watch over it."

10. Lands' End catalog: "Lands' End Sport: Six pages dedicated to your VITALITY. BALANCE. SPIRIT."

11. Department store commercial: "25–40% off every stitch of clothing." (A qualification that flashes on the screen only briefly in the ad notes that the discounts do not apply to underwear, socks, hosiery, and other "accessories.")

12. An American Dairy Council ad features Olympic track-star Marion Jones wearing a milk moustache. The copy reads, "Wanna race? Milk has nine essential nutrients active bodies need. It can't be beat and neither can I."

13. An ad for Five Star grease gun cartridges shows a sultry woman leaning forward, exposing an impressive cleavage. The ad reads, "This is Debbie. She wants you to have this pair in your car." The rest of the ad talks about buying the grease gun cartridges she holds in her hands.

14. Ad for Kay jewelry: "Every kiss begins with Kay."

15. An ad for lipstick and nail color shows an attractive twenty-something at her office desk smiling and talking on a cell phone. The text reads, in part, "Wild about: Closing the deal. Poker night. Anything chocolate."

16. Head & Shoulders dandruff shampoo ad: "You only have one chance to make a first impression."

17. Commercial: "Springfield, Missouri: It's everyone's definition of fun."

18. Airline ad: "Nonstop to Orlando from $99." At the bottom of the page the following restrictions, among others, are noted: "Seats are limited and fares may not be available on all flights. All fares are one-way. . . . 10-day advance purchase required. Prices do not include PFC, segment tax or Sept. 11 security fee of up to $10.30 per segment."

19. AT&T commercial: "Reach out and touch someone."

20. Verbal Advantage ad: "Let me give you the secrets of fearless conversation! I promise you the ability to walk into a room full of strangers—and talk to anyone with total confidence, authority and flair."

21. Ad for Lincoln's sport utility vehicle: "Urban Assault Luxury Vehicle. Lincoln Navigator. American Luxury."

22. Imodium A-D ad: A man with a mortified look on his face is shown in a hot tub sitting between two attractive women. The ad copy reads, "Where will you be when your diarrhea comes back?"

23. Ad for Chanel perfume: "Chanel No. 5 is sensual but shy. Not for all women, but perfect for some."

24. A magazine ad for Hamburger Helper shows a mother in her kitchen, a smiling pigtailed child, and a plate of Hamburger Helper Cheeseburger Macaroni. The mother says, "Tonight, I will turn this hamburger into a great meal." The child says, "Tonight, you're getting a big hug." The caption below

the plate of macaroni reads, "Tonight, you're having a home-cooked meal. One pound. One pan. One happy family."

25. An ad for Tag Body Spray shows an attractive young man in his underwear, socks, and T-shirt, being strip-searched by three attractive female airport security guards. The ad copy reads, "Warning: Introducing new pocket-size Tag Body Shots. Load it, lock it, and rock it at your own risk. Consider yourself warned."

26. An ad for Ford trucks shows a rugged, balding man in his late forties, wearing a white T-shirt and a slightly tattered casual jacket. The text of the ad reads, in part, "Tore down the front wall first. Renovated everything, down to the doorknobs. But it wasn't until he hung up the sign with his name on it that he gave his resignation to his boss."

27. A Bud Light commercial shows a young couple walking by a pool on a warm summer night. The girl says, "Great night for a swim" The guy replies, "I don't have my bathing suit." The girl says, "Neither do I." They give each other a consenting smile, and in the next scene we see both of them skinny-dipping in the pool. What they don't realize is that the pool has a glass bottom that opens on a bar below where guys are enjoying the view, yelling and taking photos. The tag line says, "For the great taste that will never fill you up or let you down, make it a Bud Light."

SUMMARY

1. We are assailed daily by messages from the media. While some media sources target specific audiences, the mass media deliver their messages to a large and diverse audience with varying interests, levels of education, political viewpoints, and so forth.

2. To assign meaning to a message, we need to know something about the context of the message—the background of the information, the intentions or perceived intentions of the speaker, and the wider implications and circumstances that surround it. Without context, messages can be meaningless and useless. Unfortunately, the news media extract information from the wider context, leaving us with some facts but little knowledge.

3. In place of context, which would require thorough, extensive investigation and demand much of the audience, the media substitute appeals to our noncritical natures and common emotions, selecting stories of crime, scandal, violence, and whatever else will disturb, frighten, or shock audiences. Heartwarming stories about animals and children are common as well, as are stories of rescues and warnings about hidden dangers. Stories critical of corporations and the media do not usually appear in the mainstream press. In general, stories are selected for their entertainment value.

4. The media employ a number of techniques to exaggerate the importance of some stories and to play down others. Often these techniques result in

a distortion of reality, especially since extensive coverage is reserved for big events that are uncommon or trivial matters that are inconsequential. Persistent issues and trends receive relatively little coverage.

5. Although "objectivity" is difficult to attain, some members of the news media attempt to be objective by reporting news without commentary or analysis. This approach to the news often leads to problems when the media pass along information that is not credible or that has not been verified. Although some critics contend that the news media are biased toward a political viewpoint, most media organizations, preferring not to alienate current or potential customers, choose not to stir up controversy with pronounced political viewpoints. Some news personnel have on occasion blatantly offered their opinions on issues. In fact, some audiences now, unfortunately, look more and more to news reporters for their opinions and insights.

6. The media-literate critical thinker is aware of the techniques used in the news media to entertain an audience in an effort to keep them reading and watching. A media-literate consumer of news knows that stories have been stripped of their contexts and can separate fact from opinion in news stories.

7. The point of studying advertising ploys and strategies is to become a more critical, insightful, and selective consumer of the barrage of advertising appeals we experience.

8. Advertising permeates our environment. Using a host of ploys that appeal to both our physiological needs—food, drink, sleep—and our psychological needs—affiliation, affection, acceptance, self-esteem, status—advertisers invest vast amounts of money to break through our rational defenses to sell us their products.

9. Some of the more common strategies of advertisements include humor, catchy slogans and jingles, anxiety ads, emotive language, weasel words, fine-print disclaimers, puffery, sex appeals, feel-good ads, image ads, and celebrity endorsements.

CHAPTER 15

SCIENCE AND PSEUDOSCIENCE

Science is the most powerful intellectual tool ever discovered. It has transformed the way we live, work, travel, and communicate. It has given us computers, telephones, televisions, VCRs, DVD players, refrigerators, and a thousand other conveniences of modern life. It has improved health care, raised living standards, and significantly increased average life expectancy worldwide. Most significant, science has added enormously to the sum of human knowledge and has, after ages of more or less blind groping, finally provided human beings with a proven method for answering age-old questions about ourselves and the awe-inspiring physical universe in which we live.

Despite the profound impact science has on our daily lives, studies show that a large percentage of Americans are "scientifically illiterate."[1] Evidence of this can be seen in scientific literacy surveys (see box, "What Americans Believe . . ."), in the dismal performance of American high school students on international math and science tests,[2] and in the upsurge in interest in "New Age" or occult phenomena such as ESP, astrology, reincarnation, ghosts, psychic prediction, levitation, psychic surgery, the Bermuda Triangle, the lost continent of Atlantis, the prophecies of Nostradamus, healing crystals, pyramid power, out-of-body experiences, and trance channeling.

In this chapter we offer a brief introduction to science and scientific reasoning, discuss the limitations of science, explain how to distinguish real science from pseudoscience, and explore in detail one example of pseudoscientific thinking: astrology.

> All our science, measured against reality, is primitive and childlike—and yet it is the most precious thing we have.
>
> —Albert Einstein

> The true men of action in our time, those who transform the world, are not the politicians and statesmen, but the scientists.
>
> —W. H. Auden

THE BASIC PATTERN OF SCIENTIFIC REASONING

Science is a method of inquiry that seeks to describe, explain, and predict occurrences in the physical or natural world by means of careful observation and rigorous experiment.[3] Although there is no single "scientific method" that

What Americans Believe about Science and the Paranormal

The term **paranormal** refers to mysterious, unusual, or supernatural phenomena that supposedly transcend the limits of existing science and are due to hidden or occult causes.[4] Here is a sampling of things Americans believe about science and the paranormal:

18 percent of adult Americans believe that the sun revolves around the earth, rather than vice versa.[5]

More than 50 percent of adult Americans don't know that the earth takes a year to orbit the sun.[6]

63 percent of adult Americans don't know that the last dinosaur died before the first human arose.

57 percent of adult Americans don't know that electrons are smaller than atoms.[7]

47 percent of adult Americans believe that God created human beings at one time within the past 10,000 years pretty much in their present form.[8]

93 percent of adult Americans believe in some form of paranormal phenomena.[9]

48 percent of adult Americans believe in ESP.

25 percent of adult Americans believe in astrology.[10]

28 percent of adult Americans believe in communication with the dead.[11]

---

all scientists use, most scientific reasoning does follow a certain general pattern. That pattern can be summarized as follows:

The Basic Pattern of Scientific Reasoning

1. Identify the problem.
2. Gather relevant data.
3. Formulate hypotheses to explain the data.
4. Test the hypotheses by observation or experiment.

Identifying the Problem   Try to remember the last time you thought really hard about something. We'd be willing to bet there was some *problem* you were trying to solve: Should I change my major? Quit my dead-end job? Move into my own apartment? Talk to my friend about his drinking problem? Tell my boyfriend about my planned sex-change operation? In fact, as John Dewey and other philosophers have pointed out, most of the serious thinking we do is problem-solving thinking.

Science, by its very nature, is a kind of problem-solving activity. It always begins with a question or puzzle that researchers believe can be answered by means of observation or experiment: Do oral contraceptives cause breast cancer? Does drinking red wine lower the risk of heart attack? Did the universe begin with a big bang? What are the fundamental building blocks of matter? Were dinosaurs wiped out by the impact of a large asteroid? How do honeybees communicate? What genes determine eye color? Did life once exist on Mars? What causes those amazing bubbles to percolate up from the bottom of a glass of beer? Science seeks to answer such puzzles by means of careful observation and rigorous testing.

Gathering Relevant Data   The ultimate test of a scientific theory or hypothesis is whether it fits the observable facts. No matter how popular, comforting, or long accepted a scientific idea may be, it must be rejected if it fails to agree with the clear evidence of our senses.

Sometimes it is possible to confirm or refute a scientific hypothesis by means of a single decisive observation or experiment. That was the case, for example, when Galileo, according to a famous but possibly apocryphal story, refuted Aristotle's claim that heavy objects fall faster than light objects by dropping two iron balls of different weights from the Leaning Tower of Pisa and noting that the two balls struck the ground at the same instant. In most cases, however, a scientific hypothesis can be effectively confirmed or refuted only by collecting a great deal of observational evidence. To find out, for example, whether coffee drinking contributes to coronary heart disease, scientists would need to collect information on the coffee-drinking habits and other health-related characteristics of literally thousands of people over a period of many years. The patient, methodical collection of facts is what consumes most of the time and energy of most working scientists.

> *The great tragedy of Science — the slaying of a beautiful hypothesis by an ugly fact.*
>
> —Thomas Henry Huxley

Formulating Hypotheses   Contrary to a popular misconception, scientists don't just go around collecting facts blindly or indiscriminately. All scientific investigation is guided by certain presuppositions that influence the kinds of observations and experiments scientists think are worth making. Among these presuppositions are a class of tentative, or "working," assumptions scientists call **hypotheses**. Let's consider a few examples.

Suppose you are a doctor investigating an outbreak of serious stomach-flu-like symptoms onboard a commercial jet airliner. Five passengers, all from the same family and all seated in the first-class cabin, became sick during a long overseas flight. Your job is to find out why. How would you begin?

> *Often the most difficult step in the discovery of what is true is thinking of a hypothesis which may be true.*
>
> —Bertrand Russell

Clearly, you wouldn't begin just by collecting facts at random: noting the color of the sick passengers' socks, the number of coins in their pockets, their favorite sports teams, the kinds of toothpaste they prefer, and so on. Based on your knowledge of how things normally work in the world, you would assume that those facts aren't pertinent to your investigation. Instead, you would start by looking for *relevant* facts, guided by a kind of working hypothesis such as the following:

H_1: The passengers became sick because of the food they ate on the plane.

Suppose you do some quick checking, however, and discover that two of the five sick passengers were fasting and ate nothing on the plane. Naturally, you would then set aside your initial hypothesis and formulate another, such as the following:

> H_2: The passengers became sick because they all came down with the stomach flu.

> *Science is nothing but trained and organized common sense, differing from the latter only as a veteran may differ from a raw recruit.*
>
> —Thomas Henry Huxley

You might then call for some medical tests, which, let's suppose, confirm that the passengers did indeed come down with a severe case of viral gastroenteritis, more commonly known as stomach flu.

As this example makes clear, there is a complex interplay between observations and hypotheses in science. Hypotheses inevitably *guide* observations because scientists wouldn't have a clue where to begin their investigations without at least some initial assumptions about what sorts of data are worth collecting. Observations, in turn, are used to *test* hypotheses—to modify, confirm, or refute them in the light of empirical evidence and experimentation. It is this complex interplay between careful observation and rigorous testing that is the touchstone of modern science.

Testing the Hypotheses   Scientific hypotheses are tested by *considering their implications* and then *testing those implications* by means of observation or experiment. Consider, again, the problem of the sick airline passengers.

Recall that we were able to quickly rule out our initial hypothesis—that the passengers became sick because of the food they ate on the plane—simply by noting that two of the passengers who became sick did not eat on the plane. In effect, we reasoned like this:

1. If the passengers became sick because of the food they ate on the plane, then all the passengers who became sick must have eaten on the plane.
2. But it is not the case that all the passengers who became sick ate on the plane.
3. So, it is not the case that the passengers became sick because of the food they ate on the plane.

Let H stand for the hypothesis that the five passengers became sick because of the food they ate on the plane. Let I stand for the implication of H, that all the five passengers did, in fact, eat on the plane. The pattern of our reasoning is thus:

1. If H, then I.
2. Not I.
3. So, not H.

As you will recall from Chapter 3, this is a deductively valid pattern of reasoning called *modus tollens. Modus tollens* arguments are widely used in scientific reasoning as a way of *disconfirming,* or falsifying, scientific hypotheses.

A different pattern of scientific reasoning is often used to *confirm* scientific hypotheses. Consider the reasoning we used to verify our second hypothesis—the stomach flu hypothesis—in our example above:

1. If the five passengers became sick because they came down with the stomach flu, then medical tests should confirm that diagnosis.

2. Medical tests do confirm that diagnosis.

3. So, the five passengers did become sick because they came down with the stomach flu.

Here the pattern of reasoning is

1. If *H,* then *I.*

2. *I.*

3. So, *H.*

This is a pattern of reasoning called *affirming the consequent.* As we saw in Chapter 3, arguments of this pattern are *not* deductively valid. For example:

1. If JFK died in a bungee-jumping accident, then JFK is dead.

2. JFK is dead.

3. So, JFK did die in a bungee-jumping accident.

In this argument the premises are both true and the conclusion is clearly false. Thus, arguments of this pattern are not deductively valid.

Does this mean that scientific reasoning is inherently flawed? No. Arguments of this pattern can provide *persuasive evidence* for a conclusion, even though they are not deductively valid. For example:

If it rained, then the streets are wet.

The streets are wet.

Therefore, it rained.

Clearly, this argument does not *prove* that it rained. It might be the case that the streets are wet because some pranksters from the local volunteer fire department hosed them down during the night. But given the fact that rain and wet streets are regularly associated in our experience, the fact that the streets are wet does provide strong *presumptive* evidence that it rained. By a similar process of reasoning, scientists are often able to provide strong (but not logically conclusive) evidence for a hypothesis by a process of (1) deducing specific implications from the hypothesis (i.e., asking what *would be true* if the hypothesis were true); (2) testing those implications by observation or experiment; and (3) finding that those implications consistently turn out to be true across a variety of demanding test conditions.

Because of the inherent theoretical and practical difficulties in confirming scientific hypotheses, scientific conclusions can never be 100 percent certain. No matter how much evidence we amass for a scientific "law" of the form "All A's are B's," it is always possible that tomorrow we will discover an A that is *not* a B. No matter how carefully we make our observations or conduct our experiments, it is always possible that some hidden cause or overlooked variable will bias our conclusions. For those reasons scientific conclusions are always tentative and open to revision.

Does this mean that everything is up for grabs in science? By no means. Many scientific conclusions *can* be affirmed with a high degree of confidence.

The scientific temper is cautious, tentative, and piecemeal.
—Bertrand Russell

One way in which scientists are able to achieve such confident conclusions is by conducting controlled studies.

A **controlled study,** as we noted briefly in Chapter 11, is a rigorous, carefully structured test in which scientists use a baseline comparison, or control group, to answer questions of the form "Does A cause B?" Suppose you want to discover, for example, whether vitamin C prevents colds. Here is the most reliable way to find out:

1. Randomly select a large number of people from the whole population.
2. Randomly divide them into two groups: an *experimental group* and a *control group.*
3. Treat the two groups exactly alike, except that you give the experimental group a specified dosage of vitamin C and you give the control group a *placebo*—that is, a sugar pill or some other known inactive substance.
4. Conduct the study *double-blind.* That is, you make sure that neither the scientists nor the subjects know which of the subjects is getting the vitamin C and which is getting the placebo.
5. Check to see if there is a *statistically significant difference* in the frequency with which the two groups get colds. If the experimental group gets significantly fewer colds than the control group, it is reasonable to conclude that vitamin C does help prevent colds.[12]

Each of these five steps is generally necessary to establish the effectiveness of a treatment beyond a reasonable doubt.

Randomly selecting a *large* number of subjects from the population as a whole is necessary to ensure that you have a sample that is representative of the population as a whole.

Using a *control group* is necessary to determine that it is the substance being tested, and not some other factor, that explains any apparent causal effects.

Using a *placebo* is necessary because studies have shown that many people will experience improvement in their condition even if they are given a sugar pill or some other treatment that is known to be worthless. The only way to control for this "placebo effect" is to give one group the real stuff (the substance being tested) and another group a placebo, without telling either group which they are receiving.

Making the study *double-blind* is necessary to make sure, first, that the *scientists* don't bias the results by consciously or unconsciously treating one group differently from the other and, second, that the *subjects* don't bias the results by knowing which group is receiving the real stuff and which isn't.

Last, checking to see if there is a *statistically significant difference* in the frequencies of the measured effect is necessary to ensure that any observed differences are not simply due to chance.

The type of controlled study just described is called a **randomized experimental study** because it involves deliberate "interventions," or tests, on

> *The power which a man's imagination has over his body to heal it or make it sick is a force which none of us is born without.*
>
> —Mark Twain

groups that have been randomly selected. Sometimes, for ethical or other reasons, it is not possible to conduct studies of this kind. For example, suppose you wanted to find out if low-level lead poisoning causes hearing loss in young children. Clearly, it would be unethical to deliberately expose children to potentially harmful levels of lead. Nevertheless, there are two types of controlled tests you could use to try to answer your question scientifically. Specifically, you could perform either a nonrandomized prospective study or a nonrandomized retrospective study.

In a **nonrandomized prospective study,** you begin with a group of people that has *already been exposed* to a suspected causal agent (in our example, low levels of lead poisoning). This group (or a representative sample) serves as the experimental group. You then find a group of people that has not been exposed to the suspected causal agent but matches the first group in all other relevant respects. (For the study to be reliable, great care must be taken to ensure that the two groups really are alike in all relevant respects.) This second group serves as the control group. You then track the two groups over time. If the experimental group exhibits the suspected effect at significantly higher rates than the control group, this provides evidence for the suspected cause-and-effect relationship.

In a **nonrandomized retrospective study,** you start with a group of people that *already exhibits a certain effect.* You then find a control group that is as similar as possible to the first group except that its members do *not* exhibit the observed effect. You then work backward to try to determine the cause of the observed effect. In the lead-poisoning example, for instance, if a researcher were to find that children with hearing loss suffer from low-level lead poisoning at significantly higher rates than children in the control group, this would provide evidence that such poisoning does cause hearing loss in children.

We are constantly bombarded by claims about "miracle" or "alternative" cures. Does shark cartilage cure cancer? Do magnets ease back pain? Does zinc cure colds? Do copper bracelets alleviate motion sickness? To answer these questions, you might try one or more of the following ever-popular techniques:

Popular Methods for Assessing "Miracle" or "Alternative" Cures

The method of personal experience:	"I tried it, and it worked."
The method of anecdotal evidence:	"Someone else tried it, and it worked."
The method of paid testimonials:	"A famous actor or sports hero was paid to say it works."
The method of folklore:	"An ancient practice or folklore says it works."[13]

Each of these methods, however, has been proven time and again to be unreliable. Sick people often feel better for all sorts of reasons that have nothing to do with any treatments they may be receiving. So, the only way to know

He who proves things by experience increases his knowledge; he who believes blindly increases his errors.

—Chinese proverb

• Critical Thinking Lapse •

Shortly before his death, science writer Carl Sagan published an article in *Parade* magazine, in which he bemoaned the fact that American high school students perform poorly on international math and science tests. A tenth-grade teacher in Minnesota handed out copies of the article to her class and asked what they thought. Here's what some of the students wrote in response (all quotes are verbatim):

- Not a Americans are stupid We just rank lower in school big deal.
- Maybe that's good that we are not as smart as the other countries. So then we can just import all of their products and then we don't have to spend all of our money on the parts for the goods.
- And if other countries are doing better, what does it matter, their most likely going to come over the U.S. anyway?
- Not one kid in this school likes science. I really didn't understand the point of the article. I thought it was very boreing. I'm just not into anything like that.
- I think your facts were inconclusive and the evidence very flimsy. All in all, you raised a good point.[14]

beyond a reasonable doubt that a "cure" is effective is through careful, controlled scientific testing.

EXERCISE 15.1

In small groups, design reliable scientific studies to test the following hypotheses. Be prepared to share your study designs with the class as a whole.

1. Magnets can ease chronic back pain.
2. Sleeping with a night-light can cause near-sightedness in young children.
3. Drinking two or three cups of green tea a day reduces the risk of heart attack.
4. Teen pregnancy-prevention programs that emphasize abstinence are less effective than programs that emphasize both abstinence and safer-sex education.
5. The chemical defoliant Agent Orange caused birth defects in the children of American soldiers who served in Vietnam.

THE LIMITATIONS OF SCIENCE

Science is the most reliable method we have for discovering empirically verifiable truths about the physical universe. There are, however, many important questions that science cannot answer. Among these are fundamental questions of *meaning* and *value*.

Questions of Meaning   Science deals with empirically observable facts. But many of life's most important questions deal not with empirically observable facts but with the meaning or significance of those facts. Thus, for example, science cannot answer fundamental questions such as these:

- Does the universe have a purpose?
- Does my life have a purpose?
- What things in life are truly meaningful and important?
- Does my suffering have meaning?
- Does anything I do have enduring meaning or significance?

Although science can provide evidence relevant to these questions, these are not scientific questions because they are not questions of objective, empirically verifiable fact.[15]

Questions of Value   Questions of value, or *normative questions,* are questions about what is good or bad, right or wrong, better or worse, beautiful or ugly, desirable or undesirable. Here are some examples of questions of value:

> *Science can only ascertain what is, but not what should be.*
> —Albert Einstein

- Is abortion always wrong?
- Is capital punishment justifiable?
- Should gay marriage be legal?
- Is it ever right to lie?
- Should embryonic stem cell research be permitted?
- What is a just society?
- Is freedom more important than equality?

These are important questions we can argue about well or badly, reasonably or unreasonably. But they are not scientific questions because they cannot be settled by any conceivable empirical observation or experiment.

Some people claim that science can, in fact, answer questions of meaning and value. Specifically, they claim that modern science shows us that the universe has *no* meaning or purpose and that values are only subjective. Often they defend this claim with some version of the following argument:

1. Either beliefs are mere subjective opinions or they are facts.
2. All facts are scientific facts.
3. Beliefs about meanings or values are not scientific facts.
4. Therefore, beliefs about meanings or values are mere subjective opinions.

This argument can be challenged in several ways. Here, let's focus just on (2), the claim that

All facts are scientific facts.

A little reflection shows that this claim cannot possibly be true. The statement "All facts are scientific facts" is not itself a scientific fact. It cannot be validated by any scientific observation or procedure. Consequently, the statement is *self-refuting*—that is, false even in its own terms. The statement cannot be true because it undermines itself.

Statements such as "All facts are scientific facts" or "Science is the only reliable guide to truth" are not, in fact, scientific claims but expressions of an uncritical form of science-worship called *scientism*. **Scientism** is the view that science is the only reliable way of knowing.[16]

Scientism must be carefully distinguished from science. Whereas science is cautious and empirical, scientism is arrogant and dogmatic. For example, defenders of scientism often claim that science has shown that all the following beliefs are false or unwarranted:

- God exists.
- There is life after death.
- The universe has a purpose.
- Religious experience is sometimes a valid way of knowing.
- Some things are objectively right or wrong.

These claims may be true or false, warranted or unwarranted. Our point is simply that they are philosophical or religious claims, not scientific ones. No amount of scientific evidence will ever prove that the universe has no purpose. You will never hear a scientist exclaim, "Aha! The litmus paper turned blue. I *told* you there are no objective moral values!" Science limits itself to what can be observed, measured, and tested. It doesn't pretend to answer fundamental questions of meaning or value.

How to Distinguish Science from Pseudoscience

Pseudoscience is false science—that is, unscientific thinking masquerading as scientific thinking. It is thinking that appears to be scientific but is, in fact, faithless to science's basic values and methods.[17] Because pseudoscientific thinking often looks and sounds like real science, it can be hard for nonscientists to tell them apart. Luckily, there are certain marks of pseudoscience that any educated person can use to distinguish it from true science,[18] including the following:

Six Marks of Pseudoscience
1. It makes claims that are not testable.
2. It makes claims that are inconsistent with well-established scientific truths.

3. It explains away or ignores falsifying data.
4. It uses vague language.
5. It is not progressive.
6. It often involves no serious effort to conduct research.

Scientists, of course, aren't perfect. Consequently, even genuine science will sometimes display one or two of these marks (though rarely in a serious or systematic way). But if an allegedly "scientific" discipline displays several of these marks (or even one in a particularly blatant way), that is a strong indication that it is pseudoscience rather than science.

Absence of Testability   Science seeks to answer questions about the natural world, not through myth, intuition, or guesswork, but through careful observation and experiment. Thus, by the very nature of the scientific enterprise, all genuinely scientific claims must be testable.

A scientific claim is *testable* when we can make observations that would show the claim to be true or false. In thinking about this criterion, we must avoid two common mistakes.

First, scientific claims need not be *directly* testable. Obviously, we can never go back in time to obtain direct observational evidence that birds evolved from dinosaurs. However, there is a great deal of *indirect* evidence that supports this hypothesis, including DNA evidence, structural similarities (homologies) between birds and certain species of dinosaurs, and transitional fossil forms. The fact that scientists can argue for or against this hypothesis by appealing to such indirect evidence is enough to make the hypothesis a genuinely scientific one.

Second, scientific claims need not be *immediately* testable. For example, when Einstein proposed in 1916 that clocks run faster in space than they do on Earth, it wasn't possible to test this hypothesis experimentally with the technology available at the time. It wasn't until many decades later that the invention of jet aircraft and high-precision atomic clocks allowed scientists to test Einstein's hypothesis and prove that it was true.[19]

Although scientific claims need not be directly or immediately testable, they must at least be *testable in principle;* that is, there must be at least some observations we can realistically imagine making that would show the claim to be true or false. If we can't conceive of any observations that would count for or against the claim, it is not a claim about empirically observable reality, and hence not a claim that can be studied scientifically.

Here are some examples of claims that are *not* scientifically testable:

There are invisible, completely undetectable gremlins that live deep in the interior of the earth.

An exact duplicate of you exists in a parallel universe that is completely inaccessible to us.

All reality is spiritual; matter is only an illusion.

> *A theory's validity depends on whether or not it can be verified.*
> —John Paul II

The earth was once visited by superintelligent aliens who left no trace of their visit.

Every time a bell rings, an angel gets its wings.

Each of these claims may, for all we know, be true. But they are not scientific claims because there is no possible observation or experiment that would tell us whether they are true or false.[20]

To be scientific a claim must be testable in two senses: it must be verifiable in principle and falsifiable in principle. A claim is *verifiable in principle* when we can imagine some possible observation that would provide good reason to believe that the claim is true. A claim is *falsifiable in principle* when we can imagine some possible observation that would provide good reason to believe that the claim is false.

Pseudoscientists commonly make claims that violate the second of these two conditions. That is, they often make claims that are not falsifiable even in principle.

A good example of this comes from the field of ESP research. ESP (extrasensory perception) is the alleged ability to sense or perceive things without the aid of the five senses. Believers in ESP often point to experiments that seem to provide evidence for claims of the form

X has genuine powers of ESP.

Unfortunately, every time scientists have sought to repeat such experiments under tightly controlled conditions, no evidence of ESP abilities has been found. To explain this failure, believers in ESP often offer the following two excuses:

- ESP works sometimes but not others.
- ESP doesn't work when skeptics are present.[21]

These excuses may sound plausible—until you notice the kind of "heads-I-win, tails-you-lose" logic behind them. For those who offer such excuses, there can be evidence *for* ESP but not evidence *against* it. By resorting to such rationalizations, believers in ESP render their claim unfalsifiable and hence unscientific.

Catch-22 cop-outs like this are commonplace in pseudoscience. For example, when researchers in the 1970s failed to confirm poorly controlled experiments suggesting that plants were sensitive and aware, die-hard believers in plant consciousness retorted that this was because the skeptical researchers weren't emotionally "in tune" with the plants.[22] Similarly, when scientists in the 1960s failed to find evidence supporting James V. McConnell's startling claim that cannibalistic flatworms acquired their fellow worms' knowledge, McConnell's colleague Allan Jacobson defended McConnell's work by charging that the scientists lacked feelings for the worms.[23]

EXERCISE 15.2

Determine whether the following items are scientifically testable. If so, how? If not, why not?

1. Joey swims well because he was a dolphin in a previous life.
2. Everyone has a guardian angel.
3. Razor blades stay sharp when placed inside a pyramid.
4. Disobeying the law is always morally wrong.
5. The entire universe sprang into existence from nothing five minutes ago, exactly as it then was, apparent fossils in the ground, wrinkles on people's faces, and other signs of age all instantly formed and thoroughly deceptive.[24]
6. The Loch Ness monster exists.
7. Human beings are the most intelligent species in the universe.
8. "The chief purpose of life, for anyone of us, is to increase according to our capacity our knowledge of God by all the means we have, and to be moved by it to praise and thanks." (J. R. R. Tolkien)[25]
9. *Tarot card reader:* You have unresolved issues in your love life.
10. There are exactly 19, 367, 401, 303 living trees in Canada.
11. All human actions and choices are fundamentally selfish.
12. Some diseases can be cured by prayer.
13. The universe and everything in it doubled in size last night while we were sleeping.

Inconsistency with Well-Established Scientific Findings   Science is cumulative and progressive. It constantly changes and grows. Sometimes these changes involve big "paradigm shifts"—whole new ways of looking at the world or a particular area of science, such as that which occurred in the seventeenth century when scientists abandoned the traditional Earth-centered view of the universe. Even in these big revolutions, however, science advances not by throwing out well-established scientific truths but by extending those truths into new domains. Science progresses by building on existing knowledge, not by starting from scratch.

In contrast, in pseudoscience one often encounters claims that conflict with well-confirmed scientific conclusions. Young-earth creationism is a case in point.

Young-earth creationists are religious conservatives who believe, as a literal reading of Genesis would have it, that the universe is only six thousand to ten thousand years old, that the theory of evolution is false, and that the fossil record and the major geological features of the earth can be explained by the Great Flood described in Genesis 6:5–8:22.

Young-earth creationism conflicts with many well-established scientific findings. In fact, as Isaac Asimov notes with only slight exaggeration, young-earth creationism cannot be accepted "without discarding all of modern

> *Science is knowledge that has had its feet held to the fire.*
> —Chet Raymo

biology, biochemistry, geology, astronomy—in short, without discarding all of science."[26] Consider just a few of the problems faced by those who insist on a literal reading of the Genesis account of Noah's ark and the Great Flood:

- How could a 600-year-old man have constructed a wooden boat larger than any supertanker? How many years would this have taken? How much wood would this have required?

- There are well over a million species of animals alive today. Millions of other animal species are now extinct. According to Genesis, Noah took into the ark seven pairs of all "clean" animals, seven pairs of all birds, and two pairs of all "unclean" animals (Gen. 7:2–5). How could all these living and now-extinct animals have fit on the ark? How could Noah, his wife, three sons, and their wives have gathered and stored enough food and water for all of these animals? (Did Noah, for example, travel to Australia to gather the fresh eucalyptus leaves that koalas need to survive? If so, how did he keep the leaves fresh on the journey home?) How could all of these creatures have gotten to the ark from the far-flung portions of the globe? How could saltwater marine species have survived in a freshwater environment? How could plants and trees have survived underwater for nearly a year? What did the animals eat when they got off the ark? How did they travel to their current habitats? Why did marsupials, but no placental mammals, manage to get to Australia?

- Young-earth creationists claim that floodwaters covered the entire earth to a depth of 3 miles. Scientists have calculated that this would require 3.4 times more water than exists in all of the earth's oceans.[27] Where did all of this water come from? Where did it all go?

- Earth's continents are covered with sedimentary deposits to an average depth of 1 mile. In some places, these deposits consist of millions of distinct, alternating layers of light and dark sediment. Geological observations indicate that such deposits take millions of years to form. How could these millions of alternating layers have been laid down in a single flood that lasted less than a year?[28]

- Earth's fossil record shows a remarkably consistent pattern: more-primitive plant and animal species in the lower geological strata, more-advanced species in the higher. Young-earth creationists seek to explain the fossil record by invoking three principles of "flood geology": (1) lower-dwelling creatures (e.g., marine invertebrates) would be deposited before higher-dwelling creatures (e.g., amphibians and reptiles); (2) less buoyant creatures would be deposited before more buoyant creatures; and (3) less mobile creatures (e.g., tortoises and snails) would be deposited before more mobile creatures (e.g., humans and horses) because the latter would be able to flee to the hilltops before being overwhelmed by the flood.[29]

This explanation, however, conflicts starkly with both the fossil record and common sense. Marine invertebrates are found at all levels of the fossil record. Flowering plants and trees are never found with more-primitive plants and trees. Modern fish are never found at the same levels as ancient extinct fish. Whales and dolphins are always found at higher levels than extinct marine reptiles. And many highly mobile creatures, such as carnivorous dinosaurs and flying reptiles, are always found at lower levels than modern mammals and birds.

In short, young-earth creationism conflicts at many points with extremely well-confirmed scientific findings. This demonstrates clearly that it is pseudoscience rather than science.

Explaining Away or Ignoring Falsifying Evidence   Science is self-correcting. It advances by continually seeking to *disprove* its own hypotheses and then learning from its own mistakes. For this reason, scientists don't fear or ignore falsifying evidence; they welcome it as essential to scientific progress. This attitude is reflected in the following story told by Oxford biologist Richard Dawkins:

> One of the formative experiences of my Oxford undergraduate years occurred when a visiting lecturer from America presented evidence that conclusively disproved the pet theory of a deeply respected elder statesman of our zoology department, the theory that we had all been brought up on. At the end of the lecture, the old man rose, strode to the front of the hall, shook the American warmly by the hand and declared, in ringing emotional tones, "My dear fellow, I wish to thank you. I have been wrong these fifteen years." We clapped our hands red. Is any other profession so generous towards its admitted mistakes? [30]

In contrast, pseudoscientists often ignore or seek to explain away evidence that conflicts with their favored theories. A good example of this involves the famed Israeli entertainer Uri Geller.

Geller, a nightclub magician, became something of a psychic celebrity in the 1970s. Audiences and even respected scientists were astounded at his apparent ability to read minds, peer inside sealed envelopes, and bend keys and spoons with the power of his mind alone. In fact, Geller was a complete fraud who used parlor tricks and sleight-of-hand to perform his "psychic" feats. He was finally exposed when hidden cameras caught him blatantly cheating. When proof of Geller's guilt was shown to his fans, some sought to explain this by claiming that Geller resorted to cheating only when his psychic powers failed! [31]

Or consider another form of psychic humbug that created a stir in the 1970s: "psychic surgery." Psychic surgeons are people who claim to be able to remove diseased tissue or dangerous tumors from a patient's body without conventional surgery. Psychologist Terence Hines describes how the procedure supposedly works:

> As the psychic surgeon performs "surgery," his hand is seen to disappear into the patient's belly and a pool of blood appears. After groping around, apparently

The hallmark of science is not the question "Do I wish to believe this?" but the question "What is the evidence?"
—Douglas J. Futuyma

Those who lose an argument win if, in the discipline or tradition with which they identify, better arguments prevail.
—Holmes Rolston III

Believers in the paranormal are like unsinkable rubber ducks.
—James Randi

inside the body cavity, the psychic surgeon dramatically pulls his hand "out" of the body, clutching what is said to be the tumor or diseased tissue that was causing the patient's problem. The offending tissue is promptly tossed in a handy nearby fire to be purified. When the patient's belly is wiped clean of the blood, no incision is found.[32]

In fact, the procedure is performed through simple sleight-of-hand, with fake blood and animal tissue typically concealed in a false plastic thumb. When laboratory tests showed that the "tumors" were actually chicken livers or other animal remains, some hard-core believers in the procedure remained unconvinced. How amazing, they said, that these miracle workers can not only perform operations without making an incision but can also transform deadly tumors into harmless animal tissue![33]

Rationalizations of this sort are completely opposed to the spirit of science. Science learns from its mistakes or failures; it does not ignore them or sweep them under the rug.

Use of Vague Language   To be scientific a claim must be testable, and to be testable it must be expressed in clear, specific language. A prediction like "A big change will occur in your life next year" is not a scientific prediction because it is so vague that almost anything could be counted as confirming it.

Pseudoscientists often use language that is too vague to be testable. Consider "psychic readers," for example. Psychic readers claim to be able to know all sorts of things about people through mysterious "psychic" abilities. Although there is no credible scientific evidence that such abilities are real, psychics employ a variety of ruses to convince people that they are. One of these ploys involves the skillful use of vague or general language.

To be successful a psychic reader must be able to convince complete strangers that he knows all about their problems and experiences. To accomplish this, psychics use a technique called "cold reading."

Cold reading is a sophisticated set of skills used by palm readers, psychics, tarot card readers, and other professional "readers" for gathering surprisingly accurate information about persons whom the reader has never met before. The method works largely through a combination of close observation; knowledge of human commonalities; flattering "feel-good" statements; the use of vague, general language; and the natural human tendency to remember hits and forget misses. Here let's focus on psychic readers' use of vague or general language.

A psychic reading usually begins with a "stock spiel"—a set of general statements that apply to practically everybody. Here is a stock spiel that has been shown to be particularly effective with college students:

> Some of your aspirations tend to be pretty unrealistic. At times you are extroverted, affable, sociable, while at other times you are introverted, wary and reserved. You have found it unwise to be too frank in revealing yourself to others. You pride yourself on being an independent thinker and do not accept others' opinions without satisfactory proof. You prefer a certain amount of change and

variety, and become dissatisfied when hemmed in by restrictions and limitations. At times you have serious doubts as to whether you have made the right decision or done the right thing. Disciplined and controlled on the outside, you tend to be worrisome and insecure on the inside. . . .

　　While you have some personality weaknesses, you are generally able to compensate for them. You have a great deal of unused capacity which you have not turned to your advantage. You have a tendency to be critical of yourself. You have a strong need for other people to like you and for them to admire you.[34]

Studies have shown that when people are presented with general personality descriptions like this, they are often amazed at their accuracy. Psychologists call this the "Barnum effect," after the nineteenth-century showman P. T. Barnum, who once famously declared, "There's a sucker born every minute."

In a manipulative technique called **fishing for details,** psychic readers use a combination of vague, exploratory language and close observation of verbal and visual clues to subtly elicit detailed information from a subject. Two types of vague expressions are especially crucial to this technique: multiple-out expressions and try-ons.

Multiple-out expressions are statements or questions that are so vague that they can easily be interpreted, often after the fact, as fitting many different outcomes.[35] For example, a reader might say, "Someone close to you is having problems in his or her love life." Her surprised client might respond, "That's amazing! How did you know my friend Marta is getting a divorce?" Of course, the reader didn't know anything about Marta or her divorce, but the expressions "close to you" and "having problems in his or her love life" are so broad and elastic that almost anyone can think of at least one person (and on reflection, probably several) who fits these descriptions.

Try-ons are subtle statements designed to prompt a reaction, but carefully phrased so that they are easily interpreted as hits but not so easily interpreted as misses.[36] For example, a reader might say, "I'm getting a feeling you may have some serious financial concerns you're dealing with." If the client does have "serious financial concerns" (note the vague language), this will naturally be counted as a hit. On the other hand, if the client does not have serious financial concerns, this may not be counted as a miss. After all, the reader hasn't positively stated that the client *does* have serious financial worries—only that he's *getting a feeling* that the client *may* have such worries.

A skilled cold reader can learn an amazing amount of information about a client simply by making a few vague statements and then watching closely how the client reacts. Extremely subtle visual clues—downcast eyes, a slight nod of the head, an almost imperceptible flushing of the cheeks—can tell an experienced cold reader whether she's on the right track. Such abilities can seem uncanny, but in reality there is nothing mysterious or "paranormal" about them. In fact, now that you know the secrets of cold reading, you too can amaze your friends with your "psychic" abilities.

> It is a typical soothsayer's trick to predict things so vaguely that the predictions can hardly fail.
> —Karl Popper

> We humans are best defined not as "the rational" but as "the self-deceiving" animal.
> —Richard Paul

Lack of Progressiveness   Science is progressive. It continually advances and grows. Pseudoscience, in contrast, is often intellectually static. It gets stuck at a certain point and stops changing and progressing.

A good example of this is the flat-earth hypothesis supported by the International Flat Earth Research Society. (Yes, there really is such a society.) Flat-Earthers believe that the earth is shaped like a pancake, with the North Pole at the center and an enormous wall of ice at the perimeter. It is this wall of ice, presumably, that prevents ships and planes from falling off the edge of the world or flying off into space.

Many centuries ago belief in a flat earth was perfectly reasonable. After all, the earth *looks* flat, even from a high mountaintop. Moreover, it doesn't feel like we're whirling around at 1,000 miles per hour, as scientists tell us we are. And if the earth is spinning at 1,000 miles per hour, why is it that when we shoot an arrow straight up in the air, it lands at our feet instead of many miles away?

These may have been more or less reasonable grounds for belief in a flat earth at one time. But, of course, not any longer. To paraphrase Richard Dawkins: It is absolutely safe to say that if you meet someone who claims not to believe that the earth is round, that person is ignorant, stupid, or insane (or joking, which we would hope is the case).

It is the glory of science to progress.

—C. S. Lewis

Failure to Conduct Research   Science is a body of well-confirmed facts. More important, science is a *method,* a set of proven techniques for advancing the frontiers of human understanding. As we have seen, science by its very nature is constantly asking questions, seeking solutions, collecting data, trying out hypotheses, and searching for new insights and deeper understanding. Thus, systematic, disciplined inquiry—in short, *research*—lies at the heart of the scientific enterprise.

Pseudosciences, on the other hand, often fail to engage in any serious program of research. Consider the "water cure," an alternative medical treatment touted by Dr. Fereydoon Batmanghelidj, author of the 1992 book *Your Body's Many Cries for Water.*[37]

The idea behind the water cure is simple. The root cause of most illnesses is lack of water in the body—chronic dehydration. To maintain proper hydration, people should drink eight to ten glasses of water a day, consume salt liberally, and avoid caffeine and alcohol. Among the many diseases Dr. Batmanghelidj claims can be prevented or cured by this simple natural remedy are asthma, arthritis, back pain, cancer, depression, erectile dysfunction, high blood pressure, migraines, muscular dystrophy, and multiple sclerosis.

What proof does Dr. Batmanghelidj have that drinking large amounts of water can actually prevent and cure all of these various diseases? The evidence he presents is almost purely anecdotal. Both Dr. Batmanghelidj's book and his Web site are full of testimonials by people saying, "I tried it and it worked!"

We have seen, however, that anecdotal evidence of this sort is highly unreliable. Every useless quack remedy and snake-oil treatment since the dawn of

Science is more than a body of knowledge; it is a way of thinking.

—Carl Sagan

civilization has been supported by anecdotal evidence. The only way to be sure that a treatment is effective is to test it scientifically under rigorous, controlled conditions.

Bob Butts, a prominent supporter of Dr. Batmanghelidj, has argued that it is pointless to test the water cure scientifically. "The need for testing makes about as much sense as someone suggesting that we do research to see if daylight exists," Butts claims. It is just common sense, he argues, that "the body's cure for drought is water." [38]

It may be common sense that chronic dehydration can be harmful to one's health, but it is not common sense to suppose that dehydration is the root cause of most diseases. This is, in fact, quite implausible in the light of modern medical knowledge. The causes of most diseases are now well understood, and there is no reason to suspect that chronic dehydration is a significant causal factor in most of them. The water cure *may* have the amazing health benefits Dr. Batmanghelidj claims, but the only way to *know* whether it does is to subject it to rigorous scientific testing.

In summary, science can be contrasted with pseudoscience in the following ways:

Science	Pseudoscience
Makes claims that can be rigorously tested through observation or experiment.	Makes claims that cannot be tested, even in principle.
Makes claims that are consistent with well-established scientific findings.	Makes claims that conflict with well-established scientific findings.
Actively seeks out falsifying data and confronts it openly and honestly.	Ignores or explains away falsifying data.
Uses language that is clear and specific.	Uses language that is vague and imprecise.
Constantly changes and progresses.	Often fails to change or progress.
Engages in serious ongoing research.	Usually makes no serious effort to conduct research.

EXERCISE 15.3

Use what you have learned in this and previous chapters to evaluate the thinking in the following passages. Identify any marks of pseudoscientific thinking you find.

1. I know that herbal medicines work for me. Last night I had a splitting headache after work. I drank a cup of herbal tea, and before I knew it the headache was gone.

2. I'm convinced that Nostradamus, the sixteenth-century astrologer and physician, could foresee the future. Consider this prophecy, for example:

> At night they will think they have seen the sun,
> When they see the half pig man:
> Noise, screams, battles seen fought in the skies:
> The brute beast will be heard to speak.

Clearly, this is a prophecy of the bombing of Baghdad at the outset of the Gulf War. The sun is the light of exploding bombs, the half pig man is a Stealth bomber pilot wearing goggles and an oxygen mask, and the beast that speaks refers to the use of the radio.[39]

3. This paper has been sent to you for Good Luck! The original copy is in New England. It has been around the world nine times. The Luck has been sent to you. You will receive Good Luck in four days. This is no joke.

   You will receive it in the mail. Send copies to the people you think need Good Luck. Do not send cash, as fate has no price. Do not keep this letter. It must leave your hands within 96 hours. . . . Since the copy must make the tour of the world, you must make twenty copies and send them to your friends and associates. After a few days you will get a surprise. This is true even if you are not superstitious.

   Note the following: Constantine Dess received the chain in 1953. He asked his secretary to make twenty copies and send them out. A few days later he won the lottery for two million dollars. Andy Duddit, an office employee, received the letter and he forgot it had to leave his hands in 96 hours. He lost his job. Later, after finding the letter again, he mailed out twenty copies. A few days later he got a better job. Mr. Fairchild received the letter and not believing it, threw it away. Nine days later he died.

   Please send no money. Please do not ignore it! It works. . . . Good Luck is coming your way! (chain letter)

4. I see where the guy that took the famous 1934 photograph of the Loch Ness monster has confessed that the picture was a fake. But I don't believe him. How do we know the guy isn't saying that just to get his name in the newspapers again?

5. Sure, psychics disagree all the time, but so do scientists. One month they tell us coffee is bad for us, the next month they tell us it's not. So, science isn't any more reliable than what you call "pseudoscience."

6. I believe in ESP. A few years ago, I woke up in the middle of the night in a cold sweat. I had this terrible feeling my sister was in trouble. I phoned her immediately, and her husband told me she had been in a serious car accident and was in the hospital. Surely that couldn't have been a mere coincidence.

7. *Graphologist* (handwriting expert): I can tell from your firm, flowing script that you like feeling happy, but don't like feeling lonely, depressed, or anxious. In fact, the more miserable you are, the more you dislike it.[40]

8. *Stefan:* Nothing bad ever happens to a person unless he or she deserves it.
   Lucy: O yeah? What about babies who die from AIDS? What have they done to deserve that?
   Stefan: Obviously, they did something bad in a previous life.

9. *Seventeeth-century cardinal* (explaining why he refuses to look into Galileo's telescope): I have no reason to look in your telescope; I know what I shall see. Aristotle has said there are no moons around planets other than our own, and I trust the authority of Aristotle more than I trust that newfangled instrument of yours.

10. If astrology were valid, twins would presumably have similar fates, since the stars and planets were all in the same positions at the time of their births. Yet plainly there are cases in which one twin dies in childhood and the other lives to a ripe old age. Astrologer Robert Parry offers the following response to this obvious objection: "Twins may not always share the same characteristics, of course, but their lives do generally develop at a similar pace. The differences when they occur are subtle ones, which is exactly what astrology would expect. Even in your example, where one twin dies while the other lives, clearly the same event, namely death, has entered both lives at the same time. One twin dies, while the other is touched radically by the sorrow and tragedy of the death of the other. Surely this is an argument for, rather than against astrology."[41]

11. *Earl:* Aliens abduct millions of people every year. They take them up to their spaceships and conduct all kinds of weird genetic and reproductive experiments on them.
    Zoe: Why don't these alien spacecraft ever show up on our radar?
    Earl: They have cloaking devices. Their technology is vastly superior to ours.
    Zoe: How come these aliens never set off burglar alarms or appear on home surveillance cameras? Why don't husbands or wives ever wake up and notice their spouses are missing?
    Earl: I told you, they're much too advanced ever to be detected by us. They probably just beam people up to their spaceships and put android look-alikes in their places.

12. God always answers prayers. But sometimes He gives us what is good for us, not what we ask for.

13. Of course dowsing works. I've seen my grandfather do it several times. Every time his well on his farm runs dry, he takes a forked stick and walks out into his pasture. When the stick dips toward to the ground, he knows just where to dig. Works every time.

14. Many so-called scientific studies have cast doubt on magnet therapy—a form of alternative treatment that claims that magnets can relieve pain and a host of other bodily ills. But why should we trust these studies? Doctors, scientists, and pharmaceutical companies stand to lose billions if this simple, natural remedy were shown to be effective.

15. Whenever harmonious music is being played in the presence of your crystal or amethyst, the mood and thoughts of the composer become deeply embedded

Never ignore, never refuse to see what may be thought against your own thought.
—Friedrich Nietzsche

within the very heart of the crystal and if you "listen" to the crystal afterward with your inner ear, you will often be able to pick up the esoteric meaning of the music itself. (from a healing-crystals Web site)

A CASE STUDY IN PSEUDOSCIENTIFIC THINKING: ASTROLOGY

> *You can make a better living in the world as a soothsayer than as a truthsayer.*
>
> —G. C. Lichtenberg

Can the stars and the planets affect people's personality and destiny? For thousands of years, believers in the ancient divinatory art of astrology have claimed that they can. Even in our own advanced scientific age, belief in astrology remains surprisingly strong. Polls show that about 25 percent of adult Americans believe that astrology works.[42] More than twelve hundred U.S. newspapers have a daily column on astrology. There are ten times more astrologers in the United States than there are astronomers.[43] And more money is spent each year in the United States on astrology than is spent on all astronomical research combined (excluding NASA).

Belief in astrology is very ancient. It began more than four thousand years ago in Mesopotamia (modern-day Iraq and Syria) and then spread throughout the ancient world. The form in which astrology exists today in the Western world is based largely on the work of Ptolemy, a Greek astronomer and astrologer who lived in Alexandria in the second century A.D.

Astrologers claim that human personality, behavior, and destiny are all strongly influenced by the position of the sun, moon, planets, and stars at the time of one's birth. Here, in a nutshell, is how astrology supposedly works.

Each year the sun appears to travel a certain path around the earth. This path is called the *ecliptic.* Astrologers take a 16-degree-wide belt of sky centering on the ecliptic and divide it into twelve equal 30-degree parts. These are the familiar *signs of the zodiac:* Aquarius, Pisces, Libra, Capricorn, and so forth. These signs are so named because they correspond roughly with the star-groupings, or constellations, that bear the same names. A person's "sun sign" is the sign of the zodiac the sun appeared to be in on the day of his or her birth. Thus, for example, anyone born between December 23 and January 19 is a Capricorn because the sun appears to be in the same part of the sky as the constellation Capricorn during that period.[44]

Sun signs are the basis for "pop astrology," the kind of astrology you find in newspaper horoscopes and popular astrology Web sites. Professional astrologers tend to be highly skeptical of these one-size-fits-all daily horoscopes. For really serious astrology, they insist, you need to take into account not only a person's sun sign but also the precise time and place of his or her birth, the positions of the planets, and a host of other factors.

Despite its antiquity and widespread acceptance, astrology has absolutely no scientific basis. Let's look at six reasons why this is so:[45]

1. Astrologers fail to identify a plausible physical force or mechanism that could explain astrology's alleged influences.
2. Astrologers fail to provide a convincing response to the problem of precession.
3. Astrologers fail to deal adequately with the discovery of three planets and other recent astronomical discoveries.
4. Astrologers often use vague, untestable language.
5. Astrologers fail to offer a convincing response to the problems of time twins and mass disasters.
6. Scientific tests do not support astrology's claims.

Astrologers Fail to Identify a Plausible Physical Force or Mechanism

Astrologers claim that extremely remote celestial objects have powerful effects on human personality, destiny, and behavior. But how, exactly? What forces or mechanisms could possibly explain such remarkable effects?

For the ancients the answer was simple: magic. The stars and planets were believed to be divine and were often associated with particular mytho-logical beings. The planet Venus, for example, was named after the Roman goddess of love and beauty. Accordingly, it was believed that anyone born under the influence of the planet Venus must be romantic, sensitive, emotional, and artistic. Similarly, anyone born under the influence of the planet Mars was thought to be aggressive and courageous, since Mars was the Roman god of war.

We, of course, no longer believe in these mythical associations. So what mechanisms or forces could possibly explain astrology's alleged influences?

Astrologers have proposed five possible explanations:

- gravity
- tidal forces
- electromagnetic forces
- magnetic fields
- emitted particles

Unfortunately, none of these mechanisms is an even remotely plausible candidate. Gravity, tidal forces, and electromagnetic forces are all far too weak to have any significant effect on human behavior over the vast distances of space. In fact, many ordinary objects around you exert far stronger forces on you than remote planets and stars. For example, the book you are now holding exerts about *one billion times* as much tidal force on you as does the planet Mars.[46] Magnetic fields and emitted particles are even less plausible mechanisms because not all astrologically significant celestial objects have magnetic fields (Venus and the moon do not, for example), and none of the planets in our solar system emits any particles.[47]

Of course, it is possible that there is some mysterious, not-yet-discovered force that could explain astrology's alleged influences on human life. But as astronomer George Abell points out, this force would have to be one with very strange properties:

> It would have to emanate from some but not all celestial bodies, have to affect some but not all things on earth, and its strength could not depend on the distances, masses, or other characteristics of those [celestial bodies] giving rise to it. In other words it would lack the universality, order, and harmony found for every other force and natural law ever discovered that applies in the real universe.[48]

Although the existence of such a force cannot be completely ruled out, it seems very unlikely given what we know about the fundamental laws and forces of nature.

The Problem of Precession   Scientists have long known that, owing to the gravitational pull of the sun and the moon, the earth slowly "wobbles" in its orbit, much like a spinning top or gyroscope. As a consequence the apparent positions of the stars relative to the sun slowly change over time. This is a phenomenon astronomers call *precession*. This shift in the apparent positions of the stars is extremely slow—only about 1 degree every seventy-one years—but in the two thousand years since the signs of the zodiac became fixed, the change has been significant. The position of the sun relative to the constellations has now shifted almost a whole astrological sign to the east. So, for example, if your horoscope says you are an Aries, it is very likely that the sun was actually in the constellation of Pisces on the day of your birth. Professional astrologers are well aware of this fact but are divided over the best way to deal with it. Most astrologers simply shrug off the problem, claiming that "constellations are simply not that important."[49] This response, however, is inconsistent with the vital role constellations have always played in astrological theory, and it leaves it utterly mysterious how an arbitrary division of signs can fundamentally affect human character and destiny. Other astrologers claim that the constellations "remember" the influences they had two thousand years ago! They fail to explain, however, why the constellations don't remember the influences they had in even earlier epochs.[50]

Astrology Is Not Progressive   We have seen that pseudoscience, unlike real science, is often static; it fails to change in the light of advancing knowledge. Let's consider two examples of astrology's stagnant character: (1) its inability to deal convincingly with the discovery of three more planets and other recently discovered celestial objects and (2) its failure to take into account the arbitrary nature of constellations.

Funeral by funeral, scientific theory advances.
—Paul Samuelson

For thousands of years, astrologers consistently taught that there are only seven celestial bodies in the solar system other than Earth: the sun, the moon, Mercury, Venus, Mars, Saturn, and Jupiter. In recent centuries, however, astronomers have discovered the planet Uranus in 1781, Neptune in 1846, and the "dwarf planet" Pluto in 1930, as well as a multitude of moons and many large asteroids and comets. These discoveries pose two major problems for astrology.

First, if astrology were true, why weren't astrologers able to deduce the existence of Uranus, Neptune, and Pluto long before scientists discovered them? If, as astrologers now claim, these planets have effects on human life, then astrologers' predictions must have been systematically in error for the past two thousand years.[51] Why during these centuries wasn't there even a single astrologer who noticed these errors and predicted the eventual discovery of unknown planets to account for them?[52]

Second, why is it that only stars, planets, the sun, and our own moon have any astrological influences? Since the time of Galileo (1564–1642), scientists have discovered more than fifty additional moons in our solar system. Two of these moons (Ganymede and Titan) are larger than the planets Pluto and Mercury. In addition, many thousands of asteroids have been discovered. Some of these asteroids are larger than all but a few of the moons in our solar system. (One asteroid has even been found to have its own satellite.) Why does remote Pluto, for example, have astrological influences when closer and, in a few instances, more massive moons and asteroids do not?[53]

Another problem for astrology is its failure to deal convincingly with our modern scientific understanding of constellations. Ancient astrologers believed that the constellations really were fixed, neutrally observable "pictures in the sky." We now know that this is totally false. Other cultures see quite different pictures from those we see; the appearance of the constellations changes over time (one million years ago the Big Dipper looked like a spear to our ancestors on the African savanna); and stars that appear to us to be close together in space may in fact be millions of light-years apart from one another.

Why is this a problem for astrology? Because the personality characteristics astrologers associate with particular sun signs presuppose that the constellations are real rather than merely perceiver-relative human constructions. Consider the following list, which shows the constellations of the zodiac, their namesakes, and selected sun-sign personality characteristics:

> *You can only predict things after they've happened.*
> —Eugene Ionesco

Constellation and Symbol	Namesake	Selected Characteristics
Aries	ram	headstrong, impulsive, quick-tempered
Taurus	bull	plodding, patient, stubborn
Gemini	twins	vacillating, split personality
Cancer	crab	clinging, protective exterior shell
Leo	lion	proud, forceful, born leader
Virgo	virgin	reticent, modest
Libra	scales	just, harmonious, balanced
Scorpius	scorpion	secretive, troublesome, aggressive
Sagittarius	archer	active, aims for target
Capricorn	goat	tenacious
Aquarius	water carrier	humanitarian, serving mankind
Pisces	fish	attracted to sea and alcohol[54]

Notice the kind of thinking implicit in these associations: "The constellation Taurus sort of looks like a bull. Bulls are stubborn and plodding. Therefore, Tauruses must be stubborn and plodding." This makes clear at a glance the kind of magical thinking that has always been the true basis of astrology.

> *Science is what we have learned about how not to fool ourselves.*
>
> —Richard Feynman

Astrology Uses Vague, Untestable Language   One of the clearest signs that astrology is a pseudoscience is its frequent use of vague, untestable language. Here, for example, is a recent daily horoscope for Taurus people offered on the Excite.com astrology Web site:

> *Taurus* (April 20–May 20): Your plans with friends could go awry. If you're stubborn enough to keep going, you may still achieve your goals. The longer you hang on, the more likely you are to achieve your goals.

> *The astrologers have an easy game when they warn us, as they do, of great and imminent changes and revolutions; their prophecies are present and palpable; no need to go to the stars for that.*
>
> —Michel de Montaigne

This passage contains two deceptive uses of language. First, it uses the weasel words *could* and *may*. *Weasel words,* as you will recall, are words used to water down a claim so that it ends up saying much less than it may appear to say. In saying only that "your plans with friends *could* go awry" and that "you *may* achieve your goals," the writer is making claims that are so vague and highly qualified that almost nothing could be counted as disproving them. Second, the passage uses general Barnum-type language that can readily be interpreted as applying to almost anyone. (Isn't it virtually true by definition that the longer you keep going the more likely you are to achieve your goals?) By using vague and deceptive language like this, a skillful horoscope writer can fool millions into believing that he or she can really foresee the future.

Of course, astrologers do sometimes make statements that are specific enough to be checked. For example, according to the astrology.com Web site, the principal writer of this chapter, as an Aquarian, should have the following preferences in music:

> **Music:** The Water Bearer's favorite goal is to change the world. You've already worn out several copies of the *Hair* soundtrack, as you like to listen to music based on an era where everyone was trying to make the world a better and more unified place. From the Grateful Dead to the Allman Brothers, you are now likely to be an avid fan of Phish—or any party band for that matter. Aquarians are social and appreciate a good sing-along classic.[55]

> *Astrology rests on a proven principle, namely that if you know the exact positions where the moon and the various planets were when a person was born, you can get this person to give you money.*
>
> —Dave Barry

As a matter of fact, my tastes run more to classical and folk music—though I confess I do sometimes find myself humming some of the racier lyrics from *Hair.*

EXERCISE 15.4

I. Visit the astrology Web site at *www.astrology.com* (or a similar Web site) and check out the supposed preferences for food, music, sports, and television for people with your sun sign. Then check out the alleged preferences for your parents. Do you find any difference in the accuracy of the profiles? If so, what might explain the difference?

II. Can people accurately pick out their own daily horoscopes? Here is a simple way to find out. The day before your next class meeting, a student volunteer will copy down the twelve daily horoscopes from a major daily newspaper or an astrology Web site. The horoscopes should be typed or pasted randomly on a single page, numbered 1–12, with all references to specific zodiac signs removed. Here's an example of how the page might look:

Please write your zodiac sign here: _____
Circle the number that best describes the type of day you had yesterday.
(1) Love is a whirlwind. This is a day when you'll explain, announce, and persuade. On the job, realize that you have more to offer.
(2) A lucky meeting produces revenue. There are monetary limits on fun, but this should only be an incentive to the creative imagination.
(3) A dashing, desirous urgency manifests itself in marvelous romantic gestures. Ignore one who tries to compete with you. . . .[56]

[And so on, for all twelve horoscopes.]

Make enough copies for each student in the class, then administer the test and tabulate the results.

The Problems of Time Twins and Mass Disasters   Most astrologers claim that a person's destiny is strongly influenced by the position of the stars and the planets at the moment of that person's birth. Since ancient times critics have noted two obvious objections to such a claim. First, if astrology were true, shouldn't *time twins* (i.e., biologically unrelated persons born at exactly the same time and place) have very similar destinies?[57] Second, how can astrologers explain *mass disasters*—tragic events such as earthquakes or hurricanes in which hundreds or thousands of people may die at the same time? Are we to believe, for example, that everyone who drowned aboard the *Titanic* had the same foreboding horoscope?

Astrologers commonly respond to the time-twins objection by claiming that there are many well-documented cases in which time twins have been found to have led remarkably similar lives.[58] One often-cited example involves actor Rudolph Valentino. When Valentino died, the movie industry launched a nationwide search for a double. One of the most convincing candidates turned out to have been born in the same area and on the same day as Valentino.[59]

Isolated examples like this, however, don't prove anything. One would expect to find a certain number of "amazing parallels" like this purely by chance. The relevant question is whether time twins exhibit similarities in personality, destiny, career choice, and so forth *that cannot be explained by mere chance*. Studies of time twins have found no evidence that this is the case.[60]

Astrologers often attempt to explain mass disasters by claiming that whole *nations* have horoscopes just as individuals do and that sometimes the horoscopes of nations override those of individuals.[61] This response is unconvincing for several reasons. First, many mass disasters (e.g., some hurricanes, earthquakes, and plane crashes) involve people from many different nations. Second, there are many relevant differences between nations and individuals. For example, nations, unlike individuals, often have fluid borders and no clear "date of birth." Third, there is no agreement among astrologers about how to determine when a nation's horoscope will override those of individuals. Fourth, numerous studies have found no evidence that astrologers can accurately predict major national events.[62]

Scientific Tests Do Not Support Astrology's Claims   In science the bottom-line question is always: *Does it work?* Dozens of scientific studies of astrology have been conducted over the past few decades. The clear verdict of these studies is that astrology does *not* work. Let's look at a few representative studies.

Many astrologers claim there is a correlation between sun sign and physical appearance. According to astrologer Sandra Shulman, for example, those born under the sign of Aries tend to be roundheaded and snub-nosed, with reddish or light brown hair.[63] To test such claims, researchers R. B. Culver and P. A. Ianna surveyed hundreds of college students. They studied more than thirty physical characteristics, including height, weight, hair color, skin complexion, and head size. Not a single physical feature they examined had any correlation with sun sign.[64]

Most astrologers also claim that some sun signs make for compatible personal relationships and others do not. If that were true, reasoned psychologist Bernard I. Silverman, then pairs with compatible sun signs should show higher rates of marriage and lower rates of divorce than pairs with incompatible sun signs. When Silverman looked at the birth dates of 2,978 Michigan couples who were getting married and 478 couples who were getting divorced, however, he found no correlation between sun sign and rates of marriage or divorce.[65]

Another claim commonly made by astrologers is that a person's sun sign strongly influences his or her choice of a career. Many astrologers claim, for example, that Leos tend to become politicians. To test such claims, scientist John D. McGervey looked at the birth dates of 16,634 scientists and 6,475 politicians. He found no correlation between sun sign and either of these two career choices.[66] Studies of some sixty other careers and occupations have likewise found no correlation between astrological sign and choice of profession.[67]

In addition, most astrologers also claim that personality is strongly influenced by sun signs. Psychologist W. Grant Dahlstrom and his associates tested this claim by administering the Minnesota Multiphasic Personality Inventory (MMPI) to 2,600 adults. They found no significant correlations between sun sign and any of the many personality traits measured by the MMPI.[68]

It might be objected that statistical studies of this kind are not fair tests of astrology because sun signs alone are not enough for an accurate astrological reading. Virtually all astrologers admit, however, that sun signs have at least some influence on personality, career choice, and so on. If that were true, then some systematic statistical correlations should be discoverable.

In fact, several scientific studies have been done that involved complete astrological birth charts, not just subjects' sun signs. One of the best known of these studies was conducted by San Diego State University physicist Shawn Carlson.

Carlson gave thirty of the world's most prominent astrologers the complete natal horoscopes of 116 subjects. He then asked the astrologers to match these horoscopes against three California Personality Inventory (CPI) psychological profiles. One profile was the subject's actual psychological profile; the other two were chosen at random. The result: the astrologers did no better than chance.[69]

A few scientific studies have found evidence that *weakly* supports certain claims of astrology. For example, Michael Gauquelin, a respected French researcher, published a study in 1955 that indicated a statistically significant correlation between certain positions of the planet Mars and the births of sports champions. More recent studies, however, have generally failed to replicate Gauquelin's findings, and serious questions have been raised about the reliability of his data.[70]

In short, scientific tests do *not* support astrology's claims. For these and other reasons we have noted, astrology must be regarded as a pseudoscience.

My business is to teach my aspirations to conform themselves to fact, not to try to make facts harmonize with my aspirations.

—Thomas Henry Huxley

EXERCISE 15.5

I. Discuss the following questions in small groups. Be prepared to share the highlights of your discussions with the class as a whole.

1. Do you agree that astrology is a pseudoscience? Why or why not?

2. If astrology has no scientific basis, why do so many people believe in it? What accounts for its persistent appeal?

II. In small groups, design a scientific study to test the hypothesis that time twins tend to have similar personalities and destinies.

III. In small groups, research and present to the class one of the following topics. Is the phenomenon an example of pseudoscience? Why or why not?

alien abductions	creation science	palmistry
ancient astronauts	dowsing	precognition
Atlantis	healing crystals	pyramid power
Bermuda Triangle	homeopathy	reflexology
Bible code	Loch Ness monster	reincarnation
Bigfoot	magnet therapy	Roswell crash
channeling	moon madness	therapeutic touch
clairvoyance	Nostradamus	UFOs

IV. Write a short argumentative paper (the precise length will be determined by your instructor) on one of the topics listed in Exercise III. Consult Chapters 12 and 13 for guidelines on writing argumentative papers.

SUMMARY

1. *Science* is a method of inquiry that seeks to describe, explain, and predict occurrences in the physical or natural world by means of careful observation and experiment. Science is the most powerful intellectual tool ever discovered, and it profoundly influences almost every aspect of our daily lives. Yet surveys show that a large percentage of Americans know distressingly little about science or its methods and values.

2. Although there is no single "scientific method" that all scientists use, most scientific reasoning does follow a basic pattern. That pattern consists of four steps:
   - Identify the problem.
   - Gather relevant data.
   - Formulate hypotheses to explain the data.
   - Test the hypotheses by observation or experiment.

3. Science is the most reliable method we have for discovering empirically verifiable truths about the physical or natural world. But there are many important questions that science cannot answer. Among these are questions of meaning and questions of value.

4. *Pseudoscience* is false science—that is, unscientific thinking masquerading as scientific thinking. We looked at six common marks of pseudoscience:
   - It makes claims that are not testable.
   - It makes claims that are inconsistent with well-established scientific truths.
   - It explains away or ignores falsifying data.
   - It uses vague language.
   - It is not progressive.
   - It often involves no serious effort to conduct research.

5. We looked in detail at an example of pseudoscientific thinking: astrology. We argued that astrology is a pseudoscience for the following reasons:
   - Astrologers fail to identify a plausible physical force or mechanism that could explain astrology's alleged influences.

- Astrologers fail to provide a convincing response to the problem of precession.
- Astrologers fail to deal adequately with the discovery of three planets and other recent astronomical discoveries.
- Astrologers often use vague, untestable language.
- Astrologers fail to offer a convincing response to the problems of time twins and mass disasters.
- Scientific tests do not support astrology's claims.

NOTES

CHAPTER 1

1. Our discussion of critical thinking standards is indebted to Richard Paul, *Critical Thinking: What Every Person Needs to Survive in a Rapidly Changing World* (Rohnert Park, CA: Center for Critical Thinking and Moral Critique, 1990), pp. 51–52.
2. Martin Heidegger, *Being and Time,* trans. John Macquarrie and Edward Robinson (San Francisco: HarperSanFrancisco, 1962), pp. 376–77. Originally published in 1927.
3. William Strunk Jr. and E. B. White, *The Elements of Style,* 3rd ed. (New York: Macmillan, 1979), p. 79.
4. William H. Herndon, quoted in David Hackett Fischer, *Historians' Fallacies: Toward a Logic of Historical Thought* (New York: Harper & Row, 1970), p. 291.
5. Harold Kushner, *When All You've Ever Wanted Isn't Enough: The Search for a Life That Matters* (New York: Pocket Books, 1986), p. 15.
6. Used by permission of Kenneth R. Merrill.
7. Erma Bombeck, *All I Know about Animal Behavior I Learned in Loehmann's Dressing Room* (New York: HarperPaperbacks, 1995), p. 66.
8. Bertrand Russell, *Unpopular Essays* (New York: Simon & Schuster, 1950), pp. 75–76.
9. Cited in Thomas Gilovich, *How We Know What Isn't So: The Fallibility of Human Reason in Everyday Life* (New York: Free Press, 1991), p. 77. The same survey found that only 2 percent of respondents rated themselves below average in their leadership ability. Another survey found that 86 percent of Australians rate their job performance as above average. David G. Myers, *The Pursuit of Happiness* (New York: Avon, 1993), p. 111.
10. Adapted from J. E. Russo and P. J. H. Schoemaker, *Decision Traps: Ten Barriers to Brilliant Decision Making and How to Overcome Them* (New York: Simon & Schuster, 1989), p. 71.
11. Answers: 1. 39 years; 2. 4,187 miles; 3. 12.3% (2005); 4. 39 books; 5. 2,160 miles; 6. 390,000 pounds; 7. 36,132,147 (U.S. Census Bureau 2005 estimate); 8. 1756; 9. 5,959 miles; 10. 36,198 feet.
12. For a discussion of common critical thinking errors in poker, see Gregory Bassham and Marc C. Marchese, "Don't Play on Tilt! Avoiding Seven Costly Critical Thinking Errors in Poker," in Eric Bronson, ed., *Poker and Philosophy* (Chicago: Open Court, 2005), pp. 81–92.
13. Doyle Brunson, *Poker Wisdom of a Champion* (Cooper Station, NY: Cardoza Publishing, 2003), pp. 90–91.
14. Quoted in Paul, *Critical Thinking,* pp. 91–92.
15. See Stanley Milgram, *Obedience to Authority: An Experimental View* (New York: Harper & Row, 1974).
16. Joel Rudinow and Vincent E. Barry, *Invitation to Critical Thinking,* 4th ed. (Ft. Worth, TX: Harcourt College Publishers, 1999), p. 20.
17. Grant H. Cornwell, "From Pluralism to Relativism and Back Again: Philosophy's Role in an Inclusive Curriculum," *Teaching Philosophy* 14:2 (June 1991), pp. 143–153. Used with permission.
18. There is a third way in which moral relativism can lead to conflicting moral duties, namely, when a relativist belongs to a culture that holds conflicting moral beliefs. As a little Socratic questioning quickly makes clear, most people unwittingly hold conflicting moral beliefs. To take a simple example: a child might believe both that "I should always do what my teacher tells me" and that "I should always do what my parents tell me," without realizing that these two rules can conflict. A whole society, of course, can also hold inconsistent moral beliefs and, indeed, is even more likely to do so than an individual, since a society has no single, unifying mind to iron out conflicts. At one time, for instance, a majority of Americans believed both that "unjustified discrimination is wrong" and that "women should not be permitted to vote," which we recognize to be inconsistent, though few people at the time did. Because a relativist must share the moral beliefs of his society (or at least those beliefs he is aware of), he may find himself committed to inconsistent beliefs.
19. *Weekly World News,* March 11, 2000.
20. This list of critical thinking dispositions is drawn largely from three sources: Vincent Ryan Ruggiero, *Beyond Feelings: A Guide to Critical Thinking,* 5th ed. (Mountain View, CA: Mayfield, 1998), pp. 13–14; John Chaffee, *The Thinker's Way* (Boston: Little, Brown, 1998), pp. 34–37; and Paul, *Critical Thinking,* p. 54.

CHAPTER 2

1. More precisely, a statement (or proposition) is the truth claim asserted by a sentence or part of a sentence that is capable of standing alone as a declarative sentence. Thus, the French sentence *Le ciel est bleu* and the English sentence *The sky is blue* have the same meaning, and hence express the same statement, even though they are different sentences in different languages. For purposes of this text, the distinction between declarative sentences and statements will largely be ignored.
2. *Washington Post,* December 26, 1999, p. B3.
3. This list is adapted from Sherry Diestler, *Becoming a Critical Thinker: A User-Friendly Manual,* 2nd ed. (Upper Saddle River, NJ: Prentice Hall, 1998), pp. 8, 10.
4. "Truck Driver Takes to Skies in Lawn Chair," *New York Times,* July 3, 1982; "Lawn-Chair Pilot Faces $4,000 in Fines," *New York Times,* December 19, 1982.
5. John M. Murrin et al., *Liberty, Equality, Power: A History of the American People,* 2nd ed. (Fort Worth, TX: Harcourt Brace, 1999), p. 1067.
6. Stephen Nathanson, *Should We Consent to Be Governed? A Short Introduction to Political Philosophy* (Belmont, CA: Wadsworth, 1992), p. 70.
7. Harold Kushner, *When All You've Ever Wanted Isn't Enough: The Search for a Life That Matters* (New York: Pocket Books, 1986), p. 156.
8. Adapted from an example in Wilson Follett, *Modern American Usage* (New York: Hill and Wang, 1966), p. 93.
9. Nadine Strossen, "Regulating Racist Speech on Campus: A Modest Proposal?" *1990 Duke Law Journal* (June 1990), p. 489.
10. *Portland Oregonian,* August 23, 1999.

CHAPTER 3

1. These exercises are loosely adapted from similar exercises in Kathleen Dean Moore, *Reasoning and Writing* (New York: Macmillan, 1993), p. 103.
2. Adapted from John Hoagland, *Critical Thinking,* 2nd ed. (Newport News, VA: Vale Press, 1995), p. 68.
3. In logic a *particular statement* refers to *some but not all members* of a particular class. For example, "Tom Cruise is an actor" and "Some mushrooms are poisonous" are particular statements. A *general statement* refers to *all* members of a particular class—for example, "All dogs are mammals."
4. There are cases in which an arguer mistakenly believes that his premises provide only probable support for the truth of his conclusion when in fact they provide logically conclusive support. Such cases are rare, however, and for purposes of this text they will be ignored.
5. David Weiss, "Man Struck by Train Says He, Brother Fell Asleep on Tracks," *Wilkes-Barre Times Leader,* November 21, 2001, p. 13A.
6. In this section and the following, we are indebted to Patrick J. Hurley, *A Concise Introduction to Logic,* 9th ed. (Belmont, CA: Wadsworth, 2006), pp. 32–35.
7. Some critical thinking texts define *hypothetical syllogism* more narrowly, as an argument that has the following form: "If A then B; if B then C; therefore, if A then C." We prefer to call arguments of this pattern *pure hypothetical syllogisms* or *chain arguments.*
8. Latin for "denying mode" or "the way of denying."

9. A more precise definition is offered in Chapter 9.
10. Notice the pattern of this argument: "Either A is true or B is true. But A isn't true; therefore, B is true." Arguments of this pattern are known as *disjunctive syllogisms* and are one variety of arguments by elimination.
11. Thus, not all arguments that refer to numbers or quantities are arguments based on mathematics. Statistical arguments, for example, as we see shortly, are usually best treated as inductive.
12. Dave Barry, *Dave Barry Turns 50* (New York: Crown Publishers, 1998), p. 176.
13. Robert Fulghum, *It Was on Fire When I Lay Down on It* (New York: Ivy Books, 1989), p. 3.
14. It should be noted that *cogent* is used here in a technical sense that does not conform perfectly with ordinary usage. (In ordinary usage, *cogent* means something like "forcible or properly convincing.") An inductive argument can certainly be powerful and convincing (and in that sense a "good" inductive argument) even if some of its premises are false. A lawyer, for example, might present to a jury an inductive argument with seven absolutely knockdown reasons why Sturdley is guilty of robbing his local Piggly-Wiggly store, plus an eighth premise that is false. Overall, the lawyer's argument would be properly convincing but not *cogent* in the sense we have defined. Our thanks to Sean Martin and his colleagues for drawing our attention to this issue.
15. This example is borrowed from David A. Conway and Ronald Munson, *The Elements of Reasoning,* 2nd ed. (Belmont, CA: Wadsworth, 1997), p. 40.
16. Daniel Butler, Alan Ray, Leland Gregory, *America's Dumbest Criminals* (Nashville, TN: Rutledge Hill Press, 1995), pp. 147–48 (slightly adapted).
17. This is a stock example that exists in many versions. This version is borrowed from Hurley, *A Concise Introduction to Logic,* p. 142.

CHAPTER 4

1. *Parade,* December 27, 1998, p. 8.
2. Adapted from an example in Andrea Lunsford and Robert Connors, *The St. Martin's Handbook,* 2nd ed. (New York: St. Martin's Press, 1992), p. 288.
3. S. Morris Engel, *With Good Reason: An Introduction to Informal Fallacies,* 5th ed. (New York: St. Martin's Press, 1994), p. 119.
4. Ibid., p. 121.
5. Richard L. Epstein, *Workbook for Critical Thinking* (Belmont, CA: Wadsworth, 1999), p. 19.
6. Quoted in Clifton Fadiman, ed., *The Little, Brown Book of Anecdotes* (Boston: Little, Brown, 1985), p. 504.
7. Quoted in Sherry Diestler, *Becoming a Critical Thinker: A User-Friendly Manual* (Upper Saddle River, NJ: Prentice Hall, 1998), p. 282.
8. Fadiman, *The Little, Brown Book of Anecdotes,* p. 140.
9. Ibid., p. 171.
10. William Shakespeare, *Two Gentlemen of Verona,* Act 2, Scene 4.
11. Quoted in Anders Henriksson, "The Ultimate Rewrite: A Plague of Boobs," *The Wilson Quarterly* (Fall 1983), p. 5.
12. Leon Jaroff, "The Magic Is Back," *Time,* October 10, 1988, p. 20.
13. "Steve Goldstein, "Soviets Bask in Success of First Shuttle," *Philadelphia Inquirer,* November 16, 1988, p. A3.

14. William Lutz, "The New Doublespeak," *Newsweek,* August 12, 1996, p. 57.

CHAPTER 5

1. It follows from this definition that an argument is not fallacious simply because it contains false premises. Some logicians prefer to define *fallacy* more broadly as "any faulty or defective argument." Given the eclectic mix of argumentative errors and deceptive tactics traditionally classified as "fallacies," neither definition is completely adequate. We prefer our narrower definition because it fits more closely with traditional usage.

2. Many critical thinking texts distinguish between "formal" and "informal" fallacies. The distinction is roughly this: *formal fallacies* are fallacious arguments that involve *explicit* use of an invalid argument form, whereas *informal fallacies* are fallacious arguments that do not. According to this definition, most of the arguments we discuss in this chapter and the next are informal fallacies. In this text we avoid the distinction between formal and informal fallacies because (a) students find it confusing and (b) in practice the distinction often breaks down. For more on the traditional distinction between formal and informal fallacies, see Patrick J. Hurley, *A Concise Introduction to Logic,* 9th ed. (Belmont, CA: Wadsworth, 2006), pp. 110–11.

3. These helpful distinctions are borrowed from Trudy Govier, *A Practical Study of Argument,* 5th ed. (Belmont, CA: Wadsworth, 2001), pp. 174–75.

4. An argument's premises provide "probable reasons" for a conclusion if the premises, if true, make the conclusion likely.

5. Scott Adams, *The Dilbert Principle* (New York: Harper Business, 1996), p. 9.

6. Quoted in Clifton Fadiman, ed., *The Little, Brown Book of Anecdotes* (Boston: Little, Brown, 1985), p. 357.

7. The traditional name of this fallacy is *ad hominem* abusive. (*Ad hominem* is a Latin phrase meaning "against the person.")

8. The traditional name for this fallacy is *ad hominem* circumstantial. Some critical thinking texts define the fallacy slightly more broadly than we do.

9. The traditional name for this fallacy is *tu quoque* (pronounced "too-kwo-kway"), which is Latin for "you too." The fallacy is often treated as a variety of the personal attack fallacy.

10. Quoted in the *Wilkes-Barre Times Leader,* January 27, 2000.

11. Quoted in Eleanor and Reginald Jebb, *Belloc, The Man* (Westminster, MD: The Newman Press, 1957), p. 19.

12. Often called appeal to fear or appeal to force. The traditional Latin name for this fallacy is *argumentum ad baculum* (literally, "argument to the stick").

13. The traditional name for this fallacy is *argumentum ad misericordiam* (Latin for "argument to mercy").

14. Adapted from Alan Brinton, "Pathos and the 'Appeal to Emotion': An Aristotelian Analysis," *History of Philosophy Quarterly* 5 (1989), p. 211.

15. See the definition of *red herring* and the supporting passage cited from the third edition of Nicholas Cox's *The Gentleman's Recreation* (1686) in *The Compact Edition of the Oxford English Dictionary* (New York: Oxford University Press, 1971).

16. This example is adapted from Hurley, *A Concise Introduction to Logic,* p. 152.

17. Thomas V. Morris, *Making Sense of It All: Pascal and the Meaning of Life* (Grand Rapids, MI: William B. Eerdmans Publishing, 1992), p. 38.

CHAPTER 6

1. Alvin Plantinga, *Warrant and Proper Function* (New York: Oxford University Press, 1993), p. 77.

2. Notice that this is consistent with what we said in Chapter 5 about the fallacy of attacking the motive—the fallacy of criticizing a person's motivation for offering a particular argument or claim, *rather than examining the worth of the argument or claim itself.* In these examples, questioning the testifier's motives is necessary to evaluate the worth of the argument.

3. *Weekly World News,* October 10, 1999.

4. Quoted in Dr. Laurence J. Peter, *Peter's Quotations* (New York: Morrow, 1977), p. 296.

5. Other names for this fallacy include *false dilemma, false dichotomy,* the *either-or fallacy,* and the *black-and-white fallacy.* Our discussion of this fallacy is indebted to Patrick Hurley, *A Concise Introduction to Logic,* 9th ed. (Belmont, CA: Wadsworth, 2006), pp. 149–50.

6. *USA Today News,* July 22, 2000; available online at *www.usatoday.com/news/nwveird.htm.*

7. Notice that the only thing wrong with these arguments is that they have a false premise: they falsely claim that there are only two relevant alternatives when in fact there are more than two. Strictly speaking, therefore, the fallacy of false alternatives, like the fallacy of begging the question, is not a fallacy. We follow convention, however, in treating them as fallacies.

8. House of Commons Debates of Canada, June 10, 1982. Quoted in Douglas N. Walton, *Begging the Question* (New York: Greenwood Press, 1991), p. 239.

9. For a fuller discussion of the post hoc fallacy and other forms of the questionable cause fallacy, see pages 323–330.

10. This example is adapted from Hurley, *A Concise Introduction to Logic,* p. 142.

11. This example is adapted from a similar example in C. Stephen Layman, *The Power of Logic* (Mountain View, CA: Mayfield, 1999), p. 180.

12. According to a 1996 poll, only 39 percent of scientists believe in a personal God, compared with more than 90 percent of the general population. See Edward J. Larson and Larry Witham, "Scientists Are Still Keeping the Faith," *Nature* 386 (1997), pp. 435–36.

13. The argument does commit a fallacy. Specifically, it commits the fallacy of hasty conclusion. The *fallacy of hasty conclusion* occurs when an arguer jumps to a conclusion without adequate evidence. Most of the fallacies we discuss in this chapter are subvarieties of the fallacy of hasty conclusion.

14. This threefold analysis is adapted from Ralph H. Johnson and J. Anthony Blair, *Logical Self-Defense,* U.S. ed. (New York: McGraw-Hill, 1994), p. 183.

15. From a newspaper call-in column, *Wilkes-Barre Times Leader,* January 23, 2000.

16. For a fuller discussion of reasoning by analogy, see pages 312–323.

17. Adapted from an oft-quoted saying of Yogi Berra. See Clifton Fadiman, ed., *The Little, Brown Book of Anecdotes* (Boston: Little, Brown, 1985), p. 61.

18. This example is adapted from an anecdote told by Bertrand Russell in his book *Human Knowledge: Its Scope and Limits* (New York: Simon & Schuster, 1948), p. 180.

19. This example was inspired by a remark made by Ronald Reagan.

20. Quoted in David Halberstam, *The Fifties* (New York: Fawcett Columbine, 1993), p. 10.

21. Quoted in Stephen E. Ambrose, *Citizen Soldiers* (New York: Simon & Schuster, 1997), p. 105 (slightly adapted).

22. Quoted in Al Franken, *Rush Limbaugh Is a Big Fat Idiot and Other Observations* (New York: Island Books, 1996), p. 292.

23. Our thanks to Brooke Moore and Richard Parker for helpful suggestions on this exercise.

CHAPTER 7

1. More precisely still, a premise is *linked* just in case (1) the amount of support it provides for the conclusion would be affected (i.e., either weakened or strengthened) by the omission of some other premise in the argument, or (2) its omission from the argument would affect the amount of support provided by some other premise in the argument. Similarly, a premise is *independent* when neither of these two conditions obtains. For a fuller discussion, see Gregory Bassham, "Linked and Independent Premises: A New Analysis," in Frans H. van Eemeren et al., eds., *Proceedings of the Fifth Conference of the International Society for the Study of Argumentation* (Amsterdam: Sic Sat, 2003), pp. 69–73. For purposes of this introductory text, these technical refinements can be safely ignored.

2. Thomas Lickona, *Educating for Character: How Our Schools Can Teach Respect and Responsibility* (New York: Bantam, 1991), p. 77.

3. Our discussion in this section is indebted to C. Stephen Layman, *The Power of Logic* (Mountain View, CA: Mayfield, 1999), pp. 73–74.

4. This example is adapted from an argument discussed (but not endorsed) by C. S. Lewis in his book *God in the Dock: Essays on Theology and Ethics* (Grand Rapids, MI: William B. Eerdmans Publishing, 1970), p. 105.

5. This argument is stated but not endorsed by Pierce and VanDeveer.

6. This argument is stated but not endorsed by Morris.

7. This argument is a restatement of an argument originally presented by seventeenth-century French philosopher René Descartes.

8. *Washington Post,* December 26, 1999.

9. We owe this example to the Plain English Homepage at *www.plainenglish.co.uk/examples.html.*

10. Thanks to our colleague Len Gorney for passing along this (slightly adapted) example to us.

11. This example is borrowed from William Strunk Jr. and E. B. White, *The Elements of Style,* 3rd ed. (New York: Macmillan, 1979), p. 25.

12. David Hume, *Dialogues Concerning Natural Religion,* ed. Norman Kemp Smith (Indianapolis: BobbsMerrill Educational Publishing, 1947), p. 143.

13. See pages 46–48 above for a discussion of the principle of charity.

14. "No Sex in Show Me State?" *Wilkes-Barre Times Leader,* November 6, 1994.

15. Our formulation of these rules is indebted to Robert Paul Churchill, *Logic: An Introduction,* 2nd ed. (New York:

St. Martin's Press, 1990), pp. 61–63; and David A. Conway and Ronald Munson, *The Elements of Reasoning,* 2nd ed. (Belmont, CA: Wadsworth, 1997), pp. 9–10.

16. This example is borrowed from Thomas V. Morris, *Making Sense of It All: Pascal and the Meaning of Life* (Grand Rapids, MI: William B. Eerdmans Publishing, 1992), p. 55.

17. Charles E. Sheedy, *The Christian Virtues,* 2nd ed. (Notre Dame, IN: University of Notre Dame Press, 1951), p. 15.

18. Theodore Schick Jr., "Fate, Freedom and Foreknowledge," in William Irwin, ed., *The Matrix and Philosophy: Welcome to the Desert of the Real* (Chicago: Open Court, 2003), pp. 94–95.

19. *Baton Rouge Advocate,* April 4, 1998. Our thanks to Professor Barbara Forrest for this example and the accompanying standardization.

20. Bob Butts, letter to the editor, *Wilkes-Barre Times Leader,* September 16, 1998.

CHAPTER 8

1. Some of these examples are borrowed from Tom Morris, *Philosophy for Dummies* (Forest City, CA: IDG Books Worldwide, 1999), pp. 92–94.

2. One exception should be noted here. In some arguments the premises may still provide good reason for the conclusion even though the argument contains a premise that is false. This occurs when the false premise is *superfluous,* that is, not needed to prove or establish the conclusion. Having noted this complication, we shall ignore it in what follows.

3. This follows from the definition of a valid argument—one in which it is impossible to have both all true premises and a false conclusion. Thus, if any premises in an argument deductively entail the conclusion, the argument as a whole remains valid no matter how many false or irrelevant premises the argument may contain.

4. If an argument is inconsistent, at least one of its claims must be false. Strictly speaking, therefore, consistency is included in the standard of accuracy and is not a separate standard in its own right. Inconsistency is such an important and pervasive form of inaccuracy, however, that it is useful for our purposes to treat it as a separate standard.

5. It should be noted that these guidelines are not intended to be comprehensive. Many specific guidelines for evaluating arguments are presented throughout the text.

6. Our discussion of this principle is indebted to Brooke Noel Moore and Richard Parker, *Critical Thinking,* 5th ed. (Mountain View, CA: Mayfield, 1998), pp. 71–79.

7. Answer: 11. (Many people overlook the *f*'s in the word *of.*) This exercise is borrowed from Scott Plous, *The Psychology of Judgment and Decision Making* (New York: McGraw-Hill, 1993), p. 9.

8. Our discussion of this principle is indebted to Brooke Noel Moore and Richard Parker, *Critical Thinking,* 5th ed. (Mountain View, CA: Mayfield, 1998), p. 84.

9. For a helpful general discussion, see Theodore Schick Jr. and Lewis Vaughn, *How to Think about Weird Things: Critical Thinking for a New Age,* 2nd ed. (1999), chap. 3.

10. Tom Morris, *Philosophy for Dummies* (Indianapolis: Wiley, 1999), p. 51.

11. This exercise is inspired by one in John Chaffee, *The Thinker's Way* (Boston: Little, Brown, 1998), p. 64.

12. "Gun Safety Training"; available online at *www.darwinawards .com.*

13. This exercise is adapted from Moore and Parker, *Critical Thinking,* p. 74.
14. *Weekly World News,* September 3, 1999.
15. Stan Daniels, letter to the editor, *Wilkes-Barre Times Leader,* June 10, 1996.
16. Leonard Pitts, "Don't Use God's Law to Beat Up on Gays," *Wilkes-Barre Times Leader,* June 8, 1997.
17. Constance Hilliard, "We're Spendthrift 'Environmentalists,'" *USA Today,* December 8, 2000.
18. Editorial, "Campus Rules Overreach," *USA Today,* March 3, 2004.
19. Richard Delgado, "Hate Cannot Be Tolerated," *USA Today,* March 3, 2004.
20. Editorial, "Drop Out of the College," *New York Times,* March 14, 2006.
21. Charles Krauthammer, "The Case for Profiling," *Time,* March 10, 2002.
22. John Tierney, "On Campus, a Good Man Is Hard to Find," *New York Times,* March 25, 2006.
23. Editorial, "Don't Blame the Burgers," *USA Today,* January 31, 2005.
24. "I'm a Man, I Can Handle It." Available online at *www.darwinawards.com/darwin/index_darwin1997.html.*
25. Editorial, *USA Today,* April 8, 1994.

CHAPTER 9

1. The method is named after its inventor, English logician John Venn (1834–1923).
2. These numbers aren't normally included in Venn diagrams. They are added here temporarily to make it easier to refer to the relevant areas.
3. In math, shading an area generally means that the area is *not* empty. In logic, shading has just the opposite meaning.
4. "The 1999 Darwin Award Wannabes"; available online at *www.tiac.net/users/cri/darwin99a.html.*
5. Many logic and critical thinking texts adopt the convention that ambiguous generalizations like these should always be translated as "all." Although this convention certainly simplifies matters for students, it is more important, we think, to respect the principle that speakers' intentions be interpreted plausibly and charitably.
6. Our discussion of stylistic variants of standard categorical forms is indebted to C. Stephen Layman, *The Power of Logic* (Mountain View, CA: Mayfield, 1999), pp. 129–31.
7. Strictly speaking, quantifying expressions such as *many, most,* and *nearly all* aren't really stylistic variants of *some* because they convey more-specific quantitative information than *some* does. For example, "Nearly all Canadians are friendly" clearly says something much stronger than "Some [i.e., at least one] Canadian is friendly." With rare exceptions, however, these verbal differences are irrelevant for purposes of categorical logic. Thus, so long as due care is exercised, quantifying expressions such as *many, most,* and *nearly all* can be safely translated as *some.*
8. William H. Halverson, *A Concise Logic* (New York: Random House, 1984), p. 83.
9. The 1999 Darwin Award Wannabes"; available online at *www.tiac.net/users/cri/darwin99a.html.*
10. "Underpants Fail to Mask Robber's Identity," AOL News, October 13, 2001.

CHAPTER 10

1. In this chapter we will not consider arguments with more than three variables because such arguments become impractical to analyze by means of truth tables. The number of columns needed is determined exponentially. With two variables we need four columns, two squared. With three variables we need eight columns, two cubed. With four variables we would need sixteen columns, two to the fourth power. This quickly becomes work that is more suitable for a computer than a human being.
2. A horseshoe, ⊃, is also an acceptable symbol for this operation.
3. Counterfactual conditionals, such as "If Caesar had fought in the Revolutionary War, he would have used firearms," are another matter altogether. Consideration of counterfactuals would take us beyond the aims and scope of this chapter.

CHAPTER 11

1. In Chapter 3 we discussed six patterns, but here our discussion focuses on four.
2. For a thorough explanation of how this figure is calculated, see A. Agresti and B. Finley, *Statistical Methods for the Social Sciences,* 2nd ed. (San Francisco: Dellen, 1986), p. 103.
3. These are the figures used and made available by the Gallup Poll. See Charles W. Roll and Albert H. Cantril, *Polls: Their Use and Misuse in Politics* (New York: Basic Books, 1972), p. 72.
4. Statistics can also be used to make inductive generalizations, especially when they argue to a conclusion about most members of a class. Some, but not all, statistical arguments are also inductive generalizations. And, clearly, not all inductive generalizations are statistical arguments.
5. It is also possible to have negative arguments from analogy. For example, x and y are not similar in ways a, b, and c. So, they are probably not similar in d either.
6. This example is adapted from Jostein Gaarder's *Sophie's World: A Novel about the History of Philosophy* (New York: Berkley Books, 1994), p. 328.
7. Clifton Fadiman, ed., *The Little, Brown Book of Anecdotes* (Boston: Little, Brown, 1985), p. 61.
8. This analysis ignores prizes less than The Grand Prize. For more information, visit Powerball.com.

CHAPTER 12

1. Gary Ink, "Book Title Output and Average Prices: 1996 Final and 1997 Preliminary Figures," *The Bowker Annual Library and Book Trade Almanac,* 43rd ed. (New Providence, NJ: R. R. Bowker, 1998), p. 521.
2. "Leading U.S. Daily Newspapers" and "U.S. Commercial Radio Stations, by Format, 1992–98," *The World Almanac and Book of Facts, 1999* (Mahwah, NJ: World Almanac Books, 1999), pp. 185, 186.
3. Sigmund Freud, "Femininity," in *New Introductory Lectures on Psychoanalysis* (New York: Norton, 1965).
4. *Answers to the Most Asked Questions about Cigarettes* (Washington, DC: The Tobacco Institute, n.d.).
5. In 1981 a *Washington Post* Pulitzer Prize–winning article about an eight-year-old heroin addict had been fabricated.

6. Although the terms are often used interchangeably, a *journal* is a periodical limited to a particular subject (medicine, politics, literature, sociology, etc.) and aimed at an audience familiar with the subject. A *magazine* includes articles on various subjects and is aimed at a more general readership.

7. William Carlos Williams, "The Virtue of History," in *In the American Grain* (New York: New Directions, 1925, 1956), p. 201. Hamilton, in fact, was forty-nine when he died.

8. *New York Times,* February 25, 1997.

9. "Of Studies," in *Essays or Counsels Civil and Moral* (1625).

10. *The Affluent Society* (Boston: Houghton-Riverside, 1958), p. 21.

CHAPTER 14

1. For recommendations on evaluating information in journals of opinion, see Chapter 12.

2. "Homesick Man Who Flew as Cargo Recounts Journey"; available online at *www.cnn.com/2003/US/Southwest/09/10/stowaway.flight.ap* (adapted).

3. Stanley J. Baran, *Introduction to Mass Communication,* 3rd ed. (New York: McGraw-Hill, 2004), p. 27 (citing *Los Angeles Times* reporter Steve Lopez).

4. Inspired by an exercise in Stephen S. Carey, *The Uses and Abuses of Argument: Critical Thinking and Fallacious Reasoning* (Mountain View, CA: Mayfield, 2000), p. 167.

5. Paul S. Voakes, "The Newspaper Journalists of the '90's: Who They Are . . . and What They Think about the Major Issues Facing Their Profession." American Society of Newspaper Editors, 1997; available online at *www.asne.org/kiosk/reports/97reports/journalists90s/coverpage.html.*

6. Neal Gabler, "The Media Bias Myth," *Los Angeles Times,* December 22, 2002.

7. Baran, *Introduction to Mass Communication,* p. 50.

8. Advertising Age 2006 Fact Pack, p. 11.

9. Baran, *Introduction to Mass Communication,* p. 378.

10. George Gerbner, "The Stories We Tell," *Media Development* (April 1996), pp. 13–17.

11. Max Sutherland, *Advertising and the Mind of the Consumer* (St. Leonards, Australia: Allen & Unwin, 1993), pp. 6–12.

12. New York: Picador, 2002.

CHAPTER 15

1. Carl Sagan, *The Demon-Haunted World: Science as a Candle in the Dark* (New York: Random House, 1995), p. 6.

2. For example, in a 1998 international test, American high school students finished eighteenth out of twenty-one nations in math and science literacy, and the test didn't even include any of the traditionally high performing Asian countries. James Freeman, "To Improve Schools, Forget Computers," *USA Today Online,* September 10, 1999; available online at *www.usatoday.com/news/comment/columnists/freeman/ncjf38.htm.*

3. Sometimes, *science* is defined more broadly to include nonempirical disciplines such as logic and mathematics. When we speak of "science," we mean *empirical* science in the sense defined.

4. This definition is adapted from Paul Kurtz, "Believing the Unbelievable: The Scientific Response—A Foreword," in *Science and the Paranormal: Probing the Existence of the Supernatural,*

eds. George O. Abell and Barry Singer (New York: Scribner's, 1981), pp. vii–viii.

5. Poll cited in *Parade,* December 26, 1999, p. 7.

6. National Science Foundation poll, reported in the *Wilkes-Barre Times Leader,* May 23, 1996.

7. This and the preceding statistic are cited in Sagan, *The Demon-Haunted World,* p. 324.

8. Poll cited in the *Gallup Poll Monthly,* August 1999, p. 35.

9. 1990 Gallup Poll cited in Terry O'Neill, ed., *Paranormal Phenomena: Opposing Viewpoints* (San Diego, CA: Greenhaven press, 1991), p. 13.

10. This and the preceding statistic are cited in a poll published in the *Gallup Poll Monthly,* September 1996, p. 23.

11. 1994 Gallup Poll cited in Stuart A. Vyse, *Believing in Magic: The Psychology of Superstition* (New York: Oxford University Press, 1997), p. 17.

12. In fact, controlled studies have found no evidence that vitamin C prevents or cures colds.

13. Our discussion of these methods is indebted to Theodore Schick Jr. and Lewis Vaughn, *How to Think about Weird Things: Critical Thinking for a New Age,* 2nd ed. (Mountain View, CA: Mayfield, 1999), p. 196.

14. Sagan, *The Demon-Haunted World,* pp. 339–40.

15. When we speak of "questions of meaning or purpose," we have in mind primarily questions of existential or cosmic meaning or purpose. We don't mean to deny that there are some kinds of "meanings" and "purposes" that science is competent to deal with.

16. This is one standard sense of *scientism.* See, for example, John F. Haught, *Science and Religion: From Conflict to Conversation* (Mahwah, NJ: Paulist Press, 1995), p. 16. In a weaker sense, scientism is the view that the methods of the natural sciences should be applied in every field of human knowing. Robert Todd Carroll, "Scientism"; available online at *http://skeptic.com/scientism/html.*

17. This definition is indebted to Sagan, *The Demon-Haunted World,* p. 13.

18. Our discussion in this section is indebted to William D. Gray, *Thinking Critically about New Age Ideas* (Belmont, CA: Wadsworth, 1991), chap. 5.

19. Nigel Calder, *Einstein's Universe* (Harmondsworth, England: Penguin Books, 1980), pp. 72–83.

20. Of course, any of these statements might reasonably be believed on the basis of religious revelation, provided there is ample proof that the revelation is genuine. When we speak of "possible observations or experiments," we have in mind observations or experiments that don't rely on supernatural agencies or rest on mere appeals to authority.

21. For representative statements of these excuses, see Robert H. Ashby, *The Guidebook for the Study of Psychical Research* (London: Rider and Company, 1972), excerpt reprinted in O'Neill, *Paranormal Phenomena,* p. 132; D. Scott Rogo, "The Making of Psi Failure," *Fate* (April 1986), pp. 76–80. For a helpful critical discussion, see Ray Hyman, *The Elusive Quarry: A Scientific Appraisal of Psychical Research* (Buffalo, NY: Prometheus Books, 1989), pp. 210–15.

22. See Arthur W. Galston and Clifford L. Slayman, "The Not-So-Secret Life of Plants," *American Scientist* 67 (May 1979), pp. 337–44.

23. Barry Singer, "Double Standards," in Abell and Singer, *Science and the Paranormal,* p. 144.

24. This is Bertrand Russell's famous "five minute hypothesis." This formulation of the argument is borrowed from Tom Morris, *Philosophy for Dummies* (Foster City, CA: IDG Books Worldwide, 1999), p. 62.

25. Humphrey Carpenter, ed., *The Letters of J. R. R. Tolkien* (Boston: Houghton Mifflin, 1981), p. 400.

26. Isaac Asimov and Duane Gish, "The Genesis War," *Science Digest,* October 1981, pp. 82–87.

27. Lee Tiffin, *Creationism's Upside-Down Pyramid: How Science Refutes Fundamentalism* (Buffalo, NY: Prometheus Books, 1994), p. 28.

28. Robert J. Schadewald, "Six 'Flood' Arguments Creationists Can't Answer," in *Evolution versus Creationism: The Public Education Controversy,* ed. J. Peter Zetterberg (Phoenix, AZ: Oryx Press, 1983), p. 450.

29. See, for example, Henry M. Morris, ed., *Scientific Creationism* (San Diego, CA: Creation-Life Publishers, 1974), pp. 118–19.

30. Richard Dawkins, *Unweaving the Rainbow: Science, Delusion and the Appetite for Wonder* (Boston: Houghton Mifflin, 1998), p. 31.

31. Terence Hines, *Pseudoscience and the Paranormal* (Buffalo, NY: Prometheus Books, 1988), p. 93. See generally James Randi, *The Truth about Uri Geller* (Buffalo, NY: Prometheus Books, 1975).

32. Hines, *Pseudoscience and the Paranormal,* pp. 245–46.

33. James Randi, "Science and the Chimera," in Abell and Singer, *Science and the Paranormal,* p. 214.

34. C. R. Snyder and R. J. Shenkel, "The P. T. Barnum Effect," *Psychology Today* 8 (March 1975), pp. 52–54.

35. Hines, *Pseudoscience and the Paranormal,* p. 34.

36. Robert Novella, "Cold Reading"; available online at *www.factsource.com/cut/coldreading.html.* This article originally appeared in *The Connecticut Skeptic* 2, No. 2 (Spring 1997), p. 3.

37. Fereydoon Batmanghelidj, *Your Body's Many Cries for Water,* 2nd ed. (Falls River, VA: Global Health Solutions, 1997). For more on Dr. Batmanghelidj and the water cure, see the Global Health Solutions Web site at *www.watercure.com.*

38. Bob Butts, letter to the editor, *Wilkes-Barre Times Leader,* September 3, 1997. Butts, owner of an auto-parts store in Moosic, Pennsylvania, has spent more than $300,000 of his own money in recent years touting the water cure. For more on Butts and his crusade, see Michael Rubinkam, "The Water Man," online at *www.abcnews.go.com/sections/living/DailyNews/water000619.html.*

39. This example is inspired by an example in Gray, *Thinking Critically about New Age Ideas,* p. 110.

40. This example is adapted from an example in David A. Levy, *Tools of Critical Thinking: Metathoughts for Psychology* (Boston: Allyn & Bacon, 1997), p. 53.

41. Robert Parry, *In Defense of Astrology: Astrology's Answers to Its Critics* (St. Paul, MN: Llewellyn Publications, 1991), p. 88.

42. *Gallup Poll Monthly,* September 1996, p. 23. A 1984 Gallup Poll found that 55 percent of American teenagers believe in astrology. Paul Kurtz and Andrew Franknoi, "Scientific Tests of Astrology Do Not Support Its Claims," reprinted in *The Outer Edge: Classic Investigations of the Paranormal,* eds. Joe Nickell, Barry Karr, and Tom Genoni (Amherst, NY: Committee for the Scientific Investigation of Claims of the Paranormal, 1996), p. 36.

43. Carl Sagan, *Cosmos* (New York: Random House, 1980), p. 48.

44. An important qualification to this statement is noted below.

45. Our discussion in this section is indebted to Hines, *Pseudoscience and the Paranormal,* pp. 141–56.

46. George O. Abell, "Astrology," in Abell and Singer, *Science and the Paranormal,* p. 87.

47. Hines, *Pseudoscience and the Paranormal,* p. 147. It can also be asked why these forces have no effect on human behavior until the precise moment of birth. After all, most of these forces also operate in the womb.

48. Abell, "Astrology," p. 88.

49. Parry, *In Defense of Astrology,* p. 113.

50. Abell, "Astrology," p. 86.

51. Many astrologers are reluctant to concede that the discovery of the three new planets proves that astrologers' predictions have been systematically in error for the past two thousand years. Noted astrologer Linda Goodman, for example, argues that ancient astrologers' claims weren't mistaken because planets *have* no astrological influences until they are discovered! Cited in Hines, *Pseudoscience and the Paranormal,* p. 146.

52. It is also instructive to note how astrologers sought to determine what astrological influences the newly discovered planets possessed. They did this not by empirical investigation but by resort to Greek and Roman mythology. For example, Pluto (Hades) was the Greek god of the underworld. From this it was inferred that the planet Pluto must influence matters connected with death. See Ronny Martens and Tim Trachet, *Making Sense of Astrology* (Buffalo, NY: Prometheus Books, 1998), pp. 100–101.

53. Some astrologers do claim that asteroids (at least the larger ones) do have astrological influences. The claimed influences, however, are invariably based on myth, not empirical observation. See, for example, "Astrology on the Web," available online at *www.astrologycom.com/aster.html.*

54. Paul Kurtz, *The Transcendental Temptation: A Critique of Religion and the Paranormal* (Buffalo, NY: Prometheus Books, 1986); excerpt reprinted in O'Neill, *Paranormal Phenomena,* pp. 154–55.

55. "Aquarius: Your Preferences"; available online at *www.astrology.com/prefs_aquarius.htm.*

56. These horoscopes are taken from astrologer Joyce Jillson's syndicated column, *Wilkes-Barre Times Leader,* November 24, 2000.

57. As Saint Augustine pointed out, essentially the same problem arises with biological twins. Time twins present an even greater challenge for astrologers, however, because with time twins quibbles cannot be raised about their being born even a few minutes apart.

58. See, for example, Parry, *In Defense of Astrology,* p. 100.

59. Ibid.

60. See, for example, Christopher C. French, Antony Leadbetter, and Geoffrey Dean, "The Anatomy of Time Twins: A Re-Analysis," *Journal of Scientific Exploration* 11, No. 2 (1997), p. 147.

61. See, for example, Parry, *In Defense of Astrology,* pp. 106–7.

62. R. B. Culver and P. A. Ianna, *The Gemini Syndrome: A Scientific Evaluation of Astrology* (Buffalo, NY: Prometheus Books, 1984), pp. 169–70; R. N. Hunter and J. S. Derr, "Prediction Monitoring and Evaluation Program: A Progress Report," *Earthquake Information Bulletin* 10, No. 3 (1978), pp. 93–96.

63. Sandra Shulman, *The Encyclopedia of Astrology* (New York: Hamlyn Publishing Group, Ltd., 1976), p. 168; cited in Culver and Ianna, *Gemini Syndrome,* p. 125.

64. Culver and Ianna, *Gemini Syndrome,* pp. 125–27.

65. Bernard I. Silverman, "Studies of Astrology," *Journal of Psychology* 77 (1971), pp. 141–49; cited in Culver and Ianna, *Gemini Syndrome,* p. 131.

66. John D. McGervey, "A Statistical Test of Sun-Sign Astrology," in *Paranormal Borderlands of Science,* ed. Kendrick Frazier (Amherst, NY: Prometheus Books, 1981), pp. 235–40.

67. Culver and Ianna, *Gemini Syndrome,* pp. 127–29.

68. W. Grant Dahlstrom et al., "MMPI Findings on Astrological and Other Folklore Concepts of Personality," *Psychological Reports* 78 (1996), pp. 1059–70.

69. Shawn Carlson, "A Double-Blind Test of Astrology," *Nature* 318 (December 5, 1985), pp. 419–25. A follow-up study, addressing astrologers' objections to the design of Carlson's study, was conducted a few years later. See J. H. McGrew and R. M. McFall, "A Scientific Inquiry into the Validity of Astrology," *Journal of Scientific Exploration* 4 (1990), pp. 75–83. This study also failed to support astrology's claims.

70. See, for example, Claude Benski et al., *The Mars Effect: A French Test of Over 1,000 Sports Champions* (Buffalo, NY: Prometheus Books, 1996); P. Kurtz, J. W. Nienhuys, and R. Sandhu, "Is the 'Mars Effect' Genuine?" *Journal of Scientific Exploration* 11 (1997), pp. 19–39.

ANSWERS TO SELECTED EXERCISES

CHAPTER 2

EXERCISE 2.1

I.

1. Statement.
4. Nonstatement; suggestion.
7. Statement. (This is a brief and emphatic way of saying "This is great.")
10. Statement. (You might be lying.)
13. Nonstatement; request.
16. Statement. (This is an emphatic way of saying "This is a crock.")
19. Nonstatement; request.
22. Statement. (Spanish for "My house is your house.")
25. Nonstatement; exclamation.

II.

1. Yes.
4. Yes.
7. Yes.
10. Yes.
13. Yes.
16. Yes.

EXERCISE 2.2

I.

1. *Premise:* Pain is a state of consciousness, a mental event.
   Conclusion: It can never be directly observed.
4. *Premise 1:* Business is the art of growth.
   Premise 2: Growth is the essence of life.
   Conclusion: Business is the art of life.
7. *Premise:* Science is based on experiment, on a willingness to see the universe as it really is.

Conclusion: Science sometimes requires courage—at the very least the courage to question the conventional wisdom.

10. *Premise:* The lowest animal is a lot nicer and kinder than most of the humans beings that inhabit this earth.
    Conclusion: Animals have souls.

13. *Premise:* Oil isn't helping anyone when it sits in the ground.
    Conclusion: There is nothing wrong with burning crude oil like crazy—so long as there's a plan for energy alternatives when the cheap oil runs out.

16. *Premise:* If we encourage each other to blame God for injustices, we are giving the evil or dark side a victory by keeping God's precious children—that's all of us—away from His loving arms.
    Conclusion: Although it is part of human nature to be angry at God when bad things happen, there is no point in doing so.

19. *Premise 1:* More than 99 percent of all the creatures that have ever lived have died without progeny.
    Premise 2: Not a single one of your ancestors falls into this group.
    Conclusion: You are lucky to be alive.

II.

1. *Premise 1:* Man knows that he is dying.
   Premise 2: Of its victory over man, the universe knows nothing.
   Conclusion: When the universe has crushed him, man will be nobler than that which kills him.
4. *Premise 1:* Moral responsibility presupposes free-will.
   Premise 2: This freedom is not compatible with universal causal determination.
   Premise 3: Universal causal determinism appears to be the case.
   Conclusion: Contrary to what most people believe, human beings are not morally responsible.

7. *Premise 1:* If you're not speeding, you don't have to worry about speed traps.
Premise 2: A speed trap could save your life if some other speeder is stopped.
Conclusion: No one in his right mind should criticize the state police for the speed traps.

10. *Premise:* He that loveth not his brother whom he hath seen, cannot love God whom he hath not seen.
Conclusion: If a man say, "I love God," and hateth his brother, he is a liar.

13. *Premise:* Your alternative to accepting reality the way it occurs is continuous anxiety and desperate disappointments.
Conclusion: Whether you like it or not, you'd better accept reality the way it occurs: as highly imperfect and filled with the most fallible human beings.

16. *Premise 1:* Those who develop the first-thing-in-the-morning routine tend to be more consistent in their training.
Premise 2: Morning runs avoid the heat and peak air pollution.
Premise 3: You can enjoy your runs without carrying along all the stress that builds up during the day.
Premise 4: Early-morning runs save time by combining your morning and postrun shower.
Conclusion: Getting in your run early certainly has its advantages.

19. *Premise 1:* You'll begin to eat food in season, when it is at the peak of its nutritional value and flavor.
Premise 2: You won't find anything processed or microwavable.
Premise 3 (subconclusion): You'll cook.
Premise 4: You'll be supporting the farmers in your community.
Premise 5: You'll be helping defend the countryside from sprawl.
Premise 6: You'll be saving oil by eating food produced nearby.
Premise 7: You'll be teaching your children that a carrot is a root, not a machine-lathed orange bullet that comes in a plastic bag.
Conclusion: Shop at the farmer's market.

EXERCISE 2.4

I.
1. Nonargument; explanation.
4. Nonargument; conditional statement.
7. Nonargument; report of an argument.
10. Nonargument; illustration.
13. Nonargument; report of an argument.
16. Nonargument, report of an explanation.
19. Nonargument; unsupported assertion. (Notice that the word *because* does not function as a premise indicator in either sentence of this passage.)
22. Nonargument. (No conclusion is drawn.)
25. Nonargument; illustration.

28. Nonargument; conditional statement. (*When* here means "if.")
31. Argument.
34. Nonargument; illustration.

II.
1. Explanation.
4. Argument.
7. Explanation.
10. Explanation.
13. Explanation.
16. Explanation.
19. Explanation.
22. (Facetious) argument.
25. (Facetious) explanation.

CHAPTER 3

EXERCISE 3.1

I.
Problem 1: Moriarty.

II.
Problem 1: Mike: Grape juice.
Amy: Pepsi.
Brian: Diet Coke.
Lisa: Ice tea.
Bill: 7-Up.

EXERCISE 3.2

1. *Modus tollens.*
4. Chain argument.
7. Denying the antecedent.
10. Affirming the consequent.

EXERCISE 3.3

1. Deductive. (Argument based on mathematics; also the conclusion follows necessarily from the premises.)
4. Deductive. (Argument by elimination; also the conclusion follows necessarily from the premises.)
7. Inductive. (Given that signs can be wrong, the conclusion follows only probably from the premises.)
10. Inductive. (Argument from authority; also a prediction; also *probably* is an induction indicator word.)
13. Inductive. (The principle of charity dictates that the argument be regarded as inductive because the conclusion follows at best probably from the premises.)
16. Inductive. (Conclusion does not follow necessarily from the premises; argument from authority: "Kevin says . . . .")

19. Inductive. (The principle of charity dictates that the argument be regarded as inductive because the conclusion does not follow necessarily from the premises.)

22. Deductive. (Argument by elimination; also the conclusion follows necessarily from the premises.)

25. Deductive. (Argument based on mathematics; also conclusion follows necessarily from the premises; also *it necessarily follows* is a deduction indicator phrase.)

28. Inductive. (Argument from analogy; also the conclusion does not follow necessarily from the premises.)

EXERCISE 3.4

1. Beta.
4. Delta is not an alpha.
7. If Delta is an alpha, then Delta is a theta.
10. Some alphas are thetas. (Or: Some thetas are alphas.)

EXERCISE 3.5

I.
1. Valid.
4. Invalid (denying the antecedent).
7. Valid.
10. Invalid.

II.
1. Sound.
4. Unsound (invalid argument: affirming the consequent).
7. Unsound (invalid argument: denying the antecedent).
10. Unsound (false premise).

III.
1. Cogent.
4. Uncogent. (The argument compares two activities that are different in relevant respects. "Lying and deception" is a known and accepted strategy in poker and so is not sufficiently similar to the real-world lying and deception that can occur in business.)
7. Cogent.
10. Uncogent. (The conclusion does not follow probably from the premises.)

IV.
1. Deductive, valid.
4. Inductive, weak.
7. Inductive, strong.
10. Inductive, weak.
13. Inductive, weak.
16. Inductive, weak.
19. Inductive, strong.
22. Deductive, valid.
25. Deductive, invalid (affirming the consequent).

CHAPTER 4

EXERCISE 4.1

I.
1. *Cruising* is *vague,* unless specifically defined by law.
4. *Vague.* "A chance of rain" could mean anything from a tiny chance of rain to a virtual certainty.
7. *Ambiguous.* Whose enormous bottom is exposed to the sky, Ellen's or *Titanic's?*
10. *Ambiguous.* Who is hot, Bob or Devlin? And "hot" in what sense?
13. *Vague and overgeneral.* More specifics are needed.
16. *Ambiguous.* Does Disraeli mean he will read the manuscript in the near future or that he won't waste his time by bothering to read it?
19. *Ambiguous. She* can refer to Jana or her sister.
22. *Ambiguous.* Does "lower passage" refer to a part of the emperor's anatomy or to a tract of land?
25. *Ambiguous.* "Takes over" what, precisely?!

II.
1. Verbal. (Two senses of "religious" are used.)
4. Factual. (What time did the coach say the game starts?)
7. Factual. (Who had the higher batting average, Cobb or Hornsby?)

EXERCISE 4.2

IV.
1. Stipulative.
4. Precising.
7. Lexical.
10. Persuasive.
13. Lexical.
16. Lexical.
19. Lexical.

V.
1. Enumerative.
4. Subclass.
7. Ostensive.
10. Genus and difference.
13. Synonymous.
16. Etymological.
19. Synonymous.

VI.
1. Too broad.
4. Lacking in context.
7. Circular. (*Knowledge* is used in the definition of *knowledge.*)
10. Lacking in context.
13. Too broad.

16. Slanted. (Only a Catholic would agree that the pope is the "infallible Vicar of Christ.")
19. Obscure.

EXERCISE 4.4

I.

4. Possible choices: *begged, pleaded, requested, implored, insisted,* and *demanded. Begged, pleaded,* and *implored* suggest that the speaker is dependent on the listener or that she is desperate. *Demanded* shows that she has more power over the listener, making "please" in the sentence merely courteous or perhaps sarcastic.

7. Possible choices: *gripped, grabbed, clutched, seized,* and *squeezed.* A word like *gripped* connotes aggression or dominance; a word such as *clutched* might suggest fear or protection.

10. Possible choices: *cold, hard-hearted, apathetic, callous, insensitive,* and *unsympathetic.* These words are all close in meaning, but *callous* might imply a roughness developed after many disappointments, whereas *apathetic* suggests indifference and a lack of concern.

13. Possible choices: *accepted, okayed, endorsed, praised, admired,* and *celebrated.* These words all have different meanings, but they share the notion of approval. However, some of the words (*praised, celebrated*) suggest something far more positive than others (*accepted, okayed*).

II.

1. Emotive words and phrases in the advertisement include *charming, cozy* (code for "small"?), *older neighborhood, lower-level recreation room* (basement?), *modern,* and *tender loving care* (needs lots of work?). All of these words are used to create a warm and receptive attitude in the prospective buyer.

4. This passage does not have the obvious kinds of emotive language that critical thinking students get accustomed to looking for—the blatant emotional appeals, sarcastic slanting, and name-calling characteristic of the preceding passages. We think it's important to let students know that some writing (such as you find in literary essays) contains more-subtle emotional appeals. The emotive words and phrases in this passage include *family herd, grandma's practiced eye, desperate families, flooded, seeking, bundle, toddlers, hang, unswaddle,* and *species.* Students might be asked how Kingsolver carefully sets up her final sentence with a subtle, emotionally charged passage. They might also comment on whether the historical description of women's work is relevant to the point suggested in the final sentence. We're not sure it is.

CHAPTER 5

EXERCISE 5.1

1. Positively relevant.
4. Logically irrelevant.

7. Negatively relevant.
10. Positively relevant. (Although the premises don't provide evidence for God's existence, they do provide prudential, or self-interested, reasons for *belief* in God. Whether these prudential reasons are properly convincing is, of course, another question.)
13. The first premise is negatively relevant, and the second premise is positively relevant.

EXERCISE 5.2

I.

1. Bandwagon argument.
4. Straw man.
7. Begging the question.
10. Two wrongs make a right.
13. Equivocation.
16. No fallacy.
19. No fallacy.
22. Straw man.
25. Red herring.
28. Attacking the motive.
31. Bandwagon argument.
34. Bandwagon argument.
37. Red herring.
40. No fallacy.

CHAPTER 6

EXERCISE 6.1

I.

1. Inappropriate appeal to authority.
4. Inappropriate appeal to authority.
7. Hasty generalization.
10. Inappropriate appeal to authority.
13. Weak analogy.
16. Inappropriate appeal to authority.
19. No fallacy.
22. Hasty generalization.
25. Inappropriate appeal to authority.
28. Inconsistency.
31. False alternatives.
34. Weak analogy.
37. Hasty generalization.
40. Slippery slope.

II.

1. Loaded question.
4. False alternatives.
7. False alternatives.
10. Questionable cause.
13. Equivocation.

16. Hasty generalization.
19. False alternatives.
22. Hasty generalization.
25. Weak analogy.
28. Inconsistency.
31. Questionable cause. Possible hasty generalization and inappropriate appeal to authority.
34. Weak analogy.

CHAPTER 7

EXERCISE 7.1

I.

1. ① Bertie probably isn't home. ② His car isn't in the driveway, and ③ there are no lights on in his house.

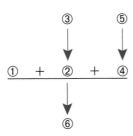

4. ① Affirmative action in higher education is morally justifiable because ② it compensates for past discrimination, ③ provides valuable role models for women and minorities, and ④ promotes multicultural understanding.

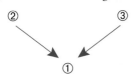

7. ① Only three people could have stolen the CD: Danny, Stacy, or Patrick. But ② Stacy couldn't have stolen the CD because ③ she was out riding her bike. ④ Patrick couldn't have stolen the CD because ⑤ he was at a friend's house. Therefore, ⑥ Danny must have stolen the CD.

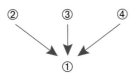

10. Several states have abolished the insanity defense against criminal responsibility. ① This may be popular with voters, but it is morally indefensible. ② Insanity removes moral responsibility, and ③ it is

wrong to punish someone who is not morally responsible for his crime. Moreover, ④ it is pointless to punish the insane because ⑤ punishment has no deterrent effect on a person who cannot appreciate the wrongfulness or criminality of his or her actions.

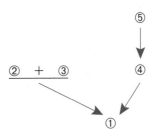

13. ① If today is Saturday, then tomorrow is Sunday. ② If tomorrow is Sunday, then we'll be having pasta for dinner. ③ If we'll be having pasta for dinner, then I should pick up some red wine today because ④ in this state wine can be purchased only at liquor stores, and ⑤ the liquor stores are closed on Sundays. ⑥ Today is Saturday. Therefore, ⑦ I should pick up some red wine today.

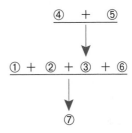

II.

1. Since ① our feelings, desires, and preferences can be either beneficial or harmful, noble or ignoble, praiseworthy or damnable, and since ② they can be either in harmony or in conflict with other people's feelings, desires, and preferences, ③ they are obviously not accurate tools for analysis of moral issues or trustworthy guidelines to action.

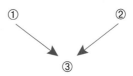

4. ① School tests should be abolished. ② Tests introduce competition where it does not belong. ③ They deny the individuality of students' talents and interests. ④ They degrade education by encouraging passivity, mindlessness, and triviality. Finally, ⑤ they send the wrong messages about what is valuable in education and in life.

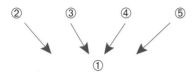

7. ① Everything eternal is necessary. But ② whatever God wills, he wills from eternity, for ③ otherwise His will would be mutable. Therefore, ④ whatever He wills, He wills necessarily.

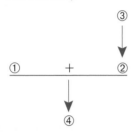

10. ① Education implies teaching. ② Teaching implies knowledge. ③ Knowledge is truth. ④ The truth is everywhere the same. Hence ⑤ education should be everywhere the same.

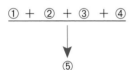

13. ① Planetary exploration has many virtues. ② It permits us to refine insights derived from such Earth-bound sciences as meteorology, climatology, geology and biology, to broaden their powers and improve their practical applications here on Earth. ③ It provides cautionary tales on the alternative fates of worlds. ④ It is an aperture to future high technologies important for life here on Earth. ⑤ It provides an outlet for the traditional human zest for exploration and discovery, our passion to find out, which has been to a very large degree responsible for our success as a species. And ⑥ it permits us, for the first time in history, to approach with rigor, with a significant chance of finding out the true answers, questions on the origins and destinies of worlds, the beginnings and ends of life, and the possibilities of other beings who live in the skies—questions as basic to the human enterprise as thinking is, as natural as breathing.

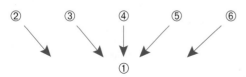

16. ① All students should study a foreign language. ② It improves mastery of English. ③ It helps to avoid

cultural provincialism by expanding the cultural experience of students. ④ It is useful for travel and commerce. ⑤ It makes it possible to do advanced work in a foreign language, including the study of the major literary works in that language. Finally, ⑥ the ability to read, speak, and think in a second language is a source of pleasure and satisfaction even if this language is not used for travel and business and even if it does not become a field of further study.

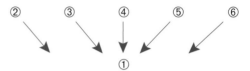

19. ① Lefty Grove was the greatest pitcher of all time, period. ② The one best indicator of a pitcher's ability is his ERA, and ③ Lefty Grove led leagues in earned run average nine times. ④ No one else even approaches this record. ⑤ The second-best indicator of a pitcher's ability is his winning percentage. Guess what? ⑥ Grove also led the league in that more times than anyone else.

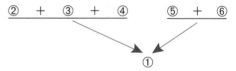

EXERCISE 7.2

1. Most Californians are friendly.

4. Human beings are the only rational creatures (on Earth).

7. Having a lot of money is not the secret to true happiness.

10. Because a well-regulated citizen militia is necessary to the security of a free state, the right of individual citizens to keep and bear arms shall not be infringed. [*Not:* The right of the individual citizens to keep and bear such arms as are necessary for the maintenance of well-regulated citizen militias shall not be infringed.]

13. Common sense tells us that long-established governments should not be changed without compelling reasons. That is why, as all experience shows, people tend to be willing to endure political abuses, while those abuses are tolerable, rather than correct them by abolishing the forms of government to which they are accustomed. But when a long series of abuses and injustices, all with the same purpose, makes clear that the government is attempting to establish a complete dictatorship, it is their right and duty to throw off the government and provide new safeguards for their future security.

EXERCISE 7.3

I.

1. *Missing premise:* All Mazda Miatas are convertibles.
4. *Missing premise:* This is not a Honda.
7. *Missing premise (subconclusion):* This is a Toyota.
10. *Missing premise:* Some Fords are Rangers.

II.

1. *Missing premise:* Most people from Singapore speak English.
4. *Missing premise (subconclusion):* It is not cold.
   Missing premise (subconclusion): It is not snowing.
   Missing conclusion: Uncle Fred will be coming over for dinner.
7. *Missing premise:* Today is Thursday.
   Missing premise: Zoe is not on the golf course.
10. *Missing premise:* Jay is a Hampton College student.
    Missing premise: Anyone who voted the straight Republican ticket in the last election and regularly attends meetings of the Young Republicans is probably a Republican.
    Missing premise: Most Republicans favor a constitutional amendment banning abortion.

EXERCISE 7.4

1.

1. Asking the question "Will this be on the exam?" indicates that your main interest is in getting through the course with a good grade rather than in learning what the instructor has to teach.
2. The question is insulting to the teacher who has worked hard to put you in a position to appreciate the material—its intrinsic interest, its subtlety, its complexity.
3. Thus, the question "Will this be on the exam?" infuriates many instructors, and rightly so. (from 1 and 2)
4. Therefore, you should not ask, nor be tempted to ask, the question "Will this be on the exam?" (from 3)

4.

1. Everyone needs thinking skills to meet the demands of career and citizenship.
2. The highest of Abraham Maslow's hierarchy of human needs, self-actualization, is unachievable without the ability to think productively.
3. [Maslow correctly identifies self-actualization as the highest human need.]
4. Thus, everyone needs thinking skills to realize his or her potential as a human being. (from 2 and 3)
5. Thus, to deny meaningful instruction in thinking to students below a certain IQ or proficiency level is to deny them an essential part of their humanity. (from 4)
6. The constitutional guarantees of freedom to speak, to choose one's own religion, and so on, lose much of their meaning when only some individuals are trained to evaluate and choose among competing views.

7. Therefore, thinking instruction in elementary and secondary education should not be limited to the honors program. (from 1, 5, and 6)

7.

1. All sorrow or pain is either for something that is truly evil or for something that is apparently evil, but good in reality.
2. There is something worse than pain or sorrow for that which is truly evil, namely, either not to reckon as evil that which is really evil or not to reject it.
3. Thus, pain or sorrow for that which is truly evil cannot be the greatest evil. (from 2)
4. There is something worse than sorrow or pain for that which is apparently evil, but really good, namely, to be altogether separated from that which is truly good.
5. Thus, pain or sorrow for what is apparently evil, but good in reality, cannot be the greatest evil. (from 4)
6. Therefore, it is impossible for sorrow or pain to be man's greatest evil. (from 1, 3, and 5)

10.

1. The economic cost of legal drugs is two-and-a-half times greater than that of illicit drugs.
2. [Thus, although legalizing drugs may take the profit motive away from the street and clandestine manufacturers, these drugs will continue to be manufactured and the economic costs of drugs will still be high (from 1).]
3. Drug use not only has impacts on the user, but also has serious implications for families, the community, consumers, and others.
4. Legalizing drugs would open the floodgates of access to these mood-altering chemicals and would send a message that drugs are not harmful.
5. Thus, legalizing drugs would increase the risk that pilots, surgeons, and school bus drivers would use drugs on the job. (from 4)
6. Thus, drug use is not a right and should never be. (from 3 and 5)
7. [It is ridiculous to say that child abuse laws should be repealed because abuse of children is escalating.]
8. Saying drugs should be legalized because drug use is escalating is like saying child abuse laws should be repealed because abuse of children is escalating.
9. [Thus, it is ridiculous to say that drugs should be legalized because drug use is escalating (from 7 and 8).]
10. Common sense and state experiments with the decriminalization of marijuana in the 1970s tell us that when there are fewer controls, there will be more incidents.
11. America's two favorite legal drugs—alcohol and nicotine—have a tremendous negative impact on the physiological, social, psychological, economic, and spiritual aspects of our lives.
12. Thus, if drugs were legalized, hospitalizations, crimes, car accidents, addicted babies, industrial accidents,

family break-ups, and other problems afflicting our society would worsen significantly. (from 10 and 11)

13. [Therefore, drugs should not be legalized (from 2, 6, 9, and 12).]

CHAPTER 8

EXERCISE 8.3

I.

1. The statement is self-refuting. If no statements are true, then the statement that no statements are true isn't true either. So, if the statement is true, it's false, which is a contradiction.

4. The statement is self-refuting. If no beliefs are justified, then the belief that no beliefs are justified isn't justified either. So, if the statement is true, it's false, which is contradictory. Looked at another way, if we should be absolute and total skeptics (i.e., hold that no beliefs are justified), we should be skeptical of the claim that we should be absolute and total skeptics, and hence *not* be absolute and total skeptics. The statement asserts that we should be absolute and total skeptics, yet implies that we shouldn't, which is contradictory.

7. If the claim here is that all children in Lake Wobegon are above average with respect to *other Lake Wobegon children,* the claim is necessarily false, for something can be above average in a comparison group only if some other things in the group are below average. The statement is not necessarily false if it means that all children in Lake Wobegon are above the *national* average.

II.

1. What about polar bears, seals, walruses, and orcas, to name a few?

4. Plausible counterexamples include Thoreau, Melville, Hawthorne, Poe, Fitzgerald, Hemingway, and Faulkner, among others.

7. Don't forget good ol' Ohio and Utah.

III.

1. Answers will vary. Pertinent counterpoints include: Not all colleges cost a fortune. Often students who were bored in high school find that they enjoy college work. Though jobs like trucking and construction may be relatively high-paying, the work may be more dangerous, less enjoyable, less prestigious, and less secure than many jobs that require a college education. The difference in earning power may also be greater than this individual supposes. Studies consistently show that college graduates make on average about 45 percent more than those who have only a high school diploma.

4. Answers will vary. Some pertinent counterpoints include: Although the meaning of the Second Amendment is hotly debated, few would argue that the "right to bear arms" extends to military-style weapons that are neither necessary for personal protection nor suitable for hunting. Moreover, the risks of legalizing such weapons would seem to outweigh the gains. The risks of foreign invasion or a breakdown of society are probably pretty remote. By contrast, the risk that such weapons could fall into the hands of criminals or be used in Columbine-type massacres, domestic disputes, and accidental shootings is high.

7. Answers will vary. Pertinent points that arguably weaken or refute the argument include: There is a likelihood that legalizing hard drugs would lead to greatly increased use and addiction rates, with all the personal and societal costs this would entail: more overdoses, hospitalizations, car accidents, industrial accidents, suicides, family break-ups, unemployable workers, lower productivity, and so forth. Legalizing hard drugs would also likely make these drugs more readily available to children and implicitly send a message that these drugs aren't harmful.

CHAPTER 9

EXERCISE 9.1

1.

Artichokes　　　　　Fruits

4.

Skateboarders　　　　Jazz fans

7.

Women　　　U.S. presidents or vice presidents

10.

World's greatest golfers　　　South Americans

EXERCISE 9.2

1. All psychiatrists are doctors.

4. All Mustangs are Fords.

7. All players due to report on Monday are persons who are pitchers or catchers.

10. All persons who may use the Teachers' Lounge are teachers.

13. All persons God loves are persons that dwelleth in wisdom.
16. All things that the wise man seeks are useful things.
19. All free persons are masters of themselves.

EXERCISE 9.3

I.

1. All maples are trees.
4. All insects are animals.
7. Some things that glitter are not gold things.
10. All persons that hit are persons who swing the bat.
13. Some birds are birds that cannot fly. (Or: Some birds are not things that fly.)
16. All places where the grass is greener are places on the other side.
19. Some polar bears are bears that live in Canada.
22. All liars are thieves.
25. Most humans are humans who live lives of quiet desperation.
28. All persons who persevere in error are fools.
31. All statements that are certain are statements identical to the statement "Nothing is certain."
34. All villains dwelling in Denmark are arrant knaves.
37. No times are times when one should fret about trifles.
40. Some men are rogues.
43. No unjust "laws" are true laws.

EXERCISE 9.4

I.

1. No barracuda are pets.
   No sharks are barracuda.
   So, no sharks are pets.

Barracuda

Invalid

Sharks   Pets

4. Some bankers are vegetarians.
   No anarchists are bankers.
   So, some anarchists are not vegetarians.

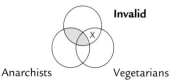

Bankers

Invalid

Anarchists   Vegetarians

7. No poker players are early-risers.
   Some firefighters are early-risers.
   So, some firefighters are not poker players.

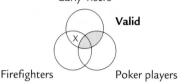

Early-risers

Valid

Firefighters   Poker players

10. No Fords are Pontiacs.
    All Escorts are Fords.
    So, some Escorts are not Pontiacs.

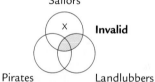

Fords

Invalid

Escorts   Pontiacs

13. No landlubbers are sailors.
    Some sailors are not pirates.
    So, some pirates are not landlubbers.

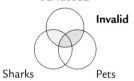

Sailors

Invalid

Pirates   Landlubbers

16. No fish are reptiles.
    All trout are fish.
    So, some trout are not reptiles.

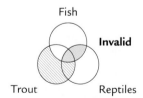

Fish

Invalid

Trout   Reptiles

19. Some butchers are not bakers.
    No butchers are candlestick makers.
    So, some candlestick makers are not bakers.

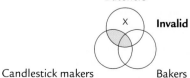

Butchers

Invalid

Candlestick makers   Bakers

II.

1. No Nobel Prize winners are rock stars.
   Some astrophysicists are Nobel Prize winners.
   Therefore, some astrophysicists are not rock stars.

Nobel Prize winners

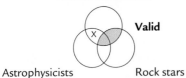

Valid

Astrophysicists   Rock stars

4. All liberals are big spenders.
   All persons identical to Senator Crumley are big spenders.
   So, all persons identical to Senator Crumley are liberals.

Big spenders

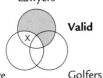

Invalid

Senator Crumley   Liberals

7. Some lawyers are not golfers.
   All lawyers are persons who have attended law school.
   So, some persons who have attended law school are not golfers.

Lawyers

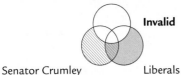

Valid

Persons who have   Golfers
attended law school

10. All political scientists are social scientists.
    Some political scientists are persons who favor campaign finance reform.
    So, some persons who favor campaign finance reform are social scientists.

Political scientists

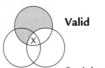

Valid

Persons who favor   Social scientists
campaign finance reform

13. All tax evaders are lawbreakers.
    No lawbreakers are model citizens.
    So, no model citizens are tax evaders.

Lawbreakers

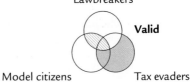

Valid

Model citizens   Tax evaders

16. No harmless acts are immoral acts.
    Some lies are not harmless acts.
    So, some lies are not immoral acts.

Harmless acts

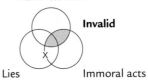

Invalid

Lies   Immoral acts

19. All persons who eat pizza every night are persons at risk for heart disease.
    Some persons who are at risk for heart disease are cab drivers.
    So, some cab drivers are persons who eat pizza every night.

Persons at risk for heart disease

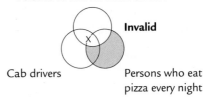

Invalid

Cab drivers   Persons who eat
                     pizza every night

CHAPTER 10

EXERCISE 10.1

I.	II.	III.
1. p	1. T	1. T
4. $p \& q$	4. T	4. T
7. $p \& q$	7. F	7. F
10. $p \& q$	10. F	10. T

EXERCISE 10.2

I.

1.

p^*	q^*	$p \& q$ C
T	T	T
T	F	F
F	T	F
F	F	F

Valid.

4.

r*	s C
T	T
T	F
F	T
F	F

Invalid.

II.

1. p
   q
   ∴ p & q

p*	q*	p & q C
T	T	T
T	F	F
F	T	F
F	F	F

Valid.

EXERCISE 10.3

I.
1. F
4. F
7. F
10. T

III.
1. p & ~q
4. ~p & q
7. p & ~q
10. ~(p & q)

IV.

1.

p	q*	~p*	~p & q C
T	T	F	F
T	F	F	F
F	T	T	T
F	F	F	F

Valid.

4.

p	q	p & q	~(p & q)*	p*	~q C
T	T	T	F	T	F
T	F	F	T	T	T
F	T	F	T	F	F
F	F	F	T	F	T

Valid.

V.

1. ~p & ~q
   ∴ ~(p & q)

p	q	~p	~q	p & q	~p & ~q*	~(p & q) C
T	T	F	F	T	F	F
T	F	F	T	F	F	T
F	T	T	F	F	F	T
F	F	T	T	F	T	T

Valid.

4. ~(p & q)
   p
   ∴ ~q

p	q	p & q	~(p & q)*	p*	~q C
T	T	T	F	T	F
T	F	F	T	T	T
F	T	F	T	F	F
F	F	F	T	F	T

Valid.

EXERCISE 10.4

I.
1. T
4. F
7. T
10. T

III.
1. (c & d) & ~k
4. (t & b) & ~w

IV.

1. p & q
   ~(q & r)
   ∴ ~r

	p	q	r	q & r	p & q*	~(q & r)*	~r C
1.	T	T	T	T	T	F	F
2.	T	T	F	F	T	T	T
3.	T	F	T	F	F	T	F
4.	T	F	F	F	F	T	T
5.	F	T	T	T	F	F	F
6.	F	T	F	F	F	T	T
7.	F	F	T	F	F	T	F
8.	F	F	F	F	F	T	T

Valid.

4. b & ~t
   ~(m & b)
   ∴ ~m & ~t

	b	m	t	~m	~t	m & b	b & ~t*	~(m & b)*	~m & ~t C
1.	T	T	T	F	F	T	F	F	F
2.	T	T	F	F	T	T	T	F	F
3.	T	F	T	T	F	F	F	T	F
4.	T	F	F	T	T	F	T	T	T
5.	F	T	T	F	F	F	F	T	F
6.	F	T	F	F	T	F	F	T	F
7.	F	F	T	T	F	F	F	T	F
8.	F	F	F	T	T	F	F	T	T

Valid.

V.

1. f & t
   ~s
   ∴ ~(f & s)

	f	t	s	f & s	f & t*	~s*	~(f & s)C
1.	T	T	T	T	T	F	F
2.	T	T	F	F	(T	T	T)
3.	T	F	T	T	F	F	F
4.	T	F	F	F	F	T	T
5.	F	T	T	F	F	F	T
6.	F	T	F	F	F	T	T
7.	F	F	T	F	F	F	T
8.	F	F	F	F	F	T	T

Valid.

4. s & ~e
~(e & t)
∴ s & t

	s	e	t	~e	e & t	s & ~e*	~(e & t)*	s & t C
1.	T	T	T	F	T	F	F	T
2.	T	T	F	F	F	F	T	F
3.	T	F	T	T	F	T	T	T
4.	T	F	F	T	F	(T	T	F)
5.	F	T	T	F	T	F	F	F
6.	F	T	F	F	F	F	T	F
7.	F	F	T	T	F	F	T	F
8.	F	F	F	T	F	F	T	F

Invalid.

EXERCISE 10.5

I.
1. T
4. T
7. T
10. F

III.
1. d v r
4. w v d
7. p v f
10. ~(t v a) & w

IV.
1.

p	q	p v q*	~p*	q C
T	T	T	F	T
T	F	T	F	F
F	T	(T	T	T)
F	F	F	T	F

Valid.

4.

	t	a	w	~t	t & a	~(t & a)*	a v w*	~t & a C
1.	T	T	T	F	T	F	T	F
2.	T	T	F	F	T	F	T	F
3.	T	F	T	F	F	(T	T	F)
4.	T	F	F	F	F	T	F	F
5.	F	T	T	T	F	T	T	T
6.	F	T	F	T	F	T	T	T
7.	F	F	T	T	F	(T	T	F)
8.	F	F	F	T	F	T	F	F

Invalid.

V.
1. d v r
~r
∴ d

d	r	d v r*	~r*	d C
T	T	T	F	T
T	F	(T	T	T)
F	T	T	F	F
F	F	F	T	F

Valid.

4. s v a
~(s & a)
a
∴ s

s	a	s & a	s v a*	~(s & a)*	a*	s C
T	T	T	T	F	T	T
T	F	F	T	T	F	T
F	T	F	(T	T	T	F)
F	F	F	F	T	F	F

Invalid.

EXERCISE 10.6

I.
1. F
4. T
7. F
10. T

III.
1. b → e
4. h → f
7. ~c → ~e
10. (s → g) → (~s → p)

IV.
1.

	p	q	p → q*	~p*	~q C
1.	T	T	T	F	F
2.	T	F	F	F	T
3.	F	T	(T	T	F)
4.	F	F	T	T	T

Invalid.

4.

	p	q	r	~p	~q	p → q*	~q v r*	~p & r C
1.	T	T	T	F	F	(T	T	F)
2.	T	T	F	F	F	T	F	F
3.	T	F	T	F	T	F	T	F
4.	T	F	F	F	T	F	T	F
5.	F	T	T	T	F	T	T	T
6.	F	T	F	T	F	T	F	F
7.	F	F	T	T	T	T	T	T
8.	F	F	F	T	T	(T	T	F)

Invalid.

V.

1. $b \to e$
   $\sim e$
   $\therefore \sim b$

	b	e	$b \to e^*$	$\sim e^*$	$\sim b$ C
1.	T	T	T	F	F
2.	T	F	F	T	F
3.	F	T	T	F	T
4.	F	F	T	T	T

Valid.

4. $g \to s$
   $\therefore \sim g \to \sim s$

	g	s	$\sim g$	$\sim s$	$g \to s^*$	$\sim g \to \sim s$ C
1.	T	T	F	F	T	T
2.	T	F	F	T	F	T
3.	F	T	T	F	T	F
4.	F	F	T	T	T	T

Invalid.

CHAPTER 11

EXERCISE 11.1

1. Strong.
4. Strong.
7. Strong.
10. Weak.

EXERCISE 11.2

I.

1. Strong. Is the sample large enough? Yes. Is the sample representative? Yes
4. Weak. Is the sample large enough? Yes. Is the sample representative? No.

II.

1. Is the sample large enough? No, there are just three cities. Is the sample representative? No, not necessarily; for example, at least two of the cities have problems with illegal immigration that may add to the crime problem.
4. Is the sample large enough? Possibly, depending on the size of the faculty. Is the sample representative? No, they are all from one department. Other departments may tenure far fewer applicants for tenure.

EXERCISE 11.4

I.

1. (c) Strong and reliable.
4. (c) Strong and reliable.
7. (c) Strong and reliable.
10. (c) Strong and reliable.

EXERCISE 11.6

1. 2: The skills involved are very different.
4. 5: There are big differences between a small family budget and a large city budget.
7. 7: The argument does not claim very much, and considering Jordan's athletic ability, love for the game, and practice, it isn't unreasonable to claim he could learn to play tennis fairly well.
10. 3: The conclusion is too strong in claiming he must be "just like" the character. There are a couple of important similarities but not enough to fully support the conclusion.

EXERCISE 11.8

I.

1. Strong.
4. Weak.

II.

1. a. Strengthen.
   b. Strengthen.
   c. Weaken.
   d. Strengthen.
4. a. Strengthen.
   b. Weaken.
   c. Weaken.
   d. Strengthen.

EXERCISE 11.10

I.

1. Bad evidence.
4. Good evidence.
7. Good evidence.
10. Good evidence.

II.

1. What else did he eat? Did anyone else become sick from eating it?
4. The percentage of women with breast implants who have connective tissue disease; the percentage of women in the general public who have connective tissue disease; the percentage of women with silicone breast implants who have connective tissue disease; the percentage of women with saline breast implants who have connective tissue disease.
7. Why do students choose to sit in the front row?
10. How do we define a "healthy heart"? Just red wine, or other alcoholic beverages?

EXERCISE 11.11

1. Relative frequency.
4. Epistemic.
7. Relative frequency.
10. A priori.

EXERCISE 11.12

I.

1. Negative.
4. Negative.

CHAPTER 12

EXERCISE 12.2

II.

1. *Facts:* Cal Thomas worked for NBC News in the late 1960s. Robert Kitner was at one time president of NBC, as was Sylvester Weaver, who went by the name of Pat. *Matters of fact:* Stories were selected based on the audience they would attract (this could be verified with interviews, for example, or with corporate correspondence). Whether or not "ratings for news started to matter, as they did for entertainment" could be verified in similar ways, though some words, such as *mattered* would need to be clarified. The decline in the ratings could easily be documented. But what about the claim that "the respect most people once had for the journalism profession" also declined? Could that be documented through surveys or opinion polls? Could such a statement be shown to be factual?

4. *Facts:* Harvard is the oldest institution of higher learning in America; thirty-three Nobel Prize winners graduated from Harvard; Bill Gates developed the programming language BASIC; Radcliff was founded in 1879 and started admitting men in 1973; Martin Luther King Jr. received a doctorate in theology from Boston University, and so forth. Some statements, however, are not immediately verifiable. For example, it would be very difficult to document the claim that MIT is "generally acknowledged to be the nation's top school for science and engineering." The imprecise language—"generally acknowledged"—makes the statement more opinion than fact. Qualifying the statement might bring it closer to a matter of fact: "MIT is regarded among college presidents as the nation's best school for engineering." At least such a claim could be verified.

EXERCISE 12.3

1. Rush Limbaugh is a radio-talk-show host and author who espouses a conservative point of view. His claim that condoms fail "around" 17 percent of the time should be cautiously considered and verified with more-reliable sources. One key to Limbaugh's bias is his characterization of liberals in the first sentence of the quoted item. (Could he be charged here with a straw man fallacy?)

4. The billboards proclaiming these "facts" are sponsored by someone who is attempting to reduce the level of immigration into the United States. The figures on the billboards may or may not be correct, but anyone hoping to use them in an argument would do well to corroborate the information with other sources. (A careful reader will notice the slippery language and less-than-reliable information. In the first billboard, how little is "very little"? In the second, "arrive" is a vague word with several possible meanings, including "visit.")

7. It may well be true that 67 percent of listeners "would prefer that the races be separated," but that doesn't prove that "67 percent of *people*" prefer the same. Are the callers to a radio talk show a representative sample of "people" everywhere? Hardly.

10. *The Onion* is an online parody newspaper that publishes satirical articles about newsworthy events (and nonevents). Its intended audience—primarily regular readers who appreciate *The Onions*'s biting satire—won't be misled by the passage. Given the patent implausibility of such an event, few others will be either.

13. *America (The Book)* is a satirical romp through American history written by Jon Stewart and the writers of Comedy Central's fake news program, *The Daily Show*. The passage is obviously a joke, but a pointed one given long-standing debates about how disinterested the founding fathers' motives were.

EXERCISE 12.4

1. Answers will vary. Here is one possibility: In her book *Starting Out Suburban: A Frosh Year Survival Guide,* Linda Polland Puner suggests that most freshmen find it difficult to be away from home for the first time. They miss some of the comforts, such as good meals and privacy. Some are lucky enough, particularly if their family lives nearby, to get home within the first month of school, but others must wait until Thanksgiving or even Christmas. Even just a semester away from home can seem very long, and the distances can seem longer than they really are.

4. Answers will vary. Here is one possibility: In her article "A Test for Assessing Phonemic Awareness in Young Children," Hallie Kay Yopp claims that researchers have found that phonemic awareness, or the ability to sound out words, is perhaps the single most important requirement for good reading skills. This ability appears to be a more important indicator of reading success than IQ scores and vocabulary and listening comprehension tests. Having a proper assessment tool in place, therefore, can help direct the teacher to awareness of potential problems and to the use of available exercises that will enable the student to acquire stronger spelling and reading skills.

EXERCISE 12.5

1. Because rules are precise and must be followed to the letter, it would be best to quote the rule or the relevant part of the rule exactly as it appears in the book. In claiming that a player should have lost a tournament, someone might write, "In hitting the ball twice, Sampras clearly violated Rule 20d, which prohibits the player from 'deliberately touch[ing] it [the ball] with his racket more than once' in a given point." The writer would need, of course, to prove that the action was "deliberate."

4. The passage could be paraphrased or summarized with some phrases quoted if necessary. The following sentence might appear in a student's paper: "Athletes who push themselves to the limit often incur injuries, but the medical community is now considering whether athletes who push too hard might be susceptible to 'a host of chronic diseases, even cancer'" (Tabor).

EXERCISE 12.6

1. Fact available in wide variety of sources; does not need to be documented.

4. This fact should be documented. It is not widely known.

7. No need to document this fact; it is widely known and available.

10. This one is tricky. For scholars of Dickens's life and work, this is a commonly known fact: Dickens's childhood experiences are indeed reflected in several of his novels. Therefore, in preparing an argument for a literature class, you would most likely find this information in several sources and would not have to cite it. However, you would not be incorrect in giving a source if you chose to do so. In your paper you might write, "According to Charles Dickens's friend and biographer, John Forster, the novelist's childhood experiences, including his father's imprisonment for debt and Dickens's subsequent work in a shoe-polish factory, influenced his work as a novelist." (You would also need, of course, to supply the appropriate reference information.)

13. This is still being debated, so it would be best to tell your reader what source you are using.

CHAPTER 14

EXERCISE 14.8

1. f
4. m
7. b

10. d
13. n
16. q
19. x
22. z
25. v
28. cc

EXERCISE 14.9

III.

1. Weasel word.
4. Catchy slogan.
7. Humor.
10. Emotive words.
13. Sex appeal and humor.
16. Anxiety ad.
19. Catchy slogan.
22. Anxiety ad.
25. Sex appeal. Possible puffery and catchy slogan.

CHAPTER 15

EXERCISE 15.2

1. Not testable. (Not realistically verifiable or falsifiable, though scientific evidence no doubt bears on the issue.)

4. Not testable. (Value statement.)

7. Not testable. (We can imagine evidence that would falsify the claim—superintelligent extraterrestrials might visit the earth, for example—but the claim is not realistically verifiable because we have no way to search the immensity of space.)

10. Not realistically verifiable. Not only would tree-counters have to resolve difficult borderline cases ("Is this a tree or a bush?" "Is this scraggly-looking tree alive or dead?"), but there is no way, even with an army of counters, that all living trees in Canada could be located (many are in remote locations, growing in tall grasses, hidden under leaves, etc.). And even if these obstacles could somehow be overcome, any ongoing count would be continually invalidated by the growth of new trees and the deaths of others. There are ways, however, in which the claim might be reasonably falsified.

13. Not testable. (If absolutely everything doubled in size—including all yardsticks and other standards of measurement—there would be no way to detect the difference.)

EXERCISE 15.3

1. Pseudoscientific thinking. The arguer relies on an appeal to personal experience ("I tried it and it worked"). The herbal tea might have worked because of the placebo effect. Alternatively, the headache might have gone away by itself.

4. Pseudoscientific thinking. The arguer is explaining away falsifying evidence.

7. Pseudoscientific thinking. The graphologist is relying on general, Barnum-type language that applies to practically everybody.

10. Pseudoscientific thinking. Parry is explaining away falsifying data.

13. Pseudoscientific thinking. It's not surprising that dowsing sometimes works because underground water is abundant. The only way to *know* whether dowsing consistently works, however, is to test it under controlled conditions.

CREDITS

6 Reprinted by permission of Kenneth R. Merrill. **14** From *Decision Traps* by J. Edward Russo and Paul J. H. Schoemaker. Copyright © 1989 by J. Edward Russo and Paul J. H. Schoemaker. Used by permission of Doubleday, a division of Random House, Inc. **21** Grant H. Cornwell, "From Pluralism to Relativism and Back Again: Philosophy's Role in an Inclusive Curriculum," *Teaching Philosophy* 14:2 (June 1991), pp. 143–153. Used with permission. **56** Adapted from John Hoaglund, *Critical Thinking,* Third Edition, Newport News, VA: Vale Press, 1999, p. 65. Reprinted with permission from the publisher. **87** "Dwayne" adapted from Daniel R. Butler, Alan Ray and Leland Gregory, *America's Dumbest Criminals,* Nashville, TN: Rutledge Hill Press, 1995, pp. 147–148. With permission from the publisher. **190** "SAT Scores," Letter to the Editor, *Wilkes-Barre Times Leader,* September 16, 1998. Reprinted with permission from Robert Butts. **192** "EBR's Students Need Your Vote," editorial, *The Baton Rouge Advocate,* April 4, 1998. Reprinted with permission from the publisher. **198** "Don't Rush to Adopt Mail Voting System," editorial, *The Baton Rouge Advocate,* February 6, 1996. Reprinted with permission from the publisher. **199** Carmen F. Ambrosino, "Legalizing Drugs Spawns Many Problems, Solves None," *Wilkes-Barre Times Leader,* February 17, 1997. Reprinted with permission from the publisher. **218** Letter to the Editor of *Wilkes-Barre Times Leader,* June 10, 1996. Reprinted with permission from Stan Daniels. **218** From Leonard Pitts, Jr., "Don't Use God's Law to Beat Up on Gays," *Miami Herald,* June 8, 1997. **219** Constance Hilliard, "We're Spendthrift 'Environmentalists,'" *USA Today,* December 8, 2000. Reprinted with permission of the author. **220** *USA Today.* (3-3-04). Reprinted with permission. **221** Richard Delgado, "Hate Cannot Be Tolerated," *USA Today,* March 3, 2004. **222** Editorial. "Drop Out of the College," March 14, 2006. Copyright © The New York Times Co. Reprinted with permission. **223** © 2005 Time Inc. Reprinted by permission. **224** Tierney, John. "A Good Man is Hard to Find," March 25, 2006. Copyright © The New York Times Co. Reprinted with permission. **225** *USA Today.* (1-31-05). Reprinted with permission. **226** *USA Today.* (4-8-94). Reprinted with permission. **229** Jack Pytleski, "Defending My Right to Claim My 'Steak' in the Animal Kingdom," *Wilkes-Barre Times Leader,* July 10, 1997. Reprinted with permission from the author. **372** Anna Quindlen, "Raised on Rock and Roll," *The New York Times,* February 25, 1987. Copyright © 1987 by The New York Times Co. Reprinted by permission. **396** Letter to the Editor, *Wilkes-Barre Times Leader,* August 1998. Reprinted with permission from George R. Race. **416** From *Amusing Ourselves to Death* by Neil Postman. Copyright © 1985 by Neil Postman. Used by permission of Viking Penguin, a division of Penguin Group (USA) Inc. **449** From "The Newspaper Journalists of the 90's." Copyright © 1996. Used with permission from the American Society of Newspaper Editors. **491** From Paul Kurtz, *The Transcendental Temptation,* Prometheus Books. Copyright © 1986 Prometheus Books. Reprinted by permission of the publisher.

INDEX

Page numbers in **bold** indicate definitions. Page numbers in *italic* indicate boxes or illustrations.